Top Rated™ Fly Fishing

Top Rated™ Fly Fishing

Salt & Freshwaters in North America

Edited by
Maurizio Valerio

THE DERRYDALE PRESS
Lanham and New York

THE DERRYDALE PRESS

Published in the United States of America
by The Derrydale Press
4720 Boston Way, Lanham, Maryland 20706

Distributed by NATIONAL BOOK NETWORK, INC.

ISBN: 1-58667-000-X (paperback : alk. paper)
Library of Congress Card Number: 00-102313

To Allison, Marco and Nini

Table of Contents

Table of Contents

Top Rated™ Fly Fishing

Acknowledgments

It is customary in this section to give credit to those who have contributed to the realization of the end product. The Top Rated™ Guides started 5 years ago as a personal crusade and has evolved into a totally challenging, stimulating and rewarding full time commitment.

My deep thanks must go first to all the Captains, Ranchers, Guides, Lodges and Outfitters who decided to trust our honesty and integrity. They have taken a leap of faith in sharing their lists of clients with us and for this we are truly honored and thankful.

They have constantly encouraged our idea. Captains have taught us the difference between skinny fishing and skinny dipping, while River Guides have patiently helped us to identify rafters, purlins, catarafts and J-rig rafts. They were also ready to give us a badly needed push forward every time this monumental effort came to a stall. We have come to know many of them through pleasant phone chats, e-mails, faxes and letters. They now sound like old friends on the phone and we are certain we all share a deep respect for the mountains, the deserts and the waters of this great country of ours.

The Top Rated / Picked-By-You Team (both in the office and abroad), with months of hard work, skills, ingenuity, good sense of humor and pride, have then transformed a simple good idea into something a bit more tangible and much more exciting. They all have put their hearts in the concept and their hands and feet in the dirt. Some with a full-time schedule, some with a part-time collaboration, all of them bring their unique and invaluable style and contribution.

My true thanks to Brent Beck, Lindsay Benson, Robert Evans, Cheryl Fisher, Brian Florence, Grace Martin, Jerry Meek, Allison C. Mickens, Tom Novak, Slim Olsen, Shelby Sherrod, Dyanne Van Swoll, Giuseppe Verdi and Mr. Peet's Coffee and Tea.

Last, but not least, my sincere, profound, and loving gratitude to my wife Allison. Her patient support, her understanding, her help and her skills have been the fuel which started and stoked this fire. Her laughter has been the wind to fan it.

To you, Allison, with a toast to the next project…just kidding!

Maurizio Valerio

Preface

The value of information depends on its usefulness. Simply put, whatever allows you to make informed choices will be to your advantage. To that end, Top Rated™ Guides aims to take the guesswork out of selecting services for outdoor activities. Did you get what you paid for? From Top Rated™ Guides' point of view, the most reliable indicator is customer satisfaction.

The information in this book is as reliable as those who chose to participate. In the process of selecting the top professionals, Top Rated™ Guides contacted all licensed guides, outfitters and businesses which provide services for outdoor activities. They sought to include everyone but not all who were contacted agreed to participate according to the rules. Thus, the omission of a guide, outfitter or service does not automatically mean they didn't qualify based on customer dissatisfaction.

The market abounds with guidebooks by 'experts' who rate a wide range of services based on their personal preferences. The value of the Top Rated concept is that businesses earn a place in these books only when they receive favorable ratings from a majority of clients. If ninety percent of the customers agree that their purchase of services met or exceeded their expectations, then it's realistic to assume that you will also be satisfied when you purchase services from the outdoor professionals and businesses included in this book.

It's a fact of life; not everyone is satisfied all of the time or by the same thing. Individual experiences are highly subjective and are quite often based on expectations. One person's favorable response to a situation might provoke the opposite reaction in another. A novice might be open to any experience without any preconceived notions while a veteran will be disappointed when anything less than great expectations aren't met.

If you select any of the businesses in this book, chances are excellent that you will know what you are buying. A diversity of clients endorsed them because they believed the services they received met or exceeded their expectations. Top Rated™ Guides regards that information as more valuable than a single observer or expert's point of view.

The intent behind Top Rated™ Guides is to protect the consumer from being misled or deceived. It is obvious that these clients were given accurate information which resulted in a positive experience and a top rating. The number of questionnaire responses which included detailed and sometimes lengthy comments impressed upon us the degree to which people value

their experiences. Many regard them as "once-in-a-lifetime" and "priceless," and they heaped generous praise on those whose services made it possible.

Top Rated™ Guides has quantified the value of customer satisfaction and created a greater awareness of top-rated outdoor professionals. It remains up to you to choose and be the judge of your own experience. With the help of this book, you will have the advantage of being better informed when making that pick.

Robert Evans, *information specialist*

The Top Rated™ Concept

Mission Statement

The intent of this publication is to provide the outdoor enthusiast and his/her family with an objective and easy-to-read reference source that would list only those businesses and outdoor professionals who have **agreed to be rated** and have been overwhelmingly endorsed by their past clients.

There are many great outdoor professionals (Guides, Captains, Ranches, Lodges, Outfitters) who deserve full recognition for putting their experience, knowledge, long hours, and big hearts, into this difficult job. With this book we want to reward those deserving professionals while providing an invaluable tool to the general public.

Top Rated™ Guides are the only consumer guides to outdoor activities.

In this respect it would be useful to share the philosophy of our Company, succinctly illustrated by our Mission Statement:

"To encourage and promote the highest professional and ethical standards among those individuals, Companies, Groups or Organizations who provide services to the Outdoor Community.

To communicate and share the findings and values of our research and

surveys to the public and other key groups.

To preserve everyone's individual right of a respectful, knowledgeable and diversified use of our Outdoor Resources".

Our business niche is well defined and our job is simply to listen carefully.

THEY "the Experts" versus WE "the People"

Top Rated books were researched and compiled by **asking people such as yourself**, who rafted, fished, hunted or rode a horse on a pack trip with a particular outdoor professional or business, to rate their services, knowledge, skills and performance.

Only the ones who received A- to A+ scores from their clients are found listed in these pages.

The market is flooded with various publications written by 'experts' claiming to be the ultimate source of information for your vacation. We read books with titles such as <u>The Greatest River Guides</u>, <u>The Complete Guide to the Greatest Fishing Lodges</u>, etc.

We do not claim to be experts in any given field, but we rather pass to history as good....listeners. In the preparation of the Questionnaires we listened first to the outdoor professionals' point of view and then to the comments and opinions of thousands of outdoor enthusiasts. We then organized the findings of our research and surveys in this and other publications of this series.

Thus we will not attempt to tell you how to fish, how to paddle or what to bring on your trip. We are leaving this to the outdoor professionals featured in this book, for they have proven to be outstanding in providing much valuable information before, during and after your trip.

True [paid] advertising: an oxymoron

Chili with beans is considered a redundant statement for the overwhelming majority of cooks but it is an insulting oxymoron for any native Texan.

In the same way, while 'true paid advertising' is a correct statement for some, it is a clear contradiction in terms for us and certainly many of you. A

classic oxymoron.

This is why we do not accept commissions, donations, invitations, or, as many publishers cleverly express it, "...extra fees to help defray the cost of publication". Many articles are written every month in numerous specialized magazines in which the authors tour the country from lodge to lodge and camp to camp sponsored, invited, or otherwise compensated in many different shapes or forms.

It is indeed a form of direct advertising and, although this type of writing usually conveys a good amount of general information, in most cases it lacks the impartiality so valuable when it comes time to make the final selection for your vacation or outdoor adventure.

Without belittling the invaluable job of the professional writers and their integrity, we decided to approach the task of **researching information and sharing it with the public** with a different angle and from an opposite direction.

Money? ... No thanks!

We are firmly **committed to preserve the impartiality** and the novelty of the Top Rated idea.

For this reason we want to reassure the reader that the outdoor professionals and businesses featured in this book have not paid (nor will they pay), any remuneration to Top Rated™ Guides or the editor in the form of money, invitations or any other considerations.

They have earned a valued page in this book solely as the result of *their hard work and dedication to their clients.*

"A spot in this book cannot be purchased: it must be earned"

Size of a business is not a function of its performance

Since the embryonic stage of the Top Rated idea, during the compilation of the first Top Rated / Picked-By-You book, we faced a puzzling dilemma.

Should we establish a minimum number of clients under which a business or outdoor professional will not be allowed to participate in our evaluating process?

This would be a 'safe' decision when it comes the time to elaborate the responses of the questionnaires. But we quickly learned that many outdoor professionals limit, by choice, the total number of clients and, by philosophy of life, contain and control the size of their business. They do not want to grow too big and sacrifice the personal touches or the freshness of their services. In their words "we don't want to take the chance to get burned out by people." They do not consider their activity just a job, but rather a way of living.

"WHY, NO MAM, WE NEVER HAVE HAD ANY OF THOSE SASQUATCH SIGHTINGS IN THESE PARTS."

But if this approach greatly limits the number of clients accepted every year we must say that these outdoor professionals are the ones who often receive outstanding ratings and truly touching comments from their past clients.

Some businesses have provided us with a list of clients of 40,000, some with 25 . In this book **you will find both the large and the small**.

From a statistical point, it is obvious that a fly fishing guide who submitted a list of 32 clients, by virtue of the sample size of the individuals surveyed, will implicitly have a lower level of accuracy if compared to a business for which we surveyed 300 guests. (Please refer to the Rating and Data Elaboration Sections for details on how we established the rules for qualifica-

tion and thus operated our selection).

We do not believe that the size of business is a function of its good performance and we feel strongly that those dedicated professionals who choose to remain small deserve an equal chance to be included.

We tip our hats

We want to recognize all the Guides, Captains, Ranches, Lodges and Outfitters who have participated in our endeavor, whether they qualified or not. The fact alone that they accepted to be rated by their past clients is a clear indication of how much they care, and how willing they are to make changes.

We also want to credit all those outdoor enthusiasts who have taken the time to complete the questionnaires and share their memories and impressions with us and thus with you. Some of the comments sent to us were hilarious, some were truly touching.

We were immensely pleased by the reaction of the outdoor community at large. The idea of "Top Rated™ Guides" was supported from the beginning by serious professionals and outdoor enthusiasts alike. We listened to their suggestions, their comments, their criticisms and we are now happy to share this information with you.

Questionnaires

"Our books will be only as good as the questions we ask."

We posted this phrase in the office as a reminder of the importance of the 'tool' of this trade. The questions.

Specific Questionnaires were tailored to each one of the different activities surveyed for this series of books. While a few of the general questions remained the same throughout, many were specific to particular activities. The final objective of the questionnaire was to probe the many different facets of that diversified field known as the outdoors.

The first important factor we had to consider in the preparation of the Questionnaires was the total number of questions to be asked. Research shows an *inversely proportionate relation* between the total number of questions and the percentage of responses: the higher the number of questions, the lower the level of response. Thus we had to balance an acceptable

return rate with a meaningful significance. We settled for a compromise and we decided to keep 20 as the maximum number.

The first and the final versions of the Questionnaires on which we based our surveys turned out to be very different. We asked all the businesses and out-door professionals we contacted for suggestions and criticisms. They helped us a great deal: we weighed their different points of view and we incorporated all their suggestions into the final versions.

We initially considered using a phone survey, but we quickly agreed with the businesses and outdoor professionals that we all are already bothered by too many solicitation calls when we are trying to have a quiet dinner at home. We do not want you to add Top Rated™ Guides to the list of companies that you do not want to talk to, nor do we want you to add our 800 number to your caller ID black list.

In using the mail we knew that we were going to have a slightly lower percentage of questionnaires answered, but this method is, in our opinion, a more respectful one.

We also encouraged the public to participate in the designing of the ques-tionnaire by posting on our website at www.topratedsurveys.com the oppor-tunity to submit a question and ...."Win a book". Many sent their suggestions and , if they were chosen to be used in one of our questionnaires, they were given the book of their choice.

Please send us your question and/or your suggestions for our future sur-veys to:

TOP RATED™ Surveys, P.O. Box 718, Baker City, OR 97814

Rating (there is more than one way to skin the cat)

We considered many different ways to score the questionnaires, keeping in mind at all times our task:

translate an opinion into a numerical value

Some of the approaches considered were simple *averages* [arithmetical means], others were sophisticated statistical tests. In the end we opted for simplicity, sacrificing to the God of statistical significance. WARNING: if $p \leq 0.001$ has any meaning in your life stop reading right here: you will be disappointed with the rest.

For the rest of us, we also made extensive use in our computation of the *median*, a statistic of location, which divides the frequency distribution of a set of data into two halves. A quick example, with our imaginary Happy Goose Outfitter, will illustrate how in many instances the *median* value, being the center observation, helps in describing the distribution, which is the truly weak point of the *average*:

Average salary at Happy Goose Outfitters $ 21,571

Median salary at Happy Goose Outfitters $ 11,000

5,000	10,000	10,000	11,000	12,000	15,000	98,000
Wrangler	Guide	Guide	Senior Guide	Asst.Cook	Cook	Boss

Do not ask the boss : "What's the average salary?"

These are the values assigned to **Questions 1-15**:

5.00 points	OUTSTANDING
4.75 points	EXCELLENT
4.25 points	GOOD
3.50 points	ACCEPTABLE
3.00 points	POOR
0.00 points	UNACCEPTABLE

Question 16, relating to the weather conditions, was treated as bonus points to be added to the final score.

Good=0   Fair=1   Poor=2

The intention here was to reward the outdoor professional who had to work in adverse weather conditions.

Questions 17 - 18 = 5 points

Questions 19 - 20 = 10 points

The individual scores of each Questionnaire were expressed as a percentage to avoid the total score from being drastically affected by one question left unanswered or marked "not applicable." All the scores received for each individual outdoor professional and business were thus added and computed.

The 90 points were considered our cutoff point. Note how the outfitters must receive a combination of Excellent with only a few Good marks (or better) in order to qualify.

Only the Outfitters, Captains, Lodges, Guides who received an A- to A+ score did qualify and they are featured in this book.

We also decided not to report in the book pages the final scores with which the businesses and the outdoor professionals ultimately qualified. In a way we thought that this could be distractive.

In the end, we must admit, it was tough to leave out some outfitters who scored very close to the cutoff mark.

It would be presumptuous to think that our scoring system will please everybody, but we want to assure the reader that we tested different computations of the data. We feel the system that we have chosen respects the

overall opinion of the guest/client and maintains a more than acceptable level of accuracy.

We know that .... "You can change without improving, but you cannot improve without changing."

The Power of Graphs (how to lie by telling the scientific truth)

The following examples illustrate the sensational (and unethical) way with which the 'scientific' computation of data can be distorted to suit one's needs or goals.

The *Herald* presents a feature article on the drastic increase of total tonnage of honey stolen by bears (mostly Poohs) in a given area during 1997.

Total tonnage of honey stolen by bears (Poohs)

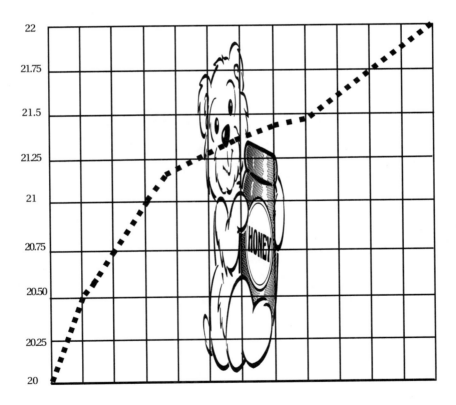

Total tonnage of honey stolen by bears (Poohs)

It is clear how a journalist, researcher or author must ultimately choose one type of graph. But the question here is whether or not he/she is trying to make "his/her point" by choosing one type versus the other, rather than simply communicate some findings.

Please note that the bears, in our example, are shameless, and remain such in both instances, for they truly love honey!

Graphs were not used in this book. We were just too worried we wouldn't use the correct ones.

The Book Making Process

Research

We **researched** the name and address of every business and outdoor professional **in the United States and** in all the **provinces of Canada** (see list in the Appendix). Some states do not require guides and outfitters or businesses providing outdoor services to be registered, and in these instances the information must be obtained from many different sources [Outfitter's Associations, Marine Fisheries, Dept. of Tourism, Dept. of Environmental Conservation, Dept. of Natural Resources, Dept. of Fish and Game, US Coast Guard, Chamber of Commerce, etc.].

In the end the database on which we based this series of Top Rated™ Guides amounted to more than 23,000 names of Outfitters, Guides, Ranches, Captains etc. Our research continues and this number is increasing every day. The Appendix in the back of this book is only a partial list and refers specifically to Top Rated Fly Fishing.

Participation

We **invited** businesses and outdoor professionals, with a letter and a brochure explaining the Top Rated concept, to join our endeavor by simply sending us a <u>**complete** list of their clients</u> of the past two years. With the "Confidentiality Statement" we reassured them that the list was going to be kept **absolutely confidential** and to be *used one time only* for the specific purpose of evaluating their operation. Then it would be destroyed.

We truly oppose this "black market" of names so abused by the mail marketing business. If you are ever contacted by Picked-By-You you may rest assured that your name, referred to us by your outdoor professional, will never be sold, traded or otherwise used a second time by us for marketing purposes.

Questionnaires

We then **sent a questionnaire** to **every single client on each list** (to a maximum of 300 randomly picked for those who submitted large lists with priority given to overnight or multiple day trips), asking them to rate the

services, the **knowledge** and **performance** of the business or outdoor professional by completing our comprehensive questionnaire (see pages 250-251). The businesses and outdoor professionals found in these pages may or may not be the ones who invest large sums of money to advertise in magazines, or to participate at the annual conventions of different clubs and foundations. However, they are clearly the ones, according to our survey, that put customer satisfaction and true dedication to their clients first and foremost.

Data Elaboration

A **numerical value was assigned to each question**. All the **scores were computed**. Both the **average** and the **median** were calculated and considered for eligibility. Please note that the total score was computed as a percentile value.

This allows some flexibility where one question was left unanswered or was answered with a N/A. Furthermore, we decided not to consider the high

and the low score to ensure a more evenly distributed representation and to reduce the influence which an extreme judgement could have either way (especially with the small sample sizes).

We also set a **minimum number of questionnaires** which needed to be answered to allow a business or an outdoor professional to qualify. Such number was set as a function of the total number of clients in the list: the smaller the list of clients, the higher was the percentage of responses needed for qualification.

In some cases the outfitter's average score came within 1 point of the A-cutoff mark. In these instances, we considered both the median and the average were considered as well as the guests' comments and the total number of times that this particular business was recommended by the clients by answering with a 'yes' question 19 and 20.

Sharing the results

Top Rated™ Guides will share the results of this survey with the businesses and the outdoor professionals. This will be done at no cost to them whether or not they qualified for publication. All questionnaires received will, in fact, be returned along with a summary result to the business, keeping the confidentiality of the client's name when this was requested. This will prove an invaluable tool to help improve those areas that have received some criticisms.

The intention of this series of books is to research the opinions and the comments of outdoor enthusiasts, and to share the results of our research with the public and other key groups.

One outfitter wrote us about our Top Rated™ Guides series, "I feel your idea is an exciting and unique concept. Hopefully our past clientele will rate us with enough points to 'earn' a spot in your publication. If not, could we please get a copy of our points/questionnaires to see where we need to improve. Sincerely…"

This outfitter failed to qualify by just a few points, but such willingness to improve leaves us no doubt that his/her name will be one of those featured in our second edition. In the end it was not easy to exclude some of them from publication, but we are certain that, with the feedback provided by this survey, they will be able to improve those areas that need extra attention.

We made a real effort to keep a position of absolute impartiality in this process and, in this respect, we would like to repeat that the outfitters have not paid, nor they will pay, one single penny to Top Rated™ Guides or the Editor to be included in this book.

The research continues.

Top Rated Icon Legend

General Services and Accommodations

INFANT CARE

TODDLER PROGRAM

KIDS PROGRAMS

BABY SITTING

FAMILY

SENIOR CITIZEN
AGE +

HANDICAP

ARCHEOLOGICAL SITES

FULL BOARD

GOURMET MEALS

HOT SPRINGS

SWIMMING POOL

General Services and Accommodations

DOME / SPIKE TENT

WALL TENTS

CABINS

LODGE

TRAILER CAMPS

SLEEP ABOARD

DROP CAMPS

HOTEL / MOTEL

BED & BREAKFAST

WOMEN ONLY TRIPS

DOG FACILITIES

General Services

Season(s) of operation

Locations

 BLUE RIBBON STREAM

 BLUE RIBBON WATERS

 RIVER DELTA

 SALTWATER

 ESTUARIES

 LAKE

 OPEN OCEAN

 POND

 LARGE RIVER

 STREAMS

 MARSH/WETLANDS

Activities/Fishing Techniques

 CATCH & RELEASE

 FLY FISHING

 SKINNY FISHING

 WHITEWATER FISHING

 BASS TOURNAMENT

 SPIN CASTING

 DEEP WATER FISHING

 TROPHY FISHING

 TROLLING

 ICE FISHING

 FLY TYING SCHOOL

 FLY FISHING SCHOOL

Activities

SUPERVISED SPORTS

SEA KAYAKING

SCUBA DIVING

RACQUETBALL COURT

TENNIS COURT

SWIMMING

ZODIAC TOURS

WHITEWATER TRIPS

ARCHERY

WAGON RIDES

SNOW MOBILE

Activities

CLAY SHOOTING

HORSEBACK

HORSE PACK TRIPS

HIKING / TREKKING

CROSS COUNTRY

SNOWSHOEING

LLAMA PACK TRIPS

WHALE WATCHING

BIRD WATCHING

Fish

 Amberjack

 Arctic Char

 Arctic Grayling

 Atlantic Cod

 Barracuda

 Small Mouth Bass

 Large Mouth Bass

 Sea Bass

 Striped Bass

 White Bass

 Bluefish

 Bluegill

 Bonefish

 Crappie

 Dolphin Fish

 Drum

 Mackerel

 Marlin

Fish

 Muskellunge

 Northern Pike

 Perch

 Permit

 Sailfish

 Atlantic Salmon

 Chum Salmon

 King-Chinook Salmon

 Pink Salmon

 Red-Sockeye Salmon

 Silver - Coho Salmon

 Shad

 Shark

 Snapper

 Snook

 Steelhead

 Swordfish

 Tarpon

Fish

Brook Trout

Brown Trout

Cutthroat Trout

Dolly Varden

Rainbow Trout

Sea Trout

Tuna

Walleye

Boat Types and Transportation

FLOAT AIRPLANE

AMPHIBIOUS VEHICLE

ALL TERRAIN VEHICLE

MAKO

ALUMINUM BOAT

BASS BOAT

CABIN CRUISER

CANOE

CATARAFT

FISHING VESSEL

FLATS' SKIFF

FLY BRIDGE

JET BOAT

Boat Types and Transportation

INFLATABLE KAYAK

LUXURY YACHT

McKENZIE / DORY

MOTOR BOAT

NORDIC TUG

OPEN CONSOLE

RAFT

HOVERCRAFT

SEA KAYAKING

ZODIAC TOURS

HORSE PACK TRIPS

LLAMA PACK TRIPS

Top Rated
Outfitters, Guides, and Lodges

Alaska

Outdoor Professionals

1. Alaska Fish & Trails Unlimited
2. Classic Alaska Charters
3. George Ortman Adventure Guiding
4. Tracy Vrem's Blue Mountain Lodge

License and Report Requirements

• State requires licensing of Outdoor Professionals.

• State requires a "Hunt Record" for big game.

• Saltwater Charter Vessels Logbook Program - Charter Vessel guided trips are required to submit pages of logbook on a weekly basis.

• Charter Vessels are required to be licensed with the Commercial Fisheries Entry Commission at Juneau, phone: (907) 789-6150.

Useful information for the state of

Alaska

State and Federal Agencies

Alaska Dept. of Fish & Game
PO Box 25526
Juneau, AK 99802-5526
phone: (907) 465-4180 Fish
(907) 465-4190 Game

Alaska Region Forest Service
709 West 9th Street
Box 21628
Juneau, AK 99802-1628
phone: (907) 586-8863
TTY: (907) 586-7816
www.fs.fed.us/r10

Chugach National Forest
3301 C Street, Ste. 300
Anchorage, AK 99503-3998
phone: (907) 271-2500
TTY: (907) 271-2332

Tongass National Forest:
Sitka Office
204 Siginaka Way
Sitka, AK 99835
phone: (907) 747-6671
TTY: (907) 747-4535
fax: (907) 747-4331

Tongass National Forest:
Federal Building
Ketchikan, AK 99901-6591
phone: (907) 228-6202
fax: (907) 228-6215

Bureau of Land Management
Alaska State Office
222 W. 7th Avenue, #13
Anchorage, AK 99513-7599
phone: (907) 271-5960
or (907) 271-plus extension
fax: (907) 271-4596
http://www.ak.blm.gov

Office Hours: 8:00 a.m. - 3:45 p.m.

National Parks

Denali National Park & Preserve
phone: (907) 683-2294

Gates of the Arctic National Park
phone: (907) 456-0281

Glacier Bay National Park
phone: (907) 697-2230

Katmai National Park
phone: (907) 246-3305

Kenai Fjords National Park
phone: (907) 224-3175

Kobuk Valley National Park
phone: (907) 442-3890

Lake Clark National Park
phone: (907) 271-3751

Wrangell-St. Elias National Park
phone: (907) 822-5234

Yukon-Charley Rivers National Park
phone: (907) 456-0593

Associations, Publications, etc.

American Fisheries Society
2720 Set Net Ct.
Kenai, AK 99611
phone: (907) 260-2909
fax: (907) 262-7646

Trout Unlimited Alaska Council
PO Box 3055
Soldotna, AK 99669
phone: (907) 262-9494

Federation of Fly Fishers
http://www.fedflyfishers.org

Alaska Fish and Trails Unlimited

Jerald D. Stansel

1177 Shypoke Dr. • Fairbanks, AK 99709
PO Box 26045, Bettles Field, AK 99726
phone: (907) 479-7630 • http://www.ptialaska.net/~aktrails/

Alaska Fish and Trails Unlimited is owned by guide and bush pilot Jerry Stansel, who has been operating and guiding in the Brooks Range Gates of the Arctic for 25 years.

His tours specialize in guided and unguided fly-in fishing, rafting, backpacking and photography trips.

Species of fish include arctic char, sheefish, lake trout, arctic grayling, whitefish, northern pike and salmon.

So come, breathe Alaska's crisp, clean air. Drink its pure, fresh water. Fly across the Arctic Circle and Arctic Divide. Fish for a variety of species, either around Fairbanks or in the Arctic.

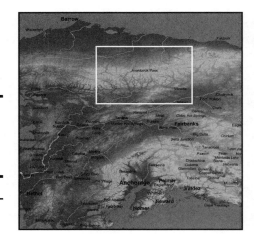

"Caught and Released over 100 lake trout, all but one over 10 lbs. Caught one pike over 48 inches!!" Keith Smith

SEASONS OF OPERATION

FISH SPECIES

 Arctic Char
 Arctic Grayling
 King-Chinook Salmon
 Red-Sockeye Salmon
 Silver - Coho Salmon
 Lake Trout
 Rainbow Trout
 Northern Pike

ACTIVITIES & TRANSPORTATION

 WHITEWATER TRIPS
 WHITEWATER FISHING
 CATCH & RELEASE
 ICE FISHING
 TROLLING
 TROPHY FISHING
 #1
 FLOAT AIRPLANE
 CANOE

LOCATIONS & SERVICES

 BLUE RIBBON WATERS
 KIDS PROGRAMS
 FAMILY
 CABINS
 DROP CAMPS
 WOMEN ONLY TRIPS
 OVERNIGHT TRIPS
 ARCHEOLOGICAL SITES

Classic Alaska Charters

Capt. Robert Scherer

P.O. Box 6117 • Ketchikan, AK 99901
phone: (907) 225-0608 • captrob@classicalaskacharters.com
www.classicalaskacharters.com

Classic Alaska Charters is unique. We consult directly with you as to your particular interests and design a vacation around you.

Alaskan fishing is among the best in the world. You'll experience unspoiled fishing grounds all to yourself at your pace. Whether an expert or novice, you'll catch the fever when you hook into a monster halibut or stand in a salmon-swollen river. Or fish all day in the safety and comfort of our motor yacht. You can also take walks along the tideflats to photograph black and brown bear, marine mammals, bald eagles, harbor seals, waterfalls and wildflowers.

Captain Rob is U.S.C.G. certified and has been professionally guiding in Alaska since 1984. He is a wildlife and nature photographer and can guide you into spectacular wilderness photo opportunities.

"Captain Rob gives a personal touch to his trips that I think is the best. I cannot wait to go back." Jerry Robertshaw

SEASONS OF OPERATION

FISH SPECIES

Chum Salmon | King-Chinook Salmon | Pink Salmon | Red-Sockeye Salmon | Silver-Coho Salmon | Steelhead

ACTIVITIES & TRANSPORTATION

LOCATIONS & SERVICES

George Ortman Adventure Guiding

George Ortman
Box 261 • Willow, AK 99688
phone/fax: (907) 495-6515

I offer the finest in wilderness fishing and travel. My expertise and knowledge will provide you with a fantastic wilderness experience. Your complete comfort, safety, and satisfaction are my priority and goal.

During the summer, we have many fishing options, such as the Kokwok, Kenektok and Izavieknik rivers. Each has its own characteristics and attractions with varying degrees of difficulty. I will organize your trip around your personal goals and fishing style. I offer substantial discounts with two destinations and many guests choose to do two rivers for a broader experience, both with fishing and seeing the country. Lake trout can be sought on Upnuk Lake where lakers over 30 pounds are regularly taken.

I provide a complete guiding service, including all gear, food, and flights from your arrival in Dillingham through departure.

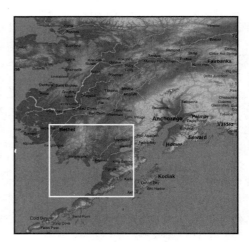

"Nothing was too much trouble for George, he is obviously a dedicated guide who is dedicated to his guests, and very much cares for the environment, the fish and the wildlife!" Doug Linburn

SEASONS OF OPERATION

SPRING · SUMMER · FALL

FISH SPECIES

Arctic Char	Arctic Grayling	Northern Pike	King-Chinook Salmon	Red-Sockeye Salmon	Silver - Coho Salmon	Steelhead	Dolly Varden	Lake Trout

ACTIVITIES & TRANSPORTATION

CATCH & RELEASE · GUIDED ACTIVITIES · FLOAT AIRPLANE · CANOE · RAFT

LOCATIONS & SERVICES

BLUE RIBBON WATERS · LARGE RIVER · LAKE · KIDS PROGRAMS · FAMILY · HANDICAP · ARCHEOLOGICAL SITES · WOMEN ONLY TRIPS

Tracy Vrem's Blue Mountain Lodge

Tracy Vrem

P.O. Box 670130 • Chugiak, AK 99567
phone: (907) 688-2419 • fax: (907) 688-0491

We're in the heart of the best fishing in the Alaska Peninsula. Blue Mountain Lodge is located in the Becherof Ugashik lakes region. These lakes are spawning grounds for millions of salmon. It's not uncommon to catch and release more than 30 fish a day, from trophy-sized grayling, to acrobatic rainbow trout, lunker arctic char, lake trout, northern pike, or all five species of salmon.

We rarely lose a day of fishing due to the weather. And, with the excellent fishing, you'll have an opportunity to sight bear, caribou and moose. A short flight to Katmai National Monument is part of our agenda.

The wood frame and aluminum-sided lodge is a far cry from being plush, but it's comfortable and unique. There is a shower and washroom; the toilet facility is an outhouse.

"...the fishing can not be described, one must experience it to believe it. On the trip home one of our group told me 'Ben, we can't tell anyone about this, they will think we are lying'!" Ben Miller

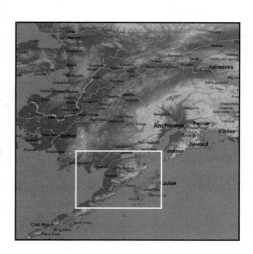

SEASONS OF OPERATION

FISH SPECIES

 Arctic Char | Arctic Grayling | Northern Pike | King-Chinook Salmon | Red-Sockeye Salmon | Silver - Coho Salmon | Pink Salmon | Dolly Varden | Rainbow Trout

ACTIVITIES & TRANSPORTATION

LOCATIONS & SERVICES

Arkansas

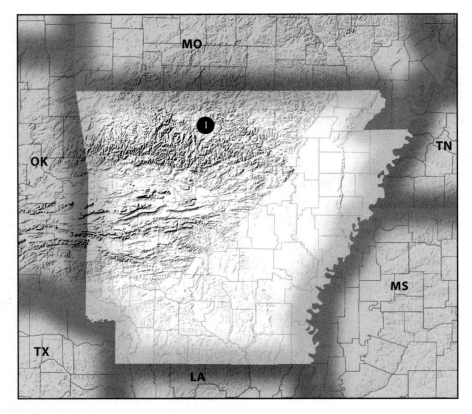

Outdoor Professionals

1 The John B. Gulley Fly Fishing Guide Service

License and Report Requirements

• State does not license or register Outfitters, Guides or Lodges.

• State has no report requirements.

Useful information for the state of

Arkansas

State and Federal Agencies

Arkansas Game & Fish Commission
#2 Natural Resources Dr.
Little Rock, AR 72205
phone: (501) 223-6300
fax: (501) 223-6425
http://www.agfc.com

Bureau of Land Management
Eastern States
7450 Boston Boulevard
Springfield, VA 22153
phone: (703) 440-1660
or (703) 440-plus extension
fax: (703) 440-1599

Office Hours: 8:00 a.m. - 4:30 p.m.

Eastern States
Jackson Field Office
411 Briarwood Drive, Suite 404
Jackson, MS 39206
phone: (601) 977-5400

Forest Service
Southern Region
1720 Peachtree Road NW
Atlanta, GA 30367
phone: (404) 347-4177
TTY: (404) 347-4278

Ouachita National Forest
Federal Building
PO Box 1270
Hot Springs, AR 71902
phone: (501) 321-5202
TTY: (501) 321-5307

Ozark-St. Francis National Forests
605 West Main Street
PO Box 1008
Russellville, AR 72811
phone: (501) 968-2354
TTY: (501) 964-7201

National Parks

Hot Springs National Park
PO Box 1860
Hot Springs, AR 71902
phone: (501) 624-3383

Associations, Publications, etc.

American Fisheries Society
Arkansas Chapter
401 Hardin Road
Little Rock, AR 72211
phone: (501) 228-3620
fax: (501) 228-3601
http://www.ark.usgs.gov

Trout Unlimited Arkansas Council
1794 Berry Street
Fayetteville, AR 72701-1641
phone: (501) 521-8664
Email: kfree94508@aol.com
http://www.flyflinger.com/arktu

Federation of Fly Fishers
http://www.fedflyfishers.org

Arkansas Bass Chapter Federation
119 Lilly Street
Searcy, AR 72143
phone: (501) 268-6659

The Ozark Society
PO Box 2914
Little Rock, AR 72203

The John B. Gulley Fly Fishing Guide Service

John B. Gulley II

1703 River Ridge Rd. • Norfork, AR 72658-9005
phone: (870) 499-7517 • fax: (870) 499-5132
email: John_Gulley@juno.com • www.flyguide.com

John Gulley's Orvis®-endorsed Fly Fishing Service is designed for the rivers and lakes of Arkansas. Arkansas trout waters are 99% tailwater fisheries, therefore, guides need to be extremely versatile in order to fish all the conditions necessary to catch trout.

Our operation includes walk-in wade fishing at private and public access points and highwater float trips. Our service also includes the opportunity for the flyfisherman to catch some of the best freshwater striper action in America.

An Arkansas native, I have more than 25 years experience in guiding flyfishermen and casting instruction. My flies include many innovative patterns that I have developed for trout, bass and stripers.

Orvis® 1999 Guide of the Year

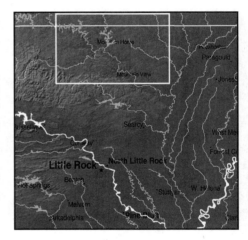

"This trip was my son's graduation present, also the first fly fishing trip for both of us. We have planned a trip next year to the same place using John Gulley. Excellent trip and guide." Pat Gavin

SEASONS OF OPERATION _____

FISH SPECIES _____

Striped Bass Steelhead Brown Trout Rainbow Trout

ACTIVITIES & TRANSPORTATION _____

CATCH & RELEASE TROPHY FISHING MOTOR BOAT FLY TYING SCHOOL FLY FISHING SCHOOL

LOCATIONS & SERVICES _____

STREAMS BLUERIBBONSTREAM GUIDED ACTIVITIES OVERNIGHT TRIPS HANDICAP

Top Rated Professionals in
California

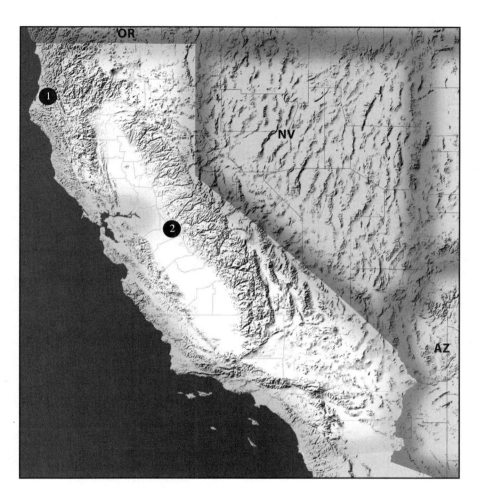

Outdoor Professionals

1. Bruce Slightom
2. Tim Bermingham's Drift Boat Guide Service

California

State and Federal Agencies

California Fish & Game Commission
License & Revenue Branch
3211 "S" Street
Sacramento, CA 95816
phone: (916) 227-2245
fax: (916) 227-2261
http://www.dfg.ca.gov

Pacific Southwest
Forest Service Region
630 Sansome St.
San Francisco, CA 94111
phone: (415) 705-2874
TTY: (415) 705-1098

Bureau of Land Management
California State Office
2800 Cottage Way
Sacramento, CA 95825
fax: (916) 978-4657
http://www.ca.blm.gov

Office Hours: 8:30 - 4:30 pm (PST)

National Parks

Lassen Volcanic National Park
phone: (530) 595-4444

Redwood National Park
phone: (707) 464-6101

Sequoia & Kings Canyon Natl. Parks
phone: (209) 565-3341

Yosemite National Park
phone: (209) 372-0200

Channel Islands National Park
phone: (805) 658-5700

Associations, Publications, etc.

California Trout, Inc.
870 Market St. #859
San Francisco, CA 94102
phone: (415) 392-8887
http://www.caltrout.org

Trout Unlimited, California Chapter
1024 C. Los Gamos
San Rafael, CA 94903-2517
phone: (415) 472-5837
http://cwo.com/~trout/index.html

Federation of Fly Fishers
http://www.fedflyfishers.org

Bass Chapter Federation
751 Melva Ave.
Oakdale, CA 95361
phone: (209) 541-3673
or (209) 847-3272

California Outdoors
PO Box 401
Coloma, CA 95613
phone: (800) 552-3625
http://www.caloutdoor.org

License and Report Requirements

• State requires licensing of Outdoor Professionals.
• State requires the filing of a "Monthly Guide Log" for all outdoor professionals,
   including river outfitters.
• River Outfitters need a "Use Permit", required for BLM, National Forest, Indian
   reservations, and National Parks.
• Boat and Waterways Dept. requires license for all motorized craft, and raft or floating
   device if carrying more than 3 persons.

Bruce Slightom

Bruce Slightom

4841 Cummings Rd. • Eureka, CA 95503
phone: (707) 442-3168 • email: Cheryls@Humboldt1.com

Bruce Slightom has been guiding fall flyfishers on the Klamath and Trinity rivers for more than 20 years.

He has been an instructor in the local university's beginning and advanced fly casting classes for 15 years. With this experience, Bruce can get you into fish as well as help anglers of all levels hone their skills.

In winter, conventional gear is used to pursue steelhead on the coastal rivers of Northern California. Based in Eureka, the Eel, Mattole, Smith and other rivers are all close by, offering a choice of rivers to fish as conditions change.

Jet boat, drift boat, raft or walk-in trips — we can go where the fish are. Not only will you catch fish but you can also take advantage of Bruce's skill in teaching how to fish.

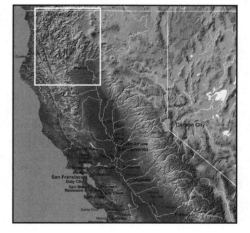

"Great person, excellent guide...have fished with Bruce for years!" Leon Vhalde

SEASONS OF OPERATION

FISH SPECIES

 Steelhead   King-Chinook Salmon   Rainbow Trout

ACTIVITIES & TRANSPORTATION

LOCATIONS & SERVICES

Tim Bermingham's Drift Boat Guide Service

Tim Bermingham

840070 Melones Dam Rd. • Jamestown, CA 95327
phone/fax: (209) 984-4007
email: info@driftfish.com • http://www.driftfish.com/index.html

Tim Bermingham has fished California inland waters for more than 30 years.

Raised in Merced, he knows the Merced River better than anybody. Fishing mainly on the Merced River during spring, summer and fall, we also have jet or driftboat trips on the Tuolumne, Stanislaus and Mokelumne rivers, and the Smith and Mattole rivers in northwest California during the winter.

We boast a 100% success rate; not one of my clients has ever failed to land fish. Rainbow, brook or brown trout, salmon, steelhead, largemouth, smallmouth and striped bass success is a sure bet.

Fly, spin or baitfishing, all tackle provided. All you need is a California fishing license. Join us for an exciting fly fishing adventure.

"Tim's a master of the drift boat experience. My son and I had a great time."
John Larson

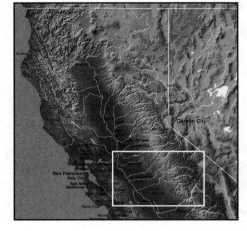

SEASONS OF OPERATION

FISH SPECIES

 Small Mouth Bass
 Large Mouth Bass
 Striped Bass
 Steelhead
 King-Chinook Salmon
 Brook Trout
 Brown Trout
 Rainbow Trout

ACTIVITIES & TRANSPORTATION

 Catch & Release
 Whitewater Fishing
 Jet Boat
 McKenzie Dory

LOCATIONS & SERVICES

 Large River
 Guided Activities
 Overnight Trips

Colorado

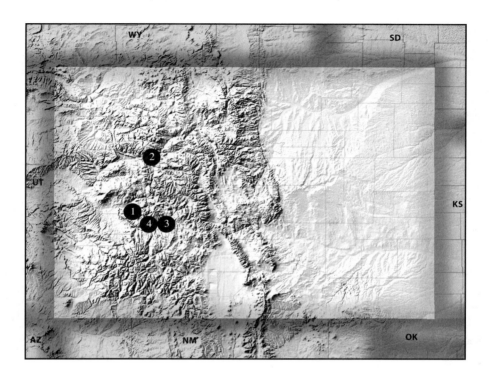

Outdoor Professionals

- **1** Dragonfly Anglers
- **2** Fly Fishing Outfitters
- **3** Mike Wilson's High Mountain Drifters
- **4** The Troutfitter

License and Report Requirements

- State requires licensing of Outdoor Professionals.

- State requires an "Inter-Office Copy of Contract with Client" be submitted each time a client goes with an Outfitter. Colorado Agencies of Outfitters Registry sends this copy to client to fill out and return to their agency.

- Colorado State Forest Service requires a "Use Permit" for all guided activities on federal land.

Colorado

State and Federal Agencies

Colorado Agencies of Outfitters Registry
1560 Broadway, Suite 1340
Denver, CO 80202
phone: (303) 894-7778

Colorado Dept. of Natural Resources
1313 Sherman, Room 718
Denver, CO 80203
phone: (303) 866-3311

Forest Service
Rocky Mountain Region
740 Simms Street
PO Box 25127
Lakewood, CO 80225
phone: (303) 275-5350
TTY: (303) 275-5367

Arapaho-Roosevelt National Forests
Pawnee National Grassland
phone: (970) 498-2770

Grand Mesa-Umcompahgre
Gunnison National Forests
phone: (970) 874-7641

Pike-San Isabel National Forests
Comanche & Cimarron National
Grasslands
phone: (719) 545-8737

San Juan-Rio Grande National Forest
phone: (719) 852-5941
fax: (719) 852-6250

White River National Forest
phone: (970) 945-2521
fax: (970) 945-3266

Bureau of Land Management
Colorado State Office
2850 Youngfield St.
Lakewood, CO 80215-7093
phone: (303) 239-3600

fax: (303) 239-3933
Tdd: (303) 239-3635
Email: msowa@co.blm.gov
Office Hours: 7:45 a.m. - 4:15 p.m.

National Parks

Mesa Verde National Park, CO 81330
phone: (303) 529-4465

Rocky Mountain National Park
phone: (303) 586-2371

Associations, Publications, etc.

American Fisheries Society
Colorado & Wyoming Chapter
PO Box 6249
Sheridan, WY 82801
phone: (307) 672-7418
fax: (307) 672-0594

Trout Unlimited Colorado Chapter
1487 Cross Creek Court
Lafayette, CO 80026-8000
phone: (800) 525-3786
fax: (303) 277-6246
http://www.cotrout.org

Federation of Fly Fishers
http://www.fedflyfishers.org

CO Bass Chapter Federation
2713 Garden Drive
Ft. Collins, CO 80526
phone: (303) 221-3608

Colorado Outfitters Association
PO Box 893
Alamosa, CO
phone: (719) 589-4186
fax: (719) 589-4186
email: redmt@fone.net

Dragonfly Anglers

Rod and Roger Cesario

307 Elk Ave., P.O. Box 1116 • Crested Butte, CO 81224
phone: (800) 491-3079 • (970) 349-1228 • (970) 349-9836 • Lic. #711

Dragonfly Anglers offers guided fly fishing trips for the beginner to the experienced fisherman in Gunnison County and Western Colorado. We fish large rivers, small streams, private water and everything in between.

Also available are guided overnight or day trips to the gold medal Black Canyon of the Gunnison River. Custom overnight trips to our remote lodge in northwestern Gunnison County offer an unforgettable fly fishing experience and provides a different river or stream each day.

Dragonfly Anglers is licensed, bonded and insured and operates under special-use permits from USDA Forest Service, Gunnison National Forest and BLM.

"Rod Cesario is an outstanding guide. We had a very tough weather conditions... but his skill and knowledge made the adverse conditions secondary... one of the most memorable days fishing!"
Charles Wilkins

SEASONS OF OPERATION

FISH SPECIES

Brook Trout · Brown Trout · Cutthroat Trout · Rainbow Trout

ACTIVITIES & TRANSPORTATION

LOCATIONS & SERVICES

Fly Fishing Outfitters

Bill Perry

1060 Beaver Creek Blvd. • *Avon, CO 81620*
phone: (800) 595-8090 • *(970) 476-FISH (3474)* • *fax: (970) 845-8025*
email: fish@vail.net • *www.flyfishingoutfitters.net* • *Lic. #1337*

Fly Fishing Outfitters offers year-round guided fly fishing trips in the heart of Colorado ski country. Our store is conveniently located 100 miles west of Denver, along the banks of the Eagle river in the Vail valley. We are in close proximity to some of the most productive and scenic trout waters in the west.

Fly Fishing Outfitters finds the very best fishing the area has. We are fortunate to have private access agreements in place with several area ranches. This includes more than 100 miles of private access, on the Blue, Colorado, Eagle, Roaring Fork, and Yampa Rivers. Brush, Gypsum, and Sweetwater Creeks all have miles of private access for our guests who prefer smaller creeks.

Fly Fishing Outfitters also has arrangements to stay and guide on several of the best lodge and ranch properties in the west. Please inquire about your trip of a lifetime.

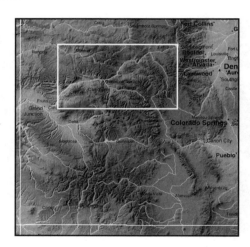

"Bill Perry ranks at the top. Very, very enjoyable each and every trip!" Steve Russell, Lincoln, NE

SEASONS OF OPERATION

FISH SPECIES

 Brook Trout Brown Trout Cutthroat Trout Rainbow Trout

ACTIVITIES & TRANSPORTATION

 CATCH & RELEASE WHITEWATER FISHING WHITEWATER TRIPS McKENZIE / DORY RAFT

LOCATIONS & SERVICES

 BLUERIBBONSTREAM LAKE LARGE RIVER POND STREAMS GUIDED ACTIVITIES LODGE HOTEL / MOTEL GOURMET MEALS

Mike Wilson's High Mountain Drifters

Mike Wilson
115 South Wisconsin St. • Gunnison, CO 81230
phone: (800) 793-4243 • (970) 641-4243

High Mountain Drifters is the Gunnison Basin's leading fly shop and guide service. We fish the most diverse and exclusive waters in the area and pride ourselves in making every trip fun.

We have male and female guides available, and they are young, experienced and enthusiastic. We offer the highest quality and most miles of private water in the valley. Trips are available for all ages and abilities. Our trips start at 9 a.m. and full day trips get back when you want them to, not at 5 p.m.

We offer free casting clinics every Saturday morning taught by the valley's only two certified casting instructors. We are a full-service, year-round shop and a dealer for Winston, Scott, Redington, Sage, Hexagraph and Cortland rods. We also carry Simms, Fly-Tech, Patagonia and Filson clothing and waders. Our catalog is available upon request.

"We have a lot of guides in this area, but I would use Mike Wilson's exclusively. They are the best!" Ray Schnickels

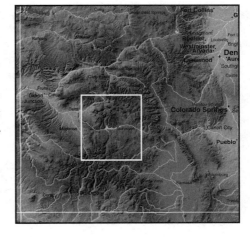

SEASONS OF OPERATION

FISH SPECIES

Northern Pike | Brook Trout | Brown Trout | Cutthroat Trout | Lake Trout | Rainbow Trout

ACTIVITIES & TRANSPORTATION

LOCATIONS & SERVICES

The Troutfitter

Dominque Eymere and Bradley Sorock

313 Elk Ave., PO Box 2779 • Crested Butte, CO 81224
phone: (970) 349-1323 • fax: (970) 349-5066 • Lic. #1655
email: info@troutfitter.com • www.troutfitter.com

The Troutfitter is located in the beautiful historic town of Crested Butte, Colorado. We offer walk/wade trips on a variety of exclusive private stretches of water.

We take that extra step to make your trip a pleasurable experience, including a catered lunch from a fine local dining establishment, two-to-one client/guide ratio, and pristine fishing water which we limit to four fishermen per day.

Our guides meet rigorous requirements of experience and are friendly, outgoing and personable.

All trips include any rental needs, including waders, boots, fly vests, and quality flyrods from G-Loomis and St. Croix.
Come fish with us.

"Would highly recommended Don for beginner. He is a very patient and a great teacher." Lee Lynch

SEASONS OF OPERATION

FISH SPECIES

ACTIVITIES & TRANSPORTATION

LOCATIONS & SERVICES

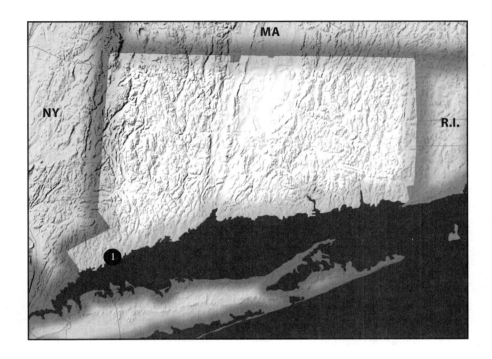

Outdoor Professionals

1 Westport Outfitters

License and Report Requirements

• Charter boat/part license is required on Saltwater fishing only.

• Fishing/Hunting guides licenses are not required at this time.

Useful information for the state of

Connecticut

State and Federal Agencies

Connecticut Dept. of Environmental Protection
79 Elm Street.
Hartford, CT 06106
Wildlife Division: (860) 424-3011
Fishing Division: (860) 424-3474
Marine Fisheries: (860) 434-6043
Bur. of Outdoors/Recreation: (860) 424-3200

Connecticut Dept. of Economic & CommunityDevelopment
505 Hudson Street
Hartford, CT 06106
http://www.state.ct.us/tourism

Connecticut River Valley & Shoreline Visitors Council
393 Main Street
Middletown, CT 06457
phone: (860) 347-0028 or 486-3346

Coastal Fairfield Visitor Bureau
297 West Avenue
Norwalk, CT 06850
phone: (800) 866-7925 or (203) 899-2799
http://www.visitfairfieldco.org

National Forest - Eastern Region
Milwaukee District Office
310 W. Wisconsin Ave., Suite 450
Milwaukee, WI 53203
phone: (414) 297-3646

Bureau of Land Management
Eastern States
7450 Boston Boulevard
Springfield, VA 22153
phone: (703) 440-1660
or (703) 440- Plus Extension
fax: (703) 440-1599

Office Hours: 8:00 a.m. - 4:30 p.m.

Associations, Publications, etc.

Federation of Fly Fishers
http://www.fedflyfishers.org

Trout Unlimited Connecticut Council
(please refer to local listings)

Connecticut Bass Federation
(please refer to local listings)

Westport Outfitters

Captain Jeff A. Northrop

570 Riverside Avenue • Westport, CT 06880
phone: (203) 226-1915 • fax: (203) 454-0857
www.saltwater-flyfishing.com

Capt. Jeff A. Northrop, considered by many as the man who pioneered Northeast saltwater flats fishing, has been stalking the Northern shallows for the past 32 years. Capt. Jeff is credited with introducing the Northeast to "flats style fly fishing and flats boats".

We have specialized in saltwater fly fishing and light tackle spin fishing since 1968. Our marina, located on the Saugatuck River, places us within 15 minutes of the Norwalk Island chain, home of world record striped bass!! Starting in the early spring you can expect to stalk migrating bass in and around the mouths of the seven rivers that flow into the Island chain. When June arrives the bass are joined on the flats by huge daisy chaining bluefish. In the fall, the striped bass and bluefish, along with bonito and false albacore, feed nonstop in anticipation of the migration south.

My guides and I hope you will come and enjoy a day of fishing with us this season.

"October fishing in Norwalk Islands is excellent. We enjoyed the fishing, guide & area!"
Captain Chuck Wiggins, McAfee, NJ

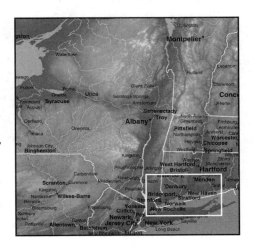

SEASONS OF OPERATION

FISH SPECIES

 Striped Bass Bluefish Mackerel Tuna

ACTIVITIES & TRANSPORTATION

LOCATIONS & SERVICES

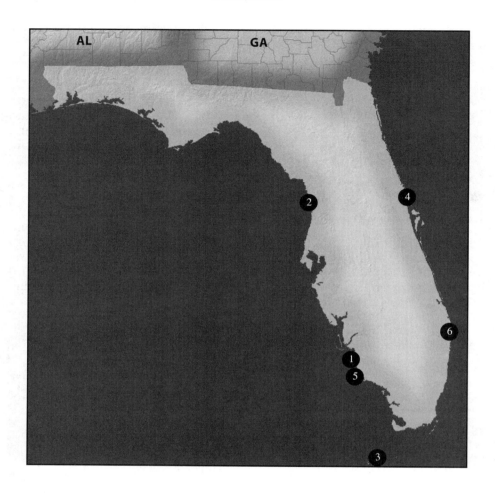

Outdoor Professionals

1. Captain Doug Hanks
2. Captain Mike Locklear
3. Fly Fishing Paradise
4. Gone Fishing
5. Look-N-Hook Charters
6. Salt & Fresh Water Fishing Charters

Useful information for the state of

Florida

State and Federal Agencies

Florida Fish & Wildlife Conservation
Commission
620 S. Meridian St.
Tallahassee, FL 32399-1600
phone: (850) 488-4676
or (850) 488-1960

Forest Service Southern Region
1720 Peachtree Road NW
Atlanta, GA 30367
phone: (404) 347-4177
TTY: (404) 347-4278

Apalachicola, Ocala, Osceola National
Forests
325 John Knox Rd., Ste. F100
Tallahassee, FL 32303
phone: (850) 942-9300
TTY: (850) 942-9351

Bureau of Land Management
Eastern States
7450 Boston Boulevard
Springfield, VA 22153
phone: (703) 440-1660
fax: (703) 440-1599

Eastern States Jackson Field Office
411 Briarwood Drive, Suite 404
Jackson, MS 39206
phone: (601) 977-5400
fax: (601) 977-5440

National Parks

Biscayne National Park
phone: (305) 247-2044

Everglades National Park
phone: (305) 242-7700

Associations, Publications, etc.

American Fisheries Society
Florida Chapter
100 8th Avenue, SE
St. Petersburg, FL 33701

Trout Unlimited Florida Council
4006 S. Florida Avenue
Lakeland, FL 33813
phone: (941) 646-1476

Federation of Fly Fishers
http://www.fedflyfishers.org

International Game Fish Association
300 Gulf Stream Way
Dania Beach, FL 33004
phone: (954) 927-2628
fax: (954) 924-4299
email: igfahq@aol.com
http://www.igfa.org

Florida Bass Chapter Federation
44 Muskogee Road
San Mateo, FL 32187
phone: (904) 328-6035

Florida Sportsmen's Conservation
Association
PO Box 20051
West Palm Beach, FL 33416-0051
phone: (561) 478-5965
fax: (561) 688-2553

Marine Industries Association of South
Florida
phone: (954) 524-0633

Outdoor Guides Association
PO Box 12996
Tallahassee, FL 32317
http://www.di.com/oga

License and Report Requirements

• State requires licensing of Saltwater Outdoor Professionals.
• Florida Fish & Wildlife Conservation Commission requires a "trip ticket" from Captain whose clients leave fish on board and Captain sells to the public. "Trip ticket" includes length of stay out, county and area, but no client names. "Trip tickets" must be turned in each month.

Captain Doug Hanks

Captain Doug Hanks
3600 Cottage Club Lane • Naples, FL 34105
phone: (941) 263-7478 • fax: (941) 263-4621

Captain Doug Hanks operates his backcountry guide service in the Everglades National Park.

Anglers travel from all locales to experience fishing in this unique environment. Alligators, manatees and abundant bird life inhabit the remote Mangrove Swamp.

The diverse wildlife only adds to the real attraction — the spectacular fishing.

Fishermen can expect to catch snook, redfish and tarpon using traditional or flyfishing tackle.

Captain Doug Hanks supplies all tackle and licenses. All equipment is top-quality, including his specialized Silverking flats skiff.

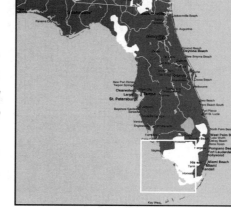

"Capt. Doug is a very capable guide who provided me with an outstanding fishing trip and new insights to the Florida Everglades / 10,000 Islands!" George Atkinson

SEASONS OF OPERATION

FISH SPECIES

 Drum
 Snook
 Tarpon

ACTIVITIES & TRANSPORTATION

 CATCH & RELEASE
 SKINNY FISHING
 FLY FISHING
 SPIN CASTING
 FLATS' SKIFF

LOCATIONS & SERVICES

 ESTUARIES
 RIVER DELTA
 SALTWATER
 GUIDED ACTIVITIES
 DAY TRIPS

Captain Mike Locklear

Captain Mike Locklear
5011 S. Craig Point • Homosassa, FL 34446
phone/fax: (352) 628-4207
e-mail: captmike@xta/wind.net • www.leisuretimetravel.com/locklear.htm

Enjoy light tackle or flyfishing the gin-clear flats of the Gulf near the Homosassa River with Captain Mike Locklear, a local professional guide of more than 20 years.

Experience the beauty of the river's lush sub-tropical landscape to and from your fishing destination. Our natural coast is protected by barrier islands and shallow waters so that even on windy days the seas seldom get too rough to fish.

Mike will direct you to a fun day on the water while pursuing different varieties of game fish such as redfish, speckled trout, tarpon and more. Enjoy a comfortable boat of modern technology while professionally guided. All gear, tackle and licenses provided. Nice efficiencies and motel rooms located next to the river.

"Excellent fishing + excellent time = Mike Locklear."

SEASONS OF OPERATION _____

FISH SPECIES _____

 Drum   Permit   Sea Trout   Tarpon

ACTIVITIES & TRANSPORTATION _____

 CATCH & RELEASE   FLY FISHING   SPIN CASTING   SKINNY FISHING   FLATS/ SKIFF

LOCATIONS & SERVICES _____

 SALTWATER   ESTUARIES   FAMILY   GUIDED ACTIVITIES   DAY TRIPS

Fly Fishing Paradise

Capt. Dexter Simmons

P.O. Box 145 • Sugarloaf, FL 33044
reservations and information: (305) 745-3304
email: captdexter@prodigy.com • http://www.keywestfishing.com

Fly fish or use light tackle to fish the saltwater flats of Key West, the Marquesas, the Florida Keys, the Bahamas, the Caribbean or Central America.

Catch and release tarpon, bonefish, permit, barracuda, shark, cobia and mutton snapper aboard "FlatsMaster" (an 18-foot Action Craft flats skiff) with Capt. Dexter Simmons.

Full day, half day and week-long charters available. Overnight excursions to the Marquesas, Bahamas, Belize, Yucatan or Central America offer an angling adventure. Deluxe accommodations available.

Top-notch fly fishing and light tackle gear, and friendly, helpful instruction included.

"A true well-educated fisherman and conservationist. I highly recommend him"
Jack Copass

SEASONS OF OPERATION

FISH SPECIES

Barracuda · Bonefish · Permit · Snapper · Shark · Tarpon

ACTIVITIES & TRANSPORTATION

LOCATIONS & SERVICES

Gone Fishing

Captain Karty and Angie Sills

3320 Mango Tree Dr. • Edgewater, FL 32141
phone: (904) 423-FISH (3474)

Discover the famous Indian River and Mosquito Lagoon with me, Captain Karty Sills on Florida's East Central Coast. Your trip begins with a majestic sunrise.

Feel the excitement of pursuing redfish, snook, trout, and tarpon on the flats and in the backcountry among the pristine Mangrove Island.

You will enjoy the beautiful habitats of birds, dolphin, alligators and manatees. I offer guided flats fishing for one or two, flyfishing for one, and river fun fishing on a pontoon boat for up to six.

Treat yourself to a gourmet shore lunch. I provide everything you need except sunglasses, sunscreen and sodas.

"Karty is an accommodating, talented and down to earth fisherman and guide. He was worth the money!" J.J. Jones

SEASONS OF OPERATION

YEAR AROUND

FISH SPECIES

 Drum   Sea Trout   Snook   Tarpon

ACTIVITIES & TRANSPORTATION

 FLY FISHING   SPIN CASTING   SKINNY FISHING   FLATS' SKIFF

LOCATIONS & SERVICES

 ESTUARIES   KIDS PROGRAMS   FAMILY   GUIDED ACTIVITIES   DAY TRIPS   FISH CLEANING

Look-N-Hook Charters

Capt. Jim and Shari Nickerson

3100 4th St. N.E. • Naples, FL 34120-1339
phone: (941) 353-5448 • fax: (941) 353-5879
email: tarpon500@aol.com

Capt. Jim is an experienced backcountry guide who specializes in sight fishing for snook, redfish, and tarpon on a fly or spin rod in Everglades National Park and Ten Thousand Islands. Established in 1989, Look-N-Hook is endorsed by Orvis and is a member of Yamaha's elite guide program.

Look-N-Hook, Capt. Jim's 17-foot Action Craft flats skiff, roams the nation's ninth largest national park in search of prized game fish. Enjoy the calm waters and the tranquil beauty shared by nature's creatures such as manatee, dolphin, alligator and a variety of birds. It is truly a fisherman's dream and a nature lover's paradise.

The boat is limited to two anglers, but Capt. Jim will accommodate larger groups by booking additional boats. Half-day and full-day trips available.

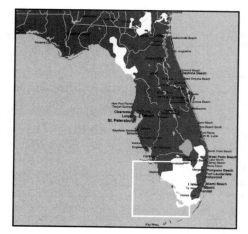

"Wonderful trip, great guide, great fishing...couldn't have asked for a better time!" Phillip Schwartz

SEASONS OF OPERATION

FISH SPECIES

 Drum Snook Sea Trout Shark Tarpon

ACTIVITIES & TRANSPORTATION

 Catch & Release Fly Fishing Spin Casting Skinny Fishing Trophy Fishing #1 Flats Skiff

LOCATIONS & SERVICES

 Estuaries Family Guided Activities Day Trips

Salt & Fresh Water Fishing Charters

Captain Charlie Clyne

1879 E. Terrace Dr. Lake Worth, FL 33460
phone: (800) 226-1766 • (561) 588-1766 • cell: (561) 762-7146
fax: (561) 585-8191 • www.captain@flinet.com

Captain Charlie Clyne has more than 30 years' experience in saltwater and freshwater fishing.

Feel free to ask questions as he has a wealth of knowledge about fish patterns, behavior and local idiosyncrasies for the areas you will be fishing. Fishing expert Curt Gowdy (The American Sportsman) fishes with Captain Charlie at least once a week.

Captain Charlie holds a commercial fishing occupation license for Palm Beach County and the city of Lake Worth, and belongs to the 1,300 member West Palm Beach Fishing Club. Captain Charlie offers both saltwater and freshwater fishing charters aboard one of his two available vessels. Love flyfishing? That's Captain Charlies personal favorite.

SEASONS OF OPERATION

FISH SPECIES

 Amberjack
 Snook
 Tarpon

ACTIVITIES & TRANSPORTATION

 CATCH & RELEASE
 FLY FISHING
 SPIN CASTING
 SKINNY FISHING
 FLATS SKIFF

LOCATIONS & SERVICES

 RIVER DELTA
 KIDS PROGRAMS
 FAMILY
 GUIDED ACTIVITIES
 DAY TRIPS
 WOMEN ONLY TRIPS

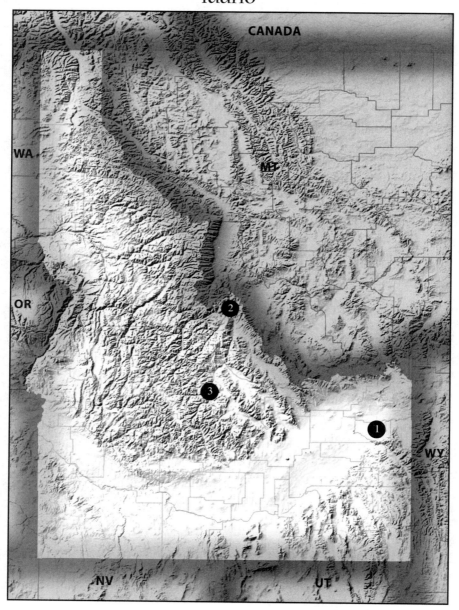

Outdoor Professionals

1. Heise Expeditions
2. Solitude River Trips
3. Wilderness Outfitters

Idaho

State and Federal Agencies

Idaho Fish & Game Dept.
600 South Walnut
Boise, ID 83707
phone: (208) 334-3700
fax: (208) 334-2114

Outfitter & Guides Licensing Board
1365 N. Orchard, Room 172
Boise, ID 83706
phone: (208) 327-7380
fax: (208) 327-7382

Forest Service
Northern Region
Federal Bldg.
PO Box 7669
Missoula, MT 59807-7669
phone: (406) 329-3616
TTY: (406) 329-3510

Clearwater National Forest
phone: (208) 476-4541

Idaho Panhandle, Coeur d'Alene, Kaniksu,
St. Joe National Forests
phone / TTY: (208) 765-7223

Nez Perce National Forest
phone: (208) 983-1950

Bureau of Land Management
Idaho State Office
1387 S. Vinnell Way
Boise, ID 83709-1657
phone: (208) 373-3896
or (208) 373-plus extension
fax: (208) 373-3899
Office Hours 7:45 a.m. - 4:15 p.m.

Associations, Publications, etc.

Trout Unlimited Idaho Council
212 N. Fourth Street #145
Sandpoint, ID 83864-9466
phone: (208) 263-4433
fax: (208) 265-2996

American Fisheries Society
Edward D. Koch
3765 La Mesita Way
Boise, ID 83072
phone: (208) 378-5293
Email: ted_koch@mail.fws.gov

Federation of Fly Fishers
http://www.fedflyfishers.org

Idaho Bass Chapter Federation
President: Allan Chandler
9906 W. Deep Canyon Drive
Star, ID 83669
phone: (208) 859-5433 (day)
Email: chandlr@micron.net

Idaho Outfitters & Guides Association
PO Box 95
Boise, ID 83701
phone: (208) 342-1438
fax: (208) 338-7830
Email: info@ioga.org • http://www.ioga.org

License and Report Requirements

• State requires licensing of Outdoor Professionals.
• State requires that every Outfitter be it bird, fish, big game, river rafting, trail riding or packing file a "Use Report" annually.
• Bureau of Land Management requires Special Use Permit for commercial guiding on BLM property.
• Currently, no requirements for Guest/Dude Ranches.

Heise Expeditions

Mike Quinn

5116 E. Heise Rd. • Ririe, ID 83443
phone: (800) 828-3984 • (208) 538-7453 • fax: (208) 538-6039

Heise Resort is nestled in the heart of the world's finest cutthroat trout fishing, just 20 miles east of Idaho Falls. Airport transportation can be arranged; car rentals are available.

Our professional guides are customer-oriented to provide everything necessary for an exciting and enjoyable trip. Experience the beauty, serenity and uniqueness of Idaho's "blueribbon" cutthroat fishing on the South Fork of the Snake River. With hot springs, lodging, golf course and beautiful scenery, you'll get hooked on what we have to offer.

For over 100 years, the family-owned Heise Resort has set traditions of excellence which have kept customers coming back. Blending history with modern recreation, Heise Expeditions continues to provide that unique experience with nature that will keep you coming back.

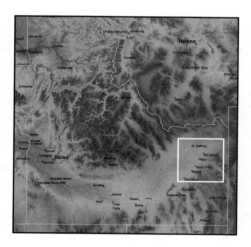

"I simply had an excellent time." Robert Kelton

SEASONS OF OPERATION

FISH SPECIES

ACTIVITIES & TRANSPORTATION

LOCATIONS & SERVICES

Solitude River Trips

Al and Jeana Bukowsky
main office: P.O. Box 907 • Merlin, OR 97532
summer (June-August): P.O. Box 702 • Salmon, ID 83467
phone: (800) 396-1776 • www.rivertrips.com

Although just floating the river is an exhilarating and enlightening experience, flyfishermen will find the Middle Fork of the Salmon River a heaven on Earth.

Since 1973, a catch-and-release, single, barbless hook-only policy has been in effect. The native cutthroat trout, the predominant species, has thrived and, along with a few native rainbow and Dolly Varden trout, provides some of the finest fishing in the country. The trout average 12 to 15 inches in length, with some up to 19 inches. You don't even have to be an expert to catch these beautiful fish.

Our guides offer patient fly-casting instruction for the novice, while also providing helpful tips for the most experienced angler.

The plentiful trout make the Middle Fork a great place to learn, or to simply improve one's fishing skills.

"Top river float in the West for dry fly action on native Cutthroat...great staff and food." Gene and Debbi Hering

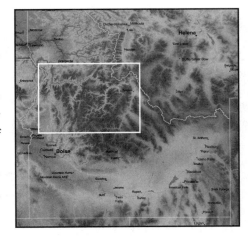

SEASONS OF OPERATION

FISH SPECIES

ACTIVITIES & TRANSPORTATION

LOCATIONS & SERVICES

Wilderness Outfitters

Scott, Shelda, Justin and Jerrod Farr

P.O. Box 64 • Challis, ID 83226
phone: (208) 879-2203 • fax: (208) 879-2204
email: farr@cyberhighway.net • www.fsr.com/wildernessoutfitters/

If you are a hard-core fly fisherman in search of solitude and trout that has seldom, if ever, laid eyes on an artificial fly, search no further. The resources at our back door can provide all these things and more.

Our streams and high mountain lakes can offer this scenario without so much as a ripple of concern.

Our expertise and equipment will provide the means to access your dreams without undue impact on these pristine places.

We operate from a private ranch located at the mouth of Loon Creek on the Middle Fork of the Salmon River. We are accessible by raft, horseback, hiking or aircraft.

"...we horsebacked to a 'secret' mountain lake that was teeming with 16"-24" Cutthroats that were absolutely breathtaking in their color! A true wilderness trout adventure!!" Paul B. Dorsch, Jr. Finleyville, PA

SEASONS OF OPERATION

FISH SPECIES

Cutthroat Trout | Dolly Varden | Rainbow Trout

ACTIVITIES & TRANSPORTATION

CATCH & RELEASE | FLY FISHING | SPIN CASTING | WHITEWATER FISHING | HOT SPRINGS | HIKING/TREKKING | HORSEBACK | RAFT | HORSE PACK TRIPS

LOCATIONS & SERVICES

LAKE | STREAMS | KIDS PROGRAMS | FAMILY | SENIOR CITIZEN | AGE + FULL BOARD | DOME/5 PERSON TENT | WALL TENTS | WOMEN ONLY TRIPS

Maine

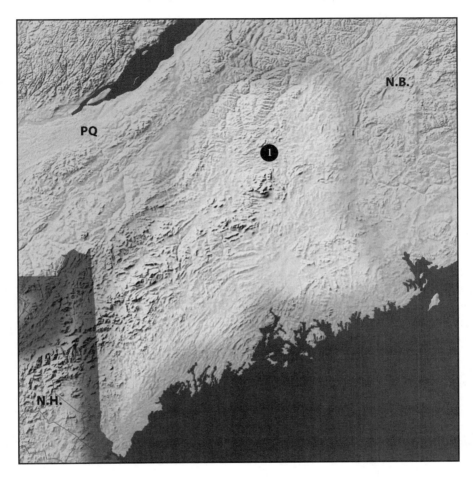

Outdoor Professionals

1 Libby Sporting Camps

License and Report Requirements

• State requires licensing of Outdoor Professionals.

• Monthly Head Fee Guides Report required for Whitewater River Companies.

• No report required for Hunting and Fishing Professionals.

Useful information for the state of

Maine

State and Federal Agencies

Maine Dept. of Fish & Wildlife
284 State St. Station #41
Augusta, ME 04333
phone: (207) 287-8000
fax: (207) 287-6395

Forest Service
Eastern Region
310 West Wisconsin Ave. Rm 500
Milwaukee, WI 53203
phone: (414) 297-3646
TTY: (414) 297-3507

White Mountain National Forest
Federal Building
719 Main Street
Laconia, NH 03246
phone: (603) 528-8721

Bureau of Land Management
Eastern States
7450 Boston Boulevard
Springfield, VA 22153
phone: (703) 440-1660
or (703) 440- Plus Extension
fax: (703) 440-1599

Office Hours: 8:00 a.m. - 4:30 p.m.

Eastern States
Milwaukee District Office
310 W. Wisconsin Ave., Suite 450
(P.O. Box 631 53201-0631)
Milwaukee, WI 53203
phone: (414) 297-4450
fax: (414) 297-4409

National Parks

Acadia National Park
phone: (207) 288-3338

Associations, Publications, etc.

Trout Unlimited Maine Council
President: Dick Walthers
75 Bow Street
Otisfield, ME 04270
phone: (207) 743-7461

Federation of Fly Fishers
http://www.fedflyfishers.org

Atlantic Salmon Commission
650 State St.
Bangor, ME 04401-5654
phone: (207) 941-4449
fax: (207) 941-4443

American Bass Assoc. of Maine
20 Marshwood Estates
Eliot, ME 03903
phone: (207) 748-1744

Sportsman's Alliance of Maine
RR 1, Box 1174
Church Hill Road
Augusta, ME 04330-9749
phone: (207) 622-5503
fax: (207) 622-5596

Maine Bass Chapter Federation
RR 1. Box 332
Hollis Center, ME 04042
phone: (207) 929-8553

Maine Professional Guide Association
phone: (207) 549-5631 or 549-4579

The Maine Sportsman
phone: (207) 846-9501

Libby Sporting Camps

Matthew and Ellen Libby

P.O. Box V, Dept. 0 • Ashland, ME 04732
radio phone: (207) 435-8274 • fax: (207) 435-3230
email: libbycam@libbycam.sdi.agate.net

The Libby family has operated a lodge and guide service in the Aroostook and Allagash River headwaters of Maine since 1890. The camp is located 150 miles north of Bangor in the heart of a 4-million acre wilderness near the Canadian border. Hunting for trophy deer, bear and moose is second to none in the state. An abundance of grouse rounds out the hunter's dream.

The six guest cabins are comfortable, clean, spacious and private. The food is home-cooked and served family-style in the dining room overlooking the lake. The cabins are handcrafted — from the peeled log timbers and immense fieldstone fireplace in the lodge to the handmade quilts on the beds.

Perfect accommodations for families, business groups and honeymooners.

"If you fish you have to fish at Libby's at least once in your life. It is an outstanding experience in every way." Tom Baynes

SEASONS OF OPERATION

FISH SPECIES

ACTIVITIES & TRANSPORTATION

LOCATIONS & SERVICES

Top Rated Professionals in
Montana

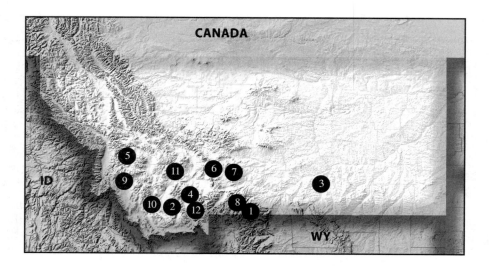

Outdoor Professionals

1. Beartooth Plateau Outfitters
2. Broken Arrow Lodge
3. Eagle Nest Lodge
4. East Slope Anglers
5. Esper's Under Wild Skies Lodge & Outfitters
6. Grossenbacher Guides
7. Hatch Finder's
8. Rocky Fork Guide Service
9. The Complete Fly Fisher
10. The Reflective Angler
11. Tite Line Fishing
12. Wild Trout Outfitters

License and Report Requirements
• State requires licensing of Outdoor Professionals.
• State requires an "Annual Client Report Log" for all Hunting and Fishing Outfitters.
• State does not regulate River Guides.
• Guest/Dude Ranches need to get an Outfitter license only if they take guest to fish or hunt on land that they do not own.

Useful information for the state of
Montana

State and Federal Agencies

Montana Board of Outfitters
Dept. of Commerce
Arcade Building - 111 North Jackson
Helena, MT 59620-0407
phone: (406) 444-3738

Montana Dept. of Fish, Wildlife & Parks
1420 East 6th
Helena, MT 59620
phone: (406) 444-2535

Forest Service
Northern Region
Federal Building
PO Box 7669
Missoula, MT 59807-7669
phone: (406) 329-3616
TTY: (406) 329-3510

Bitterroot National Forest
phone: (406) 363-3131

Custer National Forest
phone / TTY: (406) 248-9885

Flathead National Forest
phone: (406) 755-5401

Gallatin National Forest
phone / TTY: (406) 587-6920
fax: (406) 587-6758

Helena National Forest
phone: (406) 449-5201

Kootenai National Forest
phone: (406) 293-6211

Lewis & Clark National Forest
phone: (406) 791-7700

Lolo National Forest
phone: (406) 329-3750

Bureau of Land Management
Montana State Office
Granite Tower
222 North 32nd Street
P.O. Box 36800
Billings, MO 59107-6800
phone: (406) 255-2885
fax: (406) 255-2762
Email - mtinfo@mt.blm.gov
Office Hours: 8:00 a.m. - 4:30 p.m.

National Parks

Glacier National Park
phone: (406) 888-5441

Associations, Publications, etc.

Fishing Outfitters Assoc. of Montana
PO Box 67
Gallatin Gateway, MT 59730
phone: (406) 763-5436

Federation of Fly Fishers
PO Box 1595
502 South 19th, Ste. #1
Bozeman, MT 59771
phone: (406) 585-7592
fax: (406) 585-7596
http://www.fedflyfishers.org

Trout Unlimited Montana Council
Council Chairman: Michael A. Bushly
2611 - 5th Avenue South
Great Falls, MT 59405-3023
phone: (406) 727-8787
fax: (406) 727-2402
Email: mbushly@cmrussell.org
http://www.montanatu.org

Montana Bass Chapter Federation
12345 O'Keefe Road
Missoula, MT 59812
phone: (406) 728-8842

Beartooth Plateau Outfitters, Inc.

Ronnie L. Wright

P.O. Box 1127 • Cooke City, MT 59020-1127
phone: (800) 253-8545 • (406) 838-2328 June-Sept. • (406) 445-2293 Oct.-May

Beartooth Plateau Outfitters specializes in "away from the crowd" horseback pack trips into the back country of Yellowstone Park and the spectacular, unspoiled Absaroka-Beartooth Wilderness, as featured on "the Fishin' Hole", hosted by Jerry McKinnis-ESPN-TV.

Our pack trips into the Absaroka-Beartooth Wilderness offer literally hundreds of high, pristine, alpine lakes full of a wide variety of trout (cutthroat, brook, golden and rainbow), and arctic grayling. Our Yellowstone Park pack trips offer secluded fishing in famous trout waters such as: the Lamar River and Slough Creek.

We'd like to invite you to let us be your hosts and show you the Yellowstone Park backcountry and the Absaroka-Beartooth Wilderness high lake area. Orvis® Fly Fishing Expedition Outfitter.

"Ronnie & his staff have mastered the art and science of a low impact pack trip into the wilderness. They pay attention to every little detail, and customer safety and satisfaction is their top priority." John Frost, Norfork, MA

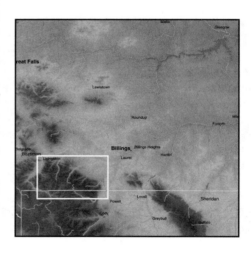

SEASONS OF OPERATION

FISH SPECIES

    ...

Arctic Grayling | Brook Trout | Cutthroat Trout | Lake Trout | Rainbow Trout

ACTIVITIES & TRANSPORTATION

Catch & Release | Fly Fishing | Spin Casting | Hiking/Trekking | Bird Watching | Horseback | Horse Pack Trips

LOCATIONS & SERVICES

Blue Ribbon Stream | Lake | Kids Programs | Family | Cabins | Dome/Spike Tent | Full Board | Wall Tents | Overnight Trips

Broken Arrow Lodge

Erwin and Sherry Clark

2200 Upper Ruby Rd., P.O. Box 177 • Alder, MT 59710
phone: (800) 775-2928 • phone/fax: (406) 842-5437
www.recworld.com/state/mt/hunt/broken/broken.html

With private access and minimal fishing pressure, the Ruby offers some of the finest fishing in Montana and tends to be the most popular with our guests.

The Ruby is a friendly stream, easily waded. The small streams in the backcountry are easily accessible and offer great fishing for cutthroats along with breathtaking scenery and abundant wildlife. Lake fishing on Clark Canyon provides an opportunity to catch the "big fish," rainbows and browns average 4-1/2 pounds. A short distance from the lodge, float trips on the Big Hole, Madison, Yellowstone, Beaverhead and Jefferson rivers are available on request and provide exhilarating experiences with beautiful scenery, quality fishing and the thrill of floating the river. We recommend mid-June until late September for the most rewarding fishing trip.

We offer the option to fish on your own or with a guide.

"The hospitality was wonderful...we felt like we were visiting friends." Mary Ann McGuire

SEASONS OF OPERATION

FISH SPECIES

 Brook Trout   Brown Trout   Cutthroat Trout   Rainbow Trout

ACTIVITIES & TRANSPORTATION

LOCATIONS & SERVICES

Eagle Nest Lodge

Keith Kelly

P.O. Box 509 • Hardin, MT 59034
phone: (406) 665-3711 • fax: (406) 665-3712

Eagle Nest Lodge is one of the world's premier fly-fishing destinations and has the distinction of being one of the first Orvis®-endorsed operations.

A family business since its conception in 1982, Eagle Nest is owned and managed by the Kellys. The services, lodging and dining of this Montana sporting lodge have satisfied the most discerning anglers for more than a decade.

Eagle Nest is secluded on the banks of the Bighorn River, a fishery heralded as one of the world's finest for the remarkable number of trophy browns and rainbows it holds. Out of the Big Horn Mountains flows the Tongue River, a stream that boasts fantastic scenery in addition to solitude and an abundance of cutthroat, rainbow and brown trout.

"The Bighorn River is a fly-fishing experience every angler should take advantage of...I give Eagle Nest, its staff and guides, my total endorsement." Leigh H. Perkins, Chairman, ORVIS

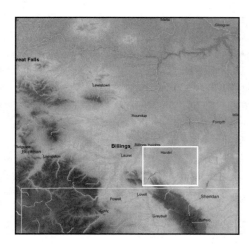

SEASONS OF OPERATION

FISH SPECIES

Brown Trout	Cutthroat Trout	Rainbow Trout

ACTIVITIES & TRANSPORTATION

LOCATIONS & SERVICES

East Slope Anglers

Brad Parsch and Wayne Rooney

P.O. Box 160249 • Big Sky, MT 59716
phone: (888) Fly Fysh (359-3974) • (406) 995-4369
www.eastslopeanglers.com

Our fishing guides are among the best available. They have the knowledge to be successful and the ability to impart their knowledge in a helpful and friendly manner. From beginner to expert, we can make your fishing experience a rewarding one. Youngsters are welcome.

Float trips are day-long on one of the float-fishing rivers in the area. Wade trips can be arranged for a half or full day with a maximum of three fishermen per guide. Full-day trips include lunch and can involve any number of waters in the area. We also provide instruction by the hour.

One-day and overnight horseback trips to less accessible waters around Big Sky are also available through East Slope Anglers. These trips can be enjoyed with non-fishing members. Most trips involve rides to alpine lakes and the use of float-tubes.

"I couldn't believe the number of fish we caught and released. Would give my un-qualified recommendation to anyone to use these services!" Don Tillery

SEASONS OF OPERATION

YEAR AROUND

FISH SPECIES

 Brook Trout Brown Trout Cutthroat Trout Lake Trout Rainbow Trout

ACTIVITIES & TRANSPORTATION

 CATCH & RELEASE WHITEWATER FISHING FLY TYING SCHOOL FLY FISHING SCHOOL McKENZIE / DORY RAFT HORSE PACK TRIPS

LOCATIONS & SERVICES

 STREAMS LAKE POND KIDS PROGRAMS FAMILY HANDICAP WOMEN ONLY TRIPS  DAY TRIPS OVERNIGHT TRIPS

Esper's Under Wild Skies Lodge & Outfitters

Vaughn and Judy Esper

P.O. Box 849 • Philipsburg, MT 59858
phone: (406) 859-3000 • fax: (406) 859-3161

Under Wild Skies Lodge and Outfitters is located in the Deerlodge National Forest at the boundary of the Anaconda Pintler Wilderness.

Our guest ranch offers something for everyone. For the fisherman we have two lakes on the ranch. The Middle Fork of Rock Creek, which traverses the property, offers four species of trout. Take a scenic wilderness horseback ride for a day or overnight pack trip into the majestic Pintler mountains, or just relax in the casual elegance of the lodge.

At Under Wild Skies we take pride in our facilities, services and the meticulous attention we pay to every detail of your stay. You come as a guest and leave as a friend.

"Under Wild Skies, Vaughn and Judy Esper, were the best experience I ever had in fishing, horseback riding and general exploring of the Anaconda/Pintler Wilderness area." Brad Windsor

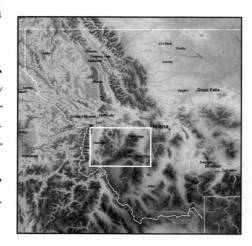

SEASONS OF OPERATION

FISH SPECIES

 Brook Trout Cutthroat Trout Dolly Varden Rainbow Trout

ACTIVITIES & TRANSPORTATION

 CATCH & RELEASE FLY FISHING   MOTOR BOAT CANOE HORSE PACK TRIPS

LOCATIONS & SERVICES

 BLUE RIBBON STREAM LAKE POND KIDS PROGRAMS FAMILY LODGE FULL BOARD GOURMET MEALS DROP CAMPS

Grossenbacher Guides

Brian and Jenny Grossenbacher

P.O. Box 6704 • Bozeman, MT 59771
phone: (406) 582-1760 • fax: (406) 582-0589

At Grossenbacher Guides, we guarantee customer service and satisfaction.

We not only work hard to get you into fish, but also to fill your expectations of a paramount flyfishing adventure.

Our philosophy, *The Total Flyfishing Experience*, follows the belief that a great day of fishing not only includes plenty of fish, but also an appreciation for the surrounding ecosystems, regional history and geology.

We place a premium on education; whether it's an improvement on your cast, a faster way to tie knots, or a brief lesson in ornithology, you will take home more than just memories of a great trip.

"In a word, he was 'outstanding'. Brian could give lessons to most of the services industry, as far as attention to detail, interpersonal skills and customers service." Kevin Critzer

SEASONS OF OPERATION _____

FISH SPECIES _____

Brown Trout   Rainbow Trout

ACTIVITIES & TRANSPORTATION _____

LOCATIONS & SERVICES _____

Hatch Finder's Fly Shop

Dean A. Reiner

120 South M St. • Livingston, MT 59047
phone: (406) 222-0989
email: hatchfinders@mcn.net • www. mcn.net/~hatchfinders

Spring and summer fishing on the Yellowstone River can be the challenge of a lifetime. Prolific caddis hatches in May produce the first major dry fly fishing of the year. The river comes alive with aggressive fish beginning with the salmon fly hatch in early July followed by hoppers in August and September.

DePuy's and Armstrong's Spring creeks are the mecca of fly fishing summer or winter. Hatches occur daily along 2.5 miles of the creek. Nymphing and dry fly fishing are not for the faint of heart.

Float trips by drift boats seat two fishermen at a time. Large parties can easily be accommodated. Enjoy the beautiful Paradise Valley where wildlife abounds and the scenery is breathtaking.

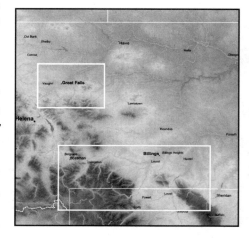

"Dean did an outstanding job overall to make my trip a lasting great memory."
Capt. Rodney Smith

SEASONS OF OPERATION

FISH SPECIES

Brown Trout	Rainbow Trout

ACTIVITIES & TRANSPORTATION

LOCATIONS & SERVICES

Rocky Fork Guide Service

Ernie Strum
HC 50, Box 4849 • Red Lodge, MT 59068
phone: (406) 446-2514

It is our business and great pleasure to offer fly fishing trips tailored to the client's desires.

You'll float the Yellowstone, Stillwater or other rivers, fishing from a drift boat and stopping at productive spots to wade and fish from shore. Or, you may prefer a hiking/wading day on a smaller mountain stream, high lake or private pond ... it's up to you.

We'll provide transportation, a hearty shore lunch, tackle and flies if desired, and as much instruction and advice as you wish. Our guides are experienced, licensed and insured.

Outfitter Ernie Strum is a Federation of Fly Fishers-certified casting instructor.

"...great people who are extremely knowledgable and proficient in the art and skill of fly fishing. I would certainly recommend Rocky Fork Guide Service most highly." L. Rex Smith

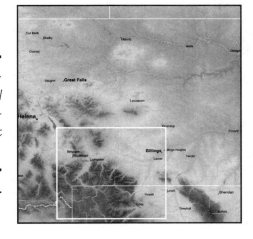

SEASONS OF OPERATION

SPRING | SUMMER | FALL

FISH SPECIES

Brook Trout | Brown Trout | Cutthroat Trout | Rainbow Trout

ACTIVITIES & TRANSPORTATION

CATCH & RELEASE | WHITEWATER FISHING | FLY FISHING SCHOOL | McKENZIE / DORY | RAFT

LOCATIONS & SERVICES

BLUE RIBBON STREAM | POND | LAKE | KIDS PROGRAMS | FAMILY | GUIDED ACTIVITIES | DAY TRIPS

The Complete Fly Fisher

David W. and Stuart Decker
Box 127 • Wise River, MT 59762
phone: (406) 832-3175 • fax: (406) 832-3169
email: comfly@montana.com • www.completeflyfisher.com

There are few places on this earth where legendary water, wild trout and five-star hospitality come together to provide the perfect balance. Where solitude, relaxation, challenge and excitement coexist. This is where life and angling combine to create the Complete Fly Fisher.

What makes one fly fishing experience different from another? Well, there's the river and we've got some of the world's best. There's the level of experience of the angler, or the guide, and we've definitely got the best.

But what really sets your time at The Complete Fly Fisher apart is the hospitality. Our staff and our guides are totally committed to anticipating your needs.

We've fine-tuned the perfect fly fishing experience.

"Dave and Stuart Decker run one of the most professional operations I've ever seen...it will be an annual event for many years to come." Josh Gelman

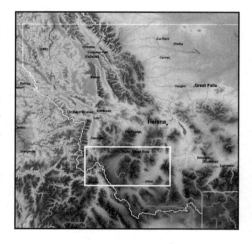

SEASONS OF OPERATION

FISH SPECIES

 Arctic Grayling
 Brook Trout
 Brown Trout
 Cutthroat Trout
 Rainbow Trout

ACTIVITIES & TRANSPORTATION

 CATCH & RELEASE
 WHITEWATER FISHING
 FLY TYING SCHOOL
 FLY FISHING SCHOOL
 HORSEBACK
 HORSE PACK TRIPS
 RAFT

LOCATIONS & SERVICES

 BLUE RIBBON STREAM
 LARGE RIVER
 KIDS PROGRAMS
 FAMILY
 HANDICAP
 LODGE
 FULL BOARD
 HOT SPRINGS
 OVERNIGHT TRIPS

The Reflective Angler

Eric and Al Troth

P.O. Box 6401 • Bozeman, MT 59771 (winter)
P.O. Box 1307 • Dillon, MT 59725 (summer)
phone: (406) 582-7600 (Bozeman) • (406) 683-2752 (Dillon)

We stalked to within two rod lengths of a large brown trout feeding on mayflies beneath a bank of willows. A perfect cast and the water exploded with a splash as the 20-incher seized the fly. It was the beginning of an unforgettable memory.

I seek to provide the extra dimension and personal attention that makes your trip truly satisfying. I share waters that I know intimately from more than 20 years' experience, and I specialize in instructing the fine points of dry fly and nymphing techniques.

Our daily float/wade excursions to southwestern Montana's blue-ribbon Beaverhead and Big Hole Rivers begin in Dillon (a range of accommodations are available). I cater to individuals, pairs and small parties and personally guide all trips.

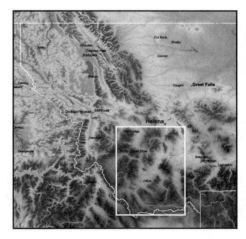

"A first class guide whose main year round profession is guiding fly fishermen. An excellent teacher! He ties and provides all flies for various waters and situation. The BEST!"

SEASONS OF OPERATION

FISH SPECIES

 Brown Trout   Rainbow Trout

ACTIVITIES & TRANSPORTATION

LOCATIONS & SERVICES

Tite Line Fishing

John Seidel

1520 Pancheri Dr. • Idaho Falls, ID 83402
toll free: (877) LV2-FISH • phone: (208) 529-4343 • fax: (208) 529-4397
email: jseidel@hydeboats.com

Tite Line Fishing offers the absolute best in fly fishing on the Missouri River, and some of the best fishing in all of Montana and the western United States.

Our professional resident guides will put you where the fish are. Their enthusiasm helps make them experts on the river's hatches and effective fly patterns. We practice catch and release.

From the beginning angler to the seasoned, Tite Line Fishing will ensure your trip is a lifetime experience. The Missouri River is populated by 5,500 trout per mile with the average length 16 to 17 inches.

In addition to the trout, you will find a variety of Montana wildlife and breathtaking scenery.

"One of the very best guided floats I've been on ... very enjoyable, what more could one want!" Robert S. Pulcipher

SEASONS OF OPERATION

FISH SPECIES

Brown Trout   Rainbow Trout

ACTIVITIES & TRANSPORTATION

LOCATIONS & SERVICES

Wild Trout Outfitters

J.D. Bingman

P.O. Box 160003 • Big Sky, MT 59716
phone: (406) 995-4895 • Fly Shop: (406) 995-2975 • 1-800-4AFISH2 (423-4742)
fax: (406) 995-3678 • www.gomontana.com/WildTrout.html

Wild Trout Outfitters offers the following exciting trout fishing experiences:

Walk/Wade Trips: This is a trip for anglers of all skill levels. It is an excellent opportunity to gain confidence in areas such as casting, knot tying, stream entomology and wading safety. **Float Trips:** Riding downstream in a safe, comfortable drift boat, two anglers with a guide have an excellent opportunity for trophy trout fishing, all the while enjoying a tremendous view of the river and surrounding landscape. **Float Tube Fishing:** This is an excellent way to access the numerous alpine lakes. Float tube fishing for the "Gulpers" of Hebgen and Quake lakes can produce huge rainbow and brown trout. **Full Day Horsepack Trips:** A horseback fishing trip is one of the most memorable fly-fishing adventures you can have. Horsepack fly-fishing trips offer an unparalleled opportunity to fish the crystalline mountain lakes and streams.

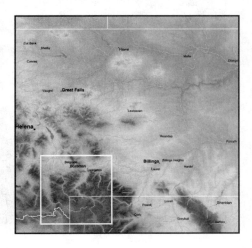

"J.D. Bingman is fun to be with – more fun to fish with. He's fished the Madison River so many times, he knows the fish by name…." John F. Fisher, Sedona, AZ

SEASONS OF OPERATION

FISH SPECIES

Arctic Grayling | Brook Trout | Brown Trout | Cutthroat Trout | Rainbow Trout

ACTIVITIES & TRANSPORTATION

CATCH & RELEASE | FLY FISHING | WHITEWATER FISHING | WHITEWATER TRIPS | HORSE PACK TRIPS | McKENZIE / DORY

LOCATIONS & SERVICES

BLUE RIBBON STREAM | LAKE | STREAMS | GUIDED ACTIVITIES | DAY TRIPS

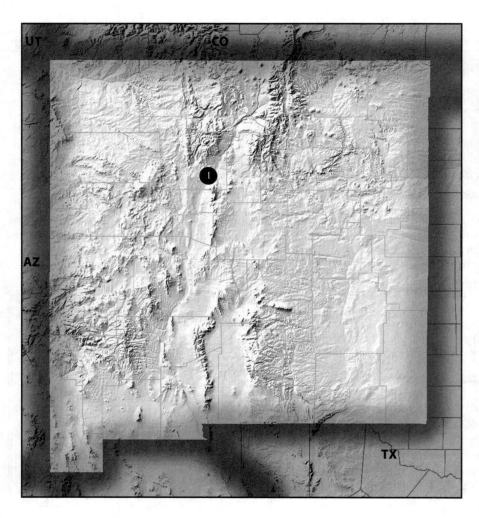

Outdoor Professionals

 **The Reel Life**

License and Report Requirements

- State requires that Hunting Outfitters be licensed.
- State requires the filing of an "Annual Report of Outfitters' Clients" for hunting only.
- "Use Permit" required for Fish and River Outfitters using BLM and Forest Service lands. They are not required to file any reports.

Useful information for the state of

New Mexico

State and Federal Agencies

New Mexico Fish and Game
PO Box 25112
Santa Fe, NM 87504
phone: (505) 827-7911
fax: (505) 827-7915

General Info & Proclamation Requests
(800) 862-9310

Forest Service
Southwestern Region
Federal Building
517 Gold Avenue SW
Albuquerque, NM 87102
phone: (505) 842-3300
TTY: (505) 842-3898

Carson National Forest
phone: (505) 758-6200

Cibola National Forest
phone / TTY: (505) 761-4650

Gila National Forest
phone: (505) 388-8201

Lincoln National Forest
phone: (505) 434-7200

Santa Fe National Forest
phone: (505) 438-7840

Bureau of Land Management
New Mexico State Office
1474 Rodeo Road
Santa Fe, NM 87505

Mailing Address:
P.O. Box 27115
Santa Fe, NM 87502-0115

Information Number: (505) 438-7400
fax: (505) 438-7435
Office Hours: 7:45 a.m. - 4:30 p.m.

National Parks

Carlsbad Caverns National Park
3225 National Parks Hwy.
Carlsbad, NM 88220
phone: (505) 785-2232
Email: cave_interpretation@nps.gov

Associations, Publications, etc.

American Fisheries Society
New Mexico Chapter
C. Marc Wethington
New Mexico Dept. of Fish & Game
PO Box 6429
Navajo Dam, NM 87419
phone: (505) 623-8818 or (505) 827-7915

Federation of Fly Fishers
http://www.fedflyfishers.org

Trout Unlimited Rio Grande Chapter
President: Michael Norte
7849 Quintana NE
Albuquerque, NM 87109
phone: (505) 844-0935

New Mexico Bass Chapter Federation
PO Box 717
Socorro, NM 87801
phone: (505) 835-1200

New Mexico Council of Outfitters & Guides, Inc.
160 Washington SE #75
Albuquerque, NM 87108
phone: (505) 764-2670

The Reel Life

Manuel J. Monasterio
1100 San Mateo Blvd. NE, Ste. 10 • Albuquerque, NM 87110
510 Montezuma • Santa Fe, NM 87501
phone: (888) 268-3474 • (505) 268-1693

New Mexico is one of fly fishing's best-kept secrets. Excellent weather, beautiful scenery and plentiful trout waters provide truly memorable, year-round fly fishing. Whether you are conducting business in Albuquerque, sight-seeing in Santa Fe or skiing in Taos, our experienced guides can meet you at or drive you to the most productive stretch of water. Choose from world-class, private spring creeks on the Rio Penasco; private stretches on medium-sized tailwaters such as the Cimarron, Costilla or Culebra; and scenic western freestone rivers like the Pecos or Rio Grande; or phenomenal high lakes.

Anglers seeking solitude will enjoy our overnight llama pack trips. Our Albuquerque shop is located 10 minutes from the airport, and our new Santa Fe location is a short walk from the historic plaza district. Both shops offer an extensive selection of Orvis® tackle, clothing and gifts.

"An excellent experience. The guide was very attentive to our needs. I'd go with this outfitter in a heartbeat!" Kevin Sedota

SEASONS OF OPERATION _____

FISH SPECIES _____

Northern Pike | Brown Trout | Rainbow Trout

ACTIVITIES & TRANSPORTATION _____

CATCH & RELEASE | FLY FISHING | LLAMA PACK TRIPS | FLY TYING SCHOOL | FLY FISHING SCHOOL

LOCATIONS & SERVICES _____

RUBBER BOOTS/STREAM | LARGE RIVER | GUIDED ACTIVITIES | DROP CAMPS | DAY TRIPS | OVERNIGHT TRIPS

New York

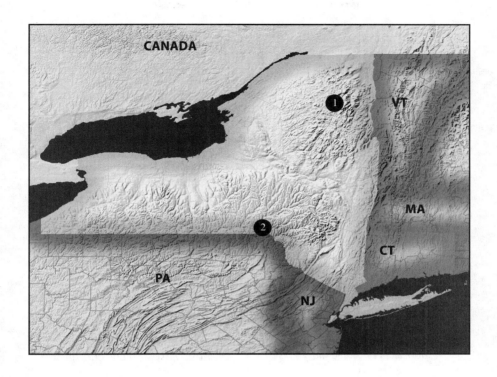

Outdoor Professionals

1. The Hungry Trout Motor Inn
2. West Branch Angler and Sportsman's Resort

Useful information for the state of
New York

State and Federal Agencies

Dept. of Environmental Conservation
50 Wolf Rd.
Albany, NY 12233
phone: (518) 457-3400

Bureau of Land Management
Eastern States
7450 Boston Boulevard
Springfield, VA 22153
phone: (703) 440-1660
or (703) 440- Plus Extension
fax: (703) 440-1599

Office Hours: 8:00 a.m. - 4:30 p.m.

Eastern States
Milwaukee District Office
310 W. Wisconsin Ave., Suite 450
(P.O. Box 631 53201-0631)
Milwaukee, WI 53203
phone: (414) 297-4450
fax: (414) 297-4409

Fire Island National Seashore
120 Laurel Street
Patchogue, NY 11772

Finger Lakes National Forest
5218 State Route 414
Hector, NY 14841
phone: (607) 456-4470
fax: (607) 546-4474

Associations, Publications, etc.

Trout Unlimited New York Council
2711 Girdle Road
Elma, NY 14059
phone: (716) 655-1331 or (914) 892-8630

American Fisheries Society
Cornell Biological Field Station
R.D. 1
Bridgeport, NY 13030
phone: (315) 633-9243

Federation of Fly Fishers
http://www.fedflyfishers.org

Great Lakes Sport Fishing Council
PO Box 297
Elmhurst, IL 60126
phone: (630) 941-1351
fax: (630) 941-1196
email: glsfc@netwave.net
http://www.execpc.com/glsfc

New York Bass Chapter Federation
274 N. Goodman Street
Rochester, NY
phone: (716) 271-7000

New York State Outdoor Guides Assoc.
(NYSOGA)
PO Box 4704
Queensbury, NY 12804
phone: (518) 359-7037
phone/fax: (518) 798-1253

License and Report Requirements

• State requires licensing of Guides.

• State requires that Guides be re-certified each year.

• State has no report requirements.

The Hungry Trout Motor Inn

Jerry and Linda Bottcher
Rt. 86 • Whiteface Mountain, NY 12997
phone: (800)-766-9137 • (518) 946-2217 • fax: (518) 946-7418
email: hungrytrout@whiteface.net • www.hungrytrout.com

The Hungry Trout Motor Inn rests on the banks of the legendary West Branch of the Ausable River in New York's Adirondack Mountains.

Fifteen minutes from Lake Placid, The Hungry Trout has been headquarters for anglers and bird hunters wishing upscale lodging, gourmet dining and access to private water and superb grouse hunting. The Hungry Trout Fly Shop is a leading outfitter in the area and offers professional fishing and grouse hunting guide service throughout the season.

Starting in late fall, you can combine trout fishing and grouse hunting on the same day as the Adirondacks harbor some of the best grouse cover in New York State. The Inn has first-class packages that combine lodging, dining and guide service.

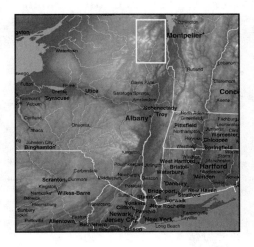

"Rachel is one of the guides we've had and the best thing is we always catch fish!" Kim and Judy Straw

SEASONS OF OPERATION

SPRING · SUMMER · FALL

FISH SPECIES

Small Mouth Bass · Large Mouth Bass · Northern Pike · Brook Trout · Brown Trout · Rainbow Trout

ACTIVITIES & TRANSPORTATION

FLY FISHING · HIKING / TREKKING · CANOE

LOCATIONS & SERVICES

BLUE RIBBON STREAM · POND · LARGE RIVER · FAMILY · LODGE · CABINS · FULL BOARD · SWIMMING POOL · WOMEN ONLY TRIPS

West Branch Angler and Sportsman's Resort

Harry Batschehet and Ray Finney
150 Faulkner Rd., PO Box 102 • Deposit, NY 13754
phone: (607) 467-5525 • fax: (607) 467-2215
email: wbangler@spectra.net • www.westbranchangler.com

The West Branch Angler and Sportsman's Resort is nestled in the beautiful Catskill Mountains on the famous West Branch of the Delaware River.

Our resort offers the fly angler cozy, upscale accommodations with 17 fully self-contained cabins, set on the banks of this magnificent tailwater fishery.

We have a world-class fly shop on premises. We can provide experienced fishing guides and canoe and boat rentals. Additionally, we have a spectacular restaurant and bar services, and we provide family activities with our swimming pool, trout pond, sporting clays, hiking and mountain biking.

Our winter activities include snowshoeing and cross country skiing.

"West Branch was an excellent, clean place. Food was good and the price reasonable." Ed Foss

SEASONS OF OPERATION

FISH SPECIES

Small Mouth Bass · Brown Trout · Rainbow Trout

ACTIVITIES & TRANSPORTATION

LOCATIONS & SERVICES

Oregon

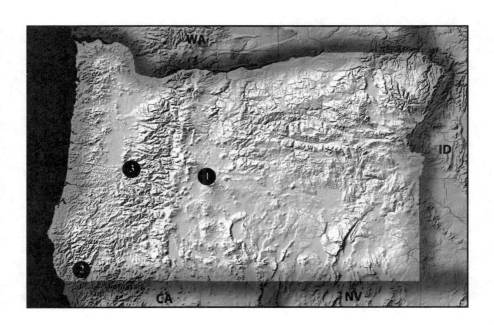

Outdoor Professionals

- **1** Fishing on the Fly
- **2** Sweet Old Boys Guide Service
- **3** Tightlines

License and Report Requirements

- State requires licensing of Outdoor Professionals.

- State requires a "Year-End Report" for Outfitters hunting and/or fishing on BLM land.

- U.S. Coast Guard licensing required for guides and captains that fish in "Near Coastal Waters".

Useful information for the state of
Oregon

State and Federal Agencies

Oregon Dept. of Fish & Wildlife
PO Box 59
Portland, OR 97207
phone: (503) 872-5268

Oregon Marine Board
435 Commercial St. NE
Salem, OR 97310
phone: (503) 373-1405
or (503) 378-8587

Columbia River Gorge Ntl. Scenic Area
902 Wasco Avenue, Ste 200
Hood River, OR 97031
phone: (541) 386-2333

Forest Service
Pacific Northwest Region
333 SW 1st Avenue
PO Box 3623
Portland, OR 97208
phone: (503) 326-2971
TTY: (503) 326-6448

Rogue River National Forest
phone: (541) 858-2200

Siskiyou National Forest
phone: (541) 471-6500

Siuslaw National Forest
phone: (541) 750-7000

Umpqua National Forest
phone: (541) 672-6601

Winema National Forest
phone: (541) 883-6714

Bureau of Land Management
Oregon State Office
1515 SW 5th Ave.
P.O. Box 2965
Portland, OR 97208-2965

phone: (503) 952-6001
or (503) 952-Plus Extension
fax: (503) 952-6308
Tdd: (503) 952-6372

Electronic mail
General Information:
or912mb@or.blm.gov
Webmaster: orwww@or.blm.gov

National Parks

Crater Lake National Park
phone: (541) 594-2211

Associations, Publications, etc.

American Fisheries Society
19948 S. Leland Road
Oregon City, OR 97045
phone: (503) 731-1267
fax: (503) 235-4228

Oregon Trout, Inc.
117 SW Front Ave.
Portland, OR 97204
phone: (503) 222-9091

Trout Unlimited Oregon Council
22875 NW Chestnut Street
Hillsboro, OR 97124-6545
phone: (541) 640-2123
fax: (503) 844-9929

Federation of Fly Fishers
http://www.fedflyfishers.org

Oregon Bass Chapter Federation
2475 N. Baker Drive
Canby, OR 97013
phone: (503) 266-7729

Oregon Outdoor Association
PO Box 9486
Bend, OR 97708-9486
phone: (541) 382-9758

Fishing on the Fly

Tim Dority
P.O. Box 242 • Bend, OR 97709
phone: (541) 389-3252 • fax: (541) 317-1483

Almost any time is trout time on the Deschutes. This river's wild trout populations are among the best in the nation. Known locally as redside, this unique race of rainbow provides reel-screaming action from the instant the hook is set. If you succeed in landing one you'll see the characteristic broad red band that makes them one of the loveliest game fish in North America.

Nothing quite matches the thrill of hooking a steelhead on a fly. Steelhead begin arriving in the Deschutes in midsummer. These tenacious fish provide fly anglers with unparalleled excitement through December. Jet boat excursions near the mouth of the river are offered beginning in August, and drift boat trips are available later in the year.

Fishing on the Fly specializes in teaching the art of flyfishing, be it nymph or dry fly techniques, entomology or stream reading and tactics.

"I would not hesitate to book with them again. Great fishing and super instruction." Cleo Childres

SEASONS OF OPERATION

FISH SPECIES

 Steelhead Rainbow Trout

ACTIVITIES & TRANSPORTATION

 CATCH & RELEASE FLY FISHING WHITEWATER FISHING FLY FISHING SCHOOL JET BOAT McKENZIE / DORY

LOCATIONS & SERVICES

 LARGE RIVER GUIDED ACTIVITIES DAY TRIPS

Sweet Old Boys Guide Service

Marsden P. (Tiny) Case
1790 Laurel Rd. • Cave Junction, OR 97523
phone: (541) 592-4552

We fish the Rogue River from Cole Rivers Hatchery above Shady Cove to Graves Creek Landing, depending on the season and water conditions.

Using a drift boat and up-to-date fishing equipment, we provide you with the opportunity to catch steelhead, salmon and trout. Flyfishing available by request for all three.

You need to bring an Oregon fishing license and tags (day license with tag is available), camera (chance for wildlife pictures), lunch, drink, a hat and sunscreen. You should dress in layers, as some mornings are cool.

Fish fall salmon August through October; spring salmon mid-May through July; winter steelhead November through April; summer steelhead July through October, and trout year-round.

"You will fish all types of water, all types of gear for a full day. If any guide will catch fish it will be Martin!" John H. Garner

SEASONS OF OPERATION

FISH SPECIES

 King-Chinook Salmon

Silver - Coho Salmon

Steelhead

Rainbow Trout

ACTIVITIES & TRANSPORTATION

LOCATIONS & SERVICES

Tightlines

Jeff and Laura Helfrich

47611 McKenzie Highway • Vida, OR 97488
phone/fax: (541) 896-3219 • email: FishOR9446@aol.com

A family business since the early 1920's, Tightlines offers one to four day driftboat fishing adventures on the wild and scenic McKenzie and Rogue Rivers.

Home of the McKenzie River Driftboat, (dory), the pristine clear waters of the McKenzie hide rainbow trout up to 20". Both experienced and beginners enjoy the dry fly hatches of the McKenzie as most patterns are no smaller than size 12. We operate flycasting camps on the Lower McKenzie as the water here is excellent for beginners.

The Rogue River is known as one of the premier steelhead salmon streams in the West. Drifting 43 miles of river we stay in a different lodge each of the three nights. Fantastic food meets you at each nights stay, combine this with fishing all day and you have a wonderfully relaxing vacation.

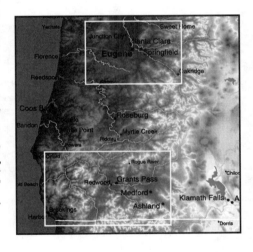

"Jeff is the best boatman I have had the opportunity to fish with. Always considerate, safe & most importantly...on the fish!" Dick Johnson, Pleasant Hill, OR

SEASONS OF OPERATION

FISH SPECIES

Small Mouth Bass | King-Chinook Salmon | Silver - Coho Salmon | Cutthroat Trout | Rainbow Trout | Steelhead

ACTIVITIES & TRANSPORTATION

LOCATIONS & SERVICES

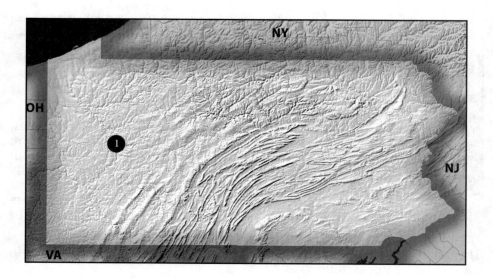

Outdoor Professionals

① Serene Fly-Fishing Adventures

License and Report Requirements

• State requires licensing of Outdoor Professionals.

• State requires the filing of the "Charter Boat/Fishing Guide Report".

Useful information for the state of

Pennsylvania

State and Federal Agencies

Pennsylvania Game Commission
2001 Elmerton Ave.
Harrisburg, PA 17110
hunting: (717) 787-4250
fishing: (717) 657-4518

Division of Tourism
Commonwealth of Pennsylvania
phone: (800) 847-4872

Forest Service
Eastern Region
310 West Wisconsin Avenue, Room 500
Milwaukee, WI 53203
phone: (414) 297-3646
TTY: (414) 297-3507

Allegheny National Forest
222 Liberty Street
PO Box 847
Warren, PA 16365
phone: (814) 723-5150
TTY: (814) 726-2710

Bureau of Land Management
Eastern States
7450 Boston Boulevard
Springfield, VA 22153
phone: (703) 440-1600
or (703) 440- Plus Extension
fax: (703) 440-1599

Office Hours: 8:00 a.m. - 4:30 p.m.

Eastern States
Milwaukee District Office
310 W. Wisconsin Ave., Suite 450
(P.O. Box 631 53201-0631)
Milwaukee, WI 53203
phone: (414) 297-4450
fax: (414) 297-4409

Associations, Publications, etc.

Trout Unlimited Pennsylvania Council
President: Melvin S. Brown
239 Station Road
Fairfield, PA 17320
phone: (717) 642-2449
fax: (717) 642-2475
Email: mel.brown@quebecorusa.com

Federation of Fly Fishers
http://www.fedflyfishers.org

Pennsylvania Bass Chapter Fed., Inc.
769 N. Cottage Road
Mercer, PA 16137
phone: (412) 475-2422
http://www.pabass.com

Great Lakes Sport Fishing Council
PO Box 297
Elmhurst, IL 60126
phone: (630) 941-1351
fax: (630) 941-1196
email: glsfc@netwave.net
http://www.execpc.com/glsfc

North American Native Fisheries Assoc.
123 W. Mt. Airy Ave.
Philadelphia, PA 19119

Serene Fly-Fishing Adventures

Pete Serene
RD 2, Box 139 G • Kittanning, PA 16201
phone: (724) 783-6346 • (724) 783-6678
email: mms1@alltel.net • www.alltel.net/~mms1/index.html

We offer guided flyfishing on all of Pennsylvania's top streams, from Erie tributaries for steelhead to theW.B. Delaware for wild trout and everything in between. I have 25 years' flyfishing experience and specialize in central Pennsylvania's limestone streams. We also have special package trips to Michigan's famous Pere Marquette River for salmon in the fall and steelhead in the spring.

Float in a Hyde driftboat when possible or wade. One- to seven-day packages include use of a 24-foot motorhome, which provides all the comforts of home. Lunches are provided. With friendly instruction and tips, we work hard to provide a pleasant and relaxing atmosphere in order for you to get the maximum satisfaction out of your flyfishing experience.

Let me take you on a trip that you will always remember.

"Pete's primary goal is to catch fish and have fun doing it. Pete also ties custom flies. My son and I are hooked!" Bill Herhorn

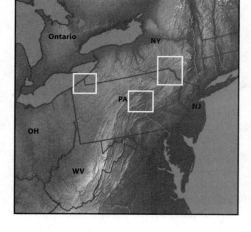

SEASONS OF OPERATION

FISH SPECIES

King-Chinook Salmon · Brown Trout · Rainbow Trout · Steelhead

ACTIVITIES & TRANSPORTATION

LOCATIONS & SERVICES

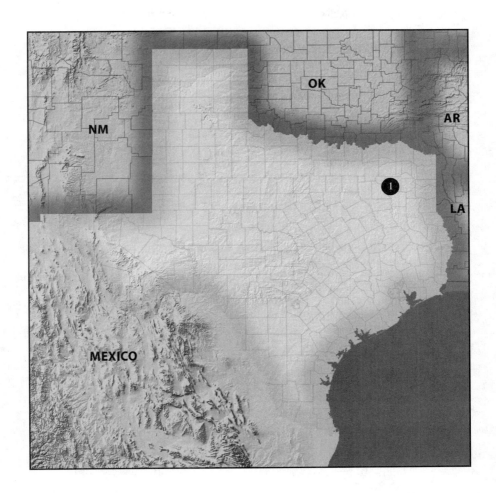

Outdoor Professionals

1 G & W Guide Service

License and Report Requirements

• State does license or register Outfitters, Guides, or Lodges.

• State has no report requirements.

Useful information for the state of

Texas

State and Federal Agencies

Texas Parks & Wildlife Dept.
4200 Smith School Rd.
Austin, TX 78744
phone: (512) 389-4800

Forest Service
Southern Region
1720 Peachtree Road NW
Atlanta, GA 30367
phone: (404) 347-4177
TTY: (404) 347-4278

Angelina, Davy Crockett, Sabine, Sam Houston National Forests
Homer Garrison Federal Bldg.
701 North First Street
Lufkin, TX 75901
phone/TTY: (409) 639-8501
fax: (409) 639-8588

Padre Island National Seashore
9405 S. Padre Island Drive
Corpus Christi, TX 78418
phone: (512) 937-2621

Bureau of Land Management
New Mexico State Office
(serves Kansas, Oklahoma & Texas)
Mailing Address:
P.O. Box 27115
Santa Fe, NM 87502-0115
http://www.nm.blm.gov

Information Number: 505-438-7400
fax: (505) 438-7435
Public Lands Information Center (PLIC):
(505) 438-7542

Office Hours: 7:45 a.m. - 4:30 p.m.

National Parks

Big Bend National Park
Big Bend National Park, TX 79834
phone: (915) 477-2251

Guadalupe Mountains National Park
HC 60, Box 400
Salt Flat, TX 79847-9400
phone: (915) 828-3351

Associations, Publications, etc.

American Fisheries Society, Texas Chapter
Texas Parks & Wildlife Department
Visitor Services Manager
Texas Freshwater Fisheries Center
5550 Flat Creek Road
Athens, TX 75751
phone: (903) 676-2277
fax: (903) 676-3474

Trout Unlimited Guadalupe River Chapter
President: Billy Trimble
3601 Lovage Drive
Austin, TX 78727-3058
phone: (512) 218-1876
http://www.grtu.org

Federation of Fly Fishers
http://www.fedflyfishers.org

Texas Bass Chapter Federation
1529 Sunview Drive
Dallas, TX 75253
phone: (214) 352-7531

G & W Guide Service

Brian Gambill
1100 N. Shore • Little Elm, TX 75068
phone: (972) 294-3202

Flyfisher Brian Gambill, who has more than 15 years of guiding experience, was one of the first flyfishing guides on Lake Fork, a premier trophy bass lake located east of Dallas near Quitman.

With a maximum depth of 70 feet and an average depth of 25 feet, the 27,690 acre lake regularly produces fish in the 5- to10-pound range.

Specialty flies, lunch and drinks are provided. Equipment rental is available at a nominal rate.

"Brian ties all his own flies and he develops patterns to help his business. He has developed techniques to fish 12 ft., 20ft. whatever it takes to be effective on a flyrod." Paul Koenig

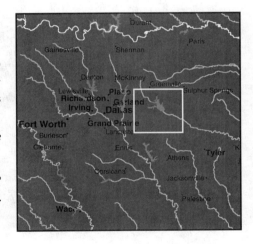

SEASONS OF OPERATION

FISH SPECIES

ACTIVITIES & TRANSPORTATION

LOCATIONS & SERVICES

Top Rated Professionals in
Utah

<u>Outdoor Professionals</u>

1 Alpine Anglers Fly Shop & Boulder Mountain Adventures

116

Useful information for the state of
Utah

State and Federal Agencies

Utah Dept. of Natural Resources
1636 W. North Temple
Salt Lake City, UT 84116
phone: (801) 538-4700

Forest Service
Intermountain Region
324 25th Street
Ogden, UT 84401-2310
phone: (801) 625-5306
TTY: (801) 625-5307

Ashley National Forest
phone: (435) 781-5157

Dixie National Forest
phone: (801) 865-3700

Fishlake National Forest
phone: (801) 638-1033

Manti-LaSal National Forest
phone / TTY: (801) 637-2817

Uinta National Forest
. phone: (801) 342-5100

Wasatch-Cache National Forests
phone: (801) 524-3900

Bureau of Land Management
Utah State Office
P.O. Box 45155
Salt Lake City, UT 84145-0155
Information Number: (801) 539-4001
fax: (801) 539-4013
Office Hours: 8:00 a.m. - 4:00 p.m.

National Parks

Arches National Park
Moab, UT 84532
phone: (801) 259-8161

Bryce Canyon National Park
Bryce Canyon, UT 84717
phone: (801) 834-5322

Canyonlands National Park
Moab, UT 84532
phone: (435) 259-7164

Capitol Reef National Park
Torrey, UT 84775
phone: (435) 425-3791

Zion National Park
Springdale, UT 84767
phone: (435) 772-3256

Associations, Publications, etc.

Trout Unlimited Rio Grande Chapter
President: Michael Norte
7849 Quintana NE
Albuquerque, NM 87109
phone: (505) 844-0935

Federation of Fly Fishers
http://www.fedflyfishers.org

New Mexico Bass Chapter Federation
PO Box 717
Socorro, NM 87801
phone: (505) 835-1200

License and Report Requirements

- State does not license or register Outfitters, Guides, Captains or Lodges.
- State Parks & Recreation Division requires that River Rafting Guides and Outfitters register and file a "River Outfitting Company Registration".
- BLM, Forest Service and National Park Service require a "Use Permit" and "User Fee" for Boating, Fish and River Outfitters using their lands. Guides and Outfitters required to file a "Year End Report of Activities".

Alpine Anglers & Boulder Mountain Adventures

Rich and Lori Cropper

310 W. Main, P.O. Box 750308 • Torrey, UT 84775
phone: (435) 425-3660 • (888) 484-3331

Experience the flyfishing trip of a lifetime in scenic southern Utah.

Brookies, cutthroat, splake and tiger trout fill the waters of more than 80 high mountain lakes, streams and beaver ponds on beautiful Boulder Mountain.

We offer day trips and overnight flyfishing pack trips. Our flyshop will outfit you with top-of-the-line flyfishing equipment.

Friendly, knowledgeable guides provide a rewarding experience for the novice as well as the seasoned angler.

"Fishing was great...we've never experienced fishing in a float tube before. What fun we had." Wendy and Chat Hailstone

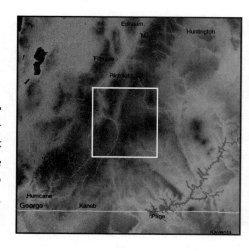

SEASONS OF OPERATION

FISH SPECIES

 Brook Trout Brown Trout Cutthroat Trout Rainbow Trout

ACTIVITIES & TRANSPORTATION

LOCATIONS & SERVICES

118

Top Rated Fly Fishing

Vermont

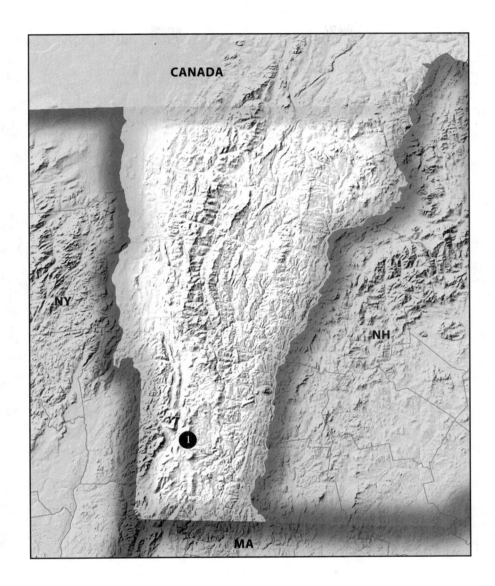

Outdoor Professionals

1 The Battenkill Anglers

Useful information for the state of
Vermont

State and Federal Agencies

Vermont Fish & Wildlife Dept.
103 South Main St.
Waterbury, VT 05671-0501
phone: (802) 241-3700

Eastern Region National Forest
310 West Wisconsin Ave., Room 500
Milwaukee, WI 53203
phone: (414) 297-3646
TTY: (414) 297-3507

Green Mountain, Finger Lakes National
Forests
231 North Main Street
Rutland, VT 05701
phone: (802) 747-6700
fax: (802) 747-6766

Bureau of Land Management
Eastern States
7450 Boston Boulevard
Springfield, VA 22153
phone: (703) 440-1600
or (703) 440-plus extension
fax: (703) 440-1599

Office Hours: 8:00 a.m. - 4:30 p.m.

Eastern States
Milwaukee District Office
310 W. Wisconsin Ave., Suite 450
(P.O. Box 631 53201-0631)
Milwaukee, WI 53203
phone: (414) 297-4400
fax: (414) 297-4409

Associations, Publications, etc.

Trout Unlimited Vermont Council
President: Matthew J. Glerum
PO Box 88
Manchester, VT 05254-0088
phone: (802) 362-8512
Email: glerumm@orvis.com

Federation of Fly Fishers
http://www.fedflyfishers.org

Vermont Bass Chapter Federation
19 Pinewood Rd.
Montpelier, VT 05602
phone: (802) 223-7793

Vermont Outdoor Guides Association
PO Box 10
North Ferrisburg, VT 05473
(800) 425-8747

License and Report Requirements

• State does not license or register Outfitters, Guides, or Lodges.

• State has no report requirements.

The Battenkill Anglers

Tom Goodman
Box 6204, Main Street • Manchester Center, VT 05255
phone: (802) 362-3184 • www.battenkill.apexhosting.com

The Battenkill Anglers focus on learning techniques, strategies and tactics for taking trout, as well as the secrets of some of New England's finest trout rivers. We adhere to no schedule and our guides are not salespeople. All of our instructor/guides are full-time professional fly fishers who have been hand-picked for their devotion to the study of taking trout on artificial flies. Our guides have academic backgrounds in stream ecology and entomology, which qualifies them to give you an experience with depth in the science of angling for trout, and really put you in touch with the pulse of our rivers.

Fly fishing for trout is an ancient craft, a blend of art and science that offers many options to the student.

The Battenkill Anglers can help you achieve your angling goals in the classroom or on one of our rivers.

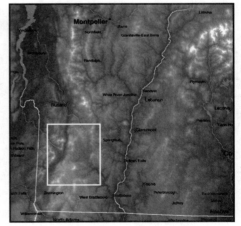

"My trip was made memorable because of Tom. I would highly recommend Tom to everyone without exception and without qualification!" Wayne Rooney

SEASONS OF OPERATION

FISH SPECIES

ACTIVITIES & TRANSPORTATION

LOCATIONS & SERVICES

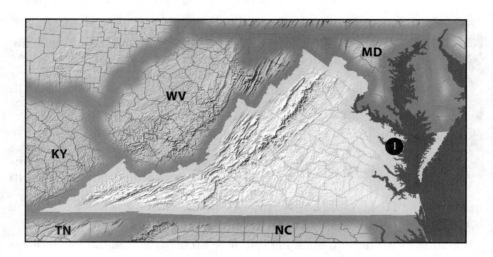

Outdoor Professionals

1 Chesapeake Bay Charters

License and Report Requirements

• State does not license or register Outfitters, Guides, Captains or Lodges.

• State has no report requirements.

Useful information for the state of

Virginia

State and Federal Agencies

Dept. of Game & Inland Fisheries
4010 W. Brood St.
Richmond, VA 23230
phone: (804) 367-1000

Forest Service
Southern Region
1720 Peachtree Road NW
Atlanta, GA 30367
phone: (404) 347-4177
TTY: (404) 347-4278

George Washington & Jefferson National
Forests
5162 Valley Pointe Parkway
Roanoke, VA 24091
phone: (540) 265-5100
Toll Free: (888) 265-0019

Bureau of Land Management
Eastern States
7450 Boston Boulevard
Springfield, VA 22153
phone: (703) 440-1660
or (703) 440-plus extension
fax: (703) 440-1599

Office Hours: 8:00 a.m. - 4:30 p.m.

Eastern States
Jackson Field Office
411 Briarwood Drive, Suite 404
Jackson, MS 39206
phone: (601) 977-5400
fax: (601) 977-5440

National Parks

Shenandoah National Park
Rt. 4, Box 348
Luray, VA 22835
phone: (703) 999-2243

Associations, Publications, etc.

Trout Unlimited Virginia Council
302 Danray Drive
Richmond, VA 23227
phone: (804) 264-6941
or
202 Deerfield Lane
Lynchburg, VA 24502

Federation of Fly Fishers
http://www.fedflyfishers.org

American Fisheries Society
Steve McMullin,
Dept. of Fisheries & Wildlife Sciences
100 Cheatham Hall
Virginia Tech
Blacksburg, VA 24601-0321
phone: (540) 231-8847
fax: (540) 231-7580

Virginia Bass Chapter Federation
113 Lavergne Lane
Virginia Beach, VA 23454
phone: (804) 428-4280

American Bass Assoc., Inc.
PO Box 896
Gate City, VA 24251
phone: (540) 386-2109

Future Fisherman Foundation
1033 N. Fairfax St., Ste. 200
Alexandria, VA 22314
phone: (703) 519-9691
http://www.asafishing.org

Chesapeake Bay Charters

Capt. Leroy G. Carr

Rt. 3, Box 217F, 205 Riverview Rd. • Heathville, VA 22473
phone: (home) (804) 453-4050 • (boat) (804) 450-4050

The Blue Streak provides fishing charters and cruises in Chesapeake Bay, Virginia and Maryland. Our objective is to offer personal and courteous service for cruising and/or fishing.

From May through December catches include striped bass, blues, spot, Spanish mackerel, trout, flounder, croaker and occasionally, black drum, channel bass, cobia and shark. Cruise options include, but are not limited to Tangier Island or Smith Island and lunch or dinner cruises.

The Blue Streak is a 36-foot flybridged sport fishing boat, Coast Guard licensed, fully fitted with electronics, twin engines and all safety equipment. We belong to the National Charter Boat Association and serve on the board of directors for Virginia Charter Boat Association.

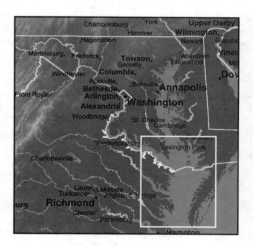

"The only one I will go fishing with on the Chesapeake Bay." James F. Bailey, Jr.

SEASONS OF OPERATION

 SPRING SUMMER FALL

FISH SPECIES

 Striped Bass Drum Mackerel Shark Sea Trout

ACTIVITIES & TRANSPORTATION

 CATCH & RELEASE FLY FISHING DEEP WATER FISHING SPIN CASTING TROLLING FLY BRIDGE

LOCATIONS & SERVICES

 ESTUARIES RIVER DELTA KIDS PROGRAMS FAMILY  GUIDED ACTIVITIES DAY TRIPS

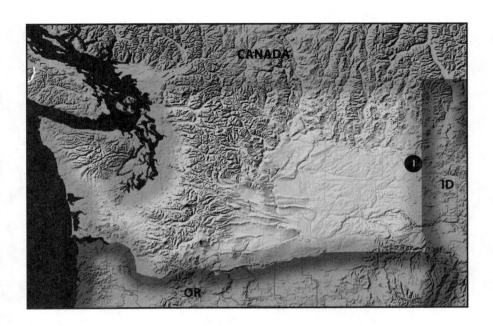

Outdoor Professionals

 Tom Loder's Panhandle Outfitters

License and Report Requirements

• State requires licensing of Outdoor Professionals.
• State requires that licensed steelhead guides report any catches.

Useful information for the state of

Washington

State and Federal Agencies

Washington Fish & Wildlife
600 North Capitol Way
Olympia, WA 98501
phone: (360) 902-2200
fax: (360) 902-2300

Forest Service
Pacific Northwest Region
333 SW 1st Avenue
PO Box 3623
Portland, OR 97208
phone: (503) 808-2971

Colville National Forest
phone: (509) 684-7000

Gifford Pinchot National Forest
phone: (360) 891-5000

Mt. Baker-Snoqualmie National Forest
phone: (206) 775-9702

Okanogan National Forest
phone: (509) 826-3275

Olympic National Forest
phone: (360) 956-2300

Wenatchee National Forest
phone: (509) 662-4335

Bureau of Land Management
Oregon State Office
(serves Washington also)
1515 SW 5th Ave.
P.O. Box 2965
Portland, OR 97208-2965
phone: (503) 952-6001
fax: (503) 952-6308

General Information
Email :or912mb@or.blm.gov
Webmaster: orwww@or.blm.gov
Office Hours: 7:30 a.m. - 4:30 p.m.

Spokane District Office
1103 N. Fancher
Spokane, WA 99212
phone: (509) 536-1200
fax: (509) 536-1275
Email: or130mb@or.blm.gov

National Parks

Mount Rainier National Park
phone: (206) 569-2211

North Cascades National Park
phone: (206) 856-5700

Olympic National Park
phone: (206) 452-4501

Associations, Publications, etc.

Washington Outfitters & Guides Association
23836 SE 124th Street
Issaquah, WA 98029
phone: (425) 392-6107

Paddle Trails Canoe Club
8909 27th Ave. NE
Seattle, WA 98115

Washington Kayak Club
3048 62nd Ave. SW
Seattle, WA 98116
phone: (206) 933-1178

Washington Bass Federation
President: Jim Owens
16569 - 162nd Place SE
Renton, WA 98058
(425) 271-6569
http://www.wabass.org

Tom Loder's Panhandle Outfitters

Tom Loder

12601 Thunder Mountain • Valleyford, WA 99036
phone: (888) 300-HUNT (4868) • fax: (509) 922-8289
email: panhandle-outfitters@usa.net • http://www.panhandle-outfitters.com

We are Orvis® endorsed fly-fishing outfitters with guide service on all the famous Rocky Mountain Rivers centered around the Panhandle of northern Idaho. These include Idaho's "wild & scenic" St. Joe and famed Clearwater Rivers and Montana's "blue ribbon" Kootenai, and legendary Clark Fork Rivers. In Washington, we fish the Snake and Grande Ronde Rivers for steelhead, plus the Spokane River and several lakes and spring creeks.

Our trips on Idaho's St. Joe River provide some of the highest quality and most scenic cutthroat fishing in the West. We offer over 70 miles of uncrowded river solitude with guides attentive to your personal needs. From our deluxe camp enjoy the soothing rush of the river, friendly campfires, relaxing hot showers and home-style Dutch oven cuisine. Refresh your senses with day trips, deluxe camp, or multiple river package trips for individuals, families or groups.

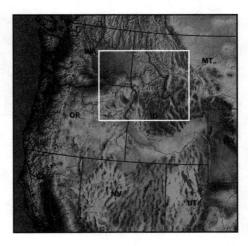

"I wanted my trip to be a learning experience above everything else. Tom did an outstanding job, with respect!"
Paul Brandt, Spokane, WA

SEASONS OF OPERATION

FISH SPECIES

 Brook Trout
 Brown Trout
 Cutthroat Trout
 Rainbow Trout
 Steelhead

ACTIVITIES & TRANSPORTATION

LOCATIONS & SERVICES

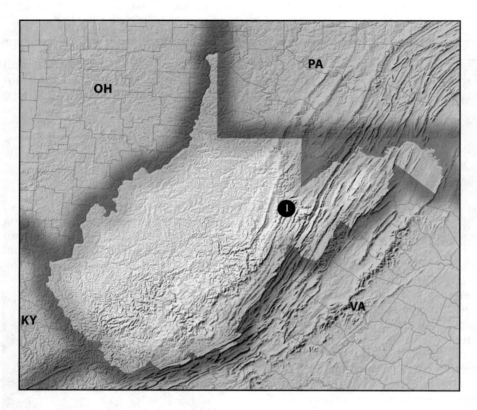

Outdoor Professionals

1 Kelly Creek Flyfishers

License and Report Requirements

• State requires licensing of Outdoor Professionals.

• State requires that Commercial Whitewater Guides file a "Monthly Report of Customers".

Useful information for the state of

West Virginia

State and Federal Agencies

Dept. of Natural Resources
1900 Kanawha Blvd. East
State Building 3
Charleston, WV 25305
Fisheries: (304) 558-2771
Law Enforcement: (304) 558-2771

Forest Service
Eastern Region
310 West Wisconsin Avenue, Room 500
Milwaukee, WI 53203
phone: (414) 297-3646
TTY: (414) 297-3507

Monongahela National Forest
USDA Building
200 Sycamore Street
Elkins, WV 26241-3962
phone/TTY: (304) 636-1800

Bureau of Land Management
Eastern States
7450 Boston Boulevard
Springfield, VA 22153
phone: (703) 440-1660
or (703) 440- Plus Extension
fax: (703) 440-1599

Office Hours: 8:00 a.m. - 4:30 p.m.

Eastern States
Milwaukee District Office
310 W. Wisconsin Ave., Suite 450
(P.O. Box 631 53201-0631)
Milwaukee, WI 53203
phone: (414) 297-4450
fax: (414) 297-4409

Associations, Publications, etc.

American Fisheries Society
PO Box 1278
Elkins, WV 26241
phone: (304) 636-6586
fax: (304) 636-7824

Trout Unlimited West Virginia Council
637 Grand Street
Morgantown, WV 26505-6911
phone: (304) 293-7749

Federation of Fly Fishers
http://www.fedflyfishers.org

West Virginia Bass Chapter Federation
President: John Burdette
25 West Main Street
Buckhannon, WV 26201
phone: (304) 472-3600 or 472-6221

The American Bass Association of
West Virginia
2620 Fairmont Ave., Ste. 110
Fairmont, WV 26554
phone: (304) 366-8183

Kelly Creek Flyfishers

Gary Lang

Rt. 1, Box 328-41 • Elkins, WV 26241
phone: (304) 636-7642

WestVirginia is overlooked by most Eastern flyfishers. While we have some fairly high country, our latitude saddles us with several weeks of 80-degree daytime temperatures in midsummer. For this reason, many of the area's stocked streams suffer from significant trout mortality.

The majority of our summer fishing is for native brook trout on small headwater creeks. There are now several high-quality catch and release areas established on larger streams which maintain a carryover fishery. It is on these headwater creeks and catch and release areas where we guide.

With the benefit of our crew's combined 75 years' experience, a fishing vacation inWestVirginia rivals anything in the East.

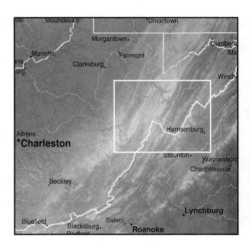

SEASONS OF OPERATION

FISH SPECIES

 Brown Trout
 Rainbow Trout

ACTIVITIES & TRANSPORTATION

LOCATIONS & SERVICES

Wyoming

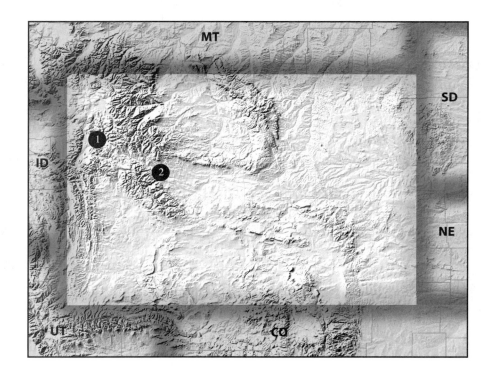

Outdoor Professionals

1. John Henry Lee Outfitters, Inc.
2. Paintrock Adventures

License and Report Requirements

- State requires licensing of Outdoor Professionals.
- State requires that Big Game Outfitters file a "Year-End Report".
- Fishing Outfitters need to get a permit to operate on Federal land.
- Outfitters and Guest/Dude Ranches must file a "Use" or "Day Report" with the Wyoming Forest Service if they Fish, Hunt or Raft on Forest Service or BLM land.
- Licensed guides must be signed on and validated by a state licensed outfitter/guide service.

Wyoming

State and Federal Agencies

Wyoming Dept. of Admin. & Information
State Board of
Outfitters & Professional Guides
1750 Westland Rd.
Cheyenne, WY 82002
(800) 264-0981
phone: (307) 777-5323
fax: (307) 777-6715

Wyoming Game & Fish Dept.
5400 Bishop Blvd.
Cheyenne, WY 82002
phone: (307) 777-4600

Forest Service
Intermountain Region
Federal Building
324 25th Street
Ogden, UT 84401-2310
phone: (801) 625-5306
TTY: (801) 625-5307

Bridger-Teton National Forests
Forest Service Building
340 North Cache
PO Box 1888
Jackson, WY 83001
phone: (307) 739-5500
TTY: (307) 739-5064

Bureau of Land Management
Wyoming State Office
(serves Nebraska also)
Information Access Center
5353 Yellowstone
P.O. Box 1828
Cheyenne, WY 82003
phone: (307) 775-6BLM or 6256
fax: (307) 775-6082

Office Hours: 7:45 a.m. - 4:30 p.m.

National Parks

Grand Teton National Park
PO Drawer 170
Moose, WY 83012
phone: (307) 739-3399

Yellowstone National Park
PO Box 168
Yellowstone National Park, WY 82190
phone: (307) 344-7381

Associations, Publications, etc.

Trout Unlimited Wyoming Council
1250 Foothill Blvd.
Rock Springs, WY 82901-4403
phone: (307) 382-8051
fax: (307) 382-2985
Email: vancep@sweetwater.net
http://www.firehole.com/troutunlimited

Federation of Fly Fishers
http://www.fedflyfishers.org

Wyoming Bass Chapter Federation
106 Folsom Drive
Rock Springs, WY 82901
phone: (307) 382-4742

Wyoming Outfitters & Guides Assoc.
PO Box 2284
239 Yellowstone Ave., Suite C
Cody, WY 82414
phone: (307) 527-7453
fax: (307) 587-8633

Jackson Hole Outfitters & Guide Association
850 W. Broadway
Jackson Hole, WY 83001
phone: (307) 734-9025

John Henry Lee Outfitters, Inc.

John Lee
Box 8368 • Jackson, WY 83001
phone: (800) 352-2576 • (307) 733-9441 • fax: (307) 455-3215
email: infojhl@johnhenrylee.com • http://www.johnhenrylee.com

Come and experience a float-fishing trip with breathtaking views of the Teton Range and the serenity of the wilderness.

We offer guided fishing trips on the Snake, Green and New Fork rivers. In addition, we offer guided walk-in trips to Yellowstone with fishing on the Madison, Firehole, or Yellowstone River.

Backcountry fishing trips vary from seven to ten days in Yellowstone National Park or in the Bridger Teton Wilderness.

These areas are considered by many to be the best cutthroat trout fishing in the world. Fish the headwaters of the Yellowstone or Thoroughfare River for an experience you'll always remember.

"We can honestly say we enjoyed every minute of each trip and would highly recommend this outfitter to anyone." Jeani Smith

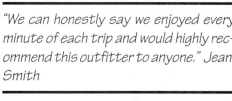

SEASONS OF OPERATION

SPRING   SUMMER   FALL

FISH SPECIES

Brook Trout   Brown Trout   Lake Trout   Cutthroat Trout   Rainbow Trout

ACTIVITIES & TRANSGPORTATION

CATCH & RELEASE   FLY FISHING   HIKING / TREKKING   HORSE PACK TRIPS   FLY FISHING SCHOOL   McKENZIE / DORY

LOCATIONS & SERVICES

BLUE RIBBON STREAM   POND   LAKE   KIDS PROGRAMS   FAMILY   HANDICAP   WALL TENTS   FULL BOARD   OVERNIGHT TRIPS

Paintrock Adventures, L.L.C.

Todd Jones

P.O. Box 52 • Hyattville, WY 82428
phone: (307) 469-2274 • fax: (307) 469-2215
email: todd@paintrock.com • http://www.paintrock.com

Ride horseback with us into Cloud Peak Wilderness and see the endless beauty of this great ecosystem aboard your well mannered horse. Activities include float tubing, trail riding, fly fishing (both lake and stream), hiking, and just plain relaxing. Catch (and release) of the day could be the prized golden trout, cutthroat, brook, mackinaw and splake.

Our camps are very comfortable and the food cowboy five star. This is a fantastic trip for the whole family. Be prepared to catch a lot of fish! Your adventure starts on Sunday evening and ends Friday afternoon. Trips are available July and August. We practice light on the land camping techniques with a definite western flavor.

What is included? Meals, full accommodations, professional guides, airport transportation, and a memorable vacation!

"There are no words to describe this trip except 'Trip of a Lifetime'. If you love to fly fish and catch all the species of trout, this is the trip to take. Todd Jones holds the highest integrity and honesty!" Bill Aderholz, Dayton, VA

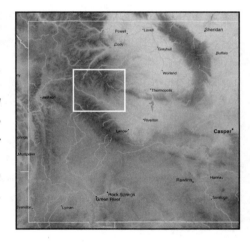

SEASONS OF OPERATION

FISH SPECIES

 Arctic Grayling Brook Trout Brown Trout Cutthroat Trout Lake Trout Rainbow Trout

ACTIVITIES & TRANSPORTATION

LOCATIONS & SERVICES

Canada

Canada

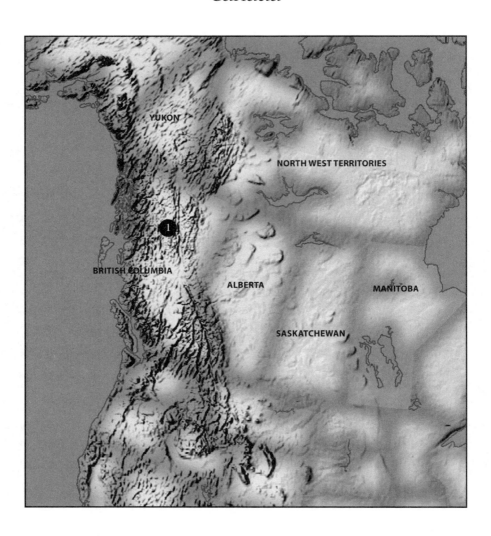

Outdoor Professionals

1 Love Bros. & Lee, Ltd.

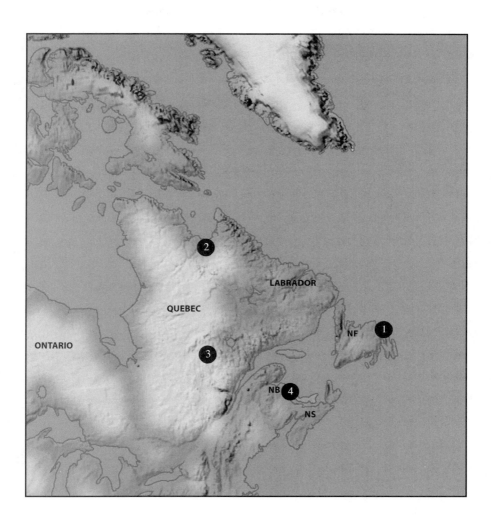

Outdoor Professionals

1. Gander River Outfitters, Inc.
2. George River Lodge, Inc.
3. Les Enterprises du Lac Perdu, Inc.
4. M&M's Whooper Hollow Lodge

Useful information for the provinces of
Canada

British Columbia:
Ministries and Agencies

Department of Fisheries & Oceans
200 Kent Street
Ottawa, Ontario Canada K1A 036

British Columbia Ministry of the
Environment, Lands & Parks
Wildlife Division
PO Box 9374
Victoria, B.C. Canada V8V 1X4
phone: (250) 387-9789
Fisheries Division phone: (250) 387-9581

Ministry of Small Business Tourism &
Culture
1117 Wharf St.
Victoria, B.C. Canada V8V 2Z2
phone: (604) 387-1683

Associations, Publications, etc.

Federation of Fly Fishers
http://www.fedflyfishers.org

Guide Outfitters Association of British
Columbia
7580 River Road, Suite 250
Richmond, B.C. Canada V6X 1X6
http://www.goabc.org

American Fisheries Society
Tim L. Slaney, Aquatic Resources Ltd.
9010 Oak Street
Vancouver, B.C. Canada V6P 4B9
Email: 76043.2377@compuserve.com

License &Report Requirements

• All outfitters/guides must be registered
  with province. Hunting guides must
  submit a "hunt record" of each hunt
  within ten days.
• Charter boats/guides are licensed by
  each province.

New Brunswick:
Ministries and Agencies

Dept of Natural Resources & Energy
PO Box 6000
Fredericton, NB Canada E3B 5H1

Dept. of Fisheries & Oceans
Gulf Region
Bernard LeBlanc
Box 5030
Moncton, NB Canada E1C 9B6
phone: (506) 857-7750

Huntsman Marine Science Centre
Brandy Cove Road
St. Andrews, NB Canada E0G 2X0
phone: (506) 529-1200
fax: (506) 529-1212

Associations, Publications, etc.

Federation of Fly Fishers
http://www.fedflyfishers.org

License &Report Requirements

• All outfitters, guides and charter boats
  must be registered with each
  province.

Useful information for the provinces of

Canada

Newfoundland:

Ministries and Agencies

Department of Fisheries & Oceans
200 Kent Street
Ottawa, Ontario Canada K1A 036

Department of Natural Resources
PO Box 8700
St. John's, NF Canada A1B 4J6
phone: (709) 729-4715

Wildlife Division
PO Box 8700
St. John's, NF Canada A1B 4J6
phone: (709) 729-2817

Newfoundland LabradorWildlife Fed.
phone: (709) 364-8415

Department of Tourism, Culture & Recreation
PO Box 8730
St. John's, NF, Canada A1B 4J6
phone: (709) 729-2830
fax: (709) 729-1965
email: info@tourism.gov.nf.ca

Associations, Publications, etc.

Federation of Fly Fishers
http://www.fedflyfishers.org

License &Report Requirements

- All outfitters, guides and charter boats must be registered with each province.

Québec:

Ministries and Agencies

Department of Fisheries & Oceans
200 Kent Street
Ottawa, Ontario Canada K1A 036

Dept. of Recreation, Fish & Game
Place de la Capitale 150 Blvd.
Rene-Levesque Est, Québec
Canada G1R 4Y1
phone: (418) 627-6266

Associations, Publications, etc.

Federation of Fly Fishers
http://www.fedflyfishers.org

Federation of Québec Outfitters
2485 Boul Hamel
Québec, Canada G1P 2H9
phone: (418) 877-5191

License &Report Requirements

- All outfitters, guides and charter boats must be registered with each province.

Gander River Outfitters, Inc.

Terence D. Cusack, President

P.O. Box 21017 • St. John's, Newfoundland, Canada AIA 5B2
phone: (888) SALMON3 (725-6663) • (709) 753-9163 • fax: (709) 753-9169
email: ganderRiver@GanderRiver.com • www.GanderRiver.com

Gander River Outfitters, Inc. offers a quality fishing experience from its camp on the lower Gander River. The stock counts are up and are expected to increase the next few years.

The camp has a capacity of 10-12 rods and is reached by riverboat from Gander Bay. The camp has indoor plumbing, showers, electricity and refrigeration. Our uniformed guides are all well-trained and highly motivated, and our chef will delight you with a variety of excellent meals served on our Portmeirion "Compleat Angler" china.

We consider quality and service to be conditions of doing business.

We are sure that you will enjoy the experience with us and we would be happy to discuss arranging a trip to meet your needs. We also offer hunting for Eastern moose and black bear.

"Top of the line gear. Excellent guide, catered to any kind of food. Best spot in Labrador/ Newfoundland." Terrance Giblingham

SEASONS OF OPERATION

FISH SPECIES

Atlantic Salmon — Brook Trout — Sea Trout

ACTIVITIES & TRANSPORTATION

LOCATIONS & SERVICES

George River Lodge, Inc.

Pierre et Jean Paquet

CP. 88 • St. Augustin, Québec, Canada G3A 1V9
phone: (800) 473-4650 • fax: (418) 877-4652
email: adventure@norpaq.com • www.norpaq.com

George River Lodge runs and operates three different lodges on three rivers in northern Quebec. We offer fully-guided catch and release stream flyfishing at each.

George River provides opportunities to catch Atlantic salmon, brook trout and lake trout. Club Chateauguay has two camps to cover 50 miles of stream for big brook trout and lake trout.

The Whale River Camp is situated on the headwaters of the river for land-locked salmon, brook trout, northern pike and huge lake trout.

All destinations are top-notch for fly fishermen and offer some of the best flyfishing in the world because of their remoteness.

"This is a great place with great guides and I would recommend it without reservation. " George Motsay

SEASONS OF OPERATION

FISH SPECIES

ACTIVITIES & TRANSPORTATION

LOCATIONS & SERVICES

Les Enterprises du Lac Perdu, Inc.

Michel and Mary-Anne Auclair

3, rue Zurich, Ste-Brigitte de Laval • Québec, Canada GOA 3KO
phone: (418) 825-3500 • fax: (418) 825-2113
email: Mauclair@lac-perdu.qc.ca • www.lac-perdu.qc.ca

Yes, we found the lost lake, north of the 50th parallel, deep in the heart of the Quebec boreal forest, in a savage and uncharted region.

Magnificent Lake Perdu, 12 miles long, overlooks an exclusive territory spanning more than 150 square miles, midway between Lake Mistassini and the Manic 5 hydro project.

We have been operating since 1980 and we guarantee that a stay at our lodge will provide you with the fishing thrills of a lifetime. We offer excellent trophy fishing locations for the serious angler interested in native speckle trout, lake trout, great northern pike and white fish. Our hunting and fishing lodge sits in the middle of a vast territory that will meet your highest expectations.

"A wonderful fly-in experience!! Plenty of trouts on dry flies." Ray Scott

SEASONS OF OPERATION

FISH SPECIES

Northern Pike | Brook Trout | Lake Trout

ACTIVITIES & TRANSPORTATION

LOCATIONS & SERVICES

Love Bros. and Lee, Ltd.

Ron Fleming and Brenda Nelson

RR#1, Kispiox Rd. • Hazelton, British Columbia, Canada V0J 1Y0
phone/fax: (250) 842-6350

Experience a flyfishing trip of a lifetime in northwestern British Columbia.

Our remote wilderness camp is accessible by float plane only. We offer guided flyfishing for wild rainbow or guided hunting for big game in an exclusive wilderness area, 165 airmiles north of Smithers, British Columbia.

Accommodations are fully-equipped log cabins. A shower is also available.

To ensure you have a personalized quality adventure, we take a maximum of four guests per week.

"Over the 12-13 years with Love Brothers & Lee, my experiences have been great... Brenda and Ron Fleming are the greatest." Sandy Wilkinson

SEASONS OF OPERATION _____

FISH SPECIES _____

ACTIVITIES & TRANSPORTATION _____

LOCATIONS & SERVICES _____

M&M's Whooper Hollow Lodge

Martin and Marie Budaker

108 Fulton Ave. • Fredericton, New Brunswick, Canada E3A 2B6
office/fax: (506) 472-6391 • lodge: (506) 627-9391
www.angelfire.com/biz2/mmwhooper

M&M's Whooper Hollow Lodge is nestled in a field sloping to the shores of the beautiful and legendary Dungarvon River, a tributary of the main Southwest Miramichi. Our lodge features delicious home-cooked meals and accommodations for nine guests with full bath. We take pride in our professional hunting and fishing guide service. We welcome mixed groups and are pleased to package and store your fish and game trophies.

Atlantic salmon are usually present in the Dungarvon from mid-June to mid-October. Angling packages feature one guide for every three anglers.

We accommodate a maximum of six guests for a minimum three-day stay. Book early for prime dates.

"The location of the Lodge is for those truly looking for the 'out of the way' adventure, located looking over the river. The food is always homecooking and in plenty. The family as a whole really enjoys our trips to Whooper Hollow Lodge." Paul Arnold

SEASONS OF OPERATION

FISH SPECIES

Small Mouth Bass / Atlantic Salmon / Brown Trout / Lake Trout / Rainbow Trout

ACTIVITIES & TRANSPORTATION

Fly Fishing / Spin Casting / Trophy Fishing / ATV Riding / Canoe

LOCATIONS & SERVICES

Streams / Lake / Family / Handicap / Cabins / Full Board / Day Trips / Overnight Trips

Top Rated
Photo Album

146

150

Top Rated Fly Fishing - Photo Album

Photo Credits

Appendix
&
Questionnaire
&
Indexes

APPENDIX-FISHING

This is the list of _ALL_ the fishing Guides, Captains, Lodges and Outfitters that we contacted during the compilation of our books. In all more than 12,000 just for fishing!

We invited them to participate in our survey by simply sending us their complete client list.

Some replied praising the Picked-By-You idea, but decided not to participate in our survey. Their main concern was the confidentiality of their client list. We truly respect their position, but we hope to have proven our honest and serious effort. We are sure they will join us in the next edition. Some did not respond.

Others participated by sending their complete list of clients, but did not qualify for publication. In some cases because of a low score, and in other instances because of an insufficient number of questionnaires returned by their clients.

The names of the Outdoor Professionals published in this book who have qualified with an A rating from their past clients are **bolded** in the Appendix.

United States

Alabama

Company Bay Springs Marina
Contact
City Centre
Company Bear Creek Lakes
Contact
City Russellville
Company Charlie Mac's Sport & Tackle World
Contact
City Decatur
Company Dauphin Island Marina
Contact Mike Thierry & Terry Malone
City Dauphin Island
Company Eagle Charters
Contact Harold H. Williams
City Waverly
Company Goose Pond Colony
Contact
City Scottsboro
Company John's Campground
Contact
City Centre
Company JR's Marina
Contact
City Cedar Bluff
Company Lee Sells Outfitter & Guide
Contact Lee D. Sells
City Eufaula
Company Ossa-Win-Tha Resort
Contact
City Guntersville
Company Pruett's Fish Camp
Contact
City Centre
Company Riverside Campground & Motel
Contact
City Cedar Bluff
Company Sea Reaper
Contact Capt. Jeff Hardy
City Orange Beach
Company Southern Outdoor Center, LLC
Contact Thomas Sherburne
City Auburn
Company Tee's Bait & Guide Service
Contact Tee Kitchens
City Guntersville
Company Weiss Lake Landing
Contact
City Cedar Bluff
Company Welch Guide Service
Contact Dale Welch
City Crane Hill
Company White Oak Plantation
Contact
City Tuskegee
Company

Contact Sonny Alawin
City Orange Beach
Company
Contact Brian C. Annan
City Orange Beach
Company
Contact Gloycie Ard
City Orange Beach
Company
Contact Frankie Broz
City Lillian
Company
Contact Neal T. Brube
City Orange Beach
Company
Contact Nathan W. Cox
City Orange Beach
Company
Contact Bobby F. Cudworth
City Orange Beach
Company
Contact Charles W. Day
City Foley
Company
Contact Paul D. Eberly
City Gulf Shores
Company
Contact Donald Flournoy
City Orange Beach
Company
Contact Neal T Grube
City Orange Beach
Company
Contact Larry Johnson
City Orange Beach
Company
Contact Captain Jimbo Meador
City Point Clear
Company
Contact Wynn Millson
City Orange Beach
Company
Contact Dan H Negus
City Orange Beach
Company
Contact Charles Pruitt
City Tuscaloosa
Company
Contact Captain Daniel Ratliff
City Orange Beach
Company
Contact Bill Rawson
City Orange Beach
Company
Contact Sandy G. Smith
City Orange Beach
Company
Contact Bill Staff
City Orange Beach
Company
Contact Neil Trimble
City Orange Beach
Company
Contact Joseph A. Warren
City Orange Beach

Alaska

Company "Caps" Tundra Time Adventures
Contact Chriss D. Hurley
City Anchorage
Company "Fish On" Fishing Adventures
Contact Frank Carter
City Anchorage
Company 2-E Fish Company
Contact Michael Tuhy
City Soldotna
Company 20 Mile Lodge
Contact Bruce Leadman
City Anchorage
Company 4 W Air/Justin Tyme Guide
Contact Bill Woodin
City Soldotna
Company 58 22' North Sailing Charters
Contact Delbert & Wayne Carnes
City Juneau
Company A & A Charters
Contact John Armstrong
City Homer
Company A & M Charters
Contact Allan Sherman
City Anchorage
Company A Charter You'll Never Forget
Contact Gregory L. Trigg
City Juneau
Company A J Charters
Contact Steve & Andrea Torok
City Juneau
Company A Smart Charter
Contact Gerald E. & Cathy I. Smart
City Anchorage
Company A-Hook Charters
Contact Myron Craig McDonald
City Homer
Company A-M Charters
Contact Melissa Sherman Allan
City Anchorage
Company A-Ward Charters
Contact Sandra & Alexandria Ward Robert
City Anchor Point
Company AAA Halibut & Salmon Charters
Contact Jeff & Myrna Rogers
City Palmer
Company Absolut Charters
Contact David Worgum
City Yakutat
Company Absolute Charters
Contact Sean McLean
City Seward
Company Ace Charters
Contact Steve Merritt
City Craig
Company Acord Guide Service

Contact Greg Acord
City Wasilla
Company Action Jackson & M & M
Contact Mkell Welsh
City Glennallen
Company Action Jackson Charters
Contact Charles Jackson
City Anchorage
Company Action Marine Adventure
Contact Jim L. Frary
City Anchorage
Company Adams Alaskan Safaris
Contact Captain Dale Adams
City Sitka
Company Admiral Halibut Charters
Contact William T. Jones
City Eagle River
Company Admiralty Island Charters
Contact Matt Kookesh
City Angoon
Company Adventure Bound Alaska
Contact Steven & Winona Weber
City Juneau
Company Adventure Charter
Contact Brad R. Kimberlin
City Copper Center
Company Adventures Afloat
Contact Francis A. & Linda C. Kadrlik
City Juneau
Company Afognak Wilderness Lodge
Contact Roy & Shannon Randall
City Seal Bay
Company Air Adventures
Contact Robert Brouillette
City Anchorage
Company Air Adventures
Contact Jeremy Schimmel
City Anchorage
Company Air Adventures
Contact Mike McBride
City Kenai
Company Airboat Charter
Contact Clarita B. Fears
City Fairbanks
Company AK Panhandle Charters
Contact Val Tibbetts
City Juneau
Company AK Quigley Sport Fishing Charters
Contact James Quigley
City Craig
Company AK Recreational Services
Contact Jack Willis
City Wasilla
Company AK Scenic Charters
Contact Mike & Ellen Williams
City Ketchikan
Company AK Trophy Hunting & Fishing
Contact Mel Gillis
City Anchorage
Company AK Wilderness Trips
Contact Clark & CherylWhitney
City Soldotna
Company AK. Pac. N.W. Fish Adv.

Contact Jack Oneil
City Kenai
Company Al's Charter Service
Contact Al Turner
City Ward Cove
Company Alaska Ridge Riders, Inc.
Contact Sharon Kanareff
City Healy
Company Alaska Adventure Charters
Contact John Padilla
City Sitka
Company Alaska Adventure Company
Contact Mark Underwood
City Willow
Company Alaska Adventures
Contact Charles & Eric Miknich
City Anchorage
Company Alaska Angler
Contact Chris & Adela Batin
City Fairbanks
Company Alaska Anglers
Contact David Fandel
City Kenai
Company Alaska Anglers
Contact Ed Tompkins, Sr.
City Palmer
Company Alaska Angling, Inc.
Contact Kent A. Brekke
City Petersburg
Company Alaska Aquamarine Experience, Inc.
Contact Johny Gilson
City Ketchikan
Company Alaska Blue Water
Contact Roger & Elizabeth Watney
City Anchor Point
Company Alaska Bound Adventures
Contact Robert & George Wagner
City Homer
Company Alaska Cast & Blast
Contact Kenneth Darrell McDonald
City Chugiak
Company Alaska Clearwater Charters
Contact Tom Standerwick
City Sitka
Company Alaska Clearwater Sportfishing Adv.
Contact Daniel R. Myers
City Soldotna
Company Alaska Coastal Airlines, Inc.
Contact Dave Brown
City Juneau
Company Alaska Coastal Outfitters
Contact Brad A. Dennison
City Sitka
Company Alaska Commercial
Contact Emmet Heidemann
City Eagle River
Company Alaska Connections/ Sherlter Lodge
Contact Richard Yamada
City Auke Bay
Company Alaska Dawn Charters
Contact Donald R. Byrd

City Sitka
Company Alaska Deep Sea Adventures
Contact Dustin W. Clark
City Anchorage
Company Alaska Deshka Landing Charters
Contact Gerald Gange
City Willow
Company Alaska Dream Charters
Contact
City Valdez
Company Alaska Dream Fishing
Contact William Byrnes
City Eagle River
Company Alaska Drift Boaters
Contact Ken & Tim Robertson
City Soldotna
Company Alaska Fish
Contact Andrew Szczesny
City Soldotna
Company Alaska Fish 'n Fun Charters
Contact Rhon & Sandra Lyons
City Sterling
Company Alaska Fish & Trails Unlimited
Contact Jerald D. Stansel
City Fairbanks
Company Alaska Fish Tales
Contact Burl D. Weller & Robert Bailey
City Petersburg
Company Alaska Fish-N-Fun Charters
Contact Anthony L. & Debra L. Azure
City Ketchikan
Company Alaska Fishing Centre
Contact Raymond Pelland
City Anchorage
Company Alaska Fishing Charters
Contact Delfin Cesar
City Sitka
Company Alaska Fishing Expedition
Contact John Hart
City Anchorage
Company Alaska Fishing Guide Service
Contact Michael & Jeanne Allen
City Anchorage
Company Alaska Fishing Safaris
Contact Merle R. Frank
City Anchorage
Company Alaska Fishing with Terry Adlam
Contact Terry Adlam
City Chugiak
Company Alaska Flaggs Kenai
Contact Luren Flagg
City Soldotna
Company Alaska Fly Fishing Safaris
Contact Rolf Sandberg
City Girdwood
Company Alaska Freshwater Safaris
Contact Roger A. Denny, Jr.
City Eagle River
Company Alaska Girl Adventures
Contact James & Joy Baldridge
City Kenai
Company Alaska Guides
Contact Herman Fandel
City Kenai
Company Alaska Gulf Coast Adventures, Inc.
Contact George Davis
City Cordova
Company Alaska Holiday Charter Company
Contact Victor Johnson
City Sitka
Company Alaska Hunting & Fishing
Contact Meryl & Beverly Wolford
City Homer
Company Alaska Jetboat Charters
Contact James & Lori Kedrowski
City Wasilla
Company Alaska Midnight Sun Charters
Contact Douglas Judge
City Homer
Company Alaska Native Charters
Contact Wayne Kvasnikoff
City Ninilchik
Company Alaska Native Charters
Contact William Kvasnikoff
City Ninilchik
Company Alaska Northern Adventures
Contact Thomas & Katie Prijatel

City Cordova
Company Alaska Northwind Charters
Contact Donald D. Phillips
City Soldotna
Company Alaska on the Fly
Contact Jeremy Schimmel & Rene Wilson
City Kenai
Company Alaska Pacific M.W. Fishing Adventures
Contact Jack O'Neil
City Kenai
Company Alaska Passages
Contact Brian & Julie Hursey
City Petersburg
Company Alaska Peak & Sea's
Contact Mark A. Galla
City Wrangell
Company Alaska Premier Charters, Inc.
Contact Theresa Weiser & Calvin Hayashi
City Sitka
Company Alaska Private Guide
Contact Donald Duncan
City Fairbanks
Company Alaska Professional Guides
Contact C. Vernon Humble
City Anchorage
Company Alaska Quest
Contact Gary Kroll
City Fairbanks
Company Alaska Rainbow Lodge
Contact Ron & Sharon Hayes
City King Salmon
Company Alaska Rainbow Unlimited
Contact Clifford Pulis
City Iliamna
Company Alaska River Adventures
Contact George Heim
City Cooper Landing
Company Alaska River Charters
Contact Robert L. Krize
City Fairbanks
Company Alaska River Journeys
Contact Steve Weller
City Anchorage
Company Alaska River Pros
Contact Kent & Paula Hueser
City Soldotna
Company Alaska River Safaris
Contact Ronald B. Hyde, Sr.
City Anchorage
Company Alaska Rivers Co.
Contact Gary & Leon Galbraith
City Cooper Landing
Company Alaska Salmon Guaranteed Charters
Contact Michael W. Miller
City Juneau
Company Alaska Saltwater
Contact Toney Hannah
City Anchorage
Company Alaska Saltwater Charters
Contact Dianne Dubuc
City Homer
Company Alaska Se Air Adventures
Contact Michael & Connie Mills
City Gustavus
Company Alaska Sea Hunter
Contact Mark & Cathie Prindle
City Anchorage
Company Alaska Seakatch Charters
Contact James Van Der Sanden
City Homer
Company Alaska Sheefish Haven Lodge
Contact Gail & Robert Vanderpool
City Red Devil
Company Alaska Skiff Charters, Inc.
Contact Mark & Michelle Kaelke
City Juneau
Company Alaska Sport Fishing Tours
Contact Les Coates
City Anchor Point
Company Alaska Sports & Hobby Expediters
Contact Gerald Silliman
City Eagle River
Company Alaska Sunrise Fishing Adventures
Contact Wayne Pulley
City Sterling
Company Alaska Tolovana Adventures
Contact Doug Bowers & Kathy

Liemiger
City Nanana
Company Alaska Trail & Sail Adventures
Contact Tadd Owens, Zach Steer Clint Lentfer
City Anchorage
Company Alaska Trophy Safaris, Inc.
Contact H. Dennis Harms
City Chugiak
Company Alaska Trout Outfitters
Contact Richard Andres
City Wasilla
Company Alaska Troutfitters
Contact Curt Muse & Bob Andres
City Cooper Landing
Company Alaska Victory Adventures
Contact Vickie Staples
City Anchorage
Company Alaska Walkabouts
Contact Ted Raynor
City Anchorage
Company Alaska Waters Charters
Contact Eric Morisky
City Sitka
Company Alaska Waters, Inc.
Contact Jim & Wilma Leslie
City Wrangell
Company Alaska Waterways
Contact Don Reesor
City Soldotna
Company Alaska West Air, Inc.
Contact Doug & Danny Brewer
City Nikiski
Company Alaska Whitewater Kings
Contact Dave Burk
City Gakona
Company Alaska Wild Salmon Charters
Contact Jason Yeoman
City Kasilof
Company Alaska Wilderness Tours
Contact Steven Parks
City Anchorage
Company Alaska Wilderness Tours
Contact Ty & Bill Newman
City Eagle River
Company Alaska Wilderness Trips
Contact Clark & Cheryl Whitney
City Soldotna
Company Alaska Wildland Adventures
Contact Kirk Hoessle & Fred Telleen
City Girdwood
Company Alaska Wildlife Charters
Contact Hans Zietlow & Paul Berg
City Juneau
Company Alaska Yacht Guides
Contact Bob & Ann Widness
City Ketchikan
Company Alaska Yachting & Fishing
Contact Dean Jaquish
City Wrangell
Company Alaska's Cook Inlet Lodge
Contact James Yancy
City Ninilchik
Company Alaska's Lost Rainforest Guide
Contact Lavern R. Beier
City Juneau
Company Alaska's Valhalla Lodge
Contact Capt. Kirk
City Anchorage
Company Alaska's Wilderness Lodge
Contact Tim Cudney
City Anchorage
Company Alaska/Idaho Fishing Guide
Contact Steve Toth
City Anchorage
Company Alaskan Ecoventures
Contact Glen Tilghman
City Anchorage
Company Alaskan Adventure Charters
Contact Michael Hopley
City Soldotna
Company Alaskan Adventures
Contact Ray Crandall
City Homer
Company Alaskan Adventures
Contact Sean Barrow
City Anchor Point
Company Alaskan Adventures in the Wilderness
Contact Chuck Hugny
City Tanana

Company Alaskan Angler
Contact Robert Johnson
City Soldotna
Company Alaskan Angler Charters
Contact Joseph & Cynthia Kilian, Jr.
City Valdez
Company Alaskan Angling
Contact Matt Dimmick
City Anchorage
Company Alaskan Charters
Contact H. Dale & Betty Tyree
City Anchorage
Company Alaskan Combination Charters
Contact Stewart & Jani Trammell
City Kenai
Company Alaskan Escapes
Contact Kim & Sue Betzina
City Point Baker
Company Alaskan Experience
Contact Jim Bailey
City Eagle River
Company Alaskan Fishing Eagle Charters
Contact L. Tom Smotherman
City Sitka
Company Alaskan Game Fisher
Contact Mel Erickson
City Soldotna
Company Alaskan Helicopter Fishing
Contact Tony Oney
City Anchorage
Company Alaskan Helicopter Fishing
Contact John & Anthony Oney
City Anchorage
Company Alaskan Home Fishing Lodge
Contact Robert B. Holston, Jr.
City Ketchikan
Company Alaskan Outback Outfitters
Contact
City Wasilla
Company Alaskan Outdoor Adventures
Contact Brad Adams
City Soldotna
Company Alaskan River Charters
Contact Fred Rhoades
City Anchorage
Company Alaskan River's & Sea's Fishing Guides
Contact Melvin H. Forsyth, Jr.
City Soldotna
Company Alaskan Scenic Waterways
Contact Ron Compton
City Petersburg
Company Alaskan Snow Bear
Contact Patrick Grimm
City Anchor Point
Company Alaskan Sportfisher
Contact Shawn Friendshuh
City Copper Center
Company Alaskan Sports
Contact Rodney J. Kelly
City Sitka
Company Alaskan Star Charters
Contact Ken & Toni Wyrick
City Wrangell
Company Alaskan Summertime
Contact Jon & Tena Tippit
City Seward
Company Alaskan Trophies
Contact Mark Tuter
City Soldotna
Company Alaskan Trophy Charters
Contact Donald L. Erwin
City Ninilchik
Company Alaskan Wildlife & Fishing Adventures
Contact Richard Baker
City Kenai
Company Alasking Charters
Contact Michael Dick
City Anchorage
Company Alasking Charters
Contact Chad Thurman
City Anchorage
Company Alexander Creek Lodge
Contact Kristi Sherwood
City Alexander Creek
Company Alexander Creek Lodge, Inc.
Contact Fred Sorensen
City Alexander Creek
Company Alexander Lake Lodge

Contact Dr. Gunter Weis
City Anchorage
Company Alie-Bob Charters
Contact Robert P. Mattson
City Ketchikan
Company All Alaskan Adventures
Contact Fred C. Heim
City Kenai
Company Aloha Charters
Contact Gary Jarvill
City Sitka
Company Altland's Kenai Guides
Contact William & Sandy Altland
City Kenai
Company Amaya's Alaska Adventures
Contact Alvaro Amaya
City Alexander Creek
Company Amberg Enterprises
Contact William Amberg
City Wasilla
Company Amorak Traders
Contact Craig S. Loughran
City Palmer
Company Anchor Marine Charters
Contact Richard Pendrey
City Anchor Point
Company Anchor Pass Charter Co.
Contact Randy Spearing & Craig Trulock
City Ketchikan
Company Anchor Point Lodge
Contact Dean T. Murayama & Matthew T. Sugal
City Auke Bay
Company Anderson Charters
Contact Curtis M. Anderson
City Ketchikan
Company Anderson's Guide Service
Contact Ray Anderson
City Kenai
Company Angel Haven Lodge
Contact Thomas Angel
City Skwentna
Company Angel Haven Lodge Inc.
Contact Christopher Sopp
City Anchorage
Company Angela Rose Adventures
Contact
City North Pole
Company Angler Choice Lodge
Contact Doug Unruh
City Juneau
Company Angler Paradise - Kulik
Contact Peter Ball
City Anchorage
Company Angler's Charter Service
Contact Mike White
City Sitka
Company Angler's Lodge & Fish Camp
Contact Patrick Tolar
City Sterling
Company Angler's Paradise
Contact Kip Minnery
City Anchorage
Company Anglers Emporium
Contact Joe Dibenedetto
City Anchorage
Company Anglers Paradise Lodges
Contact
City Anchorage
Company Angling Unlimited, Inc.
Contact
City Sitka
Company Aniak Air Guides
Contact Rick Townsend
City Aniak
Company Aniak River Lodge
Contact Sam Sudore
City Aniak
Company Ann's Charters
Contact David A. Bernhardt
City Sitka
Company Another Adventures
Contact Collette M. & Robert E. Golson
City Homer
Company Anytime Charters
Contact Marvin H. Walter
City Juneau
Company Anytime Cruises, Inc.
Contact James R. Chen
City Juneau
Company Apple Island Charter & Lodge

Contact Thomas D. Rightmier
City Sitka
Company Aquabionics, Inc.
Contact Jon & Lois VanHyning Jack
City Fairbanks
Company Arch Cape Charters
Contact Brenda Hays
City Homer
Company Arctic Alaska Hunts
Contact David S. Morris
City Fairbanks
Company Arctic Blue Adventures
Contact Stephen W. Gierke
City Anchorage
Company Arctic Fox Charters
Contact Larry E. Bass
City Soldotna
Company Arctic Grayling Guide Service
Contact Reed Morisky
City Fairbanks
Company Arctic Maritime, Inc.
Contact Darwon & Kay Waldsmith
City Ninilchik
Company Arctic Tern Charters
Contact Perry Flotre
City Sterling
Company Arctic Wilderness Charters, Inc.
Contact Shawn Stephen
City Anchorage
Company Argo Charters
Contact James C. Long
City Fairbanks
Company Around the Bend Outfitters
Contact Will D. Cole, et al
City Fairbanks
Company Astco
Contact Burr Henriksen
City Seward
Company Auke Bay Charters
Contact Richard A. White
City Juneau
Company Auklet Charter Services
Contact David P. Janka
City Cordova
Company Aurora Charters
Contact Rodney W. & Stacey A. Mitchell
City Valdez
Company Aurora Charters
Contact Colin B. Ingwersen
City Sitka
Company Aurora Charters
Contact Carl & Kim Hughes
City Seward
Company Aurora Charters
Contact Clifford Chamberlin
City Sterling
Company Austin's Alaska Adventures
Contact Jerry & Clara Austin
City St. Michael
Company B & C Charters
Contact Mary Baringer
City Homer
Company B & R Drift Trips
Contact Brian Greco
City Anchorage
Company B-Obe Charters
Contact Robert Shepard
City Fairbanks
Company B.K. Service's
Contact Brian Kelley
City Gakona
Company BA Charters
Contact Brett Aldridge
City Soldotna
Company Baby J Fishing Charters
Contact Tom & Darcy Stetson
City Juneau
Company Back Country Logistical Services
Contact Greg L. Finstad
City Fairbanks
Company Back Country Logistics
Contact Richard Wysong
City Talkeetna
Company Baja Alaskan Experiences
Contact Charles L. Chandler
City Juneau
Company Bald Mountain Air Service, Inc.
Contact Jeannie G. Porter
City Homer
Company Balmy Weather
Contact Donald Tirrell

City Kasilof
Company Barking Trout Guide Service
Contact John M. McClure
City Fairbanks
Company Barony Lodge - Hewitt Lake
Contact Michael Barron
City Anchorage
Company Barrel E
Contact Steven Childs
City Skwentna
Company Bay Excursions
Contact Karl Stoltzfus
City Homer
Company Bayside Charters
Contact Bert Stromquist
City Sitka
Company Bayside Inn
Contact Mallory Darcey, James Hamilton Jr.
City Larsen Bay
Company Bayside Inn
Contact Michael Massa
City Larsen Bay
Company Bayview Charters, Inc.
Contact Danny Wilson
City Kodiak
Company BDS Investments
Contact Bill Breedlove
City Sitka
Company Beagle Charters
Contact Leanne & Jeff Pilcher
City Juneau
Company Bear Air
Contact Bill & Peggy Bear
City Wasilla
Company Bear Necessity Charters
Contact James K. Davis
City Kodiak
Company Bear Paw Charters
Contact John & Denise Ogle
City Anchor Point
Company Bear Paw Lodge
Contact Thomas Kreinheder
City Anchorage
Company Beartrack Charters
Contact Todd Wich & William Helms
City Juneau
Company Beartrack Charters
Contact Ken & Darlene Wicks
City Juneau
Company Becharof Lodge
Contact Mark LaRae LaCrosse
City Egegik
Company Belinda V. Charters
Contact Shapleigh & Saundra Howell
City Bethel
Company Beluga Bob's Guide Service
Contact Robert W. Honea
City Kenai
Company Berean & Sons' Enterprises
Contact William Berean
City Big Lake
Company Bergie's Guide Service
Contact Bruce Bergman
City Bethel
Company Bering Straits Exploration & Charter Serv.
Contact Louis H. Green, Jr.
City Nome
Company Bernie Fishing Charts
Contact Bernard White
City Soldotna
Company Big Al's Charter
Contact Allen Clark
City Kodiak
Company Big Blue Charters
Contact Michael R. Keating
City Sitka
Company Big Dan's Cheap Charters
Contact Dan Martin
City Sitka
Company Big Dick's Wild Alaskan Adventures
Contact Richard L. Nadeau
City Anchorage
Company Big Dipper Guides
Contact Joseph Hanes
City Soldotna
Company Big Fisherman Charters
Contact Thomas & Bruce Knowles
City Wasilla
Company Big Jim's Charters
Contact Jim & Jane Preston
City Auke Bay

Company Big John's Charter Service
Contact John Malouf
City Anchorage
Company Big Mike's Charters
Contact Michael Boettcher
City Anchorage
Company Big Pond Sportfishing
Contact Charles A. Hoff
City Anchorage
Company Big Sky Charter & Fish Camp
Contact Joseph F. Connors
City Anchorage
Company Big T's Fishing Guide Service
Contact Timothy W. Linngren
City Soldotna
Company Big-Un's Guide Service
Contact Terry M. Brasel
City Sterling
Company Bilak's Stillwater Adventures
Contact Richard P. Bilak
City Anchorage
Company Bill Martin Fish Alaska, Inc.
Contact William R. & Mary K. Martin
City Anchorage
Company Bill Roley Guide Service
Contact Bill Roley
City Seldovia
Company Bill's Alaska Charters
Contact William Cox
City Soldotna
Company Bill's Fishing Guide Service
Contact William Deavilla
City Anchorage
Company Bill's Guide Service
Contact Keith Bockhahn
City Anchorage
Company Bill's Riverboat Service
Contact William Bohlscheid
City Anchorage
Company Billiken Charters
Contact Frank & Linda Sheppard
City Anchorage
Company Birch Bark Charters
Contact Bill Robbins
City Kodiak
Company Birch Island Lodge
Contact Stephen J. Brooks
City Haines
Company Bit O Lab Kennels
Contact James & Marilyn Bitney
City Wasilla
Company Black Dog Fishing Guides
Contact Patrick D. Carter
City Soldotna
Company Black Fox Lodge
Contact Nancy Conklinand Eddie Metcalf
City Alexander Creek
Company Black Fox Lodge/K and M Ventures
Contact Kris Draper
City Anchorage
Company Black Heart Charters
Contact Bill & Barbara Swearingiz
City Kodiak
Company Blue Jacket Enterprises
Contact Peter Kimzey
City Port Alexander
Company Blue Raven Charters
Contact Frank Demmert, Jr.
City Klawock
Company Blue Sky Charter
Contact Kevin C. Fromm
City Craig
Company Blue Sky Charters
Contact James Wilson
City Kenai
Company Blue Star Charters
Contact Brett Stillwaugh
City Ketchikan
Company Blue Water Charter
Contact Terrance L. Clark
City Homer
Company Bo's Fishing Guide Service
Contact Raymond Ansel
City Soldotna
Company Boardwalk Wilderness
Contact Douglas Ibbetson
City Thorne Bay
Company Bob's Trophy Charters
Contact David Morris
City Homer
Company Bob's Walkabout Fly

Fisher's Guide
Contact Robert P. Shafer
City Seward
Company Booth Trophy Fishing
Contact David Booth
City Soldotna
Company Borealis Charters
Contact Tom Cocklin
City Anchorage
Company Bounty Hunter Charter
Contact Joseph Laba
City Anchorage
Company Brabazon Expeditions
Contact Patrick & Kathi Pellett
City Yakutat
Company Brado's Fishing
Contact Keith Brady
City Wrangell
Company Bread 'n Butter Charters
Contact Kenneth R. & June A. Miller
City Whittier
Company Breakaway Adventures
Contact Eric Yancey
City Wrangell
Company Brightwater Alaska, Inc.
Contact Charles Ash
City Anchorage
Company Briska Charters
Contact
City Homer
Company Bristol Bay Anglers
Contact Chip Henward
City King Salmon
Company Bristol Bay Charter Adventures
Contact Patrick & Diedre O'Neill
City Soldotna
Company Bristol Bay Coastal Charters
Contact Anthony G. & Deborah A. Bartlett
City Petersburg
Company Bristol Bay Outfitters
Contact Robert Heyano & William Chaney
City Dillingham
Company Bristol Bay River Charters
Contact James V. Grimes
City Dillingham
Company Bristol Charters
Contact James Archer Corbin, Jr.
City North Pole
Company Brownie's Charters
Contact Wayne B. Brown
City Sitka
Company Bruce Nelson's Float Fishing Service
Contact Bruce Nelson
City Cooper Landing
Company Bryant's Hunting Adv.
Contact Larry Bryant
City Anchorage
Company Bubba Charters
Contact Eryl J. Peterson
City Homer
Company Buccaneer Charters
Contact Arthur Myers
City Homer
Company Bulchitna Lake Lodge
Contact William Mazoch
City Anchorage
Company Burton Charters
Contact Hugh Burton
City Sitka
Company Bush Fishing
Contact Perry S. Burress
City Nome
Company Bush Guiding
Contact Bobby Kempson
City North Pole
Company Bush Wacker Fly Fishing Service
Contact John & Cidi Godsey
City Eagle River
Company By the Sea Enterprises
Contact Avery G. Simmons
City Sitka
Company C & D Guides & Outfitters
Contact Charles Dickson
City Soldotna
Company C & E Enterprises
Contact Clifford & Emestine Alexander
City Sterling
Company C & R Outfitters
Contact Richard Bennett
City Anchorage

Company C B Three Charters
Contact Robert R. & Cheryl Wambach
City Homer
Company C-Jo Charters
Contact Joe R. Collins
City Sitka
Company C&J's Alakan Safaris
Contact James & Connie Sargeant
City Anchor Point
Company C.C. Charters
Contact Chad Christoffer
City Soldotna
Company Cache Creek Lodge
Contact Bonnie Hutcheson
City Trapper Creek
Company Cache Creek Lodge
Contact Robert Lane
City Eagle River
Company Camp Bendeleben
Contact John Elmore
City Nome
Company Campbell Air, Inc.
Contact Kevin Campbell
City Fairbanks
Company Campbell's Fishing Charters
Contact Clyde & Vicki Campbell
City Ketchikan
Company Can-Do Fishing Charters
Contact Rick V. Sauve
City Soldotna
Company Cannonball Charters
Contact Foy Nevers
City Sitka
Company Cap'n Patty Charters
Contact Michael & Patricia Wing
City North Pole
Company Cape Codder Adventures
Contact Bruce A. Reddish
City Eagle River
Company Capital City Fishing Charters
Contact Tracy A. Rivera
City Juneau
Company Capt. Black Bart's Charters
Contact James M. Cowan
City Sitka
Company Capt. Bligh Beaver Cr.
Contact Larry Wheat
City Soldotna
Company Capt. Bligh's Beaver Creek Lodge
Contact Clinton & Dolores Coligan
City Soldotna
Company Capt. Mike's Charters
Contact Michael & Mary Huff
City Homer
Company Capt. Ron's Specialty Charters
Contact Ronald W. Becker
City Anchorage
Company Captain B's Alaskan C's Adventures
Contact Captain Bryan
City Homer
Company Captain Bob's Charters
Contact Robert C. Crocker
City Anchorage
Company Captain Brown's Sound Adventures
Contact Grady Brown, Jr.
City Fairbanks
Company Captain Cook Charters
Contact Alfred M. Cook
City Juneau
Company Captain Dan's Charters
Contact Dan Gagnon
City Hoonah
Company Captain George's Charters
Contact Jr. & Ann Dimmick George Will
City Wasilla
Company Captain Jim's Great Alaska Charter Co.
Contact Jim & Ruby Alexander
City Valdez
Company Captain Pete's Alaskan Experience
Contact Captain Pete Wedin
City Homer
Company Captain Ron's Alaska Adventures
Contact Ronald & Sherry Johnson
City Homer
Company Carl's Fishing Fiesta
Contact Carl Ulrich
City Soldotna
Company Carmuk Charters

Contact Carla Szitas & Mike Norris
City Ketchikan
Company Carpe Dien Charters
Contact Robert W. Cowell
City Sitka
Company Casa De Kings Fishing Adventures
Contact Phil & Earl Mertzweiller James
City Anchor Point
Company Cascade Inn & Boat Charters, Inc.
Contact
City Sitka
Company Catch Master Charters
Contact Rick & Teresa Versteeg
City Petersburg
Company Catch-A-King Charters
Contact Richard Manning & Paul Roop
City Craig
Company Caught A Big One
Contact David Milton
City Houston
Company Celebrity Charters
Contact J. C. Morrison
City Sitka
Company Cetacea Enterprises
Contact Dan Garner
City Auke Bay
Company Chaik George Charters
Contact Garfield P. George
City Angoon
Company Chan IV Charters
Contact L.S. & Alvara Wright
City Petersburg
Company Chances R Charters
Contact Ken & Lori Elliott
City Juneau
Company Chandalar River Outfitters
Contact Keith C. Koontz
City Fairbanks
Company Chanty
Contact Cheryl Pritchard
City Sitka
Company Charley Charters
Contact Charles E. Brown
City Anchorage
Company Charlie Charters
Contact Michael Zelinski
City Homer
Company Charlie's Big Fish Charters
Contact Charlie Pearson
City Manley Hot Springs
Company Chatanika Outfitters
Contact Diane E. Burgess
City Fairbanks
Company Chatham Strait Charters
Contact Dickie L. Dau
City Juneau
Company Chazman Charters
Contact Charles A. Glagolich
City Kodiak
Company Chelatna Lake Lodge
Contact Victor Andresen
City Anchorage
Company Chelatna Lake Lodge
Contact Duke Bertke
City Anchorage
Company Chelatna Lake Lodge
Contact Dale & Logan Raley
City Anchorage
Company Chesser Enterprise
Contact Nathan Chesser
City Anchor Point
Company Chicagof Charters
Contact Paul Johnson
City Elfin Cove
Company Chieko Charters
Contact John & Vivian Kito
City Anchorage
Company Chihuly Charters
Contact Melvin Johnson
City Anchorage
Company Chihuly's Charters
Contact Mark & Susan Chihuly
City Ninilchik
Company Chihuly's Charters
Contact Mike & Shirley Chihuly
City Ninilchik
Company Childs Charters
Contact John Childs
City Fairbanks
Company Chilkat Charters
Contact Norman Hughes
City Haines

Company Chilkat Lake Lodge
Contact William S. Samalon
City Juneau
Company Chilkoot Charters
Contact Larry D. Pierce
City Haines
Company Chinook Charters
Contact Tom Ramiskey
City Ketchikan
Company Chinook Charters
Contact Johnathan Holstrand
City Homer
Company Chinook Charters
Contact Johnathan Hillstrand
City Homer
Company Chip Porter Charters
Contact Chip Porter
City Ketchikan
Company Chitina Bay Lodge
Contact George Juliussen
City Anchorage
Company Choctaw Charters
Contact Glenn Mitchell
City Skagway
Company Chuck Porter Charters
Contact Chuck Porter
City Juneau
Company Chuit River Adventures
Contact Clifford A. Morrison
City Anchorage
Company Chuitna River Guides
Contact Frank Standifer
City Tyonek
Company Cie Jae Charters
Contact Charles & Roberta Crabaugh
City Yakutat
Company Cie Jae Ocean Charters
Contact Charles Crabaugh
City Homer
Company Cinder River Lodge
Contact Gary King, Jr.
City Anchorage
Company CJ's Ventures
Contact Craig A. Jackson
City Fairbanks
Company Classic Alaska Charters
Contact Captain Robert Scherer
City Ketchikan
Company Clearwater Adventures
Contact Thomas & Jody Fica
City Homer
Company Cleaver Wallis Associates
Contact Joe & Mary W. Wallis
City Homer
Company Clive's Fishing Guide Service
Contact Clive & Marilyn Talkington
City Anchor Point
Company Clover Bay Lodge
Contact Stan & Bonnie Oaksmith
City Ketchikan
Company Clover Pass Resort
Contact Gerald F. Engelman
City Ketchikan
Company Coal Creek Wilderness Guided Adv.
Contact Russel J. Lewis
City Kasilof
Company Coastal Island Charters
Contact Michael & Lori Bauer
City Wrangell
Company Coastal Outfitters
Contact Charles & Helen Keim
City Anchor Point
Company Coastal Wilderness Charters
Contact Eric R. Swanson
City Sitka
Company Coho Charters
Contact Marilyn & Terrance Vraniak
City Fairbanks
Company Coho Guide & Air Service
Contact Peter G. Blackmon
City Anchorage
Company Come Fishing with John
Contact John M. Lambe
City Kasilof
Company Comfort Charters
Contact Philip Warren
City Homer
Company Commercial Fisherman's Charter Co.
Contact Steve Weissberg
City Sitka
Company Compass Rose Charters
Contact Jack & Lisa Wallis
City Wasilla

Company Cook Inlet Charters
Contact R. McLean
City Anchorage
Company Cooper Landing Floating
Contact Howard Mulanax
City Anchorage
Company Copper River Guide Service
Contact James & Marlene Tilly
City Iliamna
Company Cordova Airboat Tours
Contact Sharon & John Buehrle, III
City Cordova
Company Cordova Fishing Charters
Contact Craig Lynch
City Cordova
Company Cori-Ann Charters
Contact Joseph Roche
City Anchorage
Company Cottonwood Lodge
Contact William Brion
City Chugiak
Company Covert Alaskan Expeditions
Contact William Covert
City Anchor Point
Company Cra-Zee's II Charter
Contact Dexter C. Zernia
City Anchorage
Company Crackerjack Sportfishing Charters
Contact Captain Andrew Mezirow
City Seward
Company Creekside Inn
Contact Bill Avarell
City Ninilchik
Company Crowley Guide Service
Contact Gerald Crowley
City Talkeetna
Company Cruiser V Charters
Contact Stephen Novakovich
City Anchorage
Company Crystal Creek Lodge
Contact Don Michels
City Anchorage
Company Crystal Sea Charters
Contact Dale & Susan Kanen
City Craig
Company Curt's Guide Service
Contact Curt Madson
City Aniak
Company Curtis' Custom Charters
Contact Curtis H. Bates
City Kenai
Company Cusack's Alaska Lodge
Contact Bob Cusack
City Iliamna
Company Custom Charter
Contact Dale & June Robbins
City Ketchikan
Company D & G Enterprises
Contact David M. & Gail L. Floyd
City Palmer
Company D & M Charters
Contact Debbie J. Hill
City Anchorage
Company Dale's Alaskan Guide Service
Contact Dale Benson
City Anchorage
Company Dale's Guide Service
Contact Dale Hedger
City Kasilof
Company Dan Mar Charters
Contact Dan Loitz
City Ketchikan
Company Dan's Guide Service
Contact Daniel Verkuilen
City Kasilof
Company Daniel's Personalized Guide Service
Contact Daniel H. Donich
City Homer
Company Darbyshire & Associates
Contact Ralph R. & Iele G. Darbyshire
City Anchorage
Company David Ansel Enterprises
Contact David Ansel
City Soldotna
Company Day Harbor Charters
Contact David W. & Agnes A. Miller
City Seward
Company Dean's Guide Service
Contact Dean R. Moloney
City Soldotna
Company Deap Sea Charters
Contact David Rauwolf
City Ketchikan

Company Decker Guide Outfitters
Contact Mark Decker
City Girdwood
Company Deep Creek Fishing Club
Contact Steven Moe
City Ninilchik
Company Deep Sea Charters
Contact Daniel & Jane Gorham
City Homer
Company Deep Sea Charters
Contact Lin L. Keightley
City Sitka
Company Deer Creek Cottage
Contact Sidney & Kathleen Cook
City Thorne Bay
Company Deer Mountain Charters, Inc.
Contact Sr. & Robert Simmons Stephen Aldrich
City Ketchikan
Company Delsbrat Charters
Contact Robert L. Jaynes
City North Pole
Company Denali Highlands Adventures, Inc.
Contact C. Michael Yates
City Delta Junction
Company Denali River Guides
Contact Joe Halladay
City Talkeetna
Company Denny's Gone Fishin Guide Service
Contact Dennis Wells
City Chugiak
Company Dersham's Outlook Lodge
Contact Ed & Karan Dersham
City Anchor Point
Company Diamond Willow Charters
Contact Roger W. Fleming
City Delta Junction
Company Discovery Adventures, Inc.
Contact Robert & Leslie Bell
City Homer
Company Discovery Voyages
Contact Dean Rand
City Cordova
Company Dog Bay Charters of Kodiak
Contact David Bugni
City Kodiak
Company Don T. S/F Charter
Contact Don Tetzlaff
City Anchorage
Company Don's 49er Charter
Contact Donald N. Wood
City Soldotna
Company Donald F. Smith
Contact Donald Smith
City Soldotna
Company Doo Dah Charters
Contact Laurie Flanders
City Anchorage
Company Dorie-J
Contact John Johnson
City Homer
Company Doug Wilhite River Guide
Contact Doug Wilhite
City Coffman Cove
Company Dr. Hook Charters
Contact Leslie & Rory Vail
City Big Lake
Company Dream Catcher Charters
Contact Erwin Samuelson
City Cordova
Company Dream Charters
Contact Chris Nelson & Jody Kruger
City Yakutat
Company Dream Creek Guides
Contact Richard Rothley, Jr.
City Willow
Company Dugan Creek Outfitters
Contact John A. Miller
City Fairbanks
Company Duke Charter
Contact Ronald K. Anderson
City Petersburg
Company Duke's Charter Fishing
Contact Duane "Duke" Hohwart
City Craig
Company E & K's Alaskan Charters
Contact Ernest & Kimberly Kirby
City Palmer
Company E.R.S.A.
Contact Daniel Lange
City Anchorage
Company Eagle Adventures
Contact Larry & Joanne Shaker

City Kodiak
Company Eagle Charters
Contact Al Poskam
City Ketchikan
Company Eagle Claw Charters
Contact Michael Herold
City Juneau
Company Eagle Island Charters
Contact Ed Leask
City Ketchikan
Company Eagle Song Lodge
Contact David Jenny
City Eagle River
Company Eagle Song on Trail Lake
Contact Michael & Paula Williams
City Eagle River
Company Eagle Spirit Charters
Contact Ronald McKinstry
City Homer
Company Eagle-Eye Fishing Charters
Contact Daniel & Diane Ward
City Soldotna
Company Early Time Charters
Contact Norman Rowe
City Clam Gulch
Company Early Times Charters
Contact Dean Bias
City Clam Gulch
Company East Fork Ventures
Contact Robert J. Rehm
City Anchorage
Company Easy Charter
Contact William J. Holman
City Craig
Company Eclipse Alaska
Contact A.E. & Edith VonStauffenberg
City Haines
Company Edgecumbe Exploration
Contact Michael Brooks
City Sitka
Company Eide's Sportfishing Service
Contact Sterling Eide
City Kenai
Company Eight Mile Fish Lodge
Contact Larry Yahnian
City Eagle River
Company El Capitan Lodge, Inc.
Contact Scott E. Van Valin
City Ketchikan
Company Elby Charters
Contact Robert L. Buechner
City Anchorage
Company Elfin Cove Lodge
Contact Captain Dan Baxter
City Elfin Cove
Company Elite Charters
Contact Robert A. Carlson
City Anchorage
Company Elkhorn Adventures
Contact Lester Connelly
City Palmer
Company Ellis Marine
Contact John Ellis
City Wrangell
Company Ellis, Inc.
Contact Dave Ellis
City Petersburg
Company Emerald Cove Lodges
Contact Gary Pahl & Rod Hodgins
City Wasilla
Company Emerald Sea Charters
Contact Mark & Cindy Hedgecock
City Kasilof
Company Emerick Alaska Enterprises
Contact Jonathan Emerick
City Fairbanks
Company Encore Charters
Contact Gerald B. Hughes
City Ketchikan
Company Encounter Charters
Contact Jerry & Barbara Burnett
City Juneau
Company Eres
Contact Louis Butera
City Willow
Company Erion's Guide Service
Contact Tim Erion
City Ninilchik
Company Eruk's Wilderness Floats
Contact Eric Williams
City Anchorage
Company Eskimo Fishing Adventures
Contact Kay, Dorothy, Albert, Valerie Adolph
City Dillingham

Company Esposito Guide Service
Contact Frederick Esposito
City Soldotna
Company Etholen Tours
Contact Forrest Dodson
City Sitka
Company Excursions Unlimited
Contact Craig Monaco
City Sitka
Company Expert Services
Contact Francis Mitchell
City McGrath
Company Explorations Northwest
Contact Mike Halbert
City Juneau
Company Explore Alaska's Southeast
Contact Gordon J. Williams
City Angoon
Company F.I.S.H.E.S.
Contact Floyd Peterson
City Hoonah
Company F/V Eleanor S.
Contact Richard Boyce
City Haines
Company F/V Orion
Contact Thomas W. Rockne
City Petersburg
Company F/V Puffin Lady
Contact Fred Sturman
City Soldotna
Company Fair C's Charters
Contact Darryl Cooper
City Ninilchik
Company Fairchase Charters
Contact Keith A. Kline
City Kenai
Company Fairweather Adventures
Contact James S. Kearns
City Gustavus
Company Fairweather Charters
Contact Frank & Donna Libal
City Homer
Company Fairweather Charters
Contact Kenneth K. Imamura
City Juneau
Company Fakon Charters
Contact Tony Arsenault
City Homer
Company Falls Creek Alaskan Tours
Contact Michael & Margie Barry
City Chugiak
Company Family Charters, Inc.
Contact Arthur Lariviere
City Anchorage
Company Fantasea Charters
Contact Keith & Janice Washburn
City Anchorage
Company Fantasy Fishing Adventures
Contact Philip & Sharon Needham
City Homer
Company Fantasy North
Contact Kenneth A. Cope
City Anchorage
Company Far North Adventures, Inc.
Contact Hal A. LaPointe
City Anchorage
Company Far Out Camping
Contact Clarke Smith
City Anchorage
Company Far Out Camping
Contact Elizabeth Smith
City Anchorage
Company Far Out Camping
Contact Myron Fultz
City Anchorage
Company Farris's Kvichak River Lodge, Inc.
Contact Donald G. & Steve D. Farris
City Anchorage
Company Fejes Guide Service L.T.D.
Contact Samuel T. Fejes, Jr.
City Anchorage
Company Fenton Bros. Guided
Contact Douglas Vincent
City Soldotna
Company Fin-N-Fur Charters, Inc.
Contact Kenneth & Darlene Buttolph
City Fairbanks
Company Fine Charter
Contact Douglas Vincent
City Craig
Company Fireweed Lodge
Contact Bob Anderson
City Klawock
Company Fireweed Lodge Lake

Creek
Contact Werner & Irene Frauenfelder
City Anchorage
Company First Frontier Adventures, Inc.
Contact Gary Price & Fred Christiansen
City Old Harbor
Company First Out-Last In Charter
Contact Craig Loomis
City Haines
Company Fish Alaska Mills Enterprises
Contact C. Larry Mills
City Soldotna
Company Fish Assassin Charters
Contact Clyde M. Campbell IV
City Ketchikan
Company Fish Doctor Guide Service
Contact Bill Whitney
City Soldotna
Company Fish Happens Guide Service
Contact James Stogsdill
City Soldotna
Company Fish Hawk Charters
Contact Richard & Rita Hemmen
City North Pole
Company Fish Hawk Sea Ventures
Contact Lon & Nancy Walters
City Seldovia
Company Fish Man Taxidermy
Contact Michiel L. West
City Soldotna
Company Fish'n With Ed
Contact Ed Pearson
City Kasilof
Company Fish On Charters
Contact Patrick Moore
City Anchorage
Company Fish On Charters
Contact Bradley & Brandon Snodgrass
City Palmer
Company Fish Pirate Charters
Contact Ed Stahl
City Ketchikan
Company Fish R Plenty
Contact Thomas Dotson
City Anchorage
Company Fish Slammer Charters
Contact Kenneth Meserve & Jeff Skaflestad
City Hoonah
Company Fish Tale Charters
Contact Dale Griner
City Anchor Point
Company Fish Tales Charters
Contact Jerry & Leslie Gustafson
City Salchia
Company Fish-N-Chips Charters
Contact David Ardinger
City Kodiak
Company Fish,P.R.N.
Contact Larry Flynn
City Anchorage
Company Fisherman's Choice Charters
Contact Raymond & Debra Blodgett
City Houston
Company Fishers of Men-Outfitters & Guide Service
Contact Mark Conway
City Soldotna
Company Fishin Finders
Contact Karl Finlanbinder
City Homer
Company Fishin World
Contact Frank Huffman
City Anchorage
Company Fishing Experience
Contact Frank Severy
City Anchorage
Company Fishing Rod's Kenai Charters
Contact Rodney W. Jones
City Anchorage
Company Fishing Spirit
Contact Jill Alford
City Anchorage
Company Fishing Unlimited, Inc.
Contact Lorane Owsichek
City Anchorage
Company FishTale River Guides
Contact Andrew Couch
City Palmer
Company Fishward Bound Adventures

Contact Timothy Evers
City Ninilchik
Company Fitzgerald Guide Service
Contact Kevin Fitzgerald
City Talkeetna
Company Flat Fun Charters
Contact Carl & Kathleen High
City Homer
Company Flat Horn Lake Lodge
Contact Norman Kayton
City Anchorage
Company Flat Horn Lake Lodge
Contact Chris Tonkinson and Richard Kerr
City Anchorage
Company Flatlanders
Contact Jim Long
City Homer
Company Floating-N-Fishing
Contact Les Lloyd
City Anchorage
Company Fly Fish with Sandra
Contact Sandra L. Arnold
City Anchorage
Company Fly Rodder's Heaven
Contact Joel Malta
City Anchorage
Company Fly-In Wilderness Fishing
Contact Bob Elliott
City Fairbanks
Company Fly-Inn Fishing & Safaris
Contact Drew Dix
City Manley Hot Springs
Company Flyfishing Kodiak
Contact Jim Lambert
City Kodiak
Company Flying Bear Charters
Contact Bruce Randall
City Ninilchik
Company Forget-Me-Not Charters
Contact Tom Leslie
City Wrangell
Company Forget Me Not North & South
Contact Stu Merchant
City Klawock
Company Forget-Me-Not Charters
Contact Raymond Stein
City Sitka
Company Fowler's Kenai Charters
Contact Robert Fowler
City Soldotna
Company Fox Bay Lodge
Contact Nikolavs Steigler & Doris Ehrenstein
City King Salmon
Company Fred Bouse's Gulkana Salmon Charters
Contact Fred Bouse
City Fairbanks
Company Fred Cook Guide Service
Contact Fred Cook, Jr.
City Anchorage
Company Freddy J's Fish Camp
Contact Alfred G.Yawit, Jr.
City Ninilchik
Company Free Spirit Charters
Contact L.J.Chmielowski
City Juneau
Company Freebird Guide Service
Contact Peter H. Mueller
City Sterling
Company Frontier Charters
Contact Anthony Perez
City Anchorage
Company Frontier Charters
Contact Mike Fleenor
City Ketchikan
Company Frontier Excursions
Contact Robin Stickler
City Sitka
Company Frontier Fly Fishing
Contact Joe Schuster
City Anchorage
Company Frontier Rivers
Contact Glen Byrns
City Sterling
Company Fun Fishin' Alaska
Contact Lewis & Linda Dillon
City Soldotna
Company G & C Enterprises
Contact Geoffrey Brown
City Anchorage
Company G & D Recreational Sportfishing
Contact Gerald Delkettie

City Anchorage
Company G & J Fishing Ventures
Contact Michael Gunderson & Carl Jensen, Jr.
City Cordova
Company G E M Pac
Contact C.L. Traylor
City Wrangell
Company G.I.L.T.P.
Contact David H. Couch
City Sitka
Company Gabbert's Fish Camp
Contact Jim Sprague
City Palmer
Company Gabbert's Fish Camp
Contact Russina & Mike Gabbert
City Anchorage
Company Gabbert's Fish Camp
Contact Paul and Gilbert Gabbert Keith
City Alexander Creek
Company Galatea Charters
Contact J. Mark Quam
City Hoonah
Company Game Fish Alaska
Contact Tokpela Gunton
City Palmer
Company Gate Way Travel
Contact Andre R. Sanders
City North Pole
Company Gentlemen's Sport Guiding
Contact James A. & Gale M. Eastwood
City Petersburg
Company Gentlemen's Sport Guiding
Contact Bradley R. Elfers
City Juneau
Company George Ortman Adventure Guiding
Contact George Ortman
City Willow
Company George Siavelis Registered Guide
Contact George Siavelis
City Aniak
Company Get Hooked Alaska Charters
Contact Graig & Nancy Curtiss
City Petersburg
Company Glacerview Charters
Contact David Vanliere
City Homer
Company Glacier Bay Eagles Nest Lodge
Contact Larry Berryhill
City Gustavus
Company Glacier Bear Lodge, Inc.
Contact James Ross
City Yakutat
Company Glacier Guides, Inc.
Contact Jimmie C. Rosenbruch
City Gustavus
Company Glacier Wind Charters
Contact Shawn McConnell
City North Pole
Company Glacier's Edge Sportfishing
Contact Clifford & Barbara Young
City Eagle River
Company Glen Adventures
Contact Glen W. Ramos
City Palmer
Company Glennallen Sporting Goods
Contact Mike & Linda Lanegan
City Glennallen
Company Go Fishing Alaska
Contact Patrick LeBreton
City Alexander Creek
Company Goins Fishing Charter
Contact Gary L. Goins
City Anchorage
Company Gold Coast Lodge
Contact David Allan Ausman
City Ketchikan
Company Golden Eagle Charters
Contact Ronald & Pamela Gillham
City Soldotna
Company Gone Fishin Charters
Contact Russell Miller
City Ninilchik
Company Good Time Charters
Contact Jeff & J. Chett Cundiff
City Anchor Point
Company Goodhand Charters
Contact John Goodhand
City Ester
Company Goodnews River Lodge

Contact Frank Byerly
City Goodnews Bay
Company Gotta Fish Charters
Contact Debra C. Mackie
City Soldotna
Company Great Alaska Drift Boat
Contact John Drumm
City Talkeetna
Company Great Alaska Fish Camp
Contact Daniel Watts
City Anchorage
Company Great Alaska Fish Camp/Int. Safari
Contact Alan Tappan
City Sterling
Company Great Alaska Fish CampTotem Charters
Contact Gary & Melinda Chamberlin
City Sterling
Company Great Chase Charters
Contact James & Penny Fruge
City Hoonah
Company Great Land Charters
Contact Glen A. Douglas
City Wrangell
Company Great Northern Charters
Contact Ronald D. Kinman
City North Pole
Company Greater Northwest Charters
Contact Bruce Schwartz
City Soldotna
Company Greatland Guide Servce
Contact Alan Goins
City Anchorage
Company Greatland Guide Service
Contact Maria Goins
City Soldotna
Company Greene Water Charters
Contact Harold H. Greene
City Sitka
Company Greg's EZ Limit Guide
Contact Greg Brush
City Soldotna
Company Grey Eagle Charters
Contact George Hiller
City Eagle River
Company Grizzly Charters
Contact Robert Higgs
City Homer
Company Grizzly Charters
Contact John & Jo Earls
City Homer
Company Grubstake Griff's Guides & Outfitter
Contact Michael P.Griffin
City Sterling
Company Guide's Life Enterprises
Contact Richard & Dale Swartzlender
City Kasilof
Company Gulkana Fish Guides
Contact L.A. & Shirley LeMaster
City Gakona
Company Gulkana River Experience
Contact IMike Knaner & Tyler Meinhold
City Fairbanks
Company Gumption Freight
Contact Mitch Falk
City Auke Bay
Company Gunnar Svindland's Charters
Contact Gunnulf Svindland
City Kodiak
Company Gurtler Ent./Manley Boat Charters
Contact Frank & Dian Gurtler
City Manley Hot Springs
Company Gustavus Marine Charters
Contact Michael J. Nigro
City Gustavus
Company Gusto Charters
Contact Ronald Downing
City Homer
Company Gusto Charters
Contact John Owen & Pamela Miedtke
City Gustavus
Company Guth's Lodge at Iliamna
Contact Guth, Inc.
City Soldotna
Company Guy Turner's Northbound Adventures
Contact Guy Turner
City Anchorage
Company Gwin's Lodge, Inc.

Contact George Siter
City Eagle River
Company Gypsy Eagle
Contact Patrick J. Stewart
City Homer
Company H & E Charters
Contact Ben Eveland
City Kasilof
Company H and J Fish Co.
Contact Harold & Janet Haynes
City Ketchikan
Company H. Kernans Guiding Service
Contact Harold Kernan
City Kenai
Company Haida Chief
Contact Kurtis Klese
City Ketchikan
Company Haida Way Lodge Charters
Contact Shaanseet, Inc.
City Craig
Company Haines Tackle Co.
Contact C.P.DeFranco
City Haines
Company Hair of the Bear Charters
Contact Brad Langvardt
City Kenai
Company Halcyon Charter
Contact Bruce Tedtsen
City Gustavus
Company Halo Wawa
Contact Mark Nugent
City Ketchikan
Company Hanada Charters
Contact Todd & Karinda Person
City Juneau
Company Hands On Charters
Contact J. Jason Page
City Auke Bay
Company Hank Hankerd Ltd.
Contact Hank Hankerd
City St. Michael
Company Hanna's Darby
Contact John & Nancy Hanna
City Fairbanks
Company Hannah's Fishing Charters
Contact Keith D.C. Greba
City Sitka
Company Happy Hooker Fishing Lodge
Contact James & Gregorita Smith
City Ninilchik
Company Happy Hooker Sport Fishing
Contact Charles J. Horvath
City Juneau
Company Harbor Mountain Charters
Contact James D. Roesch
City Sitka
Company Hardy's Alaskan Adventures
Contact Joe & Billie Hardy
City Soldotna
Company Harelequin Lodge
Contact Dean Taylor
City Yakutat
Company Harlequin
Contact Larry Dietrick
City Juneau
Company Harmony Point Lodge
Contact Tim & Ila Dillon
City Seldovia
Company Harry Gaines Kenai River
Contact Reuben Hanke
City Kenai
Company Harry Gaines Kenai River
Contact James Rose
City Anchorage
Company Harry's Halibut Charter
Contact Harry Frisbie Jr. & Sr.
City Anchorage
Company Hart Charters
Contact Robert R. Hart
City Homer
Company Hart's Fishing Charters
Contact Richard Hart
City Haines
Company Harv's Charters
Contact Harvey Haynes
City Chugiak
Company Harvs Halibut Charters
Contact Jon Faulkner
City Soldotna
Company Hawk Eye Charters
Contact Albert Bixby & Pam Woolcott
City Juneau

Company HD Charters
Contact Howard Driskell
City Anchorage
Company Headwaters Expeditions, Inc.
Contact Wayne R. Dawson
City Aniak
Company Heidys Alaskan Hideaway Cruises
Contact Boyd & Linda Heidy
City Craig
Company Herring Bay Charters
Contact Robert L. Miller III
City Ketchikan
Company Hewitt Lake Lodge
Contact Martin Wegscheider
City Anchorage
Company Hi-Lo Charters
Contact Bryan Lowe
City Kenai
Company HIC Tours
Contact James R. Ross & John Matsko
City Yakutat
Company Hidden Bay Charters
Contact John Lurhs
City Ketchikan
Company High Adventure Air Charter
Contact Greg & Sandra Bell Mark
City Soldotna
Company High Adventure Air Charter
Contact Jesse Updike
City Kenai
Company High Adventure Air Charter
Contact Nathan Warren
City Soldotna
Company High Adventure Air Charter
Contact Kevin Waldrip
City Soldotna
Company High Country Experience
Contact Jeff & Kris Pralle
City Wasilla
Company Highline Charters
Contact William Webb, Jr.
City Kenai
Company Highliner
Contact Reginald Oleyer
City Anchorage
Company Hill's Charter Fishing Service
Contact Richard Hill
City Soldotna
Company Hindman Charters
Contact Richard S. & Terry H. Hindman
City Petersburg
Company Hoffman & Daughters
Contact Robert B. Hoffman, Jr.
City Anchorage
Company Holiday Charters
Contact Ruby & Geraald Gwillim
City Ward Cove
Company Homer Halibut Charters
Contact Timothy Carr
City Homer
Company Hong Kong Drifter
Contact Thomas Kilfoyle
City Kasilof
Company Hook and Eye Charters
Contact Sean Reilly
City Petersburg
Company Hook-Em Charters
Contact Michael E. White
City Sitka
Company Hook-M-Up Tours, Inc.
Contact Roy Wooderson & Jerry Peterson
City Aniak
Company Hooka-Tooka-Salmon Charters
Contact Lyle D. Ludvick
City Sterling
Company Hooksetter's Guide Service
Contact William Fortney
City Kenai
Company Hoonah Charters
Contact Gordon & Christina Pederson
City Hoonah
Company Hoover's Guide Service
Contact Richard Hoover
City Wasilla
Company Hope Fishing & Sightseeing Charters

Contact Barbara J. Wright
City Hope
Company Hot Spot Charters
Contact David L. Magnus
City Sitka
Company Hotline Charters
Contact Richard W. Frost
City Homer
Company Howard Charters
Contact Christoper B. Howard
City Pelican
Company Howl-It Charters
Contact Steven E. Howlett
City Kenai
Company Hungry Fisherman Charters
Contact Richard & Nancy Diemer
City Kodiak
Company Hunky Dory Enterprises
Contact James Kent
City Craig
Company Hunt Alaska
Contact Virgil L. Umphenour
City Fairbanks
Company Hyak Alaska Charters
Contact Gary McWilliams
City Wrangell
Company Ice Water Adventures
Contact Paul Hansen
City Anchor Point
Company Icelinus Charters
Contact Jeffrey Alden
City Anchorage
Company Icy Beaver Rentals
Contact Don & Terry Johnson
City Myers Chuck
Company Icy Strait Adventures
Contact Joe & Sandra Craig
City Douglas
Company Icy Straits Charters
Contact Robert Clark
City Hoonah
Company Icy Straits Charters
Contact Jamie F. Coby
City Gustavus
Company Iilsgidaay's (Shiny Lady's) Charters
Contact Lisa Marie Lang
City Hydaburg
Company Iliamna Bearfoot Adventures
Contact Greg & Sally Hamm
City Willow
Company Iliaska Lodge, Inc.
Contact Ted Gerken
City Iliamna
Company Independent
Contact Brysan Mulkey
City Skwentna
Company Indian Creek Lodge
Contact Ken R. Jones
City Houston
Company Indian Creek Lodge
Contact William Dixson
City Anchorage
Company Indian Creek Lodge
Contact Kenneth Jones and Valerie Abney
City Anchorage
Company Iniakuk Lake Wilderness Lodge
Contact
City Fairbanks
Company Inian Island Charters
Contact Fred C. Howe
City Elfin Cove
Company Inland Ocean Charters
Contact John T. Robson
City Ketchikan
Company Inland River Charters
Contact Kenneth V. & L. Colleen Conner
City North Pole
Company Inlet Charters
Contact Gary Ault
City Homer
Company Inlet Charters
Contact Harris Miller
City Soldotna
Company Inlet Charters
Contact Instinctive Outdoors
City Marvin Park
Contact Anchor Point
Company Interior A.K. Adventures
Contact Logan G. Ricketts
City Fairbanks
Company Interior Fishing Guide

Contact Chet R.T. Higa
City Eureka
Company International Excursions
Contact Pat Cooper
City Soldotna
Company Irish Lord Charters
Contact Robert Carroll
City Kasilof
Company Irish Lord Charters
Contact Monty H.& Florita F. Richardson
City Seward
Company Irish Rover Charters
Contact Anastatia Gleeson & Charles Ash
City North Pole
Company Irishlord Charters
Contact Jason Sintek
City Kasilof
Company Island Adventures
Contact Gregg Parsley
City Craig
Company Island Adventures
Contact Michael McVey
City Sitka
Company Island Adventures
Contact Paul A. Chervenak
City Kodiak
Company Island Alaska Charters
Contact Patrick L. Smith
City Craig
Company Island Coast Charters
Contact Kenneth J. Rear
City Sitka
Company Island Eagle Charters
Contact Edward C. Leask
City Metlakatla
Company Island Memories
Contact Sandra L. Vinberg
City Kodiak
Company Island Point Lodge, Inc.
Contact Kevin & Frank Stelmach
City Petersburg
Company Island Vacation Services
Contact Susan W. Motter
City Anchorage
Company Island Wings Air Service
Contact Michelle Masden
City Ketchikan
Company Islander Charters
Contact Ole & Sandy Bartness
City Juneau
Company Ivory Gull Charters
Contact Mark A. Wartes
City Fairbanks
Company J & J Charters
Contact Jay B. Myer
City Sitka
Company J & K Outfitters
Contact P.Michael Kush
City Anchorage
Company J & M Charters
Contact Jack Jaynes
City Wasilla
Company J & S Charters
Contact John Hartrick
City Wasilla
Company J-Hook Fisheries
Contact D.L. Corwelius
City Kodiak
Company J&J Charters/Bottom Line Charters
Contact James Russo
City Eagle River
Company J.B.'s Guide Service
Contact John Gilcrease
City Anchorage
Company Jack's Kings & Silvers
Contact Jack & Betty Petersen
City Anchorage
Company Jackpot Charters
Contact Kenneth Kulm
City Wrangell
Company Jackpot Charters
Contact Linda Price
City Sitka
Company Jacobsen's Guide Service
Contact Leif Jacobsen
City Soldotna
Company Jake's Alaska Wilderness Outfitters
Contact John"Jake"Caudet
City Anchorage
Company Jake's Nushagak Salmon Camp
Contact John J. Gaudet

City Anchorage
Company Jambro, Inc.
Contact Thomas James
City Homer
Company Jason's Custom Charters
Contact Jason Loren Carter
City Tenakee Springs
Company JC Rose Guiding
Contact James C. Rose
City Eagle River
Company JD's Adventures
Contact James D. Palin
City Dillingham
Company Jeff Allen Guide Service
Contact Jeff Allen
City Soldotna
Company Jepco Charters
Contact Jep Hansen
City Soldotna
Company Jerry Metcalf Fishing Guide
Contact Jerry Metcalf
City Soldotna
Company Jerry's Charters
Contact Jerry S. Montgomery
City Homer
Company Jim Mackey's Guide Service
Contact James T. Mackey
City Kasilof
Company Jim Rivers Co.
Contact James L. Irvin
City Kenai
Company Jim Rusk Fishing
Contact James Rusk
City Sterling
Company Jim's Guide Service
Contact James McCormick
City Kenai
Company Jim's Jaunts
Contact James R. Hamp
City Haines
Company Jimmie D. Charters
Contact James Decker
City Nikiski
Company Jimmie Jack Charters, LLC.
Contact James Drath & James Drath, Sr.
City Wasilla
Company JKB Outfitters & Guides
Contact John K. Kajiwara
City Anchorage
Company Jodan Partnership
Contact Joann Bailey & Daniel Glaab
City Sitka
Company Jodi Ann Charters
Contact Jerry Virchow
City Sitka
Company Joe Schuster Guide/Outfitter
Contact Joe Schuster
City Anchorage
Company Joe's Alaskan Fishing Adventure
Contact Joseph & Patti Szczesny
City Soldotna
Company Joel McKellar
Contact Joel McKellar
City Chugiak
Company John & Don's Guide Service
Contact John Gamble & Don VanDenboss
City Girdwood
Company John H. Latham, Reg. Guide & Outfitter
Contact Frances C. Latham
City Yakutat
Company Johnny's East River Lodge
Contact Janice Lowenstein
City Yakutat
Company Johnson & Sons Enterprises
Contact Leonard Johnson
City Anchorage
Company Johnson Bros. Sportfishing Guides
Contact James K. Johnson
City Soldotna
Company Johnson's Salmon Service
Contact Brian Johnson
City Eielson AFB
Company Jolly Rogers Charters
Contact Dennis Rogers
City Sitka
Company Jon James Adventures
Contact Jon James
City Anchorage
Company Jones Junkets

Contact Robert Jones
City Ninilchik
Company Joseph M. Dubler Guiding 1
Contact Joseph M. Dubler
City Palmer
Company Joyce Marie Charters
Contact Thomas Mahoney
City Ninilchik
Company Judy Ann AK Charters
Contact Dan Schapt
City Sterling
Company Judy Ann's Alaskan
Contact Daniel Schaff
City Anchorage
Company Jughead Salmon Charters
Contact John Metcalf
City Anchorage
Company K & K River Drifters
Contact Fred B. Hall
City Kasilof
Company K-Bay Charters
Contact Steve Morphis and Kenneth Copple
City Homer
Company Kachemack Bay Water Taxi
Contact Daniel Heitman
City Homer
Company Kachemak Marine Services
Contact Dan Klein
City Anchor Point
Company Kachemak Recreational Services
Contact Richard A. Baltzer
City Homer
Company Kahlitna Fish Camp
Contact Roy Keen
City Palmer
Company Kaleidoscope Cruises
Contact Barry E. Bracken
City Petersburg
Company Kalgin Island Seaside Lodge
Contact David Chessik
City Kenai
Company Kaliakh River Adventures
Contact D. Scott & Candace Ranney
City Homer
Company Kamp Kiseralik
Contact Kakarmiut Corp.
City Akiak
Company Kanektok River Safaris, Inc.
Contact Qanirtuug, Inc.
City Quinhagak
Company Karasti Trophy Lodge
Contact James R. & Alice L. Karasti, Sr.
City Ekwok
Company Karluk Spit Lodge
Contact Arthur Panamaroff
City Larson Bay
Company Kasilof Drifters
Contact William Borgen
City Kasilof
Company Katamiland, Inc.
Contact Raymond F. Petersen
City Anchorage
Company Katmai Fishing Adventures
Contact Nanci A. Morris
City King Salmon
Company Katmai Guide Service
Contact Joseph R. Klutsch
City King Salmon
Company Kayak Express
Contact Peter B. Wright
City Juneau
Company KC's Charter Fishing
Contact Kyle D. & Connie E. Sinclair
City Anchorage
Company Keetah Fish Camp
Contact Dennis & Barbara Roper
City Soldotna
Company Keith Gain
Contact Eric Nordenson
City Seldovia
Company Kellum Enterprises
Contact Daryl E. Kellum
City Point Hope
Company Kelsey's Guide Service
Contact Lanny K. Kelsey
City Anchorage
Company Kemperman
Contact William L. Kemperman
City Thorne Bay
Company Ken's Charters
Contact Kenneth & Barbara Klein
City Ketchikan

Company Kenai Angler
Contact Thomas Jessing
City Sterling
Company Kenai Coast Charters
Contact Robert K. Reiman
City Anchorage
Company Kenai Fjords Outfitters, Inc.
Contact Russ Smith
City Homer
Company Kenai Fjords Outfitters, Inc.
Contact Terry Reece
City Anchorage
Company Kenai Fly Fisher
Contact Stan Smith
City Anchorage
Company Kenai King Drifters
Contact David Musgrave
City Indian
Company Kenai King Fishing Charters
Contact Peter E. Deluca
City Soldotna
Company Kenai Lake Adventures
Contact Michael Bethe
City Anchorage
Company Kenai Lake Adventures & Air Service
Contact Kenneth Bethe
City Cooper Landing
Company Kenai River Guide Service
Contact Raymond McGuire
City Anchorage
Company Kenai River King
Contact Daniel Paulk
City Soldotna
Company Kerr's Slow Boat Charters
Contact Clint J. & Johnny M. Kerr
City Fairbanks
Company Ketch-All-Charters
Contact Michael S. Krieger
City Ketchikan
Company Ketcham's Fishing Charter
Contact Dennis L. Ketcham
City Ketchikan
Company Ketchum Air Service, Inc.
Contact Craig Ketchum
City Anchorage
Company Kev's Fishing Charter
Contact Kevin Pickett
City Soldotna
Company Kevin's King Salmon Inc.
Contact Kevin Zimmerman
City Ninilchik
Company Key-O's Guide Service
Contact Lynn Keogh
City Anchorage
Company King Bear Lodge
Contact Kenneth Christoffersen Sr. & Jr.
City Eagle River
Company King Bear Lodge
Contact Andrew Piekaeski
City Eagle River
Company King Bear Lodge
Contact James Ivey
City Skwentna
Company King Bear Lodge
Contact Danny Germany
City Chugiak
Company King Charters
Contact Mark E. Buchner
City Valdez
Company King Fisher Charters
Contact Terry & Kathie King
City Soldotna
Company King Guiding Service
Contact Jan King
City King Salmon
Company King Halibut Charters
Contact Lucien LaFlamme
City Anchorage
Company King KoInn
Contact Matt Norman & Biz Smith
City Anchorage
Company King Master Charters
Contact Helmer W. & Annette C. Olson
City Petersburg
Company King of Kings Guide Service
Contact Richard & Bonnie Andersen
City Anchor Point
Company King of the River Fishing Charters
Contact Dean Schlehofer
City Anchorage
Company King Pint Lodge
Contact Ronald Dionne

City Wasilla
Company King Point Lodge
Contact Jeff Woodward & Bruno Krebs
City Anchorage
Company King Point Lodge
Contact Patrick Nelson
City Eagle River
Company King Size Adventures
Contact Kenneth Bingaman
City Soldotna
Company King's Budget Charters
Contact Jeffrey King
City Soldotna
Company King's Sportfishing
Contact Joanne G. Fitzerald
City Soldotna
Company Kingfisher Charters
Contact Ken Heaps
City Fairbanks
Company Kingfisher Charters
Contact Seth Bone
City Sitka
Company Kings Run Charters
Contact Lawrence B. & Suzan E. Cobb
City Ninilchik
Company Kirawan Custom Cruises
Contact Frederick N. & Marti A. Anderson
City Homer
Company Kitchen Pass Charters
Contact Steven M. & Arnel A. Whitney
City Anchorage
Company Kittiwake Charters
Contact Don Ingledue
City Juneau
Company Klondike Mike's Drift Fishing
Contact Michael Johnson
City Soldotna
Company Klutina Lake Lodge
Contact Mike & Samuel Jordan
City Anchorage
Company Knight Island Adventures
Contact Kenneth Storlie
City Fairbanks
Company Knik Guide Service
Contact John Whitlatch
City Plmer
Company Kniktuk Outfitters, Inc.
Contact Cynthia A. Wener
City Delta Jct.
Company Kodiak Discoveries
Contact Thomas H. Stick
City Kodiak
Company Kodiak Island Charters
Contact Chris & Jainan Fiala
City Kodiak
Company Kodiak Kingbuster Sportsfishing
Contact John & Joy Parker
City Kodiak
Company Kodiak Lucky Hook Charters
Contact Fred O'Hearn
City Kodiak
Company Kodiak Sports & Tour
Contact Scott R. Phelps
City Port Lions
Company Kodiak Western Charters
Contact David Harville & Eric Stirrup
City Kodiak
Company Kodiak Wilderness Lodge
Contact Jim Hamilton & Mitch Hull
City Kodiak
Company Kodiak-Katmai Outdoors, Inc.
Contact Clint & Sharol Hlebechuk
City Kodiak
Company Kraft Adventures
Contact Keith Maltison
City Anchorage
Company Krestof Charters
Contact David Pearson
City Sitka
Company Krog's Kamp
Contact Mel & Bob Krogseng
City Soldotna
Company KS Fisheries
Contact Geoff Widdows
City Yakutat
Company Kurtti Marine
Contact Robert Kurtti
City Wrangell
Company Kuskokwim Wilderness

Adventures
Contact Jill & Bev Hoffman Michael
City Bethel
Company L & M Charters
Contact Michael & Linda Slifer
City Sitka
Company L & S Company
Contact Lawrence & Shirley Rodger
City Skwentna
Company l'But Kick'n Charters
Contact Dennis D. Hubble
City Anchorage
Company Lady Luck Charters
Contact Glen M. Clough
City Old Harbor
Company Laine's Guide Service
Contact Laine W. Lahrdt
City Kasilof
Company Lake Clark Air, Inc./The Farm Lodge
Contact Sr. & Jean P. Alsworth Glen R.
City Port Alsworth
Company Lake Creek Lodge
Contact Brenda & John Shrader
City Palmer
Company Lake Iliamna Adventures
Contact John Baechler
City Iliamna
Company Lake Trout with Bob
Contact Robert Plouffe
City Glennallen
Company Lakeside Lodge
Contact Norm & Brad Johnson
City Port Alsworth
Company Lannigan, Inc.
Contact David & Vicki Lannigan
City Juneau
Company Larry Waltrip, Guide
Contact Larry Waltrip
City Soldotna
Company Iaska Anglers
Contact Steve Voth
City Anchorage
Company Last Frontier Adventures
Contact Nick Pendergast
City Soldotna
Company Last Frontier Charters
Contact Ralph C. & Jacqueline J. Burnett
City Thorne Bay
Company Last Frontier Fishing Comp.
Contact Joe Cannava & Chris Cromer
City Soldotna
Company Lazy-Sun Charters
Contact Timothy Joseph Billings
City Anchor Point
Company LeConte Outfitters
Contact David & Wanda Helmick
City Petersburg
Company Leisure Fishing Charters
Contact George Wm. Wiese
City Fairbanks
Company Leisure Time Charters
Contact Albert Stuefloten
City Ninilchik
Company Lemire Charters
Contact Steven J. Lemire
City Klawock
Company Lenny Dipaolo's Guided Fishing
Contact Lenny Dipaolo
City Kasilof
Company Leonard's Landing Lodge, Inc.
Contact Dawn Otto
City Yakutat
Company Leprechaun Custom Charters
Contact Joan L. Herbage
City Juneau
Company Lewis Charters
Contact Daniel Lewis
City Anchorage
Company Lewis Charters
Contact Nevin Dahl
City Anchorage
Company Lick Creek Guiding Services
Contact Michael Sexton
City Anchorage
Company Lighthouse Charter Service
Contact James R. Peters
City Juneau
Company Lighthouse Charters
Contact Burgess Bauder
City Sitka

Company Line Stripper Fishing Adventures
Contact Daniel E. Welch
City North Pole
Company Linus Charters
Contact Dennis McElroy
City Ketchikan
Company Lisa Mae Charters
City Sitka
Company Lisianski Charter
Contact Denny & Paul Corbin
City Pelican
Company Lisianski Inlet Lodge
Contact Gail D. Corbin
City Pelican
Company Little Hobo Charters
Contact Michael G. Paterson
City Ketchikan
Company Local Yocal
Contact James J. Slone
City Kenai
Company Lodge Across the Bay
Contact George & Nancy Curtiss
City Petersburg
Company Log Cabin Resort & RV
Contact Verne L. & Martin J. Fabry
City Klawock
Company Lone Wolf Charters
Contact John J. Bosarge
City Soldotna
Company Lonesome Dove Charters
Contact Patrick F. Laws
City Ketchikan
Company Long Island Charters
Contact Jim Hanson
City Sitka
Company Loomis Charters
Contact Robert Loomis
City Haines
Company Lorato Charters
Contact Thomas & Lori Stewart
City Kodiak
Company Lori's Charters
Contact Lori Blank
City Ninilchik
Company Lost Marlin Charters
Contact Kevin M. & Lynetta J. Siska
City Juneau
Company Lowe's Guide Service
Contact John Lowe
City Anchorage
Company Lower Cook Inlet Charters
Contact
City Soldotna
Company Luck of the Irish Charters
Contact Patrick & Peggy Bookey
City North Pole
Company Lucky Pierre Charters
Contact Dave Mastolier
City Homer
Company Lucky Pierre Charters/PWS
Contact Gary Mastolier
City Homer
Company Lucky Strike Charters
Contact Lewis Stamm
City Ketchikan
Company M & M Guiding
Contact Marty Myre
City Anchorage
Company M-N-L Charters
Contact Mark H. Bailleson
City Port Lions
Company M/V Irish
Contact Robert Sean Martin
City Homer
Company M/V Juno Charter
Contact Donald D. Holmes
City Petersburg
Company M/V Serrant
Contact Mark A. & Karla Jo Clemens
City Seward
Company Maaluqs Lodge
Contact Lukia Lelkok, Sr.
City Ekwok
Company Mac's Charters
Contact Herman M. Meiners, Jr.
City Juneau
Company Macaw Point Marine
Contact Marvin & Suzanne Proctor
City Sitka
Company MacDougall Lodge
Contact Joshua Tompkins
City Palmer
Company Mackinaw Charters
Contact Glen Szymoniak

City Homer
Company Mad Viking Charters
Contact John & Marilyn Kvarford
City Seldovia
Company Madd Gaffer Charters
Contact James Bostrom
City Anchor Point
Company Maestro's Guide Service
Contact Michael R. Cunningham
City Anchorage
Company Magic Man Charters
Contact Stan Malcom
City Petersburg
Company Magie's Guide Service
Contact Mike Pierce
City Anchorage
Company Magnum Charters
Contact Gary & Emily Salter
City Kodiak
Company Magnum Charters
Contact William & Sharon Kacenas
City Ketchikan
Company Mahay's Riverboat Service
Contact Stephen T. & Kristene O. Mahay
City Talkeetna
Company Mahay's Riverboat Service
Contact Eric Johnson
City Talkeetna
Company Majestic Mountain Alaskan Adv., Inc.
Contact Jeff & Cyndi Chadd
City Glennallen
Company Majestic River Charters
Contact Michael R. & Priscilla Pate
City Soldotna
Company Major Scales Charters
Contact Dale A. Curtis
City Ketchikan
Company Makai Charters
Contact Troy B. Thain
City Craig
Company Many Rivers Alaska
Contact Robert Maker
City Anchorage
Company Many Rivers Alaska
Contact Robert Maker & Steve Olson
City Anchorage
Company Many Rivers Alaska
Contact Steven Olson
City Wasilla
Company Mar Nee' Rods
Contact Mark Lutsch
City Sterling
Company Maranatha Lodge
Contact Roger & Vera Skogen
City Koliganek
Company Marina Air, Inc.
Contact Rick Gold
City Fairbanks
Company Marine Air Service
Contact Joseph N. & Deborah Darminio
City Kodiak
Company Mark Madura Inc.
Contact Mark Madura
City Anchorage
Company Mark's Fishing
Contact Mark Reilly
City Kasilof
Company Mark's Guide Service
Contact Mark Sandland
City Anchorage
Company Marlin's Fly & Tackle
Contact Marlin Benedict
City Wrangell
Company Marlow's Kenai River Drifters
Contact Neil L. Marlow
City Soldotna
Company Marmot Bay Charters
Contact Kevin W. Adkins
City Port Lions
Company Marmot Bay Excursions
Contact Andrew & Cheryl Christofferson
City Ouzinkie
Company Marta R. Charters
Contact James N. Ryman
City Sitka
Company Martin's Fishing Guide Service
Contact Gregor P. Martin, Sr.
City Anchorage
Company Mary Time Charters
Contact Doug & Mary Blossom

City Clam Gulch
Company Masu Fishing
Contact James Nardelli
City Halibut Cove
Company Maverick Charters
Contact Paul K. Matter
City Sitka
Company McComon's Guide Service
Contact David McComon
City Cooper Landing
Company McCord Lodge
Contact Brent & Kevin Arndt
City Kodiak
Company McCormick Charters
Contact Craig & Linda McCormick
City Haines
Company McDougall Lodge
Contact David McHoes
City Skwentna
Company McDougall Lodge
Contact John Bitney
City Anchorage
Company McDougall Lodge
Contact Earl Wright
City Big Lake
Company McDougall Lodge
Contact Kazuko Floyd
City Anchorage
Company McDougall Lodge
Contact Frank Ciccone
City Anchorage
Company McFarland's Floatel
Contact Jim & Jeannie McFarland
City Thorne Bay
Company McPuffin Charters
Contact Fred Shultz & Dave Skidmore
City Ketchikan
Company Meggie Rose, Inc.
Contact Megan & Cassie Carlsen David
City Kodiak
Company Meyers Chuck Lodge
Contact Clifford E. Gardner
City Ketchikan
Company Michael L. Duvall Charters
Contact Michael Duvall
City Juneau
Company Mick's Adventures
Contact Robert Allen Mick
City Anchorage
Company Mickey Fin Charters
Contact Lyall Hadsel
City Juneau
Company Midnight Sun Trophy Pike Adventures
Contact Dean Nelsen & Leon Randermann
City Kenai
Company Midnight Sun Yacht Charters
Contact Captain Ted C. Pratt
City Ketchikan
Company Mike Cusack's King Salmon Lodge, Inc.
Contact Mike Cusack
City Anchorage
Company Mike's Good Time Charters
Contact Michael Butcher
City Big Lake
Company Mike's Salmon X-Press
Contact Michael T. Turner
City Anchorage
Company Miller's Riverboat Service
Contact Gary L. Miller
City Houston
Company Millers Charters
Contact Mark & Partheniu Miller
City North Pole
Company Mission Lodge at Aleknagik
Contact Dale DePriest
City Anchorage
Company Misty Fjords Air & Business
Contact David P.Doyon
City Ketchikan
Company Mitkof Island Charters, Inc.
Contact Gregg Magistrale
City Petersburg
Company Moby King Charters
Contact Robert R. Estes
City Sterling
Company Moe-Z Charters
Contact Michael Comstock
City Homer
Company Moegy's Guide Service
Contact Lee & Mary Moeglein

City Wasilla
Company Montana Trout Lodge
Contact David H. Couch
City Sitka
Company Moose Horn Lodge
Contact Ron Helliwell
City Wasilla
Company Moose John Outfitters
Contact
City Girdwood
Company Moosehorn Lodge
Contact Eric Napflin
City Wasilla
Company Moosehorn Roadhouse
Contact James Butts
City Trapper Creek
Company Moquin Marine Charters
Contact Eugene Louis Moquin
City Gustavus
Company Morning Glory
Contact Ked Schoming
City Palmer
Company Morning Mist Charters
Contact Wayne & Barbara Fleek
City Anchorage
Company Morning Peace River Guides
Contact Pete Brown
City Aniak
Company Morrison Guide Service
Contact Michael E. Morrison
City King Salmon
Company Mosby Charters
Contact Lewis Mosby
City Anchorage
Company Mother Goose Lodge
Contact Donald Wallis
City Skwentna
Company Mother Goose Lodge
Contact Vernon Logan
City Skwentna
Company Mountain Monarchs of Alaska
Contact David J. Leonard
City Kenai
Company Mountain Point Bed & Breakfast
Contact Jeffrey & Marilyn Meucci
City Petersburg
Company Mountain Point Charter & Boat Rental
Contact Stella Callentine
City Ketchikan
Company Mr. B's
Contact Richard S. Bartolowits
City Clam Gulch
Company Mr. C's
Contact Chuck Martin
City Wrangell
Company Muddy River Boat Works
Contact Thomas E. Jackson
City Haines
Company Muskeg Excursions
Contact Johnnie R. & Fran C. Laird
City Wrangell
Company My-Time Cruises
Contact James Young
City King Salmon
Company Mykwasina Charters
Contact Mark T. Johnson
City Ketchikan
Company Narrow's Edge
Contact Robert & Beth Oyler
City Petersburg
Company Natalia Charters
Contact Bruce Schactler
City Kodiak
Company Natron Air
Contact Virgil Mosiman
City Soldotna
Company Natron Air
Contact Chuck Osmond
City Soldotna
Company Nedrow Enterprises
Contact Monte "Wes" & Sandra Kay Nedrow
City Kodiak

Company Nekton Charters
Contact
City Sitka
Company New Englander on the Kenai, Guide Svc
Contact Ronald & Deborah Kim Verney
City Soldotna
Company Newhalen Lodge, Inc.
Contact Bill Sims
City Anchorage
Company Nick's Guide Service
Contact Dominic Hallford
City Soldotna
Company Nikiski Boat Works
Contact Bill Boutilier
City Nikiski
Company Nine Lives Charters
Contact Michael Dobson
City Juneau
Company Ninilchik General Store
Contact Duane Giarratana
City Ninilchik
Company Ninilchik Saltwater
Contact Steven Smith
City Ninilchik
Company Ninilchik Saltwater Charters
Contact Peter & Susan Ardison
City Ninilchik
Company Ninilchik Village Charters
Contact Stephen Vanek, Jr.
City Ninilchik
Company Noah's Guide Service
Contact Jeremy Baum
City Soldotna
Company Noatak Canyon Outfitters
Contact David M. Aldridge
City Anchorage
Company Norbert's Wagger Sport
Contact Norbert Chaudhary
City Ketchikan
Company Nordic North
Contact Charles Hostetler & Phillip Weidner
City Anchorage
Company Nordic Raven Charters
Contact James L. Dybdahl
City Hoonah
Company North Country River Charters
Contact William C. O'Halloran
City Fairbanks
Company North Lake Alaskan
Contact Michael Parker
City Anchorage
Company North Pacific Business
Contact Leonard & Michaela Kelley Kaylen
City Anchorage
Company North Pacific Charters
Contact Dan Leathers
City Ketchikan
Company North Pacific Marine Services
Contact Patrick A. Day
City Valdez
Company North Pole Wilderness Guide Outfitters
Contact Darrell Needham
City North Pole
Company North River Guides
Contact William E. Anker & Darrell Needham
City North Pole
Company North Star Charters
Contact David L. Lucher
City Anchorage
Company North Star Charters
Contact Herman Nelsen
City Seward
Company North Star Sailing Adventures
Contact Mark Canil & Mark Vevera
City Palmer
Company Northern Comfort, Inc.
Contact Edgar & Stephen Pyle William Walker
City Valdez
Company Northern Drift Exposure
Contact Robert Peacock
City Wasilla
Company Northern Exposure
Contact Jacquie and Marcus Gaskins
City Anchorage
Company Northern Lights Charters

Contact Ken & Dawn Teune
City Ward Cove
Company Northern Lights Haven Lodge
Contact Vernon H. Schumacher
City Yakutat
Company Northern Magic Charters
Contact Dave Tousignant
City Valdez
Company Northern Star Charters
Contact Stewart W. Willis
City Elfin Cove
Company Northern Ventures
Contact Chad Smith
City Wrangell
Company Northern Wilderness Adventures, Inc.
Contact Nick Pierskalla
City Wasilla
Company Northland Wilderness Expeditions
Contact Alan Robertson
City Wasilla
Company Northstar Adventures Inc.
Contact Bix Bonney
City Soldotna
Company Northstar Charters
Contact Richard R. Straty
City Auke Bay
Company Northstar Fishing Adventures
Contact Michael L. Chaussee
City Soldotna
Company Northward Bound
Contact James Harrower
City Anchorage
Company Northwest Charters
Contact Stanley K. Divine
City Kodiak
Company Northwest Outfitters
Contact Jens & Leslie Klaar
City Anchor Point
Company Northwoods Lodge
Contact Robert Clark
City Skwentna
Company Northwoods Lodge
Contact Eric & Shan Johnson
City Skwentna
Company Norton Bay Charters
Contact Abraham Anasogak, Sr.
City Koyuk
Company Norton Sound Guide Service
Contact
City Unalakleet
Company Nyliaq Alaska Charters
Contact Richard M. Tate
City Fairbanks
Company O'Brien Enterprises
Contact Stephen F. O'Brien
City Manley
Company Odeeo Charters
Contact Randall Odens
City Anchorage
Company Offshore Salmon Charters
Contact Phil Klobertanz
City Homer
Company Ole Creek Lodge
Contact Don & Marjorie Hangen
City Fairbanks
Company Olga Bay Lodge, Inc.
Contact James David Jones
City Kodiak
Company Olson Yukon River Tours
Contact Marvin James McGuffey
City Emmonak
Company Orca Charters
Contact Maurice W. Widdows
City Yakutat
Company Orca II Fish Guides
Contact Jonathan D. Wackler
City Soldotna
Company Orion River Specialists
Contact James Coyle
City Trapper Creek
Company Orion River Specialists
Contact James Coyle & Russel E. Stec
City Talkeetna
Company Orion River Specialists
Contact Matthew Holsinger
City Wasilla
Company Osborn River Service
Contact John G. Osborn
City Nome
Company Osprey Alaska
Contact Richard Fowler

City Cooper Landing
Company Osprey Alaska, Inc.
Contact Charles & Irene M.Lukey
City Cooper Landing
Company Osprey Enterprises
Contact Kenneth L. Herrick
City Petersburg
Company Ostrov Wygodnny Enterprises
Contact Albert Wilson & Kim Elliott
City Sitka
Company Otter Cove Bed & Breakfast
Contact Ginnie S. Porter
City Pelican
Company Ouktok Outfitters
Contact James M. Knopke
City Chugiak
Company Outdoor Adventure Program
Contact
City Elmendorf AFB
Company Outdoor Alaska
Contact Don Goffinet
City Ketchikan
Company Outdoor Enterprises
Contact Gerald Thompson
City Juneau
Company Outer Limits Charters
Contact J.M. Gilman
City Anchorage
Company Outercoast Charters
Contact Larry Trani
City Sitka
Company Outlook Enterprises
Contact Jerry L. Smith
City Anchorage
Company Outlook Lodge
Contact Robert Dersham
City Anchor Point
Company Ouzel Expeditions
Contact Ron Zandman-Zenan
City Anchorage
Company Ouzel Expeditions
Contact Bill Stoabs
City Anchorage
Company Ouzel Expeditions
Contact Herb Wottlin, Jr.
City Seward
Company Ouzel Expeditions, Inc.
Contact Paul & Sharon Allred
City Girdwood
Company Ouzel Expeditions, Inc.
Contact Randall Knauff
City Anchorage
Company Overland Express
Contact Johann Overland
City Anchorage
Company P&D Riverboat Services
Contact Paul & Diana Pfeiffer
City Anchorage
Company Pacific Charters
Contact Joe & Diane Svymbersky
City Fritz Creek
Company Pacific Gold Charters
Contact James Harrigan
City Sitka
Company Pacomia Northstar Guide Service
Contact James M. Harrigan
City Anchorage
Company Painter Creek Lodge, Inc.
Contact Joe Maxey & Jon Kent
City Anchorage
Company Pala II Charters
Contact Claude Henning
City Sitka
Company Palco Enterprises
Contact Richard L. Teague
City Sitka
Company Paradise Cove Lodge
Contact Dick Carlson
City Anchorage
Company Paradise Lodge
Contact John Lewis
City Talkeetna
Company Parker Recreational Services
Contact Ken Parker
City Auke Bay
Company Parker/Boyce Guide Service
Contact James M. Boyce & Bruce E. Parker
City Sitka
Company Parsley's Charter

Contact John Parsley
City Palmer
Company Pasco's Inlet Charters
Contact Jeffrey Pasco
City Ninilchik
Company Patrick's AK Fishing
Contact Patrick Johnson
City Soldotna
Company Paul's Deep Creek Charters
Contact Paul Goedert II
City Ninilchik
Company Paul H. Gabbert
Contact Gary Sevesind
City Alexander Creek
Company Paul's Sport Fishing Guide Service
Contact Paul F. Asicksik, Sr.
City Shaktoolik
Company Paxson Alpine Tours
Contact Kris & Murray Howk
City Paxson
Company Peace of Selby, Inc.
Contact Art & Dee Mortvedt & Be Sheldan
City Manley Hot Springs
Company Pelican Charters
Contact Norm Carson
City Pelican
Company Peninsula Adventures
Contact John & Dawn Lesterson
City Sterling
Company Peninsula Charters
Contact Bob Pennini
City Clam Gulch
Company Pennock Island Charters
Contact Vic Utterback
City Ketchikan
Company Peregrine Charters
Contact Robert Gibson & Jackie Feigon
City Aniak
Company Perfect Charters
Contact Steve Carlson
City Anchorage
Company Pete's Guide Service
Contact Peter W. Evans
City Soldotna
Company Peterson's Adventures
Contact Jeff Peterson
City Old Harbor
Company Peterson's Guide & Charter Service
Contact William W. Peterson
City Sitka
Company Petre's Fishing Charters
Contact Dennis & Chris Petre
City Salcha
Company Phantom Charters
Contact George Kirk
City Kodiak
Company Phantom Mtn. Adventures
Contact William L. & Shelley A. Stewart
City Palmer
Company Picnic Cove Charters
Contact John Timmer
City Sitka
Company Piedra Enterprises
Contact Charles Piedra
City Pelican
Company Pilgrim's Retreat
Contact Joe Page & Kathy J. McKelvey
City Talkeetna
Company Pillar Creek Guide & Outfitter
Contact Joseph Katancik
City Kodiak
Company Pioneer Charters
Contact David G. Logan
City Juneau
Company Pioneer Lodge, Inc.
Contact Steven H. & Gwendolyn A. White
City Willow
Company Piper Enterprises
Contact Charles Piper
City Homer
Company Plum Bluff Charters
Contact Gary R. Buzunis
City Ninilchik
Company Pocket Change
Contact William C. Lyle
City Fairbanks
Company Point Adventure Lodge, Inc.

Contact Mark Kneen
City Iliamna
Company Point's North Alaska Wild. Outfitters
Contact Mike McDaneld
City Big Lake
Company Poisne
Contact Sam Hryhorysak
City Kasilof
Company Poitry In Motion
Contact Steven Poitry
City Kasilof
Company Polaskan Charters
Contact Ray Majeski
City Sitka
Company Popeye Charters, Inc.
Contact Vincent & Jean Mitchell
City Valdez
Company Port Lions Lodge
Contact Steve & Peggy Andresen
City Wasilla
Company Portage Ch. General Store & Lodge
Contact Chris & Leona Carr
City Portage Ck.
Company Potter's Services
Contact Gerald O. Potter
City Homer
Company Prestages Sportfishing Lodge
Contact John & Betsy Prestage
City King Salmon
Company Preview Air Service
Contact Richard Trzesniowski
City Anchorage
Company Prime Time Charters
Contact Peter C. Unger
City Anchorage
Company Prime Time Charters
Contact David Pinquoch
City Wasilla
Company Prince of Wales Lodge
Contact Will Jones, Sr.
City Craig
Company Prince William Sound Adventures
Contact Gary & Libbie Graham
City Cordova
Company Professional Chartering
Contact Robert Tait
City Anchorage
Company Profish-N-Sea Charters
Contact Steven R. Zernia
City Anchorage
Company Ptarmigan Air
Contact Steven Williams
City Anchorage
Company Puffin Charters, Inc.
Contact James L. & Barbara M. Cheatham
City Juneau
Company Puffin Family Charters
Contact Leslie A. Pemberton
City Anchorage
Company Pullin Ventures
Contact Denver & Tom Pullin
City Ketchikan
Company Pybus Point Lodge
Contact Alan Veys
City Juneau
Company Qatuk's Kobut River Charters
Contact Virgil F.Coffin
City Noorvik
Company Quarterback Charters
Contact Karl & Robyn Amundsen
City North Pole
Company Quarterdeck and Mercer's
Contact Roger Mercer
City Seward
Company Quiet Cove Charters
Contact Thomas R. Kinberg
City Sitka
Company Quinnat Landing Resort
Contact David McGuire & Joe Chandler
City Anchorage
Company Quinns Caravan Charters
Contact Michael & Jill Quinn
City Kake
Company Qwik Fish Guide Service
Contact Jerry E. Hartman
City Soldotna
Company R & D Charters
Contact Dan Murphy
City Soldotna

Company R & R Charters
Contact Ray Jackson
City Kodiak
Company R R Charters
Contact Guy J. Bonhrand
City Yakutat
Company R-N-A Charters
Contact Ron & Cindy Matteson
City Wasilla
Company R-W's Fishing
Contact Ken Weilbaches
City Soldotna
Company R.J. Charters
Contact Rick Wood
City Soldotna
Company Rain-Bou Outfitters & Guide
Contact Glenn M. Oliver
City Anchorage
Company Rainbird Charters
Contact Dwight N. Bloom
City Auke Bay
Company Rainbow Bay Resort
Contact Jerry S. Pippen
City Pedro Bay
Company Rainbow Expeditions
Contact John Nicholson
City Anchorage
Company Rainbow River Lodge
Contact Chris Goll
City Anchorage
Company Rainbow Tours
Contact Jack Montgomery
City Homer
Company Raindancer Sport Fishing Charters
Contact John M. Brooks
City Sitka
Company Raindog Charters
Contact Scott W. Raneg
City Cordova
Company Randa's Guide Service
Contact Denis H. Randa
City Soldotna
Company Rather Rough-It Adventures
Contact Carl A. Bowman, Jr.
City Copper Center
Company Raven Charters
Contact Scott P.McLeod
City Sitka
Company Raven's Fire, Inc.
Contact Barbara Bingham
City Sitka
Company Ray Atkins Guiding & Flying Service
Contact Ray Atkins
City Cantwell
Company Real Alaska
Contact Agnes Alexie
City Nondalton
Company Real Alaska Adventures, Ltd.
Contact Stephen Conner
City Petersburg
Company Red Dog Charters
Contact Mert Stromire & T. Fitzgerald
City Chugiak
Company Red Dog Sports
Contact Mert Stromire
City Glennallen
Company Red Wing Charters
Contact Harold Corson
City Anchorage
Company Reel Adventures
Contact Gary Fuller
City Sterling
Company Reel Affair Charters
Contact Timothy Twaddle
City Sitka
Company Reel Alaska
Contact Ryon & Angela Morin
City Ketchikan
Company Reel Charters
Contact Patrick J. Lorentz
City Anchorage
Company Reel Class Charters
Contact Captain Derek W. Floyd
City Sitka
Company Reel Magic Charters
Contact Mark Hammer
City Sitka
Company Reel Pleasure Charters
Contact Wally Turner
City Fairbanks

Company Reeliable Fishing Charters
Contact Daniel B. Nore
City Juneau
Company Remember Alaska
Contact David & Nadine Hillstrand
City Homer
Company Remote Sportsmans Rentals
Contact Willy Keppel
City Bethel
Company Resurrection Bay Charters
Contact Darrell T. Robinson
City Seward
Company Revilla Fishing Charters
Contact Dewie & Debra Hamilton
City Ward Cove
Company Richards Kenai River Charters
Contact David Richards
City Soldotna
Company Richmond's Alaskan Guide Service
Contact Phillip Michael Richmond
City Big Lake
Company Rick Mah Charters
Contact Rick Mah
City Sitka
Company Riddle's Guide Service
Contact Stephen S. & Donna L.Riddle
City Kenai
Company Ringo's Guide Service
Contact Brian Ringeisen & Karrie Burns
City Sterling
Company Riptide Outfitters
Contact R. Steve Scheldt
City Thorne Bay
Company Rising Wind Dojo
Contact Philip Fyfe
City Dillingham
Company River & Sea Outfitters
Contact Dave Forsted
City Soldotna
Company River Fox Charters
Contact Robert Herz
City Eagle River
Company River Song Lodge
Contact Philip Tremrco
City Anchorage
Company River Wranglers
Contact Kevin & Suzanne McCarthy
City Gakona
Company Riverside Guides & Outfitters
Contact Jeff Bevans
City Anchorage
Company Riversong Adventures
Contact Carl L. Dixon
City Anchorage
Company Riversong Lodge
Contact Robert Carey
City Skwentna
Company Riversong Lodge
Contact Mitchell Coe
City Levelock
Company Riversong Lodge
Contact Tim Lynes
City Anchorage
Company Robert J. Juba
Contact Robert Juba
City Anchorage
Company Roberts River Rafting Adventures
Contact Monte Roberts
City Soldotna
Company Rocky Point Charters
Contact Walt Payne
City Petersburg
Company Rocky Point Resort
Contact Clarence F.Whittle
City Petersburg
Company Rod 'n Real Charters
Contact Rod & Randy Berg
City Soldotna
Company Rod and Real Charters/BC Charters
Contact Joseph Conkright
City Anchorage
Company Rod Bender's
Contact Lance Domonoske
City Sterling
Company Roe's Charter Service
Contact Richard M. Roe
City Ninilchik
Company Rohrer Bear Camp, Inc.
Contact Richard A. Rohrer

City Kodiak
Company Ron's Riverboat Service
Contact Ronald & Marilyn Wilson
City Wasilla
Company Rosalyn's Fishy Business
Contact Rosalyn Stowell
City Fairbanks
Company Ross Marine Recreations
Contact C. Alan Ross
City Craig
Company Royal Charters & Tours
Contact Royal Tauno Hill, Sr.
City Hoonah
Company RR Charters
Contact Richard "Rick" Richardson
City Soldotna
Company Rue's Charters
Contact David Rue
City Ambler
Company Rum Runner Charters
Contact Chris & Teri Conder
City Auke Bay
Company Runnin Bear Charters
Contact Rance J. Dailey
City Sitka
Company Rust's Flying Service
Contact Todd & Hank Rust
City Anchorage
Company Rustic Fly & Spin
Contact Helen Kurtz
City Palmer
Company Ruth Ann's All-Brite Charters
Contact Don & Ruth Ann Albright
City Craig
Company RW Guides Service
Contact Garry Keller
City Soldotna
Company RW's Fishing
Contact William Davis and Ron Weilbacher
City Soldotna
Company RW's Guide Service
Contact Gary Byerly
City Soldotna
Company S.E. Salmon Excursions
Contact Steven K. Scott
City Ketchikan
Company S.S.S. Charters
Contact Michael & Susan Boarland
City Chugiak
Company Sage & Spirit
Contact Karen Frost
City Girdwood
Company Sage and Spirit
Contact William & Karen Frost
City Girdwood
Company Sage Charters
Contact Dan P. Bilderback
City Cordova
Company Salmon & Sons River Guide Service
Contact Kevin Hall
City Wasilla
Company Salmon Falls Resort
Contact Alvin & Shirley White
City Ketchikan
Company Salmon Run Charters
Contact Dale Mulford
City Haines
Company Salmon Stone
Contact Lawrence F. Heilman
City Beluga River
Company Saltery Lake Lodge
Contact Bill Franklin & Doyle Hatfield
City Kodiak
Company Saltwater Adventures
Contact Greg Krenpasky
City Anchorage
Company Saltwater Sportsman Charter Service
Contact Timothy Schwartz
City Sitka
Company Salty Dog Charters
Contact Tim Rebischke
City Anchorage
Company Salty's Touring & Guiding Service
Contact Clyde Saltz
City Soldotna
Company Samantha B Charters
Contact Tom Young
City Sitka
Company Sandi-Kay Charters
Contact Ray J. Zernia
City Anchorage

Company Sanity Charters
Contact Ken L. Larson
City North Pole
Company Santilli Enterprises
Contact Stephen L. Santilli
City Anchorage
Company Sappah & Son Guide Service
Contact Terry L. Sappah
City Sterling
Company Sappah & Son Guide Service
Contact Terry Sappah
City Anchorage
Company Scana Fish Guides
Contact Bret Herrick
City Anchor Point
Company Scenic Bays Charters
Contact Bruce Bays
City Anchor Point
Company Scenic Day Charters
Contact Mike Cottrell
City Petersburg
Company Schmidt Enterprises
Contact Linda Bergdoll-Schmidt
City Sitka
Company Screaming Reel Charters
Contact Thomas O. Drennan
City Petersburg
Company Sea Bear Charters
Contact John B. Phillips
City Homer
Company Sea Breeze Charters
Contact Dennis Lanham
City Sitka
Company Sea Crest Charters
Contact Rocky L. Ertzberger
City Ward Cove
Company Sea Cruise Alaska
Contact George Eliason
City Sitka
Company Sea Dawn
Contact Donald T. McCarthy
City Sitka
Company Sea Fever Charters
Contact L.A. & Joann Wilson
City Juneau
Company Sea Fish Alaska
Contact Joe R. Garrison
City Sitka
Company Sea Flight Charters
Contact Leah W. Jenkin
City Homer
Company Sea Haven Beachcombers
Contact Alan Andersen
City Sitka
Company Sea King Charters
Contact Gary S. Bernhardt
City Sitka
Company Sea Otter Lodge
Contact Tim & Lynne Graves
City Ketchikan
Company Sea Otter Sound Fish Camp
Contact Allen & Barbara Richter
City Naukati
Company Sea Quest Charters
Contact Samuel & Marvol Barnard
City Ketchikan
Company Sea Quest Charters
Contact George Huntington
City Sitka
Company Sea Scape Adventures
Contact Richard E. VanMeter
City Sitka
Company Sea Sound Charters
Contact William C. Steffen
City Cordova
Company Sea Star Charters
Contact Erin L. & Kelly Railing
City Homer
Company Sea Trek Charters
Contact Ken Nelson
City Sitka
Company Sea Venture Charters
Contact Gary Plumb
City Ketchikan
Company Sea-AK Charters
Contact Bruce A. Smith
City Gustavus
Company Sea-Nic Fishing & Wildlife
Contact Darrell P. Riggs
City Sitka
Company Sea-Trek Charters
Contact Darwin E. Jones
City Petersburg
Company Seafood Safaris

Contact Jon Todd Weck
City Sitka
Company Seaguy's
Contact Leroy Edenshaw
City Hydaburg
Company Sealand Charters
Contact Rick Hinson
City Valdez
Company Sealaska Cruises, Inc.
Contact Richard F. Billings
City Sitka
Company Seamans Alaskan Fishing Adventure
Contact Joseph & Lora Seaman
City Kenai
Company Seamist Charter & Guide Service
Contact Malcolm Doiron
City Ward Cove
Company Seaview Charters
Contact James M. Heston
City Valdez
Company Seaweaver Charters
Contact James S. Franzel
City Sitka
Company Seawind Cruises
Contact Ken & Barb Gehring
City Douglas
Company Secret Cove Charters
Contact Dan Oneil
City Petersburg
Company See Alaska Charters
Contact Anthony Leichty
City Craig
Company See Alaska Tours & Charters
Contact Randy & Judy Henderson
City Petersburg
Company See Alaska with Jim H. Keeline, Inc.
Contact Jim H. Keeline
City Icy Bay
Company See Fish Ventures Inc.
Contact Tabor Ashment
City Homer
Company See Fish Ventures, Inc.
Contact Sharm Setterquist
City Homer
Company Seethe North Tour Service
Contact Sok Chang
City Anchorage
Company Seldovia Fishing Adventures
Contact David & Peggy Cloninger
City Seldovia
Company Seldovia Sports Charters & Ecotours
Contact William N. & Shirley H. Spencer
City Seldovia
Company Semmer Charters
Contact William J. Semmer
City Kodiak
Company Serendipity Boat Charters
Contact Jim Catlin
City Manley
Company Serenity Charters
Contact James Whigman
City Girdwood
Company Service Transfer
Contact Michael K. Snowden
City Sitka
Company Shadow
Contact Kenneth L. Malay
City Wasilla
Company Shamanz Charters
Contact Rober & Rose Shymanski
City Wrangell
Company Shandy & Sons Charters
Contact David Shandy
City Ninilchik
Company Shandy & Sons Charters
Contact Anthony Shandy
City Chugiak
Company Share Alaska Charters
Contact Harry A. Sevirina & Larry A. Cutbirth
City Anchorage
Company Shawner Charters
Contact Richard Nitz
City Anchorage
Company Shearwater Lodge & Charters
Contact Steven F. Hemenway
City Elfin Cove
Company Shelikof Expedition

Company
Contact David J. Krause
City Sitka
Company Shella's Fishing Charters
Contact Shella R. Maddox
City Kenai
Company Shelter Cove Lodge
Contact John Patterson & Larry Christian
City Craig
Company Shgen-Doo Charters
Contact Gabriel George
City Angoon
Company Shoestring Charters
Contact Don L. & Lisa M. Butler
City Fairbanks
Company Shuregood Adventures
Contact Donald W. & Christine M. Graves
City Dutch Harbor
Company Sid's Guide Service
Contact Sidney M. Wolford
City Homer
Company Sights Southeast
Contact Stephen Berry
City Petersburg
Company Silver Fox Charters
Contact Peter D. & Linda L. Udelhoven
City Homer
Company Silver Fox Charters
Contact Wayne E. Conley
City Delta Junction
Company Silver King Charters
Contact Leo E. Evans
City Sitka
Company Silver King Charters
Contact Donald E. Westlund
City Ketchikan
Company Silver King Charters
Contact Bob & Joanne Saxton
City Soldotna
Company Silver King Marine
Contact Mike & Astrid Bethers
City Auke Bay
Company Silver KingLodge
Contact Robert Saxton
City Soldotna
Company Silver Lining Charters
Contact Earl D. Cagle
City Seward
Company Silver Salmon Creek Lodge
Contact David Coray
City Soldotna
Company Silver Wind Charters
Contact Steve & Helen Keller
City Wrangell
Company Silversides Sportfishing
Contact Eli R. Ribich
City Petersburg
Company Silvertip Fishing Service
Contact Ronald Lundamo
City Ketchikan
Company Simpson Charters
Contact Joe Simpson
City Ninilchik
Company Sitka Alaska Fish Buster Charters
Contact James L. Lecrone
City Sitka
Company Sitka Sea Charters
Contact Charles E. Wilbur
City Sitka
Company Sitka Sea Roamer
Contact Mike Reif
City Sitka
Company Sitka Sound Charters
Contact John B. Morrell
City Sitka
Company Sitka Springtime Sitka Fishing Charters
Contact John C. Yerkes
City Sitka
Company Sitka Super 8
Contact Ronald Rivett
City Sitka
Company Sitka's Secrets
Contact Kent Hall & Bev Minn
City Sitka
Company Siwash Safaris, Inc.
Contact Paul Ellis
City Anchorage
Company Skagway Sport Fishing
Contact
City Juneau
Company Skip Dove - Kenai River Guide

Contact Skip & John Dove
City Soldotna
Company Skookum Charters
Contact Kent John
City Sterling
Company Skwentna Goods
Contact Kevin & Susan Boyce
City Skwentna
Company Skwentna Landing Corp.
Contact
City Skwentna
Company Skwentna River Fishing
Contact Roy Mackie
City Skwentna
Company Skwentna Roadhouse
Contact Raymond Doyle
City Skwentna
Company Skwentna Roadhouse & Lodge
Contact J.W. Cox
City Anchorage
Company Sky's the Limit Adventures
Contact Michael Sizelove
City Anchorage
Company Slammin Salmon
Contact Gary E. & Sussanne Hull
City Soldotna
Company Slammin Salmon Charters & Excursions
Contact James & Jacque Vaughan
City Craig
Company Slammin' Sam's Charters
Contact Samuel & Lesly Peters
City Klawock
Company Sleeping Lady Charters
Contact John Phelps
City Anchorage
Company Sleeping Lady Charters
Contact Roy Chambers
City Eagle River
Company Sleeping Lady Charters
Contact John Phelps & Bill Masker
City Eagle River
Company Sleeping Lady Charters
Contact Bill Masker & John Phelps
City Anchorage
Company Slipper Skipper Charters
Contact Harold Bailey
City Wrangell
Company Small Fry Charters
Contact Tim Fulton
City Sitka
Company Smith Enterprises
Contact Robert C. Smith
City Sitka
Company Smitty's Salmon Safari
Contact Larry Snyder
City Anchorage
Company Snoopy III Charters
Contact Norman & Mildred Lang
City Valdez
Company Snoopy' Adventures
Contact Keith & Debbie Stephens
City Juneau
Company Snow's Cove, Inc.
Contact Michael W. Holman
City Ketchikan
Company Snowline Marine Adventures
Contact Edward G. Klinkhart
City Anchorage
Company Sockeye Charters
Contact Thomas H. Hagberg
City Anchor Point
Company Somerset Charters
Contact Troy Curtiss
City Petersburg
Company Son-Of-A-Gun Charters/Alaskan Ocean
Contact Kemper L. Sackman & Doug Morgan
City Homer
Company Sorry Charlie Charters
Contact Michael & Laurie Coates
City Homer
Company Sound Adventure Charters
Contact John & Anne Herschleb
City Girdwood
Company Sourdough Charters
Contact Vincent Strahmann
City Soldotna
Company Sourdough Charters
Contact Ron Somerville
City Juneau
Company South Forty Enterprises
Contact Jr & Paula Terrel Richard D.

Hofmann
City Juneau
Company Southeast Alaska Adventures
Contact A. Clark & Josephine M. Emery
City Auke Bay
Company Southeast Alaska Guiding
Contact Hans Baertle & Mike Sofoulis
City Douglas
Company Southeast Alaska Ocean Adventures
Contact Noel Johnson
City Sitka
Company Southeast Alaska Outdoor Adventures
Contact Mike & Paul A. Yanak
City Sitka
Company Southeast Alaska Sports Fishing
Contact Larry McQuannie
City Ketchikan
Company Southeast Coastal Charters
Contact Domenick Monaco
City Sitka
Company Southeast Excursions Alaska
Contact James E. Elstad
City Sitka
Company Southeast Guide Service
Contact Scott Newman
City Petersburg
Company Southside Wilderness Lodge
Contact Mike & Jean Young
City Thorne Bay
Company Specialized Guide Service
Contact Gerald Willard
City Wasilla
Company Spirit of Alaska Wilderness Adventures
Contact Steele Davis
City Kodiak
Company Spirit Walker Expeditions
Contact
City Gustavus
Company Sport Fishing Guide Service
Contact Allan L. Howard
City Soldotna
Company Sports Den Fishing Team
Contact James Golden
City Soldotna
Company Sportsman's Inn/Baranof Expeditions
Contact James M. Boyce
City Sitka
Company Spruce Island Charters
Contact Herman L. Squartsoff
City Ouzinkie
Company Star Charter
Contact H. Giese
City Ninilchik
Company Star Dust Charters
Contact Floyd Raduege
City Homer
Company Starfish
Contact Jere & Karen Christner
City Sitka
Company Starfish Charters
Contact John Joyner
City Ketchikan
Company Steckel's Sportfishing
Contact John Steckel
City Soldotna
Company Steller Charters
Contact William Foster
City Sitka
Company Stikine Straits Sport Charters
Contact Alan J. Sorum
City Wrangell
Company Stocker's Guide
Contact Jim Stocker
City Palmer
Company Streak'n Charters
Contact Danny Kern
City Anchorage
Company Strieby's Guide Service
Contact Jerry Strieby
City Soldotna
Company Stump Jumper Charter
Contact John Pangbom
City Wasilla
Company Summer Breeze
Contact John & Pam Jensen
City Petersburg

Company Sunnahae Lodge
Contact Jerald R. Mackie
City Craig
Company Sure Strike Charters
Contact Kirk Agnitsch
City Craig
Company Susan Charters
Contact Joe McClure
City Kodiak
Company Susitna Basin Airboat Adventures
Contact Richard Ames
City Anchorage
Company Susitna River Guides
Contact Wetzel Betts
City Wasilla
Company Susitna River Safaris
Contact Thomas Kean
City Chugiak
Company Susitna Riverover Charters
Contact Daniel Tucker & Frank Prat
City Wasilla
Company Susitna Riverover Charters
Contact Frank Pratt, III
City Anchorage
Company Susitna Safaris
Contact Douglas and Conrad
City Wasilla
Company Susitna Safaris
Contact
City Wasilla
Company Swelltime Charters
Contact James R. Lee
City Anchorage
Company Swifter Drifter
Contact Tyland Vanlier
City Soldotna
Company Swiftwater Lodge
Contact Greg W. Turner
City Auke Bay
Company SWS Charters
Contact Steve Terrell
City Gakona
Company T's Charter Boat Service
Contact Trish Leverenz
City Big Lake
Company Tackle Shack
Contact Donald & Rose McNellis
City Willow
Company Tacklebuster Charters
Contact Weldon S. Chivers
City Kenai
Company Tacklebuster Halibut
Contact Michael Johnson
City Homer
Company Tacom Alaskan Adventures
Contact Tony Monzingo
City Anchorage
Company Tads Alaskan Trophy Fishing
Contact Tad Waldrip
City Soldotna
Company Tail Out Guide Services
Contact Andrew J. Carmichael
City Kasilof
Company Take-A-Chance Charters
Contact Simeon Dushkin
City King Cove
Company Takedown Alaskan Guide Service
Contact Charles & Sandra Hoskins
City Anchorage
Company Talaview Resorts
Contact Rjay Lloyd & Rex Maughan
City Anchorage
Company Talisman Charters
Contact Robert S. Johnson
City Sitka
Company Talkeetna Rafting
Contact Murray Nash
City Talkeetna
Company Talkeetna River Boat
Contact Frank Shores
City Talkeetna
Company Talkeetna River Guides
Contact Gerald L. Sousa
City Talkeetna
Company Talkeetna Riverboat
Contact Mac Stevens, Jr.
City Talkeetna
Company Talkneetna Riverboat
Contact Kelly Ernst
City Talkeetna
Company Tall Tales Charters
Contact Charles E. & Joanne Collins
City Anchor Point

Company Talofa Associate
Contact Joe C. Ashcraft
City Ketchikan
Company Tain Air Service, Inc.
Contact Alan C. Helfer
City Soldotna
Company Talstar Lodge
Contact Gary Layton
City Soldotna
Company Talstar Lodge
Contact Michael Patton
City Palmer
Company Talstar Lodge/Self
Contact Wylie Betts
City Wasilla
Company Tanaku Lodge
Contact Dennis Meier & Jim Benton
City Elfin Cove
Company Tanana River Charters
Contact Kenneth E. Edwards
City Healy
Company Tangent Charters
Contact Greg & Deborah Scheff
City Wrangell
Company Taquan Air Service, Inc.
Contact Jerry A. Scudero
City Ketchikan
Company Tartan Charters
Contact William L. Urquhart
City Ketchikan
Company Tatonduk Flying Service
Contact Robert Everts
City Fairbanks
Company Tchaika Fishing Guide Services
Contact James E. Bullock, Jr.
City Gakona
Company Team Navy Charters
Contact Daniel W. Knight & Richard M.Collins
City Ketchikan
Company Ted's Trophy Fishing
Contact Ted Forgi
City Soldotna
Company Tenacious Charters
Contact Michael T. Lockabey
City Wrangell
Company Tenakee Hot Springs Lodge
Contact Samuel & Juan McBeen
City Tenakee Springs
Company Terrapins
Contact Ronald E. Dick
City Sitka
Company Terry's Unforgettable Charters & Expd.
Contact Terry Durkin
City Petersburg
Company The Bawana Group
Contact Ernie Norton, Jr.
City Anchorage
Company The Bwana Group
Contact Phil Weber
City Anchorage
Company The Cove Lodge
Contact John Thomas & Gordon Wrobel
City Elfin Cove
Company The King and I
Contact Michael L. Ashton
City Wrangell
Company The Lodge at Hidden Basin
Contact Theresa J. Brigman
City Kodiak
Company The Nets End
Contact Josh Rago
City Juneau
Company The O'Fishial Charters of Alaska
Contact William A. & Kathy A. Coe
City Anchorage
Company The Spruce Fly
Contact John Martin
City Homer
Company The Walking River Guide
Contact Warren P. Huff
City Fritz Creek
Company The Whales Eye Lodge & Charter
Contact Rick & Karen Bierman
City Auke Bay
Company Thomas Bay Lodges
Contact Frank H. & Ruth A. Kerr
City Petersburg
Company Thomas Fishing Lodge
Contact Dennis & Evelyn Thomas

City Crooked Creek
Company Thompson Charters
Contact Jim Thompson
City Petersburg
Company Thompson's Halibut
Contact Marvin Parks
City Anchor Point
Company Thompson's Halibut
Contact Jimmy Thompson
City Soldotna
Company Thompson's Halibut Charters
Contact Billy E. & Billy Jo Thompson
City Soldotna
Company Three Eagle Charters
Contact Thomas J. Dawson
City Juneau
Company Three Eagles Enterprises
Contact Donald J. Henry, Jr.
City Sitka
Company Tide Runners
Contact Jay & Jane Griffel
City Kenai
Company Tides-In Charters
Contact Glenn Melvin
City Anchorage
Company Tidewater Charter
Contact Reginald Krkovich
City Juneau
Company Tightline Charters
Contact David & Marilyn Denney
City Kenai
Company Tightlines
Contact Ronald Diltz
City Eagle River
Company Tikchik Narrows Lodge, Inc.
Contact
City Anchorage
Company Tikchik Riverboat Service
Contact Shane Woodworth
City Dillingham
Company Tim Bergs Alaskan Fishing
Contact Guy Cox
City Ninilchik
Company Tim's Charters
Contact Timothy J. Carsini
City Valdez
Company Timberline Guide Service
Contact Gregory A. Andersen
City Anchorage
Company Time-N-Tide Charters
Contact Paul Donnelly
City Anchor Point
Company Tippecanoe
Contact Raymond B. & Heather L. Kelley
City Willow
Company TNT Alaskan Adventures
Contact Tamara Pellegrom
City Kenai
Company Tod River Outfitters
Contact Joyce & John Erickson
City Hoonah
Company Todd's Iguigig Lodge
Contact Larry & Elizabeth Todd
City Wasilla
Company Togiak River Fishing Adventures
Contact Bud Hodson & Ron McMillan
City Anchorage
Company Tok Guide Service
Contact Jeffrey Van Zandt
City Tok
Company Tom Cat Charters
Contact Tom Klemz
City Sterling
Company Tom's Alaskan Outdoor
Contact Thomas Robertson
City Anchorage
Company Tom's Outdoor
Contact Thomas Castillo, Jr.
City Eagle River
Company Tomilson Unicorp./Miss Holly
Contact Russ Tomilson
City Homer
Company Tongass Adventures
Contact Mark S. Guillory
City Sitka
Company Tongass Maritime Excursions
Contact Michael & Claudia Herrick
City Auke Bay
Company Toni Lake
Contact Don Mobley
City Skwentna

Company Top of the World Sportfishing
Contact Greg A. Jerich
City Anchorage
Company Totem Bay Outfitters
Contact Debbie White & Ronnie Jackson
City Craig
Company Tovya Fishing Charters
Contact Ray Kolean
City Ketchikan
Company Towhead Lake Charters
Contact Larry Asplund
City Skwentna
Company Toxic Too Charters
Contact Daniel Chalup
City Homer
Company Tozi Enterprises
Contact Bill & Cathy Fliris
City Tanana
Company Tracy Vrem's Blue Mountain Lodge
Contact Tracy Vrem
City Chugiak
Company Trail Ridge Air
Contact Geoff Armstrong
City Anchorage
Company Trail Ridge Air, Inc.
Contact Glenn Curtiss
City Anchorage
Company Trail Ridge Air, Inc.
Contact James Jensen
City Anchorage
Company Trapper Jim's Lodge
Contact James & Jolatne Soplanda
City Anchor Point
Company Treasure Island Charters
Contact Ronald & Janice Phillips
City Wrangell
Company Tri River Charters
Contact Bob & Maxine Stickles
City Talkeetna
Company Tri-River Charters
Contact Robert Meals
City Talkeetna
Company Triple H. Lodge
Contact Thomas L. Hoseth
City Dillingham
Company Triton Charters
Contact Hans von Rekowski
City Sitka
Company Trophies Only
Contact Richard & Lorraine King
City Ekwok
Company Trophy Charters
Contact Glenn Keller
City Ketchikan
Company Trophy King Lodge
Contact Reubin Payne
City Anchor Point
Company Trophy King Lodge
Contact David Cozzini
City Ninilchik
Company Troublesome Creek Fish Co.
Contact Joe & Chris Crum
City Anchor Point
Company True North Charters
Contact Carl W. Mielke
City Juneau
Company Tsimshian Halibut Charters
Contact John Hill
City Homer
Company Turn-Again Sports
Contact Kenneth Manning
City Girdwood
Company Tuuqak Charters
Contact Steven R. & Linda S. Carpenter
City Soldotna
Company Two Rivers Charters
Contact John W. Kalmbacher
City Fairbanks
Company Tyee Charter Service
Contact Jay Lloyd
City Juneau
Company Tyee Outfitters
Contact Jay Skordahl
City Sitka
Company Ugashik Lake Lodge
Contact Gus Lamoureux
City Anchorage
Company Ultima Thule Outfitters
Contact
City Chitina
Company Ultimate Charters
Contact Roy & Millie Self

178

City Sterling
Company Ultimate Rivers
Contact
City Anchorage
Company Unalakleet Lodge
Contact Mary A. Brown
City Unalakleet
Company Under Sail Adventures
Contact William B. & Kathleen Fliger Bailey
City Nikniski
Company Unreel Guide Service
Contact John Iverson
City Soldotna
Company Unuk River Post
Contact Williaml Neumann & Charlie Pinkepank
City Ketchikan
Company Up the Creek/Talketna
Contact William Bentley
City Talkeetna
Company Uppa Charlie's Up River Adventures
Contact Evan & Annie B. Chocknok
City New Stuyahok
Company Uyak Air Service
Contact Oliver"Butch"Tovsen
City Kodiak
Company V2 Expeditions
Contact Leonard D. & Deborah K. Verrelli
City Juneau
Company Valarie's Fishing Guide Service
Contact Valarie L. Early
City Soldotna
Company Valdez Sea Adventures
Contact Wallace A. Evans
City Fairbanks
Company Valentine
Contact Chad F.& Miriam K.Valentine
City Talkeetna
Company Valhalla Charters
Contact Bruce L. Blandford
City Valdez
Company Valley King Charter
Contact Charles Lee
City Palmer
Company Valley River Charters
Contact Mathew L. Peterson & Jonathan Lindsey
City Wasilla
Company Valley Rod Shop/Valley
Contact Rene Roberts
City Anchorage
Company Van Saun Charters
Contact Rod Van Saun
City Anchorage
Company Vector Guide Service
Contact John Gumpert
City Anchorage
Company Ventna Adventure Charters
Contact Bobby Padie
City Houston
Company Ventures North
Contact Chris & Linda Erickson
City Juneau
Company Viapan Camp
Contact Edwin Taylor & Tamara Smid
City Beluga
Company Wagners Guide Service
Contact Vince & Leslie Wagner
City Kenai
Company Wallona Transport
Contact Leroy Wallona
City Dillingham
Company Wally's Guide Service
Contact Walter L.Martin
City Kenai
Company Walt Morris
Contact Walter Morris
City Anchorage
Company Water Dog Fishing Charters
Contact Mark Stubbefield
City Juneau
Company Water Ouzel Express
Contact Jerry G. Barber
City Sitka
Company We Tie Co. AK Fly Mfg.
Contact Jack W. Spangler
City Anchor Point
Company Webster's Outdoor Adventures
Contact Jeff & Cathy Webster
City Soldotna

Company Weeping Trout Sports Resort
Contact Roger & Debra Schnabel
City Haines
Company Weight-N-Sea Charters
Contact Sean Mitchel
City Ketchikan
Company Weigner's Backcountry Guiding
City Sterling
Company Weise Adventures
Contact James R. Weise
City Anchorage
Company Wes' Guide Service
Contact Wesley T. Yamaoka
City Soldotna
Company West Fjord Charters
Contact Gary & Neoma Scheff
City Craig
Company West Rentals
Contact Galen D. West
City Sitka
Company Wet & Wild Kenai Fishing
Contact Jeff Moore
City Sterling
Company Whale of a Tale Charters
Contact Marcellus Fegley
City Sitka
Company Whale Pass Lodge
Contact Robert & Denise May
City Port Lions
Company Whaler's Cove Lodge
Contact Richard L. Powers
City Angoon
Company Whales Resort, Inc.
Contact William R. Fannemel
City Ketchikan
Company Whales Tale Marine Service & Charters
Contact Albert R. Manchester
City Gustavus
Company Whalesong Charters
Contact Garry & Kim Brand
City Craig
Company Whisper Marine Charters
Contact Douglas R. Ogilvy
City Gustavus
Company White Cloud Charters
Contact Al C.& Vickie F. Levine
City Seward
Company White Savage/Joyce Marie Charters
Contact Ricky Thompson
City Ninilchik
Company Whitmore Enterprises
Contact Shawn M. Whitmore
City Soldotna
Company Wild Bill's Guide Service
Contact William C. Burnett
City Soldotna
Company Wild Creek Lodge, Inc.
Contact
City Kodiak
Company Wilderness Charters
Contact Christopher White
City Auke Bay
Company Wilderness Enterprises
Contact Joe & Vici Letarte
City Fairbanks
Company Wilderness Experiences
Contact Lamont E. Albertson
City Aniak
Company Wilderness Place Lodge
Contact Ed & Judy Sharpe
City Anchorage
Company Wilderness Place Lodge
Contact Brant Bounous
City Anchorage
Company Will's Copper King Charters
Contact William Bailey
City Ninilchik
Company Willie"D"& Me Charter Service
Contact Jacqueline & Wilfred Dentz
City Anchorage
Company Williwaw River Tours
Contact David Dowling
City Anchorage
Company Willow Creek Outfitters
Contact Dean Langton
City Willow
Company Wilson's Guided Sportfishing
Contact James E. Wilson
City Soldotna

Company Winchester Fishing Co.
Contact Jim Winchester
City Iliamina
Company Windsinger Lodge
Contact Pahl & Bill Gottschalk Sandra
City Wasilla
Company Windy Way Charters
Contact Allen Girens, Jr.
City Craig
Company Wings
Contact Robert Gretzke
City Anchorage
Company Witer King Charters
Contact Ralph E. Lohse
City Cordova
Company Wits End
Contact Corinne Heidemann
City Eagle River
Company Wolf Country Fishing
Contact Scott & Roberta Ravenscroft
City North Pole
Company Wolverine Creek Wilderness Cabins
Contact Thomas H. Rench
City Wasilla
Company Women Sail Alaska
Contact Theresa Tavel & Karen Walter
City Juneau
Company Women's Flyfishing
Contact Celilia Kleinbauf
City Anchorage
Company Wood River Lodge
Contact John D. Ortman
City Anchorage
Company Wood's Alaska Sport Fishing
Contact Jack Wood
City King Salmon
Company Wooden Wheel Cove Lodge
Contact Robert & Patty Gray
City Pt. Baker
Company Woods Sport Fishing
Contact John Wood
City King Salmon
Company World Class Sportfishing
Contact Mike Arthur
City Sitka
Company Y-Knot Charter Service
Contact Richard D. & Betty J. George
City Anchorage
Company Ya Shur Charters
Contact Capt. H.G. Hollo
City Homer
Company Yakutat Bay & River Charters
Contact Flank Deveraux
City Yakutat
Company Yakutat Lodge
Contact Ken & Jill Fanning
City Yakutat
Company Yakutat Outfitters
Contact Robert Fraker
City Yakutat
Company Yentna Station Roadhouse
Contact Dan Gabryszak
City Houston
Company Yes Bay/Mink Bay Lodges
Contact Kevin M. Hack
City Ketchikan
Company Yeshna Guided Tours
Contact Steven Hay
City Haines
Company Yukon Don's, Inc.
Contact Yukon Don & Kristan Tanner
City Wasilla
Company Yukon Fish Guiding Service
Contact Gregory Landeis
City Soldotna
Company Yukon River Tours
Contact Paul & Mary E. Starr
City Tanana
Company Zachar Bay Lodge
Contact Martin & Linda Eaton
City Kodiak
Contact Kenneth T. Alt
City Fairbanks
Contact Allen & Leslie Barnett
City Sitka
Company
Contact Michael Bellenir
City Chugiak
Company

Contact Donald A. Bentley, Jr.
City Ninilchik
Company
Contact William C. Blake
City Anchorage
Company
Contact Louis Butera
City Palmer
Company
Contact George Campbell
City Haines
Company
Contact Gary Chamberlain
City Gustavus
Company
Contact Douglas Cole
City Trapper Creek
Company
Contact Creig Corlis
City Palmer
Company
Contact Patricia Culleeny
City Anchorage
Company
Contact Frank Danford
City Anchorage
Company
Contact Gerald Denison
City Palmer
Company
Contact V.E. DeWitt
City Craig
Company
Contact Larry Edwards
City Skwentna
Company
Contact Cammeron Edwards
City Skwentna
Company
Contact Dave Forster
City Soldotna
Company
Contact Michael Funke
City Anchorage
Company
Contact Ken Graves
City Auke Bay
Company
Contact Gary Hammes
City Fairbanks
Company
Contact Mark Hermon
City Palmer
Company
Contact Jamie Hickman
City Soldotna
Company
Contact Pat Johnson
City Soldotna
Company
Contact Joseph Juckel
City Anchorage
Company
Contact John Kalmbach
City Skwentna
Company
Contact Billy Kidd
City Trapper Creek
Company
Contact Tom Laffey
City Anchorage
Company
Contact John Lohrey
City Anchorage
Company
Contact Joseph Malatesta
City Soldotna
Company
Contact Jr. Malesic
City Anchorage
Company
Contact Monte McFarland
City Sitka
Company
Contact Edward Q. Merritt
City Whittier
Company
Contact Bill Gablehouse & Ron Merritt
City Wrangell
Company
Contact David C. Miller
City Ketchikan
Company
Contact Robert Mills
City Gustavus
Company

Contact Patrick Mooney
City Anchorage
Company
Contact Michael & Lillian Moore
City Trapper Creek
Company
Contact Eric Morgan, Sr.
City Chuathbaluk
Company
Contact Ronald Pannell
City Trapper Creek
Company
Contact Walter Phillips
City Trapper Creek
Company
Contact David G. Pingree
City Chiniak
Company
Contact Glenn Rowe
City Fairbanks
Company
Contact Max Schwab
City Talkeetna
Company
Contact Tom Shones
City Palmer
Company
Contact John St. Beverly
City Trapper Creek
Company
Contact Bob Stuvek
City Anchorage
Company
Contact Donald E. Teeple
City Anchorage
Company
Contact Glen S. Thurman
City Manley Hot Springs
Company
Contact James C. Tudor
City Naknek
Company
Contact Richard Voth
City Eagle River
Company
Contact Richard J. Walsh
City Petersburg
Company
Contact James White
City Dutch Harbor
Company
Contact Robert Whitenberg
City Anchorage
Company
Contact Merle G. Wilson
City Tenakee Springs
Company
Contact James Woods
City Skwentna
Company
Contact Danny Zarlengo
City Junea

Arizona

Company Alaska Tuff, Inc.
Contact Charles McGurrem
City Phoenix
Company Beartracks Lodge
Contact Frank Barrett & Dan Reiling
City Tempe
Company Blue Rivers Guide Service
Contact
City Flagstaff
Company Hartman Outfitters Corp.
Contact Roger L. Hartman
City Flagstaff
Company Lake Powell Charter
Contact Ray V. Young
City Page
Company Lazy H Guide Service
Contact Tom Holmquest
City Chandler
Company Lee's Ferry Lodge
Contact Maggie Sacher
City Marble Canyon
Company Little Grizzly Creek Ranch, Inc.
Contact Leo Douglas Sysel
City Paradise Valley
Company Meadowlark Ranch
Contact Brad Custer

City Phoenix
Company Trophy King Lodge
Contact Sandy Kellin
City Carefree
Company Troutback Flyfishing Guide Service
Contact
City Springerville
Company United States Outfitters of Arizona
Contact Van Hale
City Eager
Company
Contact Larry Alexander
City Mesa
Company
Contact George A. Amadei
City Lake Havasu City
Company
Contact M.D. Anderson
City Heber
Company
Contact Kay C. Arnold
City Page
Company
Contact Ted J. Auer
City Glendale
Company
Contact David J. Baca
City Mesa
Company
Contact Charles B. Beamer
City Flagstaff
Company
Contact James E. Beauchamp
City Phoenix
Company
Contact James B. Bedlion
City Flagstaff
Company
Contact William H. Bishop
City Lakeside
Company
Contact Tom S. Boggess III
City Phoenix
Company
Contact Steve Bond
City Phoenix
Company
Contact Wallace C. Boulden
City Chandler
Company
Contact Loren E. Bradley
City Springerville
Company
Contact Rodney E. Brock
City Glendale
Company
Contact Thomas A. Brown
City Flagstaff
Company
Contact Jimmie D. Burton
City Chandler
Company
Contact Robert W. Callahan
City Forest Lakes
Company
Contact Fred P.Campbell
City Clifton
Company
Contact Ronald G. Cannon
City Phoenix
Company
Contact Hellen J. Carter
City Phoenix
Company
Contact Olin E. Castleberry
City Phoenix
Company
Contact Arthur W. Chamberlin
City Roosevelt
Company
Contact Joseph Chimienti
City Tucson
Company
Contact Neal G. Cissel
City Scottsdale
Company
Contact Douglas W. Clapson
City Mesa
Company
Contact Donald C. Clauser
City Lake Havasu
Company
Contact James W. Cliburn
City Page

Company
Contact Darr A. Colburn
City Flagstaff
Company
Contact Darius A. Copley
City Tucson
Company
Contact Norman G. Crawford, Jr.
City Benson
Company
Contact Anthony C. Crilley
City Happy Jack
Company
Contact David L. Crockett
City Tucson
Company
Contact Lance E. Crowther
City Show Low
Company
Contact Edward L. Davenport
City Tucson
Company
Contact John DePonte, III
City Tucson
Company
Contact Robert J. Dillman
City Young
Company
Contact Chris J. Dunn
City Cottonwood
Company
Contact Ervin R. Earl
City Apache Jct.
Company
Contact Ron L. Eichelberger
City Peoria
Company
Contact Nathan E. Ellison
City Globe
Company
Contact Jeffrey S. English
City Marble Canyon
Company
Contact Corwin E. Estes
City Eagar
Company
Contact Miles S. Etchart
City Litchfield Park
Company
Contact Mark D. Excine
City Lakeside
Company
Contact Barry D. Fenstermache
City Phoenix
Company
Contact Daniel F.Finucane
City Page
Company
Contact Leon D. Fleming
City Sonoita
Company
Contact Dave Foster
City Marble Canyon
Company
Contact Richard I. Francis
City Cibola
Company
Contact Henry L. Gassaway
City Roosevelt
Company
Contact Thomas H. George
City Willcox
Company
Contact Steven M. George
City Willcox
Company
Contact Charles L. Gibbs
City Tucson
Company
Contact Rick A. Gillespie
City Phoenix
Company
Contact Jerry G. Gragg
City Peoria
Company
Contact Paul D. Grissom
City Roosevelt
Company
Contact Terry C. Gunn
City Marble Canyon
Company
Contact Van D. Hale
City Eagar
Company
Contact Ronald D. Hall
City Page

Company
Contact Allen M. Haws
City Snowflake
Company
Contact Gary C. Heckler
City Scottsdale
Company
Contact Homer E. Helmuth
City Tempe
Company
Contact Daniel C. Hicks
City Vail
Company
Contact Greg H. Hines
City Gilbert
Company
Contact Paul J. Hobel
City Phoenix
Company
Contact Michael R. Hoffman
City Scottsdale
Company
Contact Wayne Holmes
City Sedona
Company
Contact Thomas L. Holmquist
City Gilbert
Company
Contact James W. Houchin
City Glendale
Company
Contact David R. Howell
City Phoenix
Company
Contact Sandy K. Johnson
City Mesa
Company
Contact Royce R. Johnson
City Miami
Company
Contact Theda A. Johnston
City Apache Junction
Company
Contact Richard S. Jones
City Phoenix
Company
Contact Jimmy Joy
City Blue
Company
Contact Mark Kaesemeyer
City Marble Canyon
Company
Contact Mike L. Kannapel
City Mesa
Company
Contact Cameron W. Karber
City Phoenix
Company
Contact Walter J. Kellmer, Jr.
City Tucson
Company
Contact Jonathon L. Kibler
City Higley
Company
Contact Daniel P.Knight
City Florence
Company
Contact Doyle S. Kridelbaugh
City Phoenix
Company
Contact Jeffrey A. Kush
City Chandler
Company
Contact Terry A. LaFuze
City Phoenix
Company
Contact Theodore K. Larson
City Lakeside
Company
Contact Robert M. Lee
City Lake Havasu
Company
Contact George O. Lening
City Cibola
Company
Contact John J. Leuy
City Tucson
Company
Contact Marion B. Lewis
City Taylor
Company
Contact Victor G. Liebe
City Flagstaff
Company
Contact William D. Maloney
City Prescott

Company
Contact Samuel L. Manning, Sr.
City Lake Havasu City
Company
Contact William R. Marshall
City Payson
Company
Contact Brian E. Marshall
City Payson
Company
Contact William D. Martin
City Kingman
Company
Contact William H. McBurney
City Prescott
Company
Contact James K. McCasland
City Prescott
Company
Contact John E. Murray
City Phoenix
Company
Contact Dennis L. Notson
City Payson
Company
Contact Gilbert R. O'Connor
City Casa Grande
Company
Contact Michael J. O'Halo
City Winslow
Company
Contact George J. Oberdin
City Bullhead City
Company
Contact James J. Ocker
City Lake Havasu
Company
Contact Walter E. Oxley, Jr.
City Glendale
Company
Contact Billy W. Palmer
City Globe
Company
Contact George B. Peat
City Page
Company
Contact Charles M. Peters
City Taylor
Company
Contact Doug J. Phillips
City Yuma
Company
Contact Gregory R. Pishkur
City Flagstaff
Company
Contact Kenneth R. Preder
City Eagar
Company
Contact Gerald D. Puckett
City Page
Company
Contact David Pulsifer
City Springerville
Company
Contact James B. Reece
City Chandler
Company
Contact Raymond F.Rende
City Roosevelt
Company
Contact Michael L. Riddle
City Phoenix
Company
Contact Clement V. Rogers
City Phoenix
Company
Contact Robert R. Rogers
City Phoenix
Company
Contact Joe A. Rosania
City Show Low
Company
Contact Mike Roth
City Taylor
Company
Contact Jerry C. Ruehle
City Bullhead City
Company
Contact Don J. Sanders
City Yuma
Company
Contact John K. Sasser
City Phoenix
Company
Contact Todd L. Schneider
City Mesa

Company
Contact Bill Schultz
City Marble Canyon
Company
Contact Craig R. Schultz
City Phoenix
Company
Contact William J. Schultz
City Flagstaff
Company
Contact Danny R. Shaw
City Greenehaven
Company
Contact John J. Shaw
City Glendale
Company
Contact Les R. Shelton
City Flagstaff
Company
Contact Frederick W. Smith
City Marble Canyon
Company
Contact Paul Smith
City Mesa
Company
Contact Lawrence F.Snead
City Phoenix
Company
Contact Johnny C. Spear
City Clay Springs
Company
Contact Curtis B. Rambo, Sr.
City Tonto Basin
Company
Contact Scott W. Stevens
City Skull Valley
Company
Contact David N. Stewart
City Scottsdale
Company
Contact David O. Stewart
City Flagstaff
Company
Contact Russell Sullivan
City Marble Canyon
Company
Contact Frank V. Talbott
City Apache Junction
Company
Contact Dennis Taylor
City Lake Havasu
Company
Contact Rick Tourney
City Roosevelt
Company
Contact Thomas J. Upshir
City Glendale
Company
Contact Jeffrey A. Voss
City Marble Canyon
Company
Contact Terry A. Walker
City Glendale
Company
Contact James F.Warner
City Goodyear
Company
Contact Billie Weaver
City St. Johns
Company
Contact William H. Weigele
City Tempe
Company
Contact Michael P.Whelan
City Cottonwood
Company
Contact Dale L. Whitmore
City Marble Canyon
Company
Contact John E. Williams
City Phoenix
Company
Contact Thomas E. Williams
City Apache Junction
Company
Contact Wally L. Wolfe
City Martinez Lake
Company
Contact Arthur G. Woods
City Phoenix
Company
Contact Bill H. Workman
City Mesa
Company
Contact Donald E. Wyckoff
City Rimrock

Company
Contact Gary T. Yamaguchi
City Phoenix

Arkansas

Company Alaska Charter Service
Contact Julian J. Gustin
City Fayetteville
Company Anderson House Inn
Contact
City Heber Springs
Company Batty's Resort
Contact
City Mountain Home
Company Bob Snyder's Web Page
Contact
City Old Joe
Company Breckenridge Guide Service
Contact Russell & Russ Breckenridge
City Henderson
Company Chamberlain's Trout Dock
Contact
City Cotter
Company Chandler's Guide Service
Contact Terry C. Chandler
City Hot Springs
Company Cotter Trout Dock
Contact
City Cotter
Company Dripping Springs Trout Dock
Contact
City Pangburn
Company Gene's Trout Dock
Contact
City Mountain Home
Company Hurst Fishing Service
Contact
City Cotter
Company Jack's Fishing Resort
Contact
City Mountain View
Company Jenkins Fishing Service & Motel
Contact Eric S. & Terry G. Jenkins
City Calico Rock
Company Joseph R. Harris
Contact
City Vilonia
Company Kenai Lake Adventures
Contact Kevin McCarthy
City Little Rock
Company Norfork Trout Dock
Contact
City Norfork
Company P.J.'s Fly Fishing & Resort Lodge
Contact Paul & Joyce Campbell
City Norfork
Company Pace & Harkins Fishing Service
Contact
City Flippin
Company Peal's Resort
Contact
City Mt. Home
Company Rainbow Trout Resort
Contact
City Mountain Home
Company Red's Guide Service
Contact Mike VanScoyoc
City Mountain Home
Company Rivercliff Trout Dock
Contact
City Bull Shoals
Company Rose Fishing Service
Contact
City Norfork
Company Tall Timbers Resort
Contact Richard E. Lee
City Oakland
Company The John B. Gulley
Flyfishing Guide Service
Contact John B. Gulley, II
City Norfork
Company The Ozark Angler
Contact
City Heber Springs
Company Woodsman's Sport Shop & Fishing Serv.

Contact
City Norfork
Company
Contact Ben Adams
City Springdale
Company
Contact Donald Adkerson
City Gassville
Company
Contact Gerald C. Adkerson
City Cotter
Company
Contact Mathew D. Alaniz
City Fayetteville
Company
Contact Corbet A. Albright
City Pearcy
Company
Contact Norman J. Alexander
City Fayetteville
Company
Contact Rodney F. Anderson
City Gassville
Company
Contact James D. Anderton
City Heber Springs
Company
Contact Albert L. Andrews
City Bentonville
Company
Contact James Apata
City Gassville
Company
Contact Jim H. Apel
City Tucker
Company
Contact Ron C. Armalost
City Bull Shoals
Company
Contact Robert V. Armstrong
City Bull Shoals
Company
Contact Tom J. Aston
City Witts Springs
Company
Contact Gregory K. Ault
City Jessieville
Company
Contact Clarence Auston
City Lakeview
Company
Contact Gary H. Baggett
City Heber Springs
Company
Contact Lonnie D. Bagwell
City Mountain Home
Company
Contact Robert H. Bailey
City Oxford
Company
Contact Samuel A. Balsano
City Gamaliel
Company
Contact Eddie B. Bansemer
City Mountain Home
Company
Contact Wesley E. Barnes
City Summit
Company
Contact Frank Barton
City Little Rock
Company
Contact Shannon Bassham
City Mountain Home
Company
Contact Edward Bayghan
City Mountain Home
Company
Contact Jerry D. Bean
City Lonsdale
Company
Contact Eddie D. Beard
City Lakeview
Company
Contact John Bell
City Cotter
Company
Contact Justin J. Bell
City Ft. Smith
Company
Contact Gary Belletini
City Bull Shoals
Company
Contact Ralph O. Benefield
City Calico Rock
Company

Contact Steven Berg
City Flippin
Company
Contact Farrell Billings
City Fayetteville
Company
Contact James Bishop
City Tumbling Shoals
Company
Contact Frank Blawton
City Flippin
Company
Contact William B. Blevins
City Heber Springs
Company
Contact Thomas R. Bly
City Heber Springs
Company
Contact William O. Bodeker
City Horseshoe Bend
Company
Contact Eric M. Bogy
City Pine Bluff
Company
Contact William L. Bohunnon
City Diamond City
Company
Contact Alan E. Boland
City Flippin
Company
Contact Lance Booth
City Mount Ida
Company
Contact Darrell W. Bowman
City Mountain Home
Company
Contact Will R. Branscum
City Newark
Company
Contact Scott Branyan
City Rogers
Company
Contact Randy Brott
City Cotter
Company
Contact Robert S. Brown
City N. Little Rock
Company
Contact Mike C. Brown
City Tumbling Shoals
Company
Contact Mike W. Brumley
City Benton
Company
Contact Glen E. Bucher
City Flippin
Company
Contact Dennis A. Buck
City Hatfield
Company
Contact Steve Buckingham
City Hot Springs
Company
Contact Barry E. Bullock
City Pine Bluff
Company
Contact Charles F. Bump
City Royal
Company
Contact Donald W. Bunch
City Fayetteville
Company
Contact Jack A. Burbridge
City Fairfield Bay
Company
Contact Clyde W. Burchard
City Mountain Home
Company
Contact David A. Butterfield
City Mountain Home
Company
Contact Jerry D. Bynum
City Cabot
Company
Contact James M. Byrd
City Hope
Company
Contact John D. Cagle
City Flippin
Company
Contact Doyal W. Cain
City Royal
Company
Contact Jess Cain
City Fairfield Bay
Company

Contact David E. Capps
City Yellville
Company
Contact Richard H. Carpenter
City Midway
Company
Contact John P. Carter
City Caddo Gap
Company
Contact Greg Cash
City Glenwood
Company
Contact Kurt A. Caudill
City Yellville
Company
Contact Arlie D. Caudill
City Midway
Company
Contact Ronald W. Chaney
City Harrison
Company
Contact Rick L. Chaney
City Yellville
Company
Contact Bruce Chankler
City Gassville
Company
Contact Ed S. Chapko
City Rogers
Company
Contact Roy E. Chapman
City Eureka Springs
Company
Contact Charles R. Chapman
City Bull Shoals
Company
Contact Ralph R. Chatelain
City Bull Shoals
Company
Contact Bobby D. Cheatham
City Jacksonville
Company
Contact Bobby J. Cheek
City Gassville
Company
Contact Keith Chism
City Calico Rock
Company
Contact Clifford L. Chism
City Gassville
Company
Contact Raymond Choate
City Calico Rock
Company
Contact Mark R. Christian
City Flippin
Company
Contact Walter J. Clark
City Stuttgart
Company
Contact George Clark
City Norfork
Company
Contact George J. Clark
City Norfork
Company
Contact Roy E. Clark
City Eureka Springs
Company
Contact Jonathan C. Clayton
City Rogers
Company
Contact William A. Cobb
City Cotter
Company
Contact Steve Cockerel
City Mountain Home
Company
Contact Michael D. Cogburn
City Benton
Company
Contact Donald E. Collins
City Pleasant Grove
Company
Contact Ron G. Colvin
City Eureka Springs
Company
Contact Paul W. Combs
City Heber Springs
Company
Contact Jeff L. Condery
City Henderson
Company
Contact John E. Connelly
City Bull Shoals
Company

Contact Marvin D. Coombe
City Marshall
Company
Contact William H. Cooper
City Gassville
Company
Contact Larry E. Cooper
City Hot Springs
Company
Contact Robert L. Copeland
City Bull Shoals
Company
Contact Douglas R. Coppemoll
City Mountain Home
Company
Contact Calvin R. Cowart
City Gassville
Company
Contact Lonnie B. Cox
City Cotter
Company
Contact L.R. Cox
City Bull Shoals
Company
Contact James R. Cox, Sr.
City Norfork
Company
Contact Frank M. Cox
City Calico Rock
Company
Contact Lonnie L. Cox
City Flippin
Company
Contact Frankie J. Cox
City Norfork
Company
Contact Edward M. Craft
City Heber Springs
Company
Contact Donald D. Cranor
City Mountain Home
Company
Contact Richard Crawford
City Heber Springs
Company
Contact Frank Cresswell
City Higden
Company
Contact Gary & Scott Cresswell
City Heber Springs
Company
Contact Michael R. Crisenberry
City Flippin
Company
Contact Toby A. Crosby
City Mountain Home
Company
Contact Frederick T. Crouch
City Heber Springs
Company
Contact James Crownover
City Gassville
Company
Contact Wayne D. Crumpton
City Royal
Company
Contact Elmer Crumpton
City Hot Springs
Company
Contact Chris D. Curley
City Yellville
Company
Contact Rex A. Curley
City Cotter
Company
Contact Danny L. Curtis
City Calico Rock
Company
Contact Jimmy D. Curtis
City Midway
Company
Contact Timothy C. Curtis
City Bull Shoals
Company
Contact Stephen K. Daffron
City Flippin
Company
Contact Tom W. Darr
City Mountain Home
Company
Contact Tony Davenport
City Yellville
Company
Contact Alvin R. Davis
City Harriet
Company

Contact	City
Gerald D. Davis	Flippin
Danny E. Deatherage	Hot Springs
Irvin & Richard B. Deatley	Mountain Home
Ray Dickerson	Norfork
Darren Dilday	Flippin
Foster M. Divis	Lewisville
John W. Dixon, III	Conway
John W. Dixon, Jr.	Calico Rock
Gary W. Dodd	Pearcy
Charles Donham	N. Little Rock
M.R. Dorsey	Hot Springs
Parker L. Dozmier	Hot Springs
Timothy W. Drewry	Leslie
Jerry D. Dudley	Fayetteville
Leon W. Due	Flippin
Andy Due	Harrison
Jackie D. Due	Bull Shoals
Tommy G. Due	Flippin
James P.Due	Flippin
Jimothy J. Duff	Lakeview
Steven E. Eager	Fayetteville
Randy P.Eckley	Flippin
Terry G. Edwards	Rogers
Dave H. Elling	Bull Shoals
Bobby L. Ellis	Gassville
DeWayne L. Eubanks	Cotter
Eddie W. Eversmeyer	Mountain View
Joe A. Farkas	Rogers
Richard K. Farquhar	Bull Shoals
Michael J. Farris	Brockwell
Bobby D. Feagin	Springdale
John P.Flaherty	Bull Shoals
Bill W. Fletcher	Mountain Home
Russell L. Flippin	Cotter
Robert L. Flippin	Cotter
Gary E. Flippin	Gassville
Michael R. Flippin	Flippin
Gary T. Foster	Flippin
Forrest J. Fowler	Heber Springs
Gary R. Fox	Mount Ida
James E. Fraize	St. Charles
Bob Franks	Calico Rock
Greg Fulton	Hot Springs
Dale Fulton	Cotter
Rick Gardner	Mountain Home
Bobby G. Garland	Lakeview
Danny Garrett	Bull Shoals
Carroll T. Gartrell	Rogers
Donald K. Gauger	Gamaliel
Wiliam L. Gilbert	Flippin
Phillip A. Gladden	Hot Springs
James D. Goldsmith	Flippin
Roy L. Golightly	Norfork
Charles I. Goodwin	Lakeview
Darryl Graham	Rogers
Jonathon S. Graves	Jessieville
Floyd Graves	Mountain Home
Harry S. Grimes	Quitman
Fred A. Grueber	Gassville
Jay D. Gudermuth	Heber Springs
Lloyd Gunsolus	Norfork
Marvin H. Gwin	Mabelvale
Duane E. Hada	Ft. Smith
Buddy Haislip	Fairfield Bay
Roy J. Hall	Calico Rock
John T. Hall	Hot Springs
Doyle Hall	Yellville
James Hall	Yellville
Homer W. Hamilton	Mountain Home
David Haney	Mountain Home
Adam F. Hardcastle	Eureka Springs
Albert Harless	Flippin
Robert E. Harper	Bull Shoals
Bob Harrington	Mountain View
Jack L. Harrison	Boswell
Michael A. Haverland	Flippin
Jeffrey Hawthorne	Heber Springs
Walter Hedges	Fayetteville
Rick E. Helmus	Flippin
James E. Henderson	Green Forest
Dwight Henry	Flippin
Stevie D. Henry	Marshall
Bill F.Heuel	Perryville
Robert Hightower	Heber Springs
Doug Hill	Royal
James G. Hinkle	Mountain Viewe
Darrell Hipp	Heber Springs
Leon Hobgood	Heber Springs
Roy C. Hobson	Flippin
Oliver D. Hoffmann	Conway
Michael Holcer	Norfork
Wayne K. Holeton	Oakland
Gary L. Holland	Casscoe
John E. Honeycutt	Heber Springs
Ted C. Hood, Jr.	Heber Springs
Wilburn H. Hooten	Heber Springs
Donely R. Hoover	Austin
Ray Horn	Heber Springs
James R. Howe	Smackover
Jason Hudgens	Pineville
Steve Hudgens	Norfork
Otis Humphrey	Flippin
Kenten H. Hunnell	Lakeview
John P.Ingram	Quitman
William L. Ingram	Hot Springs
Danny P.Inskeep	Clarkridge
Bryon Jackson	Calico Rock
Lawrence D. Jefferson	Horseshoe Bend
Jackie L. Jefferson	Flippin
James B. Jensen	Oakland
Kenneth R.Jewett	Little Rock
Jimmy L. Johnson	Alexander
J.B.Johnson	Heber Springs
Larry Johnson	Norfork
Carl H. Jones	Flippin
Jack Jones	Heber Springs
Charles E. Jones	Mountain Home
Leonard R. Jones	Cotter
Gerald D. Jones	Mountain Home
Loren D. Jones	Mountain View
James A. Jordan	Mountain Home
Floyd Juern	Diamond City
John M. Keehnel	Mountain Home
Pat Kelley	Yellville
Ashley A. Kelley	Lakeview
Michael E. Kelly	Yellville
Vaughn Killebrew	Flippin
Jerry D. Killebrew	St. Joe
Arnold Knight	Mountain Home
Mark A. Koehler	Springdale
Dennis Kreutzer	Benton
Greg Kroll	Lakeview
Donald F. Kruse, Jr.	Lakeview
Don L. & Eddie D. Lack	Fillipin
Lonnie S. Lack	Flippin
Troy Lackey	Gassville
Richard V. Lane	Flippin
Dennis N. Langston	Norfork
Ricky W. Latting	Mountain Home
Jerry D. Lawrence	Flippin
Ken Lawson	Gamaliel
Robert Leard	Mountain Home
Dave Lekin	Mountain Home
Thomas Leonard	Flippin
Walter D. Leonard	Lakeview
Eddie D. Lester	Calico Rock
David Lewis	Calico Rock
Elroy M. Lewis, Jr.	Mountain Home
Greg Lfoulk	Flippin
James R. Lindsey	Calico Rock
Jimmy W. Lipscomb	Lakeview
James Loosey	Norfork
Jeremiah S. Love	Searcy
Mike Lucas	Bull Shoals
Robert D. Lutz	Bull Shoals
James P.Martin	Mountain View
Mark Martin	Mountain View
Dan Martin	Lowell
Gregory Mathews	Cotter

Contact Kenneth H. Maxwell **City** Mountain Home Company	**Contact** Leland Nave **City** Pineville Company	**Contact** Harlin D. Ponnell **City** Flippin Company	**Contact** John E. Scott **City** Calico Rock Company	**Contact** James Stevens **City** Gassville Company
Contact Greg W. Mayfield **City** Calico Rock Company	**Contact** Michael Neher **City** Flippin Company	**Contact** Gerald W. Pope **City** Summit Company	**Contact** Carl E. Seago **City** Heber Springs Company	**Contact** Charles R. Stewart **City** Bull Shoals Company
Contact Kim McCluskley **City** Fayetteville Company	**Contact** Steven C. Newbrey **City** Pineville Company	**Contact** Tina Posey **City** Austin Company	**Contact** James D. Seaman **City** Gassville Company	**Contact** Jackie Stinnet **City** Gassville Company
Contact Douglas W. McCormick **City** Manila Company	**Contact** Damon M. Newpher **City** Shirley Company	**Contact** Larry C. & Michele M. Price **City** Calico Rock Company	**Contact** Stephen R. Sharp **City** Jonesboro Company	**Contact** Ronald L. Stokes **City** Mountain Home Company
Contact Randel A. McCoy **City** Calico Rock Company	**Contact** Patrick A. Nichols **City** Harrison Company	**Contact** Cid A. Price **City** Alma Company	**Contact** Jerry C. Shaum **City** Shirley Company	**Contact** Paul Storm **City** Norfork Company
Contact Jeffrey F. McCoy **City** Big Flat Company	**Contact** Verron L. Nieghbors **City** Hot Springs Company	**Contact** Don R. Rand **City** Royal Company	**Contact** Robert D. Shaw **City** Lakeview Company	**Contact** Bobby G. Strother **City** Oden Company
Contact Mark McDole **City** Mountain Home Company	**Contact** Richard L Niffenegger **City** Drasco Company	**Contact** Richard M. Rangel **City** Norfork Company	**Contact** Steve W. Shawl **City** Fairfield Bay Company	**Contact** Jimmy L. Sweat **City** Mountain View Company
Contact Bryan S. McDowell **City** Flippin Company	**Contact** Donald R. Noles **City** Benton Company	**Contact** Joseph L. Reagan, Jr. **City** Mountain Home Company	**Contact** Gary Shelton **City** Searcy Company	**Contact** Melvin D. Taylor **City** Norfork Company
Contact Del D. McFarland **City** Summit Company	**Contact** Paul Nordrum **City** Mountain View Company	**Contact** Virgil M. Reeves **City** Yellville Company	**Contact** Robert L. Shuler **City** Flippin Company	**Contact** Aaron B. Teague **City** Calico Rock Company
Contact Charles G. McGowen **City** Mountain Home Company	**Contact** Linda J. Norton **City** Heber Springs Company	**Contact** Al H. Reinhart **City** Flippin Company	**Contact** Thomas I. Sigler **City** Mountain Home Company	**Contact** William M. Tenison **City** Fayetteville Company
Contact Donald T. McKellup **City** Harrison Company	**Contact** Steve F. O'Dell **City** Jacksonville Company	**Contact** Robert L. Rickerson **City** Diamond City Company	**Contact** Michael Simunoil **City** Norfork Company	**Contact** Edward J. Tercoe **City** Heber Springs Company
Contact Ralph D. McNair **City** Flippin Company	**Contact** Richard A. O'Neale **City** Midway Company	**Contact** Robert F. Rillings **City** Fayetteville Company	**Contact** Lee G. Sisk **City** Big Flat Company	**Contact** Jim P. Thorwarth **City** Hot Springs Company
Contact Larry J. McNair **City** Mountain Hme Company	**Contact** John T. Ogle **City** Rogers Company	**Contact** Tommy N. Rodgers **City** Gassville Company	**Contact** David Small **City** Mountain Home Company	**Contact** Mark V. Thow **City** Mount Ida Company
Contact Jim D. McSwain **City** Calico Rock Company	**Contact** Dane S. Ovalls **City** Royal Company	**Contact** Rick Rogers **City** Mountain Home Company	**Contact** Perry J. Smith **City** Gassville Company	**Contact** Jimmy Tilley **City** Big Flat Company
Contact Brad H. Medlock **City** N. Little Rock Company	**Contact** Robert D. Owens **City** Story Company	**Contact** Dean C. Rogers **City** Yellville Company	**Contact** Cary C. Smith **City** Flippin Company	**Contact** Elmo Tilley **City** Bull Shoals Company
Contact Carl E. Meeks **City** Gassville Company	**Contact** Andy Packmore **City** Heber Springs Company	**Contact** Ronald D. Rosborough **City** Hot Springs Company	**Contact** Jimmy G. Smith, Jr. **City** Cabot Company	**Contact** Lonnie Tilley **City** Mountain Home Company
Contact Gerald V. Melton **City** Mountain Home Company	**Contact** Andy J. Packmore **City** Ft. Smith Company	**Contact** Gerald D. Rose **City** Midway Company	**Contact** Buddy Smith **City** Rogers Company	**Contact** Randy D. Tilley **City** Bull Shoals Company
Contact Harley F. Meredith **City** Hot Springs Company	**Contact** Winston Parkinson **City** Bull Shoals Company	**Contact** Alvin L. Ross **City** Flippin Company	**Contact** Phil S. Smith **City** Flippin Company	**Contact** Greg W. Tilley **City** Marshall Company
Contact James L. Nichols **City** Mountain Home Company	**Contact** Thomas A. Parks **City** Cotter Company	**Contact** Robert F. Ross **City** Gilbert Company	**Contact** James F. Snyder **City** Fayetteville Company	**Contact** Damon R. Tillman **City** West Fork Company
Contact Everett G. Middleton **City** Flippin Company	**Contact** Pete Paszli **City** Hot Springs Company	**Contact** Dewey S. Rudolph **City** Ozark Company	**Contact** Leon H. Sommerville, Jr. **City** Harriet Company	**Contact** Harry L. Tillolson **City** Bismarck Company
Contact Richard B. Mikuska, Jr. **City** Garfield Company	**Contact** Louie Patrizi **City** Bull Shoals Company	**Contact** Stanley J. Rura **City** Bull Shoals Company	**Contact** James T. Southard **City** Calico Rock Company	**Contact** Bobby L. Tolliver **City** Mountain Home Company
Contact Alvin R. Milam **City** Ward Company	**Contact** Buddy M. Patterson **City** Calico Rock Company	**Contact** Robert Russell **City** Dolph Company	**Contact** Michael B. Sparks **City** Palestine Company	**Contact** Rang G. Tolliver **City** Cotter Company
Contact Wayne D. Miles **City** Flippin Company	**Contact** Leon Payton **City** Heber Springs Company	**Contact** John H. Rust **City** Flippin Company	**Contact** Robert E. Spearman **City** Ft. Smith Company	**Contact** Jim Traylor **City** Bull Shoals Company
Contact Jon K. Miller **City** Gassville Company	**Contact** James H. Peck **City** Little Rock Company	**Contact** Paul M. Saba **City** Bull Shoals Company	**Contact** Garry N. Sperry **City** Gamaliel Company	**Contact** Winfred O. Traywick **City** Ashdown Company
Contact John H. Miskelly **City** Mountain Home Company	**Contact** Todd Percival **City** Cotter Company	**Contact** Frank S. Saksa **City** Mountain Home Company	**Contact** Robert P. Spezio **City** Flippin Company	**Contact** Donald J. Trimble **City** Flippin Company
Contact Robert R. Mixon **City** Pearcy Company	**Contact** James M. Perdue **City** Midway Company	**Contact** Ted Salzman **City** Mountain Home Company	**Contact** Lowell E. Spitzer **City** Lakeview Company	**Contact** Kenny Trivitt **City** Cotter Company
Contact Jeff Moore **City** Bull Shoals Company	**Contact** Patrick A. Perdue **City** Bull Shoals Company	**Contact** Jimmie D. Sanders **City** Greenland Company	**Contact** Carl R. Spongberg **City** Rogers Company	**Contact** Harold F. Trivitt **City** Cotter Company
Contact Edward Moore **City** Bentonville Company	**Contact** Jimmy L. Phillips **City** Gentry Company	**Contact** Rickey P. Sattenwhite **City** Batesville Company	**Contact** Terry W. Stacy **City** Calico Rock Company	**Contact** Dale Tucker **City** Bonnerdale Company
Contact Terry L. Morris **City** Gassville Company	**Contact** Joseph D. Pieratt **City** Magnolia Company	**Contact** Ronald J. Schneider **City** Mountain Home Company	**Contact** Ronald Stark **City** Oakland Company	**Contact** Louis M. Turner **City** Magnolia Company
Contact Chuck B. Morrow **City** Flippin Company	**Contact** Robert W. Pilger **City** Norfork Company	**Contact** Regan I Scott **City** Wilbum Company	**Contact** William F. Statler **City** Salem Company	**Contact** Tom A. Turney **City** Mountain Home Company
Contact Hal H. Murray **City** Batesville Company	**Contact** Rodney L. Plummer **City** Fox Company	**Contact** Warren J. Scott **City** Fordyce Company	**Contact** Kevin K. Stephens **City** Mayflower Company	**Contact** Lon J. Unger **City** Flippin Company
Contact Jerry E. Myers **City** Mountain Home Company	**Contact** Frederick S. Polich **City** Bull Shoals Company	**Contact** Carl Scott **City** Calico Rock Company	**Contact** Virgil Stephenson **City** Heber Springs Company	**Contact** Carl B. VanNetter **City** Calico Rock Company

Contact Willie W. Wade
City Enola
Company

Contact Charles F. Wagnon
City Mountain Home
Company

Contact Mick Wagoner
City Flippin
Company

Contact Eldawan Wagoner
City Flippin
Company

Contact John A. Wahler
City Bull Shoals
Company

Contact Edward R. Waits, III
City Pine Bluff
Company

Contact Donnie L. Wallace
City Gassville
Company

Contact Russell Wallace
City Flippin
Company

Contact Murray R. Wallace
City Rogers
Company

Contact Miles E. Wallace
City Hot Springs
Company

Contact Normal L. Wallace
City Flippin
Company

Contact Patrick Walter
City Bull Shoals
Company

Contact Phil Wantland
City Fayetteville
Company

Contact Howard D. Wards
City Melbourne
Company

Contact Calvin D. Warner
City DeWitt
Company

Contact G.H. Warren
City Hot Springs
Company

Contact Haron H. Watkins
City Searcy
Company

Contact Jerry D. Watts
City Big Flat
Company

Contact Jarrod D. Watts
City Harriet
Company

Contact Thurl L. Watts
City Calico Rock
Company

Contact Donald G. Watts
City Marshall
Company

Contact Billy Weaver
City Eureka Springs
Company

Contact Elvin L. Weaver
City Gassville
Company

Contact Randall L. Weaver
City Gassville
Company

Contact Patrick S. Weir
City Lakeview
Company

Contact Thurman Welch
City Fifty-Six
Company

Contact Terry W. Wells
City Mountain Home
Company

Contact Michael r. Wheeler
City Heber Springs
Company

Contact Carl J. Whisenhunt
City Flippin
Company

Contact Slim R. White
City Flippin
Company

Contact Lance J. Whiteaker
City Calico Rock
Company

Contact Paul D. Whitney
City Calico Rock
Company

Contact Jim T. Wiebe
City Mountain View
Company

Contact Ralph Wiegand
City Gassville
Company

Contact Matt Wilbur
City Norfork
Company

Contact David G. Wilkes
City Flippin
Company

Contact Charlie E. Willet
City Gassville
Company

Contact William P. Williams
City Mayflower
Company

Contact Ricky E. Williamson
City Booneville
Company

Contact Jerry Wilson
City Flippin
Company

Contact Kalen Wilson
City Springdale
Company

Contact Curtis L. Wing
City Rogers
Company

Contact Jim Wingard
City Calico Rock
Company

Contact Arvle L. Winkler
City Siloam Springs
Company

Contact Clyde W. Wofford
City Midway
Company

Contact Phillip D. Woodford
City Little Rock
Company

Contact Randy L. Woods
City Flippin
Company

Contact Morrell J. Woods
City Norfork
Company

Contact Christopher L. Wooten
City Pineville
Company

Contact Carl J. & David Wooten
City Calico Rock
Company

Contact James Worster
City Yellville
Company

Contact Roy B. Wright
City Pangburn
Company

Contact Mike Wurm
City Hot Springs
Company

Contact Joseph R. Zink
City Mountain Home

California

Company Al's Four Season Taxidermy
Contact
City Redding

Company Alagnak Lodge
Contact Vin Roccanova
City Sacramento

Company Alaska Angling Adventures
Contact Rafi Jeknavorian
City N. Hollywood

Company All-Seasons Catalina Mako Charters
Contact
City Avalon

Company Amigos De Baja
Contact
City Huntington Beach

Company Arcularius Ranch
Contact Bill & Diane Nichols
City Mammoth Lakes

Company Ardison Charters
Contact Jason Young
City Scotts Valley

Company Avila Beach Sportfishing

Contact
City Avila Beach
Company Aztec
Contact Curt Wegener
City San Diego

Company B & B Fishing Adventures, Inc.
Contact E.F.'Bus'Bergmann III
City Atwater

Company Baja AirVentures
Contact Kevin Warren
City Chula Vista

Company Battle Creek Outfitters
Contact Ronald F. Gayer
City Bakersfield

Company Battle River Wilderness Retreat
Contact Tim Conway
City Sacto

Company Bear Ridge Fishing
Company
Contact John & Lynn Pizza
City Santa Rosa

Company Big Bluff Ranch
Contact
City Red Bluff

Company Big Dog's Alaska Guide Service
Contact Gary & Bev Lindstrom
City Smith River

Company Bigfoot Campground Guide Service
Contact
City Junction City

Company Blue Ribbon Fishing Charters
Contact
City South Lake Tahoe

Company Bob's Guide Service
Contact Robert A. Wigham
City Redding

Company Bongo's Sportfishing Headquarters
Contact
City Newport Beach

Company Bruce Slightom
Contact Bruce Slightom
City Eureka

Company Bryan-Sherman Packing
Contact Mike Bryan & Bink Sherman
City Etna

Company Cameron & Smith Fly Fishing
Contact
City Pacific Grove

Company Casa De Kings
Contact Steve Nowak
City Stockton

Company Channel Islands Sportfishing Center
Contact
City Oxnard

Company Charger
Contact Rick Craddick
City San Diego

Company Chartle Sportfishing
Contact Joseph F. Stoops
City Santa Cruz

Company Clearwater Guides
Contact
City Truckee

Company Clearwater House on Hat Creek
Contact Richard Galland
City Cassel

Company Clearwater Trout Tours
Contact
City Cassel

Company Compensator/Western Charter Company
Contact
City San Diego

Company Concepts in Fly Fishing
Contact James Mershan Ferris
City Santa Ana

Company Craig's Guide Service
Contact Craig L. VanHousen
City Kelseyville

Company Curtis Guide Service
Contact Curtis S. Fletscher
City San Jose

Company D.J.'s Guide Service
Contact Darrin Johnston
City Quartz Hill

Company Daily Double
Contact Ralph Botticelli

City San Diego
Company Damm Drifter Guide Service
Contact Darol L. Damm
City Crescent City

Company Dana Wharf Sportfishing
Contact
City Dana Point

Company Davey's Locker Sportfishing
Contact
City Balboa

Company Dean James Guide Service
Contact Dean S. James
City Healdsburg

Company Denardi Outfitting
Contact
City Yreka

Company Diamond H Hunting Preserve
Contact
City Burlingame

Company Dos Mas
Contact Bud Aronis
City San Diego

Company Durand's Fishing Guide
Contact
City Redding

Company Eagle Charters
Contact Levi E. Hubbard
City Redondo Beach

Company Farewell Harbour Resort
Contact Paul Weaver
City Carlsbad

Company Fish First! Guide Service
Contact
City Albany

Company Fishtales
Contact Thomas D. Stanton
City Hayfork

Company Fly Fishing Outfitters
Contact
City San Francisco

Company Free Willy Prof. Fishing Guide Service
Contact
City Redding

Company God's Country Guide Service
Contact Gerald B. Gray
City Trinity Center

Company Gold Coast Sportfishing
Contact
City Oxnard

Company Golden West Sports Tours
Contact
City San Francisco

Company Greg Nicol Guide Service
Contact Greg Nicol
City Smith River

Company H & M Landing
Contact
City San Diego

Company Hagen's Guide Service
Contact Donald Hagen
City Gasquet

Company Hansen-Silver Guest Ranch
Contact Brett W. Hansen
City Westlake Village

Company Hat Creek House
Contact DUane milleman
City Cassel

Company Helgren's Sportfishing Trips
Contact
City Oceanside

Company Henderson Springs
Contact Mark Henderson
City Big Bend

Company High Sierra Fly Fishing
Contact David Moss
City Mammoth Lakes

Company Holiday
Contact Glory Giffin
City San Diego

Company Huck Finn Sportfishing
Contact
City El Granada

Company Inset Guide Service
Contact
City Redding

Company J. Fair's Hand Tied Flies
Contact
City Susanville

Company Jerry's Guide Service
Contact Gerald R. Bertagna
City Oroville

Company Jim Munk Bass Guides
Contact James and Nancy Munk
City Middletown

Company Keller's Kenai Sport Fishing
Contact Patrick Keller
City Rohnert Park

Company Kemoo Trout Farm
Contact
City West Point

Company Kevin's Guide Service
Contact Kevin Hicks
City Smith River

Company King Salmon Charters
Contact Capt. Dennis Pecaut
City Eureka

Company Kingfish Guide Service
Contact
City Tahoe City

Company Kutzkey's Guide Service
Contact Albert Kutzkey
City Yreka

Company Lake Amador Resort
Contact Robert Lockhart
City Sutter Creek

Company Lake Tahoe Adventures
Contact
City So. Lake Tahoe

Company Lava Creek Lodge
Contact
City Fall River Mills

Company Lee Palm Sportfishers
Contact
City San Diego

Company Long Beach Sportfishing
Contact
City Long Beach

Company Long Fin Charters
Contact Tom Ward
City Orange

Company Los Angeles Harbor Sportfishing
Contact
City San Pedro

Company Mac-A-Tac Fishing Charters
Contact
City Tahoe City

Company Maestro Safaris
Contact
City San Diego

Company Mammoth Adventure Connection
Contact
City Mammoth Lakes

Company Mark Glassmaker Fishing
Contact Mark Glassmaker
City Movato

Company McBroom & Company: Packers & Guides
Contact
City Etna

Company Mickey's Big Mack Charters
Contact
City Tahoe City

Company Mickey's Big Mack Charters
Contact Mickey E. Daniels
City Tahoe City

Company Mike Bogue's Guide Service
Contact Michael E. Bogue
City Redding

Company Monterey Sport Fishing
Contact
City Monterey

Company Morning Star
Contact Ben Griffith
City San Diego

Company Mt. Lassen Trout
Contact
City Red Bluff

Company Mt. Shasta Fly Fishing Guide Service
Contact
City Mt. Shasta

Company Multiple Use Managers, Inc.
Contact Gordon Long
City West Point

Company New Easy Rider Sportfishing
Contact
City Berkeley

Company New Lo-An
Contact Nick Cates & Buzz Brizendine

City San Diego
Company Newport Landing Sportfishing
Contact
City Balboa
Company No See Um Lodge, Inc.
Contact John W. Holman
City Redding
Company North Bay Adventures
Contact Michael R. Addiego
City San Carols
Company O'Rourke's Outdoor Adventures
Contact Richard O'Rourke
City La Porte
Company Oakridge Inn
Contact Vijay Patel
City Oak View
Company Oasis Springs Flyfishing Lodge
Contact Warren Quan
City Oakland
Company Pacifica
Contact Guy Ashley
City San Diego
Company Phil's Smiling Salmon Guide
Contact Philip Desautels
City Smith River
Company Point Loma Sportfishing
Contact
City San Diego
Company Pronto
Contact Alan Fay
City San Diego
Company Randy's Fishing Trips
Contact
City Monterey
Company Red's Kern Valley Marina
Contact
City Lake Isabella
Company Redwood Empire Outdoor Adventure
Contact
City Miranda
Company Restoration Through Recreation
Contact Rocky & Sharon McElvea
City Rocklin
Company Rich Brown Guide Service
Contact
City Redding
Company Rick's Lodge
Contact
City Fall River Mills
Company Ring's Fishing Guide Service
Contact Floyd Ring
City Cypress
Company Riptide Sportfishing
Contact CaptainWilliam "Smitty" Smith
City San Francisco
Company SBL Company
Contact
City Palo Cedro
Company Sea Star Charters
Contact
City Oceanside
Company Shadow Lake Ranch
Contact
City Bella Vista
Company Shasta Tackle & Sportfishing
Contact
City Bella Vista
Company Sierra Club Outings
Contact
City San Francisco
Company Skipper's 22nd Street Landing
Contact
City San Pedro
Company Skyline Park
Contact
City Napa
Company Sorensen's Resort
Contact
City Hope Valley
Company Spring Creek Specialist
Contact James Marc
City Larkspur
Company Springfield Trout Farm
Contact
City Sonora
Company Sundown
Contact Jack Smith

City San Diego
Company Ted Fay Fly Shop
Contact
City Dunsmuir
Company The Fly Shop
Contact
City Redding
Company The Sea Ranch Lodge
Contact Rosemary McGinnis
City The Sea Ranch
Company Thy Rod & Staff
Contact
City Truckee
Company Tide Change
Contact Gary Adams
City San Diego
Company Tim Bermingham's Drift Boat Guide Service
Contact Tim Bermingham
City Jamestown
Company Timbuctoo Sporting Estate
Contact
City Smartville
Company Time Flies
Contact
City Arcata
Company Tom Jasper River Guide Service
Contact Thomas E. Jasper
City Smith River
Company Trinity Canyon Lodge
Contact
City Helena
Company True North Charters
Contact Donald E. & Sandra Terrell
City Grass Valley
Company Turner's Guide Service
Contact Scott Turner
City Sutter
Company Virg's Landing
Contact
City Morro Bay
Company Warrens Guide Service
Contact Tom Rogers
City Crescent City
Company Western Wildlife Services
Contact
City Millville
Company Wild Sport Services
Contact Randolph B. Rigdon
City Smartville
Company Wild West Adventures
Contact Gary Robbins
City Sylmar
Company Wilderness Place Lodge
Contact Justin Trombello
City San Francisco
Company Wilderness Place Lodge
Contact Dean Gilardi
City Larkspur
Company Wolfe's Guide Service
Contact
City Alton
Company Wolverine Lodge
Contact Renee & Fred Bettschen
City Palm Springs
Company
Contact William Adelman
City Richmond
Company
Contact Roger W. Adrian
City Weaverville
Company
Contact Terry Alcorn
City Tulelake
Company
Contact Neil Amundson
City Crescent City
Company
Contact Philip Anastasia
City Carmel Valley
Company
Contact Randy Andersen
City Carlotta
Company
Contact Thomas April
City Mammoth Lakes
Company
Contact David Armocido
City Colusa
Company
Contact Michael Arujo
City Santa Monica
Company
Contact Ron Babbini
City Healdsburg

Company
Contact Victor Babbitt
City S. Lake Tahoe
Company
Contact Mike Barats
City San Jose
Company
Contact George Barber
City Shady Cove
Company
Contact Jerry Bass
City Yuba City
Company
Contact Mike Baxter
City Santa Cruz
Company
Contact Robert Bearding
City Somes Bar
Company
Contact Kurt Belcher
City Cathedral City
Company
Contact Nick Belkofer
City Chester
Company
Contact Raymond Bell
City Fairfield
Company
Contact Larry Bennett
City Fortuna
Company
Contact Craig Bentley
City Biggs
Company
Contact Victor Bergstrom
City Coleville
Company
Contact Howard L. Bernth
City Santa Barbara
Company
Contact Leroy Bertolero
City El Macero
Company
Contact Steve L. Bertrand
City Carmichael
Company
Contact Michael Bias
City Elk Grove
Company
Contact Richard Bishop
City Yuba City
Company
Contact Harry L. Blackburn
City Mammoth Lakes
Company
Contact Carl A. Blackledge
City Santa Rosa
Company
Contact James M. Blakesley
City Cottonwood
Company
Contact Gregory H. Bock
City Fullerton
Company
Contact Robert H. Bonslett
City Roseville
Company
Contact Gary Boyd
City Granada Hills
Company
Contact Marvin H. Braden
City Petaluma
Company
Contact Ted Bradley
City Redding
Company
Contact David C. Brown
City Cassel
Company
Contact Ed Brown
City Lewiston
Company
Contact Patrick T. Buckley
City Castaic
Company
Contact R. A. Bumbaugh
City Redding
Company
Contact Gary T. Burch
City Petaluma
Company
Contact George L. Burdick
City Klamath
Company
Contact Kenneth R. Burkey
City Leggett

Company
Contact Edwin S. Burlarley
City Oakdale
Company
Contact John T. Burllile
City Lakespur
Company
Contact Pat Burton
City Lewiston
Company
Contact Doug Byrd
City Red Bluff
Company
Contact Gilbert Camargo
City Ione
Company
Contact Edward B. Campbell
City Susanville
Company
Contact John Cantrell
City Big Bear Lake
Company
Contact William P. Carnazzo
City Newcastle
Company
Contact Carl M. Carrillo
City Santa Barbara
Company
Contact Daniel J. Carter
City Kelseyville
Company
Contact John E. Carter, Jr.
City Bakersfield
Company
Contact David Castellanos
City Smith River
Company
Contact Paul J. Catanese
City Douglas City
Company
Contact Ron Cervenka
City Saugus
Company
Contact Tim A. Chambers
City Sebastopol
Company
Contact John R. Chargulaf
City Msuli
Company
Contact Henry J. Chojnakci
City Redding
Company
Contact Thomas N. Christiana
City Mammoth Lakes
Company
Contact Allen Clyde
City Clovis
Company
Contact Casj Colby
City Oroville
Company
Contact Don Collis
City Alturas
Company
Contact Amos C. Cross
City Napa
Company
Contact Jim Crouse
City S. Lake Tahoe
Company
Contact Bob Crupi
City Castaic
Company
Contact Mark E. Crutcher
City Potter Valley
Company
Contact Jenise Cunningham
City Clovis
Company
Contact Ronald Cushman
City Tulelake
Company
Contact Ralph Cutter
City Truckee
Company
Contact John D. D'Angelo
City Lake Almanor
Company
Contact Clifford Dahlquist
City Santa Rosa
Company
Contact John R. Dall
City Canyon Country
Company
Contact Ed Darrach
City Manteca

Company
Contact Robert Deeter
City Fort Bragg
Company
Contact George L. Dejavier
City Antioch
Company
Contact Mark Delnero
City Lodi
Company
Contact David Demoss
City Douglas City
Company
Contact William Dennis
City Smith River
Company
Contact Randy Depee
City Crescent City
Company
Contact Dave & Kent Dohnel
City Bishopo
Company
Contact Jeremy Drakeford
City Helena
Company
Contact Frank C. Duarte
City Chico
Company
Contact Edgar B. Duggan
City Willow Creek
Company
Contact Douglas Dumas
City Colfax
Company
Contact James A. Dunn
City Yuba City
Company
Contact George V. Dupoy
City S. Lake Tahoe
Company
Contact George A. Durand
City Redding
Company
Contact Ronald Ebert
City Granite Bay
Company
Contact Terry L. Edelmann
City Whitmore
Company
Contact Kenneth S. Elrod
City Burney
Company
Contact Chistopher A. Engel
City Ft. Klamath
Company
Contact Donald G. Englebrecht
City Broderick
Company
Contact Robert C. Ennis
City Cottonwood
Company
Contact Maynard M. Enos
City Livermore
Company
Contact Jay Fair, Sr.
City Susanville
Company
Contact Leroy M. Fegley
City Healdsburg
Company
Contact John Y. Findleton
City Sacramento
Company
Contact David Finn
City Camp Connell
Company
Contact Michael Fisher
City Nevada City
Company
Contact Edward J. Fitch
City Janesville
Company
Contact William Fitspatrick
City Santa Rosa
Company
Contact Rick Flamson
City Mammoth Lakes
Company
Contact Michael J. Forchini
City Healdsburg
Company
Contact Monte R. Ford
City Live Oak
Company
Contact Anthony T. Freeman
City Santa Rosa

Company
Contact Paul A. Freitas
City Windsor

Company
Contact Charles Fullerton
City Sacramento

Company
Contact Tony Furia
City Santa Rosa

Company
Contact Steve Gappa
City Corning

Company
Contact Mike Gardner
City Placentia

Company
Contact Tony Giorgi
City Geyserville

Company
Contact Jeff Glavaris
City Cottonwood

Company
Contact John D. Gleason
City Quincy

Company
Contact Liam I. Gogan
City Douglas City

Company
Contact John B. Goodwin, Jr.
City San Jose

Company
Contact Fred Gordon
City Dunsmuir

Company
Contact Robert L. Gover
City Alturas

Company
Contact Dan Gracia
City San Mateo

Company
Contact Mark Gray
City Garberville

Company
Contact Todd W. Gregorio
City Fair Oaks

Company
Contact David P. Grein
City Biggs

Company
Contact Gary E. Gunsolley
City Bishop

Company
Contact Stephen Gunther
City Forks of Salmon

Company
Contact Capt. Don Haid
City Costa Mesa

Company
Contact Bruce D. Hamby
City Ripon

Company
Contact Bradley L. Haney
City Castic

Company
Contact Eric Hanson
City Chico

Company
Contact Harry Harper
City Shasta Lake

Company
Contact John S. Harrington
City Mammouth Lakes

Company
Contact Gary D. Harrison
City Canyon Country

Company
Contact John Harsin
City Redding

Company
Contact Ronald W. Hart
City Mt. Shasta

Company
Contact Willy Haurtmann
City Redding

Company
Contact Neal Hayden, Jr.
City Stockton

Company
Contact Michael I. Hays
City Eureka Rd.

Company
Contact Wesley M. Hee
City Fort Bragg

Company
Contact Jack Hegdahl
City Linden

Company
Contact Clifford L. Hembree
City Susanville

Company
Contact Larry Hemphill
City Yuba City

Company
Contact John Henderson
City San Diego

Company
Contact Mike S. Hendry
City Orland

Company
Contact Raith Heryford
City Yuba City

Company
Contact Mark Heskett
City Torrance

Company
Contact Joe E. Heuseveudt
City Truckee

Company
Contact Thewalt J. Hibbard
City Stockton

Company
Contact Robert E. Hickox
City Petaluma

Company
Contact Kevin Hicks
City Gasquet

Company
Contact Scott Higgins
City Red Bluff

Company
Contact Edward G. Hilario
City Redding

Company
Contact Clay Hollistar
City Redding

Company
Contact Gordon L. Holt
City Eureka

Company
Contact Bill D. Howe
City Bishop

Company
Contact Bruce P. Huff
City Markleeville

Company
Contact Dennis W. Hunerberg
City Red Bluff

Company
Contact Patrick F. Jaeger
City Mammouth Lakes

Company
Contact William W. Jespersen
City Montague

Company
Contact Mark O. Jimenez
City Chester

Company
Contact Harry Jioras
City Oak View

Company
Contact Randall H. Johnson
City Tahoma

Company
Contact Brent Johnson
City Grass Valley

Company
Contact Thomas R. Jolin
City Lakeport

Company
Contact King S. Floyd, Jr.
City Hainthonne

Company
Contact Alexander M. Judice, Jr.
City Eureka

Company
Contact Roger Keeling
City Chester

Company
Contact Michael D. Kelly
City Occidental

Company
Contact Richard T. Kennedy
City Grass Valley

Company
Contact Keith F. Kerrigan
City Truckee

Company
Contact Joseph E. Kimsey
City Dunsmuir

Company
Contact David Kistle
City Vacaville

Company
Contact John M. Klar
City Eureka

Company
Contact William L. Klemin
City Stirling City

Company
Contact William R. Knox
City Susanville

Company
Contact Shane R. Kohlbeck
City Redding

Company
Contact Gary R. Kubowitz
City Mt. Shasta

Company
Contact Tim W. Kutzkey
City Montague

Company
Contact Luigi G. Laghi
City San Francisco

Company
Contact Roberta C. Lagomarsini
City Stockton

Company
Contact Thomas J. Lake
City Cedarville

Company
Contact Roger W. Langley
City Anderson

Company
Contact Mark Lathrop
City Red Bluff

Company
Contact John Stuart Lax
City Hollister

Company
Contact Jeffrey C. Lee
City Murietta

Company
Contact Arthur Lew
City Truckee

Company
Contact Daniel G. Liechty
City Arnold

Company
Contact Burt B. Llewellyn
City Scotts Valley

Company
Contact Mike Lockyer
City Klamath

Company
Contact Herbert London
City Bishop

Company
Contact Douglas W. Lovell
City Berkeley

Company
Contact Peter J. Lucia
City Napa

Company
Contact William J. Luckey
City Concord

Company
Contact Daniel R. Luckman
City Laytonville

Company
Contact Kenneth F. Mackert
City Winters

Company
Contact Michael G. Mallamo
City Larkspur

Company
Contact Terry W. Manthey
City Lakeport

Company
Contact Aaron Martens
City West Hills

Company
Contact Albert T. Martin
City Hayward

Company
Contact Donald D. Martin
City Buena Park

Company
Contact Richard Martin
City Los Banos

Company
Contact Ludwig Martinson
City Santa Rosa

Company
Contact Thomas A. Mathena
City Eureka

Company
Contact Bill Matthews
City Redondo Beach

Company
Contact David G. Matthews
City Salinas

Company
Contact Frank Mattison
City Sacramento

Company
Contact Joseph W. McCarthy
City Prunedale

Company
Contact Walter McEntyre
City Oroville

Company
Contact Michael McKay
City Arcata

Company
Contact Raymond McReynolds
City Yuba City

Company
Contact Ronald S. Mickele
City Castro Valley

Company
Contact Louis Milani, Jr.
City Colusa

Company
Contact Michael Monroe
City Sacramento

Company
Contact Sandra C. Moon
City Salyer

Company
Contact Andre Moore
City Walnut Creek

Company
Contact Michael W. Moore
City Live Oak

Company
Contact Michael Morgan
City Bishop

Company
Contact Don Morgan
City Vina

Company
Contact Robert A. Morris
City Pasadena

Company
Contact John W. Morrison
City Marysville

Company
Contact Mark R. Morrison
City Santa Margarita

Company
Contact Clifford Mosley
City Citrus Heights

Company
Contact Richard L. Mossholder
City Klamath

Company
Contact Keith L. Mount
City Bridgeport

Company
Contact William C. Munroe
City Manteca

Company
Contact Daniel A. Murphy
City Groveland

Company
Contact Mark P. Naillon
City San Jose

Company
Contact William Nakaki
City Tracy

Company
Contact Donald K. Nelson
City Mammouth Lakes

Company
Contact John W. Nelson
City Live Oak

Company
Contact Ron R. Newcomb
City Fremont

Company
Contact Rick Nielsen
City Oroville

Company
Contact Marc Nimitz
City Garberville

Company
Contact Robert M. Norman
City Santa Rosa

Company
Contact Francis J. O'Brien, III
City Redding

Company
Contact Chris O'Neill
City Fair Oaks

Company
Contact John B. Ogden
City McArthur

Company
Contact Brian F. Olson
City Truckee

Company
Contact Mike W. Osborne
City Gualala

Company
Contact Steven Osterman
City Mammoth Lakes

Company
Contact Rod Pacheco
City Salinas

Company
Contact Dennis Palla
City Douglas City

Company
Contact John Paslaqua
City San Jose

Company
Contact Barbara Payne
City Santa Rosa

Company
Contact Don R. Payne
City Modesto

Company
Contact Dennis Perea
City Burnt Ranch

Company
Contact Michael J. Peters
City Mammoth Lakes

Company
Contact Robert K. Peterson
City Trinidad

Company
Contact Jack Pinch
City Arnold

Company
Contact Clarence Pinkerton
City Lakeshore

Company
Contact Mark Pinto
City Stockton

Company
Contact Frank R. Pisciotta
City Truckee

Company
Contact John R. Pizza
City Santa Rosa

Company
Contact William Plunkett
City Crescent City

Company
Contact A. Dee Potter
City Weaverville

Company
Contact Mark L. Pounds
City Red Bluff

Company
Contact Phillip P. Powell
City Chico

Company
Contact Gene W. Prevette
City Union City

Company
Contact Sorin S. Pricopie
City Beverly Hills

Company
Contact Frank N. Prim
City Petaluma

Company
Contact Peter Pumphrey
City Stockton

Company
Contact Billy J. Quinn, Sr.
City Shingletown

Company
Contact Ron Rabun
City Dunsmuir

Company
Contact Beryl A. Rea
City Bishop

Company
Contact Ronnie S. Reese
City Citati

Company
Contact Robert E. Reid
City Anderson

Company
Contact Mitchell R. Riddle
City Markleeville

Company
Contact Raymond M. Robinson
City Crescent City

Company
Contact Daryl Rogers
City Redding
Company
Contact Dean Rojas
City Ramona
Company
Contact Richard Rombal
City Rancho Cucamo
Company
Contact Dana Rosen
City Agoura
Company
Contact Bryan D. Rosenquist
City Vallejo
Company
Contact Christopher P.Rothes
City Truckee
Company
Contact Martin Rovenstone
City San Miguel
Company
Contact Fred Rowe
City Bishop
Company
Contact Annette Russ
City Chico
Company
Contact Bill Russell
City Redding
Company
Contact Ron S. Saiki
City Sunnyvale
Company
Contact Ted Samford
City Emigrant Gap
Company
Contact Jim Sammons
City San Diego
Company
Contact Joseph M. Santone
City Fort Jones
Company
Contact Michael D. Saverino
City Mission Viejo
Company
Contact David Schachter
City Eureka
Company
Contact David B. Schemenauer
City Mammoth Lakes
Company
Contact Richard K. Schwalm
City Camarillo
Company
Contact Richard J. Scriven
City Meridian
Company
Contact Robert Scrogin
City Santa Rosa
Company
Contact David P.Shafer
City Carmichael
Company
Contact Phil P.Sharpe
City Gold River
Company
Contact Bink Sherman
City Montague
Company
Contact Jack Short
City Napa
Company
Contact William M. Siemantel
City Castaic
Company
Contact Don R. Simic
City Chico
Company
Contact Mark Simonds
City Redding
Company
Contact Virgil P.Sipes
City Oroville
Company
Contact Mark T. Slack
City Eureka
Company
Contact Robert A. Slamal
City Riverside
Company
Contact Charles B. Smith
City Chico
Company
Contact Carl S. Smith
City Loomis

Company
Contact Brett Smith
City Pacific Grove
Company
Contact Christopher T. Smith
City Burney
Company
Contact Jeffery S. Solis
City San Diego
Company
Contact Jay R. Sorensen
City Stockton
Company
Contact Stephen Sorensen
City Kerman
Company
Contact Rick Soto
City Sacramento
Company
Contact Paul J. Souza
City American Canyon
Company
Contact Pete J. Sparacio
City Hayfork
Company
Contact George L. Stelmach
City Norco
Company
Contact Robert L. Stephens
City Los Molinos
Company
Contact Peter Sturges
City Forks of Salmo
Company
Contact Michael A. Swaney
City Sebastopol
Company
Contact Dennis F.Swope
City Cassel
Company
Contact Wayne J. Syn
City Orland
Company
Contact Fernando C. Tabor
City Petaluma
Company
Contact Henry E. Tabor
City Lakeport
Company
Contact Richard Taddei
City Greenville
Company
Contact Robert C. Tanner
City Mammoth Lakes
Company
Contact Neal A. Taylor
City Santa Barbara
Company
Contact Michele Tennies
City Auburn
Company
Contact Delbert Thyarks
City Annapolis
Company
Contact Carl Ray Tomlinson
City San Jose
Company
Contact Patrick T. Tully
City Foresthill
Company
Contact William L. Turner
City Biggs
Company
Contact Gregory R. Turner
City Prunedale
Company
Contact Edward A. VanDyke
City Smith River
Company
Contact Victor Vardenega
City Fremont
Company
Contact Rene Villanueva
City Elk Grove
Company
Contact Tim Voaklander
City San Diego
Company
Contact Mark Wakeman
City Blue Lake
Company
Contact Steven B. Walser
City Sonora
Company
Contact John E. Watson
City S. Lake Tahoe

Company
Contact Jonathan D. Watson
City Santa Rosa
Company
Contact Michael J. Watson
City Somes Bar
Company
Contact Bob Webster
City Weaverville
Company
Contact Richard G. Weir
City Palermo
Company
Contact Randy Weir
City Ventura
Company
Contact F.W.Butch Wiggs
City Prather
Company
Contact Clifton M. Wilkins
City Fillmore
Company
Contact Herbert W. Wilson
City Red Bluff
Company
Contact Dennis Winchester
City Independence
Company
Contact Jerry S. Windsor
City Weimar
Company
Contact Murrey Wolfe
City Alton
Company
Contact Capt. James Wood
City Costa Mesa
Company
Contact Donald R. Wurz
City Redding
Company
Contact Chris D. Young
City Wedderburn

Colorado

Company & N Outfitters, Inc.
Contact Timothy Henley McCollum
City Norwood
Company 2V Outfitters, LTD.
Contact Stephen Greenway
City Glade Park
Company 4 UR Ranch, Inc.
Contact Rock Swenson
City Creede
Company 5 Springs Ranch Guide & Outfitter
Contact Louis Rabin
City Steamboat Springs
Company 7M Guide Service
Contact Seven Mazzone
City Durango
Company 7W Guest Ranch
Contact Russ Papke
City Gypsum
Company Adventure Experiences, Inc.
Contact Tim Kempfe
City Almont
Company Agape Outfitters & Guide Service
Contact Donna & Wayne Peck
City Creede
Company AJ's Gun Club
Contact Anthony J. Kippes
City Iliff
Company Alameno Outfitting & Guide Service
Contact Frank Alameno
City Rifle
Company Alaska Wildland
Contact William Fischer
City Vail
Company Alkali Outfitters
Contact Jerry Satterfield
City Parachute
Company Allen's Guide Service
Contact Don Allen
City Peyton
Company Almont Outfitters, Inc./ Scenic River
Contact Matthew L. Brown
City Gunnison

Company Alpine Angling & Adventure Travel
Contact Anthony Fotopulos & Bruce Stolbach
City Carbondale
Company Alpine Outfitters
Contact Chris Cassidy
City Fruita
Company Altenbern Hunting
Contact Clay A. Altenbern
City De Beque
Company American Outfitters
Contact James M. Knight
City Montrose
Company Anasazi Angler
Contact
City Durango
Company Andy Julius Outfitter & Guide
Contact Leal Andrew Julius
City Silt
Company Angler's Covey, Inc.
Contact Kent A. Brekke
City Colorado Springs
Company Apache Park Ranches
Contact Erna Sears
City Aurora
Company Archery Unlimited Outfitters
Contact Marshall Ledford
City Durango
Company Arkansas River Fly Shop
Contact Rodney A. Patch
City Salida
Company Arkansas River Tours
Contact Robert Hamel/Margie Geurs
City Cotopaxi
Company Aspen Canyon Ranch, LLC
Contact Steven Roderick
City Parshall
Company Aspen Trout Guide & Outfitter, Inc.
Contact Scott Alan Nichols
City Aspen
Company Aspen Wilderness Outfitters, Ltd.
Contact Tim McFlynn
City Apen
Company Astraddle A Saddle, Inc.
Contact Gary Bramwell
City Pagosa Springs
Company B & J Hunting Camp
Contact Robert W. Wells
City Meeker
Company B & W Guide Service
Contact Lawrence Beagley
City Grand Junction
Company B R Rhyne Guide & Outfitting
Contact Bruce L. Rhyne
City Craig
Company Back Country Guides & Outfitters
Contact William A. Yeagher
City Steamboat Springs
Company Backcounty Angler
Contact Gregg S. Jorgensen
City Pagosa Springs
Company Badger Creek Outfitter
Contact Joe E. Nelson
City Salida
Company Bar Diamond Ranch/ Ferrier Outfitters
Contact Dellis Ferrier
City Hotchkiss
Company Bar Lazy L Family, Inc.
Contact Gary Yeager
City Steamboat Springs
Company Bar T Outfitters
Contact Phillip & Joanne Talmadge Mark
City Silverthorne
Company Bar Z X Ranch & Lodge
Contact Dean Lampton
City Paonia
Company Barrett Park Outfitters
Contact Jack Steenbergen
City Gunnison
Company Beacon Landing Motel & Marina
Contact David A. & Betty J. McCloskey
City Granby
Company Bear Cat Outfitters
Contact Seth E. Peters
City Craig

Company Bear Creek Ranch
Contact Edward Wintz
City Creede
Company Bear Paw Outfitters
Contact Sam & Susan Ray
City Pagosa Springs
Company Beaten Path Outfitters
Contact Jeffery Wayne Baylor
City Las Animas
Company Beaver Canyon Guide & Outfitter
Contact Greg Pink
City Montrose
Company Beaver Creek Stables
Contact Steve Bruce Jones
City Eagle
Company Beaver Mountain Outfitters
Contact C. Duain Morton
City Dolores
Company Behram Outfitting
Contact Russell Behrman
City Maybell
Company Best Guide & Outfitters
Contact Donald L. Ankrum
City Guffey
Company Big Bones Unlimited/ Catspaw Ranch
Contact Dennis E. Schutz
City Chromo
Company Big Cimarron Outfitter
Contact Matt Wade Munyon
City Olathe
Company Big Game Hunts, LLC
Contact Ralph A. Babish
City Hayden
Company Big Horn Outfitters
Contact Lester Dean Hawkins
City Pagosa Springs
Company Big Horn Outfitters
Contact R. Vernon Mann
City Del Norte
Company Big Rack Outfitters
Contact Eric Lee Hamilton
City Craig
Company Bighorn Outfitting
Contact Dan C. Cooper & Dan Moyer
City Nucla
Company Black Elk Outfitters, LTD
Contact Dell H. Bean
City Ft.Collins
Company Black Mesa Lodge
Contact Tom McLeod
City Crawford
Company Black Mountain Invest. Ltd.
Contact Nowell R. May
City McCoy
Company Black Timber Outfitters
Contact Carrol M. Johnson & Kent Fischer
City Cedaredge
Company Blue Mountain Outfitters
Contact Shawn M. Bentley
City Pagosa Springs
Company Blue Quill Angler
Contact
City Evergreen
Company Blue Quill Anglers, Inc.
Contact Mark A. Harrington
City Evergreen
Company Brady Guide Service
Contact Jeffrey L. Brady
City Rangely
Company Breckenridge Outfitters
Contact Crosby Beane & Ian Davis
City Breckenridge
Company Broken Antler Outfitters
Contact Jacob H. Kauffman
City Granby
Company Bruton's Guide Service
Contact C. Warren Bruton
City Mesa
Company Bryce Outfitting
Contact Jim Bryce
City Delta
Company BSL Enterprises
Contact Scott Taylor
City Eagle
Company Bucks Livery, Inc.
Contact Ben Breed
City Durango
Company Buckskin Trails
Contact Glenn W. Pritchard
City Craig
Company Buffalo Creek Outfitters, Inc.

Contact Mike L. Prescott
City Walden
Company Buffalo Horn Ranch, Inc.
Contact James & Gail Walma
City Meeker
Company Buford Guide Service
Contact Tom Tucker
City Meeker
Company Buggywhip's Fish & Float Service
Contact Jim Blackburn
City Steamboat Springs
Company Bugle Masters
Contact Troy J. Hicks
City Cortez
Company Buglin' Bill Outfitters
Contact Bill Allen
City Crawford
Company Bull Mountain Outfitters
Contact Harry Wayne Garver
City Somerset
Company Bull Mountain Outfitters, Inc.
Contact Vicki L. Hale
City Livermore
Company Cabin Creek Outfitters
Contact Tony Tingle
City Meeker
Company Canyon Marine Whitewater Exp.
Contact Gregory Wright Felt
City Salida
Company Capitol Peak Outfitters, Inc.
Contact Steve Rieser
City Carbondale
Company Cedar Breaks Guides & Outfitters
Contact Monte Lew Miller
City Strasburg
Company Cedar Mountain Guide Service
Contact Daniel L. Weber
City Craig
Company Chad Hopwood Construction
Contact Chad Hopwood
City Littleton
Company Challenge Outfitters
Contact David L. Eider
City Vale
Company Challenge Outfitters
Contact Mike Martindale
City Oak Creek
Company Cherokee Trading Post & Outfitters
Contact David Slater
City Monte Vista
Company Chuck Davies Guide Service, Inc.
Contact Mark Davies
City Loma
Company Chuck McGuire Flyfishing
Contact Charles D. McGuire
City Kremmling
Company Chuit River Lodge
Contact Jeffrey Hauck
City Steamboat Springs
Company Cimarron Ridge/High Country Outfitters
Contact Thomas L. Bailey
City Montrose
Company Circle Four Hunting
Contact Thomas I. & Thomas R. Lindley
City Steamboat Springs
Company Collegiate Peaks Outfitters
Contact David Douty
City Buena Vista
Company Colorado Angler
Contact Rhonda D. Sapp
City Denver
Company Colorado Big Game Connections, Inc.
Contact Robert Gee
City Woodland Park
Company Colorado Blue Outfitters
Contact David G. Hargadine
City Kremmling
Company Colorado Diamond D Outfitters
Contact Thomas D. Dunn
City Coaldale
Company Colorado Elite
Contact John D. Verzuh
City Grand Junction
Company Colorado Fishing

Adventures
Contact Gary J. Willmart
City Colorado Springs
Company Colorado Fishing Guides
Contact
City Eagle
Company Colorado Mule Deer
Contact Linda L. Strong
City Steamboat Springs
Company Colorado Outfitters, Inc.
Contact Kelly Brooks
City Paonia
Company Colorado River Guides, Inc.
Contact Brenda D. Worley
City Oak Creek
Company Colorado Trophy Guides
Contact John & Jim Stehle
City Commerce City
Company Colorado Wilderness Safaris, Inc.
Contact Paul E. Mitzel, Jr.
City Gunnison
Company Columbine Outfitters, LLC
Contact Greg Ward
City Silverthorne
Company Comanche Wilderness Outfitters, Inc.
Contact Scott A. Limmer
City Fort Collins
Company Cottonwood Meadows Guide Service
Contact Randy P. Keys
City Antonito
Company Cougar Mountain, Inc.
Contact Si H. Woodruff
City Meeker
Company Craig Outfitting Servic
Contact Philip S. Craig
City Durango
Company Crawford Ranch
Contact Gayle R. Crawford
City Meeker
Company Creative Outdoor Sprts
Contact Frank E. Meek
City Steamboat Springs
Company D & S Guide & Outfitter
Contact Dennis E. Rodebaugh
City Meeker
Company DAL Outfitters, Inc.
Contact David Lowry
City Silverthorne
Company Dan's Fly Shop
Contact Dan Hall
City Lake City
Company Daniel J. Humphrey Guides
Contact Daniel J. Humphrey
City Montrose
Company Dave Parri's Outfitting & Guide Service
Contact David Parri
City Hot Sulphur Springs
Company Dee Norell Ranch
Contact Franklin Dee Norell
City Rifle
Company Deep Creek Outfitters
Contact Darla Ranwick Cluster
City Steamboat Springs
Company Deer Valley Ranch
Contact Harold Lee DeWalt
City Nathrop
Company Del's Triangle 3 Ranch
Contact Ray Heid
City Clark
Company Devil's Thumb Fly Fishing Adv. Center
Contact
City Tabernash
Company Diamond Lodge Guest Ranch
Contact C. Steve Paul
City Durango
Company Diamond X Bar Outfitting
Contact Robert M. Campbell
City Moffat
Company Diamond-D-Ranch & Outfitters
Contact Obbie L Dickey
City Del Norte
Company Dick Pennington Guide Service, LLC
Contact Alan & Dick Pennington
City Grand Junction
Company Dick Piffer Guide & Outfitter
Contact Richard Piffer
City Carbondale

Company Discount Fishing Tackle, Inc.
Contact Michael L. Gray
City Denver
Company Don Hawkins Outfitting
Contact Don Hawkins
City Delta
Company Double Diamond Outfitters
Contact Jack Wheeler
City Meredith
Company Double Dollar Cattle LLC
Contact Wayne Iacovetto
City Eaton
Company Double H Bar Outfitting
Contact Rick Hummel
City Grand Junction
Company Double LJ Outfitters, Inc.
Contact Layne K. Wing
City Yampa
Company Dragonfly Anglers
Contact Rod and Roger Cesario
City Crested Butte
Company Drowsy Water Ranch
Contact Kenneth H. Fosha
City Granby
Company Dry Creek Anglers
Contact Charles Grobe
City Hayden
Company Dry Fork Outfitters
Contact Donald J. Kroese, Jr.
City Craig
Company Dunckley Peak Pack Service
Contact William L. Terrill
City Craig
Company Duranglers Flies & Supplies
Contact Thomas Knopick
City Durango
Company Durango Fly Goods, LLC
Contact Michael J. Stowers
City Durango
Company Durango Outfitters, Inc.
Contact Dennis Norton
City Durango
Company Eagle River Anglers
Contact Robert Nock
City Eagle
Company Eagle Spirit Outfitters
Contact Miles Hogan
City Steamboat Springs
Company Eagle's Nest Outfitting
Contact Kai Mark Turner
City Meeker
Company Eagles Nest Outfitting
Contact Billy S. Howard
City Meeker
Company East Divide Outfitters
Contact Dennis A. Yost
City Glenwood Springs
Company Echo Canyon River Expeditions
Contact David Burch
City Canyon City
Company Elk Country Outfitters
Contact David Butterfield
City Montrose
Company Elk Creek Lodge
Contact Chris Lockwood
City Meeker
Company Elk Creek Marina, Inc.
Contact John Loken
City Gunnison
Company Elk Mountain Outfitter & Guides
Contact John Pickering
City LaJunta
Company Elk Mountain Outfitters, Inc.
Contact Gerald Seifert
City Silt
Company Elk River Guest Ranch
Contact William Hinder
City Clark
Company Elkhorn Outfitters, Inc.
Contact Richard J. Dodds
City Craig
Company Elkhorn Outfitters, Inc.
Contact
City Fort Collins
Company Elkshead Guides & Outfitters
Contact John M. Connon
City Bayfield
Company Elktrout Lodge
Contact Marty Cecil
City Kremmling

Company Estes Angler
Contact
City Estes Park
Company Fantasy Ranch Outfitters, Inc.
Contact James R. Talbot
City Crested Butte
Company Ferro's Blue Mesa Outfitters
Contact John Ferro
City Gunnison
Company Fly Fishing Outfitters
Contact Bill Perry
City Avon
Company Fly Fishing Outfitters
Contact
City Vail
Company Flyfishing Durango, Inc.
Contact Bill Leahy
City Durango
Company Flyfishing Outfitters, Inc.
Contact William C. Perry
City Vail
Company Flyfishing Services, Inc.
Contact
City Littleton
Company Flying Diamond Outfitters, LLC
Contact John R. Adams
City Steamboat Springs
Company Flying Eagle Outfitters
Contact Mark O. Anderson
City New Castle
Company Flying Raven Ranch
Contact Matt Redd
City Powderhorn
Company Flynn & Sons Outfitters
Contact Delnor F. Flynn
City Crawford
Company Foutz Outfitting Service
Contact Charles F. Foutz
City Ignacio
Company Front Range Outfitters
Contact Ronald E. Sniff
City Pueblo
Company Front Range Outfitters
Contact Mark Ross
City Canon City
Company Frosty Acres Ranch
Contact Doug & Janet Camilletti
City Craig
Company Frying Pan Anglers
Contact Ray Clarence Palm
City Basalt
Company Fryingpan River Ranch
Contact James B. Rea
City Meredith
Company Full Draw Outfitters
Contact Fred Eichler & Don Ward
Blye Chadwick
City Fort Collins
Company Gateview Ranch
Contact Yosef Lutwak
City Gunnison
Company Glacier Bay Outfitters
Contact John M. Snyder
City Littleton
Company Golden Gate Outfitters
Contact Randy L. Christensen
City Rollinsville
Company Gore Livestock, Inc.
Contact Warren D. Gore
City Glade Park
Company Gorsuch Outfitters
Contact Scott David Gorsuch
City Vail
Company Grand Wapiti Outfitters
Contact Lyle D. Horn
City Granby
Company Great Scott Adventures
Contact Scott Harkins
City Telluride
Company Groundhog Outfitters
Contact James J. Wagoner
City Dolores
Company Gunnison River Pleasure Park
Contact LeRoy Henry Jagodinski
City Lazear
Company Gunnison River Telluride Flyfishers
Contact Henry E. Hotze
City Montrose
Company Gypsum Creek Outfitters, Ltd.
Contact John Jodrie

City Gypsum
Company Hansen Cattle Ranch, Inc.
Contact Richard Hansen
City Crawford
Company Happy Trails Outfitters
Contact Gary L. Calhoun
City Edwards
Company Hawk Creek Outfitting, Co.
Contact Billy R. Jackson
City Glenwood Springs
Company Heart of the Rockies Outfitters
Contact Wayne E. Spencer
City Salida
Company Hi Country Outfitters
Contact Richard R. Cooper
City Lake City
Company High Country Outfitters, LLC
Contact Kathy Johnson
City Cortez
Company High Lonesome Outfitter & Guides
Contact Thomas W. Bowers
City Yampa
Company High Lonesome Outfitters of Colorado
Contact Mark Lumpkins
City Bailey
Company High Lonesome Ranch
Contact John H. Doden
City DeBeque
Company High Meadows Ranch
Contact Dennis Stamp
City Steamboat Springs
Company High Mountain Drifter Guide
Contact
City Gunnison
Company High Mountain Hookers
Contact
City Gunnison
Company High Park Outfitters
Contact Dan Aubuchon
City Trinchera
Company Highlanders Outfitting & Guide, Co.
Contact Rhonda Kellerer
City Bayfield
Company Hills Guide Service
Contact Clifford E. & Janice Hill
City Collbran
Company Hillview Outfitters
Contact Willard E. Forman
City Dillon
Company Hook, Line & Leader
Contact David F. Wahl
City Denver
Company Horizon River Adventures, Inc.
Contact Vilis J. Zigurs
City Carbondale
Company Hot"T"Camp
Contact Jack Flowers
City Montrose
Company Hubbard Creek Outfitters & Pack Station
Contact Larry Allen
City Hotchkiss
Company Indian Peak Outfitters
Contact Ardis M. Wright
City Granby
Company Indian Summer Outfitters
Contact Rick House
City Pagosa Springs
Company Inland Drifters, LLC
Contact Kimberly Moore
City Glenwood Springs
Company J & J Outfitters of Colorado, Inc.
Contact Gerald L. Woolsey
City Craig
Company J & Ray Colorado High County, Inc.
Contact Ronald Franks
City Montrose
Company J & V Guides & Outfitters
Contact Glenn Jones & Lonny Vanatta
City Steamboat Springs
Company J Bar B Guiding & Outfitting
Contact James D. Beall
City Craig
Company J.C. Trujillo Guide & Outfitter
Contact J.C. Trujillo

City Steamboat Springs
Company Jamie Prather Guide & Outfitters
Contact Jamie Prather
City Craig
Company Jim Jarvis' Guide & Outfitting Service
Contact James Howard Jarvis
City Montrose
Company JML Outfitters
Contact Marguerite M. & Marie Haskett
City Englewood
Company John's Outfitter & Guide Service
Contact John R. Harmon
City McCoy
Company JT Outfitters
Contact Jeff Burtard
City Carbondale
Company Judd Cooney Outfitting & Guiding
Contact Judd Cooney
City Pagosa Springs
Company K & D Majestic Outfitters
Contact Daniel S. Ruscetti
City Trindad
Company K & K Outfitters
Contact Marion Bricker
City Granby
Company K.E. Schultz Guide & Outfitting Service
Contact Kurt E. Schultz & Art Gurule
City Silt
Company King Creek Outfitters
Contact Mike Rodriguez
City Littleton
Company King of King's Guide Service
Contact Paul Pearson
City Cortez
Company King's Guide Service
Contact Douglas R. King
City Grand Junction
Company Kinsley Outfitters
Contact Peter Berntsen
City Boulder
Company Koo-Sto Wilderness Outfitters
Contact Phillip L. Foster
City Boulder
Company KW Wapiti Outfitters, LLC
Contact John Knoll
City Evergreen
Company L & K Guide Service
Contact Lonnie Edward & Kim Peters
City Craig
Company Lamicq Guides & Outfitters, Inc.
Contact John & Diane Lamicq
City Grand Junction
Company Lancaster Outfitters
Contact Patrick L. Lancaster
City Elizabeth
Company Latigo Ranch
Contact James A. Yost
City Kremmling
Company Lazy 3X Ranch
Contact David H. Farny
City Telluride
Company Lazy C2 Bar Ranch
Contact James Kelly Sewell
City Slater
Company Lazy F Bar Outfitters
Contact Bill Guerrieri
City Gunnison
Company Lazy FF Outfitters
Contact Kirk A. Ellison
City Creede
Company Leonard Outfitting
Contact Randy Leonard
City Montrose
Company Little Big Horn Lodge
Contact Harry L. Ergott, Jr.
City Cmarron
Company Loner Guide Service, Inc.
Contact Bradley T. Weinmeister
City Johnstown
Company Lost Creek Guides
Contact Lance D. Edinger
City Meeker
Company Lost Solar Outfitters, Inc.
Contact Thoma Marucco & Gary Stoaks
City Golden
Company Lost Solar, Inc.
Contact Thomas J. Marucco

City Denver
Company Louisiana Purchase Ranch Outfitters
Contact M. Lee Tingle
City Meeker
Company Lov Ranch
Contact James William Brennan
City Rifle
Company Luark Ranch & Outfitters
Contact Pat Edward Luark
City Burns
Company Lunney Mountain Outfitters
Contact Brett J. Harvey
City Meeker
Company M H M Outfitters
Contact George A. Malarsie
City Durango
Company Mamm Peaks Outfitters
Contact Jeffrey George Mead
City Grand Junction
Company Manhattan Creek Outfitters, Inc.
Contact Linda S. Wright-Winterfeld
City Red Feather
Company Matt Bridges Guide & Outfitting
Contact Matthew Bridges, Jr.
City Pagosa Springs
Company McDonald's Outfitter & Guide Service
Contact W. Harry McDonald
City Lake City
Company McFly's Trophy Guide Service
Contact William Jordan McStay
City Dillon
Company Medano Pass Guide & Outfitter
Contact Donny Carr
City Colorado Springs
Company Medicine Bow Outfitters
Contact Jared Fiorell
City LaPorte
Company Middle Creek Ranch Company
Contact Roy Rozell
City Oak Creek
Company Mika Ag Corp.
Contact R. Doris Karlsson
City Denver
Company Mike Wilson's High Mountain Drifters, Inc.
Contact Mike Wilson
City Gunnison
Company Mill Creek Outfitters
Contact Charles E. Wisecup
City Oak Creek
Company Miller Mountain Lemon Lake
Contact Lawrence R. Miller
City Durango
Company Mineral Mountain Guide & Outfitters
Contact John H. & Bobbie Martin
City Powderhorn
Company Monarch Guides
Contact Ken Kays Kupilik
City Kremmling
Company Monument Hill Outfitters
Contact Don Polzin
City Durango
Company Mountain Angler, Ltd.
Contact
City Breckenridge
Company Mountain Enterprises
Contact Gary & Robin Edwards
City Fort Collins
Company Mountain Man Tours
Contact Greg J. Coln
City Creede
Company Mountain Top Ranches
Contact Mary & Bob Roesler
City Hotchkiss
Company Mountain Trails Outfitters
Contact Butch Rawls
City Del Norte
Company Mountain West Outfitting, Inc.
Contact Aaron R. Neilson
City Lakewood
Company Mt. Blanca Game Bird & Trout
Contact Bill Binnian
City Blanca
Company Myers Hunting Services,

Inc.
Contact Donald G. Myers
City Hamilton
Company Natural Adventures, Inc.
Contact Thomas E. Tietz
City Littleton
Company Norm Harder Outfitter
Contact Norm Harder
City Cortez
Company North Star Ooutfitters, Inc.
Contact Robert F. Moreland
City Boulder
Company Northwest Colorado Scenic Tours
Contact Charles L. Mead
City Craig
Company Nova Guides, Inc.
Contact Steven Jay Pittels
City Vail
Company OFC Outfitting
Contact Michel C. Maurello
City Gypsum
Company Oldland & Uphoff
Contact Reuben G. Oldland
City Rifle
Company Oswald Cattle Company
Contact Stephen Oswald
City Cotopaxi
Company Ouray Livery Barn
Contact Howard Lewis Linscott
City Ridgway
Company Outdoor Connections
Contact Nicholas J. Kamzalow
City Craig
Company Over The Hill Outfitters
Contact John Neely
City Durango
Company Oxbow Outfitting Co.
Contact Jonathan J. Feinberg
City Aspen
Company Oxbow Outfitting Co.
Contact Donald L. DeLise
City Woody Creek
Company P.T.Outfitters
Contact Paul E. Menhennett
City Kremmling
Company Peacock Ranch Outfitters
Contact Darren Peacock
City Mack
Company Peters Hunting Service
Contact Harley Peters
City Rangely
Company Pierce Brothers Outfitting
Contact William Leon & Howard Pierce
City Grand Junction
Company Pikes Peak Outfitters
Contact Gary Jordan
City Woodland Park
Company Pines Ranch Partnership
Contact Dean Rusk & Richard Steamer
City Westcliffe
Company Piney River Ranch
Contact Kara Heide
City Vail
Company Plateau Creek Outfitters
Contact Joe E. Garcia
City Elizabeth
Company Pollards Ute Lodge
Contact Troy R. Pollard
City Meeker
Company Ponderosa Outfitters
Contact Norman Bruce Ayers
City Eaton
Company Poudre River Outfitters
Contact Rex L. Schmidt
City Silvercreek
Company Powderhorn Outfitters
Contact Vincent Woodrow Tanko
City Denver
Company Powderhorn Primitive Outfitters
Contact Cameron Lewis
City Gunnison
Company Prather Outfitters
Contact Ned & Lyle Prather
City DeBeque
Company Private Land Outfitters
Contact Travis Rowley
City Montrose
Company Prof. Big Game Guide & Outfitters
Contact Jack Cassidy
City Fruita
Company Purgatoire Outfitters

Contact Jay Waring
City Las Animas
Company Purnell's Rainbow Inn
Contact David P.Purnell
City Westcliffe
Company Purple Sage Outfitters
Contact Linda A. & Wesley W. DuBose
City Meeker
Company Pyramid Llama Ranch
Contact Ann Patricia & Kevin Copeland
City Hayden
Company Pyramid Outfitters
Contact Steve Whiteside
City Hayden
Company Quaking Aspen Guides & Outfitters, Inc.
Contact Dave Mapes
City Gunnison
Company Quarter Circle Circle Ranch
Contact John Judson
City Gunnison
Company Quarter-Circle Circle Ranch
Contact
City Gunnison
Company R & J Outfitters
Contact Robert Parker
City Lamar
Company R&R Hunting
Contact Gary J. Rowley
City Craig
Company R & R Ranch
Contact Ralph R. Royster
City Maybell
Company R.J.'s Greystone Guide & Outfitting
Contact Ronald Tull Jones
City Craig
Company Raftopoulos Ranches
Contact John & Steve Raftopoulos
City Craig
Company Ramble House
Contact
City Creede
Company Ranching for Wildlife
Contact Jarrell Massey
City Meeker
Company Rawhide Adventures
Contact Fred & Rod Ellis
City Meeker
Company Razor Creek Outfitters
Contact Ron K. Brink
City Powderhorn
Company Red Feather Guides & Outfitters
Contact John Todd Peterson
City Walden
Company Red Mountain Guest Ranch
Contact William Ridgeway
City Durango
Company Rendezvous Outfitters & Guides, LTD
Contact William R. Eby
City Gunnison
Company Rick Edinger & Sons
Contact Rick D. Edinger
City Meeker
Company Rick Warren Guide & Outfitting
Contact Ricky Warren
City Craig
Company Riddle's Custom Service
Contact Jack Riddle
City Ignacio
Company Ridgetrack Guide & Outfitting
Contact Craig & Cathy Krumwiede
City Fort Collins
Company Rim Rock Outfitters
Contact Monty G. Elder
City Rangley
Company Rimrock/Little Creek
Contact Alan Baier
City Fruita
Company Rivers Bend Outfitting
Contact Kip Gates
City Meeker
Company Riverside Anglers
Contact Peter McNeil & Dave Ziegler
City Hot Sulphur Springs
Company Roaring Fork Anglers
Contact
City Glenwood Springs
Company Rocky Mountain Adventures, Inc.
Contact G. David Costlow

City Fort Collins
Company Rocky Mountain Fisherman
Contact Monte G. Andres
City Granby
Company Rocky Mountain Outfitters
Contact Gary W. Bohochik
City Salida
Company Rocky Mountain Ranches
Contact Lawrence J. Bishop
City Denver
Company Rocky Mountain Rides
Contact Dave Hemauer
City Pagosa Springs
Company Rod & Reel Fly Shop
Contact Edward L. Wagner
City Creede
Company Rod Wintz Guide Service/Wason Ranch
Contact Rod Wintz
City Creede
Company Ron-D-View Ranch & Outfitting
Contact Ron Pfeffer
City Ignacio
Company Ross & Nelson Outfitters & Guides
Contact Jim Ross & Joe Nelson
City Craig
Company Route to Trout
Contact Anthony Joseph Colaizzi, Jr.
City Grand Junction
Company Roy Savage Ranches
Contact Roy E. Savage
City Rifle
Company Royal Gorge Outfitters
Contact Bill Edrington & Bill Carson
City Canon City
Company Rudy Steele Guides & Outfitters, Inc.
Contact Rudy Steele
City Glenwood Springs
Company S & K Outfitting & Guide Service
Contact Paul E. Gingery & K. Kyle Revell
City Littleton
Company Saddle Tramp Outfitters
Contact Thomas Bullock
City New Castle
Company San Juan Back Country
Contact Delbert & Laura Smith
City Silverton
Company San Juan Ranch Outfitters
Contact Scott MacTiernan
City Ridgway
Company San-Pahgre Outdoor Adven./Outfitting
Contact Stuart D. Chappell
City Montrose
Company Schlegel Ranch Co.
Contact Wesley H. Schlegel
City Burns
Company Seven Lakes Lodge
Contact Steve Cobb
City Meeker
Company Shamrock Ranch Outfitters
Contact Bruce Wilson
City Coalmont
Company Shavano Outfitters
Contact Jim E. James
City Salida
Company Sherrod Ranch
Contact Donald Lee Sherrod
City Steamboat Springs
Company Silver Fox Outfitters
Contact Kevin Martin & Ronald Roll
City Gunnison
Company Silver Peaks Outfitters
Contact Scott E. Williams
City Cortez
Company Silver Spur Outfitters
Contact Trent Snyder
City Silt
Company Silverado Outfitters, Inc.
Contact Larry Kibel
City Silverton
Company Singletree Outfitting
Contact Fain D. Richardson
City Meeker
Company Slater Creek Cattle Company, Inc.
Contact Larry L. Lyster
City Craig
Company Snowmass Anglers

Contact   Ivan L. Perrin
City   Snowmass Village
Company   Snowmass Falls Outfitters, LTD
Contact   Thomas M. Turnbull
City   Snowmass Village
Company   Snowmass Oxbow Outfitting
Contact   Bill Lund
City   Snowmass Village
Company   Sombrero Ranches, Inc.
Contact   Rex Ross Walker
City   Boulder
Company   Southfork Stables, Inc.
Contact   Kimberly Kay Baird
City   Durango
Company   Southpark Outfitters
Contact   Max Oertle
City   Fairplay
Company   Southwest Adventures
Contact   Corey Veach
City   Cortez
Company   Space Command US Air Force
Contact   Charlie Stockstill
City   Englewood
Company   Sporting Classics @ the Broadmoor Resort
Contact   Colleen Betzing
City   Colorado Springs
Company   Sporting Country Guide Service
Contact   John A. McRoy
City   Granby
Company   Sportsman of Lake City, Inc.
Contact   Paul Hudgeons
City   Lake City
Company   St. Peter's Fly Shop
Contact   Frank Praznik
City   Fort Collins
Company   St. Vrain Angler Stores, Inc.
Contact   Dale Darling
City   Longmont
Company   Stajduhar Ranches & Outfitting
Contact   John & Steven Stajduhar
City   Fruita
Company   Star Outfitters
Contact   Jeffry J. Corriveau & Dennis R. Craig
City   Craig
Company   Steamboat Lake Fishing Co., Inc.
Contact   Hans Berend
City   Steamboat Springs
Company   Steamboat Lake Outfitters, Inc.
Contact   Donald Wayne Markley
City   Clark
Company   Stetson Ranches, LLC
Contact   Franklin Stetson
City   Steamboat Springs
Company   Steward Ranch Outfitters
Contact   Laverne Gwaltney
City   Durango
Company   Stone Creek Outfitters
Contact   Bob Helmer & Clay Bassett
City   Ignacio
Company   Straightline Products, Inc.
Contact   Larry Mann
City   Steamboat Springs
Company   Straightline Sports
Contact
City   Steamboat Springs
Company   Summit Guides
Contact   Dale K. Fields
City   Dilon
Company   Sundown Outfitters
Contact   David N. Cordray
City   Pagosa Springs
Company   Sunrise Outfitters, Inc.
Contact   Leroy F. Schroeder
City   Rifle
Company   Sunset Ranch, Inc.
Contact   Patsy Wilhelm
City   Steamboat Springs
Company   T & J Outfitters
Contact   Sue Jameson & Walter Tycksen
City   Pleasant View
Company   T. Mike Murphy & Sons
Contact   T. Mike Murphy
City   Durango
Company   Talaheim Lodge
Contact   Tobin Osteen

City   Boulder
Company   Taylor Creek Ranch
Contact   Vic Taylor
City   Steamboat Springs
Company   Tayor Creek, Inc.
Contact   William D. Fitzsimmons
City   Basalt
Company   Telluride Anglers
Contact
City   Telluride
Company   Tenderfoot Outfitter & Guide
Contact   Steve & Jim Pike Paul
City   Gunnison
Company   Texas Creek Outfitters
Contact   David M. Butcher
City   Texas Creek
Company   The Craig Wild Bunch, Inc.
Contact   Many Funkhouser
City   Craig
Company   The Executive Angler
Contact   Kevin Leigh Derks
City   Denver
Company   The Gone Fishing Company
Contact   Chad Butler
City   Aurora
Company   The Gunnison Country Guide Service
Contact   John C. Nelson
City   Gunnison
Company   The Mountain Angler
Contact   Jackson Streit/John P.Streit
City   Breckenridge
Company   The Outfitter Sporting Goods, Inc.
Contact   Larry Seaman
City   Dolores
Company   The Peak Fly Shop
Contact
City   Colorado Springs
Company The Troutfitter Sports Co.
Contact Dominique Eymere & Bradley Sorock
City   Crested Butte
Company   Three Rivers Resort & Outfitting
Contact   Mark A. Schumacher
City   Almont
Company   Thunder River Guides
Contact   James K. Boyles, Jr.
City   Carbondale
Company   Timberline Outfitters
Contact   Perry Abbott
City   Bayfield
Company   Timberline Outfitters & Guide Service
Contact   Douglass C. Frank, Jr.
City   Lake City
Company   TN Bar Cattle Co., Inc.
Contact   Curtis Kuester
City   Salida
Company   Tom Fritzlan & Family
Contact   Tom Fritzlan
City   Rifle
Company   Tom Payne Outfitting
Contact   Tom Payne
City   Creede
Company   Toneda Outfitters
Contact   Ed R. Wiseman
City   Moffat
Company   Tony Hoza Guide & Outfitter
Contact   Anthony Hoza
City   Norwood
Company   Trail Ridge Outdoors
Contact   Thomas Clinkenbeard
City   Loveland
Company   Trail Skills, Inc.
Contact   Robert Getz
City   Del Norte
Company   Trappers Lake Lodge
Contact   Ross Wheeler
City   Meeker
Company   Tri-State Outfitters
Contact   Richard Petrini
City   Yampa
Company   Triple G, Inc.
Contact   Paul Alan Echtler
City   Wolcott
Company   Triple Tree Ranch
Contact   Margaret Deutsch
City   Crawford
Company   Trophy Class Outfitters
Contact   Mike Lawson
City   Glade Park

Company   Trophy Mountain Outfitters
Contact   Dean F. Silva
City   Monte Vista
Company   Trophy Time Outfitters
Contact   Sean M. Pond
City   Bedrock
Company   Troutfitters of Aspen/ Guides West
Contact   Gary Hubbell
City   Carbondale
Company   Tuff Trout Ranch, LLC
Contact   David A. Gitlitz
City   Englewood
Company   Twin Buttes Ranch
Contact   Steve Titus
City   Durango
Company   Twin Mountain
Contact   W.A. Roesch
City   Del Norte
Company   Uncompahgre Outfitters, Inc.
Contact   Chris Hutchison
City   Olathe
Company   USAF Academy Outdoor Adventure
Contact   Mike Bosso
City   USAF Academy
Company   Vail Fishing Guides
Contact   Mark C. Lokay
City   Vail
Company   Vail Rod & Gun Club
Contact   Michael James Jouflas
City   Vail
Company   Valley Hunting Service
Contact   Cliff Bankston
City   Norwood
Company   Valley View Ranch
Contact   James Peterson
City   Gunnison
Company   Vickers Enterprises, Inc
Contact   Larry Vickers
City   Lake City
Company   Vision Quest - Guided Hunts
Contact   Chris Furia
City   Trinidad
Company   Vista Verde Guest Ranch
Contact   John S. Munn
City   Steamboat Springs
Company   W 3 Outfitters
Contact   Dale R. Hopwood
City   Fruita
Company   Wallace Guides & Outfitters
Contact   Bill & Fred Wallace
City   Collbran
Company   Wanderin' Star Charters, Inc.
Contact   Gary & Kayron McCoy
City   Westminster
Company   Wapiti Company
Contact   Mark Malesic
City   Pagosa Springs
Company   Wapiti Outfitter & Guides, Inc.
Contact   Jon Garfall
City   Gunnison
Company   Wapitti Valley Guide & Outfitting
Contact   Jonathan D. Baysinger
City   Craig
Company   Wardell's Guide Service
Contact   Layne Wardell
City   Rangely
Company   Wason Ranch
Contact
City   Creede
Company   Waterfall Ranch Outfitter
Contact   Edwin A Zink
City   Durango
Company   Watson Ranches
Contact   James Lee Watson
City   Meeker
Company   Weimer Hunting Camp
Contact   Jody C. Weimer
City   Nucla
Company   Wellsweep Ranches
Contact   David R. Seely
City   Craig
Company   Western Colorado Outfitters
Contact   Gordon Blay
City   Montrose
Company   Western States Ranches
Contact

City   Meeker
Company   Western Waters
Contact   Edward J. Lawn
City   Vail
Company   Western Wilderness Outdoor Adv.
Contact   Judy Kay Stewart
City   Grover
Company   Wetherill Ranch
Contact   George Hughes
City   Creede
Company   Whistling Elk Outfitters, Inc.
Contact   John C. Ziegman
City   Rand
Company   White River Ranch
Contact   David J. Prather
City   Meeker
Company   Wild Country Outfitters
Contact   Lloyd & Michael R. Madden Clinton L
City   Clifton
Company   Wildass Outfitters
Contact   Robert W. Henry & Chester W. Mayer
City   Glade Park
Company   Wilderness Trails Ranch
Contact   Gene Roberts
City   Durango
Company   Williams Guide Service
Contact   Patrick C. Williams
City   Fort Collins
Company   Williams Peak Ranch Co.
Contact   Michael Miniat
City   Parshall
Company   Wilton Earle & Sons
Contact   Leon Earle
City   Craig
Company   Winterhawk Outfitter, Inc.
Contact   Larry L. Amos
City   Silt
Company   Winterhawk Outfitters
Contact
City   Silt
Company   Wit's End Guest Ranch & Resort
Contact   Jim & Lynn Custer
City   Bayfield
Company   Wolf Creek Outfitters, LLC
Contact   Jason Ward
City   Pogosa Springs
Company   Woodstock Guide & Outfitting
Contact   Jack Sours
City   Rifle
Company   Yampa River Outfitters
Contact   Randall W. Baird
City   Craig
Company   Younger Brothers Guiding & Outfitting
Contact   Glen Younger
City   Grand Junction
Company
Contact   Barbara A. Baird
City   Rifle
Company
Contact   Dennis Betz
City   Greeley
Company
Contact   Jim Bradwell
City   Chromo
Company
Contact   Kent Calhoun
City   Delta
Company
Contact   Edwin D. Coleman
City   Delta
Company
Contact   Rodney S. Cook
City   Maybell
Company
Contact   James R. DeKam
City   Parachute
Company
Contact   Pauline "PS" Freberg
City   Denver
Company
Contact   Dennis Fredrickson
City   Craig
Company
Contact   Joseph C. Fyvie
City   Mancos
Company
Contact   Ivan Green
City   Fruita
Company
Contact   Tim Kostur & Tim Hiett

City   Hayden
Company
Contact   David Joseph Johnson
City   Meeker
Company
Contact   Malcolm Carter Jolley, Jr.
City   Glenwood Springs
Company
Contact   James L. Jones
City   Moncos
Company
Contact   Stephen R. Jusseaume
City   Littleton
Company
Contact   John M. Kane
City   Norwood
Company
Contact   Richard A. Lillard
City   Crawford
Company
Contact   Mike W. Luark
City   Gypsum
Company
Contact   Dean Mantle
City   Rifle
Company
Contact   John L. Markham
City   Nederland
Company
Contact   Denise Mead
City   Hamilton
Company
Contact   William A. Montieth
City   Hayden
Company
Contact   David P. Morlan
City   Meeker
Company
Contact   Dan Newman
City   Bayfield
Company
Contact   M. Don Oliver
City   Durango
Company
Contact   Kenneth G. Osborn
City   Hamilton
Company
Contact   Glen Papez
City   Meeker
Company
Contact   Wayne Pennell
City   Rangely
Company
Contact   Andy Peroulis
City   Craig
Company
Contact   Robert Cole Proctor
City   Meeker
Company
Contact   Rick L. Quinn
City   Meeker
Company
Contact   De Lyle Rowley
City   Montrose
Company
Contact   Jim W. Schaffer
City   Del Norte
Company
Contact   Nick D. Speicher & Sam Smith
City   Lajara
Company
Contact   James G. Snyder
City   Silt
Company
Contact   James J. Tresch
City   Niwot
Company
Contact   Mark Turner
City   Idaho Springs
Company
Contact   Steve Whinnery
City   Powderhom
Company
Contact   Bruce A. White
City   Craig
Company
Contact   Lyle Willmarth
City   Hot Sulphur Springs

Connecticut

Company A'Vanga
Contact Capt. Byron Smith, Jr.
City New London
Company After You, Too
Contact Captain Frank Blume
City Colchester
Company Alexander Creek Lodge
Contact Alan Budney
City Newington
Company Alexander Creek Lodge, Inc.
Contact Henry Budney
City Newington
Company Anna-R Sportfishing Charters
Contact Captain Franklin A. Rathbun
City W. Mystic
Company Billfish Sport Fishing
Contact
City Enfield
Company Black Hawk II
Contact Captain Peter & Carol Clark
City Niantic
Company Captain's Choice
Contact Capt. Alan Artkop
City Clinton
Company Carol Marie
Contact Capt. Terry Thomas
City Bridgeport
Company Catch'Em
Contact Capt. Richard J. Siedzik
City Westbrook
Company Connecticut Woods & Water
Contact Capt. Dan Wood
City Waterford
Company Duffy D
Contact Capt. Jack Dougherty
City Noank
Company Eden Charters
Contact Captain Paul Retano
City Old Saybrook
Company Father & Son Fishing Tours
Contact Mark Krodel
City Salem
Company First Light
Contact Capt. Bob Romeo
City Noank
Company Flyfishing Charters
Contact
City Westport
Company Good Company II
Contact Captain Joe Garofano, Jr.
City Waterford
Company Gypsy VI
Contact Capt. Jack Miserocchi
City Westbrook
Company Hahn Bros./Brothers Too
Contact Captains Dave & Joe Hahn
City Waterford
Company Hel-Cat II
Contact Capt. Brad Glas
City Groton
Company Isle of Rhodes
Contact Captain Alan Rhodes
City Waterford
Company J & B Tackle/Dot-E-Dee Charters
Contact Capt.Kerry Douton/Capt. Jack Douton
City Waterford
Company Lady Margaret
Contact Capt. Claude M. Adams
City Niantic
Company Lauren B Charters
Contact Captain Steve Burnett
City Mystic
Company Magic Sportfishing
Contact Dave Keeney
City Hampton
Company Marlin
Contact Capt. Alex Korenkiewicz
City New London
Company Mataura Lite
Contact Capt. Ben McLoughlin
City Noank
Company My Bonnie
Contact Capt. Sal Tardella
City Norwalk
Company Nancy B
Contact Capt. Howard J. Beers
City Waterford
Company Osprey Sportfishing
Contact Capt. Joseph A. Wysocki
City Niantic

Company Playin' Hooky
Contact Capt. Robert DeMagistris
City New London
Company Reelin'Sportfishing
Contact Capt. Ernest Celotto
City Groton
Company Rick Miller Fly Fishing
Contact Rick Miller
City Stamford
Company Sea Sprite
Contact Capt. Peter Wheeler
City Old Saybrook
Company Seahawk III
Contact Capt. Judd Barnes
City Westbrook
Company Smola Flyfishing
Contact
City Enfield
Company Steve Bellefleur Saltwater Fly Fishing
Contact Captain Steve Bellefleur
City Stonington
Company Sunbeam Fleet
Contact Capt. John Wadsworth
City Waterford
Company Tigra II
Contact Capt. Peter Kriewald
City Norwalk
Company Trophy Hunter
Contact Captain Ron Helbig
City Noank
Company Venwood Lake Hunting & Fishing
Contact
City Killingworth
Company Wanderer
Contact Capt. Claude Adams III
City New London
Company Wavedancer
Contact Capt. John Stolte
City Clinton
Company Westport Outfitters
Contact Captain Jeff A. Northrop
City Westport
Company West Wind III
Contact Capt. Cecil V. Brooks, Jr.
City New London
Company White Lightning
Contact Capt. Ted Harris
City New London
Company
Contact Captain Todd Currier
City Niantic
Company
Contact Captain Peter Fisher
City New London

Delaware

Company
Contact Howard E. Cleaver
City Clarksville
Company
Contact Stephen A. Dixon
City Newark
Company
Contact Frederick A. Phillips
City Camden
Company
Contact Charles E. Powell
City Middletown
Company
Contact Jeffrey W. Powell
City Middletown

District of Columbia

Company
Contact John B. Beach
City Washington

Florida

Company 'Tween Waters Inn
Contact Jeff Shuff
City Captiva
Company A & A Charter Company
Contact
City Islamorada
Company A to Z Backwater Fishing
Contact Capt. Jon Shaffer
City Naples
Company A. C. Charters, Inc.
Contact
City Fernandina Beach
Company A.V.I.P.Charters, Inc.
Contact
City Deerfield Beach
Company Acme Wiley Corp.
Contact
City N. Palm Beach
Company Action Belize
Contact
City Naples
Company Affordable Fly Fishing
Contact Capt. Bob Prestyly
City Marco Island
Company Airboat Guide Service
Contact Tim Spaulding
City Ochope
Company Ale House Charters, Inc.
Contact
City Jupiter
Company Allocation, Inc.
Contact
City Palm Beach Shores
Company Ambush Charters, Inc.
Contact
City Naples
Company Amorous Nan, Inc.
Contact
City Key West
Company Anastasia
Contact William Frank Davis
City Destin
Company Angler's Marina
Contact
City Clewiston
Company Aquanaut Scuba Center, Inc.
Contact
City Destin
Company Aquatic Adventures, Inc.
Contact
City Pembroke Pines
Company Aquia Beach Marina, Inc.
Contact
City Marco Island
Company Archibalds, Inc.
Contact
City Islamorada
Company Atlantic White Waters Charters, Inc.
Contact
City Palm Bay
Company Atlantis Dive Center, Inc.
Contact
City Key Largo
Company B & B Rigging, Inc.
Contact
City Largo
Company B & G Charters, Inc.
Contact
City Palm Beach Shores
Company B-C Guide Service
Contact Bob Gross
City Cape Coral
Company B-Love Corp.
Contact
City Lantana
Company B. L. & L. Ent., Inc.
Contact
City Deland
Company B.P.Charters
Contact
City Islamorada
Company Back Country, Inc.
Contact
City Vero Beach
Company Backcountry Specialty Charters
Contact Capt. Steve
City Naples
Company Bagwell Ent., Inc.
Contact
City Miami
Company Bailey Ent. of Destin
Contact
City Destin

Company Barnett Charter, Inc.
Contact
City Pensacola
Company Barron River Charter
Contact Capt. Sophia Stiffler
City Everglades City
Company Barron River Resort
Contact
City Everglades City
Company Bass Buddies Guide Service
Contact
City Orlando
Company Bass Haven Lodge
Contact Cher Hooten
City Welaka
Company Bass World Lodge
Contact
City Georgetown
Company Bay Breeze Yacht Charters
Contact Mike K. Vargo
City Sanibel Island
Company Bayou Runner
Contact
City Panama City Beach
Company Beacon Charters, Inc.
Contact
City Plantation
Company Bendback Charters, Inc.
Contact
City Chokoloskee Island
Company Big Bass Lodge
Contact
City Moore Haven
Company Big Time
Contact
City Mexico Beach
Company Bigbee Marine, Inc.
Contact
City Merritt Island
Company Bimini Twist
Contact
City Naples
Company Black Bean, Inc.
Contact
City Key West
Company Black Jack Charters
Contact Capt. Steve Guinan
City Tequesta
Company Blazon
Contact
City N. Ft. Myers
Company Blue Claw LC
Contact
City Jupiter
Company Blue Fin Charter Boat
Contact
City Naples
Company Blue Marlin Ent., LC
Contact
City Jupiter
Company Blue Runner II, Inc.
Contact
City Destin
Company Blue Sea Charters, Inc.
Contact
City Deerfield Beach
Company Blue Water I, Inc.
Contact
City N. Palm Beach
Company Bluewater World Corp.
Contact
City Key Largo
Company Boat Leasing Co.
Contact
City Destin
Company Bomar Unlimited, Inc.
Contact Robert L. Paulson, II
City Marathon
Company Bonefide Charters
Contact
City Key Largo
Company Boneshaker Ent.
Contact
City Pt. Salerno
Company Bounty Hunter, Inc.
Contact
City Destin
Company Breakaway Lodge
Contact Bob Beville
City Apalachicola
Company BRRS
Contact
City Stuart
Company Budget Boat Rentals, Inc.
Contact
City Clearwater

Company Bulldog Marine LLC
Contact
City Islamorada
Company C & J Ent. Co., Inc.
Contact
City Key West
Company C & W Ent. of Destin
Contact
City Destin
Company C.B.'s Saltwater Outfitters
Contact Aledia Tush
City Sarasota
Company Calusa Lodge
Contact
City Moore Haven
Company Camp Mack
Contact
City Lake Wales
Company Canaveral Marine Services, Inc.
Contact
City Winter Park
Company Cape Point Charters
Contact
City Jupiter
Company Capt. Kidd II
Contact
City Sebastian
Company Capt. Nick Lopez's Charter Boats
Contact
City Oldsmar
Company Capt. Pete Greenan's Gypsy Guide Service
Contact
City Sarasota
Company Captain Chris River Charter
Contact
City Stuart
Company Captain Daves Charter
Contact
City Summerland Key
Company Captain Doug Hanks
Contact Captain Doug Hanks
City Naples
Company Captain Gannons Charters, Inc.
Contact
City Hudson
Company Captain John Kumiski's Guide Service
Contact Captain John Kumiski
City Chuluota
Company Captain Lloyd L. Collins Guide Service
Contact Captain Lloyd L. Collins
City Cedar Key
Company Captain Mike Locklear
Contact Capt. Mike Locklear
City Homosassa
Company Capts. Lady
Contact
City Ft. Myers Beach
Company Casuarina Bay Corp.
Contact
City Tavernier
Company Champagne Lady, Inc.
Contact
City Destin
Company Championship Promotion, Inc.
Contact
City Key West
Company Charles H. Dessommes, Jr.
Contact
City Pensacola
Company Charles J. Ungerman, Inc.
Contact
City Jupiter
Company Charter Boat Rita Key, Inc.
Contact
City Destin
Company Charter Boat Summer Wind
Contact
City Destin
Company Cheeca Lodge
Contact
City Islamorada
Company Cheney Brothers, Inc.
Contact
City W. Palm Beach
Company Chokoloskee Island Charters
Contact
City Chokoloskee

Company Class Act
Contact
City Destin
Company Clearwater Marine Ent, Inc.
Contact
City Clearwater
Company Coast Fishing Venture
Contact
City Palm Beach Shores
Company Conch House Charters Co.
Contact
City Key West
Company Cool Change Charter, Inc.
Contact
City Eastpoint
Company Coquina Reef Marine, Inc.
Contact
City Valparaiso
Company Craig Fountain, Inc.
Contact
City Miami
Company Craigearn, Inc.
Contact
City Palm Beach
Company Crompton Yacht Charters, Inc.
Contact
City Palm Beach
Company Crown Charters, Inc.
Contact
City Key West
Company Cuda
Contact
City Sarasota
Company Cuda Charter Boat, Inc.
Contact
City Naples
Company Cypress Isle RV Park & Marina
Contact
City Lake Placid
Company D. G. H. Corp.
Contact
City Palm Beach Gardens
Company Daisy Mae VI, Inc.
Contact
City Clearwater
Company Dapa the Tackle Box
Contact
City Marathon
Company Darrah Ent., Inc.
Contact
City Hudson
Company Dave Marler Boats, Inc.
Contact
City Destin
Company Dawn Patrol Charter Fishing
Contact Capt. Bill Walsh
City Marco Island
Company Dba Sunshine Tours
Contact
City Marco Island
Company Deep Water Cay Club
Contact
City Ft. Lauderdale
Company Del-Term Leasing Corp.
Contact
City Panama City
Company Destin Offshore Marine
Contact
City Destin
Company Destin Recreation USA IC
Contact
City Destin
Company Devil Woman Charters, Inc.
Contact
City Sarasota
Company Diamond H Ranch
Contact Linda Cain Sasser
City Lake Wales
Company Diving Locker Charter Service
Contact
City N. Miami
Company Dixie Queen Charters, Inc.
Contact
City Clearwater
Company Dolphin Deep Sea Fishing, Inc.
Contact
City Tarpon Springs
Company Dominic's Guide Service
Contact
City Melbourne
Company Double Eagle II

Contact
City Clearwater
Company Double Play Sport Fishing
Contact
City St. Petersburg
Company Doug Swisher Fly Fishing
Contact Capt. Doug Swisher
City Naples
Company Dragon Drift Fishing, Inc.
Contact
City Ft. Lauderdale
Company Dream Merchant Fishing Charters
Contact
City Ft. Lauderdale
Company DS Charters Ent., Inc.
Contact
City Ft. Myers Beach
Company Dubose Charters, Inc.
Contact
City Panama City
Company Duchess Charter Fishing
Contact
City Miami Beach
Company Duchess Charters, Inc.
Contact
City Panama City Beach
Company Durden Leasing, Inc.
Contact
City Panama City Beach
Company Dutra Travel, Inc.
Contact
City Ft. Lauderdale
Company Dynamic Angling, Inc.
Contact
City Panama City Beach
Company E. W. Leasing, Inc.
Contact
City Stuart
Company Easy Times Charters, Inc.
Contact
City Tampa
Company Elusive Endeavors
Contact Capt. Scott Kolpin
City Summerland Key
Company Emmanuel, Inc.
Contact
City Destin
Company Endeavor of Bay Cnty., Inc.
Contact
City Panama City Beach
Company Ernie Glover, Inc.
Contact Ernie Glover
City Moore Haven
Company Everglades Angler
Contact
City Naples
Company Everglades Explorers
Contact Jim Borovicka
City Ft. Lauderdale
Company Everglades Guide
Contact Tom Glaze
City Miami
Company Executive Sportfishing Charters
Contact
City Palm Beach Shores
Company F / V Layes Days, Inc.
Contact
City Pensacola
Company Faball Ent. of MD, Inc.
Contact
City Pt. St. Lucie
Company Factory Bay Boat Rentals, Inc.
Contact
City Marco Island
Company Fantasea Scuba
Contact
City Destin
Company Faro Blanco Resort
Contact Gregg Kenney
City Marathon
Company Fearless B
Contact
City Palm Beach Shores
Company Fin & Feather Guide Service
Contact Steve Ambrose
City Naples
Company Finest Kind Charters, Inc.
Contact
City Mexico Beach
Company First Class Charters
Contact
City Naples

Company First Light Ent.
Contact
City Destin
Company Fish Busters, Inc.
Contact
City Carrabelle
Company Fish Finder
Contact
City Naples
Company Fish On Charters
Contact Capt. Mel Dragich
City Fort Pierce
Company Fish on Charters, Inc.
Contact
City Duck Key
Company Fish Tales Charters, Inc.
Contact
City Islamorada
Company Fishfinders, Inc.
Contact
City Naples
Company Fishin Fever
Contact
City Ft. Walton Beach
Company Fishin Fever III
Contact
City Ft. Myers
Company Fishing Machine
Contact
City Duck Key
Company Fishing Unlimited, Inc.
Contact Jeff Gossweiler
City Key Largo
Company FL Fisherman II
Contact
City Madeira Beach
Company FL Keys Fishing, Inc.
Contact
City Key West
Company FL Saltwater Guides, Inc.
Contact
City Clearwater
Company Flamingo Lodge
Contact
City Flamingo
Company Florida Down Under, Inc.
Contact
City Sarasota
Company Florida Marine Tech, Inc.
Contact
City Riviera Beach
Company Fluke, Inc.
Contact
City Stuart
Company Fly Fishing Paradise
Contact Capt. Dexter Simmons
City Sugarloaf
Company Flying Fish Fleet
Contact
City Sarasota
Company Flyliner Charters
Contact
City Fort Walton Beach
Company Freedom No Limit, Inc.
Contact
City Seminole
Company Ft. Myers Beach Final Frontier Charters
Contact
City Ft. Myers Beach
Company Gangler's North Seal River
Contact Wayne Gangler
City Hernando
Company George W. Davis & Sons, Inc.
Contact
City Panama City Beach
Company Glen Hunter Guide Service
Contact Glen Hunter
City Okeechobee
Company Glenn Black Charters, Inc.
Contact
City Juno Beach
Company Gold Reserve
Contact
City Naples
Company Gollywhopper
Contact
City Mexico Beach
Company Gone Fishing
Contact Capt. Karty & Angie Sills
City Edgewater
Company Gotta Go Charters
Contact
City Panama City Beach
Company Grand Slam Outfitters, Inc.

Contact Capt. Bruce Miller
City North Key Largo
Company Greg Marler Charter Boats, Inc.
Contact Donna Ferns
City Destin
Company Guided Charters
Contact Capt. Steve Ahlers
City Boca Grande
Company Gulf Offshore Transportation
Contact
City Panama City
Company Gulf Shore Charter, Inc.
Contact
City Naples
Company Gulfside Charters, Inc.
Contact
City Panama City Beach
Company Gulfstream II Charters
Contact Captains Maxie & Suzanne Foster
City Palm Harbor
Company GWC Corp.
Contact
City Boynton Beach
Company H & G Leasing, Inc.
Contact
City Panama City Beach
Company H. L. S., Inc.
Contact
City Maitland
Company Haf N Haf Charters, Inc.
Contact
City Pt. Orange
Company Hamilton Fishing Charters, Inc.
Contact
City W. Palm Beach
Company Hamp & Son, Inc.
Contact
City Key Largo
Company Happy Hooker
Contact
City Ft. Myers
Company Happy Hooker
Contact Capt. Dennis Meehan
City Fort Pierce
Company Harborage, Inc.
Contact
City Miami
Company Harlot
Contact
City Stuart
Company Hat Trick
Contact
City Merritt Island
Company Hawk's Cay Resort & Marina
Contact Christopher R. Ferguson
City Duck Key
Company Head & Tail Charters, Inc.
Contact
City N. Miami
Company Heather IV Fishing Corp.
Contact
City Islamorada
Company Helen's International
Contact
City Pompano Beach
Company Henderson's on Lake Istokpoga
Contact
City Lake Placid
Company Herman Bunch Charters
Contact
City Ramrod Key
Company Hey Bubba, Inc.
Contact
City Destin
Company Hi-Roller
Contact
City Ponce Inlet
Company Hoof Hearted Fishing, Inc.
Contact Captain George L. Roux, III
City St. Petersburg
Company Hook Me Up
Contact
City Boca Raton
Company Horizon Yacht Service
Contact
City Naples
Company Horsepower LW, Inc.
Contact
City Islamorada
Company Huntington Marine, Inc.

Contact
City Naples
Company Inlet Lagoon Charters
Contact Capts. Craig and Dustin Boorman
City Stuart
Company Intl. Charter Service
Contact
City Naples
Company Irish Mist Charters, Inc.
Contact
City Key West
Company Island Adventures, Inc.
Contact James Hail
City Marco Island
Company Island Water Tours
Contact
City Ft. Myers Beach
Company It Fits Charters, Inc.
Contact
City Jupiter
Company J & L Boat Co., Inc.
Contact Robert L. Miley
City Panama City Beach
Company J & R Outfitters
Contact Floyd O'Bannon
City Indiantown
Company J. D. Serenity, Inc.
Contact
City Tavernier
Company Jeni Lyn, Inc.
Contact
City Marathon
Company Jester Charters, Inc.
Contact
City Cape Canaveral
Company Jigg's Landing
Contact Ray & Shirley Courson
City Bradenton
Company Joely Corporation
Contact
City Summerland Key
Company Johns Pass Boat Rentals, Inc.
Contact
City Madeira Beach
Company Jonathan L. Blum & Co., Inc.
Contact
City Coral Gables
Company Joseph D. Thomas Ent., Inc.
Contact
City Pt. Orange
Company Joyce Rehr's Fly Fishing & Light Tackle
Contact
City Sanibal Island
Company JPS Marine Services, Inc.
Contact
City Boca Raton
Company JPT Ent., Inc.
Contact
City Miami
Company Judith M
Contact Capt. Linwood Martin
City Fort Pierce
Company Just Do It
Contact
City Miami
Company Just for Fun Sport Fishing, Inc.
Contact
City Longwood
Company K & E Charters, Inc.
Contact
City Marathon
Company Ka-De Charters of Marco, Inc.
Contact
City Marco Island
Company Kelley Fleet, Inc.
Contact
City Miami Shores
Company Ken Burnette Hunting & Fishing Guide
Contact
City Lakeport
Company Kesagami Wilderness Lodge
Contact Marsha Gibbs & Bob Mattson
City Naples
Company Key Largo Sport Fishing
Contact
City Key Largo
Company Keys Angler Fish Fleet
Contact
City Islamorada
Company Keys Dive Center

Contact Thomas M. & Pamela Timmerman
City Tavernier
Company Kingfisher of Destin, Inc.
Contact
City Destin
Company L. K. Ent. of Vero, Inc.
City Vero Beach
Company Lady Brett, Inc.
Contact
City Naples
Company Lady Helen Fishing Charter, Inc.
Contact
City Ft. Lauderdale
Company Lady K
Contact
City Boynton Beach
Company Lady K, Inc.
Contact
City Destin
Company Lake Hatchineha Marina
Contact
City Haines City
Company Lake Seminole Fish Camp
Contact
City Seminole
Company Lang Sailing Center, Inc.
Contact
City Key West
Company Last Dollar, Inc.
Contact
City Key Largo
Company Laz-Z Sportfishing Charters, Inc.
Contact
City Coral Gables
Company Lils Charters, Inc.
Contact
City Lake Park
Company Linda D., Inc.
Contact
City Key West
Company Lion Fishe, Inc.
Contact
City Ft. Lauderdale
Company Lions Pride Bollinger Keys Ent.
Contact
City Islamorada
Company Lisa B Fish & Dive Trips
Contact
City Naples
Company Look-N-Hook Charters
Contact Capt. Jim & Shari Nickerson
City Naples
Company LTI Financial Service Corp.
Contact
City Juno Isles
Company Lucky Fleet, Inc.
Contact Francis T. & Peggy A. Kirwin
City Key West
Company Lucky Strike
Contact
City Ft. Pierce
Company Ma Anna Charters, Inc.
Contact
City N. Miami Beach
Company Mamas Money II
Contact
City Ponce Inlet
Company Mangrove Outfitters Guides
Contact Capt. Andrew Bostick
City Naples
Company Mangrove Outfitters Guides
Contact Capt. Robert Collins
City Naples
Company Mangrove Outfitters Guides
Contact Capt. Glen Puopolo
City Naples
Company Mar-Tim, Inc.
Contact
City Ponce Inlet
Company Matecumbe Water Sports
Contact
City Islamorada
Company Mauna Kea Ent., Inc.
Contact
City Ft. Lauderdale
Company McCloy Financial Service, Inc.

Contact
City Ft. Lauderdale
Company Meb, Inc.
Contact
City Jensen Beach
Company Meeres Jaeger, Inc.
Contact
City Ft. Lauderdale
Company Metfran, Inc.
Contact
City Marathon
Company MHJ Fisheries, Inc.
Contact
City Stuart
Company Michael Delph
Contact
City Key West
Company Michael S. Vaughn
Contact Helicon
City Cudjoe Key
Company Miss Gail Charters, Inc.
Contact Tammi Molinet
City Ft. Lauderdale
Company Miss Islamorada, Inc.
Contact
City Islamorada
Company Miss Joann Fishing Charters
Contact Capt. Russ Gober
City Goodland
Company Miss Kathleen
Contact
City Melbourne
Company Miss Moose Charters
Contact Captain Tom Rice
City Lynn Haven
Company Miss Tradewinds, Inc.
Contact
City Islamorada
Company Molester Sportfishing & Yachting
Contact
City Miami
Company Mondo Cane
Contact
City Miami Beach
Company Moodys Deep Sea Fishing, Inc.
Contact
City Destin
Company Morris Chartering, Inc.
Contact
City Islamorada
Company Mossy Cove Fishing Resort
Contact
City Lorida
Company Motivation
Contact
City Jensen Beach
Company Mustache Man & Co., Inc.
Contact
City Palm City
Company Native Charters
Contact Capt. Wayne Whidden
City Naples
Company Native Guide
Contact Dr. Steve Mack
City Miami
Company Nautical Wheeler
Contact Nicholas Aldacosta & Annette Walsh
City Marathon
Company Neko
Contact
City Sarasota
Company Neva-Miss
Contact David B. Pinkham
City Bradenton
Company Night Flight Fishing Charters
Contact
City Naples
Company Norfleet Fish Camp
Contact
City Aripeka
Company Oak Haven Fish Camp
Contact
City Tampa
Company Ocean Entertainment, Inc. 01
Contact
City Ponce Inlet
Company Ocean Isle Charters, Inc.
Contact
City Key Largo
Company Ocean Ventures, Inc.
Contact

City Panama City Beach
Company Off Duty
Contact
City Stuart
Company Offshore Adventures Charter Service
Contact
City Marco Island
Company One of a Kind
Contact
City Destin
Company Oodles Ent., Inc.
Contact
City Stuart
Company Orlando Princess
Contact
City Merritt Island
Company Otter Time Charters
Contact
City W. Palm Beach
Company Otto Greene Guide
Contact A. Otto Greene
City Everglades City
Company Panama City Beach Sports, Inc.
Contact
City Panama City
Company Panama City Scuba World, Inc.
Contact
City Panama City Beach
Company Panhandle Divers, Inc.
Contact
City Panama City
Company Pantropic Power Prod., Inc.
Contact
City Miami
Company Paradise Marine
Contact
City Marathon
Company Paradise USA, Inc.
Contact
City Islamorada
Company Pass-A-Grille Deep Sea Fishing
Contact
City St. Petersburg Beach
Company Peg Leg II Tours
Contact
City Naples
Company Pegasus Marine, Inc.
Contact John Bates
City Marathon
Company Pequod Fishing Charters, Inc.
Contact
City Palm Beach Shores
Company Phoenix Sport Fishing, Inc.
Contact
City Destin
Company Pocomoonshine Lake Lodges, Inc.
Contact
City Islamorada
Company Port of the Islands
Contact
City East Naples
Company Posada Del Sol Resort
Contact
City North Palm Beach
Company Predator Holding Co., Inc.
Contact
City Ft. Lauderdale
Company Prince Albert
Contact Kent A. Walker
City Naples
Company Purcell Charter Services
Contact
City Marathon
Company R. D. O. Express Charters, Inc.
Contact
City Big Pine Key
Company R. McAlister's Guide Services Unltd.
Contact Royce McAlister
City Lakeland
Company Rainbow III
Contact
City Daytona Beach
Company Rarin T Go Charters, Inc.
Contact
City Deerfield Beach
Company Raw Marine, Inc.
Contact
City Jupiter

Company Ray Zager & Company, Inc.
Contact
City Ponte Vedra Beach
Company Razorback Camp
Contact John J. and Buck Mclin
City Plant City
Company Reef Runner
Contact
City Panama City Beach
Company Reef Runner Charters
Contact Captain John Gargan, Jr.
City Islamorada
Company Reel Fun
Contact Capt. Dennis Meehan
City Fort Pierce
Company Reel Fun
Contact
City Marco Island
Company Reel Krazy
Contact Capt. Steve Gober
City Goodland
Company Reel Life Charters, Inc.
Contact Michael P. Currie
City Key West
Company Reel Suprise
Contact Capts. John Dahl & George Stransky
City Fort Pierce
Company Reel Tease
Contact
City Singer Island
Company Reel Wife Corporation
Contact
City Islamorada
Company Relentless Fishing
Contact
City Islamorada
Company Resort Yachts of America
Contact
City Ft. Lauderdale
Company Rip, Inc.
Contact
City Key Biscayne
Company River Ranch Resort
Contact
City Lake Wales
Company Robbies Marine Ent., Inc.
Contact
City Islamorada
Company Robert Branham, Inc.
Contact
City Plantation
Company Roboat, Inc.
Contact
City Ft. Lauderdale
Company Robroy Ind.
Contact
City Destin
Company Rocket
Contact Capt. Robert Nemson
City Fort Pierce
Company Roland Martin's Lakeside Resort
Contact
City Clewiston
Company Ron's Guide Service
Contact
City Lakeport
Company Rumblefish Marine Services
Contact
City Marathon
Company S. W. Anderson, Inc.
Contact S. W. Anderson
City Panama City Beach
Company Sabalo Fishing Charters
Contact
City Sarasota
Company Salt & Fresh Water Fishing Charters
Contact Captain Charles Clyne
City Lake Worth
Company Saltwaters Charter, Inc.
Contact
City Pensacola
Company Sandbob, Inc.
Contact
City Ft. Lauderdale
Company Sandskipper Charters, Inc.
Contact
City Cooper City
Company Sanibel Light Tackle Outfitters, Inc.
Contact Tom Rizzo & J. Boardman Capts. Al Helo
City Sanibel Island

Company Scamp Charter Services, Inc.
Contact
City Ft. Walton Beach
Company Scandia Enterprises
Contact
City Summerland Key
Company Sea Bandit, Inc.
Contact
City Singer Island
Company Sea Boots II
Contact James E. & Barbara Sharpe James E. & Barbara Sharpe
City Summerland Key
Company Sea Diver, Inc.
Contact
City Panama City Beach
Company Sea Dragon
Contact
City Marathon
Company Sea Elf, Inc.
Contact
City Key Largo
Company Sea Hunt Adventures, Inc.
Contact
City Naples
Company Sea Lady Charters & Sales, Inc.
Contact
City St. Petersburg
Company Sea Lover, Inc.
Contact
City Ponce Inlet
Company Sea Mist Ent.
Contact
City Boynton Beach
Company Sea Spirit
Contact
City Titusville
Company Sea Squirt
Contact Capt. Peter Taves
City Fort Pierce
Company Seabreeze
Contact
City Captiva
Company Seaquest
Contact
City Boca Raton
Company Sedlak, Inc.
Contact
City Jupiter
Company Serenity
Contact
City Destin
Company Serenity IV
Contact
City Ft. Lauderdale
Company Seyah Charters, Inc.
Contact
City Winter Park
Company Shady Oaks
Contact Ben Heilman
City Lake Wales
Company Show & Tell Charters
Contact Capt Joe McNichols
City Naples
Company Singer Island Marin Co.
Contact
City Palm Beach
Company Six Chuter Charters
Contact Shaun R. Chute
City Marco Island
Company Skipper Charters
Contact
City Islamorada
Company Skysail Management, Inc.
Contact
City N. Palm Beach
Company Special Marine Services, Inc.
Contact
City Panama City Beach
Company Sporting Classics Outfitters
Contact
City Tampa
Company Stafford Burgis/Glen Hunter
Contact Glen Hunter Guide Service
City Lakeport
Company Strike Zone Charters, Inc.
Contact
City Big Pine Key
Company Sun Princess
Contact
City Ft. Myers
Company Sundancer

Contact
City Ponce Inlet
Company T-Bone Charter Co., Inc.
Contact
City Ft. Myers
Company Tag Team, Inc.
Contact
City Plantation
Company Tagem, Inc.
Contact
City Tavernier
Company Tammi Lea Charters, Inc.
Contact
City Ft. Lauderdale
Company Taylor Time Ent., Inc.
Contact
City Orlando
Company The Oasis
Contact
City Lake Wales
Company The Rod & Gun Club
Contact Pat Bowen
City Everglades City
Company The Shark of Key West, Inc.
Contact
City Key West
Company Therapy Charter Fishing Yacht
Contact
City Miami Beach
Company Thompson & Co. of Tampa, Inc.
Contact Robert M. Franzblau
City Tampa
Company Thunnus Fisheries, Inc.
Contact Andre J. Fortin
City Key West
Company Ticket Charters, Inc.
Contact
City Cape Canaveral
Company Tiger Shark Ent.
Contact
City Tampa
Company Tight Lines Charters, Inc.
Contact
City Cudjoe Key
Company Tiki Charters
Contact
City Marathon
Company Tom & Jerry's Pro Guide Service
Contact
City Leesburg
Company Tomac Fisheries, Inc.
Contact
City Talahassee
Company Torbert Boat Charters, Inc.
Contact
City Homestead
Company Tortugas Unltd., Inc.
Contact
City Miami
Company Treasure Island II, Inc.
Contact
City Panama City Beach
Company Triple L. Charters, Inc.
Contact
City Pt. Orange
Company Trophy Bass Guide Service
Contact
City Welaka
Company Tropical Angler
Contact
City Marco Island
Company Tuff Ship
Contact Capt. Mike Patterson
City Islamorada
Company Uncle Joe's Marina
Contact
City Moore Haven
Company United Auto Underwriters
Contact
City Miami
Company Vols, Inc.
Contact
City Naples
Company Wally & Willerd Sports
Contact
City Islamorada
Company Walt Reynolds Fishing
Contact Captain's Cove Motel and Marina
City Clewiston
Company Waterproof
Contact
City Ponce Inlet

Company Weeki Wachee Marina
Contact Jim & Pat Lanier
City Weeki Wachee
Company Weketchum Guide Service
Contact Captain Bill O'Bry
City Inglis
Company West Fork Outfitters
Contact David G. Walker
City Gibsonton
Company Wet Venture Corp.
Contact
City N. Ft. Myers
Company White Water
Contact
City Palm Bay
Company Wiebelized, Inc.
Contact
City Key Largo
Company Wilder I Charters, Inc.
Contact
City Grant
Company Windes Brothers & Assoc.
Contact
City Destin
Company Windwalker II, Inc.
Contact
City Destin
Company Wm. Semple Co.
Contact Wm. R. Semple
City Tarpon Springs
Company WMJB Marine, Inc.
Contact
City Hypoluxo
Company World Wide Sportsman
Contact
City Islamorada
Company Yankee Roamer, Inc.
Contact
City Key West
Company Yella-Dot Charters, Inc.
Contact
City Pt. Salerno
Company
Contact Glenn D. Abend
City Key West
Company
Contact Michael Ackerman
City Key Largo
Company
Contact Christine M. Adamson
City Tequesta
Company
Contact Capt. Robert P. Adkins
City Ft. Pierce
Company
Contact A. M. Adkison
City Panama City Beach
Company
Contact David Aimentrout
City Apalachicola
Company
Contact Harry B. Akers, III
City Palm Beach Gardens
Company
Contact Walter E. Albrecht
City Key West
Company
Contact Everett Russell Albury
City Islamorada
Company
Contact Richard J. Aldacosta
City Naples
Company
Contact Sharon Alexander
City Key West
Company
Contact Eric Alexander
City Naples
Company
Contact Jerry Alexander
City Crawfordville
Company
Contact Steven Alexander
City Key West
Company
Contact Joseph & Barbara Alexander
City Key West
Company
Contact Robert Edward Allen
City Bokeelia
Company
Contact Michael & Linda G. Allevo
City Naples
Company
Contact Larry E. Altman
City Perry

Company
Contact Jerry Anders
City Marco Island
Company
Contact Kenneth E. Anderson
City Old Town
Company
Contact Glenn A. Andrews
City Marco Island
Company
Contact Richard Andrews
City Crystal River
Company
Contact Nicolace Edward Anthony
City Vero Beach
Company
Contact Everett L. Antrim
City Hudson
Company
Contact H. L. Archer, Jr.
City Panama City
Company
Contact Billy P. Archer
City Panama City
Company
Contact Fred S. Arledge
City Lake Mary
Company
Contact Hunter T. Armour
City Pensacola
Company
Contact Darcy Arrington
City Ft. Myers
Company
Contact Harold Artrip
City Key West
Company
Contact Christopher H. Asaro
City Boca Raton
Company
Contact Larry R. Askew
City Summerland Key
Company
Contact Sergio Atanes
City Tampa
Company
Contact James M. Atkins
City Steinhatchee
Company
Contact David Atkinson
City Islamorada
Company
Contact Albin Autenrieth
City St. Petersburg
Company
Contact Capt. David R. Autry
City N. Ft. Myers
Company
Contact David Ayala
City Key Largo
Company
Contact Todd A. Baad
City Summerland Key
Company
Contact Clyde J. Backus
City Islamorada
Company
Contact Steven A. Baden
City Palmetto
Company
Contact Lucious M. Baggett, III
City Englewood
Company
Contact Leslie D. Bagley
City Key Largo
Company
Contact James W. Bailey
City Key West
Company
Contact William C. Bailey
City Key West
Company
Contact Howard S. Bailey
City Ft. Myers
Company
Contact Russell J. & Maria E. Baiocco
City Palm Beach Shores
Company
Contact Capt. Duane Baker
City Tavernier
Company
Contact Lee W. Baker
City Islamorada
Company
Contact Robert Baker
City Islamorada

Company
Contact Jack Baldwin
City Naples
Company
Contact Carl V. Ball, III
City Ft. Lauderdale
Company
Contact Ronald Bamfield
City Grove City
Company
Contact Thomas W. Banks
City Destin
Company
Contact Theodore Barber
City Panama City Beach
Company
Contact Wayne A. Barder
City Nokomis
Company
Contact David B. Barker
City Winter Park
Company
Contact Bert Barkus
City Royal Palm Beach
Company
Contact James W. Barlett
City Miami
Company
Contact Curtis Barlow
City Islamorada
Company
Contact Stanley G. Barnard, Jr.
City Pensacola
Company
Contact Gary R. Barnett
City Vero Beach
Company
Contact Neil R. Baron
City Miami
Company
Contact Emmet D. Barr
City Key West
Company
Contact Richard Barrett
City St. Petersburg
Company
Contact Jeffrey W. Barta
City Satellite Beach
Company
Contact Arthur L. Barton
City Key West
Company
Contact Donald Barton
City Summerland
Company
Contact Donald R. Basmajian
City Key West
Company
Contact Joseph E. Bason
City Suwannee
Company
Contact Alan J. & Brenda A. Bassford
City St. Petersburg
Company
Contact Roger O. Batchelor
City Crystal River
Company
Contact John V. & Fong Chiang Battillo
City Key West
Company
Contact Thomas E. Bauer
City Palm Bay
Company
Contact Robert Baumann
City Miami
Company
Contact Paul R. Baumann
City St. James City
Company
Contact G. Edward Bayer
City Marathon
Company
Contact Albert J. Bazo
City Ocala
Company
Contact Horace Beagles
City Panama City Beach
Company
Contact Kenneth B. Beaird
City Destin
Company
Contact Robert F. Beale
City Ft. Lauderdale
Company
Contact Joseph L. Bean
City Marathon

Company
Contact John M. Bearden
City Bokeelia
Company
Contact George Beardslee
City Pinellas Park
Company
Contact Michael L. Beaubien
City Panama City Beach
Company
Contact Richard E. Beaugh, Jr.
City Gulf Breeze
Company
Contact Melvin W. Beck
City Naples
Company
Contact Simon Becker
City Key West
Company
Contact Capt. Simon Becker
City Key West
Company
Contact Michael S. Bednar
City Long Key
Company
Contact Dale A. Beebe
City Destin
Company
Contact David A. Beelinger
City Largo
Company
Contact James L. Bell
City Islamorada
Company
Contact Kenneth E. Bell
City Crystal River
Company
Contact Marc E. Bellefleur
City Islamorada
Company
Contact Jeff Belsik
City Grassy Key
Company
Contact William E. Bender
City Islamorada
Company
Contact Jim Bennett
City Duck Key
Company
Contact James M. Bennett
City Holiday
Company
Contact Lawrence M. Bennett
City Key Largo
Company
Contact Brian Bennett
City Key West
Company
Contact Scott Bennett
City Key Largo
Company
Contact James Bennett
City Islamorada
Company
Contact Richard P. Benson
City Key Largo
Company
Contact Richard A. Bergman
City Homosassa Springs
Company
Contact Joseph F. Bernhard
City Palmetto
Company
Contact Richard B. & Marsha Berthold
City Seminole
Company
Contact Mark Russell Bess
City Lehigh Acres
Company
Contact Stephen H. Beyer
City Alva
Company
Contact Steven F. Billing
City Ft. Lauderdale
Company
Contact Legal Bills
City Orlando
Company
Contact Vincent Biondoletti
City Islamorada
Company
Contact Dale L. Bittner
City Key West
Company
Contact John T. Black
City Lynn Haven

194

Contact Veran O. Blackburn
City Mexico Beach
Company
Contact Brock T. Blackmore
City Tampa
Company
Contact Ronald F. Blago
City Englewood
Company
Contact Waymon D. & Powell L. Blakely
City Panama City Beach
Company
Contact Mark T. Blaze
City Stuart
Company
Contact Douglas W. Blevins
City Panama City Beach
Company
Contact Dennis L. Blue
City Pt. Charlotte
Company
Contact Michael Bobrich
City Sugarloaf Key
Company
Contact Neil Bohannon
City Key West
Company
Contact Matthew R. Bohn
City Deerfield Beach
Company
Contact James R. Bollinger
City Riverview
Company
Contact Gary M. Bonacci
City Cape Coral
Company
Contact Joseph A. Bonaro
City Sarasota
Company
Contact R. & C. Bonvecio
City Palm Beach Gardens
Company
Contact Gary m. Borland
City N. Palm Beach
Company
Contact David Borras
City Islamorada
Company
Contact Dean Bos
City Naples
Company
Contact Andrew Bostick
City Marco Island
Company
Contact John R. Botting
City Marathon
Company
Contact Richard Bouley
City Key West
Company
Contact Todd Bowen
City Key West
Company
Contact Franklin L. Bowen, Jr.
City Pensacola
Company
Contact Charles M. Bowers
City Summerland Key
Company
Contact Donald N. Bowers
City Key Largo
Company
Contact Stephen F. Bowler
City Pt. Richey
Company
Contact Richard W. Bowles
City Gainesville
Company
Contact Winn F. Box
City Treasure Island
Company
Contact Glenn M. Boyette
City Placida
Company
Contact Harold H. Bracher
City Big Pine Key
Company
Contact Anderson Brackett
City Cudjoe Key
Company
Contact James L. Bradley
City St. Petersburg
Company
Contact Charles C. Brannen

City Bradenton
Company
Contact Donald Braswell
City Marathon
Company
Contact Clinton R. Braswell
City Merritt Island
Company
Contact C & S Ent. of Brevard
City Cape Canaveral
Company
Contact Craig Brewer
City Islamorada
Company
Contact Capt. Craig Brewer
City Islalmorada
Company
Contact James N. Brienza
City Key West
Company
Contact Edward A. Briglio
City Steinhatchee
Company
Contact Richard L. Brito
City Ft. Lauderdale
Company
Contact James D. Broad
City Big Pine Key
Company
Contact Anthony & Janis Brock
City Ochopee
Company
Contact Tommy G. Brock
City Tampa
Company
Contact James C. Brody
City Islamorada
Company
Contact Patrick Brooke
City Steinhatchee
Company
Contact David G. Brooker
City Vero Beach
Company
Contact Gary E. Brooks
City Venice
Company
Contact Norman S. Brown
City Naples
Company
Contact Richard E. Brown
City Gulf Hammock
Company
Contact William D. Brown
City Edgewater
Company
Contact Capt. Tina Brown
City Marathon
Company
Contact Robert B. Brown, III
City Coral Gables
Company
Contact Henry T. Brown
City Islamorada
Company
Contact Mark Brown
City Sarasota
Company
Contact Herbert M. Brown, Jr.
City Clearwater
Company
Contact Capt. Hunter Brown
City Sugarloaf
Company
Contact Jeff Brown
City Naples
Company
Contact Donald L. Brownewell
City Holmes Beach
Company
Contact Thomas L. & Cordelia J. Browning
City Destin
Company
Contact Charles L. Browskowski
City Cape Coral
Company
Contact Gustav J. Brugger
City Sebastian
Company
Contact Brian J. Bruhmuller
City Panama City Beach
Company
Contact Howard V. Bryant
City Tampa
Company

Contact Jackie Bryant
City Lecanto
Company
Contact Sidney H. Bryant
City Islamorada
Company
Contact Richard A. Buckheim
City Big Pine Key
Company
Contact Cliff Budd
City Jupiter
Company
Contact Thomas J. Buettner
City Dunedin
Company
Contact Randall W. Bunch
City Osprey
Company
Contact Gary D. Bunner
City Treasure Island
Company
Contact Clive A. Burgess
City Holmes Beach
Company
Contact Jeffrey W. Burns
City Summerland Key
Company
Contact Joe Burnsed
City Sanibel
Company
Contact Jimmy J. Burnsed
City Sanibel
Company
Contact Robert J. Burnside
City Clearwater
Company
Contact James W. Burnside
City Key Largo
Company
Contact John M. Burson
City Pt. Charlotte
Company
Contact Steven Burton
City Homosassa
Company
Contact Tommy Busciglio, Jr.
City Marathon
Company
Contact Robert F. Bushholz
City Jensen Beach
Company
Contact Richard Busino
City Lutz
Company
Contact Karen M. Bychinski
City Panacea
Company
Contact John Andrew Bylaska
City Pt. Charlotte
Company
Contact James C. Byram
City Bradenton
Company
Contact Jeffrey Mark Byrnes
City Islamorada
Company
Contact Peter J. & Margo L. Bystedt
City Dunedin
Company
Contact Phyllis C.
City Pt. Salerno
Company
Contact Joseph Cacaro
City Marco Island
Company
Contact Richard Cain
City Ft. Myers Beach
Company
Contact Charles Edward Cale
City Islamorada
Company
Contact William I. Calia
City Ft. Lauderdale
Company
Contact Don G. Campbell
City Cedar Key
Company
Contact Morris Campbell, III
City Englewood
Company
Contact Donald P. Campbell
City Wimauma
Company
Contact Edgar Campbell
City Cedar Key
Company

Contact Chad E. Campbell
City Largo
Company
Contact Jeffrey Cardenas
City Key West
Company
Contact Timothy L. Carlile
City Sugarloaf Shores
Company
Contact Capt. John Carlisle
City Chokoloskee
Company
Contact John & Carla Carlisle
City Chokoloskee
Company
Contact Walter E. Carlson
City Steinhatchee
Company
Contact Butler Snapper Carlton
City Everglades City
Company
Contact John J. Carney
City N. Palm Beach
Company
Contact John D. Carpenito
City Ft. Myers
Company
Contact Joseph Carpentieri
City Pt. Charlotte
Company
Contact Budd Carr
City Duck Key
Company
Contact Richard Carr
City Greenville
Company
Contact Richard Keith Carroll
City Jensen Beach
Company
Contact John Carson
City Bradenton
Company
Contact Robert L. Carter
City Vero Beach
Company
Contact Kirk San Cartier
City Cape Coral
Company
Contact David R. Case
City Sanibel
Company
Contact David Cassidy
City Naples
Company
Contact Capt. Frank Catino
City Satelllite Beach
Company
Contact Frank P. Catino
City Satellite Beach
Company
Contact Richard A. Catri
City Melbourne Beach
Company
Contact Jerry Cawthon
City Perry
Company
Contact Dee Cee
City Islamorada
Company
Contact Nick S. Centenaro
City Naples
Company
Contact George M. Challancin
City Belle Glade
Company
Contact James G. Chapman
City Panama City Beach
Company
Contact Phillip G. Chapman
City Lakeland
Company
Contact Laban C. Chappell
City Talahassee
Company
Contact Robert S. Chappell
City Crystal River
Company
Contact Bruce Chard
City Big Pine Key
Company
Contact Clifford E. Charlie
City Sugarloaf Shores
Company
Contact Queen Conch Charters
City Cape Coral
Company

Contact Key Limey Charters
City Key West
Company
Contact Thomas J. Chaya
City Anna Maria
Company
Contact Mark Chesser
City Marathon
Company
Contact Bob J. Chipman
City Everglades City
Company
Contact James Christman
City Nokomis
Company
Contact Robert W. Christop
City Miami Beach
Company
Contact Capt. Shaun R. Chute
City Marco Island
Company
Contact George Cipko
City Crystal River
Company
Contact Donald R. Clark
City Islamorada
Company
Contact Bruce R. Clark
City Bonita Springs
Company
Contact Craig Clark
City Key West
Company
Contact Clifton H. Clement
City St. Petersburg
Company
Contact Marion Clements
City Tavernier
Company
Contact Michael R. Clendening
City New Pt. Richey
Company
Contact Gary R. Cobb
City Bradenton
Company
Contact John Cochran
City Key Largo
Company
Contact David Cochran
City Key West
Company
Contact Timothy D. Cochran
City Marianna
Company
Contact Vaughn J. Cochran
City Summerland Key
Company
Contact Thomas M. Cockrell
City Bradenton
Company
Contact Alan W. Coe
City Ft. Pierce
Company
Contact Martin P. Cohen
City Sarasota
Company
Contact Kenneth Cohen
City Islamorada
Company
Contact Larry Cohen
City Key West
Company
Contact Michael H. Colby
City Clearwater
Company
Contact Charles E. Cole
City Ft. Myers
Company
Contact Dalton R. Cole
City New Smyrna Beach
Company
Contact Clyde Gregory Cole
City Wewahitchka
Company
Contact Winston D. Coleman
City Bokeelia
Company
Contact Raymond A. Coleman
City Boca Grande
Company
Contact Douglas D. Collett
City Homasassa Springs
Company
Contact Kenneth Collette
City Ft. Lauderdale
Company

Contact Charles C. Collins
City Palmetto
Company

Contact Michael Collins
City Islamorada
Company

Contact Capt. Ken Collins
City N. Palm Beach
Company

Contact Ronald Collins
City Marathon
Company

Contact Geoffrey Colmes
City Islamorada
Company

Contact William D. Coman
City Alligator Pt.
Company

Contact Jerry V. Combs
City Mexico Beach
Company

Contact Joseph Comparetto
City Marathon
Company

Contact Robert A. Condo, Jr.
City Cudjoe Key
Company

Contact James N. Conley, Jr.
City Orlando
Company

Contact Michael A. Conner
City Miami
Company

Contact Linda L. Connors
City Pensacola
Company

Contact Scott S. Coogle
City Key West
Company

Contact Joe M. Cook
City Boca Grande
Company

Contact Jeff Cook
City Destin
Company

Contact Wayne Cook
City Apalachicola
Company

Contact Jonathan N. Cooper
City Plantation
Company

Contact Donald J. Cooper
City Miami
Company

Contact Charles P. Cooper
City Destin
Company

Contact David S. Coover, Jr.
City St. Petersburg
Company

Contact Capt. Thomas B. Copeland
City Key Largo
Company

Contact Gary Coppenbarger
City Naples
Company

Contact Diego L. Cordova
City Marathon
Company

Contact Aaron Cothron, Jr.
City Suwannee
Company

Contact David B. Coudal
City Nokomis
Company

Contact Kamalame Cove
City Coral Gables
Company

Contact Pat J. Cowan
City Key Largo
Company

Contact Dana J. Cowart
City Brandon
Company

Contact Earl T. Cowles
City Goodland
Company

Contact Clifton R. Cox
City Destin
Company

Contact Roger R. Craft
City Panacea
Company

Contact Roger G. Crafton
City Boca Grande
Company

Contact Asbell Crawford
City Key Largo
Company

Contact Jeff Creamer
City Apalachicola
Company

Contact Ralph L. Creech, Jr.
City Cocoa Beach
Company

Contact Carl D. Crevier
City Tampa
Company

Contact James Crispino
City Pt. Canaveral
Company

Contact Ashmore Croft
City Islamorada
Company

Contact Bruce E. Cronin
City Key West
Company

Contact Paul C. Cronk, Jr.
City Steinhatchee
Company

Contact Dennis Crosby
City Apalachicola
Company

Contact Lance Crouch
City Indian Hbr. Beach
Company

Contact Kevin J. Crown
City Miami
Company

Contact Wilfred J. Croze, Jr.
City Crystal River
Company

Contact Jeffrey W. Culbreth
City Destin
Company

Contact Dale Curmanskie
City Miami
Company

Contact Joseph L. Currier
City Pt. Charlotte
Company

Contact James Curry
City Naples
Company

Contact Marshall Cutchin
City Key West
Company

Contact Wendel G. Dafcik
City Naples
Company

Contact Capt. Kurt Dafcik
City Naples
Company

Contact Rebecca A. Daniels
City Naples
Company

Contact Louis Daniels
City Everglades City
Company

Contact Douglas B. Dardeau
City Ft. Walton Beach
Company

Contact Merritt N. Darna
City Boca Grande
Company

Contact George A. David
City Palmetto
Company

Contact Jonathan L. Davis
City Palmetto
Company

Contact Ellis W. Davis
City Panama City
Company

Contact Frank E. Davis
City Boca Grande
Company

Contact Capt. Eric T. Davis
City Sebastian
Company

Contact Herbert A. Davis
City Marathon
Company

Contact Robert V. Dawson
City Destin
Company

Contact Christopher C. Dean
City S. Miami
Company

Contact Capt. Chris Dean
City Miami
Company

Contact Derl F. Debusk
City Crystal River
Company

Contact Ralph Delph
City Key West
Company

Contact Larry G. Demere
City Chokoloskee
Company

Contact Richey T. Depoyster
City Jupiter
Company

Contact Capt. Richard DeVito
City Stuart
Company

Contact Richard L. Devitt
City Homosassa
Company

Contact Gardner E. Dickinson
City Tequesta
Company

Contact John N. Dickinson
City Miami
Company

Contact Douglas R. Dietz
City Destin
Company

Contact Michael J. Digiacomo
City Ft. Myers
Company

Contact James D. Dill
City Marathon
Company

Contact Paul W. Dimaura
City Islamorada
Company

Contact Patrick M. Dineen
City Destin
Company

Contact Inc. Cape Divers
City Cocoa
Company

Contact Sylvester Dixon
City Englewood
Company

Contact Terry Dixon
City Key West
Company

Contact John D. Dixon
City Pt. St. Joe
Company

Contact Edward H. Dobie
City Stuart
Company

Contact Robert T. Dolan
City Key Largo
Company

Contact Isador A. Donatiello, Jr.
City Islamorada
Company

Contact John L. Donnell
City Tavernier
Company

Contact Richard Donofrio
City Marco Island
Company

Contact Allan B. Dopirak
City Crystal Beach
Company

Contact Buddy Dortch
City Panama City
Company

Contact James C. Dotson
City Sanibel
Company

Contact David E. Dotterwich
City Boca Raton
Company

Contact James Dougherty
City Key Largo
Company

Contact C. E. & D. M. Douglass
City Naples
Company

Contact Robert Dove
City Islamorada
Company

Contact Doyle Doxsee
City Marco Island
Company

Contact Gilbert Drake
City Key West
Company

Contact Gerald A. Drangmeister
City Marathon
Company

Contact Michael Duclon
City Tarpon Springs
Company

Contact Edward D. Duffy
City Naples
Company

Contact Robert & Gale Dumouchel
City Sugarloaf Key
Company

Contact Reuben Dunagan
City Key West
Company

Contact Bobby Joe Duncan
City Apalachicola
Company

Contact Paul W. Duncan
City Homasassa
Company

Contact Leo F. Dunn
City Sanibel
Company

Contact Merrily Dunn
City Sarasota
Company

Contact James J. Dupre
City Gainesville
Company

Contact Capt. Jim Dupre
City Gainesville
Company

Contact Cecil E. & Linda H. Dupree
City Panama City
Company

Contact Peter T. Durmer
City Sugarloaf Shores
Company

Contact Glenn P. Dyches
City Pensacola
Company

Contact Louis E. Dykes
City Santa Rosa Beach
Company

Contact Charles D. Eargle
City Inverness
Company

Contact Carl Earhart
City Key Largo
Company

Contact Carl M. Earhart
City Key Largo
Company

Contact Charles E. Eastman, Jr.
City Sebastian
Company

Contact Jonathan A. Eaton
City Cape Coral
Company

Contact Daniel J. Ebbecke
City Brooksville
Company

Contact Robert R. Edge, Jr.
City Homasassa
Company

Contact Carlos E. Edmonds
City St. George Island
Company

Contact Jack H. Edwards
City Tampa
Company

Contact Timothy R. Edwards
City Carrabelle
Company

Contact Daniel W. Egert
City Ocala
Company

Contact Edward W. Ehlers
City Islamorada
Company

Contact Michael G. Ehlers
City Islamorada
Company

Contact Capt. Dave "Flash" Eimers
City Naples
Company

Contact Michael D. Eller
City Destin
Company

Contact James O. Ellis
City Steinhatchee
Company

Contact Gary Ellis
City Islamorada
Company

Contact David Elmers
City Naples
Company

Contact Glenn Weston Elsasser
City Lecanto
Company

Contact Frank J. Emkey
City Key Largo
Company

Contact Earnest Ray Endicott
City Pt. Orange
Company

Contact James P. Enoch
City Everglades City
Company

Contact Mark A. Erickson
City Melbourne Beach
Company

Contact Eric F. Ersch
City Satellite Beach
Company

Contact Carlos Escarra
City Naples
Company

Contact David H. Esquinaldo
City Key West
Company

Contact Antonio Estenoz, Jr.
City Key West
Company

Contact Michael P. Estes
City Key West
Company

Contact Stephen C. Etts
City Steinhatchee
Company

Contact Craig Eubank
City Key West
Company

Contact James V. Evans, Jr.
City Destin
Company

Contact Frederick L. Everson
City Brandon
Company

Contact John Falcucci
City Islamorada
Company

Contact Douglas F. Faraone
City St. Petersburg
Company

Contact Karen Farley
City Marathon
Company

Contact Michael D. Farmer
City Islamorada
Company

Contact Jon V. Farmer
City Suwannee
Company

Contact David Farneski
City Treasure Island
Company

Contact Byron L. Farrell
City Marco Island
Company

Contact David H. Fawcett
City Stuart
Company

Contact Robert A. Fazioli
City Bradenton
Company

Contact Raymond W. Fecher
City Big Pine Key
Company

Contact Russell M. Feddersen
City Cape Coral
Company

Contact John F. Felber
City Key West
Company

Contact Robert Fernicola
City Key Largo
Company

Contact William F. Ferrell
City Marathon
Company

Contact Phillip Fessenden
City Panama City Beach
Company

Contact Marshall Field
City Hobe Sound
Company

Contact Neill C. Finkel, III
City Ft. Walton Beach
Company

Contact Ozzie C. Fischer
City Ft. Myers
Company

Contact Douglas Fischer
City Ft. Myers
Company
Contact Edward Fischl
City Bonita Springs
Company
Contact Captain Bert Fisher
City Clewiston
Company
Contact Timothy G. Fitzsimmons
City Cape Haze
Company
Contact Harry & Jennie Flechsig
City Engelwood
Company
Contact Matthew L. Fleming
City Crystal River
Company
Contact Todd A. Fopiano
City Hollywood
Company
Contact William C. Forbes
City Delray Beach
Company
Contact Bob Bell Ford
City Jupiter
Company
Contact Robert W. Fordyce, III
City Homestead
Company
Contact Dennis F. Forgione
City Miami Beach
Company
Contact Capt. Charlie Fornabio
City Wabasso
Company
Contact Denny Keith Forster
City Tampa
Company
Contact Shawn S. Foster
City Cocoa Beach
Company
Contact William Fotre
City Naples
Company
Contact Larry L. Fowler
City Orlando
Company
Contact Michael E. Fowler
City Titusville
Company
Contact James M. Fox
City Islamorada
Company
Contact Ted Fox
City Naples
Company
Contact John W. Franck
City Palm Bay
Company
Contact Harlin Franklin
City Key West
Company
Contact Capt. Hamilton M. Franz
City Jacksonville
Company
Contact Rick R. Frazier
City St. Petersburg
Company
Contact Gordon L. French
City Naples
Company
Contact Earl J. Friday
City Miami
Company
Contact Daniel N. Frudaker
City Panama City
Company
Contact Robert M. Fuery
City Captiva
Company
Contact Cory A. Fulford
City Cantonment
Company
Contact James R. & Kimberly S. Fuller
City Panama City
Company
Contact John M. Fussell
City Ft. Myers
Company
Contact Mark L. Futch
City Boca Grande
Company
Contact Stephen Futch
City Pt. Charlotte
Company

Contact William E. Futch
City Oak Hill
Company
Contact John M. Gaffney
City Sanibel
Company
Contact Robert P. Gaines
City Englewood
Company
Contact Wayne C. Galting
City Marathon
Company
Contact B. Galyon, III
City Islamorada
Company
Contact Thomas F. Gannon, III
City N. Miami Beach
Company
Contact Philip J. Gansz
City W. Palm Beach
Company
Contact Richard Gardner
City Marathon
Company
Contact Karell Gardner
City Steinhatchee
Company
Contact Capt. Frank Garisto
City Key Biscayne
Company
Contact Frank Garisto
City Key Biscayne
Company
Contact Capt. Len N. Garner
City Islamorada
Company
Contact Stephen Garrett
City N. Miami
Company
Contact William R. Gartrell
City Sanibel
Company
Contact Thomas E. Garvey
City Palm Beach Shores
Company
Contact William F. Gately
City Madeira Beach
Company
Contact Kevin Gunner Gause
City Tarpon Springs
Company
Contact David R. Gause
City Tarpon Springs
Company
Contact John R. Gay
City Panacea
Company
Contact George J. Geiger
City Sebastian
Company
Contact David W. Geller
City Lake Worth
Company
Contact Scott & Esperanza Genereux
City Key West
Company
Contact Douglas J. Genever
City Ft. Pierce
Company
Contact Joe V. Genovese
City St. Petersburg
Company
Contact William K. Gentile
City Jensen Beach
Company
Contact Gregg R. Gentile
City Pt. St. Lucie
Company
Contact Kelly George
City Naples
Company
Contact Troy Gerard
City Edgewater
Company
Contact Ton Gen Getalot
City Tarpon Springs
Company
Contact Brad R. Gibbs
City Key Largo
Company
Contact Pasco Gibson
City Bagdad
Company
Contact David W. Gibson
City Ft. Myers
Company

Company
Contact Frank E. Giles
City Bradenton
Company
Contact Leo C. Gillespie
City W. Palm Beach
Company
Contact Tyler R. Gilmer
City Ft. Myers
Company
Contact Inc. William H. Gilmore
City Clearwater
Company
Contact James R. Gilroy
City Crystal River
Company
Contact Fritz G. Gisewhite
City Sanibel Island
Company
Contact Paul Glanville
City Islamorada
Company
Contact James W. Glass
City Naples
Company
Contact John M. Glorieux
City Ft. Lauderdale
Company
Contact Russ Gober
City Goodland
Company
Contact Mark A. Godfrey
City Panama City Beach
Company
Contact Capt. Jerry Goering
City Ft. Lauderdale
Company
Contact James C. Goetz
City Long Key
Company
Contact David E. Goldberg
City Hollywood
Company
Contact Gary C. Golden
City Largo
Company
Contact Bob & Donna Goldstein
City Marco Island
Company
Contact Jose F. Gonzalez
City Miami
Company
Contact Craig Goodie
City Marco Island
Company
Contact Capt. Warren L. Gorall
City Stuart
Company
Contact Capt. E. A. Gorenflo
City Islamorada
Company
Contact Robert L. Gorta
City Largo
Company
Contact Roy R. Gottschalk
City Cape Coral
Company
Contact Patrick T. Gould
City Naples
Company
Contact James W. Grace
City Naples
Company
Contact Alfred P. Grace
City Islamorada
Company
Contact William F. Grace
City Islamorada
Company
Contact Dennis A. Gragg
City St. James City
Company
Contact William L. Graham
City Palm Bay
Company
Contact David L. Graham
City Tarpon Springs
Company
Contact Gordian R. Granrath
City Marathon
Company
Contact Neil Grant
City Big Pine Key
Company
Contact Capt. R. K. Grant
City Marco Island
Company

Company
Contact Richard Grathwohl
City Marathon
Company
Contact Kenneth L. Graves
City St. Petersburg
Company
Contact Stephen K. Gray
City Summerland Key
Company
Contact Danny M. Gray
City Sarasota
Company
Contact Robert L. & Margaret A. Gray
City Pensacola
Company
Contact Brett H. Green
City Ft. Myers
Company
Contact Peter Greenan
City Sarasota
Company
Contact Thurman G. Greene
City Vero Beach
Company
Contact Lawrence J. Greenwell
City Tavernier
Company
Contact Michael Charles Greig
City Cortez
Company
Contact Rocky Griffith
City Destin
Company
Contact John Joseph Griffith
City Tampa
Company
Contact Michael Griffith
City Naples
Company
Contact R. P. & Ashley S. Griffith
City Key West
Company
Contact Capt. Andy Griffiths, Jr.
City Key West
Company
Contact Harry P. Grigsby
City Key Largo
Company
Contact Roy L. Griscom
City Holmes Beach
Company
Contact Richard K. Gross
City Bradenton
Company
Contact John T. Grove
City Vero Beach
Company
Contact John W. Guastavino
City Key Largo
Company
Contact Paul Guenther
City Cape Coral
Company
Contact Kevin Michael Guerin
City Duck Key
Company
Contact James P. Guilford
City Tampa
Company
Contact William T. Guinn
City Panama City
Company
Contact Judy S. & John G. Guinta
City Crawfordville
Company
Contact Marcel C. Gutierrez
City Tampa
Company
Contact Bob Hackney
City Key Largo
Company
Contact Edward C. Hadley
City Cape Canaveral
Company
Contact Steve R. & Kelly Ann Haeusler
City Destin
Company
Contact Robert P. Hagle
City Pineland
Company
Contact Richard A. Hagood
City Islamorada
Company

Contact Irwin H. & Roberta A. Hahn, Jr.
City St. Petersburg
Company
Contact Gene W. Hail
City Marco Island
Company
Contact Capt. Jimbo Hail
City Marco Island
Company
Contact Michael G. Haines
City Miami
Company
Contact Michael W. Hakola
City New Smyrna Beach
Company
Contact William Haley
City Naples
Company
Contact Gary S. Hall
City Naples
Company
Contact Gene Hall
City Key West
Company
Contact Capt. Randy Hamilton
City Marco Island
Company
Contact Harvey L. Hamilton
City Bokeelia
Company
Contact Joseph R. Hamilton
City Marco Island
Company
Contact Howard H. Hamilton
City Suwannee
Company
Contact Mack L. & Lisa Hamilton
City Naples
Company
Contact Earl J. Hamilton, Jr.
City Ft. Walton Beach
Company
Contact Grape Hammock
City Lake Wales
Company
Contact Dennis W. Hammond
City Rockledge
Company
Contact Richard C. Hamp
City Bokeelia
Company
Contact Tim Hampson
City Key Largo
Company
Contact William D. Hampton
City Crystal River
Company
Contact Richard Hanner
City Panama City Beach
Company
Contact Robert L. & Constance Hanshaw
City Destin
Company
Contact Charles David Hanson
City Bonita Springs
Company
Contact Jason S. X. Haralambous
City Summerland Key
Company
Contact David Harding
City Naples
Company
Contact Ronald E. Hardy
City Panama City Beach
Company
Contact Alvern Odell Hargrove
City Micanopy
Company
Contact Harlee S. Harn
City N. Ft. Myers
Company
Contact Gary S. Harney
City Sugarloaf Shores
Company
Contact Franklin D. Harp
City Brooksville
Company
Contact Lindsay Harper
City Key West
Company
Contact Dempsey Harper
City Suwannee
Company
Contact Dewey Harrington

City Naples
Company
Contact Stanley B. & Beatrice K. Harris
City Marathon
Company
Contact John T. & Mary K. Harris
City Ft. Pierce
Company
Contact Ray M. Harris
City Silver Springs
Company
Contact Gary K. & Sara D. Harris
City Destin
Company
Contact Roger Harris
City Punta Gorda
Company
Contact Marc A. Harris
City Treasure Island
Company
Contact Gary R. & Robin Harris
City St. Petersburg
Company
Contact Kenneth S. Harris
City Key West
Company
Contact Michael Harrison
City Edgewater
Company
Contact Charles W. Harrison
City Boca Grande
Company
Contact Jeffrey A. Hart
City Palm Harbor
Company
Contact George Harvey
City Perry
Company
Contact A. John Harvey, III
City Jupiter
Company
Contact William Hatfield
City Palm City
Company
Contact Douglas B. Hatten
City St. Petersburg
Company
Contact Jay Haughton, III
City Panama City Beach
Company
Contact Anthony Haupt
City Panama City
Company
Contact Dennis Hausman
City Apalachicola
Company
Contact Richard D. Haveland
City Key West
Company
Contact Paul Hawkins
City St. Petersburg
Company
Contact Capt. Paul Hawkins
City St. Petersburg
Company
Contact K. E. & Segno Hawkins, Jr.
City Hollywood
Company
Contact David Stewart Hayden
City Rotonda West
Company
Contact Steven R. Hayes
City Vero Beach
Company
Contact Marcene & Frank Hayman
City Crestview
Company
Contact Capt. Bill Hegland
City Marathon
Company
Contact Robert Hehenberger
City Largo
Company
Contact Thomas Alan Heisler
City Jupiter
Company
Contact Richard Hellmuth
City Islamorada
Company
Contact Douglas L. Hemmer
City St. Petersburg
Company
Contact Mark Henninger
City Summerland Key
Company

Contact Inc. Duke Henry
City Talahassee
Company
Contact Woodrow W. Henry
City Naples
Company
Contact Thomas C. Henry
City Jupiter
Company
Contact Clyde Hensley
City Key West
Company
Contact William D. Hernandez
City Crystal Beach
Company
Contact Joseph A. Herzog
City Islamorada
Company
Contact Lewis M. Herzog
City Boca Grande
Company
Contact Gilbert C. Hess
City Dunnellon
Company
Contact Philip C. Hewitt
City Royal Palm Beach
Company
Contact Glen H. Hewlett
City Marathon
Company
Contact Ricky Hice
City Panama City Beach
Company
Contact Tim Hickey
City Captiva
Company
Contact Highlander
City Pt. Orange
Company
Contact Bobby F. Hilbrunner
City Sarasota
Company
Contact Robert L. Hill
City Pt. Charlotte
Company
Contact Les J. Hill
City Pt. Charlotte
Company
Contact Charles K. Hilliard
City Jupiter
Company
Contact Bruce A. Hitchcock
City Boca Raton
Company
Contact Charles F. Hobart
City Perry
Company
Contact Clifton C. Hodges
City Titusville
Company
Contact David W. Hoenig
City Marco Island
Company
Contact Larry A. & Mary C. Hoffman
City St. Petersburg
Company
Contact Brock Hook / Hanspeter Hoffman
City Marathon
Company
Contact Capt. Barry Hoffman
City Tavernier
Company
Contact Andrew J. Hoffman
City Odessa
Company
Contact Barry Hoffman
City Tavernier
Company
Contact Robert S. Hogan
City Oak Hill
Company
Contact Thomas Doyle Hogan
City Vero Beach
Company
Contact Stephen Hogan
City Englewood
Company
Contact Scott Hogan
City Key West

Company
Contact John Holahan
City Islamorada
Company
Contact Raymond Danny Holcomb
City Tampa
Company
Contact Clifford E. Holland
City Panama City
Company
Contact Larry B. Holland
City Goodland
Company
Contact John C. Holley
City Destin
Company
Contact William Holloway
City Islamorada
Company
Contact Baughn Holloway
City Captiva
Company
Contact Grady W. Holman
City Apalachicola
Company
Contact Richard K. Holt
City Bradenton
Company
Contact Kenneth Holzhauer
City Cape Coral
Company
Contact James R. Hooten
City Walda
Company
Contact Timothy A. Hoover
City Marathon
Company
Contact William G. Hope, III
City Brooksville
Company
Contact James A. Hopkins
City Naples
Company
Contact Joe Hopkins
City Marathon
Company
Contact Justin R. Hopper
City Key Largo
Company
Contact John Hopwood
City Tavernier
Company
Contact Dale M. Houchin
City Ft. Myers
Company
Contact Richard B. Houde
City Key West
Company
Contact Richard M. Howard
City Clearwater
Company
Contact Leon D. Howell
City Homestead
Company
Contact Vanley D. Hubbard
City Boca Grande
Company
Contact Kenneth H. Hudak
City Beverly Hills
Company
Contact Jackie W. Hudson
City Bonita Springs
Company
Contact Dustin Huff
City Duck Key
Company
Contact Steve W. Huff
City Everglades City
Company
Contact James W. & Maridean L. Huffman
City Riviera Beach
Company
Contact William L. Huffman
City New Pt. Richey
Company
Contact Richard E. Humphreys
City Hobe Sound
Company
Contact Henry B. Hunt
City Panama City
Company
Contact James F. & Frances A. Hunter
City Marathon
Company
Contact Richard Hyland

City Rotonda West
Company
Contact Thomas L. Hylton
City Clearwater
Company
Contact Patrick W. Hynes
City Key West
Company
Contact Steven Impallomeni
City Key West
Company
Contact Vicki R. Impallomeni
City Key West
Company
Contact James W. Ingalls
City Boca Raton
Company
Contact Billy Ingram
City Panama City Beach
Company
Contact Nelson A. Italiano, II
City Boca Grande
Company
Contact Calvin Jackson
City Marathon
Company
Contact David W. Jacobs
City Southport
Company
Contact Steven P. Jacobs
City Panama City
Company
Contact Lawrence P. Jagodzinski, Jr.
City Indian Rocks Beach
Company
Contact William E. James
City Lutz
Company
Contact Mark A. James
City Spring Hill
Company
Contact Gary C. & Pamela Jarvis
City Destin
Company
Contact Walter Jenkins
City Marathon
Company
Contact Gregory A. Jensen
City Cape Coral
Company
Contact Kenneth C. Jessup
City Tampa
Company
Contact Johnny K. Johnson
City Boca Grande
Company
Contact Gregory A. Johnson
City Pt. Orange
Company
Contact Dale R. Johnson
City Palm Bay
Company
Contact Bruce H. Johnson
City Monticello
Company
Contact Romana G. Johnson
City Plant City
Company
Contact Walter P. Johnson
City Steinhatchee
Company
Contact James E. Johnson
City Tavernier
Company
Contact Joe S. Johnson
City Palm Coast
Company
Contact James T. Johnson
City Summerland Key
Company
Contact Jeffrey E. Johnson
City Tavernier
Company
Contact Austin L. Joiner
City Placida
Company
Contact Jody Joiner
City Islamorada
Company
Contact James G. Joiner
City Placida
Company
Contact David Joiner
City Boca Grande
Company
Contact Austin L. Joiner, Jr.
Company

City Pt. Charlotte
Company
Contact Pamela Lee Jones
City Miami
Company
Contact Steven H. Jones
City Ft. Myers
Company
Contact Kathleen E. Jones
City Destin
Company
Contact Gerald L. Jones
City Marathon
Company
Contact Russell D. Jones
City Titusville
Company
Contact Vincent Patrick Jones, Jr.
City Pensacola
Company
Contact Ronald Jones
City Punta Gorda
Company
Contact Tom Jones
City Islamorada
Company
Contact Donald L. Joyner
City Big Pine Key
Company
Contact Cecil Oglesby, Jr.
City Everglades City
Company
Contact Robert S. Collins, Jr.
City Naples
Company
Contact Wilbur L. Edrington, Jr.
City Seminole
Company
Contact Joseph Saladino, Jr.
City Marathon
Company
Contact Frank Difilippo, Jr.
City Panama City Beach
Company
Contact S. & Nancy Owens Woodrow, Jr.
City Mexico Beach
Company
Contact Arthur L. Jones, Jr.
City Pensacola
Company
Contact Ragan D. Moss, Jr.
City Sarasota
Company
Contact Wilford F. Williams, Jr.
City Key West
Company
Contact Capt. Dan Juettner
City Ft. Myers
Company
Contact Inc. Lady Kady
City Gulf Breeze
Company
Contact Joel & Agnas M. Kalman
City Key Biscayne
Company
Contact Steve Kapp
City Apalachicola
Company
Contact Donald W. Kay
City Winter Springs
Company
Contact Richard B. Keating
City Marathon
Company
Contact Mitchell Keene
City Englewood
Company
Contact John & Hester Keener
City Destin
Company
Contact Cecil Keith, Jr.
City Islamorada
Company
Contact J. Kelle
City Ponce Inlet
Company
Contact Robert E. Keller
City Dunedin
Company
Contact Robert S. Keller
City Islamorada
Company
Contact Benjamin T. Kelley
City Panama City
Company

Contact	City	Company
Patrick S. Kelly	Lakeland	
Paula T. Kelly	Key West	
Jack C. Kelly	Key West	
Carl F. Kelly, Jr.	Rotonda West	
Greg Kembro	Apalachicola	
Fred Kembro	Apalachicola	
Ron Kennedy	Goodland	
Daniel Key	Sugarloaf Key	
Bill Kieldsen	Key West	
Larry R. Kiker	Ft. Myers Beach	
John Steven Kilpatrick	Chiefland	
Capt. Doug Kilpatrick	Summerland	
Harry D. King	Ft. Pierce	
Louis A. King, III	Pensacola	
Donnie G. King	Panama City	
Joyce F. Kinglsey	Tavernier	
John Kipp, III	Islamorada	
Walter Kirchner	Key West	
Patricia Kird	Goodland	
James E. Kirk	Marco Island	
Dennis M. Kirk	Pt. Charlotte	
Milton C. Kitchen	Crystal River	
Edward P. Kitta, Sr.	Merritt Island	
Robert Klein	Tavernier	
Timothy Klein	Islamorada	
Allen C. Kline	Homosassa	
Capt. Allen C. Kline	Homosassa	
Walter C. Klingel, Jr.	Boca Grande	
James F. Klopfler	Sarasota	
Mark Knapke	Dunedin	
William Knauber	Marco Island	
John W. Knight, Jr.	Boca Grande	
David M. Knight	Destin	
Eugene M. Knight	Arcadia	
William L. Knowles	Islamorada	
Richard G. Knox	New Pt. Richey	
Kenneth C. Knudsen	Islamorada	
Steve Korody	Marco Island	
David A. Kostyo	Miami	
Victoria Kover	Key West	
John J. Kowalski	New Pt. Richey	
Capt. Ron Kowalyk	Fort Myers	
Ronald L. Kowalyk	Ft. Myers	
Inc. Reef Kracker	Anna Maria	
Michael Krenzer	Marco Island	
Betty J. Kroll	Naples	
Mark Krowka	Davie	
Michael W. Kuenstle	Gainesville	
Randall S. Lacey	Islamorada	
Frederick J. Laier	Cape Coral	
James L. Lamb	Sarasota	
Danny A. Lampe	Key West	
Robert Lamperti	Marathon	
Steve Lancaster	Ruskin	
John R. & David Langfitt	Winter Park	
Louis G. Lapointe	Marathon	
Thomas B. Larkins	Bradenton	
Tim Larrimore	St. James City	
John F. Law, III	Panama City	
Sean Lawrence	Miami Springs	
Orren T. Lay	Punta Gorda	
Harold M. Lee	Panama City	
Derill E. Lee, Jr.	Naples	
Ruben J. Lee	Panama City	
Michael D. Lefiles	Ft. Pierce	
Connan J. Lehmkuhl	Key West	
Robert W. Lemay	Pembroke Pines	
Edward Lentz	Edgewater	
Arthur R. & Scott M. Leon	Pembroke Pines	
Steven Leopold	Islamorada	
Joe Lepree	Islamorada	
Ozzie Lessinger	Captiva	
Harold D. Lester	Pt. Orange	
Camp Lester	Lake Wales	
Dennis R. Lett	Sebastian	
Wiley D. Levins	Crystal River	
David L. Lewis	Key West	
Ronald Lewis	Edgewater	
George J. Lewis	Miami	
Kearsley J. Lewis	Inglis	
Robert Libauer	Key Largo	
James E. Liberato	Jensen Beach	
Mark R. Liberman	Sarasota	
Fred L. Lifton	Marco Island	
Richard C. Lightner	Key West	
Carlos A. Lima	St. Petersburg	
Terry Scott Lindsey	Panama City	
B. Lisa	Naples	
Wade D. Littlefield	Pt. Charlotte	
Ernest J. & Suzanne H. Litty, Jr.	Jupiter	
Capt. Jack Lloyd	Naples	
Walton T. Locke, Jr.	Pt. Charlotte	
Theodore Locker	Placida	
Kevin A. Long	Naples	
E. L. Long	Destin	
James E. Long	Homosassa Springs	
James V. Lopez	Islamorada	
Patrick J. Lovetro	Ft. Myers	
David J. Lowell	Islamorada	
H. Durance Lowendick	Cape Coral	
Capt. James Lozar	Islamorada	
Kevin Lubold	Englewood	
W. Lee Lucas	Duck Key	
Theodore K. Lund	Satellite	
Paul Lundquist	Sarasota	
Jeffrey S. Lyle	Tampa	
William F. Lyles	Homosassa	
Charles F. & Dan F. Mabius	Panama City	
Lewis W. MacDonald	N. Ft. Myers	
Edward J. Macko	St. James City	
Gordon H. Maclane	Panama City	
Gary Maconi	Key West	
Joseph W. Madden	Pensacola	
O. Dean Madison	Titusville	
Stephen C. Magee	Sugarloaf Key	
Richard Mager	Key West	
Michael C. Maher	Vero Beach	
Nicholas Malinovsky	Sugarloaf Key	
Benjamin F. Malinowski	Steinhatchee	
Michael George Malinowski	Hypoluxo	
Ronald J. Mallet	Davie	
Dan W. Malon	Tampa	
Kevin A. Malone	Ft. Lauderdale	
Capt. Dan Malzone	Tampa	
Glen Philip Manchester	Ft. Pierce	
Douglas Wayne Mandel	Pensacola	
Capt. Michael D. Mann	Melbourne	
Michael D. Manning	Pt. Richey	
Paul Marchan	Key West	
Davis L. Markett, Jr.	Tampa	
Leroy L. Marks	Pensacola	
T.P. Marquis	Big Pine Key	
Burton R. Marsh	Ft. Myers	
Linwood A. Martens	Ft. Pierce	
Capt. Roger Martin	Islamorada	
Richard D. Martin	W. Melbourne	
Kenneth Martina	Apalachicola	
Robert Marvin	Naples	
Capt. Bob Marvin	Naples	
Joseph A. Marzella	Bokeelia	
Thomas Mascari	Miami	
Walter B. Massey, III	Pensacola	
Mikel D. Masters	Clearwater	
Alton Matchett	Pensacola	
Richard A. Matre	Treasure Island	
John Bradford May	Quincy	
Ronald Maze	Englewood	
Dennis W. McAllister	Marco Island	
Capt. Denny McAllister	Marco Island	
Jonathan S. McBride	Tavernier	
Daniel J. McCarthy	Key Largo	
Gordon B. McCormack	Panama City Beach	
August R. McCullough, Jr.	St. Petersburg	
Robert McDaris	Talahassee	
William G. McDevitt	Estero	
William J. McDonald	Destin	
Michael J. McDonald	Bonita Springs	
Kevin P. McDonough	Longwood	
Sean A. McGarry	Ft. Myers	
Phillip McGinn	Key West	

Company
Contact John T. McGowen
City Panama City Beach
Company
Contact Jay McGowen
City Satellite Beach
Company
Contact Dan McGrew
City St. James City
Company
Contact David P. McGriff, III
City Perry
Company
Contact Phillip McKenna
City Miami
Company
Contact James B. McKillip
City Key West
Company
Contact Albert E. McKinley, III
City Ft. Myers Beach
Company
Contact Donovan McKinney
City Chokoloskee
Company
Contact Sandy McKinney
City Key West
Company
Contact Joe R. McKinney
City Panama City
Company
Contact Robert M. McMahon
City Deerfield Beach
Company
Contact Jean McMillian
City St. George Island
Company
Contact Corey L. McMillin
City Chokiloskee
Company
Contact Gerard F. McNeil
City Naples
Company
Contact Timothy H. McOsker
City Englewood
Company
Contact Bruce A. McVey
City Brooksville
Company
Contact Joseph W. Meadows
City Plant City
Company
Contact Gregory D. Meeks
City Panama City Beach
Company
Contact Ralph M. Melby
City Homestead
Company
Contact Robert A. Melvin, IV
City Boca Grande
Company
Contact William Melvin
City Boca Grande
Company
Contact Joseph E. & Sandra Mercurio
City Key West
Company
Contact Jess P. Mesmer
City Ft. Myers
Company
Contact George E. Metcalf
City Panacea
Company
Contact Stephen P. Metzger
City Key Largo
Company
Contact Steven B. Mevers
City Cape Coral
Company
Contact Ward Michaels
City Orlando
Company
Contact Carol L. Mick
City Hudson
Company
Contact James William Midelis, Jr.
City Ft. Pierce
Company
Contact Inc. Capt. Mike III
City Islamorada
Company
Contact Jason Mikel
City Destin
Company
Contact Douglas P. Mikesell
City Venice

Company
Contact Douglas L. Milanak
City Pensacola
Company
Contact Capt. Matt A. Miller
City Islamorada
Company
Contact William D. Miller
City Tampa
Company
Contact Capt. Carl I. Miller
City Bradenton
Company
Contact Gen. Glen Miller
City Tavernier
Company
Contact John Miller
City Chokoloskee
Company
Contact Bruce Miller
City Naples
Company
Contact Gail Ann Miller
City Key West
Company
Contact Capt. Bruce Miller
City Key Largo
Company
Contact Max B. Miller
City Everglades City
Company
Contact Leonce J. Miller
City Sanibel
Company
Contact Richard A. Miller
City Tavernier
Company
Contact George H. Miller
City Key West
Company
Contact Robert A. Miller
City Seminole
Company
Contact Patrick G. Millican
City Oldsmar
Company
Contact Katherine M. Minardi
City Astatula
Company
Contact Capt. Larry Miniard
City Jacksonville
Company
Contact David Minton
City Marathon
Company
Contact David S. Mistretta
City Indian Rocks Beach
Company
Contact Dvaid W. Mitchell
City Key West
Company
Contact Robert Mitchell
City Islamorada
Company
Contact Clare Mitchell
City Miami
Company
Contact Chris Mitchell
City Boca Grande
Company
Contact Richard A. Mitchell
City Islamorada
Company
Contact Charles J. Mizenis
City Wabasso
Company
Contact Richard A. Moeller
City Islamorada
Company
Contact Leonard Moffo
City Big Pine Key
Company
Contact Lawrence R. Mohrmann
City Homasassa Springs
Company
Contact David M. Monda
City Sarasota
Company
Contact Phillip M. Money
City Panama City
Company
Contact Daniel M. Montagna
City Clearwater
Company
Contact Robert M. Montgomery
City Miami

Company
Contact Gene D. Montgomery
City Pt. Charlotte
Company
Contact Robert N. Montuoro
City Vero Beach
Company
Contact Eugene Moore
City Summerland Key
Company
Contact David Moore
City Panama City
Company
Contact Tyson S. Moore
City Pt. Orange
Company
Contact W. B. Moore
City Carrabelle
Company
Contact James L. Moore
City Miami
Company
Contact Scott K. Moore
City Holmes Beach
Company
Contact Michael G. & Lisa M. Moore
City Panama City
Company
Contact Robert Moore
City Pt. Charlotte
Company
Contact Tyson Moore
City Pt. Orange
Company
Contact Andrew Moret
City Islamorada
Company
Contact Lewis W. Morgan, Jr.
City Rotonda West
Company
Contact Robert L. Morgan
City Steinhatchee
Company
Contact Eugene F. Moriarty
City Islamorada
Company
Contact Donald M. Morrell
City Panama City
Company
Contact Jerald L. Morris
City Key Largo
Company
Contact Wilbur B. Mosseller
City Edgewater
Company
Contact Capt. Doug Motley
City Naples
Company
Contact Allen & Beulah Moudy
City Ft. Lauderdale
Company
Contact Elias S. Mourra
City Spring Hill
Company
Contact Brian J. Mowatt
City Pt. Charlotte
Company
Contact Joel Thomas Moye
City Pensacola
Company
Contact Richard H. Muldrow
City Ocala
Company
Contact John A. Mullen
City Cocoa
Company
Contact Capt. Stacy Mullendore
City Naples
Company
Contact Donald D. Mullis
City Pt. St. Joe
Company
Contact Michael Mumma
City Sarasota
Company
Contact Paul Muniz
City Key West
Company
Contact Gil Muratori
City Miami
Company
Contact John Murkerson
City Ft. Myers
Company
Contact Jerry M. Murphy
City Pembroke Pines

Company
Contact Daniel R. Murray
City Holiday
Company
Contact James A. Myers
City N. Ft. Myers
Company
Contact Boyd Myers
City Stuart
Company
Contact Joseph D. Myrick
City Carrabelle
Company
Contact Grandon E. Naeve
City Nokomis
Company
Contact Theodore N. Naftal, Jr.
City Marco Island
Company
Contact Richard C. Nagel
City Riviera Beach
Company
Contact Abbie Napier
City Cedar Key
Company
Contact Timothy D. Nease
City Islamorada
Company
Contact Brad Neat
City Key Largo
Company
Contact Paul & Helen Nelson
City Pt. Orange
Company
Contact Richard T. Nelson
City Pembroke Pines
Company
Contact William Owen Nelson
City Ft. Walton Beach
Company
Contact Danny Nelson
City Apalachicola
Company
Contact Fred S. Nichols
City Lakeland
Company
Contact Niel Nielsen, III
City Islamorada
Company
Contact Russell C. Nixdorf, Jr.
City Jupiter
Company
Contact Mervin Noble
City Naples
Company
Contact Dennis Noble
City Everglades City
Company
Contact Greg C. Noble
City Santa Rosa Beach
Company
Contact Roger B. Nodruff
City Ft. Myers
Company
Contact Capt. Chuck Nolan
City Islamorada
Company
Contact Thomas J. Nolt
City Tavernier
Company
Contact Richard W. Norling
City Key Largo
Company
Contact David Norman
City Marathon
Company
Contact William T. Norred
City Ft. Walton Beach
Company
Contact Sidney Noyes
City Marathon
Company
Contact William E. O'Connell
City Marathon
Company
Contact John R. O'Leary
City Edgewater
Company
Contact Brian O'Meara
City Key West
Company
Contact James O'Neil
City Key Biscayne
Company
Contact James P. O'Neill
City Bradenton

Company
Contact Albert & Josephine Oakley
City Ft. Lauderdale
Company
Contact Michael D. Obeginski
City Ft. Myers
Company
Contact Douglas T. Objartel
City Cape Coral
Company
Contact Sean Okeefe
City Key West
Company
Contact William E. Oliver
City Summerland
Company
Contact Erik Olsen
City Vero Beach
Company
Contact Michael Oney
City Deerfield Beach
Company
Contact Robert Orlando
City Cape Coral
Company
Contact Kenneth S. Orthner
City Largo
Company
Contact Alv Osteen
City Ft. Walton Beach
Company
Contact Robert J. Ostrom
City Lakeland
Company
Contact Henry K. Otto, Jr.
City Key West
Company
Contact Thomas E. Owen
City Bradenton Beach
Company
Contact James L. Owens
City Crystal River
Company
Contact John Owens
City Key West
Company
Contact C.F. Gonzales, MD, PA
City Crystal River
Company
Contact Harry Padgett, Jr.
City Crystal River
Company
Contact Philip R. Pallot
City Mims
Company
Contact Thomas B. Palmer
City Spring Hill
Company
Contact Robert D. Panazze
City Tampa
Company
Contact Donald E. Parady
City Englewood
Company
Contact Kenneth & Lorraine Parker
City Key West
Company
Contact William E. Parker
City Merritt Island
Company
Contact Capt. Darrick Parker
City Miami
Company
Contact Terry L. Parsons
City Sebastian
Company
Contact Capt. Terry Parsons
City Sebastian
Company
Contact James C. Parsons, Jr.
City Pt. St. Lucie
Company
Contact Manning A. Parsons
City Steinhatchee
Company
Contact Morgan Partners
City Destin
Company
Contact Hargis & Janet Patroni
City Pensacola
Company
Contact Michael J. Patterson
City Tavernier
Company
Contact Frank N. Pawela
City Tavernier

Company
Contact Alex T. Payne
City Ft. Myers
Company
Contact John G. Pearson
City Englewood
Company
Contact Samuel P. Pecorino
City Crystal River
Company
Contact Capt. Jay Peeler
City Goodland
Company
Contact Jack C. Peerson, III
City Destin
Company
Contact John G. Peerson
City Destin
Company
Contact Capt. Russ Pellow
City Islamorada
Company
Contact Gregory F. Penix
City Lakeland
Company
Contact Daniel Pennington
City Ft. Lauderdale
Company
Contact Joe Penovich
City Cape Canaveral
Company
Contact Nelson Perez
City Marathon
Company
Contact Troy Perez
City Cocoa
Company
Contact Roderick L. Perkins
City Key West
Company
Contact John Perry
City Ellenton
Company
Contact James Perry
City Middle Torch Key
Company
Contact Inc. Pescador III
City Destin
Company
Contact Edward R. Peters
City New Pt. Richey
Company
Contact James H. Petersen
City Sugarloaf Key
Company
Contact George Pfeiffer
City Pensacola
Company
Contact Paula J. Phair
City Holiday
Company
Contact Stanley E. Phillips
City Destin
Company
Contact Leslie E. Phillips
City Panama City
Company
Contact Simon Phillips
City Islamorada
Company
Contact Rex Phipps
City Eastpoint
Company
Contact James Pic
City Panama City
Company
Contact Philip Pica
City Naples
Company
Contact Willard J. Pickrel
City Inverness
Company
Contact Thomas G. Pierce
City Key West
Company
Contact Joseph E. Pinder
City Key West
Company
Contact Ricky R. Pitts
City Ft. Myers Beach
Company
Contact Adolph W. Pitts, Jr.
City Cantonment
Company
Contact Robert D. Pitts
City Tampa

Company
Contact Capt. Jeff S. Player
City Naples
Company
Contact William Poertner, III
City Overland Park
Company
Contact Greg Poland
City Miami
Company
Contact Jane S. Polazzo
City Youngstown
Company
Contact Anthony Polizos
City Everglades City
Company
Contact Michael Pollack
City Key West
Company
Contact George M. Pollis
City Jensen Beach
Company
Contact Capt. Al Polofsky
City Islamorada
Company
Contact Capt Albert Ponzoa
City Marathon
Company
Contact Gregory T. Poole
City Indialantic
Company
Contact Charles H. Poor, Jr.
City Panama City Beach
Company
Contact Capt. Joseph A. Porcelli
City Deland
Company
Contact Sidney S. Potter
City Destin
Company
Contact John F. Potter
City Key West
Company
Contact Henry M. Powell
City Key Largo
Company
Contact Bryan K. Pradines
City W. Palm Beach
Company
Contact John C. Preeg
City Naples
Company
Contact James S. Prentice
City Gainesville
Company
Contact Arthur Price
City New Pt. Richey
Company
Contact Robert G. Elliott / Patrick Price
City Pensacola Beach
Company
Contact David Prickett
City Chokoloskee
Company
Contact Capt. Dave Prickett
City Chokoloskee Island
Company
Contact Capt. Dan Prickett
City Chokoloskee Island
Company
Contact Catherine A. Proveaux
City Crystal River
Company
Contact Lawrence M. Proveaux
City Cedar Key
Company
Contact Lawrence B. & Barbara C. Pruett
City Cocoa Beach
Company
Contact Robert M. Puccinelli
City Largo
Company
Contact Richard A. Pugh
City Ft. Myers
Company
Contact Glenn Puopolo
City Naples
Company
Contact Robert D. Purcell
City Marathon
Company
Contact David P. Purdo
City Islamorada
Company

Contact Danwin M. Purdy
City Sugarloaf Shores
Company
Contact Andrew M. Purtill
City Ft. Lauderdale
Company
Contact Rodrick Purves
City Key West
Company
Contact Richard L. Putnam
City Panama City
Company
Contact Placida Queen
City Venice
Company
Contact Larry L. Quick
City Davie
Company
Contact Denis Quilligan
City Tampa
Company
Contact Kathleen Quinn
City Key West
Company
Contact Richard Quirk
City Islamorada
Company
Contact William T. Rabitio
City Marathon
Company
Contact Roy T. Raffield
City Panama City
Company
Contact Michael Theo. Raffield
City Lynn Haven
Company
Contact Michael F. Ragan
City Seminole
Company
Contact Gregory W. Rahe
City Key West
Company
Contact Victor Ramos
City Miami
Company
Contact John A. Ramsey
City Carrabelle
Company
Contact Morton H. Rappaport
City Jupiter
Company
Contact Roy E. & Myrtle I. Ray
City Youngstown
Company
Contact Joseph Re
City Tavernier
Company
Contact Frank W. Ready
City Destin
Company
Contact Bart Ream
City Cape Coral
Company
Contact Ronald Rebeck
City Debary
Company
Contact Capt. Adam Redford
City Miami
Company
Contact William F. Reed
City Grove City
Company
Contact David E. Reese
City Pensacola
Company
Contact Capt. Gary Rehm
City Islamorada
Company
Contact Robert Reineman
City Islamorada
Company
Contact Joseph T. Reis
City Tarpon Springs
Company
Contact Ross M. Rembert
City Pensacola
Company
Contact John Renner
City Delray Beach
Company
Contact Frank Reno
City Marathon
Company
Contact Matthew J. Repic
City Florida City
Company

Contact Scott Fagan / James Revelle
City Ft. Pierce
Company
Contact Ronald J. Reynolds
City Brandon
Company
Contact Kirk Reynolds
City Destin
Company
Contact Ray Rhash
City Marathon
Company
Contact Brian David Rhodes
City Islamorada
Company
Contact Russell G. Rhodes
City Destin
Company
Contact Manuel R. Riano
City Miami
Company
Contact Arno J. Rice
City Islamorada
Company
Contact Edward Richards
City Homosassa
Company
Contact Ronald R. Richards
City Spring Hill
Company
Contact John L. Riddick
City Tavernier
Company
Contact Phillip W. Ridge
City Marco Island
Company
Contact Sandra C. Rieger
City Stuart
Company
Contact Michael B. Riggs
City Boca Grande
Company
Contact William Del Rio
City Summerland Key
Company
Contact Leonard P. Rising
City Ellenton
Company
Contact Kenneth & Rebecca Riso
City N. Palm Beach
Company
Contact Rodney D. Ristau
City New Pt. Richey
Company
Contact Norman Ritchey
City Big Pine Key
Company
Contact Richard C. Robeen
City Ft. Walton Beach
Company
Contact William P. Roberts
City Cedar Key
Company
Contact Jack Roberts
City Tavernier
Company
Contact James Robertson
City Rotonda West
Company
Contact Neville D. Robeson
City Ft. Myers
Company
Contact Vernon Robey
City Summerland Key
Company
Contact Christopher J. and Thomas H. Robinson, Jr.
City Eastpoint
Company
Contact Joseph A. Robinson
City Islamorada
Company
Contact Thomas D. Robinson
City Naples
Company
Contact John C. Robinson
City Cudjoe Key
Company
Contact Robert Rodgers
City Tavernier
Company
Contact Michael Rodriguez
City Hollywood
Company
Contact Reinaldo Rodriguez
City Ft. Myers

Company
Contact Raymond B. Rodriguez
City Boca Grande
Company
Contact Bob Rogers
City Key West
Company
Contact David Rojas
City Destin
Company
Contact James E. Rollins
City Palm City
Company
Contact Todd R. Romine
City Bradenton
Company
Contact John Walter Romish
City Inverness
Company
Contact Chris H. Roningen
City Englewood
Company
Contact Richard Earl Ross, Jr.
City W. Palm Beach
Company
Contact Peter S. Ross
City Islamorada
Company
Contact David Rountree
City St. Petersburg
Company
Contact John M. Roush
City Homosassa
Company
Contact Frank L. Roush
City Homosassa
Company
Contact Louis L. Roux
City Apalachicola
Company
Contact Capt. Diego Rouylle
City Marathon
Company
Contact Capt. Tom Rowland
City Ramrod Key
Company
Contact Thomas Rowland
City Key West
Company
Contact Kenneth E. Roy
City Crystal River
Company
Contact Capt. John C. Royall
City Merritt Island
Company
Contact John Rudzin
City Marathon
Company
Contact Capt. Frederick Ruoff
City Islamorada
Company
Contact Rocky L. Russ
City Boca Grande
Company
Contact Richard Russell
City Marco Island
Company
Contact William D. Russell
City Matlacha
Company
Contact Jim Russell
City Tampa
Company
Contact Craig A. Rust
City Cocoa
Company
Contact Kenneth A. Ruszenas
City W. Palm Beach
Company
Contact Phares B. Rutt
City Nokomis
Company
Contact Harold W. & Phyllis Ryals
City Panama City
Company
Contact William G. Saalman, III
City St. Petersburg
Company
Contact Robert Sabatino
City Captiva Island
Company
Contact Michael P. Sabo
City Destin
Company
Contact Richard L. Saddler
City Key West

Company
Contact Robert T. Sadousky
City Perry

Company
Contact Joseph F. Salomone
City Islamorada

Company
Contact Capt. Frank Salomonsen
City Cudjoe Key

Company
Contact Frank Salomonsen
City Cudjoe Key

Company
Contact Warren R. Sanders
City Daytona Beach

Company
Contact James T. Sanders, Jr.
City Ft. Myers

Company
Contact Vinny Sangermano
City Key West

Company
Contact Troy P. Sapp
City Lutz

Company
Contact W. E. Saunders
City Key West

Company
Contact Albert F. Savill
City Key West

Company
Contact Chris Savoy
City Key West

Company
Contact Devin D. Scarborough
City Hudson

Company
Contact Capt. JEsse Scarbrough
City Key West

Company
Contact Rodney B. Schiffner
City Englewood

Company
Contact Randall Schilling
City Panama City Beach

Company
Contact Victor Schilling
City Winter Park

Company
Contact Mark L. Schindel
City Sarasota

Company
Contact Capt. Dave Schlager
City Islamorada

Company
Contact Capt. Art Schmadtke
City Naples

Company
Contact Mark T. Schmidt
City Summerland Key

Company
Contact Arthur Henry Schmidt, II
City Homosassa Springs

Company
Contact Thomas W. Schmitz
City Destin

Company
Contact Edward Schneider
City Marco Island

Company
Contact Marian Schneider
City Placida

Company
Contact Jack Schneider
City Marathon

Company
Contact Randy L. Schwab
City Indian Rocks Beach

Company
Contact Matthew W. Schwarck
City Marathon

Company
Contact Capt. Bill Schwicker
City Big Pine Key

Company
Contact Charles A. Scott
City Lynn Haven

Company
Contact Frederic E. Scott
City Boca Grande

Company
Contact Michael Seeman
City Bonita Springs

Company
Contact Christopher H. Seger
City Sarasota

Company
Contact Daniel Seijas
City Hernando

Company
Contact Thomas W. Seiling
City Marathon

Company
Contact Danny W. Sellers
City St. Marks

Company
Contact John F. Sells
City Captiva

Company
Contact Jon Sen
City Merritt Island

Company
Contact Jay Senne
City Grant

Company
Contact John E. Settle
City Crystal River

Company
Contact Fred Severino
City Cedar Key

Company
Contact G. T. & Wilma Sewell
City Panama City

Company
Contact Erwin Albert Sexton
City Crystal River

Company
Contact Thomas M. Shadley
City Naples

Company
Contact Keith E. Shaffer
City Key West

Company
Contact Eric L. Shapiro
City Tampa

Company
Contact Marvin J. Shaw
City OldTown

Company
Contact Capt. Leonard M. Shaw
City Tavernier

Company
Contact Terrence J. Shea
City Marco Island

Company
Contact Gregory E. Sheretz
City Key West

Company
Contact Edward T. Shields
City Ft. Walton Beach

Company
Contact John D. Shields
City Naples

Company
Contact James C. Shipley
City Seminole

Company
Contact R. D. Boudreau / R. J. Shirer
City Destin

Company
Contact Russell M. Shirley
City S. Pasadena

Company
Contact Christopher Shoemaker
City Cape Coral

Company
Contact Edward C. Shortwell, III
City Hobe Sound

Company
Contact Wayne Shuff
City Plant City

Company
Contact Peter M. Sieglaff, Jr.
City Boca Grande

Company
Contact Vera J. Sierra
City Holmes Beach

Company
Contact Harvey Roy Silvers
City Sanibel

Company
Contact Daryl & Cindy Simeon
City Key West

Company
Contact Dexter Simmons
City Key West

Company
Contact Charles K. Sine
City Hobe Sound

Company
Contact David T. Sisung
City Islamorada

Company
Contact Charles Skinner
City Sanibel

Company
Contact Gary L. Skrobeck
City Islamorada

Company
Contact John W. Skrycki
City Loxahatchee

Company
Contact Roy Slagado
City Anna Maria

Company
Contact Mark Slatko
City Surfside

Company
Contact Timothy J. Slaught
City Homosassa

Company
Contact Ernie D. Small
City Singer Island

Company
Contact Randolph W. Small
City Islamorada

Company
Contact Glenn Smith
City Goodland

Company
Contact William E. Smith
City Suwannee

Company
Contact Gerald R. Smith
City Boca Grande

Company
Contact Robert Smith
City Sarasota

Company
Contact Edward G. Smith
City Seminole

Company
Contact Timothy A. Smith
City Rotonda West

Company
Contact Thomas E. Smith
City Parrish

Company
Contact Jep D. Smith
City Carrabelle

Company
Contact Thomas D. Smith
City Key Largo

Company
Contact Philip H. Smith
City Marco Island

Company
Contact Jeffrey A. Smith
City Naples

Company
Contact Randolph W. Smith
City Pembroke Pines

Company
Contact Paul Smith
City Pineland

Company
Contact Ronald Smith
City Cape Coral

Company
Contact Billy Snider
City Sugarloaf Shores

Company
Contact Henry M. Snow
City Marathon

Company
Contact Anthony M. Soldano
City Key West

Company
Contact R. S. South
City N. Ft. Myers

Company
Contact Michael H. Sovan
City Englewood

Company
Contact John Spear, Jr.
City Marathon

Company
Contact Sumpn Special
City Islamorada

Company
Contact Gary L. Sperl
City Islamorada

Company
Contact John W. Spinks
City Pt. Charlotte

Company
Contact Daniel R. Spisak
City Englewood

Company
Contact Gary Pitts, Sr.
City St. George Island

Company
Contact Bryan Michael Stafford
City Spring Hill

Company
Contact Bruce Stagg
City Key Largo

Company
Contact Leonard N. Stamos
City St. Petersburg Beach

Company
Contact Richard Stanczyk
City Islamorada

Company
Contact Fred Standard
City Crystal River

Company
Contact Maxie L. Stanford
City Ft. Myers

Company
Contact Harold Staples, Jr.
City Destin

Company
Contact Dan Starkey
City Daytona Beach

Company
Contact Don R. Starner
City Boca Grande

Company
Contact Greg Stearn
City Islamorada

Company
Contact Capt. Ned C. Stearns
City Marathon

Company
Contact Dean E. Steffen
City Flamingo

Company
Contact Charles J. Steger
City Key West

Company
Contact Arthur Stelfox
City Marathon

Company
Contact Lee D. Stelter
City Destin

Company
Contact Jay F. & Wylie M. Stephens
City Pensacola

Company
Contact Thomas J. Stephens
City Steinhatchee

Company
Contact Robert A. Stevenson
City Ft. Lauderdale

Company
Contact Wilmer D. Stewart
City Boca Grande

Company
Contact Steven Stier
City Naples

Company
Contact Sophia M. Stiffler
City Everglades City

Company
Contact Sophia Stiffler
City Everglades City

Company
Contact Richard J. Stiglitz
City Marathon

Company
Contact Charles A. Stivers
City Tavernier

Company
Contact James G. Stone
City Gulf Breeze

Company
Contact John V. Stoppelbein, III
City Goodland

Company
Contact Anthony Stout
City Cape Coral

Company
Contact Wallace O. Stovall, Jr.
City Tarpon Springs

Company
Contact Thomas Strayer
City N. Ft. Myers

Company
Contact Rosalie H. Stribling
City Dunedin

Company
Contact Gene K. Strickland
City Talahassee

Company
Contact Jones Natteal Strother
City Crystal River

Company
Contact Gene E. Struthers
City Tarpon Springs

Company
Contact Warren A. Sturgis
City Madeira Beach

Company
Contact Norman R. Suarez
City Pensacola

Company
Contact John J. Sullivan
City Homestead

Company
Contact Rocky A. Sullivan
City Ft. Myers

Company
Contact Barry W. Sullivan
City Destin

Company
Contact Robert F. Sullivan
City Boca Grande

Company
Contact Patti A. Sunderland-Osier
City Merritt Island

Company
Contact Capt. John Sutter
City Islamorada

Company
Contact Michael Sweeterman
City Englewood

Company
Contact Charles M. Talkington
City Plant City

Company
Contact Thomas J. Tallias
City Boca Grande

Company
Contact Thomas J. Tamanini
City Odessa

Company
Contact Brett V. Taporowski
City Big Pine Key

Company
Contact Clifford Tatje
City Islamorada

Company
Contact Allen Taube
City Key West

Company
Contact Charles W. Taverner
City Chokoloskee

Company
Contact Capt. Peter C. Taves
City Lakeland

Company
Contact Capt. James Taylor
City Key Largo

Company
Contact Capt. Ben Taylor
City Tavernier

Company
Contact Billy Joe Teems
City Destin

Company
Contact Paul Tejera
City Tavernier

Company
Contact Richard L. Terhune
City Jensen Beach

Company
Contact Wade Tesar
City Panama City Beach

Company
Contact Martha L. Tew
City Panama City

Company
Contact John P. Thomas
City Largo

Company
Contact Jack K. Thomas
City Sanibel

Company
Contact Frank J. Thomas
City Islamorada

Company
Contact James M. Thomas
City Ft. Lauderdale

Company
Contact Gary Thompson
City Copeland

Company
Contact Keith A. Thompson
City Marco Island

Company
Contact Andrew Thompson
City Homestead
Company
Contact Ernest F. Thompson
City Naples
Company
Contact Melvin D. Thorpe
City Suwannee
Company
Contact Duane L. Tibbetts
City Homosassa
Company
Contact Robert Tiburzi
City Islamorada
Company
Contact William M. Timllin
City Navarre
Company
Contact Thomas A. Tinacci
City Siesta Key
Company
Contact Robert Tittle
City Marathon
Company
Contact Phil Tollman
City Stuart
Company
Contact Erik Tomlinson
City Pt. St. Joe
Company
Contact Mario C. Del Toro
City Islamorada
Company
Contact Capt. W.J. Torpey
City Sanibel
Company
Contact William J. Torpy, Jr.
City Sanibel
Company
Contact Jeffrey A. Totten
City Englewood
Company
Contact Capt. Randy S. Towe
City Islamorada
Company
Contact James W. Townsend
City Clearwater
Company
Contact Thomas H. Tripp
City Key West
Company
Contact Ernest A. Troad II
City Homestead
Company
Contact Robert Trosset
City Key West
Company
Contact Mark A. Tryon
City Gulf Breeze
Company
Contact John J. Turcot
City Titusville
Company
Contact Thomas H. Turke
City Tampa
Company
Contact Kip Turner
City Charlotte Harbor
Company
Contact John D. Turner
City Destin
Company
Contact Chris & Jaclyn Turner
City St. Petersburg Beach
Company
Contact Paul J. Turner
City Titusville
Company
Contact Clyde E. Upchurch
City Islamorada
Company
Contact Duane Urban
City St. James City
Company
Contact Norman F. & Jo Ann Ussery
City Panama City Beach
Company
Contact Arthur Vacca
City Key West
Company
Contact Ada Valiente-Garcia
City N. Miami Beach
Company
Contact Capt. Wally Valleau
City Marco Island

Company
Contact Charles Valleau
City Marco Island
Company
Contact Ray A. Van Horn
City Tarpon Springs
Company
Contact Michael J. Van Nostrand
City Hollywood
Company
Contact Kent Van Winkle
City Miami
Company
Contact Dzadovsky & Vandelaar
City Key Largo
Company
Contact Henry C. Vanderhoeven
City Edgewater
Company
Contact Earl N. Vanhart
City Sebastian
Company
Contact Hank Vankesteren
City Cape Coral
Company
Contact Donna Vankirk
City Marathon
Company
Contact Robert Varga
City Ft. Lauderdale
Company
Contact Ralph Varnes
City Apalachicola
Company
Contact Louis H. & Janet E. Vasel
City Marco Island
Company
Contact Brian G. Vaughan
City Naples
Company
Contact Don S. Vaughn
City Davie
Company
Contact Ronnie L. Vaught
City Cedar Key
Company
Contact Charles Veach
City Key West
Company
Contact Bill Veal
City Steinhatchee
Company
Contact Fred A. Vendenbroeck
City Punta Gorda
Company
Contact Fred F. Verzone
City Valrico
Company
Contact John S. Vest
City Bonita Springs
Company
Contact Barbara A. Vick
City N. Palm Beach
Company
Contact Peter Villani
City Naples
Company
Contact Gilbert A. Viola
City Ft. Myers
Company
Contact Brian D. Vis
City Englewood
Company
Contact Virgil Vollmar
City Bokeelia
Company
Contact William L. Wade
City Vero Beach
Company
Contact Robert Wagner
City Steinhatchee
Company
Contact Capt. Hans K. Wagner
City Marathon
Company
Contact William A. Wagner, Jr.
City Duck Key
Company
Contact Paul Dale Wagner
City Destin
Company
Contact Capt. Ron Wagner
City Islamorada
Company
Contact Ron Wagner
City Islamorada

Company
Contact Karl Wagner
City Marathon
Company
Contact Allen B. Walburn
City Naples
Company
Contact Barbara A. Waldrop
City Destin
Company
Contact Edward Walker
City Palm Harbor
Company
Contact William S. Walker
City Destin
Company
Contact W. Scott Walker
City Duck Key
Company
Contact Charles R. Walker, Jr.
City Pinellas Park
Company
Contact Robert W. Wall
City Vero Beach
Company
Contact William J. Walsh
City Marco Island
Company
Contact Thomas J. Walsh
City St. James City
Company
Contact Edgar O. Walter
City Destin
Company
Contact Richard A. Walter
City Anna Maria
Company
Contact Bobby & Elizabeth Walter
City Destin
Company
Contact Ronald Walters
City Eastpoint
Company
Contact David Walters
City Homosassa
Company
Contact Mark Ward
City Naples
Company
Contact Darrell Ward
City Apalachicola
Company
Contact Ron Ward
City Summerland Key
Company
Contact Michael N. Ware
City Panama City
Company
Contact Gary S. Ware
City Panama City
Company
Contact Robert A. Waterhouse
City Big Pine Key
Company
Contact Earl E. Waters, II
City Homosassa
Company
Contact Winzalo T. Watkins, Jr.
City Crystal River
Company
Contact Capt. Danny Watkins
City Clewiston
Company
Contact William E. Watts
City Crawfordville
Company
Contact Steven L. Waugh
City Ft. Myers
Company
Contact Anclote Marine Ways
City Tarpon Springs
Company
Contact Russell Webb
City Cape Coral
Company
Contact Joseph D. Webb, Jr.
City Anna Maria
Company
Contact Capt. John Weeks
City Naples
Company
Contact Charles N. Weeks
City Bonita Springs
Company
Contact Johnnie Weeks
City Naples

Company
Contact Michael E. Weiler
City Brandon
Company
Contact Jodi Lee Weis
City Marco Island
Company
Contact Stephanie Schlmarman Weis
City Marco Island
Company
Contact Jody Lee Weis
City Marco Island
Company
Contact Kenneth L. Weiss
City Treasure Island
Company
Contact John H. Wells
City Crystal River
Company
Contact James C. Wells
City Marathon
Company
Contact Robert M. Welniak
City Destin
Company
Contact William E. Wert
City Islamorada
Company
Contact Michael & Helen Wertheimer
City Palm Bay
Company
Contact Capt. Jody P. Wesley
City Freeport
Company
Contact Charles Wetterman
City Key Largo
Company
Contact Albert P. Whaley
City Talahassee
Company
Contact David L Wheat
City Warrington
Company
Contact David L. Wheat
City Warrington
Company
Contact Wayne K. Whidden
City Naples
Company
Contact William L. White
City Bradenton
Company
Contact Duane E. White
City Naples
Company
Contact W. B. Whitmore, Jr.
City Sarasota
Company
Contact William Whitney
City Duck Key
Company
Contact Clark L. Whitt
City Key West
Company
Contact Robert L. Whittle
City Ft. Myers
Company
Contact Gary Paul Whorton
City Ramrod Key
Company
Contact David A. Wiater, Jr.
City Marco Island
Company
Contact Jerome G. Widrig
City Talahassee
Company
Contact Capt. Joe Wierback
City Naples
Company
Contact Capt. Joe Wierback
City Naples
Company
Contact William F. Wietcha, II
City Miami
Company
Contact Charles E. Wightman
City Islamorada
Company
Contact Oscar R. Wijtenburg
City Islamorada
Company
Contact Capt. Oscar Wijtenburg
City Islamorada
Company
Contact David Wiley

City Ramrod Key
Company
Contact Maurice G. Wilkins
City Marathon
Company
Contact Raymond J. Williams
City Homasassa Springs
Company
Contact Marvin L. Williams
City Crystal River
Company
Contact Jerry Bryant & Chris Williams
City Lake City
Company
Contact Capt. Dick Williams
City Chokoloskee
Company
Contact Larry I. Williams
City Cedar Key
Company
Contact Richard J. Williams
City Islamorada
Company
Contact James H. Williams, Jr.
City Key West
Company
Contact Alec H. Williams
City Homosassa
Company
Contact Larry D. Williams
City Destin
Company
Contact James H. Williams
City Palmetto
Company
Contact Arthur J. Williams
City Tavernier
Company
Contact Allan L. Williamson
City Clearwater
Company
Contact Brian P. Williamson
City Vero Beach
Company
Contact William M. Willis
City Apalachicola
Company
Contact John S. Wilson
City Palm City
Company
Contact Joanne Wilson
City Key Largo
Company
Contact David Wilson
City Islamorada
Company
Contact Edward Wilson
City Islamorada
Company
Contact Bruce Wilson
City Islamorada
Company
Contact Allen Winchel
City Lake Worth
Company
Contact Henry I. & Edna W. Windes
City Destin
Company
Contact Kelly Windes
City Destin
Company
Contact Raymond C. & Susan K. Winston
City Panama City
Company
Contact Lee C. Winston-Burnette
City Sarasota
Company
Contact Vernon Winters
City Pt. Charlotte
Company
Contact Terrence Winters
City Pt. Charlotte
Company
Contact Lee C. Winton-Bunette
City Sarasota
Company
Contact Steven Wise
City Bokeelia
Company
Contact James p. Wisner
City Tampa
Company
Contact Robert Witt
City Crystal River
Company

Contact Alan Wittersheim
City Islamorada
Company
Contact William F. Wolfe, Jr.
City Ft. Pierce
Company
Contact James E. Wood
City Terra Ceia
Company
Contact Charles Wood
City Perry
Company
Contact Todd E. Wood
City Gulfport
Company
Contact Lem P. Woods
City Boca Grande
Company
Contact Leonard Woodward
City Destin
Company
Contact Lloyd L. Wruble
City Miami
Company
Contact Fred Wyrosdick
City Panama City
Company
Contact William D. Wyss
City Key Largo
Company
Contact Thomas H. Yager
City St. James City
Company
Contact Mark S. Yanno
City Vero Beach
Company
Contact Wilson S. Yanson, Jr.
City Lynn Haven
Company
Contact Richard Yant
City Lecanto
Company
Contact Hal Yarbrough
City St. Petersburg Beach
Company
Contact Joe Yarbrough
City S. Daytona
Company
Contact George M. Yates
City Lake City
Company
Contact Jon M. Yeager
City Palmetto
Company
Contact Gerald Youmans
City Miami
Company
Contact Richard Younger
City Ft. Myers
Company
Contact John Lindley Yow, III
City Bonita Springs
Company
Contact James A. Zacharias
City Cortez
Company
Contact Robert F. Zales
City Panama City
Company
Contact L. David Zalewski
City Redington Beach
Company
Contact Jimmy W. Zeigler
City Orlando
Company
Contact Charles F. Zodrow, Jr.
City Dunedin
Company
Contact Jon Paul Zorian
City Brandon
Company
Contact Michael Zubak
City Ocean Ridge

Georgia

Company Bienville Plantation
Contact Steve Barras
City Macon
Company Bush Ventures
Contact Peter Turcotte
City Ranger

Company Come Away Plantation
Contact Jodie M. Gunter
City Norwood
Company Cross Mountain Adventures, LLC
Contact Danny Moree
City Ray City
Company Highland Marina & Resort
Contact George Marovich
City LaGrange
Company Little Saint Simons Island
Contact
City Saint Simons Island
Company Lone Cone Outfitters, Inc.
Contact Ron M. Clements
City Hartwell
Company Mountain Wilderness Outfitters
Contact Jim Garmon
City Hiram
Company Myrtlewood Sporting Clays
Contact Robert E. Carson
City Thomasville
Company Raven Fishin' Physician
Contact Joseph Turcotte
City Ranger
Company Riverview Plantation
Contact Cader B. Cox, III
City Camilla
Company Silver Bullet Outfitters, Inc.
Contact Robert W. May
City Marietta
Company The Lodge at Cabin Bluff
Contact
City Sea Island
Company Unicoi Outfitters
Contact
City Helen
Company Wilderness Trout
Contact
City Eastonollee
Company
Contact Capt. Larry Kennedy
City Saint Simons Island

Hawaii

Company Absolute Sport Fishing
Contact
City Lahaina
Company Ace Sportfishing
Contact
City Lahaina
Company Adobie Sport Fishing
Contact
City Kailua-Kona
Company Aerial Sportfishing
Contact
City Lahaina
Company Aerial Sportfishing
Contact
City Kailua-Kona
Company Ahukini Fishing For Fun
Contact
City Kapaa
Company Alani Moku Corp.
Contact
City Kailua-Kona
Company Alibi Sportfishing
Contact
City Kailua-Kona
Company Alii Kai Sport Fishing
Contact
City Maakilo
Company Aloha Sportfishing & Charters, Inc.
Contact
City Kailua-Kona
Company Alpha-Con, Inc.
Contact
City Kailua-Kona
Company Alyce C. Sport Fishing
Contact
City Kaunakakai
Company Anini Fishing Charters
Contact
City Kilauea
Company Apple Annie's Charters, Inc.
Contact
City Kihei
Company Bali Hai Sport Fishing, Inc.
Contact

City Kailua-Kona
Company Bill Buster Charters
Contact
City Kailua-Kona
Company Blue Hawaii Sportfishing
Contact
City Kailua-Kona
Company Blue Marlin, Inc.
Contact
City Kailua-Kona
Company Blue Nun Sportfishing
Contact
City Honolulu
Company Boomerang Sportfishing
Contact
City Kailua-Kona
Company C Activities
Contact
City Kailua-Kona
Company Carol Ann Charters
Contact
City Kahului
Company Cast & Catch Freshwater Bass Guides
Contact
City Koloa
Company Catchem 1 Sportfishing
Contact
City Kailua-Kona
Company Chiripa Sportfishing, Inc.
Contact
City Kailua-Kona
Company Chupu Charters
Contact
City Haleiwa
Company Coreene-C II Sport Fishing Charters, Inc.
Contact
City Kaneohe
Company De Warrior Sportfishing
Contact
City Kailua-Kona
Company Enterprise Sportfishing
Contact
City Kailua-Kona
Company Finest Kind Sportfishing
Contact
City Lahaina
Company Fly Fish Alaska-Red Quill Lodge
Contact Harold & Katharina Dungate
City Kailua-Kona
Company Foxy Lady Sport Fishing, Inc.
Contact
City Kailua-Kona
Company Gent-Lee Fishing & Sightseeing Charters
Contact
City Lihue
Company Gold Coast Sportfishing
Contact
City Holualoa
Company Golden Eagle Marine Charter Service
Contact
City Honolulu
Company Hanamana S[ortfishing, Inc.
Contact
City Kailua-Kona
Company Hapa Laka Hawaiian Charters
Contact
City Kailua-Kona
Company Happy Times
Contact
City Kailua-Kona
Company Hawaiian Horizons, Ltd.
Contact
City Honolulu
Company High Flier
Contact Dwight & Jeff Metcalf
City Kailua-Kona
Company Holiday Charters
Contact
City Kailua-Kona
Company Holiday Long Range
Contact
City Kailua-Kona
Company Honokohau Boating Ltd.
Contact
City Honualoa
Company Hua Pala Charters
Contact
City Kailua-Kona

Company Hula Girl Sportfishing
Contact
City Kailua-Kona
Company Humdinger Sportfishing
Contact
City Kailua-Kona
Company Huntress Sportfishing
Contact
City Holualoa
Company Ihu Nui Sportfishing, Inc.
Contact
City Kamuela
Company Ilima V Charter Fishing
Contact
City Honolulu
Company Illusions, Inc.
Contact
City Kamuela
Company Impulse Chartes, Inc.
Contact
City Kailua-Kona
Company Intrepid, Inc.
Contact
City Kailua-Kona
Company Island Charters on Aukai
Contact
City Honolulu
Company Island Girl Charters, Inc.
Contact
City Kailua-Kona
Company Islander II Charters
Contact
City Lahaina
Company Jun Ken Po Sportfishing
Contact
City Kailua-Kona
Company Kahuna Kai
Contact
City Kaneohe
Company Kamome Sport Fishing
Contact
City Honolulu
Company Kona Concept, Inc.
Contact
City Kaillua-Kona
Company Kona Sunrise Charters
Contact
City Kailua-Kona
Company Kona Trading Co., Inc.
Contact
City Kailua-Kona
Company Kono Sport Fishing Charters
Contact
City Honolulu
Company Kuhele Kai
Contact
City Kihei
Company Kuu Huapala Fishing Co., Inc.
Contact
City Honolulu
Company Kuuloa Kai Charters
Contact
City Haleiwa
Company Lahaina Charter Boats
Contact
City Lahaina
Company Layla Sportfishing
Contact
City Hailua-Kona
Company Lei Aloha Charter Fishing
Contact
City Kailua-Kona
Company Lil' Hooker Sportfishing
Contact
City Kailua-Kona
Company Live Bait Sportsfishing/Deep Blue Inc.
Contact Captain Dale Simmons
City Waianae
Company Luckey Strike Charters
Contact
City Lahaina
Company Lucky Fisherman Charters
Contact
City Honolulu
Company Lynell Sports Fishing, Inc.
Contact
City Honolulu
Company Maalaea Game Fishing, Inc.
Contact
City Makawao
Company Maggie Joe
Contact
City Honolulu
Company Mana Kai Adventures

Contact
City Koloa
Company Marlin Machine Charters, Inc.
Contact
City Kailua-Kona
Company Marlin Magic Sportfishing, Inc.
Contact
City Kailua-Kona
Company Maui Big Game Fishing
Contact
City Lahaina
Company Meagan Sport Fishing
Contact
City Aiea
Company My Mistress Sportfishing
Contact
City Honolulu
Company No Mercy Sportfishing
Contact
City Kailua-Kona
Company No Strings Sportfishing, Inc.
Contact
City Kailua-Kona
Company Northern Lights Sportfishing
Contact
City Kailua-Kona
Company Ocean Activities Center
Contact
City Kihei
Company Offshore Hunters, Inc.
Contact
City Lahaina
Company Pacific Blue Sport Fishing
Contact
City Honolulu
Company Pacific Blue Water Venture, Inc.
Contact
City Kailua-Kona
Company Pacific Blue, Inc.
Contact
City Kailua-Kona
Company Pamela Big Game Fishing, Inc.
Contact
City Kailua-Kona
Company Peter Rose Corp.
Contact
City Kailua-Kona
Company Phoenix Fishing
Contact
City Honolulu
Company Rascal Charters
Contact
City Kihei
Company Reel Class Sportfishig
Contact
City Kailua-Kona
Company Reel Pleasure Sportfishing
Contact
City Kamuela
Company Renegade Sport Fishing
Contact
City Kailua-Kona
Company Rhythm & Blues Sportfishing, Inc.
Contact
City Kihei
Company Robert McReynolds Fishing Charters
Contact
City Kilauea
Company Sea Dancer Sportfishing, Inc.
Contact
City Kailua-Kona
Company Sea Genie, Inc.
Contact
City Kailua-Kona
Company Sea Hawk
Contact
City Honolulu
Company Sea Lure Fishing Charters
Contact
City Kapaa
Company Sea Strike, Inc.
Contact
City Kailua-Kona
Company Sea Verse Charters
Contact
City Kailua
Company Sea Wife Charters
Contact

City Kailua-Kona
Company Sheer Pleasure Sportfishing
Contact
City Kailua-Kona
Company Shon-A-Lei Sports & Marine
Contact
City Kaunakakai
Company Spellbound Sportfishing
Contact
City Kailua-Kona
Company Spinning Dolphin Charters of Lanai
Contact
City Lanai City
Company Sport Fishing Kauai
Contact
City Koloa
Company Sportfishing Kona, Inc.
Contact
City Kailua-Kona
Company Sports Fishing Specialties
Contact
City Kailua-Kona
Company Stars N Strikes Sportfishing
Contact
City Kailua-Kona
Company Summer Hawk Sportfishing
Contact
City Ewa Beach
Company Summer Rain Sportfishing
Contact
City Kealakekua
Company Sun Seeker Corp.
Contact
City Waikoloa
Company Sundowner Sport Fishing Charters
Contact
City Kailua-Kona
Company TJR Corp.
Contact
City Holualoa
Company Tommy Rietow
Contact
City Lanai City
Company Topsail VIII Charters, Inc.
Contact
City Kailua-Kona
Company Tropical Sun Sportfishing
Contact
City Kailua-Kona
Company True Blue Charters & Ocean Sports
Contact
City Lihue
Company Twin Charters Sportfishing
Contact
City Kailua-Kona
Company Vixon Corp.
Contact
City Kailua-Kona
Company Waikiki Marine Sales
Contact
City Honolulu
Company Wild West Charters
Contact
City Kailau-Kona
Company WMS, Inc.
Contact
City Kailua-Kona

Idaho

Company 62 Ridge Outfitters
Contact Ken & Elizabeth Smith
City Ahsahka
Company A-W Outfitters
Contact Sandy Podsaid
City Hayden Lake
Company Action Hunts
Contact Charles Loeschen
City Sandpoint
Company Alaska Skagway Outfitters
Contact Chadd Harbaugh
City New Plymouth
Company Allison Ranch, Inc.
Contact Harold Thomas
City Boise
Company Anderson Creek Outfitters
Contact Edmondson & Nanette M.

Klingback
City Garden Valley
Company Antelope Valley Outfitters, Inc.
Contact Harold E. Smith, Jr.
City Darlington
Company B-Bar-C Outfitters
Contact Michael J. Stockton
City Orofino
Company Bass Fishing with Darl
Contact Darl Ray Hagey
City Moscow
Company Beamer's Landing/Hells Canyon Tours
Contact Jim & Jill Koch
City Lewiston
Company Blue Ribbon Charters
Contact Richard D. Lindsey
City Coeur d'Alene
Company Bolinder's Country Store
Contact Terry Bolinder
City Firth
Company Boren Outdoor Adventures, Inc.
Contact Elisabeth Boren
City Boise
Company Bressler Outfitters
Contact Gary Beebe
City Victor
Company Bristol Bay Sportfishing, Inc.
Contact Bruce Johnson
City Sandpoint
Company Brundage Mountain Adventures
Contact
City McCall
Company BS Flies & Tackle
Contact Bill Schiess
City Rexburg
Company C & M Adventures
Contact Ryan Miller
City Jerome
Company C & M Adventures
Contact Tim Crist
City Twin Falls
Company C & M Adventures
Contact James Miller
City Salmon
Company Cascade Adventures
Contact Jeff S. Hennessy
City McCall
Company Castle Creek Outfitters & Guest Ranch
Contact Shane & Gwenn McAfee
City Salmon
Company Cayuse Outfitters
Contact Patti & Rich Armiger
City Kamiah
Company Cee-Bar-Dee Outfitters
Contact Darrell Weddle
City Kamiah
Company Clayne Baker's Stonefly Anglers
Contact
City Boise
Company Clearwater River Company
Contact Jim Cook
City Orofino
Company Clifford Cummings Outfitter
Contact Clifford O. Cummings, Jr.
City North Fork
Company Coeur d'Alene Outfitters
Contact Murray D."Bat"Masterson
City Athol
Company Cougar Country Lodge
Contact Jason M. Schultz
City Lewiston
Company Cross Outfitters
Contact Larry W. Cross
City Preston
Company Diamond D Ranch, Inc.
Contact Thomas & Linda Demorest
City Boise
Company Discovery River Expeditions, Inc.
Contact Lester Lowe
City Riggins
Company Dixie Outfitters, Inc.
Contact W. Emmett & Zona Smith
City Dixie
Company Drifters Outfitting
Contact John McClatchy
City Ketchum
Company Drifters of the South Fork
Contact

City Swan Valley
Company E & Z Inc./Whitewater Outfitters
Contact Zeke & Erlene West
City Kamiah
Company Elkhorn Village Stables
Contact Daniel P.Mulick
City Mackay
Company Excel Adventures
Contact Scott Childs
City McCall
Company Exodus Corporation
Contact Jr. & Tony Bradbury Richard A. Bradbury
City Riggins
Company Fall Creek Outfitters
Contact Dalbert (Del) Allmon
City Meridian
Company Fish Creek Lodging
Contact Janet Keefer
City Ashton
Company Flying B Ranch, Inc.
Contact Robert Burlingame & Donald Wilson
City Kamiah
Company George E. Duncan Outfitter
Contact George E. Duncan
City Orofino
Company Gillihan's Guide Service
Contact Robert J.Gillihan
City Big Creek
Company Gilmore Ranch Outfitters & Guides
Contact Charles D. Neill, Jr.
City Grangeville
Company Granite Creek Ranch
Contact Carl Zitlau
City Rigby
Company Guth's Iliamna River Lodge
Contact Norman Guth
City Salmon
Company Hagerman Valley Outfitters, Inc.
Contact Bret C. Silver
City Hagerman
Company Hat Point Outfitters
Contact Marlin & Susan Kennedy
City Kooskia
Company Heart Mountain Outfitters
Contact Timothy N. Thomas
City DuBois
Company Heise Expeditions
Contact Mike Quinn
City Ririe
Company Hell's Canyon Lodge
Contact Reed J. Taylor
City Lewiston
Company Hells Canyon Fishing Charters
Contact Cook & Spickelmire
City Riggins
Company Henry's Fork Anglers
Contact Mike Lawson
City St. Anthony
Company High Adventure Air Charter
Contact Monte Mason
City Twin Falls
Company High Country Outfitters
Contact Ray Seal
City Bellevue
Company High Desert Ranch, Inc.
Contact Jay Reedy & Jeffrey Widener
City Weiser
Company High Roller Excursions
Contact Lee Edding
City Lewiston
Company Hincks Palisades Creek Ranch
Contact Bret Hincks
City Palisades
Company Holiday River Expeditions of Idaho
Contact Harold (Frogg) Stewart
City Grangeville
Company Hyde Outfitters
Contact
City Idaho Falls
Company Idaho Angling Service
Contact David T. Glasscock
City Picabo
Company Idaho Fishing Charters
Contact William J. Spicklemire
City Grangeville
Company Idaho Guide Service, Inc.

Contact James L. Powell
City Meridian
Company Indian Creek Guest Ranch
Contact Jon Bower
City North Fork
Company Inland Charter Service
Contact Cal Butterfield
City Coeur d'Alene
Company Intermountain Excursions
Contact Darell Bentz
City Lewiston
Company J & J Oufitters
Contact James E. Champion
City Irwin
Company Jacobs Island Park Ranch
Contact F.Mitch Jacobs
City Hamer
Company Juniper Mountain Outfitters, Inc.
Contact Stanley & Paul Meholchick
City Caldwell
Company Kingfisher Expeditions
Contact Steve F. Settles
City Salmon
Company Klessig's Guide Service
Contact Jeffrey Klessig
City Kamiah
Company Kuykendall Outfitters, Inc.
Contact Leroy M. Kuykendall
City Peck
Company L & D Fly Fishing/Three Rivers Ranch
Contact Lonnie Lee Allen
City Ashton
Company L-B Fishing & Guide Service
Contact Ronald W. Bloxham
City Challis
Company Lake Charters, Inc.
Contact Robert A. Carbone
City Coeur d'Alene
Company Last Chance Outfitters, Inc.
Contact Lynn Sessions
City Island Park
Company Lazy J Outfitters, Inc.
Contact Larry A. Jarrett
City Kuna
Company Little Wood River Outfitters
Contact Robert L. Hennefer
City Carey
Company Lost River Outfitters
Contact Scott G. Schnebly
City Ketchum
Company Mainstream Outdoor Adventures, Inc.
Contact Charles Alan Lamm
City Lewiston
Company Middle Fork Lodge, Inc.
Contact Mary Ossenkop & Scott Farr
City Boise
Company Middle Fork Rapid Transit #1
Contact Greg Edson
City Twin Falls
Company Middle Fork River Tours, Inc.
Contact Phil B. Crabtree
City Ketchum
Company Middle Fork Wilderness Outfitters, Inc.
Contact Gary Shelton
City Ketchum
Company Moser's Idaho Adventures
Contact Gary L. Moser
City Salmon
Company Norman H. Guth, Inc.
Contact Norman Guth & Mel Reingold
City Salmon
Company North Fork Guides
Contact Kenneth R. Hill
City North Fork
Company Northwest River Company
Contact Douglas A. Tims
City Boise
Company Northwest Voyageurs
Contact Jeff W. Peavey
City Lucile
Company Oars + Dories, Inc.
Contact Curtis M. Chang
City Lewiston
Company Ospry Adv./Meadow Creek Outfitters
Contact Cheryl Bransford
City White Bird
Company Oswald Pack Camp
Contact Ralph Oswold

City Kamiah
Company Pack Bridge Outfitters
Contact Robert Hamilton
City Twin Falls
Company Pend Oreille Charters Ltd. Co.
Contact Dan Jacobson & Keith Snyder
City Sandpoint
Company Pioneer Mountain Outfitters
Contact Tom & Deb Proctor
City Twin Falls
Company Pippin Plantation
Contact
City Sagle
Company Priest Lake Guide Service
Contact Gary Brookshire
City Priest Lake
Company Priest Lake Outdoor Adventures
Contact
City Nordman
Company Rapid River Outfitters
Contact Kerry Neal Brennan
City Riggins
Company Red River Corrals
Contact Archie H. George
City Elk City
Company Reel Women Fly Fishing Adv.
Contact
City Victor
Company Ridge Runner Outfitters
Contact Chad Christopherson
City Kamiah
Company River"1"Inc.
Contact Dannie A. Strand
City Challis
Company River Quest Excursions
Contact Alan W. Odegaard
City Lewiston
Company Robson Outfitters
Contact Dale R. & Janette Robson
City Felt
Company Salmon River Outfitters
Contact Steven W. Shephard
City McCall
Company Salmon Valley Guide Service
Contact Kathleen Rae Gliksman
City Salmon
Company Sawtooth Guide Service, Inc.
Contact Robert L. Cole
City Stanley
Company Sawtooth Mountain Guides
Contact Kirk D. Bachman
City Stanley
Company Scenic River Charters
Contact Timothy L. Jewett
City Lewiston
Company Seagull Charters
Contact James H. Meneely
City Kootenai
Company See Fish Ventures, Inc.
Contact Tom Ellefson
City Coeur d'Alene
Company Selway Lodge, Inc.
Contact Rick Hussey & Patricia G. Millington
City Picabo
Company Sentinel Rock Outfitters
Contact Ray Kagel
City Leadore
Company Silver Creek Outfitters, Inc.
Contact Terry W. Ring & Roger Schwartz
City Sun Valley
Company Smith River Outfitters, Inc.
Contact Gary D. Lindstrom
City Cambridge
Company Smoky Mountain Outfitters
Contact Bruce T. Butler
City Hailey
Company Snake River Adventures
Contact Michael L. Luther
City Lewiston
Company Snake River Outfitters
Contact Norman E. Riddle
City Lewiston
Company Snake River Pack Goats
Contact Steven A. Silva
City Nampa
Company Snug Outfitters, Inc./B.

Mason Outfitters
Contact William W. Mason, Jr.
City Sun Valley
Company Solitude River Trips
Contact Al & Jeana Bukowsky
City Merlin, Oregon
Company South Fork Expeditions, Ltd.
Contact John Hill, Jr.
City Idaho Falls
Company South Fork Lodge
Contact Spence Warner
City Swan Valley
Company Southern Latitudes Fly Fishing — Chile
Contact
City Ketchum
Company Sulphur Creek Ranch
Contact Tom T. Allegrezza
City Boise
Company Sun Valley Outfitters, Inc.
Contact Todd Van Bramer
City Sun Valley
Company Swiftwater Steelhead Trips
Contact Roger J. Monger
City Orofino
Company The Last Resort
Contact Jimmie Dwayne Blair
City New Meadows
Company The Lodge at Palisades Creek
Contact Chip Kearns
City Irwin
Company The River Company
Contact Olivia Falconer James
City Sun Valley
Company Thousand Springs Tours
Contact J. Russell LeMoyne
City Hagerman
Company Three Rivers Outfitters
Contact James B. Maxwell
City Lewiston
Company Title Line Fishing
Contact John Seidel
City Idaho Falls
Company Towle Outfitters
Contact Gary R. Towle
City Boise
Company Trail Creek Outfitters, Inc.
Contact Layne Davis
City Soda Springs
Company Trophy Trout Outfitters & Guides Service
Contact Richard R. Reinwald
City Careywood
Company Trout Creek Outfitters, Inc.
Contact Ray & BarBetta Cox
City Grangeville
Company Two M River Outfitters, Inc.
Contact Michael W. Murphy
City Sun Valley
Company Wapiti Meadow Ranch & Outfitters
Contact Barry & Diana Bryant
City Cascade
Company Wapiti River Guides
Contact Gary Lane
City Riggins
Company War Eagle Outfitters & Guides
Contact Ken & Dolly Jafek
City Malta
Company Watermark Adventures
Contact Pat Harper
City Boise
Company Weitas Creek Outfitters
Contact Steve F. Jones
City Potlatch
Company White Cloud Outfitters
Contact Mike Scott & Louise Stark
City Challis
Company White Otter Outdoor Adventures
Contact Randy P. Hess
City Ketchum
Company White Outfitters
Contact Bill G. White
City Orofino
Company White Water West
Contact Gail and Stan Watt
City Pingree
Company Whitewater Adventures Idaho
Contact Kenneth C. Masoner
City Boise
Company Wild Idaho Outfitters, Inc.

Contact Frank Giles
City Challis
Company Wilderness Outfitters
Contact Scott, Shelda, Justin and Jerrod Farr
City Challis
Company
Contact John Hardin
City Hailey
Company
Contact Michael Wm. Melville
City Idaho Falls
Company
Contact Laren M. Piquet
City Driggs
Company
Contact Dusty Youren
City Garden Valley

Illinois

Company A.J. Charters
Contact Capt. A.J. Johnson
City Justice
Company Babe Wojslaw
Contact Michael Wojslaw
City Chicago Heights
Company Bain Lake Lodge
Contact Northwoods Angler Ltd.
City St. Charles
Company Beaver Island Charters
Contact Capt. Elwood V. Baker
City DeerfieldBea
Company Big Bird Charters
Contact James T. Conder
City Danville
Company Blyth's Canyon Lake Lodge
Contact Bruce & Joan Blyth
City Chicago
Company Calumet Harbor Sport Fishermen
Contact Dick Ruess
City Blue Island
Company Captain Don's Charter Service
Contact Capt. Don Anderson
City Buffalo Grove
Company Challenger
Contact Capt. Bob Jenkins
City Addison
Company Charter Boats, Inc.
Contact USMM Capt. Sam S. Romano
City Chicago
Company Chock Full of Nuts
Contact Capt. Dennis O'Braitis
City Woodstock
Company Ersboat Fishing Charters
Contact Capt. Bill Ersbo
City Zion
Company Fireside Lodge
Contact
City Joliet
Company Fish Trap Charters
Contact Capt. Wayne Young
City Watseka
Company King Salmon Guides, Inc.
Contact Todd Dirks
City Hoffman Est.
Company Lac Seul Airways Ltd.
Contact John & Pat Renfro
City Rockford
Company Lake Fork Outfitters & Guest Ranch
Contact James A. Metter
City Columbia
Company Montauk IV
Contact Capt. Steven May
City Grayslake
Company Morning Star Fishing Charters
Contact Capt. Larry Griffith
City Winthrop Harbor
Company Munroe Lake Lodge
Contact Jack Stoneman
City Libertyville
Company Noble
Contact Capt. Dale Florek
City Round Lake
Company North Point Charter Boat Assoc.
Contact
City Winthrop Harbor

Company Pantera Charters
Contact Capt. Edward O. Bullen
City Winthrop Harbor
Company Rosebob Salmon Charters
Contact Bob Holzer
City Buffalo Grove
Company Salmon Unlimited of Indiana
Contact Jessie Childress
City Park Forest
Company Smooth Rock Camp
Contact Don & Lynn Leavens
City Fulton
Company Starved Rock Lodge
Contact Charlotte Wiesbrock
City Utica
Company Ted Peck's Outdoors
Contact Ted Peck
City Rockton
Company Visions
Contact Capt. Bob Worth
City Highland Park
Company Waukegan Charter Boat Association
Contact
City Waukegan
Company Wilderness Place Lodge
Contact Kyle Bowerman
City Rockford
Company
Contact Captain William Adair
City Steger
Company
Contact Jim H. Alter
City Grayslake
Company
Contact Captain Larry Benson
City Oswego
Company
Contact Captain Richard Beverly
City Warrenville
Company
Contact Captain Joseph Dawson
City Lansing
Company
Contact Michael T. Gorgas
City Ottawa
Company
Contact Michael J. Hall
City Bolingbrook
Company
Contact Les Karaffa
City Chicago
Company
Contact Captain John Markwica
City Chicago
Company
Contact Captain Bill Meier
City St. Charles
Company
Contact Jerry Nied
City Vernon Hills
Company
Contact Terry Nied
City Libertyville
Company
Contact Jerome A. Papineau
City Bradley
Company
Contact Robert S. Potesham
City Chicago
Company
Contact Gary L. Reymann
City East Dundee
Company
Contact Gary Schrock
City Seaton
Company
Contact Butch Sterling
City Plainfield
Company
Contact William Whitlock
City Chicago
Company
Contact William G. Whitlock
City W. Chicago

Indiana

Company 4-Winds
Contact Capt. Mauri Pierce
City New Palestine

Company American Fishing Institution
Contact Clif Paulin
City Terre Haute
Company Augu Bassmasters
Contact Scott Calhoun
City Anderson
Company Blue Eagle, Inc.
Contact Russell E. & Gene Loomis
City LaPorte
Company Broad Ripple Bassmasters
Contact James Wagers
City Indianapolis
Company Brookville Striper Federation
Contact Richard Johnson
City Brookville
Company Catch 1
Contact Ronald Yagelski
City Michigan City
Company Central IN Anglers
Contact Duane Strauch
City Bowling Green
Company Change of Pace
Contact Scott A. Bolka
City Michigan City
Company Chelsea Bass Masters
Contact Wes Thomas
City Hanover
Company Circle City Bass Hookers
Contact Bill Folkening
City New Palestine
Company Crokindill
Contact Steven Kreighbaum
City Michigan City
Company Dogwood Bass Masters
Contact John E. Casper
City Washington DC
Company Dune Caper Charters
Contact Anthony E. Arvay
City Portage
Company Ecstasy
Contact Capt. Mike Barkely
City Michigan City
Company Fallcreek Bassmasters
Contact Butch Isabell
City Pendleton
Company Fish Lake Bass Club
Contact Steve Krasowski
City Mill Creek
Company Fisheries Biologist
Contact Paul Gerovac
City Porter
Company Fish Trap Charters
Contact Capt. Wayne Young
City Watseka, Illinois
Company Flapper
Contact Capt. Jeff Smith
City LaPorte
Company Flymasters
Contact Christian Pedersen
City Indianapolis
Company Hard Luck Bassmasters
Contact Jack Strum
City Oaklandon
Company High Rise
Contact Capt. Larrie Falder
City LaFontaine
Company Holly Lynn Fishing Charters
Contact Gary L. Huffman
City Freetown
Company Hoosier Bass 'n Gals
Contact
City Indianapolis
Company Hoosier Bassmasters
Contact John Albertson
City Bloomington
Company Hoosier Coho Club
Contact Dan Messina
City Michigan City
Company Hoosier Flyfishers
Contact Al Fish
City Unionville
Company Hoosier Muskie Hunters
Contact Jim Bagnoli
City Carmel
Company IN B.A.S.S. Federation
Contact Steve Cox
City Indianapolis
Company IN Bass 'n Gals
Contact Karen Welty
City Shelbyville
Company Indiana B.A.S.S. Chapter Federation
Contact Larry Watson
City Anderson

Company Indianapolis Bass Hawks
Contact John Reynolds
City Greenwood
Company Indianapolis Flycasters
Contact Daniel Allen
City Indianapolis
Company Indy Bassmasters
Contact Dennis McGee
City Indianapolis
Company Indy Procasters
Contact Tony Harlow
City Whiteland
Company Ironsides
Contact Michael E. Caplis
City Michigan City
Company John & Diosa's Wabaskang Camp
Contact John & Diosa Record
City Riley
Company Kirk Leasing Corp.
Contact
City Merriville
Company Kokomo Bass Anglers
Contact E. Prickett
City Kokomo
Company Kokomo Bass Busters
Contact Jim Wells
City Kokomo
Company Lake Michigan Sport Fishing Coal.
Contact Janet Ryan
City Chesterton
Company Lakeville Conservation Club
Contact Ronald Yoder
City North Liberty
Company LaPorte Co. Bassmasters
Contact Frank Nowak
City LaPorte
Company Legal Tender III
Contact James Read
City Chesterton
Company Manx Charters
Contact Warren Holmes
City Michigan City
Company Michiana Steelheaders
Contact
City Mishawaka
Company Michigan City Charter Boat Assoc.
Contact Ralph Miyata
City LaPorte
Company Michigan City Fish & Game Club
Contact Dr. David Merrill
City Michigan City
Company Military Bass Angler Assoc.
Contact Allan Needham
City Indianapolis
Company Miller Izaak Walton League
Contact
City Portage
Company Norjernan
Contact Ronald Halus
City Michigan City
Company North Coast Charter Assoc.
Contact Dale E. Robert
City Hammond
Company Northeastern IN Trout Assoc.
Contact
City Ft. Wayne
Company Northwest Indiana Steelheaders
Contact Mike Ryan
City Chesterton
Company Oak Lake Lodge
Contact Jerry & Wanetah Helgason
City Indianapolis
Company P.O.Pluggers Bass Club
Contact Michael Price
City Indianapolis
Company Pari of Dice Charters
Contact Capt. Howard Petroski
City Griffith
Company Perch America, Inc.
Contact Joe Bala
City Hammond
Company Peru Bassmasters
Contact Jerry Arnett
City Mexico
Company Proud Lion
Contact Richard Praklet
City Lakeville
Company Pulchritude
Contact Mike Hampel
City Michigan City

Company Quick Creek Bassmasters
Contact Dave Brumett
City Austin
Company Rainmaker Charters
Contact Richard Pegau
City Portage
Company Ross Fishing Charters
Contact Jerry R. Ross
City Michigan City
Company Rouser
Contact Capt. Larry G. Simpson
City Michigan City
Company Salmon Unlimited of Indiana
Contact Bob Vanberg
City Merrillville
Company Sandpiper Charters
Contact Paul Kropp
City Valparaiso
Company Shadowland Charters
Contact Edward W. Svec
City Chesterton
Company Southwest Indiana Bass Club
Contact Jeff Norris
City Washington DC
Company Sportsmen of Northern Indiana
Contact
City Portage
Company Stylin
Contact Darrell M. Stahoviak
City LaPorte
Company The Gambler
Contact Capt. Ron Maglio
City LaPorte
Company TR Fly Fishers Newsletter
Contact
City Ft. Wayne
Company Trophy Charters III
Contact Skip Stafford
City Michigan City
Company Trophy Hunters Charters
Contact Scott Tuthill
City Portage
Company Wabash Valley Flyfishers
Contact Chris Thomas
City Terre Haute
Company Ye Olde Tackle Box
Contact Ken McIntosh
City North Webster
Company
Contact Stephen Blakley
City Fishers
Company
Contact Capt. Jimmy Bloom
City Fort Wayne
Company
Contact Willis Bradshaw
City Granger
Company
Contact John Buoscio
City Schererville
Company
Contact George E. Cadle
City Crown Point
Company
Contact Daniel Carlson
City Crown Point
Company
Contact Dennis L. Debuysser
City South Bend
Company
Contact Donald R. DeYoung
City Dyer
Company
Contact Peter Hansen
City Miller
Company
Contact Capt. George Harris
City Marion
Company
Contact Arthur G. Helgesen
City Churubusco
Company
Contact Capt. James Hirschy
City Woodburn
Company
Contact James Lynn Huffman
City Marua
Company
Contact Richard B. Jankowski
City South Bend
Company
Contact Kenneth W. Jones
City Warsaw

Company
Contact Donald L. Malcom
City Goshen
Company
Contact Gregory D. Mangus
City South Bend
Company
Contact Capt. Jerry McClurg
City Griffith
Company
Contact Capt. Lou Pieczanka
City West Harrison
Company
Contact John A. Schaul
City Ganger
Company
Contact Donald L. Schroeder
City Goshen
Company
Contact Ernest D. Slessman
City Elkhart
Company
Contact John C. Stanley
City South Bend
Company
Contact Capt. James Tennant
City Fort Wayne
Company
Contact Ken Yarnelle
City Fremont

Iowa

Company Cobham River Lodge
Contact Richard Hebel
City Mason City
Company Dave Jauron's Guide Service
Contact Dave Jauron
City Essex
Company Deer Horn Lodge
Contact Norm & Cindy Tieck
City Sioux City
Company Eva Lake Resort Airway Ltd.
Contact David Cunning
City Mount Ayr
Company Fin Fun Charters
Contact Capts. Gale & Mike Sells
City Waterloo
Company Gold Arrow Camp
Contact Don Moore
City Cherokee
Company Highrock Lake Lodge
Contact
City Underwood
Company Lac Seul Evergreen Lodge & Golden Eagle Resort
Contact Gary & Pat Beardsley
City Johnston
Company New Highrock Lodge Ltd.
Contact Randy & Jill Darnold
City Underwood
Company Ole Caretaker Guide Service
Contact Loren "Honda" Ralfs
City Davenport
Company Talaview Resorts
Contact Jacob Hunget
City Indianola

Kansas

Company Bar-X-Bar Ranch
Contact Ed Pugh
City Wamego
Company Bud's Bait & Tackle
Contact Curtis E. George
City Sylvan Grove
Company Cat Daddy Guide & Tour
Contact Renne R. Shumway
City Topeka
Company Circle A Guide Service
Contact Richard H. Archer
City Whiting
Company Claythorne Lodge
Contact
City Columbus

Company Eagle Ridge Outfitter
Contact Timothy G. Greiner
City Milford
Company Flint Hills Wildlife, Inc.
Contact
City Atlanta
Company Guide Lines Guide Service
Contact Clyde L. Holscher
City Topeka
Company J C Higgins Guide Service
Contact James C. Higgins
City Grantville
Company Keeting's Sportman Hunting & Fishing
Contact Gerald A. Keeting
City Carbondale
Company Kohl's Clearwater Outfitter
Contact Robin J. Kohls
City Clearwater
Company Lil' Toledo Lodge
Contact Ronald L. King
City Chanute
Company Midwest Guiding
Contact Richard Rightmire, Jr.
City Hartford
Company Paradise Adventure
Contact Kurtis A. Nunnenkamp
City Altoona
Company Pike Island Lodge & Outposts
Contact Ron McKenzie
City Junction City
Company Professional Guide Service
Contact Bruce R. Coate
City Wilson
Company R & B Guide Service
Contact Ronald W. Howland
City Jewell
Company R&R Guiding
Contact Ryan Rogowski
City Junction City
Company Rader Lodge
Contact Jeffrey A. Rader
City Glen Elder
Company Shadow Oaks
Contact John D. & Pauline L. Doty
City Sedan
Company Wind Dancer Guide Service
Contact Larry L. Wright
City Concordia
Company Wolf Creek Outfitters
Contact Jeffrey D. Berkenmeier
City New Strawn
Company
Contact Bill Burwell
City Abilene
Company
Contact Dudley D. Foster
City Parsons
Company
Contact W.R. Johnson
City McPherson
Company
Contact Richard D. Rexroat
City Downs
Company
Contact Thomas J. Seneeal
City Geneseo
Company
Contact Larry W. Stewart
City South Hutchins

Kentucky

Company Cave Run Guide Service
Contact
City Frenchburg
Company Lake Barkley State Resort Park
Contact
City Cadiz
Company Nancy Guide Service
Contact
City Nancy

Louisiana

Company BKD Guide Service
Contact Capt. Kirby LaCour
City Kenner
Company Bon Chance
Contact Menton "Bobby" Chouest
City Grand Isle
Company Cameron Wildlife
Contact Sammie Faulk & Steve German
City Lake Charles
Company Captain Brian's Bayou Adventures
Contact Capt. Brian Epstein
City New Orleans
Company Cherece IV Charters
Contact Rene & Diane Rice
City Grand Isle
Company Coastal Guide Service
Contact Capt. Vince Theriot
City Grand Chenier
Company Coup Platte Hunting & Fishing
Contact Terry Trosclair
City Houma
Company Doug's Hunting Lodge
Contact
City Gueydan
Company Dufrene's Guide Service Inc.
Contact Calvin Dufrene
City Galliano
Company Eddie Halbrook Grand Bayou Reservoir Guide
Contact Eddie Halbrook
City Jonesville
Company Escape Fishing Charters
Contact Tim "Hook" Ursin, Sr.
City Slidell
Company Ferrule Fly Fishing Club
Contact Shane M. Hubbs
City Covington
Company Fish & Fowl Guide Service
Contact Michael Herrman
City Chalmette
Company Fishing Guide Service
Contact A.D. "Dee" Geoghegan
City New Orleans
Company Fishing, Inc.
Contact Bill Herrington, Sr.
City Venice
Company Go For It! Charters
Contact Gary Taylor & Jim Lamarque
City Slidell
Company Gordon's Professional Guide Service
Contact Gordon Matherne
City Des Allemands
Company Great Outdoors Guide Service
Contact Dave Wartenburg
City Slidell
Company Hall Outdoors
Contact Rick Hall
City Gueydan
Company Marshland Guide Service
Contact Capts. Vernon & Thad Robichaux
City Golden Meadow
Company Painkiller Offshore Fishing Team
Contact Karl T. Cerullo
City Metairie
Company Reel Odyssey Charters, Inc.
Contact Capt. Paul Marchand
City Dulac
Company Southern Seaplane Inc.
Contact Lyle Panepinto
City Belle Chasse
Company Touch of Class Fishing Charters
Contact Kevin Frelich
City Empire
Company Wild Wings Sporting Club
Contact
City Downsville
Company
Contact E.P. Borel
City Zwolle
Company
Contact Robert F. Byrd
City Zwolle
Company
Contact G. R. Dupuis

City Arcadia
Company
Contact Richard R. Guidry
City Many
Company
Contact Bobby L. Harvey
City Anacoco
Company
Contact Gary Hood
City Bossier City
Company
Contact Maurice L. Jackson
City Many
Company
Contact F. Dale May
City Florien
Company
Contact Capt. Jeff Poe
City Lake Charles
Company
Contact Alan D. Pullin
City Monroe
Company
Contact George D. Sherwood
City Shreveport
Company
Contact Larry W. Stinson
City Zwolle
Company
Contact Mike Wheatley
City Keatchie

Maine

Company Backwoods Adventures
Contact Todd Braley
City Palmyra
Company Barnes' Outfitters, Inc.
Contact
City Freeport
Company Bean Hole Bean Jim Guide Service
Contact James Cunningham
City Searsport
Company Bear Mountain Lodge
Contact Carroll Gerow
City Smyrna Mills
Company Bear Spring Camps
Contact Peg & Ron Churchill
City Oakland
Company Bosebuck Mountain Camps
Contact
City Wilsons Mills
Company Bowlin Camps
Contact
City Patten
Company Brown's Guide Service
Contact
City Presque Isle
Company Camps of Acadia
Contact James & Kathleen Lynch
City Eagle Lake
Company Cedar Mill Guide Service
Contact John MacDonald
City Athens
Company Cedar Ridge Outfitters
Contact Hal and Debbie Blood
City Jackman
Company Colonial Sportsmens Lodge
Contact
City Grand Lake Stream
Company Dad's Camps
Contact
City Lincoln
Company Daybreak Guide Service
Contact Steve Ratey
City Wilton
Company Eagle Lodge
Contact
City Lincoln
Company Fishing Alaska Style
Contact Robert Smith
City Augusta
Company Flint River Camp
Contact The Goodman Family
City Patten
Company Gander Creek Guide Service
Contact Ronald Dodd
City Rockport
Company Geno's Maine Guide Service

Contact Gene Rossignol
City Caribou
Company Gentle Ben's Hunting & Fishing Lodge
Contact Bruce Pelletier
City Rockwood
Company Grant's Kennebago Camps
Contact
City Rangeley
Company Gray Ghost Camps
Contact
City Rockwood
Company Greenville Inn
Contact
City Greenville
Company Greenwood Motel
Contact Tom Edwards
City Greenville Jct.
Company Hardscrabble Guide Service
Contact Andy Rowe, Jr.
City Madison
Company Harrison's Pierce Pond Camps
Contact
City Bingham
Company Hatchet Mountain Outdoors
Contact Leon Jones
City Hope
Company Highlanding Camps
Contact David Prevost
City Portage
Company Hillside Guide Service
Contact
City Aurora
Company Indian Rock Camps
Contact
City Grand Lakee Stream
Company Katahdin View Lodge & Camps
Contact Jack Downing
City Greenville
Company Kennebago River Kamps
Contact
City Washington
Company King & Bartlett Fish & Game
Contact
City New Gloucester
Company Lawrence's Camps
Contact Bob Lawrence
City Rockwood
Company Leen's Lodge
Contact
City Newport
Company Libby Sporting Camps
Contact Matthew and Ellen Libby
City Ashland
Company Lincoln's Camps
Contact Maynard Drew
City Rockwood
Company Long Lake Camps
Contact
City Princeton
Company Loon Lodge
Contact Michael & Linda Yencha
City Millinocket
Company Macannamac Camps
Contact Jack & Sharon McPhee
City Patten
Company Main Outdoors
Contact
City Union
Company Maine Guide Fly Shop & Guide Service
Contact
City Greenville
Company Maine Outdoors
Contact Don Kleiner
City Union
Company Mainely Hunting & Fishing
Contact Captain Doug Jowett
City Brunswick
Company Maynard's Cabins
Contact
City Rockwood
Company Medawisla on Second Roach Pond
Contact
City Greenville
Company Merrymeeting Bay TU
Contact
City Lewiston
Company Mill Pond Guide Service

Contact Robert Whear
City Nobleboro
Company Miller's Guide Service
Contact Raymond Miller III
City Madison
Company Miller's Guide Service
Contact Robert Miller
City Dexter
Company Moose Point Camps
Contact
City Portage
Company Moose River Landing
Contact
City Rockwood
Company Mountain Air Services
Contact
City Rangeley
Company Mountain View Cottages
Contact Clayton "Cy" Eastlack
City Oquossoc
Company Mt. Kineo Cabins
Contact Dick & Elaine Wallingford
City Rockwood
Company North Camps on Rangeley Lake
Contact
City Oquossoc
Company North Ridge Guide Service
Contact Richard Higgins
City Presque Isle
Company Northern Forest Guide Service
Contact Roland Vosine
City Millinocket
Company Nugent's Chamberlain Lake Camp
Contact
City Greenville
Company Pathfinder Guide Service
Contact Robert Foshay
City Camden
Company Pinkham's Fishing Lodge
Contact Donald Gardner & Virginia Pinkham
City Ashland
Company Port Fly Shop
Contact Jim Dionne
City Kennebunk
Company Riverkeep Camp
Contact
City Ashland
Company Robertson's Guiding Service
Contact John Robertson
City Portage Lake
Company Sally Mountain Cabins
Contact Corey & Sally Hegarty
City Jackman
Company Sebago Lake Cottages
Contact Ray & Fran Nelson
City North Sebago
Company Seboomook Wilderness Campground
Contact
City Rockwood
Company Secret Pond Camps & Guide Service
Contact Mark Carver
City Unity
Company Shorelin Camps
Contact
City Grand Lake Stream
Company Skunk Hill Guide Service
Contact Rob Robinson
City Lee
Company South Branch Lake Camps
Contact
City Seboeis
Company Southern Maine Guide Service
Contact Ronald St. Saviour
City Limerick
Company Sunset View Lodge
Contact Bob Parker
City Farmington
Company Swiss Colony Cottages
Contact Ernie & Regina Allen
City Rangeley
Company The Birches on Moosehead Lake
Contact
City Rockwood
Company The Bunny Clark
Contact Capt. Tim Tower
City Ogunquit
Company The Pines

Contact Steve & Nancy Norris
City Grand Lake Stream
Company The Terraces Cottages
Contact
City Rangeley
Company Tim Pond Wilderness Camps
Contact Harvey & Betty Calden
City Eustis
Company Tuckaway Shores
Contact Phil & Paulette Thomas
City Jackman
Company Umiakovik Fishing & Hunting Ltd.
Contact Harvey Calden
City Jay
Company Upriver
Contact Richard Beedy
City Dixfield
Company Weatherby's
Contact
City Grand Lake Stream
Company White Birch Guide Service
Contact Capt. Paul R. Bois
City Lovell
Company Wilderness Ways
Contact Kenneth Bailey
City Camden
Company Wilsons
Contact Wayne & Scott Snell Shane
City Greenville Jct.
Company
Contact Blair Barrows
City Oquossic
Company
Contact Steven D. Chafin
City Limerick
Company
Contact Gary Corson
City New Sharon
Company
Contact Alvah Harriman
City Grand Lake Stream
Company
Contact Capt. Pat Keliher
City Freeport
Company
Contact Capt. Stephen Randell
City Scarborough
Company
Contact Soren Siren
City Harmony
Company
Contact Carroll Ware
City Skowhega

Maryland

Company Afternoon Delight/Standard Bet Charters
Contact Captain Hank Devito
City Glen Burnie
Company Capt. Bruce Foster
Contact
City Grasonville
Company Fin Finder Charters
Contact Captain Sonney Forrest
City Lexington Park
Company Marauder Charters
Contact Captain John Mayer
City Bowie
Company On The Fly
Contact
City Monkton
Company Reel Bass Adventures
Contact Stephen L. Folkee
City Port Tobacco
Company Running Creek Ranch
Contact Edward E. Houghton
City Chestertown
Company S S & K Charters
Contact Willis McQueen, Jr.
City Landover
Company Southern Winds Charter Service
Contact Captain Joseph G. Richardson
City Edgewater
Company
Contact Frederick R. Abner
City Chesapeake Beach
Company
Contact Stephen H. Adams

City Deale
Company
Contact Grover C. Adams
City Solomons
Company
Contact Robert J. Adelman
City Edgewater
Company
Contact Paul W. Adolph, Jr.
City Shady Side
Company
Contact Gregory W. Allen
City Annapolis
Company
Contact Joseph M. Anderson
City Baltimore
Company
Contact Ernest F. Anderson
City District Heights
Company
Contact Wyatt A. Andrews
City Middle River
Company
Contact Wallace D. Andrzejewski
City LaPlata
Company
Contact Richard R. Arnold
City Bowie
Company
Contact Donald R. Arnold
City Crisfield
Company
Contact John J. Asanovich
City Marion
Company
Contact Thomas W. Atkins
City Beltsville
Company
Contact James D. Atkins
City Deale
Company
Contact Vincent E. Austin, Jr.
City Deale
Company
Contact Stephen S. Austin
City Hampstead
Company
Contact Mitchell W. Bademan
City Deale
Company
Contact David Anthony Badwak
City Pasadena
Company
Contact Roy F. Bain
City Joppa
Company
Contact Thomas G. Baker
City Annapolis
Company
Contact Robert H. Baker
City Edgewater
Company
Contact Marvin E. Barber
City Tall Timbers
Company
Contact Norman W. Bartlett
City Joppa
Company
Contact Frederick W. Bauer
City Huntingtown
Company
Contact William H. Bean
City Dowell
Company
Contact John S. Beardmore
City Tracys Landing
Company
Contact Ralph Beatty
City Friendship
Company
Contact Michael A. Benjamin, Sr.
City North East
Company
Contact William K. Bennett
City Pasadena
Company
Contact Richard T. Bennett
City Huntingtown
Company
Contact Paul T. Benton, III
City Chance
Company
Contact John Berezoski, Jr.
City Marion Station
Company
Contact Raymond E. Bergman

City Stevensville
Company
Contact Joseph E. Besche
City Baltimore
Company
Contact Harry J. Biondi, Jr.
City Ridge
Company
Contact John A. Boender, III
City Ocean City
Company
Contact Warren E. Boerum
City West River
Company
Contact Brady C. Bounds, III
City Lexington Park
Company
Contact James M. Bowes
City Valley Lee
Company
Contact Robert H. Bowes
City Tall Timbers
Company
Contact Mark C. Bowes
City Leonardtown
Company
Contact David M. Bradburn
City Dameron
Company
Contact Dayne A. Brady
City Willards
Company
Contact John A. Bresnahan, Jr.
City Deale
Company
Contact James C. Brincefield, III
City Annapolis
Company
Contact Dale W. Brown
City Salisbury
Company
Contact Mark J. Brown
City Baltimore
Company
Contact Robert B. Brown
City Brandywine
Company
Contact Joseph A. Bryan
City Ridge
Company
Contact Milburn A. Buckler, III
City Lusby
Company
Contact Charles R. Burton
City Upper Marlboro
Company
Contact Brenda L. Burtrand
City Chesapeake Beach
Company
Contact Jeffrey T. Butler
City Stevensville
Company
Contact Robert L. Butler
City Grasonville
Company
Contact Frederick J. Buttrum
City Glen Burnie
Company
Contact Virgil F. Buttrum
City Annapolis
Company
Contact Larry R. Butts
City Baltimore
Company
Contact David Byrd, Jr.
City Bladensburg
Company
Contact Sean Callahan
City Trappe
Company
Contact Sidney S. Campen, Jr.
City Oxford
Company
Contact Ralph Walter Capasso
City Rockville
Company
Contact Steven E. Carle
City Broomes Island
Company
Contact Francis W. Carver, Jr.
City Deale
Company
Contact Philip H. Cathell
City Berlin
Company
Contact Edward G. Cave

City Edgewater
Company
Contact James W. Chaires
City Chestertown
Company
Contact Richard H. Chaney, Jr.
City Waldorf
Company
Contact John P. Charles
City Great Mills
Company
Contact Eldred W. Cherrix
City Leonardtown
Company
Contact Anthony D. Cianciarulo, Jr.
City Mechanicsville
Company
Contact Rodney P. Clark
City Glen Burnie
Company
Contact Robert L. Clark
City Solomons
Company
Contact Charles F. Clarke
City Hollywood
Company
Contact Gregory Coffren
City St. Leonard
Company
Contact Carmine C. Coiro
City Marion Station
Company
Contact Charles J. Coiro
City Marion
Company
Contact Richard L. Coleman
City Chesapeake Beach
Company
Contact William E. Collins
City Centreville
Company
Contact John H. Collison, Jr.
City Glen Burnie
Company
Contact Norman E. Colson, Jr.
City Pasadena
Company
Contact Henry H. Conley
City Lusby
Company
Contact Claude L. Conner
City Solomons
Company
Contact Stephen J. Conover
City Baltimore
Company
Contact Harvey C. Cook
City LaPlata
Company
Contact Harold Walter Coombs
City LaPlata
Company
Contact George T. Cord, Jr.
City Phoenix
Company
Contact Paul Coughlin
City Stevensville
Company
Contact Francis D. Courtney, II
City Annapolis
Company
Contact Charlotte Cregger
City North Beach
Company
Contact George R. Crosby
City Baltimore
Company
Contact James H. Cullison, Jr.
City St. Inigoes
Company
Contact Sullie Culpepper
City Salisbury
Company
Contact Daniel C. Daffin
City St. Michaels
Company
Contact Paul H. Daisey
City Bishopville
Company
Contact James W. Danford
City Huntingtown
Company
Contact Dwight H. Daniel
City Pasadena
Company
Contact Leo P. Darr, Jr.

City Edgewater
Company
Contact Edwin M. Darwin
City Baltimore
Company
Contact Lionel W. Daugherty
City Crisfield
Company
Contact Perry R. Davidson
City Centreville
Company
Contact Charles S. Davis
City Ridge
Company
Contact Michael P. Davis
City Salisbury
Company
Contact Gilbert C. Dean
City Hurlock
Company
Contact Louie P. Deane
City Chesapeake Beach
Company
Contact Richard J. Dein
City Annapolis
Company
Contact Elliot P. Dematteis
City Annapolis
Company
Contact Joseph W. Denton
City Lusby
Company
Contact Robert A. Denyer
City Port Tobacco
Company
Contact Frank A. Ditmars
City Churchton
Company
Contact Lawrence D. Dixon
City Rockville
Company
Contact Russell L. Dobson
City Lexington Park
Company
Contact John F. Doetzer
City Easton
Company
Contact Frank Donaldson
City Annapolis
Company
Contact Walter L. Donaldson, Jr.
City Bowie
Company
Contact Walter L. Donaldson, III
City Bowie
Company
Contact Vincent A. Dortenzo
City Ocean City
Company
Contact James O. Drummond
City Cobb Island
Company
Contact William T. Drummond
City Hampstead
Company
Contact Thomas R. Drury
City St. Inigoes
Company
Contact Donna & Gregory L. Drury
City Ridge
Company
Contact Robert T. Dukehart
City Ellicott City
Company
Contact William F. Duncan, Jr.
City Newark
Company
Contact David B. Duvall
City Arnold
Company
Contact David C. Eanes, III
City Wenona
Company
Contact John S. Earman
City Huntingtown
Company
Contact James M. Eckelt
City Forest Hill
Company
Contact Charles F. Eder
City Baltimore
Company
Contact Henry G. Edwards, Jr.
City Wenona
Company
Contact Robert H. Elliott

City Worton
Company
Contact John M. Estevez
City White Plains
Company
Contact Capt. Joe Evans
City Annapolis
Company
Contact Edward J. Ewers
City Baltimore
Company
Contact Carl B. Felger
City College Park
Company
Contact Dwight D. Ferrell
City Waldorf
Company
Contact Walter W. Fithian
City Rock Hall
Company
Contact James L. Flaig
City Ocean City
Company
Contact William P. Fletcher
City Rock Hall
Company
Contact Rodney W. Fluharty
City Tilghman
Company
Contact Charles L. Fobbs
City Clinton
Company
Contact Robert G. Foley
City Glen Arm
Company
Contact Steven C. Fore
City St. Inignes
Company
Contact Louis K. Forrest, Jr.
City Lexington Park
Company
Contact David Fortner
City Denton
Company
Contact J. Naudain Francis
City Rock Hall
Company
Contact William C. Fritz
City Eden
Company
Contact George A. Fromm
City Neavitt
Company
Contact Jeffrey Paul Fuller
City Pasadena
Company
Contact Richard W. Gaines
City Queenstown
Company
Contact Dwayne L. Garrett
City Annapolis
Company
Contact Richard A. Garrett
City Annapolis
Company
Contact Russell Garufi
City Pasadena
Company
Contact James A. Gasch
City Chesapeake Beach
Company
Contact Wayne C. Gatling
City Worton
Company
Contact Darryl C. Gay
City Scotland
Company
Contact William Gee
City Lusby
Company
Contact Joseph P. Geipe, Jr.
City Glyndon
Company
Contact Charles M. Gerek
City Park Hall
Company
Contact Howard E. Gibson
City Rock Hall
Company
Contact Charles P. Gilbert
City Hollywood
Company
Contact Rob Gifford

City Frederick
Company
Contact William T. Gingell
City Chesapeake Beach
Company
Contact Robert H. Goldsteen
City Silver Spring
Company
Contact Philip H. Gootee
City Church Creek
Company
Contact William A. Gottleid
City Solomons
Company
Contact Melvin R. Gough
City Dowell
Company
Contact Robert E. Gowar
City West Ocean City
Company
Contact C. Fred Graff
City Indian Head
Company
Contact James R. Gray
City Ridge
Company
Contact Francis J. Gray, Jr.
City Dunkirk
Company
Contact Russell M. Green
City Essex
Company
Contact Charles E. Green
City Chesapeake Beach
Company
Contact Joseph Green
City Chester
Company
Contact Eldred W. Greenwell
City Leonardtown
Company
Contact Richard H. Grimes
City Shady Side
Company
Contact John P. Groch
City Cambridge
Company
Contact Thomas A. Gruber
City Lothian
Company
Contact Joseph L. Gukanovich
City Annapolis
Company
Contact Bronko B. Gukanovich, Sr.
City Stevensville
Company
Contact John G. Guy, Jr.
City Leonardtown
Company
Contact Michael L. Haddaway
City Bozman
Company
Contact Charles G. Haegerich, Jr.
City Pasadena
Company
Contact James E. Hahn
City Centreville
Company
Contact Edward G. Hahn
City Centreville
Company
Contact Ben Hald
City Chesapeake Beach
Company
Contact Gregory A. Hall
City Ocean City
Company
Contact Alfred O. Hammett
City Valley Lee
Company
Contact Alton Hancock
City Indian Head
Company
Contact James E. Haney, Sr.
City Berlin
Company
Contact Terry S. Hardesty
City Edgewater
Company
Contact Charles S. Harman
City Ocean City
Company
Contact James Harris
City Rose Haven
Company
Contact Stanley B. Harris

City Mechanicsville
Company
Contact William Harrison, Jr.
City Annapolis
Company
Contact Herman R. Harrison
City Wittman
Company
Contact Charles Harrison
City Timonium
Company
Contact William Sanford Harrison
City Edgewater
Company
Contact W. Preston Hartge
City Galesville
Company
Contact Christopher M. Haussmann
City Deale
Company
Contact William T. Heacock, Jr.
City North Beach
Company
Contact Steven D. Henderson
City Greenbelt
Company
Contact Jeffrey B. Henderson
City Shady Side
Company
Contact Barry Herbster
City Cheverly
Company
Contact Danny Hicks
City St. Michaels
Company
Contact John C. Higgins
City St. Michaels
Company
Contact Kevin Higgins
City Edgewater
Company
Contact Harry L. Hilton, III
City Chesapeake Beach
Company
Contact Marcellus L. Hippert, III
City Kensington
Company
Contact Donald H. Hislop
City Severna Park
Company
Contact James J. Hogan
City Solomons
Company
Contact Robert A. Holden, Sr.
City Leonardtown
Company
Contact Paris L. Hollins
City St. Leonard
Company
Contact Bernard C. Hollis
City Silver Spring
Company
Contact Kenneth G. Holt
City Deale
Company
Contact William L. Holt
City Shady Side
Company
Contact Jack D. Holt
City Silver Spring
Company
Contact George K. Horn
City Baltimore
Company
Contact Robert L. Horsmon
City Prince Frederick
Company
Contact Bruce S. Hughes
City Annapolis
Company
Contact Peter Ide
City Callaway
Company
Contact John D. Ihnat
City Newcomb
Company
Contact Thomas H. Ireland
City Huntingtown
Company
Contact James K. Jackson
City Temple Hills
Company
Contact George C. Jackson
City Baltimore
Company
Contact Charles Jacquette

City Stevensville
Company
Contact James D. Jahn
City St. Marys City
Company
Contact Peter A. Jay
City Churchville
Company
Contact Robert R. Jenkins
City Cambridge
Company
Contact Gregory B. Jetton
City Rock Hall
Company
Contact Thomas L. Johnson
City Edgewater
Company
Contact Francis Johnson
City Boyds
Company
Contact Alfred R. Jones
City Shady Side
Company
Contact George L. Jones
City Chester
Company
Contact John K. Josenhans
City Crisfield
Company
Contact Perry E. Joy
City Severna Park
Company
Contact Adrian L. Joy
City Lusby
Company
Contact Raymond C. Nichols, Jr.
City Ocean City
Company
Contact Milton E. Ensor, Jr.
City Reisterstown
Company
Contact John H. Bunting, Jr.
City Ocean City
Company
Contact Aaron V. Ridgell, Jr.
City Denton
Company
Contact Charles T. Howes, Jr.
City Dunkirk
Company
Contact William Kaht
City Edgewater
Company
Contact Daniel F. Kardash
City Baldwin
Company
Contact Clayton O. Katski
City Bozman
Company
Contact Marion N. Kaufman
City Chester
Company
Contact Harry M. Keene
City Easton
Company
Contact Harry D. Kendall
City Churchville
Company
Contact John E. Kerr
City Severna Park
Company
Contact Bernard M. King, Sr.
City Friendship
Company
Contact John Kipp
City Ocean City
Company
Contact Harry Ol. Klein
City Chesapeake Beach
Company
Contact Kenneth D. Kloostra
City Annapolis
Company
Contact Ronald L. Knight
City Queenstown
Company
Contact John L. Knight
City Silver Spring
Company
Contact William W. Knott
City Sunderland
Company
Contact George Kohler
City Salisbury
Company
Contact Douglas A. Kolb, Jr.

City Deale
Company
Contact Stanley J. Krol, Sr.
City Baltimore
Company
Contact Robert S. Kunowsky
City Chesapeake Beach
Company
Contact Richard T. Labrie
City Queenstown
Company
Contact Michael L. Lacey
City Upper Marlboro
Company
Contact Marianne Ladzinski
City Baltimore
Company
Contact Charles L. Lagana
City Huntingtown
Company
Contact James Landon
City Crisfield
Company
Contact Charles H. Landon, Jr.
City Crisfield
Company
Contact Jack D. Langley
City Hollywood
Company
Contact Phil L. Langley, Jr.
City Dameron
Company
Contact Harry W. Larrimore
City Tilghman
Company
Contact Ronne T. Larson
City Darnestown
Company
Contact Gerald Lastfogel
City Edgewater
Company
Contact Peter R. Latvala
City Piney Point
Company
Contact Robert E. Layne
City Baltimore
Company
Contact Robert R. Lee
City Ridge
Company
Contact David A. Lehan
City North Beach
Company
Contact John G. Leonard
City Ocean City
Company
Contact David Lessner
City Baltimore
Company
Contact James R. Lilly
City Stevensville
Company
Contact Michael J. Lipski
City Tilghman Island
Company
Contact Edward A. Loughran
City Bethesda
Company
Contact Joseph L. Lowery
City Tilghman
Company
Contact John C. & Kenneth W. MacEwen
City Deale
Company
Contact Gregory N. Madjeski
City Ridge
Company
Contact Stephen F. Madjeski
City St. Inigoes
Company
Contact George Magnanelli
City Bethesda
Company
Contact John W. Mahaney
City Benedict
Company
Contact Rudolph E. Manili
City Stevensville
Company
Contact Joseph Mann
City Baltimore
Company
Contact Kimberly H. Marowski
City Bishopville
Company

Contact William A. Marr, Jr.
City Centreville
Company
Contact Linwood Martens
City Ocean City
Company
Contact Robert F. McCready
City Salisbury
Company
Contact George A. McCullough
City Chester
Company
Contact Earl McDaniel
City Harwood
Company
Contact Joseph L. McGahey
City Rose Haven
Company
Contact Rodney J. McGarrie
City Glen Burnie
Company
Contact Clyde McGowan
City Arnold
Company
Contact John W. McKnett
City St. Leonard
Company
Contact H. Turney McKnight
City White Hall
Company
Contact James McNey
City Ocean City
Company
Contact Paul E. McWilliams, Jr.
City Harwood
Company
Contact Ronald F. Meadows
City Pasadena
Company
Contact Roy W. Meadows
City Solomons
Company
Contact Craig A. Mercier
City Pasadena
Company
Contact Victor P. Mercogliano
City Kensington
Company
Contact Charles A. Meredith
City Hurlock
Company
Contact Eldridge E. & Tyrone A. Meredith
City Grasonville
Company
Contact William W. Messick
City Cambridge
Company
Contact Bernard V. Michael
City Arnold
Company
Contact Charles P. Michalk
City Cambridge
Company
Contact Bernard H. Michels
City Ocean City
Company
Contact Mark Middleton
City Owings
Company
Contact Mark V. Millar
City Tall Timbers
Company
Contact Wayne A. Mills
City Grasonville
Company
Contact Edward R. Mock
City Mayo
Company
Contact Russell P. Mogel, Jr.
City Chesapeake Beach
Company
Contact John S. Molner
City Lutherville
Company
Contact John A. Montgomery
City Huntingtown
Company
Contact James H. Moore
City Baltimore
Company
Contact Paul J. Moore
City Silver Spring
Company
Contact F. Marty Moran
City Ocean City

Company
Contact Greg W. Morgan
City Westover
Company
Contact Douglas D. Morse
City Baltimore
Company
Contact Robert Glen Mullis
City Gaithersburg
Company
Contact Tammie J. Mumma
City Chesapeake Beach
Company
Contact Michael A. Murphy
City Easton
Company
Contact Samuel T. Murphy
City Cordova
Company
Contact Francis L. Murphy, Jr.
City Laurel
Company
Contact Kerry R. Muse
City Edgewater
Company
Contact Louis G. Napfel, Jr.
City Edgewater
Company
Contact Harrison C. Nauman, Jr.
City Deal Island
Company
Contact Wallace S. Nichols
City Randallstown
Company
Contact Charles Nicholson
City Dameron
Company
Contact Robert A. Nicholson
City Glen Burnie
Company
Contact Buddy R. Nicosia
City Joppa
Company
Contact George W. Norrington
City Shady Side
Company
Contact Lionel G. Norrington
City West River
Company
Contact Joseph J. Norris
City Ridge
Company
Contact Jerry W. Norton
City Owings
Company
Contact Darrell T. & Jeffrey T. Nottingham
City Ocean City
Company
Contact Charles M. Novak
City St. Michaels
Company
Contact Richard N. Novotny
City Baltimore
Company
Contact John P.O'Brien
City Severna Park
Company
Contact Edward A. O'Brien
City Chesapeake Beach
Company
Contact Richard T. Olson
City Oxford
Company
Contact Steven R. Owens
City St. Mary's City
Company
Contact Kevin Owens
City Harwood
Company
Contact Robert W. Parks
City Crisfield
Company
Contact Herbert O. Patterson
City Mt. Airy
Company
Contact Clifford L. Patterson, Sr.
City Wheaton
Company
Contact Kenneth Penrod
City Beltsville
Company
Contact Lee R. Peters, Sr.
City Jarrettsville
Company
Contact Francis A. Pettolina

City Ocean City
Company
Contact Arthur A. Phillips, Sr.
City Fishing Creek
Company
Contact Robert Plitko
City Salisbury
Company
Contact Leonard H. Poole
City Glen Burnie
Company
Contact Samuel J. Porter
City Scotland
Company
Contact Thomas R. Price
City Stevensville
Company
Contact Daniel G. Pritchett
City St. Leonard
Company
Contact Joseph H. Quade, Jr.
City Baltimore
Company
Contact Thomas B. Quimby
City Queenstown
Company
Contact William Boyd Radford
City Dameron
Company
Contact Stephen B. Ramsey
City Joppa
Company
Contact Lawrence K. Raum
City Huntingtown
Company
Contact William L. Ray, III
City Deale
Company
Contact Wayne Reeser
City Easton
Company
Contact Frank Rehak
City Glen Arm
Company
Contact Charles T. Reichert, Jr.
City Ellicott City
Company
Contact Thomas E. Rials, Jr.
City Chesapeake Beach
Company
Contact Jack Richardson
City Preston
Company
Contact Charles E. Ridgell
City Scotland
Company
Contact Richard J. Roberts
City North Beach
Company
Contact John E. Robinson
City Solomons
Company
Contact William Charles Rode, Jr.
City Baltimore
Company
Contact George R. Rohe
City Annapolis
Company
Contact Jonathan M. Ross
City Stevensville
Company
Contact Donald C. Rowand
City Dameron
Company
Contact Henry G. Rowe, Jr.
City Ocean City
Company
Contact Darrell Roy
City Stevensville
Company
Contact Janet L. Rupp
City Chesapeake Beach
Company
Contact Joseph F. Rupp, III
City Lusby
Company
Contact Scott C. Russell
City Ridge
Company
Contact Claude W. Sacker
City Elkridge
Company
Contact Gary L. Sacks
City Ridge
Company
Contact Joseph W. Sadler, Sr.

City Stevensville
Company
Contact Merle J. Samakow
City Taylors Island
Company
Contact Mark Sampson
City Ocean City
Company
Contact James L. Sandusky
City Havre de Grace
Company
Contact J. Elwood Scaggs
City Queenstown
Company
Contact David A. Schauber
City Church Creek
Company
Contact Bruce Scheible
City Ridge
Company
Contact Douglas W. Scheible
City Ridge
Company
Contact Andrew F. Scheible
City Scotland
Company
Contact Andrew C. Schipul
City Centreville
Company
Contact William C. Schooley
City St. Leonard
Company
Contact Larry T. Schubert
City Bowie
Company
Contact George G. Schultz
City Middle River
Company
Contact Allen V. Scott
City Lusby
Company
Contact Ronald L. Scott, Jr.
City Ft. Washington
Company
Contact John L. Seymour
City Silver Spring
Company
Contact Michael E. Shaffner
City Huntingtown
Company
Contact Bernard F. Shea
City Lusby
Company
Contact Jackie R. Shelton
City Huntingtown
Company
Contact Dennis B. Shepherd
City Owings
Company
Contact Harry E. Sheppard, III
City Baltimore
Company
Contact Charles L. Shipley
City Cordova
Company
Contact Jeffrey N. Shores
City Trappe
Company
Contact Charles H. Simms
City Ridge
Company
Contact Roland M. Simounet
City North Beach
Company
Contact Albert W. Simpson
City Ocean City
Company
Contact Charles R. Sisson
City North Beach
Company
Contact Charles D. Skinner
City Annapolis
Company
Contact Robert Slaff
City Annapolis
Company
Contact Jack Smack
City Huntingtown
Company
Contact Alton L. Smith, Jr.
City Damascus
Company
Contact Michael D. Smith
City Shadyside
Company
Contact James L. Smith

City Gambrills
Company
Contact Stanley M. Smith, Sr.
City Westover
Company
Contact James T. Somerville
City Loveville
Company
Contact John A. Spangler
City Solomons
Company
Contact Stephen W. Spedden
City St. Inigoes
Company
Contact Steven Spurry
City St. Michaels
Company
Contact Chris F. Spurry
City St. Michaels
Company
Contact Gary F. Stamm
City Ocean City
Company
Contact Michael O. Starrett
City Accokeek
Company
Contact Michael P. Stewart
City Finksburg
Company
Contact Mary Carolyn Stine
City Cobb Island
Company
Contact David W. Stover
City Huntingtown
Company
Contact George J. Stransky, Jr.
City Arnold
Company
Contact Jeffrey M. Streett
City Fallston
Company
Contact Lenwood Sturdivant
City Grasonville
Company
Contact Paul L. Sturgis
City Princess Anne
Company
Contact Christopher G. Sullivan
City Chesapeake Beach
Company
Contact James E. Swagler
City Berlin
Company
Contact Jeffrey J. Swanson
City Tall Timbers
Company
Contact Howard F. Sweet
City Earleville
Company
Contact Barry Franklin Sweitzer
City Baltimore
Company
Contact Adam F. Szczypinski
City Timonium
Company
Contact Norman W. Talbert
City Temple Hills
Company
Contact Timothy N. Tanis
City Ocean City
Company
Contact George D. Tawes
City Crisfield
Company
Contact Charles N. Tawes, Jr.
City Princess Anne
Company
Contact Harry L. Tayloe
City Lothian
Company
Contact Matthew Taylor
City Lusby
Company
Contact James B. Tennyson
City California
Company
Contact F. William Thim
City Baltimore
Company
Contact Larry C. Thomas, Sr.
City Annapolis
Company
Contact Charles F. Thomas
City Baltimore
Company
Contact Lawrence Thomas

City Baltimore
Company
Contact Ralph L. Thompson
City Edgewater
Company
Contact David W. Thompson
City Tall Timbers
Company
Contact William K. Thompson
City Monkton
Company
Contact Michael J. Tihila
City Berlin
Company
Contact Lawrence D. Tippett
City Ridge
Company
Contact George L. Todd, Sr.
City Crisfield
Company
Contact Carl M. Toepfer
City Prince Frederick
Company
Contact Capt. Randy Townsend
City Chestertown
Company
Contact Robert L. Troup
City Seabrook
Company
Contact William Edward Turner
City Chesapeake Beach
Company
Contact Stephen L. Vierkorn
City Edgewater
Company
Contact Andrew Vrablic
City Stevensville
Company
Contact William G. Wade
City Dunkirk
Company
Contact Richard C. Wader
City Gambrills
Company
Contact John W. Walker
City Henderson
Company
Contact Jamie L. Ward
City Dowell
Company
Contact Robert W. Ward
City Owings
Company
Contact Willard C. Ward
City Chesapeake Beach
Company
Contact James Thomas Watkinson
City Prince Frederick
Company
Contact Christopher D. Watkowski
City Glen Burnie
Company
Contact Jerry Weakley
City Chesapeake Beach
Company
Contact James T. Webb, Jr.
City Dunkirk
Company
Contact Edward T. Webster
City Wenona
Company
Contact William Weiland
City Chance
Company
Contact Chris A. White
City Abingdon
Company
Contact Gary M. Whitehair
City Ellicott City
Company
Contact Ronald H. Whiting
City Baltimore
Company
Contact John F. Wilkinson
City Arnold
Company
Contact George G. Willett
City White Plains
Company
Contact Wayne Willett
City White Plains
Company
Contact Charles C. Williams
City Avenue
Company
Contact Walter C. Williams

City Solomons
Company
Contact Julian B. Williams, Jr.
City Ocean City
Company
Contact Clifton H. Williams
City Chesapeake Beach
Company
Contact Leland C. Williams
City Oxon Hill
Company
Contact George Willing
City Solomons
Company
Contact Ralph L. Wilson, Jr.
City Chester
Company
Contact Thomas W. Wilson, Jr.
City Lothian
Company
Contact Stuart L. Windsor
City Parkton
Company
Contact Raymond S. Wise
City Marion Station
Company
Contact William F. Wolfe, Jr.
City Queenstown
Company
Contact Robert Bruce Wooten
City Snow Hill
Company
Contact Montro Wright
City Grasonville
Company
Contact Todd R. Yeatman
City Dameron

Massachusetts

Company Adirondack Guide Service
Contact William Faelten
City Plymouth
Company B-Fast Charters
Contact Mike Bartlett
City N. Pembroke
Company Backlash Charters
Contact
City Edgartown
Company Fishing the Cape
Contact
City Harwich
Company Flyfishing the Salt
Contact
City Northfield
Company Lissivigeen
Contact
City Barre
Company Ridge Runners & River Runners
Contact William E. Davis, Jr.
City No. Adams
Company Rivers Edge Trading Co.
Contact
City Beverly
Company Talaview Resorts
Contact Evan Liberman
City Melrose
Company Talaview Resorts
Contact Christopher Taylor
City North Billerica
Company The Yankee Fleet
Contact
City Gloucester
Company Tip of the Cape Angling Adventures
Contact
City Truro
Company
Contact Capt. Chris J. Aubut
City Westport
Company
Contact Capt. Rusty Barry
City Marshfield Hills
Company
Contact Capt. Mike Bartlett
City N. Pembroke
Company
Contact Capt. Rich Bensen
City Chatham
Company
Contact Capt. Tony Biski

City Harwich
Company
Contact Capt. Fred Christian
City Marblehead
Company
Contact R. Andrew Cummings
City East Orleans
Company
Contact Richard P. Gerber
City Beverly
Company
Contact Cooper Gilkes
City Edgartown
Company
Contact Thomas A. Hunt
City Foxboro
Company
Contact Capt. Bob MacGregor
City West Falmouth
Company
Contact Capt. Bob McAdams
City Orleans
Company
Contact Capt. Jon Perette
City N. Weymouth
Company
Contact Capt. Dave Tracy
City North Plymouth
Company
Contact Chris Windram
City Housatonic

Michigan

Company 7 Seas Charters
Contact Marvin M. Miller
City Monroe
Company Al's Charter Service
Contact Al Tyrrell
City Port Huron
Company Argo Charters
Contact Louis C. Branch
City Muskegon
Company At East Sport Fishing
Contact Richard LaChance
City Romulus
Company Baldwin Creek Guide Service
Contact
City Baldwin
Company Bar-Lyn Charters
Contact Barry Wise
City Benton Harbor
Company Bay Breeze Yacht Charter
Contact Ken Coffman
City Traverse City
Company Bay Breeze Yacht Charter
Contact Harry Ashton III
City Mancelona
Company Bay Breeze Yacht Charter
Contact Bill Allgaier
City Traverse City
Company Bay Breeze Yacht Charters
Contact Michael Mueller
City Birmingham
Company Bay Breeze Yacht Charters
Contact Robert J. Louch
City Walled Lake
Company Bay Star Ventures
Contact Paul A. Starner
City Traverse City
Company Beyer's Charter Service
Contact Ronald R. Beyer
City Wayne
Company Big Jon Pro-Team Charters, Inc.
Contact Chrissie Hills
City Ludington
Company Blue Fin Sport Fishing Charter
Contact Terry Gray
City Charlevoix
Company Blue Heron Charters
Contact James Hansen
City Holland
Company Bolhouse Charters
Contact Gary and George Bolhouse
City Grand Rapids
Company Bray's Charter Service
Contact Tommy Bray
City Detroit
Company Brown's Landing Perch

Charters
Contact Jerry Brown
City Taws City
Company Budd's Gunisao Lake Lodge
Contact Jim & Brendon Budd
City Mason
Company Canadian Whitetails
Contact
City Coldwater
Company Canvasback Charters
Contact Tim Fales
City Harrison Twp.
Company Capt. Bill's Charters
Contact Bill VanLuven
City Marysville
Company Captain Chuck
Contact Chuck Wilkinson
City South Haven
Company Climax Charters
Contact Captain Thomas A. Reid
City Climax
Company Cold Coast Charter Service Inc.
Contact Eric Walline
City Saline
Company Cooper Head Charters
Contact Wayne A. Biederman
City Port Austin
Company D & D Charters
Contact Dave DeGrow
City Freeland
Company Danish Charters, Inc.
Contact Tommy M. Danish
City Newport
Company Detour Marine Inc.
Contact
City Detour
Company Easy Touch Charters
Contact Larry K. Quake
City Three Rivers
Company Encore Charters
Contact Capt. Ed Stell
City Grand Rapids
Company Fast Water, Flat Water Guide Service
Contact
City Ironwood
Company Fish Line
Contact F.Mark Rhoades
City Saranac
Company Fisherman's Center, Inc.
Contact G.L.Phillips
City Manistee
Company Fishermen's Information Services
Contact
City S.E. Grand Rapids
Company Fred Lee's Fly Fishing Guide Service
Contact
City Scotts
Company Gates Au Sable Lodge
Contact Rusty Gates
City Grayling
Company Genesee County Parks
Contact
City Flint
Company Gray Drake Outfitters
Contact Capt. Matthew A. Supinski
City Newaygo
Company Great Lakes Schooners
Contact
City Onekama
Company Greenfield Village/Henry Ford Museum
Contact
City Dearborn
Company Hall's Guiding Service
Contact Kyle L. Hall
City Kalamazoo
Company Harbortown Charters
Contact Douglas H. Severns
City Grand Haven
Company Hendershott/Frizzell
Contact L.L. Frizzell & Laurie Hendershott
City St.Joseph
Company Hollywood Charters
Contact Ed Patzer
City Shelby Twp.
Company Huron Charter Service
Contact Allen Elzinga
City Harbor Beach
Company Huron/Clinton Metrop. Auth.
Contact

City Brighton
Company Island Queen Charters
Contact Capt. Jack Behrens
City Detour Village
Company J & K Steamship Co.
Contact John Chamberlain
City Grand Ledge
Company J-Lyn Charters
Contact Kenneth & Janice Deaton
City Almont
Company Jeannie Sea II
Contact Rex B. Davis
City Charlevoix
Company Jim's Sport Fishing Charters
Contact Jim Beyers
City New Baltimore
Company Johnson's Pere Marquette Lodge
Contact
City Baldwin
Company Just In Time Industries
Contact Ron Cutler
City Lexington
Company Kingfisher Charter Service
Contact Dave Benore
City Monroe
Company Lake Michigan Fishing Charter
Contact Dave Helder
City Holland
Company LeChasseur Sport Fishing
Contact Joe Weiss
City Monroe
Company Leelanau Yacht Charter
Contact Lee Russell
City Traverse City
Company Linden Partners, Inc.
Contact Lee Hoyt
City Flint
Company Meritime Heritage
Contact
City Traverse City
Company Milo Industries
Contact Milo R. DeVries
City Spring Lake
Company Mishanda Charters
Contact Charles Pokorny
City Port Sanilac
Company National Park Concessions
Contact
City Houghton
Company New Buffalo Steelheaders
Contact
City New Buffalo
Company North-East Flyfishing
Contact
City Onaway
Company Northern Exposure Sportsfishing Charters
Contact Captain Dave Dybowski
City Sterling Heights
Company Northwest Charters
Contact Scott J. Anderson
City Traverse City
Company O J's Northport Charters
Contact Richard Seiferlein
City Turner
Company Para-Sail Beachwatch, Inc.
Contact
City Hart
Company Para-Sail, Inc.
Contact Jeffrey Porter
City Northport
Company Pisces Charter Service
Contact Lynn N. Ray
City Acme
Company Portage Lake Charter Service
Contact James Bennett
City Onekama
Company Professional Marine Services
Contact Harold D. DeHart
City Ocqueoc
Company Putney, McNeal Enterprise, Inc.
Contact
City Frankfort
Company Reel Rascal Fishing Charters
Contact Captain Ed Thompson, Jr.
City Ludington
Company Richard Rang Lake & Stream Charters
Contact Richard Rang
City Lachine
Company Riverview of Frankenmuth

Contact Jerry Kabat
City Frankenmuth
Company S.W.A.T. Charter Service
Contact Jerry Rankey
City Munger
Company Shelter Bay Charters
Contact Mitch Mattson
City Au Train
Company Shores Charters, Inc.
Contact John Yoe
City Ludington
Company Skipper Charter Service
Contact Dave Ristow
City Ada
Company Spirit of AuSable
Contact James E. Moon
City East Tawas
Company Stead Leasing, Inc.
Contact Vladimer P.Ponican
City Warren
Company Steelhead Lodge, Inc.
Contact David Bihlman
City Frankfort
Company Streamside Outfitters
Contact
City Williamsburg
Company T-Bone's Dive Shop
Contact Chris Wooten
City Beulah
Company T.M.B. Charter Service
Contact Steve Paslaski
City Oscoda
Company Talmadge Marchbanks
Contact James P.Whaley
City Mio
Company Tamarac Sportfishing Dock
Contact John Chippi
City Ludington
Company Tammy Too Charters
Contact Milo DeVries & Kenneth Melvin
City Spring Lake
Company Teresa Ann Charter Service
Contact Richard L. Vanderwest
City Fruitport
Company The AuSable River's Original Guide Service
Contact
City Grayling
Company The Mary E. Charter Svc.
Contact Emil Dean
City Bear Lake
Company Tom Sawyer Riverboat Co.
Contact
City Sault Ste. Marie
Company Touch of Class Charter Fishing Service
Contact Kevin Hughes
City Onekama
Company TradeWinds Charter Service
Contact Bill Currie
City LaSalle
Company Trans-Michigan Scuba Charter, Inc.
Contact
City Holton
Company Trek Trail/Panangling
Contact
City Ironwood
Company Trophy Charters II
Contact Capt. Mike Stowe
City St.Joseph
Company Ward Brothers Charters
Contact Bernie Ward
City Charlevoix
Company Waters Charter Service
Contact Bud Waters
City Madison Hts.
Company Wellington Maritime
Contact John P.Wellington
City Sault Ste. Marie
Company West Michigan Dive Center
Contact
City Muskegon
Company
Contact Charles Allen
City Clinton Twp.
Company
Contact Wayne E. Allen
City Tecumseh
Company
Contact Eric A. Anderson
City Hamilton

Company
Contact Jeffery Andreen
City Grand Rapids
Company
Contact Robert Andrews
City Grand Haven
Company
Contact Ross P.Arseneau
City Harrisville
Company
Contact Barry Aspenleiter
City Petoskey
Company
Contact David S. Badalamente
City Manistee
Company
Contact Charles A. Bair
City Erie
Company
Contact Carl G. Baker
City Williamsburg
Company
Contact Donald Barber
City Harrisville
Company
Contact Todd Bather
City Tawas City
Company
Contact Steve Batka
City West Olive
Company
Contact Kenneth T. Beloskur
City Harrisville
Company
Contact Roger Belter
City Spring Lake
Company
Contact Gerald B. Bettendorf
City Jackson
Company
Contact Chuck Bettinson
City Lansing
Company
Contact Charles H. Bettison
City Lansing
Company
Contact James R. Beyers
City New Baltimore
Company
Contact David Bickerstaff
City Orchard Lake
Company
Contact Robert H. Bingle
City Fair Haven
Company
Contact Bob Bingle
City Algonac
Company
Contact Garry Biniecki
City Port Sanilac
Company
Contact Gary L. Blackmore
City Williamsburg
Company
Contact Steven Block
City Frankenmuth
Company
Contact Dennis Blue
City Onekama
Company
Contact Richard D. Bonney
City Grand Haven
Company
Contact Gordon W. Boomer
City Traverse City
Company
Contact Edward E. Born
City Gobles
Company
Contact Don Boshoven
City Comstock Park
Company
Contact Edmund J. Bowen
City Williamsburg
Company
Contact Albert W. Bowers
City Marquette
Company
Contact Dennis Bowlby
City Schoolcraft
Company
Contact Steven D. Bradley
City Frankfort
Company
Contact Erval M. Bradley
City Frankfort

Company
Contact R.J.Branham
City Warren
Company
Contact Russel J. Branham
City Warren
Company
Contact George and John Brawley
City Niles
Company
Contact Tim Brendel
City North Port
Company
Contact Walter L. Bridges
City Montague
Company
Contact Martin Bringhard
City Port Huron
Company
Contact Earl R. Brink
City Manitou Beach
Company
Contact Randy Broadworth
City Caro
Company
Contact Dale A. Brockway
City Spruce
Company
Contact Roger Lee Bronkhorst
City Holland
Company
Contact Dale W. Brown
City Gladwin
Company
Contact Timothy Bruning
City Rogers City
Company
Contact Joseph F.Bryer
City Mt. Clemens
Company
Contact Craig W. Burch
City Lexington
Company
Contact Ronald Burget
City Buchanan
Company
Contact Daniel E. Burns
City Troy
Company
Contact Stanley and Julie Buxton
City Whitehall
Company
Contact Dewey J. Cameron
City Walled Lake
Company
Contact Lynn Capps
City Harrison Twp.
Company
Contact Jennifer B. Carlson
City Leland
Company
Contact William R. Carter
City Rochester Hills
Company
Contact Dominick Castoro
City Wellston
Company
Contact John I. Chamberlain
City Lansing
Company
Contact Bruce Charleston
City Bridgeman
Company
Contact Michael J. Chimelak
City Centerline
Company
Contact Daniel Chimelak
City St. Clair Shores
Company
Contact George C. Chimelak
City Detroit
Company
Contact Mark Chmura
City Bear Lake
Company
Contact Kent W. Choate
City Battle Creek
Company
Contact Lori Chouinard
City Menominee
Company
Contact Sam Ciaramitaro
City Warren
Company
Contact James D. Clark
City East Tawas

Company
Contact Kevin D. Clark
City Plymouth
Company
Contact Roger R. Clark
City Eaton Rapids
Company
Contact Russ A. Clark
City Stevensville
Company
Contact Jim Clark
City East Tawas
Company
Contact William J. Clayton
City Grosse Ile
Company
Contact Brian Cleveland
City Spring Lake
Company
Contact Richard L. Close
City Holton
Company
Contact Mike Cnudde
City Manistee
Company
Contact Douglas R. Coar
City Kentwood
Company
Contact Laurence D. Coder
City Kawkawlin
Company
Contact Norman W. Coffman
City Saugatuck
Company
Contact William Collins
City Dearborn
Company
Contact Walter Compton
City Canton
Company
Contact Michael R. Connolly
City Alpena
Company
Contact Penalope D. Cook
City Mt. Pleasant
Company
Contact David Coon
City Caro
Company
Contact Joseph P.Copland
City Oscoda
Company
Contact Jerry L. and Carol Crake
City Brown City
Company
Contact Bernard W. Crandall
City Suttons Bay
Company
Contact Dan Cruchon
City Lexington
Company
Contact William R. Currie
City LaSalle
Company
Contact John Dall
City Frankfort
Company
Contact Rodney J. Danielson
City Ludington
Company
Contact Michael B. Davis
City Ludington
Company
Contact Phil Defenbaugh
City Monroe
Company
Contact William R. Dega
City St. Clair
Company
Contact David J. DeGrow
City Freeland
Company
Contact Jerry W. Dilts
City Benton Harbor
Company
Contact Jim Dinsmore
City Tawas City
Company
Contact Robert L. Dixon
City Ludington
Company
Contact William M. Doak
City Baroda
Company
Contact John Dobis
City Harrisville

Company
Contact Andrew R. Donato
City Marysville
Company
Contact Richard Doran
City Muskegon
Company
Contact Roger Doyle
City Shelby Township
Company
Contact William and Judy Draper
City Spring Lake
Company
Contact Willliam L. Draper
City Spring Lake
Company
Contact Harold Dubay
City Saginaw
Company
Contact Donald Dubois
City Traverse City
Company
Contact Ron Dubsky
City Romulus
Company
Contact William Duckwall
City Marquette
Company
Contact John A. Duffy
City Leland
Company
Contact William F. Dusterhoft
City Traverse City
Company
Contact Dale E. Ealy
City Acme
Company
Contact Edward R. Eichbrecht
City Columbus
Company
Contact Gary L. Eikey
City Traverse City
Company
Contact David J. Ellis
City Kalamazoo
Company
Contact John Emch
City Harper Woods
Company
Contact John Emory
City Traverse City
Company
Contact Dale W. and Kevin Ender
City St. Joseph
Company
Contact Robert J. Engel
City Douglas
Company
Contact Frank D. English
City Onekama
Company
Contact David A. Erickson
City Waterford
Company
Contact James L. Fenner
City Troy
Company
Contact Theodore A. Fenwerda
City Mears
Company
Contact Joan Ferguson
City Lansing
Company
Contact Raymond R. Fifarek
City Traverse City
Company
Contact Arthur M. Fitzgerald
City Bay City
Company
Contact John E. Fouch
City Traverse City
Company
Contact Paul K. Fox
City Byron
Company
Contact Ronald L. Frank
City Monroe
Company
Contact George R. Freeman
City Lansing
Company
Contact Fredrick W. Funkey
City Copper Harbor
Company
Contact Gary Gamble
City Niles

Company
Contact Blake H. Gardner
City New Baltimore
Company
Contact Cameron Garst
City Traverse City
Company
Contact Leo A. Gayan
City Ironwood
Company
Contact James and Diane Gentel
City Northport
Company
Contact Alfred Gering
City Romulus
Company
Contact Myron W. Gilbert
City Brooklyn
Company
Contact Dwight Gillette
City Berrien Springs
Company
Contact Mike Gnatkowski
City Ludington
Company
Contact Lawrence G. Godwin
City Lapeer
Company
Contact Bobby J. Goins
City Temperance
Company
Contact Donald Goldner
City Eau Clair
Company
Contact Dennis L. Gorsuch
City Sault Ste. Marie
Company
Contact David R. Gramza
City Manistee
Company
Contact Bruce E. Grant
City Rogers City
Company
Contact David R. Granza
City Manistee
Company
Contact Gaylord Gray
City Comstock Park
Company
Contact Frederick R. Griffin
City Avoca
Company
Contact Dennnis L. Grinold
City Lansing
Company
Contact Dennis L. Grinold
City Lansing
Company
Contact Ardie R. Grubaugh
City Orchard Lake
Company
Contact Larry H. Haeger
City Montague
Company
Contact Randall Hagerman
City East Lansing
Company
Contact Steve Hamilton
City Eaton Rapids
Company
Contact Jon C. Hamm
City Spring Lake
Company
Contact Vernon L. Hart
City Greenbush
Company
Contact Richard E. Haslett
City Madison Heights
Company
Contact Billy A. Hawthorne
City Caseville
Company
Contact George Hays
City Grand Haven
Company
Contact Aaron T. Henker
City Allen Park
Company
Contact Wallace Hodges
City Allendale
Company
Contact Douglas L. Holcer
City Clyde
Company
Contact Russell Holland
City Ypsilanti

Company
Contact Richard and Carol Hooper
City Grand Ledge
Company
Contact Jack J. Hopaluk
City Sterling Heights
Company
Contact Ronald L. Horton
City AuGres
Company
Contact Ronald Horton
City Augres
Company
Contact Rick Howard
City Traverse City
Company
Contact Jon K. Howard
City Bristol
Company
Contact John M. Huck
City Manistee
Company
Contact Roger Huelsberg
City Benton Harbor
Company
Contact Niles Huey
City Whitmore Lake
Company
Contact Terry Huffman
City Marquette
Company
Contact Donald W. Huskin
City Battle Creek
Company
Contact George Husted
City Omena
Company
Contact Bart Huthwaite
City Mackinac Island
Company
Contact Jeff Iid
City Metamora
Company
Contact Floyd G. and Patricia Ikens
City Elberta
Company
Contact James A. Jachim
City Grand Haven
Company
Contact James D. Jackman
City Calumet
Company
Contact Paul Jacobs
City Traverse City
Company
Contact Thomas M. Jacobs
City Kentwood
Company
Contact George W. Janssen
City Arcadia
Company
Contact Edward D. Jenkins
City Belding
Company
Contact Russell W. Johnson
City Ironwood
Company
Contact James D. Johnson
City Ironwood
Company
Contact Marijo Johnson
City Muskegon
Company
Contact Brett R. Johnson
City Drummond Island
Company
Contact Harvey Jones
City Lake Ann
Company
Contact Steven R. Jones
City Harrison Twp.
Company
Contact Michael R. Joyce
City Lincoln
Company
Contact Marion R. Sunday, Jr.
City Vernon
Company
Contact Charles O. Justice
City Dundee
Company
Contact William R. Kampfert
City Wayne
Company
Contact Pal B. Kamprath
City Monroe

Company
Contact Walter R. Karboske
City Ludington
Company
Contact Raymond J. Karboske
City Ludington
Company
Contact Jim J. Karr
City Grand Haven
Company
Contact Robert M. Keehne
City Shelby
Company
Contact Jerry Keeler
City Westland
Company
Contact Capt. John Keki
City Horton
Company
Contact Fred A. Kenny
City Muskegon
Company
Contact David Kessel
City Baldwin
Company
Contact David Kimar
City AuTrain
Company
Contact Ronald Kimball
City New Buffalo
Company
Contact Daniel L. Kingery
City Grand Haven
Company
Contact Robert H. Kinniburgh
City Newaygo
Company
Contact Steve Kirby
City Tawas
Company
Contact Jack Kirby
City Muskegon
Company
Contact Robert E. Klein
City Allendale
Company
Contact George L. Knight
City Kinde
Company
Contact Charles Knipschild
City Benton Harbor
Company
Contact David A. Kobasic
City Escanaba
Company
Contact Daniel J. Kopytek
City Harrison Twp.
Company
Contact Robert G. Kornosky
City Harrison Twp.
Company
Contact William Kouba
City Alpena
Company
Contact William E. Kouba
City Alpena
Company
Contact Richard Kraklau
City Benton Harbor
Company
Contact David M. Krawczyk
City Montague
Company
Contact Albert Krzyston
City Monroe
Company
Contact Thaddeus E. Kubinski
City St. Clair Shores
Company
Contact George and Gloria Kuhr
City Manistee
Company
Contact Preston Kuks
City Grand Rapids
Company
Contact Bryan A. Kwiatkowski
City Alpena
Company
Contact Albert W. Laaksonen
City Kalamazoo
Company
Contact Janette Velting and Thomas Laffan
City Kalamazoo
Company
Contact Stephen J. Lamb

City Waterford
Company
Contact Capt. Edward Lamhart
City LaSalle
Company
Contact Michael J. Lantzy
City Port Austin
Company
Contact Dennis J. Lautner
City Traverse City
Company
Contact William E. Lavender
City Midland
Company
Contact Jerry G. Lawrence
City Port Hope
Company
Contact Jerry G. Lawrence
City Rochester Hills
Company
Contact Dave Ledwa
City Lake Leelanau
Company
Contact Jerry Lee
City Livinia
Company
Contact Jim G. Leishman
City Pentwater
Company
Contact Eugene Lentz
City Frankfort
Company
Contact Alexander Lesh
City Warren
Company
Contact Ronald E. Levitan
City Redford Twp
Company
Contact David W. Lewis
City Big Rapids
Company
Contact John R. Lindenau
City Interlochen
Company
Contact Peter J. Lindquist
City Munising
Company
Contact Kenneth N. Loeser
City Pentwater
Company
Contact John P. Loman
City Bay City
Company
Contact James R. Love
City Benzonia
Company
Contact James B. Lowe
City Grand Marais
Company
Contact William L. Lowrie
City Ludington
Company
Contact Edward J. Lozowski
City Goodells
Company
Contact Paul L. Luedtke
City Frankfort
Company
Contact Alfred MacDonald
City Manistee
Company
Contact Glenn E. MacDonald
City Marine City
Company
Contact David L. MacKenzie
City Buchanan
Company
Contact David MacKenzie
City Niles
Company
Contact James M. Maki
City Marquette
Company
Contact Ted Maniurski
City Whitehall
Company
Contact David Maraccini
City Iron Mountain
Company
Contact Larry Lee Marek
City Comstock Park
Company
Contact Steven T. & Arthur T. Martin
City Troy
Company
Contact James C. Marton

City New Boston
Company
Contact John Matthews
City Utica
Company
Contact James F. Mattis
City Thompsonville
Company
Contact Mitchell K. Mattson
City AuTrain
Company
Contact Derald R. May
City Berrien Springs
Company
Contact Scott McClary
City Muskegon
Company
Contact Paul D. McClure
City Canton
Company
Contact William and Deborah McLaughlin
City Sault Ste. Marie
Company
Contact Todd G. McLean
City Traverse City
Company
Contact Daniel P. McManman
City Ironwood
Company
Contact Eddie McMillion
City Wayne
Company
Contact Thomas J. Mercier
City Dryden
Company
Contact Vern A. Metz
City Holly
Company
Contact Lyle Meyer
City Bay City
Company
Contact Dean E. Michael
City Owosso
Company
Contact Frank Michelfelder
City Ypsilanti
Company
Contact Christopher Miles
City Traverse City
Company
Contact Eric Alan and Naomi K. Mills
City Algonac
Company
Contact Michael L. Mitchell
City Westland
Company
Contact Pat Mitchell
City Boyne City
Company
Contact Patrick C. Mitchell
City Boyne City
Company
Contact Henry R. Mojeske
City Allen Park
Company
Contact Donald G. and Linda L. Moloney
City Lansing
Company
Contact Donald Moore
City Charlotte
Company
Contact Michael G. Morgan
City Brighton
Company
Contact Ralph and Steven Morrill
City Ludington
Company
Contact James and Drew Morris
City Muskegon
Company
Contact James M. Munoz
City Leland
Company
Contact Dick Murphy
City Traverse City
Company
Contact Richard C. Murphy
City Frankfort
Company
Contact Ross L. Nave
City Onaway
Company
Contact Kenneth E. Neidlinger
City St. Joseph

Company
Contact Gary Nelson
City Lansing
Company
Contact Wes I. Newberry
City Ann Arbor
Company
Contact Vicki Nichols
City South Haven
Company
Contact Raymond P. Niemi
City Ironwood
Company
Contact Nelson Nienhuis
City Spring Lake
Company
Contact Lucy L. Noonan
City Lake Leelanau
Company
Contact Richard E. Nottke
City Traverse City
Company
Contact Ray Novack
City Clinton Twp.
Company
Contact Ray J. Novack, Jr.
City Sterling Heights
Company
Contact Terry L. Novak
City Harrison Township
Company
Contact Boyd M. Nutting
City Barbeau
Company
Contact Dennis M. and Andrea K.J. Olson
City Frankfort
Company
Contact Steve Otterbein
City Traverse City
Company
Contact Charles E. Owens
City Inkster
Company
Contact Capt. Paul Pacholski
City Erie
Company
Contact Greg Packer
City Lapeer
Company
Contact Peter Palajac
City Traverse City
Company
Contact Jeffrey L. Parker
City Port Huron
Company
Contact Delbert J. Parsons
City Frankfort
Company
Contact Randy Patzkowsky
City St. Joseph
Company
Contact Glenn T. and Donna Pelkey
City Mt. Clemens
Company
Contact Thomas Perilloux
City Ludington
Company
Contact Richard E. Perry
City Bear Lake
Company
Contact James M. Perry
City Highland
Company
Contact Bruce Perry
City St. Louis
Company
Contact William P. Petz
City Rogers City
Company
Contact Mick Pfeiffer
City Traverse City
Company
Contact George J. Pierson
City Holland
Company
Contact Fred 'Fritz' Pinkerman
City Temperance
Company
Contact Daniel Plescher
City Copper Harbor
Company
Contact Alvin E. Pletzke
City Bruce Crossing
Company
Contact Ronald C. Plosnak

City South Haven
Company
Contact Charles Pokorny III
City Port Sanilac
Company
Contact James M. Powers
City Negaunee
Company
Contact Thomas J. Poynter
City Kearsarge
Company
Contact Harry Pratley
City Battle Creek
Company
Contact Duncan Price
City L'Anse
Company
Contact Robert T. Price
City Shelby Township
Company
Contact Terry Promowicz
City Flint
Company
Contact Penny L. Prough
City Bronson
Company
Contact Harry A. Putney
City Frankfort
Company
Contact Richard L. Rang
City Lachine
Company
Contact Jerry D. and Judith A. Rank
City Beulah
Company
Contact Jerry Rankey
City Munger
Company
Contact Harold Raskey
City Manistee
Company
Contact David E. Rasmussen
City White Cloud
Company
Contact Lynn Ray
City Williamsburg
Company
Contact Roger D. and Patricia M. Ray
City Lansing
Company
Contact Doug Reckling
City St. Clair Shores
Company
Contact Edward Retherford
City Alpena
Company
Contact Michael E. Rice
City Frankfort
Company
Contact David Richardson
City Sanford
Company
Contact Thomas F. Richmond
City Cadillac
Company
Contact Michael Riley
City Grindstone City
Company
Contact Larry D. Ring
City Warren
Company
Contact David W. Ristow
City Ada
Company
Contact Steven R. Robards
City St. Joseph
Company
Contact William H. and Janis Robinette
City Clinton Twp.
Company
Contact Delane Robinson
City Muskegon
Company
Contact John Rockwood
City Maple City
Company
Contact Rodney Rogus
City New Baltimore
Company
Contact Robert C. and John W. Rokos
City Traverse City
Company
Contact Robert W. Rommel
City Frankfort
Company

Contact Christian Roth
City Sterling Heights
Company
Contact Joseph and David Royzer
City Monroe
Company
Contact Peter Ruboyianes
City Ludington
Company
Contact Allan W. Rumball
City Oscoda
Company
Contact Gordon Runyon, Jr.
City Belleville
Company
Contact David E. and Nancy Rusch
City St. Louis
Company
Contact Jan Sabin
City Marquette
Company
Contact A. Sachs
City Traverse City
Company
Contact Larry Sanderson
City Alpena
Company
Contact Barbara Sanderson
City Alpena
Company
Contact George Satterfield
City Monroe
Company
Contact William H. Schadler
City Benton Harbor
Company
Contact Larry R. Scharich
City Bay City
Company
Contact Vernon A. Schatz
City Garden City
Company
Contact Patrick Schiller
City Montague
Company
Contact Tom L. Schippa
City Holland
Company
Contact Rocky L. Schippa
City Hamilton
Company
Contact Paul Schlafley
City Manistee
Company
Contact Robert Schlitts
City Traverse City
Company
Contact Richard O. Seiferlein
City Turner
Company
Contact Bob Semanski
City East Pointe
Company
Contact Lloyd B. Service
City Lansing
Company
Contact Patrick Shafer
City Muskegon
Company
Contact Bernard Shellman
City Romulus
Company
Contact Patrick H. & Janet L. Sheridan
City Lexington
Company
Contact John D. Skrobot
City Oscoda
Company
Contact Wayne Smith
City Troy
Company
Contact Daniel N. Smith
City Alpena
Company
Contact Don C. Smith, Sr.
City Oscoda
Company
Contact Robert M. Smith
City Plymouth
Company
Contact Arden T. Smith
City Cadillac
Company
Contact Earl Soderquist
City Frankfort
Company

Contact Gary L. Somers
City Barton City
Company
Contact Michael Spaulding
City Petersburg
Company
Contact John L. Spencer
City Traverse City
Company
Contact Richard L. Bartley J. Spieth
City Petersburg
Company
Contact Gary St. Martin
City N. Muskegon
Company
Contact Dick Stafford
City Gladstone
Company
Contact Arthur L. Stanton
City Rhodes
Company
Contact James A. Stayer
City Lexington
Company
Contact Ronald L. Stewart
City Oscoda
Company
Contact Edward Stowe
City Ludington
Company
Contact Michael Stowe
City Niles
Company
Contact Robert J. Strathmann
City Holt
Company
Contact David L. Streeter
City South Haven
Company
Contact Paul L. Strobel
City Pontiac
Company
Contact Terry L. Strom
City Haslett
Company
Contact David Strong
City Kalamazoo
Company
Contact Douglas W. Strzynski
City Ludington
Company
Contact Eric W. Stuecher
City Shelby Township
Company
Contact Robert F. Sugar
City Hemlock
Company
Contact James S. Swanezy
City Holland
Company
Contact Robert Swantek
City Grand Rapids
Company
Contact Dan Swartz
City Washington
Company
Contact Hitoshi Takahashi
City Midland
Company
Contact James Talbot
City Cental Lake
Company
Contact Arnold Taratuta
City Alpena
Company
Contact Clifford E. Taylor
City Ludington
Company
Contact Richard Taylor
City Fenton
Company
Contact Daniel Tebo
City Alto
Company
Contact William A. Theisen
City Sodus
Company
Contact Jeff Tropf
City Northport
Company
Contact Douglas M. Trouten
City Newport
Company
Contact Richard Tworek
City Harrison Twisp
Company

Contact Edward R. Tworek
City Mt. Clemens
Company
Contact Ruth VanAtter
City White Hall
Company
Contact Tom Vanderwest
City Muskkegon
Company
Contact Charles M. and John VanDusen
City Traverse City
Company
Contact Charlie VanDusen
City Traverse City
Company
Contact Thomas N. VanItteersum
City Onekama
Company
Contact Jack G. VanLoon
City Grand Haven
Company
Contact William VanLuven
City Marysville
Company
Contact Palmer Veen
City Pentwater
Company
Contact Douglas Veihl
City Mears
Company
Contact Mark L. Veurink
City Spring Lake
Company
Contact Robert K. Vickey
City Harrisville
Company
Contact Claude Vogelheim
City Rogers City
Company
Contact Terry R. Walsh
City AuGres
Company
Contact Lee Walter
City Traverse City
Company
Contact Henry Walters, Jr.
City Fair Haven
Company
Contact Bob Walton
City Traverse City
Company
Contact Bernie Ward III
City Charlevoix
Company
Contact Jeffrey Ward
City Holland
Company
Contact Robert S. Ward
City Belding
Company
Contact Donald L. Ward
City Charlevoix
Company
Contact Bernie Ward, Jr.
City Charlevoix
Company
Contact Robert H. Warner
City Homer
Company
Contact Kelly Warner
City Homer
Company
Contact Dewey H. Waters
City Midison Heights
Company
Contact Rodney Weiss
City Port Hope
Company
Contact Ross Wellman
City Oscoda
Company
Contact Jerry Welton
City Luna Pier
Company
Contact George E. Westcott
City Gobels
Company
Contact Ronald Westrate
City Holland
Company
Contact Peter J. White
City Ludington
Company
Contact Charles G. White
City Grand Rapids

Company
Contact Mark White
City Charlevoix
Company
Contact Robert White
City Sanford
Company
Contact Ken Whitney
City Grand Haven
Company
Contact Theodore J. Wiley
City New Baltimore
Company
Contact Lorrie Witt
City Three River
Company
Contact James E. Wohlford
City Harbor Beach
Company
Contact Richard F. Wolf, Jr.
City Belleville
Company
Contact Joe Wolff
City Farmington Hills
Company
Contact Charles A. Wood
City Alpena
Company
Contact W. D. Workman
City Benzonia
Company
Contact William C. Wright
City Lake Leelanau
Company
Contact Percy L. Wright
City AuGres
Company
Contact Paul B. Yeager
City Sparta
Company
Contact Raymond Yeager
City Ludington
Company
Contact Ken Yee
City Grand Haven
Company
Contact Edward C. Zeerip
City Grand Rapids
Company
Contact Michael Zielinski
City Gibraltar

Minnesota

Company Agency Bay Lodge
Contact Ron & Sharon Palmer
City Walker
Company Alaska Fish Guides
Contact George B. Webster IV
City Deep Haven
Company Angle Outpost Resort
Contact Dave & Jessica Fandrich
City Angle Inlet
Company Angler's Inn Resort
Contact Jerry & Marie Hemen
City Aitkin
Company Arctic Lodges Ltd.
Contact Fred & Linda Lockhart
City Burnsville
Company Arneson's Rocky Point
Contact Edward Arnesen
City Roosevelt
Company Arrowhead Lodge & Resort
Contact Kathy Wilson
City Ray
Company Arrowhead Outfitters, Inc.
Contact Howard Tieden
City Cambridge
Company Ashambie Outpost Ltd.
Contact Scott & Lynda Marvin
City Warroad
Company Ballard's Resort
Contact
City Baudette
Company Bally Creek Camp
Contact David & Cathi Williams
City Grand Marais
Company Bay Store & Resort
Contact Frank & Laura Walsh
City Oak Island
Company Berger's Trading Post
Contact Elizabeth Lessard & Glennda

Scott
City Crane Lake
Company Big Rock Resort
Contact Karl & Karen Kelnhofer
City Walker
Company Bill Zup's Camps
Contact Mark & Kathy Zup
City Crane Lake
Company Bill Zups's Fishing Camps
Contact
City Ely
Company Birch Grove Resort
Contact Elaine Goodrum
City Ray
Company Birch Knoll Ranch
Contact Duke Hust
City Wayzata
Company Black Pine Beach Resort
Contact Bob & Lynn Scharenbroich
City Pequot Lakes
Company Black's Crescent Beach
Resort
Contact Jerry & Deanna Pekar
City Osakis
Company Borde Du Lac Lodge
Contact E.K. & Maribeth Crowell
City Benedict
Company Border View Lodge
Contact Mike Trueman
City Baudette
Company Borderland Lodge
Contact Eric & Jan Thompson
City Grand Marais
Company Borderland Lodge &
Outfitters
Contact
City Crane Lake
Company Buck Point Lodge & Resort
Contact Jack & Margaret Weiler
City Osakis
Company Campbell's Cabins
Contact John & Jay Handberg Robert
City Crane Lake
Company Canadian Border Outfitters
Contact
City Ely
Company Canoe Country Cabins &
Campgrounds
Contact Bob Olson
City Ely
Company City Dock Launch Fishing
Contact Jerry & Bonnie Stewart
City Walker
Company Cossette's Cove Resort
Contact Jack & Judy Cossette
City Walker
Company Custom Cabin Rentals
Contact Mike Vosburgh
City Ely
Company Deer Horn Resort
Contact Eileen S. Trandel
City Ray
Company Dickie's Portside Resort
Contact Richard Gadbois
City Isle
Company Driftwood Lodge Resort
Contact Don & Brenda Granger
City Ray
Company Eagle Ridge at Lusten
Mountains
Contact Kristin Althaus
City Lusten
Company Early Inn Resort &
Campgrounds
Contact Doug & Karla Dagel
City Osakis
Company Edgewater Resort
Contact Tom Bosiger
City Spring Lake
Company End of the Trail Lodge
Contact Dave & Sandy Slanga
City Tower
Company Fontenelle Resort
Contact Ken Reynolds
City Hines
Company Four Seasons Resort
Contact Arden & Jeanette Thompson
City Bena
Company Francis Resort
Contact Robert & Mildred Gay
City Isle
Company Golden Eagle Lodge
Contact Dan Baumann
City Grand Marais
Company Gone Again Charter
Service

Contact Capt. Kerry E. Charlet
City Crystal
Company Grizzly Creek Lodge
Contact
City Eden Prairie
Company Gunflint Pines Resort
Contact Dick & Ronnie Smith
City Grand Marais
Company Hatchet Lake Lodge
Contact
City Elk River
Company Heart Beat Charters
Contact Capt. Duane E. Bradley
City Woodbury
Company Heath's Resort
Contact Dave & Carole Heath
City Pine River
Company Hill's Wilderness Canoe Trips
Contact
City Ely
Company Hillcrest Resort
Contact Mark & Claudia
City McGregor
Company Huddle's South Shore
Resort
Contact Roy & Kay Huddle
City Whiphol
Company Hunter's Point
Contact John & Laurie Siebolds
City Isle
Company Idlewilde Resort & Lodge
Contact Gary & Judy Stellick
City Osakis
Company Island View Lodge
Contact Jim & Candace Bischoff
City International Falls
Company Ivanhoe Resort
Contact
City Walker
Company Jack's Taxidermy/Guiding
Contact
City Staples
Company Jake's Northwest Angle
Contact Dave Colson
City Angle Inlet
Company John Herrick's Trophy
Smallmouth
Contact
City Ely
Company Judd's Resort
Contact Ron & Sharon Hunter
City Bena
Company KaBeeLo Lodge
Contact Harold & Ann Lohn
City Prior Lake
Company Karpen's Sunset Bay Resort
Contact Joe & Marty
City Isle
Company Kawishiwi Lodge &
Outfitters
Contact Frank T. Udovich
City Ely
Company KDK Charter Service
Contact Capt. David Koneczny
City Duluth
Company Lake Superior Excursions
Contact Dana & ChunAe Kollars
City Beaver Bay
Company Lakeshore Resort
Contact Chuck & Mary Ward
City Osakis
Company LaTourell's Resort &
Outfitters
Contact The LaTourells
City Ely
Company Lynn Lake Fly-In Outpost
Camps
Contact
City Long Prairie
Company McArdle's Resort
Contact Craig & Paige Brown
City Bena
Company McQuoid's Inn
Contact Terry McQuoid
City Isle
Company Mille Lacs Hunting Lodge
Contact
City Onamia
Company Moore's Lodge
Contact Al & Babs Debes
City Walker
Company Muskego Point Resort
Contact Judy & Jennifer Hughes
Grant
City Cook
Company Nor'wester Lodge &

Company Garry Garrison Guide Service
Contact Garry Garrison
City Theodosia
Company Graven's Resort
Contact Dale Graven
City Falcon
Company Greg's Guide Service
Contact Greg Clanahan
City Poplar Bluff
Company Holcomb's Guide Service
Contact Mike Holcomb
City O'Fallon
Company Holliday Landing
Contact Joe Blattel
City Greenville
Company Hunting Farm Management
Contact Jim & Beth Dwiggins
City Browning
Company Huzzah Valley Camping Resort
Contact Cottrell Family
City Steelville
Company Jerry Clouse Guide Service
Contact Jerry Clouse
City Reed Springs
Company Lea Guide Service
Contact Wallace Lea
City Forsythe
Company Light House Harbor Co., Inc.
Contact Bob Blake
City Hermitage
Company Little Man's Guide Service
Contact Terry Blankenship
City Iberia
Company Lost Creek Lodge
Contact Bill Sebastian
City Greenville
Company Lost Quarter Hunting Club
Contact Ann Walton
City Mendon
Company Marvin Deckard Professional Guide Ser.
Contact
City Clinton
Company McBride's Resort & RV Park
Contact Dennis & Sandy Picou
City Protem
Company Mike Cochran Guide Service
Contact Mike Cochran
City Gainesville
Company Miller's Motor Lodge
Contact The Millers
City Wappapello
Company Niangua River Oasis
Contact Bob & Barbara Burns
City Lebanon
Company Noland Point Fishing Resort
Contact
City Theodosia
Company Olan Yokum Guide Service
Contact
City Rockaway Beach
Company Ozark Sunrise Expeditions
Contact Ralph Flippo
City Joplin
Company Pontiac Cove Marina
Contact Tim Morgan
City Pontiac
Company Rainbow Trout Ranch
Contact
City Rockbridge
Company Ralph Flippo's Guide Service
Contact Ralph Flippo
City Greenfield
Company Rich's Guide Service
Contact Rich Wade
City Licking
Company Rich's Last Resort
Contact Rich Sphar
City Duke
Company Richard's Canoe Rental
Contact Jerry & Karen Richard
City Alton
Company Ridgewood Resort
Contact Ginny Matyska
City Isabella
Company Riverside Canoe Rental
Contact
City Caulfield
Company Ryan's Resort
Contact Ken Williams
City Lake Ozark

Company S & H Bait & Tackle Inc.
Contact Mike Holcomb
City O'Fallon
Company Show Me Safaris
Contact Mark Hampton
City Summersville
Company Spring Creek Guide Service
Contact Don Schnable & Sons
City Isabella
Company Spring Creek Resort
Contact
City Isabella
Company Steve Blake Hunting & Fishing Guide
Contact Steve Blake
City Warsaw
Company Stockton State Park Marina
Contact Doug Hufferd
City Stockton
Company Stoutsville Resort & RV Park
Contact Don & Nancy
City Stoutsville
Company Table Rock Fishing Guide Service
Contact Jim Neeley
City Ridgedale
Company Tackle & Bait Shop
Contact Jerry Nauss
City Sunrise Beach
Company Taylormade River Treks
Contact Chris & Shawn Taylor
City Tecumseh
Company The Fraley Ranch
Contact Tom & Barb Fraley
City Newburg
Company Theodosia Marina-Resort, Inc.
Contact Bret & Melonie Cook
City Theodosia
Company Thunder Bay Resort
Contact
City Isabella
Company Tri Lakes Bait & Tackle
Contact Charlie Davis & Sam Krumrey
City Reed Spring
Company Tri-Lakes Guide Service
Contact Chafin & Kendall Snider
City Kimberling
Company Twin Bridges Campground & Canoe
Contact John & Frankie Stogsdill
City West Plains
Company Twin Forks Resort
Contact
City Isabella
Company Twin Oaks Resort
Contact Mel Forester
City Wappapello
Company Vogels Homestead Resort
Contact Tim & Jennifer Long
City Lebanon
Company Wappapello Guide Service
Contact Jeff Fansler
City Wappapello
Company Wayne's Guide Service
Contact
City Warsaw
Company White Oak Ranch
Contact
City Edina
Company Wilderness Ridge Resort
Contact Jack Crider
City Duke
Company
Contact Barry L. Bales
City St. Louis
Company
Contact Richard K. Brewer
City Neosho
Company
Contact Gary W. Cook
City Nixa
Company
Contact Jeffrey E. Crites
City Cape Girardeau
Company
Contact Dennis C. Goins
City New Melle
Company
Contact Hebert L. Helms
City Eagle Rock
Company
Contact Calvin Hensley
City Eagle Rock

Company
Contact Steven D. Kinierim
City Lebanon
Company
Contact Steve W. Nelson
City Tecumseh
Company
Contact Rod R. Phillips
City Golden
Company
Contact Fredic J. Richardson
City Protem
Company
Contact Anthony J. Salamon
City St. Louis
Company
Contact Dan E. Schultz
City Pontiac
Company
Contact Glen W. Stephens
Contact Carl Junction

Montana

Company 5/S Outfitting & Guide Service
Contact Glenn E. Smith
City Trout Creek
Company 9T9 Ranch
Contact
City Ennis
Company A-1 Fishing
Contact Craig Renfro
City Lakeside
Company A-Able Fishing Charters
Contact George Goggins
City Kalispell
Company Adventures
Contact
City Bozeman
Company Al Gadoury's 6X
Contact Allan W. Gadoury
City Bozeman
Company Al Troth Fly Fishing Guide Service
Contact Alfred C. Troth
City Dillon
Company Al Wind's Trout Futures
Contact Alan Wind
City Twin Bridges
Company Alaska Flyfishing Expeditions
Contact Thomas & Virginia Leroy
City Big Sky
Company Allman's Montana Adventure
Contact Kenneth C. Allman
City Darby
Company Arctic Tern Charter
Contact William Grasser
City Sula
Company At the Summit Outfitting Service
Contact
City Hardin
Company Autumn Brown Outfitting
Contact Alvin Blakley
City Fort Smith
Company Avon Outfitters
Contact Robert D. Cunningham
City Gallatin Gateway
Company B Bar Two Outfitters
Contact Lance C. Vines
City West Yellowstone
Company Bartlett Creek Outfitters
Contact Mike Smith
City Deer Lodge
Company Battle Creek Outfitters
Contact Larry Richtmyer
City Townsend
Company Bear Creek Guest Ranch
Contact William Beck
City East Glacier
Company Beartooth Flyfishing
Contact Daniel J. Delekta
City Cameron
Company Beartooth Plateau Outfitters, Inc.
Contact Ronnie L. Wright
City Cooke City
Company Beartooth Ranch & JLX Outfitters

Company James E. Langston
City Nye
Company Beartrap Express
City Ennis
Company Beaverhead Anglers
Contact Paul George Wiedeman
City Dillon
Company Big Bear Lodge, Inc.
Contact Alan R. Harris
City Bozeman
Company Big Dipper Charters
Contact Dave Minister
City Kalispell
Company Big Rivers Guide Service
Contact Don Burks
City Livingston
Company Big Salmon Outfitters
Contact Richard Kehoe Wayman
City Ronan
Company Big Sky Expeditions
Contact
City Helena
Company Big Sky Overland Cruises
Contact
City Ovando
Company Bighorn Angler
Contact Donald R. Cooper
City Roundup
Company Bighorn River Lodge
Contact Phil Y. Gonzalez
City Fort Smith
Company Bighorn River Shop/Lazy Boot Outfitters
Contact
City Hardin
Company Bill Mitchell Outfitters, Inc.
Contact William H. & Karen Mitchell
City Hamilton
Company Birch Creek Outfitters
Contact Laddie Peverley
City Hamilton
Company Birch Creek Outfitters
Contact William W. Galt
City White Sulphur Springs
Company Birch Creek Outfitters
Contact Rick Peverley
City Victor
Company Black Butte Outfitters
Contact J.O. Hash, Jr.
City Red Lodge
Company Blackbird's Fly Shop & Lodge
Contact
City Victor
Company Blacktail Ranch
Contact Sandra Renner
City Wolf Creek
Company Blue Quill Fly Co.
Contact Robert E. Krumm
City Fort Smith
Company Blue Ribbon Guide Service
Contact Anthony A. Schoonen
City Lolo
Company Bob Jacklin's Fly Shop, Inc.
Contact Bob Jacklin
City West Yellowstone
Company Bob Marshall Wilderness Ranch
Contact Virgil B. Burns
City St. Ignatius
Company Boulder River Fly Fishing Company
Contact
City Big Timber
Company Bridger Mountain Guide Service
Contact James R. Brogan
City Malta
Company Broken Arrow Lodge
Contact Erwin and Sherry Clark
City Alder
Company Broken Heart Guest Ranch
Contact Bernard C. Nieslanik
City Haugan
Company Broken Horn Outfitters
Contact Ken D. Murdoch
City Jackson
Company Bugle Ridge Outfitters
Contact John A. Keenan
City Emigrant
Company Cameron Outfitters
Contact Del Cameron
City Stevensville
Company Camp Baker Outfitters
Contact Donald W. Johnson

City White Sulphur Springs
Company Castle Mountain Fly Fishers
Contact Dillon S. Dempsey
City White Sulphur Springs
Company Centre Island Resort
Contact David Ballinger & Laura St. John
City Bozeman
Company Continental Divide Outfitters
Contact Walter D. Easley
City Corvallis
Company Copenhaver Outfitters, Inc.
Contact Steven D. Copenhaver
City Ovando
Company Copper River Fly Fishing Lodge
Contact Jeff & Pat Vermillion
City Billings
Company Covered Wagon Outfitters
Contact Edward L. Hake
City Big Sky
Company Crain Outfitting & Guide Service
Contact Richard A. Crain
City Plains
Company Crane Mountain Guide Service
Contact Fred W. Buchanan
City Bigfork
Company Cudney's Guide Service
Contact David L. Cudney
City Emigrant
Company Curry Comb Outfitters
Contact William L. Knox
City Dell
Company Custom Adventures
Contact Roger Bowers
City St. Ignatius
Company Diamond K Outfitters
Contact Charles D. Kendall
City Big Sky
Company Diamond R Guest Ranch
Contact James A. Slack
City Kalispell
Company Douglas Fir & Furs
Contact Douglas H. Gauf
City Livingston
Company Douglas Roberts Outfitter
Contact Douglas A. Roberts
City Stevensville
Company Eagle Creek Outfitters
Contact Charles Tuchschmidt
City Bozeman
Company Eagle Nest Lodge & Outfitters
Contact Keith Kelly
City Hardin
Company East Fork Outfitters
Contact Mark A. McKee
City Sula
Company East Slope Anglers
Contact Brad R. Parsch & Wayne Rooney
City Big Sky
Company ECOLLAMA
Contact David Harmon
City Missoula
Company Elkhorn Enterprises
Contact Pete Clark
City McLeod
Company Esper's Under Wild Skies Lodge & Outfitters
Contact Vaughn and Judy Esper
City Philipsburg
Company Firehole Ranch
Contact
City Jackson Hole
Company Fischer's Fishers
Contact Dennis C. Fischer
City Lewistown
Company Fish Montana
Contact Leonard Moffo
City Pray
Company Fishing Head Quarters
Contact Brete Thibeault
City Twin Bridges
Company Five Bears Outfitters
Contact Gary Peters
City Florence
Company Flat Iron Outfitting
Contact Jerry and Brenda Shively
City Thompson Falls
Company Flathead Trophy Fly Fishers
Contact George D. Widener
City Whitefish

Company Fly Fishing Unlimited
Contact Donald R. Lyman
City St. Xavier

Company Flyfishing Adventures
Contact L. Darryl Osburn
City Hamilton

Company Four Rivers Fishing Co.
Contact Jane Waldie
City Twin Bridges

Company Fowler's Charter & Rental
Contact Harry D. Fowler
City Eureka

Company Gary Evans Madison River Guides
Contact
City Ennis

Company Glacier Fishing Charters
Contact James P. Landwehr
City Columbia Falls

Company Glacier Outfitters
Contact Gary Abbey
City Ronan

Company Glacier Raft Co.
Contact Sally Thompson
City West Glacier

Company Glacier Raft Co.
Contact Onno C. Wieringa
City West Glacier

Company Glacier Wilderness Guides, Inc.
Contact Randy M. Gayner
City West Glacier

Company Great Northern Fishing
Contact
City West Glacier

Company Great Northern Llama Co., Inc.
Contact Steve C. Rolfing
City Columbia Falls

Company Great Northern Whitewater
Contact
City West Glacier

Company Greater Yellowstone Flyfishers
Contact
City Cooke City

Company Grossenbacher Guides
Contact Brian Grossenbacher
City Bozeman

Company Hanging "J" Ranch
Contact Joyce G. Rehms
City Belgrade

Company Hank Miller Steelhead
Contact Hank Miller
City Big Sky

Company Hatch Finders
Contact Dean A. Reiner
City Livingston

Company Hawkridge Outfitters & Rodbids
Contact Howard Bethel
City Bozeman

Company Healing Waters Fly Fishing Lodge
Contact Greg & Janet Lilly
City Twin Bridges

Company High Country Connection
Contact Larry C. Trimber
City Kalispell

Company High Country Outfitters Fly Fishing Lodge
Contact
City Pray

Company High Valley Ranch
Contact Patrick E. McFall
City Ennis

Company Hole in the Wall Outfitters
Contact Todd Earp
City Alberton

Company Horse Creek Outfitters
Contact Robert Bruce Malcolm
City Emigrant

Company Horseshoe Guide Service
Contact Ted E. Dinsdale
City Roberts

Company Hubbard's Yellowstone Lodge
Contact
City Emigrant

Company J-L Outfitters
Contact Arthur J. Stevens
City Augusta

Company Jennifer Smith Fly Casting
Contact Jennifer L. Smith
City Bozeman

Company Jerry Malson Outfitting
Contact Jerry R. Malson
City Trout Creek

Company John Oppelt Flyfishing Outfitter
Contact John R. Oppelt
City Bozeman

Company John Perry's West Slope Outfit
Contact John R. Perry
City Missoula

Company Johnson Outfitters
Contact Kathryn M. Johnson
City Gardiner

Company Josephson Outfitting
Contact Ed & Lisa Josephson
City Plains

Company JR Buffalo Creek Outfitters
Contact John W. Robidou
City Gardiner

Company K Lazy Three Ranch
Contact Mary Faith Hoeffner
City Lincoln

Company Kibler Charter Fishing
Contact Myron & Mary Beth Kibler
City Sand Springs

Company Klick's K Bar L Ranch
Contact Dick Klick
City Augusta

Company Kootenai River Outfitters
Contact Gary McCabe
City Troy

Company Lapham Outfitters
Contact Max C. Lapham
City Jackson

Company Lass & Ron Mills Outfitters
Contact Lass Dudley
City Augusta

Company Last Stand Outfitters
Contact August D. Edgorf
City Hardin

Company Lee Watson Outfitters
Contact Lee W. Watson
City Livingston

Company Lew & Clark Expeditions Corp.
Contact Michael John Geary
City Helena

Company Lone Mountain Ranch
Contact Robert L. Schaap
City Big Sky

Company Lost Fork Ranch
Contact Merritt G. Pride
City Cameron

Company Madion Valley Ranch
Contact
City Ennis

Company Madson River Outfitters
Contact Robert "Dan" Hull
City West Yellowstone

Company McCabe Outfitters
Contact Gary McCabe
City Troy

Company McKenzie's Sportsmans Retreat on Rock Creek
Contact
City Rock Creek

Company McNeely Outfitting
Contact Shawn G. McNeely
City Bozeman

Company Miller Outfitters
Contact Robert E. Miller
City Great Falls

Company Missoula River Trout Shop
Contact Patrick Alan Elam
City Cascade

Company MJ Outfitting Services
Contact
City Wilsall

Company Montana Casting Co.
Contact William Joyner
City Bozeman

Company Montana Fly Fishing
Contact Michael W. Mouat
City Billings

Company Montana Fly Fishing Adventures
Contact Patrick J. Bannon
City Deer Lodge

Company Montana Flyfishing Co.
Contact Kirk Johnston
City Missoula

Company Montana Outdoor Expeditions
Contact Robert James Griffith
City Gallatin Gateway

Company Montana River Trips
Contact Daniel Groshens
City Gallatin Gateway

Company Montana Trout Club
Contact
City Twin Bridges

Company Monture Outfitters
Contact James L. Anderson
City Ovando

Company Mountain Trails Outfitters
Contact A. Lee Bridges
City Eureka

Company N-Bar Land & Cattle Company
Contact Thomas E. Elliott
City Grass Range

Company Neal Outfitters
Contact Lloyd Neal
City Augusta

Company Northwest Waters Outfitters
Contact
City Missoula

Company Osprey Expeditions
Contact
City Helena

Company Paradise Adventures
Contact Ned S. Chadbourn
City Bozeman

Company Paradise Fishing Excursions
Contact James R. French
City Paradise

Company Paradise Outfitters
Contact Stephen R. Ayers
City Billings

Company Peterson's Fairmont Corral, Inc.
Contact William H. Peterson
City Anaconda

Company Pine Ridge/Bartlett Creek Outfitter
Contact Robert M. Labert
City Billings

Company PK Outfitters/Missoulian Angler
Contact Paul W. Koller
City Missoula

Company Points Unknown
Contact
City Livingston

Company Quarter Circle E.M. Outfitters
Contact Ernest E. McCollum
City Huson

Company Rach Outfitters/Flathead Charters
Contact Jeff E. Rach
City Kalispell

Company Randy Petrich Big Game Hunts
Contact Randy Petrich
City Livingston

Company Red Mountain Outfitters
Contact Les G. Nader
City Lincoln

Company Rendezvous Outfitters
Contact Herbert A. Moore
City Gardiner

Company River Bend Flyfishing
Contact Charles Miles Stranahan
City Hamilton

Company RL Outfitters
Contact Dwain Rennaker
City Hamilton

Company Robert Dupea Outfitters
Contact Robert L. Dupea
City White Sulphur Springs

Company Rocky Fork Guide Service
Contact Ernest C. Strum
City Red Lodge

Company Ron Mills Outfitting
Contact Ronald E. Mills
City Augusta

Company Royal Trude Outdoor Adventures
Contact Mark J. Shutey
City Butte

Company Ruby Springs Lodge
Contact Paul & Jeanne Moseley
City Alder

Company Rush's Lake View Ranch
Contact Keith S. Rush
City Butte

Company Salmon Forks Outfitters
Contact William H. Tidwell
City Columbia Falls

Company Sanfort & Sun Outfitting
Contact Gregory F. Sanford
City Ennis

Company SE Alaska Outfitters
Contact Thomas T. Zwick
City Hardin

Company Selway-Magruder Outfitters, Inc.
Contact Kendall Lee Wells
City Superior

Company Seven Lazy P Guest Ranch
Contact Charles C. Blixrud
City Choteau

Company Sherwood Outfitting
Contact John Sherwood
City Columbus

Company Skyline Guide Service, Inc.
Contact Victor J. Jackson
City Belfry

Company Sleepy Hollow Lodge
Contact Larry P. Miller
City West Yellowstone

Company Snowy Range Ranch Outfitters
Contact Patrick R. Landers
City Pray

Company Snowy Springs Outfitters
Contact Shawn Little
City Kalispell

Company Southwest Montana Flies
Contact
City Wise River

Company Spotted Bear Ranch
Contact Kirk & Cathy Gentry
City Kalispell

Company Stan Fisher Outfitter & Guide
Contact Stanley Fisher
City Trout Creek

Company Summit Station Lodge
Contact
City East Glacier

Company Sun Dog Outfitters
Contact Daniel L. Lahren
City Livingston

Company Sunrise Outfitters
Contact Mark Daly
City Helena

Company Tal Camp/Alaska Flyfishing
Contact Tom Lerot
City Big Sky

Company Teller Wildlife Refuge
Contact Mary Stone
City Corvallis

Company The Clearwater Crossing Lodge
Contact Todd Earp
City Alberton

Company The Complete Fly Fisher
Contact David W. & Stuart Decker
City Wise River

Company The Lodge
Contact John Talia
City Hamilton

Company The Missouri River Trout Shop & Lodge
Contact
City Craig

Company The Montana Trout Club
Contact Greg Lilly
City Sheridan

Company The Old Kirby Place
Contact
City Cameron

Company The Reflective Angler
Contact Eric and Al Troth
City Bozeman

Company The Yellowstone Fisherman
Contact Kent B. Lombard
City Livingston

Company Think Wild Enterprises
Contact Eugene G. Clark
City White Sulphur Springs

Company Thompson Outfitters, Inc.
Contact Teddy Thompson
City Big Timber

Company Tikchik Wilderness Fishing Bear Camp
Contact Justin Johns
City Kalispell

Company Tite Line Fishing
Contact John Seidel
City Idaho Falls, Idaho

Company Triple Creek/Thunder Bow
Contact Charlotte A. Zikan
City Conner

Company Victor Colvard Guided Fly Fishing
Contact Victor H. Colvard
City Bozeman

Company Wapiti Fine Flies & Outfitting
Contact Jack Mauer
City Stevensville

Company Warrens' Bunky Ranch
Contact DeVon E. Warren
City Conner

Company Wellborn Bros.
Contact David A. Wellborn
City Dillon

Company Wellborn Bros.
Contact Joseph R. Wellborn
City Dillon

Company Western AK Sport Fishing
Contact August & Kim Egdorf
City Hardin

Company Western Guide Services
Contact Randy L. Walker
City Canyon Creek

Company Western Waters and Woods
Contact Gerald Nichols
City Missoula

Company Whitcomb Lodge
Contact
City Malta

Company Whitefish Lake Fishing
Contact Jim Crumal
City Whitefish

Company Wild River Adventures
Contact Bob Jordan
City West Glacier

Company Wild River Adventures
Contact Robert Y. Jordan
City Helena

Company Wild Trout Outfitters
Contact J. D. Bingman
City Big Sky

Company Wild Trout Outfitters
Contact John F. Herzer
City Missoula

Company Wilderness Connection, Inc.
Contact Charles G. Duffy
City Gardiner

Company Wilderness Lodge & Skyline Outfitters
Contact Cameron E. Lee
City Hungry Horse

Company Wilderness Lodge Ltd.
Contact Gregory C. Grabacki
City Heron

Company Wilderness Riders Outfitting
Contact Bruce J. Duffalo
City Lolo

Company Wildlife Outfitters
Contact Richard J. Wemple
City Victor

Company Wolverine Guide Service
Contact Richard A. Labert
City Bozeman

Company Yaak River Outfitters
Contact Patrick "Clint" Mills
City Eureka

Company Yellowater Outfitters
Contact Roy G. Olsen
City Grass Range

Company Yellowstone Catch & Release Outfitter
Contact Gary David Clount
City West Yellowstone

Company Yellowstone International Fly
Contact
City Livingston

Company Yellowstone Llamas
Contact William Gavin
City Bozeman

Company Yellowstone Raft Co.
Contact Chris Lyness & Julia Page
City Gardiner

Company
Contact Gerald R. Clark
City Ennis

Company
Contact William L. Davis
City Townsend

Company
Contact Robert E. Flynn
City Twin Bridges

Company
Contact Bill Hooker

City Ovando
Company
Contact Lee Kinsey
City Butte
Company
Contact David J. Lueck
City Alder
Company
Contact Cherster L. Marion
City Livingston
Company
Contact Kurt J. Olson
City Fort Smith
Company
Contact Jennifer Olsson
City Bozeman
Company
Contact Eric T. Swedman
City Ennis
Company
Contact Paul Updike
City Townsend
Company
Contact Sandy VanderLans
City Cameron
Company
Contact Todd Andrew Wester
City Livingston

Nebraska

Company Adriondack Zak Guide Service
Contact James L. Zak
City Chektowaga
Company Buck's Guide Service
Contact Roger A. Markham
City Fairbury
Company Cornhusker Fishing Camp
Contact
City Berwyn
Company Deception Lake Lodge
Contact
City Lyman
Company Reindeer Lake Trout Camp
Contact Ron & Cindi Holmes
City Sargent
Company Riverfront Hunting Club
Contact Raymond Olson
City Tekamah
Company Sappa Creek Hunt Preserve
Contact
City Orleans
Company
Contact Steve Lytle
City McCool
Company
Contact Bruce Pitzer
City Oakdale

Nevada

Company A. McMillan Outfitter
Contact Andrew G. McMillan
City Reno
Company Angler's Guide Service
Contact William N. Spellman
City Henderson
Company Bertrand Guide Service
Contact Kenneth E. Bertrand
City Sparks
Company Big Smoky Valley Outfitters
Contact William A. Berg
City Round Mountain
Company Bull Ridge Guide Service
Contact Charles F. Marques
City Ely
Company Burdick Guide Service
Contact Jr. Burdick Shaun A. & Walter A.
City Ely
Company Cottonwood Ranch & Wilderness Exped.
Contact E. Agee Smith
City Jarbidge
Company Desert Recreation, Inc.
Contact Fredrick A. Glaner

City Laughlin
Company Donoho's Guide Service
Contact Patrick Donoho
City Las Vegas
Company Emery's Bighorn Guide Service
Contact Weston E. Emery
City Incline Village
Company First Strike Sportfishing
Contact Jeffrey L. Vogl
City Zephyr Cove
Company Fish, Inc.
Contact James E. Goff
City Henderson
Company H.B. Guide Service
Contact Howard E. Blum
City Henderson
Company Hall's Outfitting & Guide Service
Contact Keven M. Hall
City Wells
Company Hidden Lake Outfitters
Contact Henry W. Krenka
City Ruby Valley
Company Humboldt Outfitters
Contact Mike K. Morrison
City Wells
Company Karen Jones Fishing Guide Service
Contact Karen Ann Jones
City Las Vegas
Company Lonesome Duck
Contact Steve Hilbert
City Incline Village
Company Mustang Outfitters & Big Game Hounds
Contact James S. Stahl
City Round Mountain
Company Nevada Guide Service
Contact James R. Puryear
City Reno
Company Nevada Trophy Hunts
Contact Tony Diebold
City Gerlach
Company O'Malley's Fishing Charters
Contact Leonard E. O'Malley
City Zephyr Cove
Company Reno Fly Shop, INC.
Contact John D. Stanley, Jr.
City Reno
Company Sage-N-Pine, Outfitters
Contact Paul L. Strasdin
City Fallon
Company Secret Pass Outfitters
Contact Steven R. Wines
City Ruby Valley
Company Snake Mountain Guide Service
Contact Harvey Pete
City Elko
Company Tahoe Sportfishing Co.
Contact Dean Lockwood
City Zephry Cove
Company Timberline Outfitters
Contact Nicholas G. Perchetti
City Tonopah
Company Timberline Outfitters
Contact Stanley R. Galvin, Jr.
City Tonopah
Company
Contact Sid Ashton
City Reno
Company
Contact John M. Biondo
City Reno
Company
Contact Travis S. Edgar
City Battle Mountain
Company
Contact Pete N. Gray
City Reno
Company
Contact John F. Kowalski
City Gardenville
Company
Contact Capt. Lex Moser
City Reno
Company
Contact James R. Murphy
City Sun Valley
Company
Contact Zolan Tanner
City Las Vegas
Company
Contact John L. Whitehead
City Reno

Company
Contact Keith LeClair
City North Hampton
Company
Contact Rick Lillegard
City Atkinson
Company
Contact Stephen M. Lucarelli
City Meredith
Company
Contact Daniel Marchi
City Pelham
Company
Contact Joseph Nassar
City Holderness
Company
Contact Theodore W. Pierce
City Colebrook
Company
Contact Ronald M. Sowa
City Manchester
Company
Contact John McMahon Starkey
City Ctr. Barnstead
Company
Contact Janet & William R. Thompson
City Freedom
Company
Contact Mark David Whitman
City Center Harbor

New Hampshire

Company Four Buck's Guide Service
Contact Paul Buck
City Meredith
Company Lopstick Lodge & Cabins
Contact Lisa Hopping
City Pittsburg
Company Northern Land Services, Inc.
Contact
City Bethlehem
Company Reel Time Charters
Contact
City Hampton
Company Salmon Hole Lodge
Contact Scott Smith
City Seabrook
Company Tall Timber Lodge
Contact Cindy Sullivan
City Pittsburg
Company The Bass Harasser Guide Service
Contact James I. Brown
City Manchester
Company The Timberdoodle Club
Contact
City Temple
Company
Contact Charles R. Allard
City Mirror Lake
Company
Contact Mark Allen
City New Boston
Company
Contact William F. Bernhardt III
City No. Conway
Company
Contact Angus Boezeman
City Concord
Company
Contact Joseph A. Catalano, Jr.
City Londonderry
Company
Contact Raymond F. Cotnoir
City Randolph
Company
Contact Peter M. Eldridge
City Silver Lake
Company
Contact Mark Ewing
City Hanover
Company
Contact Daniel L. Fitzgerald
City Henniker
Company
Contact Richard K. Forge
City Center Harbor
Company
Contact Curtiss W. Golder
City Wolfeboro
Company
Contact Peter A. Grasso
City Laconia
Company
Contact Douglas C. Greenwood
City Loudon
Company
Contact Larry A. Guile
City Lancaster
Company
Contact Thomas L. Hadley
City Ctr. Sandwich
Company
Contact Richard D. Hamel
City Hanover
Company
Contact Kenneth B. Hastings
City Colebrook
Company
Contact Jonathan K. Howe
City North Conway
Company
Contact Alan E. Jones
City Hampton
Company
Contact Kenneth Keating
City Keene
Company
Contact George L. Kesel
City Hopkinton

New Jersey

Company Bob Marino Outfitters
Contact Bob Marino
City Elmwood Park
Company Fish P.T. Guide Service
Contact Pete Kelley, Jr.
City Caldwell
Company Jake's Buck n Rut Hunting Camp
Contact
City Belvidere
Company Muskie Daze Guide Service
Contact John Brylinski
City Layton
Company Offshore Adventures
Contact Pete Kelley, Sr.
City Caldwell
Company On A Fly Sportfishing
Contact
City Brielle
Company Streamside Guide Service
Contact Wayne Martka
City Blairstown
Company The Blackwater Bass-Guide Service
Contact Monte J. Tabor
City Hancocks Bridge
Company Trout & Shad Chasers
Contact Edward Carbonneau
City High Bridge
Company Wilderness Expeditions, Inc.
Contact
City Hawthorne
Company
Contact Ernie Ahr
City Demarest
Company
Contact Ed Broderick
City Westfield
Company
Contact William R. Hoffman
City Delanco
Company
Contact Ben Iradi
City East Hanover
Company
Contact Eugene Neiderlander
City Delaware
Company
Contact John Punola
City Madison
Company
Contact Ed Sekula
City Netcong
Company
Contact Rocky Vertone
City Watchung

New Mexico

Company 4C's Guides & Outfitters
Contact Chet Connor
City Elephant Butte
Company Beartrack Hunting Consultants
Contact John Abernathy
City Corrales
Company Born 'N' Raised on the San Juan River
Contact Tim R. Chavez
City Navajo Dam
Company Chama River Outfitters
Contact Bob Ball
City Chama
Company Charlie's Sporting Goods
Contact
City Albuquerque
Company Copper Country Outfitters
Contact Steven C. Harvill
City Silver City
Company Cottonwood Anglers
Contact Paul (Dave) Jacquez
City Blanco
Company Derringer Outfitters & Guides
Contact David & Susan Derringer
City Quemado
Company Four Corners Guides & Outfitters
Contact Ted Stiffler
City Bloomfield
Company Gary Webb Guide & Outfitter
Contact Gary Webb
City Lake Roberts
Company Gila Hotsprings Ranch
Contact Becky Campbell
City Silver City
Company Hi Valley Outfitters, Inc.
Contact Pres. Bill Wright
City Farmington
Company High County Connections
Contact Casey Veach
City Farmington
Company High Desert Angler
Contact
City Santa Fe
Company High Mountain Outfitters
Contact Pete Trujillo
City Eagle Nest
Company Kiowa Hunting Service, Inc.
Contact Alfred H. Cata
City Raton
Company Los Rios Anglers, Inc.
Contact
City Taos
Company M-Lazy-A-Ranch Outfitter/Guide Service
Contact Robert Archibeque
City Lindrith
Company Mimbres Outfitters
Contact Mark Miller
City Mimbres
Company Moreno Valley Outfitters
Contact Robert Reese & Mike Bucks
City Eagle Nest
Company Nine Sixteen Ranch Guide/Outfitter
Contact Terrell Shelley
City Cliff
Company North American Outfitters
Contact
City Alamogordo
Company Oso Ranch & Lodge
Contact John & Pamela Adamson
City Chama
Company Outwest Anglers
Contact Brian Klein
City Navajo Dam
Company Redwing Outfitters
Contact Bob Daugherty
City Raton
Company Repair Altenatives Co.
Contact Connie & Kreg Polzin Donald
City Farmington
Company Rimrock Guides & Outfitters
Contact Bryan K. Adair
City Bloomfield
Company Rizuto's San Juan River Lodge

Contact Peggy Harrell
City Navajo Dam
Company Ross Johnson Pro. Big Game Outfitter
Contact Ross Johnson
City Magdalena
Company San Juan Troutfitters
Contact Harry Lane
City Farmington
Company Sierra Grande Outfitters, Inc.
Contact Leslie D. Ezell
City Chama
Company Soaring Eagle Outfitters
Contact
City Navajo Dam
Company Sportsman Inn Guide Service
Contact
City Navajo Dam
Company T-N-T Adventures
Contact Joe M. Torrez, Jr.
City Chama
Company Taylor Streit Fly Fishing
Contact Taylor Streit
City Taos
Company Tererro Gen. Store & Riding Stables, Inc.
Contact Huie Ley
City Tererro
Company The Lodge at Chama
Contact Frank Simms
City Chama
Company The Reel Life
Contact Manuel J. Monasterio
City Albuquerque
Company The Santa Fe Flyfishing School & Guide Ser.
Contact
City Santa Fe
Company Timberline Outfitters
Contact Jerry Cazares
City Capitan
Company United States Outfitters, Inc.
Contact George Taulman
City Taos
Company Whitten's Outfitters & Guide Service
Contact Lewis Arnold Whitten
City Cimmarron
Company
Contact Martin D. Serna
City Mora

New York

Company "Farr-Out" Charters
Contact Capt. Ron Farr
City Webster
Company A-Coho-Motion Charters/ Lodge
Contact Capt. Brian Neal
City North Rose
Company A.J.'s Outdoor Services
Contact Aaron Parker, Sr.
City Cortland
Company Adirondack Bass & Camping
Contact Mark PeDuzzi
City Jay
Company Adirondack Canoes & Kayaks
Contact Harry Spetla
City Tupper Lake
Company Adirondack Champlain Guide Service
Contact
City Willsboro
Company Adirondack Fishing Adv./ Beaver Brook
Contact Pete Burns
City Wevertown
Company Adirondack Fishing Adventures
Contact
City Athol
Company Adirondack Fly Fishing Guide Service
Contact Wes Cunningham
City Gabriels
Company Adirondack Foothills

Contact Sonny & Sheila Young
City Saranac Lake
Company Adirondack Guide Service
Contact Daniel Josephson
City Old Forge
Company Adirondack Mountain & Stream Guide
Contact Jamie Frasier
City Olmsteadville
Company Adirondack Wilderness Experiences
Contact Michael J. Olivette & Craig L. Tryon
City Cazenovia
Company Adventure Guide Service/ O.J. Sports
Contact O.J. Chartrand, Jr.
City Rensselaer
Company Alaskan Great Adventure Guide Service
Contact Gregory Lee Franz
City Cortland
Company Algonquin Guides, Ltd.
Contact Roy L. Earley, Jr.
City Scotia
Company Angler's Alibi, Alagnak River
Contact John Holman & Karl Storath
City Romulis
Company Apache Outfitters
Contact Andrew Marshall
City Albany
Company Arrowhead Guide Service
Contact R. Van Middlesworth
City Pulaski
Company Battenkill Lodge
Contact Capt. Bob Storc
City Glen Cove
Company Beagle Charters
Contact
City Albion
Company Bear Cub Adventure Tours
Contact Gary Marchuk
City Lake Placid
Company Beaverkill Valley Inn
Contact Darlene O'Dell
City Lew Beach
Company Beck's Treks
Contact Robert H. Beck, Jr.
City Old Forge
Company Bequest Guide Service
Contact Bob Sedlacek
City Whitney Point
Company Big Indian Guide Service
Contact
City Big Indian
Company Black Brook Guides
Contact Denni Aprill
City Schuyler Falls
Company Bolin Sportfishin Charters
Contact
City Hyde Park
Company C-Frog/Blackjaw Bandit Charters
Contact Capt. Jim Dennis
City Wolcott
Company Call of the Wild
Contact Boyce D."Bud"Rawson, Sr.
City Wallkill
Company Cherry Grove Charters
Contact Capt. Ken Metzger
City Wolcott
Company Chinook Harbor Restaurant & Marina
Contact
City Fair Haven
Company Club 52 West
Contact
City Rensselaer
Company Conook Charters & Hunting Guide Serv.
Contact Gregory Harmych
City Mannsville
Company D.C. Outdoor Adventures, Inc.
Contact Dennis Caracciolo
City Brentwood
Company Dobber IV Charters
Contact Capt. Robert C. Dobbelaere
City Sodus Point
Company Don's Guide Service
Contact Don Kennedy
City Schenectady
Company Drybrook Environmental Adventures
Contact Martin C. Giuliano

City West Shokan
Company E & R Sport Fishing Charters
Contact Capt. Rob Brileya
City Hudson Falls
Company Ed's Fly Fishing & Guide Services
Contact Edward D. Ostapczuk
City Shokan
Company Eldred Preserve
Contact
City Eldred
Company Enchanted Circle Catskill Guide Service
Contact Pete Zito, Cliff Schwark
City Livingston Manor
Company Ephemera Guide Service
Contact Floyd N. Franke
City Roscoe
Company Expediter Charters
Contact Capt. Mick Clark
City Montour Falls
Company Farside Adventures
Contact Glenn Clark
City Potsdam
Company Finger Lakes Outfitters
Contact Lou Baum
City Fairport
Company Fish 'N Hawk Charters
Contact Capt. Ray R. Hawksby
City Morrisonville
Company Fish Doctor
Contact Capt. Ernie Lantiegne
City Mexico
Company Fish Wish Sportfishing & Taxidermy
Contact Carl Rathje
City Pulaski
Company Fishfing Fantasy Charters
Contact Capt. Steve Smith
City Webster
Company Fishin' Fever Charters
Contact Capt. Bob Titton
City Sodus Pt.
Company Fishing Fool Charters
Contact Capt. John Guarney, Jr.
City Penn Yan
Company Fishing Unlimited
Contact Capt. John J. Pedonie
City Cohoes
Company Fly A-Salt Service
Contact Capt. Bob Robl
City Dix Hills
Company Free Spirit Adventures
Contact Gary Flanagan
City Wells
Company Gad-About Griz Charter & Guide Service
Contact Capt. Paul Sents
City Conklin
Company Get-A-Way Charters
Contact Capt. Dane L. Brown
City Walworth
Company Gibaldi Guide Service
Contact Paul Gibaldi
City Warrensburg
Company Goofy Newfy Charters
Contact Capt. Dick Butler
City Saratoga Springs
Company Gray Fox Guide Service
Contact Stan Grose
City Ilion
Company Great White Charters
Contact Capt. Jack Prutzman
City Geneva
Company Great Wilderness Adventure
Contact Jeff Heusser
City Queensbury
Company High Peak Adventures, Inc.
Contact Brian K. Malloy
City Rensselaer
Company Hogancamp's Guide Service
Contact Paul E. Hogancamp
City Marlboro
Company Hookher Sportfishing Charters
Contact Capt. Bill Maglione
City Milton
Company Huff House
Contact Joe & Joanne Forness
City Roscoe
Company Jeff Russell Drift Boat Charter Service
Contact Jeff Russell

City Malta
Company Jeff's Fishing Charter Service
Contact Jeff Smith
City Bolton Landing
Company Jerry's Sport Fish'n Charters
Contact
City Pulaski
Company K & G Sportfishing Lodge
Contact Greg & Kris Gehrig
City Oswego
Company Kidney Creek Farms & Preserve
Contact Gary Breski
City Schenectady
Company L & M Sportfishing
Contact Capt. Hank Searles
City Wolcott
Company Lake Placid Lodge
Contact Charlie Levitz
City Lake Placid
Company Lake Spider Charters
Contact Capt. Pete Bragarnick
City Williamson
Company Landing Zone Charters
Contact Capt. Dick Dennie
City Macedon
Company Le Billet D'Or
Contact Ted Meskunas
City Dannemora
Company Lennyland Outfitters
Contact Mark J. Tierney
City Montgomery
Company Let's Go Fishing!
Contact Bluegill Page
City Syracuse
Company Light Line Adventures
Contact Steven A. Lucas
City Lake Placid
Company Lighthouse Charters
Contact
City Pulaski
Company Linda-Vue Charters
Contact Capt. Walt Boname
City Clayton
Company Little John's Guide Service
Contact John A. Kopy, Jr.
City Sandy Creek
Company Lopinto Farms Lodge
Contact
City Freeville
Company Lynx Guide Services
Contact Larry E. Winslow
City Glens Falls
Company Maurice's Floating Lodge
Contact Maurice Bertini
City Astokia
Company McDonnell's Adirondack Challenges
Contact Brian McDonnell
City Saranac Lake
Company Mickey Finn Charters & Guide Service
Contact Capt. Dominick (Mickey) Scarzafava
City Middletown
Company Middle Earth
Contact Wayne Failing
City Lake Placid
Company Mike's #1 Muskie Guide Service
Contact Mike Patete
City Mentor, Ohio
Company Miles Fly Fishing Guide Service
Contact Miles Goodman
City Carmel
Company Mojo Guides
Contact Moe Neale
City Burnt Hills
Company Moose River Company
Contact Mark H. Eddy
City Old Forge
Company Mountain Man Guide Service
Contact Joe Eggleston & Tim Breen
City Gansevoort
Company Mountainaire Adventures, Inc.
Contact Douglas Cole
City Wevertown
Company Natural Anglers
Contact Capt. Barry Kanavy
City Seaford
Company Naughty Lady Charters
Contact Bill Carlozzi

City Adirondack
Company North Fork Preserve, Inc.
Contact
City Riverhead
Company North Star Guiding Service, Inc.
Contact Michael F. Newell
City West Charlton
Company Northway Adirondack Guides
Contact Michael diPalma
City Queensbury
Company Northwest Catskill Mountaineering
Contact Thomas J. Owens
City Unadilla
Company Northwoods Wilderness Guide Service
Contact John Huston
City Schroon Lake
Company Oak Leaf Game Calls & Guide Service
Contact Roger A. Sannwald
City Binghamton
Company Okra Charters
Contact Capt. Mike Wilchenski
City Sodus Pt.
Company Omega II Charter Service, Inc.
Contact Capt. Jay Levy
City Baldwinsville
Company Orvis New York
Contact
City New York
Company Out of the Blue Charter & Guide Service
Contact Bruce Tompkins
City Saugerties
Company Outdoor Activities
Contact John C. Couser
City Gardiner
Company Outlaw Charters & Ultimate Predator
Contact R. Stephen Yaw
City Ticonderoga
Company Pawling Mountain Club
Contact
City Pawling
Company Peter Zito Guide Service
Contact Peter Zito
City Hughsonville
Company Pier One Charters
Contact Capts. Frank & Charles DeNoto
City Wolcott
Company Pleasant View Camps
Contact
City Hammond
Company Prime Time Charters
Contact Capt. Gregory W. Switzer
City Sodus Pt.
Company Quality Adventures, Inc.
Contact VanAlstyne & Van Nostrand Cort
City Stottville
Company Rainbow Connection Charters
Contact Capt. Steve LeRoy
City Sodus Pt.
Company Ralphy Boy II Charter Sportfishing
Contact Capt. Dave Goethals
City Rochester
Company Reel Action Guide Service
Contact Don Wood
City Glenmont
Company Repak's Backpak & Bushwak
Contact Paul Repak
City Boonville
Company RJ's Guide Service
Contact Capt. Randy VerDow
City Palmyra
Company Rod Bender Charters
Contact Capt. Charlie Portes, Jr.
City Diamond Point
Company Rodmaster Charters
Contact
City Ontario
Company Rusadventure
Contact
City Brooklyn
Company Rustic Resort Marina
Contact
City Fair Haven
Company Salmon Grabber Charters

Contact Capt. Ed Maxon
City Sodus
Company Salmon Run Charters
Contact Capt. O. Fred Miller
City Wolcott
Company Salmon Slasher Charter
Contact
City Pulaski
Company Sand n' Surf Charters
Contact Scott & John Wood
City Diamond Point
Company Screwy Louie's Sport Shop
Contact Capt. Louie Parseault
City Fair Haven
Company Sea Pass Charters
Contact Capt. Jim Tsepas
City Williamson
Company Seagull Charters
Contact Capt. Ted Hatter
City Oswego
Company Seventh Heaven Charter Services
Contact Capt. Bob Barlow
City Liverpool
Company Shihan Pete Traina Special Protection
Contact
City Ridgewood
Company Shooter Charters
Contact Capt. Mike Harrison
City North Rose
Company Sodus Point Charters
Contact James & Pat Abel
City Sodus Pt.
Company Split Shot Guide Service
Contact Harry E. VanGelder
City Canandaigua
Company Sportfishing Charters
Contact Ed Murphy & Fred Brown
City S. Glens Falls
Company Starter Charter 1
Contact Capt. Dave Burt
City Honeoye Falls
Company Strike Zone 1
Contact Capt. Ron Clark
City Pulaski
Company Sunset Charters
Contact Capt. Chris DiDio
City Williamson
Company Sweetwater Guide Service
Contact Michael Padua
City Narrowsburg
Company Tahawus Guide Service, Ltd.
Contact Joseph Hackett
City Lake Placid
Company Tamarack Preserve, Ltd.
Contact
City Millbrook
Company Ted's Charter Fishing Service
Contact Russell & Borgh Goutos
City Diamond Point
Company The Bass Man
Contact Joseph Burke
City New York
Company The Hungry Trout Motor Inn
Contact Jerry & Linda Bottcher
City Whiteface Mountain
Company The Lady J
Contact Capt. Mary Ochsner
City Phoenix
Company The Lucky Strike
Contact Capt. Ken Turco
City Long Island
Company The Wild River Inn
Contact Todd & Ann Marie Sheltra
City Pulaski
Company Thor's Trophy Outdoor Guide Service
Contact Thor S. Yarabek
City Oswego
Company Thousand Islands Inn
Contact Allen & Susan Benas
City Clayton
Company Timber Creek Guide Service
Contact Mike Kilcher
City Guilderland
Company Trophy Seeker Charters
Contact Capt. Bruce Schaller
City
Company Upper Delaware Outfitters
Contact Bill Fraser
City Hankins

Company West Branch Angler and Sportsman Resort
Contact Harry Batschelet & Ray Finney
City Deposit
Company White Dog Trail Company
Contact Jeff Whittemore & John Wainwright
City Dolgeville
Company Whiteface Guide Service
Contact G. L. Scott
City Wilmington
Company Wilderness Bound Outing Service
Contact Jack Demers
City Wynantskill
Company Yankee Angler
Contact Bradford White
City Fayetteville
Company
Contact H."Bick"Bicknell
City Henderson Harbor
Company
Contact Jack Chantler
City Skaneateles
Company
Contact Glenn A. Debrosky
City High Falls
Company
Contact Capt. Paul Dixon
City East Hampton
Company
Contact Michael J. Empey, Sr.
City Richfield Springs
Company
Contact Patrick Gallagher
City Lake Placid
Company
Contact B. L. Haines
City Massena
Company
Contact Capt. Bill Herold
City Rye
Company
Contact John Jacobson
City Andes
Company
Contact Marty Jay
City Star Lake
Company
Contact Ron Kolodziej
City Amsterdam
Company
Contact David W. Lincoln
City Selkirk
Company
Contact Felix Nieves
City Warwick
Company
Contact Tom Robinson
City Putnam Valley
Company
Contact Cliff Schwark
City Poughquag
Company
Contact James R. Seaboldt
City Yorktown Heights
Company
Contact George F.Tompkins
City Newburgh
Company
Contact Ed Viola
City Southampton

North Carolina

Company Angler Choice Adventures
Contact Rodney Duke
City Garner
Company Double Haul Guiding
Contact
City Raleigh
Company Endless River Adventures
Contact Juliet Kastorff
City Bryson City
Company Fontana Village Resort
Contact Scott Waycaster
City Fontana Dam
Company Harkers Island Fishing Center
Contact
City Harkers Island

Company Harris Lake Gaston Guide Service
Contact
City Roanoke Rapids
Company High Hampton Inn
Contact
City Cashiers
Company Highland Hiker
Contact Randy Baron
City Cashiers
Company Howard's Guide Service
Contact
City Townsville
Company Howell's Timber Lodge
Contact
City Littleton
Company Hunter Banks Co.
Contact
City Asheville
Company R.C.'s Guide Service
Contact Richard Clegg
City Creedmore
Company White Oak Outdoors Adventures
Contact
City Apex
Contact John V. Bonander
City Charlotte
Company
Contact Joseph Little
City Matthews

North Dakota

Company Beam's On The Prairie
Contact David J. Beam
City West Fargo
Company Bonzo's Guide Service
Contact Jeff Brennan
City Garrison
Company Central Flyway Outfitters
Contact John K. Kersten
City Kramer
Company Dakota Outfitters Unlimited, Inc.
Contact Larry Brooks
City Bottineau
Company Geese R-Us
Contact Capt. Joe Walleen, Jr.
City Pick City
Company Hap's Guide Service
Contact Hap Munz
City Garrison
Company Jig'm Up Guide Service
Contact Paul Folden
City Garrison
Company Molson Lake Lodge
Contact Lyle & Dianne Fett
City West Fargo
Company Northern Flight Guide Service
Contact Mike A. Schell
City Devils Lake
Company Northland Charter
Contact Larry E. Freed
City Riverdale
Company Rodger's Guide Service
Contact Rodger Affeldt
City Garrison
Company Straight to the Limit Guide Service
Contact Tim Boline
City Devils Lake
Company Tim's Guide Service
Contact Tim Charron
City Devils Lake
Company Tom's Guide Service
Contact Tom McKinven
City Harvey
Company Upper Missouri Pro Guide Service
Contact Ralph Gravos
City Alexander
Company Walleye Guides Unlimited
Contact Daryl Kerzman
City Mandan
Company
Contact Manuel Aaron
City Devils Lake
Company
Contact Keith Christianson
City Mandan

City Mandan
Company
Contact Dave Diffely
City Parshall
Company
Contact William Egge
City Williston
Company
Contact Clayton A. Folden
City New Town
Company
Contact Richard H. Folden
City Parshall
Company
Contact Thomas G. Fossen
City Edmore
Company
Contact Merritt Grubb
City Burlington
Company
Contact Rick A. Hoistad
City Forman
Company
Contact Richard Iverson
City Minot
Company
Contact Tim Johansen
City Beulah
Company
Contact Nick Kautt
City Parshall
Company
Contact Kent Odermann
City Minot
Company
Contact Fredrick Perkins
City Minot
Company
Contact Robert Scheer
City Epping
Company
Contact Jerald Shoemaker
City Stanley
Company
Contact James Sigman
City Hazen
Company
Contact Greg Simonson
City Alexander
Company
Contact Wade Williamson
City Parshall

Ohio

Company Bass Isle Resort
Contact
City Middle Bass
Company BC Charters
Contact Capt. Bill Crozier
City Martin
Company Bluewater Charters
Contact
City Martin
Company C-Cat Sportfishing Charters
Contact
City Sandusky
Company Cadez Charter Service
Contact Captains Phil & Mark Cadez
City Sandusky
Company Captain Hook Charters
Contact Capt. William Scheid, Jr.
City Sandusky
Company Danny Buoy Fishing Charter
Contact Capt. Danny Phillips
City Cridersville
Company Dockside Accommodations
Contact John & Ann Arnold
City Sandusky
Company Double D Guide Service
Contact Capt. David Demeter, Sr.
City Marblehead
Company Drawbridge Marina
Contact Karen Druckenmiller & Ken Hershey
City Port Clinton
Company Dream-Fish
Contact Capt. Richard Baltzell
City Toledo
Company Dunlap's Charter Service

Contact Capt. Rick Dunlap
City Port Clinton
Company Expositions, Inc.
Contact Chris Fassnacht
City Cleveland
Company Eyees Right Charter Service
Contact
City Port Clinton
Company Fairfield Inn
Contact Joyce Cole
City Port Clinton
Company Fisherman's Wharf
Contact
City Port Clinton
Company Full Box/Wild Wings
Contact Capt. Delano C. Baker, Jr.
City Lodi
Company Gayles Bed & Breakfast
Contact Hank Polcyn
City Put-In-Bay
Company Happy Days Boating
Contact Kevin Gottron
City Port Clinton
Company Hawg'n Too
Contact Capt. Steve Ashley
City Elyria
Company Herb's Sportsman's Supplies
Contact
City Port Clinton
Company Hi-Way Bait Store
Contact Don Mitchel
City Marblehead
Company Holiday Village
Contact Doug Alexander
City Port Clinton
Company Houston Lake Camp
Contact Ken & Iona Kronk
City Chardon
Company Jim's Taxidermy
Contact Jim & Pat Wendt
City Port Clinton
Company Lake Erie Charter Service
Contact Captain Dave Law
City Port Clinton
Company Lakeland Motel & Charter Service
Contact Capt. Dean Clemons
City Port Clinton
Company Lucky Lady Charters
Contact
City Port Clinton
Company Marina Del Isle
Contact Kathy Richmond
City Marblehead
Company Mary's Blossom Shop
Contact Mary Snyder
City Port Clinton
Company Mike's #1 Muskie Guide Service
Contact Mike Patete
City Mentor
Company Millsite Trout
Contact
City Castalia
Company Nan-Mar-Lin Charter Service
Contact
City Port Clinton
Company Nemecek Insurance
Contact Rick Nemecek
City Port Clinton
Company North Coast Marine Services
Contact Rick Brown
City Toledo
Company Ohio Division of Wildlife
Contact Vicki Snyder
City Columbus
Company Opelt Lake Erie Charters
Contact Capt. Jeffery Opelt
City Fremont
Company Ottawa County Visitors Bureau
Contact Malinda Huntley
City Port Clinton
Company Pirate Sportfishing Charters
Contact Capt. Keith Poland
City Waterville
Company Playin' Hooky Charters
Contact Capt. Jerry Taylor
City Clyde
Company Pleasant Hill Canoe Livery
Contact
City Perrysville

Company Rickard's Bait & Tackle
Contact Sherry Catley
City Marblehead
Company Rodbender Guide Service
Contact Capt. Gene Majni
City Port Clinton
Company Sandjpiper Sportfishing Charters
Contact Capt. Robert Vicek
City Parma
Company Sandusky Charter Boat Assn.
Contact
City Sandusky
Company Saucy Tomato
Contact Capt. Leroy Wenger
City Sandusky
Company Shore Nuf Charters
Contact
City Port Clinton
Company Speerfish Charters
Contact Capt. Jim Speer
City Sandusky
Company Sportsman Charter Service
Contact
City Marblehead
Company Sunnybrook Farms
Contact
City Sandusky
Company The Clevelander
Contact
City Huron
Company The Hoaky
Contact Capt. Neil Hoak
City Huron
Company The Island House
Contact Kim Sedlack
City Port Clinton
Company The Steppin' Stone Charters
Contact Capt. Gary Rosebrock
City Ney
Company Tibbels Charter Service
Contact
City Marblehead
Company Trophy Hunter Charter Service
Contact Capt. Gary Hopp
City Cleveland
Company Victorian Inn
Contact Ann & Wayne Duez
City Marblehead
Company West Harbor Towing
Contact Art Richter
City Port Clinton
Company Wild Wings, Inc.
Contact Walter Harris
City Oak Harbor
Company Yoda Guide Service
Contact James W. Dawson & Gary J. Young
City Kimbolton
Company
Contact Tracy Addison
City Hillsboro
Company
Contact Ray Anderson, Jr.
City Oak Harbor
Company
Contact Capt. Tim Apolito
City Dayton
Company
Contact Capt. Terry Ballard
City Toledo
Company
Contact Capt. Robert Banjoff
City Amherst
Company
Contact Capt. Clarence Bartlett
City Louisville
Company
Contact Capt. Michael Bednar
City North Royalton
Company
Contact Capt. Dennis Bergeman
City Milan
Company
Contact Jim Berry
City Toledo
Company
Contact Capt. David Berry
City Youngstown
Company
Contact Capt. Richard Bird
City Lakeside
Company
Contact Capt. Claudette & Bart Blaha, Jr.

Contact Capt. Marblehead
Company
Contact Capt. Jerry Bley
City Hamilton
Company
Contact Capt. Dennis Bluhm
City Willoughby
Company
Contact Capt. James Boehlke
City Westlake
Company
Contact Capt. Clyde Boger
City Oak Harbor
Company
Contact Capt. Ross Boland
City Ney
Company
Contact Capt. Jack Bolduan
City Toledo
Company
Contact Capt. Carl Boley, Jr.
City Shreve
Company
Contact Capt. Andrew Bomba
City Marblehead
Company
Contact Capt. James Borcherding
City Luckey
Company
Contact Capt. James Bostic
City Barberton
Company
Contact Capt. Robert Bowers
City Huron
Company
Contact Capt. Richard Bowser
City Gibsonburg
Company
Contact Lee Boyer
City Toledo
Company
Contact Capt. Edward Brewer
City North Olmstead
Company
Contact Capt. Larry Brown
City Westerville
Company
Contact Capt. William Brubaker
City Carroll
Company
Contact Capt. Robert Bruns
City Ottoville
Company
Contact Capt. James Bunn
City Fredericktown
Company
Contact Capt. Ronald Burdette, Sr.
City Elyria
Company
Contact Capt. William Caban
City Poland
Company
Contact Capt. Mark Cahlik
City Port Clinton
Company
Contact Capt. Thomas Call
City Lakewood
Company
Contact Capt. Thomas Cannon
City New Albany
Company
Contact Capt. Louis Capucini
City Fremont
Company
Contact Capt. Jim Capucini
City Fremond
Company
Contact Capt. Terry Cater
City Carey
Company
Contact Capt. Robert Ceglarski
City Port Clinton
Company
Contact Capt. Patrick Chrysler
City Put-In-Bay
Company
Contact Capt. Lynn D. Clarridge
City Marysville
Company
Contact Capt. David Clevenger
City Strongsville
Company
Contact Capts. Sharon & Robert Collins
City Strongsville

Company
Contact Capt. Robert Cramer
City Napoleon
Company
Contact Capt. Larry Croskey
City Lodi
Company
Contact James Crosthwaite
City Cincinnati
Company
Contact Capt. James Crosthwaite
City Orgonia
Company
Contact Capt. John DeGirolamo
City Maple Hts.
Company
Contact Jim Donich
City Sandusky
Company
Contact Capt. Gary Drwal
City Brook Park
Company
Contact Capt. Ronald Duwve
City Toledo
Company
Contact Capt. Norman Ecksmith
City Massillon
Company
Contact Capt. Harry Eisman
City Strongsville
Company
Contact Capt. Edward Ellis
City Oregon
Company
Contact Capt. Larry Endsley
City Port Clinton
Company
Contact Capt. Mel Erb
City Sugarcreek
Company
Contact Capt. David Ernsberger
City Fremont
Company
Contact Capt. Charles Eulitt
City Findlay
Company
Contact Capt. Melvin Fenger
City Warren
Company
Contact Capt. Floyd Fisher
City Crestline
Company
Contact Capt. James Fofrich, Sr.
City Toledo
Company
Contact Capt. David Fredericks
City Port Clinton
Company
Contact Capt. Larry Freeland
City Bellbrook
Company
Contact Capt. Pasqual Friscone
City Strongsville
Company
Contact Capt. George Fuller
City Oregon
Company
Contact Capt. Mark Funderwhite
City Marblehead
Company
Contact Capt. Robert Grant
City North Olmsted
Company
Contact Capt. Richard Guest
City Fairview Park
Company
Contact Capt. Dale Guiley
City Medina
Company
Contact Capt. David Gwin
City Elyria
Company
Contact Richard Hamlin
City Port Clinton
Company
Contact Capt. Robert Hammer
City Green Springs
Company
Contact Capt. Herbert Hammond
City Delaware
Company
Contact Capt. Ronald Harper
City Brook Park
Company
Contact Capt. Charles Heckman
City Cincinnati

Company
Contact Capt. Mike Heinberger, Sr.
City Mansfield
Company
Contact Capt. Roosevelt Helms
City Port Clinton
Company
Contact Capt. Frank Henderson
City Worthington
Company
Contact Capt. Donald Henry
City Elmore
Company
Contact Hugh R. Henry
City Lakeside
Company
Contact Capt. Philip Hepkema
City Cleveland
Company
Contact Capt. John Herl
City Worthington
Company
Contact Capt. James Herl
City Port Clinton
Company
Contact Capt. Thomas Hetzel
City Port Clinton
Company
Contact Capt. Willard Hipsher, Jr.
City McCutchenville
Company
Contact Capt. Michael Hluszti
City Wellington
Company
Contact Capt. Daniel Holan
City Parma
Company
Contact Capt. Joseph Holly
City Marblehead
Company
Contact Capt. Carol Holly
City Lodi
Company
Contact Capt. Steve Horn
City 43452
Company
Contact Capt. Forrest Hornbeck, Sr.
City Marblehead
Company
Contact Capt. Michael Hritz
City Avon Lake
Company
Contact Don Hubert
City Garfield Heights
Company
Contact Capt. Scott Hubert
City Brecksville
Company
Contact Capt. Jack Huston
City Port Clinton
Company
Contact Capt. Clyde Jeffries
City Barberton
Company
Contact Capt. James Jenkins
City Port Clinton
Company
Contact Capt. Gary Jennrich
City Parma
Company
Contact Capt. Edward Jones
City Marblehead
Company
Contact Capt. Earl Jones, Jr.
City Warren
Company
Contact Capt. Arthur Jones
City Cincinnati
Company
Contact Capt. Ralph Joyce
City North Olmstead
Company
Contact Capt. George Jumper, Jr.
City Urbana
Company
Contact Michael Kane
City Cleveland
Company
Contact Capt. Vernon Ketcham
City Barberton
Company
Contact Capt. Roger King
City McComb
Company
Contact Capt. Eugene Knight
City Clarksville

Company
Contact Capt. Ronald Koenig
City Marblehead
Company
Contact Capt. Joseph Kostura
City Put-In-Bay
Company
Contact Bob Kowell
City Parma Heights
Company
Contact Capt. Kenneth Krul
City Cleveland
Company
Contact Capt. Ed LaBounty
City Graytown
Company
Contact Capt. Paul LaCourse
City Toledo
Company
Contact Washington Lacy, III
City Akron
Company
Contact Capt. Bob Lamb
City Oregon
Company
Contact Capt. Earl Lambert
City Port Clinton
Company
Contact Capt. Ronald LaMont
City Toledo
Company
Contact Capt. Leroy Lasher
City Genoa
Company
Contact Capt. Robert Lawson
City Napoleon
Company
Contact Capt. William Lenner
City Marblehead
Company
Contact Capt. Kenneth Lennox
City Port Clinton
Company
Contact Capt. Carl Lillis
City Strongsville
Company
Contact Capt. Terry Lowe
City Graytown
Company
Contact Capt. Raymond Lowe
City Perrysburg
Company
Contact Capt. Russell Loyd
City Oak Harbor
Company
Contact Capt. Leslie Lytle
City Port Clinton
Company
Contact Capt. Dennis Marek
City Parma
Company
Contact Capt. John Mather
City Huron
Company
Contact Capt. John & Louise Matta
City Port Clinton
Company
Contact Capt. Michael Matta
City Powell
Company
Contact Capt. David Matta
City Port Clinton
Company
Contact Capt. Michael Matthews
City Toledo
Company
Contact Capt. John McArthur
City Toledo
Company
Contact Capt. William Meszaros
City Northfield Ctr.
Company
Contact Capt. Jerry Meyers
City Toledo
Company
Contact Capt. Bruce Moewe
City McDonald
Company
Contact Capt. Wanda Morehead
City Newark
Company
Contact Capt. William Morris
City Port Clinton
Company
Contact Capt. Douglas Morrow
City Northwood

Company
Contact Gerald L. Murphy
City Defiance
Company
Contact Capt. William Neer
City Shiloh
Company
Contact Capt. Charles Newman, Jr.
City Port Clinton
Company
Contact Capt. Robert Nickel
City Port Clinton
Company
Contact Capt. John Nickell
City Perrysburg
Company
Contact Capt. Thomas Niese
City Leipsic
Company
Contact Kenn Nowaczyk
City Toledo
Company
Contact Capt. Michael Nowaczyk
City Oregon
Company
Contact Capt. Raymond Nowak
City Lakeside
Company
Contact Capt. Charles Nutter
City Tiffin
Company
Contact Capt. George Nyerges
City Westlake
Company
Contact Capt. David O'Neal
City Oak Harbor
Company
Contact Capt. James Osborn
City Port Clinton
Company
Contact Capt. Raymond Osolin
City Euclid
Company
Contact Lake Erie Outfitters
City Port Clinton
Company
Contact Capt. Kendall Parsley
City Columbus
Company
Contact Capt. John Patrick
City Parma
Company
Contact Capt. Thomas Penny
City Walbridge
Company
Contact Capt. James Perrine
City Cortland
Company
Contact Capt. Ronald Pflug
City Marblehead
Company
Contact Jason Phipps
City Defiance
Company
Contact Capt. James Phipps
City Defiance
Company
Contact Capt. Thomas Polta
City Warren
Company
Contact Capt. Bernard Pompiley
City Rocky River
Company
Contact Don Ralph
City Morral
Company
Contact Capt. Jon Rasmussen
City Port Clinton
Company
Contact Capt. Leonard Reino
City Gibsonburg
Company
Contact Nate's Restaurant
City Port Clinton
Company
Contact Capt. Jim Roach
City Walton Hills
Company
Contact Terry A. Robinson
City Ada
Company
Contact Capt. Larry Roe
City Sandusky
Company
Contact Capt. Albert Rowh
City Cuyahoga Falls

Company
Contact Capt. James Rushworth
City Wickliffe
Company
Contact Capt. Dean Ryberg
City Centerburg
Company
Contact Capt. James Sackett
City Ashland
Company
Contact Capt. David Sackett
City Ashland
Company
Contact Capt. Jack Salisbury
City Rocky River
Company
Contact Capt. John Scaife
City Graytown
Company
Contact Capt. Daniel Schade
City Gibsonburg
Company
Contact Capt. Park Schafer
City Huron
Company
Contact Capt. Roger Schaffer
City Norwalk
Company
Contact Capt. Daniel Schlegel
City Toledo
Company
Contact Capt. Thomas Schofield
City Huron
Company
Contact Capt. David Screptock
City Oak Harbor
Company
Contact Capt. Lynn Seery
City Dayton
Company
Contact Capt. Mathew Severns
City Caldonia
Company
Contact Capt. Robert Shetenheim
City Port Clinton
Company
Contact Capt. Bruce Sibbersen, Sr.
City Woodville
Company
Contact Capt. Robert Slye
City Galloway
Company
Contact Capt. Ottie Snyder, Jr.
City Port Clinton
Company
Contact Capt. Jerry Stayer
City N. Canton
Company
Contact Capt. Marvin Stechschulte
City Findlay
Company
Contact Capt. Richard Stedke
City Lima
Company
Contact Capt. John Stefano
City Port Clinton
Company
Contact Capt. Karl Stroh
City Navarre
Company
Contact Capt. William Sturm
City Lakeside
Company
Contact Capt. Robert Summers
City Centerville
Company
Contact Capt. Edward Taylor
City Huron
Company
Contact Capt. Austin Tester
City Marblehead
Company
Contact Capt. Dean Thompson
City Toledo
Company
Contact Capt. James Tillman
City Toledo
Company
Contact Capt. Michael Topp
City Arlington
Company
Contact Capt. Dennis Toth
City Findlay
Company
Contact Capt. Ronald Trogdon
City Mentor

Company
Contact Capt. Bob Trozel
City Athens
Company
Contact Capt. Edd Twigg
City Akron
Company
Contact Capt. Keith Unkefer
City Apple Creek
Company
Contact Capt. Frank Valencic
City N. Olmsted
Company
Contact Capt. David Vargo
City Warren
Company
Contact Capt. Raty\\ymond Vargo
City Lorain
Company
Contact Capt. Edward Volan
City Seven Hills
Company
Contact John Wagenhals
City Lakeside
Company
Contact Capt. Gary Watkins
City Port Clinton
Company
Contact Capt. Thomas Weese
City Port Clinton
Company
Contact Capt. John Welch
City Stone Ridge
Company
Contact Capt. Dan Welsh
City New London
Company
Contact Capt. Phillip Whitt
City Port Clinton
Company
Contact Capt. Anthony Wieczorek
City Swanton
Company
Contact Capt. Thaddeus Wierzba
City Port Clinton
Company
Contact Capt. Jeff Williams
City Port Clinton
Company
Contact Capt. David Wise
City West Milton
Company
Contact Capt. Bernard Wise
City Perrysburg
Company
Contact Capt. Barry Witt
City Oak Harbor
Company
Contact Capt. Clark Wolfe
City Columbus
Company
Contact Capt. John Yingling, Jr.
City Boliver
Company
Contact Capt. Robert Young, Jr.
City Winchester
Company
Contact Capt. Robert Zvosec
City Marblehead

Oklahoma

Company Canadian River Ranch
Contact
City Eufaula
Company Captain Ron's Guide Service
Contact Ron Callahan
City Kingston
Company Crazy Horse
Contact M.L. Bill Swanda
City Davis
Company Deer Run Lodge
Contact
City Durant
Company Fish Alaska
Contact Clifton Shannon
City Tulsa
Company Grass River Lodge Ltd.
Contact Ike & Liz Enns
City Broken Arrow
Company Guidin'Right

Contact
City Edmond
Company Kississing Lake Lodge
Contact Curt Enns
City Broken Arrow
Company Lake Texoma Resort Park
Contact
City Kingston
Company Woods and Water, Inc.
Contact
City Catoosa
Company
Contact Gregg W. Abel
City Allen
Company
Contact Don Anderson
City Kingston
Company
Contact Travis D. Barker
City Kingston
Company
Contact Jerry T. Beard
City Kingston
Company
Contact Danny Beck
City Norman
Company
Contact Harold Wad Bibbee, II
City Allen
Company
Contact John W. Birdwell
City Del City
Company
Contact Jimmy Bishop
City Kingston
Company
Contact Robert E. Booher
City Cartwright
Company
Contact Joe Brown
City Kingston
Company
Contact Chris L. Caldwell
City Kingston
Company
Contact Larry C. Caldwell
City Kingston
Company
Contact Robert D. Callis
City Kingston
Company
Contact Harry C. Cantreall, Jr.
City Kingston
Company
Contact Bob Claunch
City Kingston
Company
Contact Earl L. Cox, Jr.
City Bradley
Company
Contact Vernon L. Davis
City Muldrow
Company
Contact Steve R. Dickson
City Kingston
Company
Contact Ira Dodson
City Mead
Company
Contact Jerry D. Dorsey
City Yukon
Company
Contact James R. Douglas, Jr.
City Parker
Company
Contact Willard L. Driesel
City Broken Bow
Company
Contact Carey Drumheller
City Chelsea
Company
Contact Wendyl Erwin
City Kingston
Company
Contact Ramon D. Foltz
City Kingston
Company
Contact Douglas V. Gray
City Hartshorne
Company
Contact Danny Griffin
City Kingston
Company
Contact Brian Hair
City Colbert
Company

Contact Thomas L. Hallum
City Haskell
Company
Contact Gary W. Hart
City Edmond
Company
Contact Jack A. Hedgcoxe
City Allen
Company
Contact Arthur L. Herndon
City Kingston
Company
Contact John W. Hoffman
City Kingston
Company
Contact Harold Honeycutt
City Kingston
Company
Contact Lloyd D. Jennings
City Moore
Company
Contact Joe Jesmer
City Kingston
Company
Contact Eddie Dean Johnson
City Kingston
Company
Contact Phillip N. Jones
City Kingston
Company
Contact Mike Lawrence
City Mead
Company
Contact Colin J. Leflore
City Kingston
Company
Contact Curgus Lowe
City Kingston
Company
Contact Steve Martin
City Kingston
Company
Contact Nial Maytubby
City Kingston
Company
Contact John H. McDonald
City Rush Spring
Company
Contact Mark Parker
City Mead
Company
Contact Steve Pierce
City Kingston
Company
Contact Richard Price
City Kingston
Company
Contact John Pryor
City Ardmore
Company
Contact Roger Raines
City Kingston
Company
Contact Henry C. Rogers
City Kingston
Company
Contact Dennis Rollan
City Kingston
Company
Contact Jimmy Rose
City Kingston
Company
Contact Mickey D. Rose
City Kingston
Company
Contact Gary Bob Scarberry
City Oklahoma City
Company
Contact Bobby Joe Scarberry
City Moore
Company
Contact Gene Skinner
City Kingston
Company
Contact R. J. Smithey
City Kingston
Company
Contact Harold Speed, Jr.
City Hendrix
Company
Contact Elmer Spicer
City Kingston
Company
Contact Charles C. Stowe, III
City Kingston
Company

Contact Charles C. Stowe
City Kingston
Company
Contact Johnny Sword
City Kingston
Company
Contact Steve Walker
City Ada
Company
Contact Jerry L. West
City Tishomingo
Company
Contact Larry Williams
City Kingston
Company
Contact Timothy E. Williams
City Kingston
Company
Contact Mike Wornom
City Kingston

Oregon

Company A-Float on the River
Contact Larry Nelson
City Springfield
Company A. Helfrich Outfitter
Contact Aaron D. & Jonnie F. Helfrich
City Springfield
Company Aces of Angling
Contact Dennis Gerke
City Eagle Point
Company Adventure Center
Contact Kirby & Minette Schmidt
City Ashland
Company Alaska Tropic Charters
Contact Floyd M. Jones
City Portland
Company Alaska Wildland
Contact Robert Rees
City Portland
Company Alaska Wildland
Contact Charles Thomas, Jr.
City Oregon City
Company Alaska Wildland
Contact Patrick Carr
City Bend
Company Alaska Wildland
Contact George Macaluso
City Bend
Company All Seasons Guide Service
Contact Jack L. Smith
City Gresham
Company Anderson River Adventures
Contact Robert D. Anderson
City Milton-Freewater
Company Angling Concepts
Contact Mike Claffy
City Albany
Company Arrowhead River Adventures
Contact Don L.Kirkendall
City Eagle Point
Company Ashland Fly Shop Guide Service
Contact Mark E. Swisher
City Ashland
Company Baker's Guide Service
Contact Ray Baker
City Eugene
Company Beaver State Adventures
Contact Robert L. Snook
City Klamath Falls
Company Big Foot Guide Service
Contact Earl D. Lowe
City Grants Pass
Company Big Redd's River Guide Service
Contact William H. Harrison
City Brookings
Company Bill Hedlund Guide Service
Contact William E. Hedlund
City Seaside
Company Bill's Guide Service
Contact Bill M. Matejka
City Central Point
Company Bing Nelson Guide Service
Contact Bing Nelson
City Florence
Company Bob Brown's Guided Sportfishing

Contact E.B. Brown
City Netarts
Company Bob Roberts Outdoors
Contact Bobby L. Roberts
City Pendleton
Company Bob Stone's Guide Service
Contact Robert P.Stone
City Eugene
Company Bob's Economy Guide Service
Contact Bob Brown
City Hillsboro
Company Borg's Guide Service
Contact Hal L. Borg
City Medford
Company Borg's Guide Service
Contact Hal Borg
City Central Point
Company Bracke's Guide Service
Contact John Bracke
City Beaverton
Company Brett's Guide Service
Contact Brett Gianella
City Lake Oswego
Company Briggs Guide Service
Contact Bret A. Clark
City Grants Pass
Company Briggs Guide Service
Contact Jerry Briggs
City Grants Pass
Company BW Guide Service, Inc.
Contact Butch & Lance A.Wicks
City Corvallis
Company Caddisfly Angling Shop
Contact Brian R. Barnes, Jr.
City Eugene
Company Canyon Outfitters, Inc.
Contact George & Lynette Hauptman
City Halfway
Company Carney's Fishing Adventures
Contact David Carney
City Rogue River
Company Carr's Wild Trout Adventures
Contact John J. Carr
City Bend
Company Cascade Guides & Outfitters, Inc.
Contact
City Sunriver
Company Cascade River Tours
Contact Todd A. Flightner
City Maupin
Company Casey's Guide Service
Contact Casey Malepsy
City Shady Cove
Company Centerfire Outfitters, Inc.
Contact Clay Woodward & Stan Rogers
City Prineville
Company Central Oregon Adventures, Inc.
Contact Richard L. Wren
City Bend
Company Chris Young Guide Service
Contact David C. Young, Jr.
City Prospect
Company Coastal Hook-R's Guide Service
Contact Paul D. Welle
City Tillamook
Company Coastal River Adventures
Contact Michael E. Kasper, Jr.
City Newport
Company Countrysport Limited
Contact John E. Hergenhan
City Portland
Company Craig's Guide Service
Contact Craig A. Lawless
City Grants Pass
Company Crystal Creek Anglers
Contact Raymond D. Rickards
City Klamath Falls
Company Dale's Guide Service
Contact Dale A. Piontkowski
City Phoenix
Company Dan Bentsen River Trips
Contact Dan Bentsen
City Springfield
Company Danny Haak Guide
Contact Danny Haak
City Oregon City
Company Dave Austin's Guide Service
Contact Dave Austin

City North Bend
Company DDK Enterprises
Contact Douglas D. Kile
City John Day
Company Deery & Guides Fishing
Contact Kenny Deery
City Corvallis
Company Deets Guide Service
Contact Dan Dieter
City Tillamook
Company Dennis Mobley River Guide
Contact Dennis R. & Darrin L. Mobley
City Bay City
Company Deschutes Canyon Fly Shop
Contact John T. Smeraglio
City Maupin
Company Deschutes Navigation Co.
Contact Dave Green
City Madras
Company Deschutes Navigation Co.
Contact William L. Miller
City Madras
Company Deschutes River Outfitters
Contact David M. Renton
City Bend
Company Deschutes River Outfitters
Contact Greg Price
City Bend
Company Deschutes River Tours
Contact David G. Randle
City Redmond
Company Deschutes River Tours
Contact Pete Carlson
City Madras
Company Deschutes Trout Tours
Contact Paul R. Pargeter
City The Dalles
Company Doran's Guide Service
Contact Doran D. Coonse
City Prineville
Company Double J Guide Service
Contact Clifford J. Godley
City Central Point
Company Drift & Fish
Contact John J. Lefler
City Ashland
Company Driftwood Enterprises
Contact Herb Fenwick
City Sandy
Company Eagle Cap Fishing Guides
Contact
City Enterprise
Company Ed Miranda's Guide Service
Contact Ed Miranda, Sr.
City Klamath Falls
Company End of the Rogue Guide Service
Contact Shaun Carpenter
City Gold Beach
Company Estuary Anglers
Contact Mike S. McCune
City Seaside
Company Fin & Feather Fly Shop
Contact Craig H. Campbell
City Prineville
Company Fish Boss Guide Service
Contact Ronald M. Buntrock
City Gold Beach
Company Fish On Guide Service
Contact Daniel B. Leis
City Cloverdale
Company Fishing 101
Contact Louis K. Lumsden
City Medford
Company Fishing on the Fly
Contact Timothy Dority
City Bend
Company Fishing with Stan
Contact Stanley W. Stanton
City Springfield
Company Fly Fisher's Place
Contact Jeff Perin
City Sisters
Company Flyfishing Shop
Contact Stensland & Barnes Bachmann
City Welches
Company Free Spirit Guide Service
Contact Sidney D. Mathis
City Klamath Falls
Company Frontier Charters
Contact Stonie Huffman
City Roseburg
Company Gary Early's Guide Service
Contact Gary B. Early

City Brookings
Company Gary Hilton's Guide Service
Contact Gary Hilton
City Tillamook
Company Gary Klein Guide Service
Contact Gary A. Klein
City Brookings
Company Gene Garner Guide Service
Contact Richard E. Garner
City Medford
Company Gorge Fly Shop Guide Service
Contact
City Hood River
Company Great Expectations Hunting Preserve
Contact Jerry & Kitty Russell
City Kimberly
Company Growler Charters
Contact Cliff Walters
City Joseph
Company Hackle & Hide
Contact Glenn W. Young
City Aloha
Company Harper McKee's Guide Service
Contact Harper C. McKee
City Grants Pass
Company Harry Mondale Guide Service
Contact Harry F. Mondale
City Phoenix
Company Havens' Guide Service
Contact Patrick J. Havens
City Medford
Company Hell's Canyon Anglers & Outfitters
Contact James C. Schroeder
City Halfway
Company High Adv. Air Charter, Inc.
Contact Steve Barnum
City Medford
Company High Cascade Descent
Contact Todd J. Vanderzwiep
City Bend
Company High Country Outfitters
Contact Marlene, Matt & Marc McDowell Woody
City Joseph
Company Homer Baker Guide Service
Contact Homer C. Baker
City The Dalles
Company Hook, Line & Sinker
Contact Jack W. Polley
City Tualatin
Company Hugh's Guide Service
Contact Hugh E. Crawford
City Medford
Company Inkrote's Guide Service
Contact William Inkrote
City Grants Pass
Company Iron Head Guide Service
Contact Jack E. Dailey
City Reedsport
Company J & L Guide Service
Contact Gerald Stambaugh
City Brookings
Company Jammin' Salmon's Guide Service
Contact Donny Morris
City Canby
Company Jeff Carr Professional Guide & Outfitter
Contact Jeff J. Carr
City Eugene
Company Jerry Tubbs Guide Service
Contact Jerome P.Tubbs
City Springfield
Company Jerry's Guide Service
Contact Gerald R. Sanderson
City Grande Ronde
Company Jim Schollmeyer Flyfishing Guide
Contact James L. Schollmeyer
City Salem
Company Jim's Guide Service
Contact Jim McCormick
City Harbor
Company Joe Bergh's River Fishing Trips
Contact Jonas A. Bergh
City Myrtle Creek
Company Joe Miller Guide Service
Contact Joe Miller

City Gold Beach
Company John Snow's Guide Service
Contact John S. Snow
City Eagle Point
Company John's Guide Service
Contact John C. McMillan
City K. Falls
Company Joseph Fly Shoppe
Contact Robert R. Lamb
City Joseph
Company Justus Outfitters
Contact Dan Justus
City Eugene
Company Kaufmann's Fly Fishing Expeditions, Inc.
Contact Randall W. Kaufmann
City Portland
Company Ken Mountain's River Guide Service
Contact Ken Mountain
City Brookings
Company Ken Robinson River Guide
Contact Kenneth W. Robinson
City Marcola
Company Kern Grieve Guide Service
Contact Kern Grieve
City Trail
Company Kimball Creek Guide
Contact Berwyn B. Bowman, Jr.
City Gold Beach
Company King Bear Lodge
Contact John Bryant
City Portland
Company King Bear Lodge
Contact Raymond Thornton
City Portland
Company King Point
Contact Darren Beko
City West Linn
Company King Point Lodge
Contact Jeffrey Ulsky
City West Linn
Company Kingfisher Charters
Contact Terry R. & Kathie King
City Merlin
Company L & W Enterprises
Contact Wayne E. Lofton
City Hebo
Company Lacy's Whitewater & Wild Fish
Contact Craig Lacy
City Bend
Company Larry's Guide Service
Contact Larry D. Skirvin
City Springfield
Company Laurie River Lodge
Contact Brent Fleck
City Gold Beach
Company Let's Go Fish Now
Contact Jim H. Hindman, Jr.
City Grants Pass
Company Lifetime Adventures-Alaska
Contact Curtis L. Hirschkorn
City Salem
Company Little Creek Outfitters
Contact John Ecklund
City LaGrande
Company M & G Outfitters
Contact Mike W. Smith
City Bend
Company MacKenzie Trail Lodge
Contact Bill Warrington
City Portland
Company Malone Guide Service
Contact Todd B. & Travis M. Malone
City Grants Pass
Company Marc's Guide Service
Contact Mark Fenton
City Brookings
Company Mark Henry's North American Outfitters
Contact Mark J. Henry
City Salem
Company Mark Van Hook Guide Service
Contact Richard M. Van Hook
City Gold Beach
Company Marshall's Guide Services
Contact Kevin Marshall
City Corvallis
Company McKenzie River Rafting Co.
Contact Joe & Jan Estes
City Springfield
Company McLees Guided Fishing Trips

Contact Lawrence M. McLees
City Oregon City
Company Michael Talia Guide Service
Contact Michael P. Talia
City Eugene
Company Mickey Finn Guide Service
Contact Patrick L. Schatz
City Bend
Company Mid Columbia Outfitters
Contact Mike Jones
City Hermiston
Company Mike Lowery Guide Service
Contact Michael E. Lowery
City Prospect
Company Moe Fishin
Contact Larry L. Moe
City Portland
Company Morrison's Rogue River Lodge
Contact
City Merlin
Company Mossbak Guide Service
Contact Gary D. Enoch
City Grants Pass
Company Mountain View Guide Service
Contact Jack T. Rose
City Leaburg
Company Nestucca Valley Sporting Goods
Contact Ray S. Hammer
City Hebo
Company Noah's World of Water
Contact Noah Hague
City Ashland
Company Norm's Just Fishin'
Contact Norm Brady
City Portland
Company North Fork Fishing Service
Contact Glen A. Gross
City Jefferson
Company North River Guide Service
Contact William L. Conner
City Glide
Company Northwest Adventures Guide Service
Contact Joe Paul
City Grants Pass
Company Northwest Drifters
Contact Daniel C. Stumpff
City Central Point
Company Northwest Drifters
Contact Dave Andreatta & Dan Stumpf
City Gold Hill
Company Northwest Eco-Ventures
Contact Christopher D. Culver
City Eugene
Company Northwest Fly Fishing Outfitters
Contact John M. Hagan, II
City Gresham
Company Northwest Traditions
Contact Adam F. Payne
City Springfield
Company Northwest Whitewater Excursions
Contact Dennis R. Brandsma
City Eugene
Company NW River Guides
Contact Dave M. McCann
City Beaverton
Company O'Brien's Guide Service
Contact Dick O'Brien
City Corbett
Company Oachs Bros. Fishing Guide Service
Contact George A. Oachs
City Gold Hill
Company Ocean Charterboat
Contact Joseph Rohleder
City Waldport
Company Oregon Alaska Sportfishing
Contact Tim Marshall
City Tillamook
Company Oregon Alaskan Outfitters/ River Guides
Contact Don A. Lee
City Philomath
Company Oregon Fishing Adventures
Contact Gary F. Krum
City Bay City
Company Oregon Outdoors
Contact Dennis Dobson

City Tillamook
Company Oregon River Outfitters
Contact Dan E. Simmons
City Salem
Company Otter Fishing Trips
Contact Jim Matney
City Merlin
Company Otter Guide Services
Contact James R. Hall
City Nehalem
Company Outdoor Adventures Plus
Contact Larry Kirkpatrick
City Eugene
Company Owyhee Guide & Outfitters
Contact Clinton L. Fillmore
City Jordan Valley
Company Peninsula River Charters
Contact Ron Latschaw
City Grants Pass
Company Pheasant Ridge, Inc.
Contact Peter K. Rittenour
City Tygh Valley
Company Phoenix Adventures
Contact John P. Diskin
City Scottsburg
Company Portland River Company
Contact John W. Tilles
City Portland
Company Powder River Guide Service
Contact Philip G. Simonski
City Baker City
Company Pringle's Guide Service
Contact Gerald A. Pringle
City Medford
Company Raft, Inc.
Contact Don W. Strasser
City Bend
Company Raft, Inc.
Contact Michael L. Huddleston
City Bend
Company Rainbow King Lodge
Contact Thomas V. Robinson
City Lake Oswego
Company Ray's Guide Service
Contact Ray Slusser
City Merlin
Company Red Dog Outdoors
Contact Kelly R. Short
City Salem
Company Redside River Guide Service
Contact Robert C. Bryant
City Eugene
Company Richard P. Helfrich
Contact Dick P. Helfrich
City Vida
Company Rick Wren's Fishing on the Fly
Contact Evelyn Wren
City Bend
Company Rising Trout Guides & Outfitters
Contact Daniel J. Bastian
City Bend
Company River Adventure Float Trips
Contact Mel & Dianne Norrick
City Grants Pass
Company River Drifters Whitewater Tours
Contact Ann & Bill Kemnitzer
City Portland
Company River Trips Unlimited, Inc.
Contact Irv Urie
City Medford
Company River's Bend Outfitters
Contact Glenn D. Summers
City The Dalles
Company Rivers Edge Outfitters
Contact Vernon L. Patterson
City Richland
Company Rivers Path Outfitters
Contact Bill K. Kremers
City Corvallis
Company Rivers Path Outfitters
Contact Frank & Tami Armendariz
City Junction City
Company Rivers Path Outfitters
Contact Don Hill
City Springfield
Company Riversong Lodge
Contact James H. Sehl, Jr.
City Tidewater
Company Riversong Lodge
Contact Gordon Descutner
City Eugene

Company Riversong Lodge
Contact Daniel Brown
City Waldport
Company Roaring Fork Guide Service
Contact John R. Gross
City Springfield
Company Rocky Point Resort
Contact Jerry J. Felciello
City Klamath Falls
Company Rodger Carbone's Fly Fishing Guides
Contact Rodger R. Carbone
City Bend
Company Rogue Excursions Unlimited, Inc.
Contact Terry O'Connors
City White City
Company Rogue Rafting Company
Contact Devon M. Stephenson
City Shady Cove
Company Rogue River Outfitters
Contact Dennis R. Hughson
City Gold Beach
Company Rogue Sport Fishing Unlimited
Contact Michael A. Hoefer
City Gold Beach
Company Rogue Whitewater Co.
Contact Mike & Shawn Ayers
City Medford
Company Ron Adkins Guide Service
Contact Ronald G. Adkins
City Eugene
Company Ron's Guide Service
Contact Ronald W. Van Iderstine
City Springfield
Company Ron's Guide Service
Contact Ronald E. Jones
City Medford
Company Sanderson's Guide Service
Contact Bill Sanderson
City Mill City
Company Sawyer's Deschutes Guide Service
Contact Lynn A. Sawyer
City The Dalles
Company Schaefers Guide Service #1
Contact Steven D. Schaefers
City Vida
Company Schaefers Guide Service #2
Contact Schaefers & Damon
City Vida
Company Sea Gull Charters
Contact Dick Overfield
City Newport
Company Shadow Wood, Inc.
Contact Robert I. Zagorin
City Eugene
Company Sheerwater Guide Sevice
Contact Barry T. Jones
City Lake Oswego
Company Silversides
Contact Dennis S. Becklin
City Grants Pass
Company Silvey's Flyfishing Guide Service
Contact Brian D. Silvey
City Welches
Company Slam Dunkin Guide Service
Contact Jason Dunkin & Bret Gesh
City Dallas
Company Slammin Salmon Guide Service
Contact Terrence F. Luckett
City Aloha
Company SMS Guide Service
Contact Steven M. Scrimsher
City Nehalem
Company Solitude River Trips
Contact Al & Jeana Bukowsky
City Merlin
Company Specialty Adventures
Contact Greg Hublou
City Milwaukie
Company Speer's Guide Service
Contact Manuel, Rob & Gary Speer Deen
City Florence
Company Stan's Guide Service
Contact Stanley W. Sumner
City Brookings
Company Steamboat Inn
Contact Jim VanLoon
City Steamboat

Company Steelblue Chameleon Lodge
Contact Mark E. Kimball
City Pt. Orford
Company Steens Mountain Packers
Contact John and Cindy Witzel
City Frenchglen
Company Steen's Wilderness Adventures
Contact Connie & Shawn Steen Jim
City Joseph
Company Sudden Impact Guide Srvice
Contact Patrick D. Kelley
City Rufus
Company Sundance Expeditions, Inc.
Contact
City Merlin
Company Sweet Old Boys
Contact Marsden P. (Tiny) Case
City Cave Junction
Company T & S Guide Service
Contact Timothy & Shana Juarez
City Tillamook
Company Talaview Resorts
Contact John Barichello
City Oregon City
Company Talaview Resorts
Contact Roger Orben
City Melrose
Company Talaview Resorts
Contact Matthew Jewett
City Springfield
Company Ten Mile Boat Rental & Guide Service
Contact Bill J. Stubblefield
City Lakeside
Company The Adventure Center
Contact Jack K. Schmidt
City Medford
Company The Fishin' Hole
Contact Jack D. Jermain
City Shady Cove
Company The Fly Fishing Shop
Contact
City Welches
Company The Guide Shop
Contact Charles E. Peterson
City St. Helens
Company The Oregon Angler
Contact Dennis R. Hannah
City Elkton
Company Tightlines
Contact Jeff & Laura Helfrich
City Vida
Company Tim Hills Enterprises
Contact Tim Hills
City Salem
Company Todd's Guide Service
Contact R. Todd Puett
City Medford
Company Toman's King Camp
Contact Jeremy R. Toman
City Clackamas
Company Trophy King Lodge
Contact Mark Kimball
City Port Orford
Company Trophy King Lodge
Contact Jeffrey Christensen
City Oregon City
Company Trophy King Lodge
Contact Michael Boettcher
City West Linn
Company Trout Magic
Contact Raven Wing
City Bend
Company Umpqua River Adventures
Contact Douglas M. Brown
City Roseburg
Company Umpqua River Guide
Contact Terry Jarmain
City Reedsport
Company Wade River Guide Service
Contact Fred H. Wade
City Portland
Company Wally Ramsay Guide Service
Contact Wally D. Ramsay
City Ashland
Company Western Fishing Adventures
Contact Brad Staples & Denny Haak
City Oregon City
Company White Water Fishing Trips
Contact Carl R. (Skip) Zapffe

City Tygh Valley
Company Whiteley's New Frontier
Contact Scott Whiteley
City Springfield
Company Whitewater Warehouse/ Wilderness
Contact
City Corvallis
Company Wilderness Place Lodge
Contact Rod Heiser
City Bannks
Company Wilderness River Outfitters
Contact Bruce Greene
City Springfield
Company William's Outdoor Adventures
Contact William C. Sheppard
City Bend
Company Williamson River Club
Contact
City Fort Klamath
Company Willie Jo Guide Service
Contact Billy F. Smith, Sr.
City Medford
Company Winter's Guide Service
Contact Jon P. Winter
City Portland
Company Wolfe Bros. Guide Service
Contact Dennis R. Wolfe
City Camas Valley
Company Yamsi Ranch
Contact Gerda Hyde
City Chiloquin
Company Young's Fishing Service, Inc.
Contact Jack LaFond & Bill Young
City The Dalles
Company Z & S Outfitters, Inc.
Contact Carl R. Zapfee
City Tygh Valley
Company Zelazek Guide Service
Contact Dave Zelazek
City Corvallis
Company
Contact John J. Aho
City Gresham
Company
Contact Brad Allen
City Medford
Company
Contact Randy R. Allen
City Oregon City
Company
Contact Gary S. & Scott A. Amerman
City Tillamook
Company
Contact Geoffrey L. Baldwin
City Grants Pass
Company
Contact Ed Balfour
City Reedsport
Company
Contact Lyman T. Barney
City Glendale
Company
Contact Ross Bell
City Gold Beach
Company
Contact Elvin C. Beltz
City Gold Beach
Company
Contact Lou Bentsen
City Springfield
Company
Contact Eric Bigler
City Marylhurst
Company
Contact Daniel H. Bishop
City Prairie City
Company
Contact Bill Boice
City Gold Beach
Company
Contact Bill Boresek
City Eugene
Company
Contact Hal Borg
City Medford
Company
Contact Daniel G. Bork
City Mt. Angel
Company
Contact Harry E. Bramel, III
City Clackamas
Company
Contact John S. Briggs

City Gold Beach
Company
Contact Stevenson E. Brown
City Gold Beach
Company
Contact Ted Bryant
City Eugene
Company
Contact Rachael Burks
City Falls City
Company
Contact Steven D. Burt
City Albany
Company
Contact Dana Burwell
City Leaburg
Company
Contact Christopher M. Carson
City White City
Company
Contact Eugene C. Clark
City West Linn
Company
Contact James L. Van Cleve
City Astoria
Company
Contact Lloyd M. Cline
City Medford
Company
Contact Tim H. Cloe
City Portland
Company
Contact Jerome A. Daley
City Medford
Company
Contact Edison R. Davis
City Gold Beach
Company
Contact Gary Distefano
City Shady Cove
Company
Contact Dan R. Dixon
City Nehalem
Company
Contact Dennis A. Dobson
City Tillamook
Company
Contact Jack R. Duncan
City Roseburg
Company
Contact Bradley K. Edwards
City Walterville
Company
Contact Greg Eide
City Gold Beach
Company
Contact Robert D. Evans
City Medford
Company
Contact Gary Farley
City Brookings
Company
Contact Cheryl Fisher
City Baker City
Company
Contact Christopher J. Fleetwood
City Shady Cove
Company
Contact Charles H. Foster, III
City Portland
Company
Contact Garry Frahm
City Roseburg
Company
Contact David Fuller
City Grants Pass
Company
Contact Wayne C. Gardner
City Leaburg
Company
Contact John Garrison
City Sunriver
Company
Contact Perri R. Gaustad
City The Dalles
Company
Contact Gary L. Geis
City Portland
Company
Contact Gary A. Gilchrist
City Brookings
Company
Contact Herb Good
City Hood River
Company
Contact James R. Goodpasture

City Vida
Company
Contact Roger Goodwin
City Salem
Company
Contact Robert L. Green
City The Dalles
Company
Contact Albert (Skip) Greenwood
City West Linn
Company
Contact William M. Grieve
City Prospect
Company
Contact John S. Hanson
City Brookings
Company
Contact James D. Harris
City White City
Company
Contact Alan L. Harrison
City Springfield
Company
Contact Anthony J. Helfrich
City Springfield
Company
Contact James D. Helfrich
City Springfield
Company
Contact Greg A. Henderson
City Grants Pass
Company
Contact Frank M. Hendrickson
City Oakland
Company
Contact Donald L. Hermance
City Troutdale
Company
Contact Gene Highfill
City Springfield
Company
Contact Jon E. Hockema
City Gold Beach
Company
Contact David W. Hodder
City Oregon City
Company
Contact Lyle E. Hubbard
City Grass Valley
Company
Contact John E. Hutter
City Talent
Company
Contact James O. Jarboe
City Oregon City
Company
Contact Mike Jespersen
City Salem
Company
Contact David L. Johnson
City Boring
Company
Contact J.C. Johnson
City Springfield
Company
Contact Terry Johnson
City The Dalles
Company
Contact Jack T. Rose, Jr.
City Walterville
Company
Contact Donald J. Keller
City Corbett
Company
Contact Danny B. Kelsay
City Blue River
Company
Contact Kenny M. King
City Eugene
Company
Contact Darian F. 'Buzz' Kleven
City Springfield
Company
Contact Stephen Koler
City Gladstone
Company
Contact Steven M. Laing
City Eugene
Company
Contact Brent F. Lamm
City Canyonville
Company
Contact Gary Leon
City Glide
Company
Contact Wally J. Lewis

City Springfield
Company
Contact Todd B. Linklater
City Eugene
Company
Contact Benjamin R. Loveland
City Portland
Company
Contact Michael J. Lowenstein
City Tillamook
Company
Contact Frankie W. Luker
City Portland
Company
Contact Patrick S. Macy
City Eugene
Company
Contact Gary S. Marks
City Imnaha
Company
Contact Russell McCall
City Myrtle Point
Company
Contact James M. McDaniel
City Trail
Company
Contact David J. McKinnon
City Gervais
Company
Contact Brian R. McKnight
City Merlin
Company
Contact Mike V. McLucas
City Maupin
Company
Contact Merl S. McMullin
City Vida
Company
Contact William O. Miller
City Grants Pass
Company
Contact James C. Miller
City The Dalles
Company
Contact Gary Monical
City Phoenix
Company
Contact Stewart Monroe, III
City Hillsboro
Company
Contact David A. Morgans
City Portland
Company
Contact Terry L. Mulkey
City Portland
Company
Contact Larry Mullinnix
City Ashland
Company
Contact Steve Neverick
City Noti
Company
Contact Scott C. Ocacio
City Brookings
Company
Contact Chris Olsen
City Vida
Company
Contact Larry E. Page
City Portland
Company
Contact Donald L. Pedro
City Gold Beach
Company
Contact Alfred S. Perryman
City Rogue River
Company
Contact Jerry Q. Phelps
City Roseburg
Company
Contact Al Plath
City Vida
Company
Contact Charles S. Polityka
City Portland
Company
Contact Michael S. Polk
City Bend
Company
Contact Wayne E. Priddy
City Beavercreek
Company
Contact Marlon R. Rampy
City Grants Pass
Company
Contact Robert A. Reavis

City Prospect
Company
Contact Phillip B. Reed
City Newport
Company
Contact Richard J. Regula
City Wedderburn
Company
Contact Michael D. Rodgers
City Vida
Company
Contact Darin M. Rowe
City Albany
Company
Contact Randall E. Rumrill
City Grants Pass
Company
Contact Denmark S. Rushing
City Lake Oswego
Company
Contact Terry F. Sawyer
City Mitchell
Company
Contact David C. Schaefers
City Leaberg
Company
Contact Ray L. Self
City Aloha
Company
Contact Kevin P. Shea
City Sixes
Company
Contact Michael Shearer
City Glide
Company
Contact Egene R. Shropshire
City Troutdale
Company
Contact Dale D. Skiles
City Canby
Company
Contact Jody G. Smith
City Elkton
Company
Contact Ronald D. Smith
City Gold Beach
Company
Contact Robert E. Spani
City Medford
Company
Contact William A. Sparks
City Merlin
Company
Contact Robert B. Staysa, Jr.
City Days Creek
Company
Contact Del L. Stephens
City Eugene
Company
Contact Gary Stott
City Springfield
Company
Contact Thomas D. Sutton
City Shady Cove
Company
Contact Otis D. Swisher
City Medford
Company
Contact Brent R. Titus
City Grants Pass
Company
Contact David Tokay
City Klamath Falls
Company
Contact Jerry G. Toman
City Gresham
Company
Contact Eldon O. Townsend
City Lebanon
Company
Contact Brian K. Truax
City Shady Cove
Company
Contact Brad W. Vanderzanden
City Hillsboro
Company
Contact A.D. Volk
City Gold Hill
Company
Contact Kenneth L. Waler
City Portland
Company
Contact William N. Wallender
City Hillsboro
Company
Contact Samuel E. Waller

City Gold Beach
Company
Contact Frank A. Welles
City Florence
Company
Contact Craig S. Wells
City Eugene
Company
Contact Dennis H. & David L. Wessels
City Sweet Home
Company
Contact Joe D. Whaley
City Brookings
Company
Contact Gary R. Williams
City Eugene
Company
Contact Paul D. Williams
City Brookings
Company
Contact Christopher L. Winslow
City Elkton
Company
Contact Gary J. Wolgamott
City Swisshome
Company
Contact Don Wouda
City Springfield
Company
Contact Anton R. Wratney
City Bend
Company
Contact Jeffery R. Zennie
City Brookings
Company
Contact Craig R. Ziegler
City Seaside

Pennsylvania

Company Alaska Adventures
Contact Allen Miknich
City Bloomsburg
Company Alaska Wilderness Expeditions
Contact
City East Fallowfield
Company Alaska Wilderness Expeditions
Contact Timonty D. & Marsha A. White
City Coatesville
Company Allegheny Outdoors
Contact David L. Heflin
City Bradford
Company Allenberry Resort & Playhouse
Contact
City Boiling Springs
Company Anglers Academy
Contact Bob Sentiwany
City White Haven
Company Big Moore's Run Lodge, Ltd.
Contact
City Coudersport
Company Chuck Swartz's Angling Adventures
Contact Chuck Swartz
City Indiana
Company Cliff Park Inn
Contact John Curtin
City Milford
Company Elk Creek Fishing Assoc., Inc.
Contact
City Yardley
Company Falling Spring Inn
Contact Adin L. Frey
City Chambersburg
Company Golden Pheasant Inn
Contact Barbara Faure
City Erwinna
Company Hawg Hunter III Fishing Charters
Contact
City Erie
Company Highwater Guide Service
Contact Gary Walck
City East Stroudsburg
Company Jerry Hadden's Guide Service
Contact

City Susquehanna
Company North American Wilderness Adventures
Contact C.E."Woody"Main
City Brookville
Company Rally Killer Charters
Contact Capt. C.J. Crisp
City Mansfield
Company Robertson Enterprises
Contact Ken Robertson
City Graceton
Company Roebling Inn on the Delaware
Contact Don & JoAnn Jahn
City Lackawaxen
Company Ron Kistler Guide Services
Contact Ron Kistler
City Allentown
Company Serene Fly-Fishing Adventures
Contact Pete Serene
City Kittanning
Company Silver Springs Outfitters
Contact Brian R. Tartar
City Kunkletown
Company Skytop Lodge
Contact
City Skytop
Company Starlight Lodge
Contact Patrick Schuler
City Starlight
Company The Feathered Hook Fly Shop & Guide Service
Contact
City Coburn
Company The Yellow Breeches Huse
Contact Matt Zito
City Boiling Springs
Company Tom & Kathy's Bed & Breakfast
Contact
City Cross Fork
Company Wilderness Lodge & Skyline Outfit, Inc.
Contact Greg Deimler
City New Bloomfield
Company Yellow Breeches House
Contact
City Boiling Springs
Company
Contact Pete Alex, Jr.
City Erie
Company
Contact Thomas D. Allen
City Bethlehem
Company
Contact Gary G. Amboyer
City North East
Company
Contact Capt. James Bonner
City Wilmerding
Company
Contact Robert A. Carlisle
City Harrisburg
Company
Contact Raymond Cichocki
City Dupont
Company
Contact Capt. Henry Cocain
City Sharpsville
Company
Contact Edward T. Concilla
City North East
Company
Contact Douglas B. Embler
City Erie
Company
Contact Randal Fair
City Ferndale
Company
Contact Brian J. Firestine
City Denver
Company
Contact Leonard J. Fritzley
City Beaver Falls
Company
Contact Capt. Joseph J. Gibbs
City W. Middlesex
Company
Contact Robert Gronowski
City Greeley
Company
Contact Ralf R. Gross
City Centerville
Company
Contact Robert N. Halmi

City Edinboro
Company
Contact Capt. Ronald Helm
City Apollo
Company
Contact Herman Henry Holl
City Evans
Company
Contact Robert J. Jenereski
City Mars
Company
Contact Joe B. Kasper
City Morrisville
Company
Contact Patrick D. Kilgallon
City Erie
Company
Contact Dick F. Learn
City Erie
Company
Contact Joseph P.Lugar II
City Pittsburgh
Company
Contact David R. McKee
City Butler
Company
Contact Frederick J. Miles
City Hellertown
Company
Contact Charles A. Minnick
City Franklin
Company
Contact Frederick H. Morosky
City Erie
Company
Contact John L. Murter
City East Prospect
Company
Contact Dwight O. Peppler
City Meadville
Company
Contact Robert Romanishin
City Waterford
Company
Contact Dale Rutherford
City Lititz
Company
Contact John A. Scypinski
City Erie
Company
Contact Raymond Serfass
City Pocono Summit
Company
Contact Scott A. Shafer
City Dallas
Company
Contact Brian L. Shumaker
City New Cumberland
Company
Contact Timothy C. Small
City Beaver Falls
Company
Contact Thomas Snyder
City Ferndale
Company
Contact Terry L. Snyder
City Brackenridge
Company
Contact Jack D. Solanik
City Pittsburgh
Company
Contact Chuck Swartz
City Honesdale
Company
Contact Richard D. Torrelli
City Erie
Company
Contact Richard Watson
City Erie
Company
Contact Michael R. Wilkerson
City York
Company
Contact Francis J. Wright
City Philadelphia

Rhode Island

Company Addieville East Farm
Contact
City Mapleville
Company

Contact Capt. Ed Hughes
City Charlestown

South Carolina

Company Bay Street Outfitters
Contact
City Beaufort
Company Bells Marina
Contact
City Eutawville
Company Bill's Guide Service
Contact Bill Conley
City Moncks Corner
Company Billup's Landing
Contact H.D."Smitty"Smith, III
City Summerton
Company Black's Camp
Contact Pam Blackmon
City Cross
Company Bray's Island Plantation
Contact
City Sheldon
Company Buddy's Guide Service
Contact Buddy Bradham
City Moncks Corner
Company Captain Billy Spearin
Contact Billy Spearin
City Eutawville
Company Captain Wally Burbage Charters
Contact Capt. Wally Burbage
City Charleston
Company Carolina Fly Fisherman
Contact
City Greenville
Company Casey's Charter Service
Contact Furman Casey, Jr.
City Moncks Corner
Company Chelsea Plantation
Contact
City Ridgeland
Company Cooper's Landing
Contact Charles Love
City Summerton
Company Curlew Charters
Contact
City Mount Pleasant
Company Delta Guide Service
Contact Gene Dickson
City Georgetown
Company Ellis Professional Guide Service
Contact Ken Ellis
City Moncks Corner
Company Fish, Inc.
Contact
City Pickens
Company Flynn's Charter Service
Contact Gene Flynn
City Moncks Corner
Company Foothills Fly Fishing
Contact Chuck Patterson
City Greenville
Company Gap Hill Landing Tackle/Guide
Contact Rocky Wells
City Six Mile
Company Garrett's Fishing & Marine
Contact Rick Garrett
City Anderson
Company Gramling & Sons
Contact John L. Gramling
City Orangeburg
Company Jack Island Gun Club
Contact
City JohnsIsland
Company Joe's Guide Service
Contact Joe Drose
City Cross
Company Little River Plantation
Contact
City Abbeville
Company Mill Creek Marina
Contact
City Vance
Company Professional Guide Service
Contact Randy Dorman
City Manning
Company Putnam's Landing
Contact Bill & Sherri Shipley
City Chapin

Company Randolph's Landing
Contact Nate & Lynn Bristow
City Manning
Company Randy's Guide Service
Contact Randy Horne
City Summerton
Company Santee Bass & Crappie Guide Service
Contact Barney Ulmer
City Cameron
Company Santee Cooper County
Contact Mary Shriner
City Santee Cooper
Company Santee Guide Service
Contact
City Santee
Company Scenic Lake Tours
Contact Hank Byrd
City Pickens
Company The Canal Lakes Resort
Contact Ray Sedgwick
City Cross
Company The Plantation
Contact
City Windsor
Company Truman's Guide Service
Contact Truman A. Lyon
City Moncks Corner
Company Woodside Guide Service
Contact Capt. Don Williams
City Irmo
Company
Contact Capt. Bramblett Bradham
City Charleston
Company
Contact John Calvin
City Greenville
Company
Contact Dominico Carchidi
City Eutawville
Company
Contact Jim Cope
City Manning
Company
Contact Lex Costas
City Pineville
Company
Contact Eddie Covington
City Summerton
Company
Contact Warren Crabtree
City Cross
Company
Contact Tom Cravens
City Pineville
Company
Contact Inky Davis
City Manning
Company
Contact Donald Drose
City Manning
Company
Contact Chuck Duke
City Summerton
Company
Contact E.S. English
City Cross
Company
Contact Dave Foster
City Eutawville
Company
Contact Wayne Goss
City Pineville
Company
Contact Richard Gray
City Manning
Company
Contact Thomas Gregory
City Eutawville
Company
Contact Mike Hester
City Greenville
Company
Contact David Hilton
City Ridgeville
Company
Contact Randy Home
City Summerton
Company
Contact L.C. Jordan
City Florance
Company
Contact Jack Matthews
City Manning
Company
Contact Sonny McFadden

City Cades
Company
Contact Ray Mills
City Sumter
Company
Contact William Nancollas
City Summerton
Company
Contact Jodie Pack
City Rimini
Company
Contact Tracy B. Pack
City Rimini
Company
Contact Pete Pritchard
City Summerton
Company
Contact David B. Ragin
City Manning
Company
Contact Pete Richard
City Summerton
Company
Contact L.B. Rush, Jr.
City Camden
Company
Contact Captain Richard C. Stuhr
City Charleston
Company
Contact Carroll Tanner
City Manning
Company
Contact W.D. Thornhill
City Pineville
Company
Contact Ray Turner
City Cross
Company
Contact Jerry Whitfield
City Pineville
Company
Contact Don Wiles
City Summerton
Company
Contact Robert C. Winters
City Cross
Company
Contact Lloyd C. Wolfe
City Pinopolis
Company
Contact Gus Woodham
City Columbia

South Dakota

Company Anchor Inn
Contact Rodney Vollmer
City Murdo
Company Big Bend Ranch
Contact Alex Falk
City Aberdeen
Company Bolton Guest Ranch
Contact Kay Bolton
City Dallas
Company Cedar Shore Resort
Contact Jennifer Redman
City Chamberlain
Company Circle CE Ranch
Contact Dick & Sally Shaffer
City Dixon
Company Crow Creek Sioux Tribe
Contact
City Fort Thompson
Company Dakota Dream Hunts
Contact Doug & Rich Converse
City Arlington
Company Fair Valley Ranch Hunting Paradise
Contact Travis & Dianne Hendricks
City Vivian
Company Fishing with Dave
Contact David Christopherson
City Pierre
Company Funkrest Hunting Preserve
Contact Don Funk
City Madison
Company Jed's Landing Guide Service
Contact Monte Hepper
City Mobridge
Company Johnson Outfitters
Contact

City Pierre
Company Krause's Goose Camp/So. Whitlock Resort
Contact Chuck Krause
City Gettysburg
Company Lewis & Clark Trail Guide Service
Contact Todd Langeliers
City Pollock
Company Lower Brule Wildlife, Fish & Recreation
Contact
City Lower Brule
Company McClelland's Guide Service
Contact Jack McClelland
City Pierre
Company Paradise Lodge
Contact Ken & Terry Korball & Gene Korthals
City Sioux Falls
Company Pike Haven Resort
Contact John & Nancy Hoffman
City Pierre
Company Ramrod Charters
Contact Wayne Musilek & Richard W. Deaver
City Sturgis
Company Reputation Guide & Kennel
Contact Gay Lynn Lang
City Ipswitch
Company Smith Pheasant Hunting
Contact Lyle & Dan Smith
City Presho
Company South Dakota Pheasant Safaris
Contact Darwin Dapper
City Pierre
Company Stukel's Birds & Bucks
Contact Ray & Cal Stukel Frank
City Gregory
Company Sunset Lodge
Contact John Gilkerson
City Pierre
Company Sutton's Place
Contact Lyle Sutton
City Agar
Company T & R Guide Service
Contact
City Howard
Company The Outpost Lodge
Contact Tom & Jill Olson
City Pierre
Company Turneffe Flats
Contact
City Deadwood
Company Wild Flush, Inc.
Contact Mike & Terry Frederick
City Waubay
Company Willimans Wildlife Lodge & Guiding
Contact
City Chamberlain

Tennessee

Company Blue Bank Resort
Contact
City Tiptonville
Company Boyett's Resort & Craft Shop
Contact
City Tiptonville
Company Cherokee Guide Service
Contact
City Tellico Plains
Company Clinch River Outfitters
Contact
City Andersonville
Company Dry Fly Outfitters
Contact
City Benton
Company Dunaway Hunting & Fishing Club
Contact
City Chattanooga
Company Eagles Nest Resort
Contact
City Samburg
Company Hamilton's Resort
Contact Jamie & Bonnie Hamilton
City Hornbeck
Company Hurrican Dock Resort

City Pierre
City Silver Point
Company Mansard Island Resort & Marina
Contact J.D. Koenig
City Springville
Company Mountain Fly Fishing
Contact
City Blountville
Company Noland's Guides Sergice
Contact Dale A. Noland
City Sevierville
Company Sportsman's Resort
Contact
City Tiptonville
Company Watts Bar Resort
Contact
City Watts Bar Dam
Company
Contact Ken Allen
City Memphis
Company
Contact Dan A. Berry
City Memphis
Company
Contact John R. Berry
City Memphis
Company
Contact Gary R. Davis
City Germantown
Company
Contact Bill M. Greene
City Kenton
Company
Contact Jim Moyer
City Clarksville
Company
Contact Chris Nischan
City Nashville
Company
Contact James W. Rouse
City Memphis
Company
Contact John H. Viser, III
City Memphis

Texas

Company 4 Corners Outfitting
Contact Dwain Lee Gibson
City Throckmorton
Company Action Outfitters
Contact Arvin Stroud
City Brownwood
Company Air Adventures
Contact Matt Kimball
City Irving
Company B Bar B Ranch Inn
Contact
City Kingsville
Company Bass Adventures
Contact
City Willis
Company Black Creek Ranch
Contact
City San Antonio
Company Black Farms
Contact
City Crowell
Company Brush Country Outfitters
Contact
City Three Rivers
Company Burton Hunting Service
Contact Kenneth D. Burton
City Georgetown
Company Captain Charlie Paradoski Bay Guide Service
Contact Captain Charlie Paradoski
City Sugarland
Company Chuck's Guide Service
Contact Chuck Uzzle
City Orange
Company Cinco Ranch
Contact
City El Indio
Company Dave Park Outfitting
Contact David R. Park
City Fowlerton
Company Dos Vaqueros
Contact
City Refugio
Company Doug Waddell's Guide

Service
Contact Douglas Waddell
City Fayetteville
Company Executive Outfitters
Contact
City Dallas
Company Fin & Feathered Safaris
Contact
City Laredo
Company G & W Guide Service
Contact Brian Gambill
City Little Elm
Company Geneva Catfish Farm
Contact
City Geneva
Company Gold Tip Guide Service
Contact Capt. Bill Pustejovsky
City Matagorda
Company Grogan Hunting Club
Contact George D. Grogan
City Longview
Company Hill Country Flyfishers
Contact
City Winberley
Company Holmes Lake Lodge/Recluse Lake Camp
Contact Mike & Lavonne Dyste
City New Braunfels
Company Indian Hills Farm, Inc.
Contact Hersh & Karen Kendall
City Smithville
Company J. Lloyd Woods Game Leases
Contact
City Tenaha
Company Joshua Creek Ranch
Contact
City Boerne
Company Lake Country Guide Service
Contact Hollice R. Joiner
City Winnsboro
Company Landon Ranch
Contact John I. Landon
City Llano
Company LH7 Bandera Ranch
Contact
City Bandera
Company Los Cuernos Ranch
Contact
City San Antonio
Company Los Patos Lodge
Contact
City Humble
Company Lynn Manor Kennels
Contact
City Manvel
Company Mark's Guide Service
Contact Mark C. Lanham
City Huntington
Company Mickey's Fishing Charters
Contact Jerry Mickey
City Rockport
Company Palmetto Guide Service
Contact David S. Cox
City Huntsville
Company Pearl Guide Service
Contact Capt. Mark Lyons
City Ingleside
Company Possum Walk Ranch
Contact
City Huntsville
Company QUAPAW
Contact Penelope Gregory
City Junction
Company Rafter S Ranch
Contact John M. Sirman
City Corrigan
Company Rapids Camp Lodge
Contact Jerry Shults & Richard VanDruten
City Dallas
Company Rick Carter's Guide Service
Contact Ricky D. Carter
City Alba
Company Rick Rule Sportfishing
Contact
City Freeport
Company Riversong Lodge
Contact Craig Peterson
City Corsicana
Company Rod & Gun Resources, Inc.
Contact J.W. Smith & David K. Gregory
City Killeen
Company SK Corp. Mariposa Ranch

Contact
City Falfurrias
Company Smokey's Guide Service
Contact Captain Smokey Gaines
City Port Aransas
Company Sundown Outfitters
Contact Paul D. Griffith
City Kilgore
Company Tecolote Charter Services
Contact R.R. Rouquette
City Rockport
Company The Back Forty Bed & Breakfast Ranch
Contact
City Fredericksburg
Company Tommy's Guide Service
Contact Tommy W. Countz
City Matagorda
Company Top of Texas Hunting
Contact Dick Cook
City Amarillo
Company Trangle T Outfitters
Contact Ed James Tibljas
City Granbury
Company Upland Bird Country
Contact
City Corsicana
Company Viapan Camp
Contact John Brothers
City Padulah
Company Wilderness Place Lodge
Contact Ray Debardelaben
City Houston
Company Wilderness Place Lodge
Contact Nathan Labus
City Haltown
Company
Contact Chuck Abbott
City San Antonio
Company
Contact Terry L. Adair
City Buchanan Dam
Company
Contact Glen Cody Adams
City Palacios
Company
Contact Daniel Ray Adams, II
City San Antonio
Company
Contact Todd N. Adams
City Fulton
Company
Contact Danny & Todd Adams
City Fulton
Company
Contact Ricky Dan Adams
City Cedar Hill
Company
Contact Jay Lauren Adams
City Rockport
Company
Contact Darryl W. Adams
City Brownsville
Company
Contact Kenneth G. Addington
City Arlington
Company
Contact William J. Agisotelis
City Zapata
Company
Contact Maria Luis Aguilar
City Los Fresnos
Company
Contact Marion T. Akers
City Ft. Worth
Company
Contact Bart Albright
City Baytown
Company
Contact John Alelus, Jr.
City Victoria
Company
Contact Justin D. Alford
City Village Mills
Company
Contact Robert W. Allen
City Baytown
Company
Contact Richard Allenbrand
City Pottsboro
Company
Contact Wendell S. Allman
City Dallas
Company
Contact John Alvarez
City Port Isabel

Company
Contact Juan Alvarez
City Port Mansfield
Company
Contact Tom Anderson
City Alba
Company
Contact William P. Anderson, Jr.
City Rockport
Company
Contact Kenneth W. Andreas
City Bandera
Company
Contact Aubrey M. Anderson
City Richardson
Company
Contact R. L. Andrews
City San Angelo
Company
Contact Ronald L. Appelbee
City Pottsboro
Company
Contact Charles H. Armendariz
City Brownsville
Company
Contact Gary Arnett
City Sherman
Company
Contact Gary S. Ash
City Greenville
Company
Contact David A. Ashcraft
City Bedford
Company
Contact David H. Askew, Jr.
City Port Aransas
Company
Contact Frank Atkins
City Sherman
Company
Contact James O. Atkins
City Corpus Christi
Company
Contact Clarence G. Atwood, Jr.
City Houston
Company
Contact Louis Austin
City Port Isabel
Company
Contact Larry Badgett
City Denison
Company
Contact Dana Allan Bailey
City Highlands
Company
Contact William M. Bain
City Longview
Company
Contact John Baker, Sr.
City Irving
Company
Contact Kirk Balke
City Amarillo
Company
Contact Mark Banister
City Pottsboro
Company
Contact Roy Bryan Bankston
City Texas City
Company
Contact Bill J. Bannister
City Pottsboro
Company
Contact John E. Barbree
City Portland
Company
Contact Robert Law Barker
City Aransas Pass
Company
Contact James E. Barker
City Canyon Lake
Company
Contact Jack W. Barkley
City Flint
Company
Contact Sonny Barnes
City Lindsay
Company
Contact Larry Barnes
City Penson Point
Company
Contact John R. Barnes
City San Antonio
Company
Contact Dan Barnett
City Pottsboro

Contact	City
Gerald Barnett	Pottsboro
Mike Barnett	Austin
John P. Barnhill	Gillett
Eddie Barr	Galveston
Gilberto O. Barrera	Kingsville
Jack Lee Barton	Port Isabel
Billy Bass	Gilmer
Dennis E. Bassinger	Denton
Ronnie H. Bayles	Grand Saline
Rick J. Baze	Collinsville
Donnie A. Beale	Arlington
W. C. Beard	Harper
Trevor W. Beck	Beeville
Edward M. Beeson, Jr.	Denison
Ronnie W. Behnke	Corpus Christi
Louis E. Belcher	Port Aransas
Andy R. Bell	Clifton
Don Benick	Corpus Christi
Charles W. Benson	Corpus Christi
Christie D. Berger	Irving
James M. Berwick	Winnie
Howard H. Bethune	Rockport
Emer W. Billings	Pleasanton
Douglas S. Bird	Corpus Christi
Sherman Birdsong	Golden
Bert F. Birdwell	Willis
E. R. Biship	Richardson
Herschel D. Black	Del Rio
Jerry Black	Del Rio
Danny R. Blackburn	Quitman
Michael D. Blanchard	Freeport
Truman Bland	Goodrich
Billy G. Blankenship	Port Aransas
Byron W. Blansett	Deer Park
Michael R. Bledsoe	Howe
Herbert W. Bode	S. Padre Island
Gerald G. Bogan	Lewisville
Frank C. Bolbecker	Houston
Paul Lynn Bolin	Frisco
Dennis C. Bolton	Granbury
Jeffrey R. Bond	South Lake
Tex R. Bonin	Conroe
Jason A. Bonner	Jefferson
Bucky Bonner	Quitman
Weldon R. Bonner	Rockwall
James D. Bonner	Jefferson
Bradley H. Boreaux	Brownsville
Scott Boren	Mineola
David W. Boudreaux	League City
Joe Edgar Bounds	Mexia
Charles Bowers	San Angelo
Larry Boyd	Buchanan Dam
Jordas B. Boyd	Weatherford
Yancy D. Brackin	Teague
Victor K. Bradshaw	Tyler
Jeffrey S. Bradshaw	Highlands
Benny Bragg	Hemphill
William T. Bralley	Aransas Pass
Eugene D. Branch	Berclair
Kelly John Brandt	McKinney
Bruce C. Breisch	Roanoke
John M. Brennan	Port Aransas
Kenneth J. Brewer	S. Padre Island
Michael L. Bridges	Pottsboro
Rex M. Bridges	Pottsboro
W. C. Briley	Irving
William G. Briscoe	Hurst
Jimmy Ray Britt	Ft. Worth
Robert Brooks	Fulton
Terry M. Brown	Odessa
Randall E. Brown	Sanger
Jeffrey C. Brown	Coldspring
Charlie F. Brown	Iraan
Charles E. Brown	Karnes City
Milton F. Browning	Mineola
John E. Brust	Dallas
Marsel Bryson	Yantis
Jason Buchanan	Tow
Jeffrey Buchanan	Corrigan
Charles R. Buchen	Los Fresnos
Rocky Buckner	Plainview
Charles R. Bujan	Port Aransas
Gary Wayne Bullion	Alvin
Will Bullock	Port Mansfield
John E. Burchell	Crystal Beach
James O. Burden	Pottsboro
James R. Burdett	S. Padre Island
Stanley Burgay	Timpson
Robert A. Burk	Spring
Kevin W. Burleson	Ballinger
Carl Burris	Pearsall
Jim Busch	Sherman
James M. Butler	Bryan
Cecil Ray Byars	Nacogdoches
Ronald G. Byrd	Garland
N. L. Cade	Rockwall
Michael G. Cade	Mineola
Kevin W. Callam	Rockport
Alexander Callander	Pottsboro
Joe N. Camp	Gainesville
Bruce Campbell	Carrollton
Gene Campbell	Baytown
Terry Lee Campbell	Yantis
Chris C. Campbell	Mineola
William L. Campbell	Pottsboro
Johnny M. Campbell	Waco
Louis M. Canalito	Texas City
Calvin E. Canamore	Bishop
William L. Cannan, Jr.	Huntsville
Dennis R. Canoda	Emory
Matt Cantwell	Troup
Bill Carey	Pottsboro
Jerry H. Cariker	Port Bolivar
Ed Carlee	San Antonio
Monty Ray Carlton	Valley View
Carl Kent Carnes	Comanche
Brett H. Caron	George West
David B. Carr	Livingston
Randy Carroll	Winnsboro
John Carroll	Dalhart
Ben Carroll	Austin
Floyd J. Carroll, Jr.	Whitney
Garold Carson	Corpus Christi
Jason Carter	Jarrel
John R. Carter	Mabank
William E. Cashin, III	Pottsboro
Mark A. Castillo	Sinton
Connie Cates	Rockwall
Ben Causey	Sanger
George Cavazos	Mission
Allen Ross Chesney	Springtown
James R. Chestnut	Converse
John M. Childers	Pt. O'Connor
Capt. J.M. (Red) Childers	Port O'Connor
Mark A. Childress	Brownsville
James G. Chism	Houston
Arthur R. Chmielewski	Rosharon
Glenn L. Chonoski	Grapeland
Ron Christenson	Austin
Allen M. Christenson, Jr.	Austin
Dale R. Church	Gordonville
David Cibulka	Port Aransas
Duanne Clark	Aransas Pass
Frank E. Clark	Corpus Christi
Gary L. Clark	Aransas Pass
Tony D. Clark	Emory
Dennis L. Clark	Bryan
Allen Dale Clement, III	Portland
Dorance K. Clifton	Emory
Gary Ray Clouse	Rockport
Lesley D. Cobb	Riviera
Benjamin A. Cockrell	Tyler
C. A. Coder	Denison
Dale Lynn Cogburn	Waco
Paul H. Coker	Corpus Christi
B. J. Coker	Richland
Joe Coker	Alba
Richard E. Colburn	Orange
Steven N. Cole	Galveston
Bobby Lee Cole	Mesquite

Company	Company	Company	Company	Company
Contact Mel S. Collins	Contact Richard E. Crow	Contact John D. Diaz	Contact Victor Dwyer	Contact Neal L. Fisher
City Sunnyvale	City Ft. Worth	City Beaumont	City Austin	City Dallas
Company	Company	Company	Company	Company
Contact Ernest G. Collins	Contact Don Crowe	Contact Edward L. Dickert	Contact Paul Eakins	Contact Robert L. Fisher
City Broaddus	City Port Isabel	City Kirbyville	City Calliham	City Paris
Company	Company	Company	Company	Company
Contact Rick Collis	Contact Robert B. Crumpler	Contact Rutherford Dickinson	Contact Dennis W. Eason	Contact Jerry Lynn Fitts
City Alba	City Damon	City Tilden	City Deer Park	City Kirbyville
Company	Company	Company	Company	Company
Contact Wade F. Collum	Contact Roy M. Cryer	Contact Stanley Dignum	Contact Paul C. Eason	Contact R. L. Flanagan
City Rockport	City Ft. Worth	City Port Aransas	City Brookeland	City Robert Lee
Company	Company	Company	Company	Company
Contact Joe A. Collum	Contact J. A. Cunningham, III	Contact David C. Dillman	Contact Mickey Ray Eastman	Contact Bettie Fleenor
City Pottsboro	City Burnet	City Houston	City Baytown	City Corsicana
Company	Company	Company	Company	Company
Contact William C. Conlee	Contact James E. Curry	Contact Stefan Dollins	Contact Paul Eccleston	Contact Clifford D. Fleming
City Austin	City Laguna Vista	City Graham	City Corpus Christi	City S. Padre Island
Company	Company	Company	Company	Company
Contact Dan B. Conoly, Jr.	Contact Charlie Cypert	Contact Robert E. Dooley	Contact Danny Eddins	Contact Bobby J. Fly
City Floresville	City Aquilla	City Pt. O'Connor	City Portland	City Shepherd
Company	Company	Company	Company	Company
Contact John Conway	Contact Steven Cyr	Contact Thomas E. Doran	Contact Steve R. Edgmon	Contact Larry E. Folkner
City Portland	City Portland	City Rockport	City Conroe	City Zapata
Company	Company	Company	Company	Company
Contact J. Paul Cook	Contact Gary C. Dale	Contact Randy V. Dorman	Contact Gary Einkauf	Contact Noson E. Fontenot
City Stephenville	City Waco	City Jasper	City Port Aransas	City Orange
Company	Company	Company	Company	Company
Contact Russell H. Cook	Contact Charles P.Dalton	Contact Thomas H. Dosier	Contact Jan Eitelman	Contact James W. Forbes
City Rowlett	City Lake Dallas	City Sunnyvale	City Gordonville	City Center
Company	Company	Company	Company	Company
Contact William R. Cooksey	Contact Randall P.Darington	Contact Mitchell G. Douglas	Contact Robert E. Ekrut	Contact James E. Ford
City S. Padre Island	City Highlands	City Lancaster	City Austin	City New Caney
Company	Company	Company	Company	Company
Contact Cecil R. Coons	Contact Haywood B. Davenport	Contact Tommy Dowdy	Contact Ronnie Elkins	Contact Charles A. Foreman
City Port Aransas	City Kirbyville	City Mesquite	City Pt. O'Connor	City Yantis
Company	Company	Company	Company	Company
Contact Joe Cooper	Contact Cheryl Davenport	Contact Charles B. Downey	Contact Stephen C. Ellingson	Contact Roger D. Foreman
City Smithville	City Irving	City Bryan	City Dallas	City Sherman
Company	Company	Company	Company	Company
Contact Michael W. Cooper	Contact Bill A. Davidson	Contact Lloyd Dreyer	Contact Richard Elliott	Contact John M. Forrest, III
City Greenville	City Wills Point	City Port Aransas	City Waco	City Sanger
Company	Company	Company	Company	Company
Contact Donald A. Cooper	Contact Shane L. Davies	Contact Meredith A. Drummond	Contact Ralph C. Elliott	Contact James B. Foster
City Corpus Christi	City Cedar Hill	City La Feria	City Portland	City Los Fresnos
Company	Company	Company	Company	Company
Contact Gary N. Cooper	Contact James Roy Davis	Contact Kenneth R. Drummond	Contact John Ellis	Contact Bobby Fowler
City Port Aransas	City Forney	City San Antonio	City Port Isabel	City Hemphill
Company	Company	Company	Company	Company
Contact Craig Coover	Contact Brad Davis	Contact Robert Lyn Dryden	Contact James R. Epps	Contact Ed Fowler
City Irving	City Gladewater	City Farmersville	City Burleson	City Sherman
Company	Company	Company	Company	Company
Contact Larry E. Corbett	Contact Jasper G. Davis, Jr.	Contact James R. Dryden	Contact Leon C. Erwin	Contact Stephen M. Fox
City Brownsville	City Irving	City Garland	City San Antonio	City Mesquite
Company	Company	Company	Company	Company
Contact Luis G. Costas	Contact Michael L. Day	Contact Richard A. Duckworth	Contact Isael Espinosa	Contact James Fox
City San Antonio	City Carrollton	City Dallas	City Corpus Christi	City Rockport
Company	Company	Company	Company	Company
Contact Ronnie E. Coward	Contact Gregory A. Deaderick	Contact Danny Duff	Contact Roy Lee Evans	Contact Tim Wade Frank
City Corpus Christi	City Hickory Creek	City Corpus Christi	City Port Mansfield	City Corrigan
Company	Company	Company	Company	Company
Contact Randy Coward	Contact John E. Dear	Contact Stephen E. Dumler	Contact William A. Evans	Contact Jerry W. Franklin
City Pt. Lavaca	City Jasper	City Arlington	City Corpus Christi	City Baytown
Company	Company	Company	Company	Company
Contact Rodger D. Cox	Contact John D. Dearmore	Contact James R. Duncan	Contact Capt. Jon Fails	Contact Mark J. Fransen
City Longview	City Alba	City Beaumont	City Corpus Christi	City Katy
Company	Company	Company	Company	Company
Contact Raymond D. Cox	Contact Leroy H. Deboer	Contact James D. Dunlap	Contact James M. Fambro	Contact Odis Frazier
City Matagorda	City Mt. Vernon	City Laguna Park	City Del Rio	City Strawn
Company	Company	Company	Company	Company
Contact Huey Cox	Contact Fred R. Dell	Contact Billy G. Dunn	Contact Gerald W. Farmer	Contact Ralph E. Frazier, Jr.
City Carthage	City Hemphill	City Buchanan Dam	City Weatherford	City Bacliff
Company	Company	Company	Company	Company
Contact Charles G. Crafts	Contact Gene Dennis	Contact Terry W. Dunn	Contact Ralph Farmer	Contact Charles W. Freeman
City Shelbyville	City Emory	City Burleson	City Three Rivers	City Pottsboro
Company	Company	Company	Company	Company
Contact Bandit Crane	Contact Billy Roy Denton	Contact Jerry Dunn	Contact Gerald W. Farrar	Contact Dennis L. Freeze
City Alba	City Irving	City Three Rivers	City Crockett	City Aransas Pass
Company	Company	Company	Company	Company
Contact Alfred E. Crawford	Contact James D. Deordio	Contact Kit Dunnam	Contact Douglas E. Felker	Contact Richard E. French, III
City Kingsland	City Arlington	City Corpus Christi	City Blue Ridge	City Granite Shoals
Company	Company	Company	Company	Company
Contact Darwin Crawford	Contact Paul O. Descoteaux	Contact Brian Duplechain	Contact Kenneth D. Ferguson	Contact Jim & Ben Friebele
City Livingston	City Graford	City Alba	City Corpus Christi	City Rockport
Company	Company	Company	Company	Company
Contact W.A. Crawford	Contact Alan D. Devine	Contact James R. Dupnik, Jr.	Contact Fermin Fernandez	Contact Blaien S. Friermood
City Coldspring	City Shepherd	City Aransas Pass	City Buchanan Dam	City Baytown
Company	Company	Company	Company	Company
Contact Alan R. Crawford	Contact Hope P.Devlin	Contact Jay Durkin	Contact Frank D. Ferry	Contact Charles Fulghum
City Buchanan Dam	City Port Aransas	City Rowlett	City Graford	City Victoria
Company	Company	Company	Company	Company
Contact Bob Creel	Contact Matthew J. Deyo	Contact Glynn Durrett	Contact Walter N. Fields	Contact Phillip K. Fulghum
City Alba	City Sinton	City Del Rio	City Hemphill	City Seadrift
Company	Company	Company	Company	Company
Contact Alfred L. Crounse	Contact Paul A. Dhane	Contact Frank Duxstad	Contact Edgar Findley	Contact Bob Fuston
City Mineral Wells	City Gainesville	City Port Aransas	City Port Aransas	City Port Mansfield

Company	Contact	City
	Roger Futch	Orange
	Pedro Garcia, Jr.	Port Isabel
	Robert H. Gardner, Jr.	Matagorda
	Mike Garner	Bonham
	Albert A. Garrison	Wadsworth
	Ronald J. Garrison	Freeport
	Andrew Garza	Euless
	Billy Gaskins	Port Aransas
	Gregory L. Gates	Ft. Worth
	Greg Gatz	Pottsboro
	Randy Gatz	Pottsboro
	Danny Ray Gaydos	Jourdanton
	David W. Gee	Fulton
	Wallace R. Gee	Three Rivers
	Stanley W. Gerzsenyi	Alba
	Michael B. Gibbs	Port Aransas
	Shane H. Gibson	Trinity
	Jack W. Gibson, Jr.	Waller
	Scott Gilbert	Corpus Christi
	W. T. Gilbert	Hemphill
	James S. Gilbert	Corpus Christi
	Gaylen Gilbreath	Zapata
	David N. Ginn	Lindale
	Robert A. Glameyer	Anderson
	John Glass	Garland
	Eric M. Glass	S. Padre Island
	Tommy Gleason	Holliday
	James W. Glenn	Three Rivers
	Rube C. Glover, Jr.	Lone Oak
	Willis H. Godwin	Hemphill
	Kenneth W. Gold	Wimberley
	Ronny Goldwin	Rockport
	John W. Goodell, III	Burleson
	Maurice B. Gordon	Houston
	James W. Gore	Quitman
	James Gotcher	Zavalla
	Dan Goyen, Jr.	Victoria
	Brent Goyen	Victoria
	Richard M. Grabein	Hemphill
	William D. Grace	McKinney
	Dean Granger	Aledo
	Wesley M. Grant	Greenville
	Robert J. Grantland	Brownsville
	Greg Grantland	Jasper
	Gary Gray	Victoria
	Preston D. Gray	Georgetown
	Dennis J. Gray	Port Isabel
	Lynette Gray-Branch	Berlcair
	David Green	Corpus Christi
	Conlaw E. Greenwood	Huntsville
	Steven K. Gregory	Granite Shoals
	Morris G. Gregory	Rockport
	Robert Lee Gregory, Jr.	Pt. O'Connor
	Orville L. Gren	Corsicana
	John E. Gresham	Gordonville
	Kenneth L. Griffith	Dickinson
	Josef F. Grigar	Pottsboro
	Bernard L. Grimes	La Marque
	Edwin Grimsley	Burleson
	Charles Grisham	Pottsboro
	James R. Griswold	Keller
	D. Russell Grumbles	Refugio
	Darren Guernsey	Port Arthur
	Machala T-N-T Guide	Friendswood
	Bobby Fox Guinn	Pottsboro
	Roy Tate Gunn	Rockport
	Jeffrey M. Gunn	Alba
	Wansley C. Gustafson	Port Aransas
	Jason J. Haas	Orchard
	Bryan W. Hague	Emory
	L. A. Hagy	Rockport
	Rusty Haire	Aransas Pass
	Clinton J. Hall	Dickinson
	William F. Hall	Shelbyville
	Tom Hall	Aransas Pass
	Randle D. Hall	Corinth
	Tim R. Hall	Pottsboro
	Joe Haltom	Pottsboro
	Bobby Hamilton	Hurst
	Robert Hamilton	Rockport
	Jack Hamlin	Pottsboro
	Calvin Z. Hammett	Pt. Lavaca
	Sammie R. Hammontree, Jr.	Sachse
	Capt. Don Hand	Corpus Christi
	Don Hand	Corpus Christi
	Jim J. Haniotis	Shelbyville
	Donald Ray Hanselman, Jr.	Del Rio
	Steven A. Hanson	Austin
	Thomas E. Hardegree, III	Pt. O'Connor
	Glen Hardin	Brookeland
	Manuel R. Hardwick	Comstock
	E. V. Harmon, IV	Zapata
	Leveta Joy Harris	Port Aransas
	Michael W. Harris	Mesquite
	Britton L. Harris	Corpus Christi
	Norman E. Harris	Tow
	Mike Harris	Big Sandy
	Claude A. Hart	Round Rock
	W. D. Hart	Richmond
	Wood W. Hartwell, II	Corpus Christi
	Michael L. Hastings	Austin
	Roy Hathcock	Mineral Wells
	Robert E. Hauser	Hemphill
	William L. Havard	Lufkin
	Bailey Ray Hawley	Quitman
	James L. Hazlitt	Emory
	Jackie E. Headrick, Jr.	Austin
	Daniel A. Hecker	Port Mansfield
	Dean Allen Heffner	Graford
	Jeffrey K. Heimann	Port Aransas
	W. D. Heldenfels, Jr.	Rockport
	W. R. Helm	Arlington
	Robert T. Hendricks	Galveston
	Howard Henry	Valerate
	John Hensel	Hemphill
	Bill Herring	Pottsboro
	George Herzog	Portland
	Greg Hess	Lindsay
	Robert W. Hester	Palacios
	Jeffrey M. Heuman	Pilot Point
	James A. Hewitt	Liberty
	Rex Hewitt	Laguna Vista
	Scott Alan Hickman	Houston
	Steven Hicks	Pottsboro
	David Higginbotham	Laguna Vista
	James Hill	Kingsville
	Perry D. Hill	Emory
	Phillip R. Hill	S. Padre Island
	Frank E. Hinds	San Angelo
	Kenneth Hines	Midland
	Bill and Kim Hines	Fulton
	Robert Hinesley	Corpus Christi
	Rene Hinojosa	Raymondville
	John E. Hobson	Grapeland
	Gerald Way Hobson	Atlanta
	Charles B. Hodgson	Plano
	Larry T. Hoffman	Rockport
	James C. Hoke	Hemphill
	Raymond P. Holcomb	Palestine
	Brian R. Holden	Rockport
	Edgar G. Holland, III	Anahuac
	William M. Holland	Jacksboro
	Travis A. Holland	Austin
	Steven W. Hollensed	Tom Bean
	Peter Hooks	Winnsboro
	Larry Hooks	Emory
	Weldon C. Hooper	Highlands
	John P. Hope	Palestine
	Dolf A. Hopf	Santa Fe
	Gordon S. Hopkins	Hooks
	Marvin M. Horner, Jr.	Port Aransas
	Reece D. Horton	Ft. Worth
	Jon Van Hoskins	Pottsboro
	Charles B. Hough	Corpus Christi
	Capt. Byron Hough	Corpus Christi
	Cecil D. Howard	Houston
	Frederic H. Howard	Missouri City
	John Roy Howell, Jr.	Aransas Pass
	Charles R. Hoyt	Aransas Pass
	Tommy Lee Hubbard	Sunnyvale

Company
Contact Elton B. Hudson, Jr.
City Rockport
Company
Contact Maple C. Hughes, Jr.
City San Antonio
Company
Contact Bryan W. Hughes
City Dallas
Company
Contact Robert Hulen
City Port Mansfield
Company
Contact George Hull
City Port Mansfield
Company
Contact Pat Hunt
City Ingleside
Company
Contact David J. Huntress
City Fulton
Company
Contact Robert D. Hurley
City Quitman
Company
Contact David Roy Huston
City Houston
Company
Contact John C. Hutchins
City Port Aransas
Company
Contact Paul S. Hyland
City Garland
Company
Contact Phyllis Ingram
City Corpus Christi
Company
Contact Richard H. Ives
City Trinidad
Company
Contact Hugh Ivey
City Port Aransas
Company
Contact John David Jacoby
City Denton
Company
Contact William D. Jacoby
City Denton
Company
Contact Joseph F. James
City Orange
Company
Contact Randy Jameson
City Gordonville
Company
Contact Gordon D. Janssen
City Rockport
Company
Contact Richard C. Jay
City Huntsville
Company
Contact Kevin G. Jeffryes
City San Antonio
Company
Contact John R. Jensen
City Port Aransas
Company
Contact Charles Jeter
City Bridge City
Company
Contact Thomas L. Jeter
City S. Padre Island
Company
Contact William R. Jett, Jr.
City Houston
Company
Contact Floyd Lee Johnson
City Spicewood
Company
Contact Edward E. Johnson
City Richardson
Company
Contact John Johnson
City Rockport
Company
Contact Robert B. Jolliff
City Waco
Company
Contact Russell C. Jones
City Pt. O'Connor
Company
Contact Montie P. Jones
City Pottsboro
Company
Contact Billy D. Jones
City Port Aransas

Company
Contact Travis W. Jones
City Port Aransas
Company
Contact Robert S. Jones
City Rockport
Company
Contact Len T. Jones
City Aransas Pass
Company
Contact Larry G. Jordan
City Highland Village
Company
Contact Steve Jordan
City Corpus Christi
Company
Contact Roy L. Jorgensen, II
City Bellaire
Company
Contact Louis D. Riggs, Jr.
City Marshall
Company
Contact Hiram I. Walker, Jr.
City La Grange
Company
Contact Howard J. Waugh, Jr.
City Port Mansfield
Company
Contact C. B. Haire, Jr.
City City by the sea
Company
Contact Jewel R. Jones, Jr.
City Lumberton
Company
Contact William L. Bone, Jr.
City Livingston
Company
Contact Herbert R. Greene, Jr.
City Port Aransas
Company
Contact Charles R. Naiser, Jr.
City West Columbia
Company
Contact Louie F. Hill, Jr.
City Goodrich
Company
Contact Robert A. Maxwell, Jr.
City San Benito
Company
Contact Ralph R. Judd
City Whitewright
Company
Contact Howard L. Judd
City Whitewright
Company
Contact Stephen N. Justice
City Cedar Creek
Company
Contact Robert D. Kalbitz
City Baytown
Company
Contact Jimmy Lee Kanetzky
City Burnet
Company
Contact Rick W. Karpuik
City Alvin
Company
Contact Harris Katchen
City Fulton
Company
Contact Charles V. Kayser
City Jasper
Company
Contact Richard H. Keitt
City Pt. O'Connor
Company
Contact Edwin F. Keller, Jr.
City Laguna Vista
Company
Contact Chad E. Kelley
City Wichita Falls
Company
Contact William M. Kells
City Emory
Company
Contact Capt. Wallace Kelly
City Corpus Christi
Company
Contact Russell F. Kenaston
City Garland
Company
Contact Kevin L. Kendall
City Mineola
Company
Contact Eamo B. Kennedy
City Kilgore

Company
Contact Roy Lee Kennimer, Jr.
City Kilgore
Company
Contact Don M. Kennon
City Granbury
Company
Contact John M. Kernan
City Austin
Company
Contact Rickey D. Kersey
City La Porte
Company
Contact Craig Clay Kidd
City Austin
Company
Contact Travis H. Kilpack
City Corpus Christi
Company
Contact Jay Kimberly
City Georgetown
Company
Contact Troy Wayne King
City Wills Point
Company
Contact Michael D. King
City Wylie
Company
Contact Larry B. King
City Broaddus
Company
Contact Gary L. King
City Kennard
Company
Contact Clifton R. Kirby
City Pittsburg
Company
Contact Ellis Kirby
City Pittsburg
Company
Contact Monty D. Kirk
City Millsap
Company
Contact Willard Kirkpatrick
City Broaddus
Company
Contact Walter A. Kittelberger
City Port Mansfield
Company
Contact Richard K. Knight
City Irving
Company
Contact Joe Knight
City Jasper
Company
Contact Todd Knight
City Jasper
Company
Contact George T. Knighten
City La Porte
Company
Contact Louis J. Kocurek, Jr.
City Robstown
Company
Contact Dennis Kolender
City Alba
Company
Contact Mark David Koliba
City Bloomington
Company
Contact George A. Koumonduros
City Houston
Company
Contact Elroy Krueger
City Three Rivers
Company
Contact Robert T. Kruft
City Rockport
Company
Contact Jerry Kruse
City Mason
Company
Contact Louis L. Kubica
City Cedar Hill
Company
Contact Elaine C. Kuchenbecker
City Livingston
Company
Contact JOhn O. Kunkel
City Throckmorton
Company
Contact Leigh K. Kunnam
City Corpus Christi
Company
Contact Michael C. Kurtz
City Corpus Christi

Company
Contact Eric Kurz
City Rockport
Company
Contact David K. Lacy
City Jasper
Company
Contact Lloyd Leon Lacy
City Hemphill
Company
Contact David B. Laine
City Woodville
Company
Contact Frank Lammens
City Carrollton
Company
Contact Lowell Lamy
City Corpus Christi
Company
Contact Rip Lance
City Pottsboro
Company
Contact Norman K. Land
City Dayton
Company
Contact Harry E. Landers
City Galveston
Company
Contact Paul Lane
City San Angelo
Company
Contact Larry Langford
City Port Isabel
Company
Contact Anthony Langston
City La Marque
Company
Contact Jimmie D. Langston
City Galveston
Company
Contact F. H. Lannom
City Pottsboro
Company
Contact Larry Large
City Alba
Company
Contact William A. Laroche
City Denison
Company
Contact Dennis N. Lary
City Pilot Point
Company
Contact Lloyd L. Lassiter
City Rockport
Company
Contact Roy H. Latham
City Rockport
Company
Contact Roy W. Lavinder
City Quitman
Company
Contact Bill Law
City Streetman
Company
Contact Jess W. Lawrence, Jr.
City San Antonio
Company
Contact Martin Lazar
City Harker Heights
Company
Contact David Leal
City S. Padre Island
Company
Contact James E. Leavelle, II
City Houston
Company
Contact Mark E. Lee
City Crosby
Company
Contact Stewart M. Lee
City George West
Company
Contact Charles H. Leflore
City Mesquite
Company
Contact Michael J. Lemke
City Kingsville
Company
Contact Tony Lenz
City Galveston
Company
Contact Frank Jose Leoeffler, IV
City Kingwood
Company
Contact Thomas G. Lewis
City Galveston

Company
Contact Henry Lewis, Jr.
City Karnack
Company
Contact Arland Lewis
City Port Mansfield
Company
Contact David Liedtke
City Waskom
Company
Contact James A. Linn
City Colleyville
Company
Contact I.C. Little
City Arlington
Company
Contact Dwayne A. Lloyd
City White Oak
Company
Contact Greg Lock
City Temple
Company
Contact Gary W. Lock
City Rogers
Company
Contact Gary W. Locker
City Shady Shores
Company
Contact Freeman P. Lockhart
City Texarkana
Company
Contact Gary W. Long
City Yantis
Company
Contact B.J. Long
City Wills Point
Company
Contact Jon Edwin Loring, Jr.
City Galveston
Company
Contact Ted Allen Lovell
City Center
Company
Contact Ronald R. Lowe
City Milam
Company
Contact Dwayne A. Lowery
City Baytown
Company
Contact Joe Wayne Lowery
City Hemphill
Company
Contact Douglas C. Lowry
City Harlingen
Company
Contact Larry Lybrand
City Mabank
Company
Contact John R. Lynch
City Brookeland
Company
Contact Matt Danny Lynch, III
City Ennis
Company
Contact David E. Lynch
City Spring
Company
Contact Wayne P. Mace
City Denton
Company
Contact Steven G. Malaer
City Santa Ana
Company
Contact Perry Mann
City Karnack
Company
Contact Paul A. Marcaccio
City Pearland
Company
Contact Jeffrey E. Margenroth
City Pt. Lavaca
Company
Contact Harold B. Marlin
City Sulphur Spring
Company
Contact Dudley Marschall
City Riviera
Company
Contact David E. Marshall
City Lone Oak
Company
Contact James Marshall
City Princeton
Company
Contact Winfield L. Marshall
City Seabrook

Company
Contact Monte Marshall
City Port Aransas
Company
Contact Wallace E. Marshall
City Garland
Company
Contact Ronald W. Marshall
City Wylie
Company
Contact Joey Martin
City Horseshoe Bay
Company
Contact Terry W. Martin
City S. Padre Island
Company
Contact Jerry Martin
City Stephenville
Company
Contact Mark E. Martin
City Vidor
Company
Contact Lawrence W. Masoner
City Carrollton
Company
Contact Dan Matchett
City S. Padre Island
Company
Contact William B. Mathers
City Brownsville
Company
Contact Johnnie M. Mathews
City Port Aransas
Company
Contact Willie Mathis
City Jefferson
Company
Contact Larry S. Matthews
City Shelbyville
Company
Contact Albert J. Matura
City Chandler
Company
Contact David Maxwell
City Alba
Company
Contact Wally Mayer
City Port Aransas
Company
Contact Ronny Maynard
City Georgetown
Company
Contact James M. McAlexander
City Houston
Company
Contact Burl L. McBride
City Baytown
Company
Contact Charles R. McCallum
City Pottsboro
Company
Contact Lucian A. McCallum
City Houston
Company
Contact Joel W. McCandless
City Grapevine
Company
Contact Patrick McCarty
City Willis
Company
Contact Richard T. McCarty
City Alba
Company
Contact Ronnie Ray McComic
City Alba
Company
Contact James E. McCowen
City Denison
Company
Contact Paul G. McCoy
City Alba
Company
Contact Joe M. McCullough
City Denton
Company
Contact Charles M. McDonald
City Henderson
Company
Contact John W. McEachern, Jr.
City Pottsboro
Company
Contact Robert A. McFarlane
City San Antonio
Company
Contact Kenneth McGaughey
City Shepherd

Company
Contact Charles G. McGonagill
City Del Rio
Company
Contact Lloyd McIntosh
City Austin
Company
Contact John W. McKinley
City Broaddus
Company
Contact Curtis McNabb
City Rockport
Company
Contact Steve A. McVay
City Granbury
Company
Contact Henry L. McWilliams, Jr.
City Borger
Company
Contact Joe D. Mendez
City Corpus Christi
Company
Contact John Mendleski
City Corpus Christi
Company
Contact Don Merki
City Aubrey
Company
Contact Arthur Meru
City Corpus Christi
Company
Contact Russell C. Metcalf
City Richardson
Company
Contact Robert C. Meza
City Port Aransas
Company
Contact Frank Byro Milam
City Lewisville
Company
Contact Ken Milam
City Tow
Company
Contact John Milina, Jr.
City Port Aransas
Company
Contact Daryl D. Miller
City Burleson
Company
Contact Johnny Lee Miller
City Clifton
Company
Contact G. A. Miller
City Pottsboro
Company
Contact Bobby J. Miller
City Houston
Company
Contact Phillip D. Miller
City Bonham
Company
Contact William A. Mills
City Marshall
Company
Contact Billy D. Mills
City Conroe
Company
Contact Randal W. Milner
City Quitman
Company
Contact Alfred J. Minns, Jr.
City Fulton
Company
Contact Kenneth Mitchell
City Frisco
Company
Contact Raymond O. Mobley
City Paris
Company
Contact Raymond Mock
City S. Padre Island
Company
Contact Troy Monjaras
City Port Mansfield
Company
Contact Billy Dean Monroe, II
City Rockport
Company
Contact Corey Montgomery
City Uvalde
Company
Contact Ronald L. Moore
City Rockport
Company
Contact D. W. Moore
City Burleson

Company
Contact Roger R. Moore
City Texarkana
Company
Contact Gary Moore
City Grapeland
Company
Contact Jerry Moore
City Burnet
Company
Contact Clark Moore
City Nacogdoches
Company
Contact George Moore
City Emory
Company
Contact Ronald A. Morgan
City Cooper
Company
Contact Jim Morris
City Hemphill
Company
Contact Glenn D. Morris
City Elmendorf
Company
Contact Jack F. Moses
City Kenedy
Company
Contact Michael H. Mottlage
City West
Company
Contact Robert J. Mudd
City Corpus Christi
Company
Contact Danny C. Mulder
City Arlington
Company
Contact Billy L. Mullen
City Euless
Company
Contact Paul E. Munarriz
City Port Isabel
Company
Contact Matt E. Murphy
City Port Isabel
Company
Contact Robert A. Murphy
City Granbury
Company
Contact Stephen D. Murphy
City Port Isabel
Company
Contact Patrick E. Murphy
City Laguna Vista
Company
Contact Clyne John Murphy, Jr.
City Pearland
Company
Contact Jonathan T. Murray
City Hurst
Company
Contact Jimmy H. Murray
City Zapata
Company
Contact Patrick Murray
City Houston
Company
Contact Jimmy Nail
City Denison
Company
Contact John M. Nash, IV
City Seguin
Company
Contact David Wade Neal
City Corpus Christi
Company
Contact Terry Neal
City Port Mansfield
Company
Contact Joel K. Neely
City Silsbee
Company
Contact William D. Nelson
City Whitney
Company
Contact Jack Nelson
City Aransas Pass
Company
Contact David W. Nesloney
City Portland
Company
Contact Francis L. Neve, III
City Graford
Company
Contact William M. Newman
City Sanger

Company
Contact Floyd D. Newman
City Waco
Company
Contact Charles M. Newton
City Fulton
Company
Contact Mason A. Newton
City College Station
Company
Contact John Nicholas
City Menard
Company
Contact David Nichols
City Chandler
Company
Contact Don Nichols
City Katy
Company
Contact Rodney C. Nichols
City Baytown
Company
Contact Wallace R. Nichols, IV
City Dallas
Company
Contact Don T. Nicoles
City Katy
Company
Contact Kurt W. Nilsson
City Elgin
Company
Contact James D. Nolder
City Del Rio
Company
Contact Dale L. Norman
City McQuenney
Company
Contact Michael W. Norrell
City Corpus Christi
Company
Contact Jerry Norris
City Port Arthur
Company
Contact Jody Norsworthy
City Jasper
Company
Contact Robert G. Norton
City Port Mansfield
Company
Contact Ervin E. Nothnagel
City Boerne
Company
Contact Michael Nowicki
City Blanco
Company
Contact James W. Nowlin
City Waco
Company
Contact Timothy Nuber
City Houston
Company
Contact Michael D. Nugent
City Aransas Pass
Company
Contact Alfred D. Nulisch
City Bay City
Company
Contact Pat Nye
City Corpus Christi
Company
Contact Patrick J. O'Brien
City Pflugerville
Company
Contact Roger O'Neal
City Burnet
Company
Contact Bill Ockerhausen
City Mt. Pleasant
Company
Contact Lowell L. Odom
City Rockport
Company
Contact Steven J. Oeller
City Port Mansfield
Company
Contact Randy Oldfield
City Wills Point
Company
Contact Larry E. Oliver
City Garland
Company
Contact Herbert Olsen
City Jasper
Company
Contact James C. Onderdonk
City Sarita

Company
Contact William L. Oppelt
City Yantis
Company
Contact Donald L. Orcutt
City Corpus Christi
Company
Contact Kenneth R. Orr
City Richardson
Company
Contact Eugene T. Osborne
City Houston
Company
Contact C.C. Oswalt
City Quitman
Company
Contact Michael D. Oswalt
City Mesquite
Company
Contact Harold J. Owen,
City Quitman
Company
Contact Harold E. Owen, II
City Quitman
Company
Contact Michael L. Owens
City Waco
Company
Contact Donald W. Oxford
City Rio Hondo
Company
Contact Gregory L. Oxner
City Waco
Company
Contact Jackie W. Pace
City Aransas Pass
Company
Contact Mark Pack
City Mineola
Company
Contact Marvin Padier
City Port Aransas
Company
Contact Richard S. Painter
City Corpus Christi
Company
Contact Michael W. Pancratz
City Wimberley
Company
Contact Terry Panknin
City Corpus Christi
Company
Contact Scott Parker
City Baytown
Company
Contact Henry I. Parker
City Buchanan Dam
Company
Contact Jesse Parker
City Yantis
Company
Contact Tony L. Parker
City Wills Point
Company
Contact Lloyd W. Parker
City Ovilla
Company
Contact Kelly D. Parks
City Victoria
Company
Contact Charles L. Patrick
City Corpus Christi
Company
Contact Alvia E. Patterson
City Yantis
Company
Contact Clayton L. Payne
City Rockport
Company
Contact Bary A. Payne
City Rockport
Company
Contact Richard L. Peabody
City S. Padre Island
Company
Contact Richard C. Pearce
City Dallas
Company
Contact Oscar L. Pence
City Helotes
Company
Contact Lillymae Pepper
City Galveston
Company
Contact James W. Peterson
City Garland

Company
Contact Lynn Vess Smith, Jr.
City Pt. O'Connor

Company
Contact Jason E. Smith
City Calliham

Company
Contact William F. Smith
City Rockport

Company
Contact Peter M. Smith
City Zavalla

Company
Contact James C. Smith
City Conroe

Company
Contact Charles C. Smith
City Matagorda

Company
Contact William R. Smith
City Hemphill

Company
Contact Ronald Smyer
City Amarillo

Company
Contact Jack B. Smythe, Jr.
City Rockport

Company
Contact M. M. Snell
City Port Mansfield

Company
Contact Edward H. Snelson
City Huntington

Company
Contact Steve E. Snopek
City New Braunfels

Company
Contact John E. Snyder, Jr.
City Waco

Company
Contact Jeffrey R. Snyder
City San Antonio

Company
Contact Scott Soisson
City Jasper

Company
Contact Robert T. Solinski
City San Antonio

Company
Contact Dallas F. Southard
City Corpus Christi

Company
Contact Gregory J. Spears
City Graford

Company
Contact Rodney C. Spivey
City Rockport

Company
Contact Sportfishing
City Whitney

Company
Contact Paul Spracklen
City Pottsboro

Company
Contact Tal W. Sprinkles
City Pflugerville

Company
Contact Michael A. St. Pierre
City Seabrook

Company
Contact Jack Stafford
City San Saba

Company
Contact Audie J. Stafford
City Longview

Company
Contact Kerry W. Stafford
City Longview

Company
Contact Bonita Staples
City Arlington

Company
Contact Ron L. Stark
City Trenton

Company
Contact Dennis J. States
City Emory

Company
Contact Daryl Stauffer
City Clifton

Company
Contact Gary L. Steed
City Crockett

Company
Contact Charles G. Steed
City Gainesville

Company
Contact Jeffrey R. Steele
City Lancaster

Company
Contact Robert A. Steele
City Dallas

Company
Contact Gordon Steele
City Hemphill

Company
Contact Michael K. Stegall
City Orange

Company
Contact Howard E. Steussy, II
City Port Mansfield

Company
Contact Riles C. Steussy
City Port Mansfield

Company
Contact Donald K. Steussy
City Austin

Company
Contact Marsh Alan Steussy
City Port Mansfield

Company
Contact Robert M. Stevenson
City Alba

Company
Contact Gary Stewart
City Pottsboro

Company
Contact William R. Stewart
City Corpus Christi

Company
Contact James Stewart
City Port Isabel

Company
Contact William L. Stickley
City Zavalla

Company
Contact Darryl Stiers
City S. Padre Island

Company
Contact John Q. Stine
City League City

Company
Contact Russell Stockton
City Harlingen

Company
Contact Roman Stockton
City Brownsville

Company
Contact George F. Strader
City Los Fresnos

Company
Contact Samuel D. Strahan
City Euless

Company
Contact Durwood Strickland
City Millersview

Company
Contact Charles Stringer
City Gordonville

Company
Contact Claude Stroud
City Rockport

Company
Contact Gregg Strouse
City Brookeland

Company
Contact Stevie Lee Strunk
City Pipe Creek

Company
Contact Michael W. Stuard
City Valerate

Company
Contact Michael R. Stuart
City Zapata

Company
Contact Jolley J. Stuart
City Portland

Company
Contact Randall E. Sullivan
City Rockwall

Company
Contact Herman J. Sullivan
City Thornton

Company
Contact Lee Roy Summerlin
City S. Padre Island

Company
Contact Travis O. Summerlin
City Sam Rayburn

Company
Contact Carl J. Svebek
City Sam Rayburn

Company
Contact Jimmy D. Sweat
City Klondike

Company
Contact David Sweeney
City Laguna Vista

Company
Contact James E. Sykes
City Kaufman

Company
Contact Otis Tally
City Denison

Company
Contact John Clark Tanner
City Royse City

Company
Contact George W. Tate
City S. Padre Island

Company
Contact Robert Taylor
City Colmesneil

Company
Contact Mitchel B. Taylor
City Corpus Christi

Company
Contact Garlin Taylor
City Pottsboro

Company
Contact Jerry R. Taylor
City Graham

Company
Contact Robert L. Taylor
City Sam Rayburn

Company
Contact Jimy R. Teague
City Rockport

Company
Contact Phillip M. Tedder
City Rockport

Company
Contact Butch Terpe
City Wills

Company
Contact Daniel Terrell
City Cedar Creek

Company
Contact Charles R. Thetford
City Pottsboro

Company
Contact Tommy S. Thomas
City Ft. Worth

Company
Contact Ann Thomasson
City Jasper

Company
Contact Charles Thompson
City Yantis

Company
Contact Johnnie J. Thompson
City Livingston

Company
Contact Jim Thompson
City Mesquite

Company
Contact James R. Thorne
City Henderson

Company
Contact Marvin W. Thornton
City Gladewater

Company
Contact Michael G. Thurman
City Cedar Hill

Company
Contact Billy W. Tidball
City Brownsville

Company
Contact Tommy Tidwell
City Taylor

Company
Contact Charles K. Tilton
City Baytown

Company
Contact Don Tollison
City Fritch

Company
Contact Jean T. Toney
City Pottsboro

Company
Contact Hector V. Torres, Jr.
City Port Isabel

Company
Contact Jackie L. Touchstone
City Big Spring

Company
Contact James L. Trahan
City Pt. Neches

Company
Contact Eddie G. Trapp
City Cooper

Company
Contact Jim Traweek
City London

Company
Contact Robert L. Tribble
City Dallas

Company
Contact David Trimble
City Broaddus

Company
Contact Noble D. Trimble
City Palestine

Company
Contact James Truesdale
City Aransas Pass

Company
Contact Gerald Truesdell
City Kerrville

Company
Contact Robert S. Trull
City Lancaster

Company
Contact Donald F. Turner
City Yantis

Company
Contact John I. Turney
City Port Mansfield

Company
Contact David E. Turowski
City Victoria

Company
Contact Tommy T. Tyler
City Conroe

Company
Contact Thomas W. Uhls
City San Antonio

Company
Contact Pete Uptmor
City Carrollton

Company
Contact Terry J. Upton
City Aransas Pass

Company
Contact Robert G. Vail
City Bridge City

Company
Contact David H. Vance
City Winnsboro

Company
Contact Capt. Mitchell Vanch
City Corpus Christi

Company
Contact Ricky D. Vandergriff
City Bullard

Company
Contact Bernard L. Vannoy
City Corpus Christi

Company
Contact Preston Vanshoubrouek
City Kirbyville

Company
Contact Nicholas E. Varga
City Mesquite

Company
Contact Gilbert Vasquez
City Pasadena

Company
Contact David H. Vassallo
City Pottsboro

Company
Contact Scott Vaughan
City Midland

Company
Contact Gilbert C. Vela
City Port Isabel

Company
Contact Gary E. Verstuyft
City San Antonio

Company
Contact Lance C. Vick
City Mineola

Company
Contact Emilio Villarreal
City S. Padre Island

Company
Contact Gerald F. Vindick
City San Antonio

Company
Contact Dan Voiles
City Pottsboro

Company
Contact Richard Vollmer
City Yantis

Company
Contact Perry Voyles
City Graham

Company
Contact Randall K. Wade
City Paris

Company
Contact David A. Wagner
City Pearland

Company
Contact John Walker
City Brookeland

Company
Contact Richard J. Walker
City Rockport

Company
Contact Phillip Walker
City Manor

Company
Contact Bobby Ray Wall
City Yantis

Company
Contact Jimy W. Walling
City Pilot Point

Company
Contact Sid Walsh
City Corpus Christi

Company
Contact Larry Walsh
City Graham

Company
Contact John I. Waner
City Beaumont

Company
Contact Jim Wann
City Granbury

Company
Contact David J. Warcham
City Waco

Company
Contact Claude E. Ward
City Port Aransas

Company
Contact David L. Washington
City Midlothian

Company
Contact Rex M. Watkins
City Ft. Worth

Company
Contact Jay Watkins
City Rockport

Company
Contact Stephen P. Watkins
City Mineral Wells

Company
Contact L. C. Weatherford
City Pottsboro

Company
Contact Mark Webb
City La Grange

Company
Contact Richard J. Weber
City Corpus Christi

Company
Contact Nick Weeks
City Kingsville

Company
Contact Mark Lee Weems
City Port Aransas

Company
Contact Chris Weems
City Graham

Company
Contact Arthur Weiss
City Aransas Pass

Company
Contact Bill Welborn
City Mineola

Company
Contact Gerald L. Wellman
City Aransas Pass

Company
Contact Vere C. Wells
City Port Isabel

Company
Contact Carl Elmer Wentrcek
City Lakehills

Company
Contact Craig West
City Corpus Christi

Company
Contact Mark E. Westmoreland
City Freeport

Company
Contact James R. Wetzel
City Keller

Utah

Vermont

City Danby
Company Pinebrook Custom Flies
Contact John Conrad
City Moscow
Company Pirate Charters
Contact Capt. Gary Frazier
City Grand Isle
Company Possible Tours Charters
Contact Lou Kircher
City Greensboro Bend
Company Reel Vermont Fishing/
Canoe Rentals
Contact Don Heise
City Calais
Company River Excitement
Contact John Marshall
City Hartland Four Corners
Company River Run Guide Service
Contact Wesley Carkin
City Manchester
Company Salmon Seeker Charters
Contact Capt. Dan McNamara
City St. Albans
Company Salty Saltzman
Contact
City Manchester
Company Schirmer's Fly Shop
Contact Edward Schirmer
City South Burlington
Company Seadog Charters
Contact Capt. Paul Pinan
City Essex Jct.
Company Seahorse Charters
Contact Capt. John Brisson
City Burlington
Company Southern Vermont Guide
Service
Contact Michael Schnaderbeck
City West Rupert
Company Streamline
Contact Peter Cammann
City Waitsfield
Company Strictly Trout
Contact David L. Deen
City Putney
Company Sure Strike Charters
Contact Capt. Rich Greenough
City Essex Jct.
Company Taddingers
Contact
City Wilmington
Company The Battenkill Anglers
Contact Tom Goodman
City Manchester Center
Company The Inn at Manchester
Contact Stan Rosenberg
City Manchester
Company The Salmon Conserv. for
Atlantic North
Contact Charles E. Metz
City Newbury
Company The Vermont Sportsman
Contact Bob Beaupre
City Morgan
Company Triple Play Charters
Contact Capt. Hanford "Skip" Davis
City Brandon
Company Trout Tracker Charters
Contact Capt. Paul Lyman
City Brattleboro
Company Uncle Noel's Bait & Tackle
Contact Todd Sudol & Randy Savage
City St. Albans
Company Uncle Noel's Guided Fishing
Tours
Contact Noel Sudol
City Stowe
Company Vermont Bound Outfitters
Contact Jack Sapia
City Wilmington
Company Vermont Fly Fishing
Specialist
Contact
City Warren
Company Wilderness Trails, Inc.
Contact Martin Banak
City Quechee
Company William's Canoe Fishing
Contact William Richard Knight
City Stowe
Company Yankee Charters
Contact Capt. Bernie Burby
City Middlebury
Company
Contact Peter Basta
City Dorset

Virginia

Company Blue Ridge Angler
Contact
City Harrisonburg
Company Camelot Farms
Contact Danny Garrett
City Hardy
Company Chesapeake Bay
Charters
Contact Captain Leroy G. Carr
City Heathville
Company Clinch Mountain Guide
Service
Contact Mike Shaffer
City Hiltons
Company Fort Lewis Lodge, Inc.
Contact
City Millboro
Company Inn at Narrow Passage
Contact Ed Markel
City Woodstock
Company New River Small Mouth,
Inc.
Contact Dave Kees
City Rich Creek
Company Orvis Roanoke
Contact
City Roanoke
Company Primland
Contact
City Claudville
Company Sable Mountain Guides
Contact John D. Ayers
City Fredericksburg
Company Shenandoah Lodge
Contact Charlie Walsh
City Luray
Company Tackle Box Adventures
Contact Wayne Nugent
City Chester
Company The Homestead
Contact
City Hot Springs
Company Van Doren's Orvis Shoppe,
Ltd.
Contact
City Richmond
Company Wilson's Guide Service
Contact
City Palmer Springs
Company
Contact Jim Abers
City Boydton
Company
Contact Roy Amburn, Jr.
City Ashland
Company
Contact Leonard Andrews
City Richmond
Company
Contact Dan Beeler
City Chesterfield
Company
Contact Nelson B. Berry
City Vienna
Company
Contact Fred M. Biddlecomb
City Reedville
Company

Contact Sterling L. Bowles, III
City Reedville
Company
Contact Pedro Cartwright
City Virginia Beach
Company
Contact E. Wayson Christopher
City Heathsville
Company
Contact James R. Conner, Jr.
City Reedville
Company
Contact William M. Copsey
City Burke
Company
Contact Danny Crabbe
City Heathsville
Company
Contact Bob Cramer
City Dayton
Company
Contact Jeff Crockett
City Tangier
Company
Contact Theodore Morrison Curtis, Jr.
City Kilmarnock
Company
Contact John C. Dahl, III
City Accomac
Company
Contact Sherman L. Davis
City Montross
Company
Contact John S. Deering
City Arlington
Company
Contact Harold J. Deibler
City Wicomico Church
Company
Contact Richard A. Devivi
City Reedville
Company
Contact Charles E. Donaldson
City Vienna
Company
Contact Terry E. Donaldson
City Arlington
Company
Contact J. Wayne Dudley
City Vinton
Company
Contact Paul B. Ebert
City Manassas
Company
Contact Byron P. Empson
City Falls Church
Company
Contact James D. Hardy
City Reedville
Company
Contact Wilmer Heishman, Jr.
City Harisburg
Company
Contact Charles W. Hennage
City Montross
Company
Contact Gerald Holliday
City Richmond
Company
Contact Capt. Jon Holsenbeck
City Richmond
Company
Contact William Jenkins, Jr.
City Burgess
Company
Contact William P. Jenkins
City Reedville
Company
Contact Roger Jones
City Richmond
Company
Contact Paul Kenny
City Vinton
Company
Contact Chuck Kraft
City Charlottesville
Company
Contact Richard C. Larkin
City Vienna
Company
Contact James S. Loop
City Callao
Company
Contact Donald P. Markwith
City Colonial Beach

Contact John Mason
City Brookneal
Company
Contact Daniel D. McDougal
City Lottsburg
Company
Contact Robert F. McLain
City Fairfax
Company
Contact Steve Miller
City Mechanicsville
Company
Contact Kingsley V. Montgomery
City Annandale
Company
Contact Donald S. Moss
City Kinsale
Company
Contact David C. Motes
City Oakton
Company
Contact Roscoe H. Niblack
City Fairfax
Company
Contact Skip Ninninger
City Salem
Company
Contact Charles D. O'Brier
City Lottsburg
Company
Contact Robert J. Parker
City Stafford
Company
Contact William Pipkin
City Heathsville
Company
Contact Eugene Pittman
City Reedville
Company
Contact Stephen Riha
City Colonial Beach
Company
Contact David M. Rowe
City Lottsburg
Company
Contact Raymond W. Shepherd
City Burgess
Company
Contact Ray Shepherd
City Morattico
Company
Contact Otis Shook, Jr.
City Milford
Company
Contact Robert E. Sivinski
City Heathsville
Company
Contact Joel Springer
City Richmond
Company
Contact Robert F. Stoner
City Callao
Company
Contact Carolyn Sullivan
City Burgess
Company
Contact Philip M. Talbott, III
City Arlington
Company
Contact Charlie Taylor
City Herndon
Company
Contact Richard W. Thomas
City Lewisetta
Company
Contact Craig Vaughn
City Chesterfield
Company
Contact Robert C. Warren, Jr.
City Reedville
Company
Contact Edward L. Weston
City Alexandria
Company
Contact Dale Wilson
City Huddleston
Company
Contact Henry Wilson
City Palmer Springs
Company
Contact Gary Wilson
City Vinton

Washington

Company Alaska Farwest Fish Camp
Contact Peter F. Hanson
City Renton
Company Alaska Sea Adventures
Contact Robert L. Horchover
City Tacoma
Company Alaska's Enchanted Lake
Lodge
Contact Dick Matthews
City Bellevue
Company Alaskan Silver Highlander
Contact Dan Rawding
City White Salmon
Company Apple Island Charter &
Lodge
Contact Dana Anderson
City Everett
Company Aventure Excursions
Contact Ralph & Lauren Mirsky
City Vashon
Company Bar-B-Q Charters
Contact Sandra K. Petersen
City Bremerton
Company Barbless Hook Fly Fishers
Guide
Contact Jim Shuttleworth
City Bothell
Company Barrier Dam Guide Service
Contact Donald Glaser
City Salkum
Company Bear River Lodge, Ltd.
Contact John Priebe
City Redmond
Company Bear Tracks Lodge
Contact Randall McDuffie
City Seattle
Company Beartracks Lodge
Contact Frank & Karetta Barrett
City Redmond
Company Big Boys, Inc.
Contact Fred Pentt & Larry Carlson
City Hoquiam
Company Blue Ribbon Jewel Flyfishing
Guide Service
Contact
City Northport
Company Bob's Piscatorial Pursuits
Contact Robert Ball
City Forks
Company Brightwater House
Contact Richard Chesmore
City Forks
Company Bristol Bay Lodge
Contact Ronald & Margaret McMillan
City Ellensburg
Company Buck's Trophy Lodge
Contact Shelly Lawrence
City Sumas
Company Buzzy's River Adventures
Contact Phillip Franklin
City Greenwater
Company C.C. Anderson Guide
Service
Contact Claude Anderson
City Federal Way
Company Captain Cal's S.E. AK
Charter Service
Contact Cal & Marie Schipper
City Port Hadlock
Company Catch 'Em Guide Service
Contact Kenneth R. Hagen
City Enumclaw
Company Catch-a-Lot Charters
Contact Robert & Kathleen Junglov
City Edmonds
Company Choice Marine Charters
Contact Jack J. Gilman
City East Sound
Company Clancy's Guided Sports
Fishing
Contact Rhonda Chumbley
City Chehalis
Company Cooper's Fly SHop
Contact
City Ellensburg
Company Cowlitz River Sportfishing
Contact Joe Little
City Chehalis
Company Current Affairs Outfitting
Contact Douglas R. Nash
City Toledo
Company Dan's Kenai Charters
Contact Danny L. Eades

City Mt. Vernon
Company Dan's Specialty Guide Service
Contact Dan Ross
City Woodland
Company Dave Duncan & Sons
Contact John, Clint, Todd & Brad Duncan Dave
City Ellensburg
Company Deep Sea Charters
Contact Bill Geary
City Westport
Company Denny's Guide Service
Contact Denny Cook
City Graham
Company Deshka Silver-King Lodge
Contact Cathy Pearcy
City Ocean Shores
Company Deshka Silver-King Lodge
Contact Susan & William Jarvis Michael
City Bellevue
Company Don's Guide Service
Contact Don Sturdivan
City Auburn
Company Eagle Charters
Contact Stanley P. Mayer
City Vancouver
Company Ed Venture Vacation Cruises
Contact Edward H. Euren
City Seattle
Company Emerald City Charters
Contact Captain Paul LaMarche
City Seattle
Company Escapade Charters
Contact Willard L. Belenski
City Longview
Company F/V Pamela Rae, Inc.
Contact Robert M. Thorstenson, Jr.
City Seattle
Company Family Charters
Contact James & Judy Thompson
City Renton
Company Fishin' Time Guide Service
Contact John Knapp
City Belfair
Company George Ortman Adventure
Contact Thomas Castle
City Bellevue
Company Ghost Rider Charters
Contact Charles G. Elliott
City Longview
Company Glacier Bay Marine Services, Inc.
Contact
City Seattle
Company Gray Wolf Outfitters
Contact Glenn Cantwell
City Poulsbo
Company Great Alaska Fish Camp
Contact Laurence John & Kathy Haley
City Poulsbo
Company Great Alaska Safaries
Contact Ken & Laurence John
City Poulsbo
Company Great Northern Charters
Contact Terry P. Charron
City Edmonds
Company Grizzly Charters
Contact Michael Price
City Forks
Company H & L Outfitters
Contact Rick A. Lane
City Ferndale
Company High Spot Charters
Contact Doug Bull
City Friday Harbor
Company Highland Stage Company
Contact Donald & Kristen Super
City Tonasket
Company HiTime Charters
Contact Captain Toni Wisner
City Newman Lake
Company Horizon West Guides
Contact Bruce Gipple
City Vancouver
Company Huckleberry Lodge
Contact
City Port Townsend
Company Inner Harbor Lodge
Contact Mike & Sandy Hayes
City Kent
Company J.R.'s Fishing Guide Service

Contact John Riedesel
City Humptulips
Company Jamal Charters, Inc.
Contact J.S. Hanna
City Kirkland
Company John Hazel & Company
Contact John T. Hazel
City Washougal
Company Katmai Lodge
Contact Tony Sarp
City Everett
Company Kenai River Bend
Contact Mike Kelly
City Silver Creek
Company King of Kings Guide Service
Contact Richard Beven II
City Renton
Company Lake Creek Lodge
Contact Jeff Woodward
City Indianola
Company Leroy's Guide Service
Contact Leroy Phillipi
City Chehalis
Company Lulu Charter
Contact Scott Hansen
City Oroville
Company Mark Miller Guide
Contact Larry Miller
City Lynnwood
Company Mark's Guide Service
Contact Mark F.O'Neil
City Quinault
Company Michael Perussa Enterprises
Contact Michael Perussa
City Auburn
Company Mid-Columbia Guide Service
Contact Charles Stanton
City Entiat
Company Middle Fork River Expeditions, Inc.
Contact Patrick Ridle
City Seattle
Company Mike's Guide Service
Contact Michael A. Sexton
City Toledo
Company Mitchell & Roane's Alaska Fly-Outs, Inc.
Contact Steve A. Mitchell & D.C. Roane
City Spanaway
Company Motor Vessel Explorer
Contact Richard N. Friedman
City Bellingham
Company Mystic Sea Charters
Contact
City La Conner
Company Natron Air
Contact Edward & Marion Osmond
City Vancouver
Company Nautical Charters of Alaska
Contact Jerry W. McCowin II & Julie VonRuden
City Seattle
Company Norrie Johnson Guide Svc
Contact Norton Johnson
City Renton
Company North Idaho Llama Outfitters
Contact Thomas P. Taylor
City Medical Lake
Company Northern Trading Voyages
Contact Dick & Betty Feenstra
City Custer
Company Ocean Cape Charters
Contact Lars E. Johnson
City Port Hadlock
Company Olympic Peninsula Sportfishing
Contact Ted A. McManus
City Forks
Company Ouzel Expeditions
Contact Rob Wottlin
City Tacoma
Company Pasayten Llama Packing
Contact Lanette E. Smith
City Winthrop
Company Poseidon Services
Contact Joan W. Gottfried
City Seattle
Company Propp's Rod & Fly, Inc.
Contact
City Spokane
Company R-Fly Charters
Contact Randall Mark Phillips

City Spokane
Company R.Z. Guide Service
Contact Rick Zugschwerdt
City Renton
Company Raleigh's Guide Service
Contact Raleigh Stone
City Toledo
Company Rich's Fishing Guide Service
Contact Rich Bogle
City Brush Prairie
Company Ron's Alaska Lodge
Contact George Wing
City Forks
Company Ron's Guide Service
Contact Ron Rogers
City Monroe
Company Ross Marine Tours
Contact Timothy J. Ross
City Des Moines
Company Scales 'N Tales Charters, Inc.
Contact Eddy L. Sison
City Mukilteo
Company Scoot's Guide Service
Contact Donald & Diana Weigand
City Puyallup
Company Scott Stewart Fishing Service
Contact Scott A. Stewart
City Vancouver
Company Skookum Charters
Contact Kent L. John
City Hansville
Company Smokey's Alaskan Fishing Adventures
Contact Anne & Jason Scribner Ron
City Selah
Company Sound Experience
Contact Roger & Marilyn Stowell
City Spokane
Company Sound Sailing
Contact Rick Fleischman
City Seattle
Company Stubbs Guide Service
Contact Richard L. Bench II
City Renton
Company Sudsy Charters
Contact Stephen J. Hauth
City Aberdeen
Company T K Fishing Adventures
Contact Terry & Kelly Lawson
City Colville
Company T.C. Lewis Lodge
Contact Paul Peck
City Ellensburg
Company Talaview Resorts
Contact John Wick
City Bellevue
Company Three Queens Outfitting
Contact D.L. "Cougar" & Janice Osmonovich
City CleElum
Company Tom Loder's Panhandle Outfitters
Contact Tom Loder
City Valleyford
Company Trophy Guide Service
Contact Ken Orrell
City Forks
Company Venture Northwest Guide Service
Contact Dean R. Swerin
City Forks
Company Wave Dance Charters
Contact Wayne & Marla Sanger
City Mt. Vernon
Company Wilderness Place Lodge
Contact John Hewellyn
City Monroe
Company
Contact Harvey F. Van Brunt
City Vancouver
Company
Contact Jeff & Pam Fredericksen
City Vashon
Company
Contact Jeff Martin
City Seattle
Company
Contact John Noe
City Forks
Company
Contact Arlen Pearsall
City Forks
Company
Contact Michael N. Perusse

City Auburn
Company
Contact Keith D. Peters
City Port Angeles
Company
Contact Ron Romig
City Fall City
Company
Contact Zeke Smith
City Ellensburg

West Virginia

Company Appalachian Backcountry Expeditions, Inc.
Contact Bill Handy
City Daniels
Company Bass Unlimited
Contact Lawrence W. Burdette
City Charleston
Company Burnsville Docks, Inc.
Contact David Waldron
City Burnsville
Company Cantrell Canoes & Rafts/ Ultimate Rafting
Contact Richard Cantrell
City Hinton
Company Cast-Away, Inc.
Contact Robin E. Moore
City Lansing
Company Cheat Mountain Club
Contact Gladys Boehmer
City Durbin
Company Cheat Mountain Outfitting & Guide Service
Contact Treve Painter
City Huttonsville
Company Cranberry Wilderness Outfitters
Contact Keith Comstock
City Fenwick
Company Elk Mountain Guides, Inc.
Contact Charles & Clare McDaniel
City Masontown
Company Evergreen Fly Fishing Co.
Contact Franklin L. Oliverio
City Clarksburg
Company Extreme Expeditions of WV, Inc.
Contact Luther Toney
City Lansing
Company Frank's Bait Shop
Contact Frank Hartenstein
City Bradley
Company Kelly Creek Flyfishers
Contact Gary D. Lang
City Elkins
Company L & D Fishing Tours
Contact W. Lee Viands
City Charles Town
Company Mountain State Outfitters
Contact Bill Murray
City Charleston
Company New River Scenic Whitewater Tours
Contact Richard Smith
City Hinton
Company North American River Runners, Inc.
Contact Frank Lukacs
City Hico
Company Potomac Highland Outfitters
Contact Michael Messenger & Keith Busmente
City Davis
Company Prospect Hall Shooting Club
Contact
City Kearneysville
Company Royal River Outfitters
Contact Jonathan Royal Magee
City Elkins
Company The Rivermen
Contact Steve & Howard Campbell
City Fayetteville
Company Tory Mountain Outfitters
Contact JPaul S. Fowler
City Thomas
Company Twin River Outfitters
Contact Basil C. Neely, Jr.
City Daniels
Company West Virginia Lakes Fishing

& Tours
Contact II/H. T. Salmon, Jr. Robt. A. Wiseman
City Beckley
Company Whitewater Information & Rafting
Contact Tom Louisos
City Oak Hill
Company Whitewater Travel, Inc.
Contact Kyle Coon
City Fayetteville
Company Wildwater Excursions Unlimited
Contact Jon Dragan
City Thurmond
Company
Contact Paul F. Baker
City Harpers Ferry
Company
Contact Capt. James Barcus
City Grafton
Company
Contact Kramer L. McCabe
City Morgantown
Company
Contact Irwin S. Seigel
City Charlestown
Company
Contact Harley E. Travis
City Bridgeport
Company
Contact Byrd E. White III
City Beckley

Wisconsin

Company #1 Guide Service
Contact Capt. Scott Corbisier
City Sturgeon Bay
Company A & J Trophy Charter
Contact Capt. Jerry Gurske
City Sturgeon Bay
Company A Gateway Sport Fishing Charter
Contact Doc Lohman
City Racine
Company A Hot Lady Sport Fishing Charters
Contact Capts. Peter R. & Cecilia M. Budge
City Sheboygan
Company A Seagull Sport Fishing Charters
Contact Capt. Stephen Cedarburg
City Milwaukee
Company A-1 Adventures/Mauer's Charter Serv.
Contact Capt. James Mauer
City Racine
Company A-1 Mauer's Charter Service
Contact Capt. Pete Mauer
City Sturtevant
Company A1 Charters
Contact Capt. Glenwood Zellmer
City Wautoma
Company AAA Charters
Contact Capt. Ron Langevin
City Algoma
Company AAA Unpredictable Charter
Contact Capt. Jerry L. Eichmann
City Manitowoc
Company Affordable Charters
Contact Capt. Rick Lesch
City Milwaukee
Company Algoma Hardware & Sporting Goods
Contact
City Algoma
Company Amber Dawn Charters
Contact Capt. Gregory J. Meyers
City Green Bay
Company Anderson Charter Fishing
Contact Lorry Anderson
City Neenah
Company Apostle Island Charter Services
Contact Capt. Steve Prevost
City Bayfield
Company Assoc. Fishing Charters of Milwaukee

Contact
City Oak Creek
Company Barbie Doll III & IV Charter
Contact Capts. Dave & Lou Mayer
City Mayville
Company Bayfield Fishing & Sailing Charters
Contact
City Bayfield
Company Bayfield Trollers Assoc.
Contact
City Bayfield
Company Belgian Queen
Contact Capt. Rod Baudhuin
City Brussels
Company Big Family Charters
Contact Capt. Dick Lettenberger
City Manitowoc
Company Billy Goat's Bait & Tackle
Contact
City Algoma
Company Black Island Resort
Contact Mike & Barb Sergio
City Wausau
Company Black-Jac Charters
Contact Capt. Jack E. Swartz
City Kenosha
Company Blue Fin Charters
Contact Capt. Joseph Anderson
City Niagara
Company Blue Max Charters
Contact Capt. Jim Hirt
City Elkhorn
Company Blue Water Fishing
Contact Capt. Ken Mandy
City Racine
Company Blue Yonder Charters
Contact Capt. Dan Peterson
City Superior
Company Bob's Guide Service
Contact Robert F. Lipo
City Oconomowoc
Company Bob-Kat Charters
Contact Tom Markley
City Algoma
Company Borgers Sport Fishing Charters, Inc.
Contact Capt. Jaco Borger
City Kenosha
Company Bruce Brock
Contact Darrell Mittlesteadt
City Wooduff
Company Caden's Kennels & Hunt Club
Contact
City Campbellsport
Company Capt. Mike Lane's Charters
Contact Capt. Michael Lane
City Green Bay
Company Capt. Paul's Charter Fishing
Contact Capt. Roger Voight
City Gills Rock
Company Captain Angelo's Fishing Bug Charter
Contact Capt. Angelo Trentadue
City Racine
Company Captain Dale's Lake Michigan Sport
Contact Capt. Dale Coleman
City Racine
Company Captain Don's Charter Service
Contact Capt. Don Hauke
City Kenosha
Company Captain Wally's Charters
Contact Capt. Wally Lindemann
City Kenosha
Company Carpenter's Mate Charters
Contact Capt. Paul (Butch) Grasser
City Amery
Company Charter Boat Marlin
Contact Capt. George Olson
City Oak Creek
Company Charters Unlimited
Contact Capt. Charles G. Swartz
City Kenosha
Company Chatmon Sport Fishing Charters
Contact Capts. Dave Chatmon & Eric Hauke
City Kenosha
Company Clay's Joy III Charter Service
Contact Capt. Clayton N. Baker
City Racine
Company Cub II Charter Service
Contact Capt. Larry Braun
City Luxemburg
Company Dale Schroeder's Charter Service
Contact Capt. Dale J. Schroeder
City Manitowoc
Company Dan Bar's Resort
Contact
City Hayward
Company Dave's Charter Service
Contact Capt. Dave Sorenson
City Ashland
Company Day-O Charters
Contact Capt. Mike Gucinski
City Port Wing
Company Dead Reckon Lake Michigan Sport Fish
Contact Capt. John B. Zabel
City Sheboygan
Company Debra Jean Sport Fishing
Contact Capt. Jim Hoffman
City Neenah
Company Dee Jay's Charter Fishing
Contact
City Washburn
Company Diana R Too
Contact Capt. Mike Rusch
City Manitowoc
Company Dogskin Lake Lodge & Outposts
Contact
City Turtle Lake
Company Double "D" Charter Fishing
Contact Capt. M. "Doc" Matson
City Racine
Company E.Fish.N.Sea Charter Service
Contact Capt. David L. Wait
City Cloquet
Company Eagle Charters
Contact Capt. Dan Nourse
City Roberts
Company Eagle Harbor Charters
Contact Capt. Roy Elquist
City Sister Bay
Company East Wisconsin Guide Service
Contact David K. Eggert
City Appleton
Company Ebben's Great Lakes Guide Service
Contact Capt. Brian Ebben
City Green Bay
Company Endeavor Lake Michigan Fishing
Contact Capt. Dennis Frey
City Sheboygan
Company Executive Charters
Contact Capt. Richard Sleep
City Manitowoc
Company Father-N-Son's Sport Fishing Charters
Contact Capt. Jeff Seefeldt
City Sheboygan
Company Fiery Fox Charters
Contact Capts. George & Sandy Shuput
City Greenfield
Company Finn Fishing Team
Contact Capt. Daniel Hill
City Algoma
Company Finn Too Charters
Contact Capt. John H. Muench
City Algoma
Company First Mate Charters
Contact Capt. Dexter Nelson
City Superior
Company Fish Fighter Charters
Contact Capt. Doug Pilon
City Sheboygan
Company Fish Lipps II
Contact Tom & Mary Lovick
City Cornucopia
Company Fish Spotter III Charter
Contact Capts. Alan & Dennis Zamecnik
City Racine
Company Fish Trap Charters
Contact Capt. Tom Bohacek
City Manitowoc
Company Fisherman's Choice Charters
Contact Capt. Brad Seymour
City Sturgeon Bay
Company Fisherman's Cove
Contact
City Port Wing
Company Fishin' Again Charter Service
Contact Capt. Ralph J. Kubsch
City Kewaunee
Company Fishing Pox Charters
Contact Capts. Gus & Darlene Rankey
City Grafton
Company Fishing Pox I
Contact Capt. Jim Belanger
City West Bend
Company Flying "R" Charters
Contact Capt. Roy S. Rusch
City West Bend
Company Flying Finn Charters
Contact Capt. Al "Willie" Williams
City Sheboygan
Company Fox #1 Charters
Contact Capt. Dave "Fox" Wilz
City Sturgeon Bay
Company Fox Brothers Charter Fishing
Contact Daniel Fox
City Wauwatosa
Company Frances Lee Charters
Contact Capt. Charles Weier
City Two Rivers
Company Gail II Charters/Wild Blue Charters
Contact Capt. Roger Misgen
City Stone Lake
Company Galleon Charters
Contact Capt. Kenneth (Mike) Kohn
City Sheboygan
Company Garmisch U.S.A.
Contact
City Cable
Company Gitcheegummee Guide Service
Contact Captain Craig Putchat
City Washburn
Company Golden Beaver Charters/ Rathsack Charter
Contact Capt. Mike Rathsack
City Two Rivers
Company Grand Slam Charters
Contact Capt. Bob Potosnyak
City Two Rivers
Company Gremlin Charter Service
Contact Capt. Charlie Woldt
City Sturgeon Bay
Company Gull Wing Charter Service
Contact Capt. Roger Sohlstrom
City Bayfield
Company Haasch Guide Service
Contact Capt. Lee Haasch
City Algoma
Company High Adventure Air
Contact George St. Catherine
City Eagle River
Company Hobo Charters
Contact Capt. Thomas Achtmann
City Oostburg
Company Hooked! Charters
Contact Capt. Jerry Bricko
City Sheboygan
Company Hooky-Lau Charters
Contact Capt. Bruce Albright
City Rochester
Company Horseshoe Charters
Contact Capt. Robert Lechner
City Kenosha
Company Hub's Motel & Pier
Contact Derek & Tyler Hubbard Ron
City Sister Bay
Company Iverson Sport Fishing
Contact John Iverson
City Stoughton
Company J & J Charters
Contact Capt. J.W. Jonesy Nelson
City Superior
Company J E Fishing Enterprises
Contact Capt. Fritz Peterson
City Sturgeon Bay
Company Jack's Charter Service
Contact Capt. Jack Remus
City Milwaukee
Company Jamieson House Inn
Contact Heidi Hutchinson
City Poynette
Company Jaws II Charters
Contact Capt. Allen Sprang
City Two Rivers
Company Jennie Lynn Charters
Contact Capt. Norrie Reykdal
City Washburn
Company Jester Charter Service
Contact Capt. Gary L. Conger
City Appleton
Company Jimmy Fly Charters
Contact Capt. Jim Christman
City Whitelaw
Company Jonny Be Good Sport Fishing Charters
Contact Capt. Jon Verhelst
City Sheboygan
Company King Catcher Charter Service
Contact Capt. Wayne Zimmer
City Two Rivers
Company Kinn's Katch Charters
Contact Capt. Howard Kinn
City Sturgeon Bay
Company Knudson Charter Service
Contact Capt. Richard Knudson
City Kewaunee
Company Kodiak Too Sport Fishing Charters
Contact Capt. Larry Morrison
City Algoma
Company Lady Van Charter
Contact Capt. Gary Eis
City Mishicot
Company Lake Michigan Charter Service
Contact Mike Rusch
City Manitowoc
Company Lake Michigan Sport Fishing Charters
Contact Capt. Eric Hauke
City Kenosha
Company Lazy Daze Charters
Contact Capt. Jeff Baird
City Algoma
Company Lazy Laker Charters
Contact Capt. Don Mitchell
City Appleton
Company Leisure Time Charters
Contact Capt. Mike Pjevach
City Brookfield
Company Len's Muskies
Contact
City Grantsburg
Company Les Brandt's Trolling Service
Contact Les Brandt
City Washburn
Company Lighthouse Charters
Contact Capt. John Nolte
City Port Washington
Company Little Dipper Charter Service
Contact Carl L. Hatch
City Menomonee Falls
Company Lori's Pride Sport Fishing Charters
Contact Eugene Spaeth
City West Bend
Company Lou's Charter Service
Contact Capt. Lou Bickel
City Ashland
Company Lucky 7 Charter
Contact Capt. Kip Cramer
City Grafton
Company Lucky Lyle's Charter Fishing
Contact Capt. Lyle Teskie
City Gills Rock
Company Lucky Strike Charter Fishing
Contact Capt. Doug Wills
City Superior
Company Lucky's Dream Charter Service
Contact Capts. Lucky & Mary Eichmann
City Sheboygan
Company Lynn's Charter
Contact Capt. Lynn Frederick
City Sister Bay
Company Lynn-A Charter Service
Contact Capt. Jerry Cefalu
City Sturgeon Bay
Company Margaret V Charters
Contact Capts. Richard & Scott Anderson
City Racine
Company Margie Two Charters
Contact Capt. Arnold E. Franke
City Fish Creek
Company Mariner Charters
Contact Capt. Paul Goodman & Paul Mariner
City Ellison Bay
Company McDougall Lodge
Contact Jeff Andrea
City Spooner
Company Midwest Tacklesmiths
Contact Capt. Jim Wierzbicki
City Kenosha
Company Moody Blue Charters
Contact Capt. Judith Feuerstein
City New Holstein
Company Nancy Jean Charter Service
Contact Capt. Clete Challe
City Algoma
Company Nauti-Gal Charters
Contact Eileen & Patrick Kolehouse
City Oconomowoc
Company Neshoto Guide Service
Contact Chris Weier
City Two Rivers
Company New Mystery Charter
Contact Capt. Brian Eggert
City Racine
Company Nicky Boy Charter Fishing
Contact Capt. Nick Waranka
City Port Washington
Company Northern Llight Charters
Contact Capt. Larry D. Mortimer
City Port Wing
Company Northern Marine Charters
Contact
City Bayfield
Company Nourse's Sport Fishing
Contact Capt. Ken Nourse
City Bayfield
Company Ozzie's Charter Service
Contact Capt. Ozzie Streblow
City Oshkosh
Company Paust's Woods Lake Resort
Contact
City Crivitz
Company Peanuts IV Charter Service
Contact Gene Stauber
City Green Bay
Company Phoenix Charters
Contact Capt. Steven-John Bignell
City Verona
Company Pickerel Arm Camp
Contact The Edwardson's
City Janesville
Company Pier Plaza Charter Service
Contact
City Bayfield
Company Pine Acres Resort
Contact
City Crivitz
Company Pinta IV Charters
Contact Capt. Gerald Joe Pienta
City Kewaunee
Company Playin Hooky Charters
Contact Capt. John Troen
City Union Grove
Company Playin' Hooky
Contact Capt. Chuck Nelson
City Manitowoc
Company Port Pacer II Charters
Contact Capt. Jerry Myers
City West Bend
Company Predator Charter Service
Contact Capt. Ron Kline
City Kewaunee
Company Prompt Delivery
Contact Capt. Dale Ahlvin
City Sheboygan
Company Proud Mary Charters
Contact Capt. Bill Garceau
City Manitowoc
Company R.V. Charters
Contact Kevin Naze & Judy Meyers
City Algoma
Company Rainbow Charter
Contact Capt. Gary Gros
City Ellison Bay
Company Rathsack Charter Service
Contact Capt. Mike Rathsack
City Two Rivers
Company Renegade Sport Fishing Charters
Contact Capt. Tim Mueller
City Cedarburg
Company Risky Business Charters
Contact Capt. John Hoffert
City West Bend
Company Roberta's Charters
Contact Capt. Tony Ripple
City Bayfield

Company Rose Marie Charter
Contact Cat. Paul Lohman
City Racine
Company Salmon Deport, Inc.
Contact Capt. Bill Silbernagel
City Baileys Harbor
Company Sanctuary Charters
Contact Capt. Doug Carlstrom
City Sheboygan
Company Sandpiper Sport Fishing
Contact Capt. Tom Morrell
City Algoma
Company Sandpiper Trophy & Sport Fishing Serv.
Contact Capt. Larry Boraas
City Algoma
Company Sea Dog Sportfishing Charters
Contact Capt. James Schlegel
City Sheboygan
Company Sea Hag Fishing Charters
Contact Capt. Sue Kalk
City Sheboygan
Company Seagull Marina & Campground
Contact
City Two Rivers
Company Seahawk Charters
Contact Capt. Ken Klas
City Port Washington
Company Secret Bait Charters
Contact Capt. Robert J. Dumovich
City Sheboygan
Company See Shore Charters
Contact Capt. Steve Propsom
City Sturgeon Bay
Company Serendipity Farm
Contact Forrest & Suzanne Garret
City Viroqua
Company Shady Lady
Contact Capts. John & Julie Gadzinski
City Manitowoc
Company Shippa Hoy Charter Fishing
Contact Capt. Warren Nelson
City Ellison Bay
Company Silver Nailor Charters
Contact Capt. James J. Silbernagel
City West Bend
Company Smoky Lake Reserve
Contact
City Phelps
Company Snap-It Charters
Contact Capt. Snap D. J. Peterson
City Sturgeon Bay
Company Sonny"D"Charters
Contact Capt. Anthony C. DiCola
City Franklin
Company South Bay Lodge
Contact Bob Lammers
City Hingham
Company South Shore Charters
Contact
City Port Wing
Company Sport Fishing Enterprises
Contact Howard Kinn
City Sturgeon Bay
Company Star Kissed Charters
Contact Capt. Charlie Maslanka
City Hurkey
Company Stone Wing Charters
Contact Capt. Stu Terhorst
City Ellison Bay
Company Striker Charters
Contact Capt. Tom Keefe
City Racine
Company Sucharda Charters
Contact Capt. John W. Sucharda
City Kenosha
Company Superior Charter Fishing Service
Contact Capt. Alex Kotter
City Superior
Company Take 5 Charters
Contact Capt. Kenneth G. Jeske
City Franklin
Company Team Turtle Charters
Contact Capt. Van R. DeZwarte
City Plymouth
Company Ten Mile Lake Camp
Contact Richard & Michelle Carpenter
City Tomah
Company The Rose
Contact Capt. Bruce Haws
City Green Bay
Company Thunder Buck Charter

Service
Contact Capt. Butch Wisnefske
City Auburndale
Company Time Out Charters
Contact Capt. David Mulligan
City Beaver Dam
Company Tracy Lee Charters
Contact Capt. Kelly Thurow
City Saxon
Company Trail Visions
Contact
City Glendale
Company Two Rivers Sport Fishing Charters
Contact
City Two Rivers
Company Viking Charters
Contact Norm Tikkanen
City Port Washington
Company Village Charters
Contact Capt. Clyde Neumann
City Two Rivers
Company Violator Charters
Contact Capt. Jim Theyerl
City Francis Creek
Company Wally's Charter Service
Contact Wally Friedman
City Milwaukee
Company Waterwitch Charters
Contact Capt. Wayne Voigt
City Windsor
Company Westfork Guide Service
Contact
City Viroqua
Company Wild Wings Hunting & Fishing Preserve
Contact
City Campbellsport
Company Willie Bee Charters
Contact Capt. Gary Lodel
City Two Rivers
Company Wisconsin Charter Association, Inc.
Contact
City Algoma
Company Wisconsin John Guides Again
Contact
City Menasha
Company
Contact Greg R. Bohn
City Hazelhorst
Company
Contact Charles M. Green
City Wisconsin Rapids
Company
Contact Patricia A. Mercier
City Racine
Company
Contact Martin M. Papke
City Lake Tomahawk
Company
Contact Fritz Peterson
City Sturgeon Bay
Company
Contact Dale H. Stroschein
City Sturgeon Bay
Company
Contact Kelly Thurow
City Saxon

Wyoming

Company A Cross Ranch
Contact Chuck Sanger
City Saratoga
Company A J Brink Outfitters
Contact James D. Brink
City Jelm
Company Aune's Absaroka Angler
Contact C. Scott Aune
City Cody
Company Bald Mountain Outfitters, Inc.
Contact Terry Pollard
City Pinedale
Company Bear Basin Camp
Contact Francis Fox
City Crowheart
Company Big Horn River Outfitters
Contact Reggie & Gwen Treese
City Thermopolis

Company Big Sandy Lodge
Contact Bernard Kelly
City Boulder
Company Bliss Creek Outfitters
Contact Dean Johnson
City Cody
Company Bressler Outfitter, Inc.
Contact Joe Bressler
City Wilson
Company BridgerTeton Outfitters
Contact Randy Foster
City Jackson
Company Bud Nelson Outfitters
Contact Bud Nelson
City Jackson
Company C K Hunting & Fishing Camp
Contact Darrell Copeland
City Big Piney
Company Camp Creek Inn Outfitting
Contact Daniel Gustafson
City Jackson
Company Coulter Creek Outfitters
Contact Robert Johnson
City Jackson
Company Crescent H Ranch
Contact
City Wilson
Company Cross Million Ranch
Contact Larry Miller
City Crowheart
Company Dave Flitner Packing & Outfitting
Contact David Flitner
City Greybull
Company Diamond J Outfitters
Contact Joe Stuemke
City Saratoga
Company Dodge Creek Ranch
Contact Jerry Kennedy
City Rock River
Company Donkey Creek Outfitters
Contact Steve R. Bietz
City Moorcroft
Company Elk Mountain Outfitters, LLC
Contact Myron J. Wakkuri
City Wheatland
Company Elk Ridge Outfitters & Lodge
Contact Terry Reach
City Pinedale
Company Fatboy Fishing
Contact A.J. DeRosa
City Wilson
Company Five Star Expeditions, Inc.
Contact Ed Beattie
City Lander
Company Fly Shop of the Big Horns
Contact
City Sheridan
Company Full Circle Outfitters
Contact Buck Braten
City Meeteetse
Company Gilroy Outfitting
Contact Paul Gilroy
City Wilson
Company Grand Slam Outfitters
Contact Mark Condict
City Saratoga
Company Great Rocky Mountain Outfitters
Contact Robert Smith
City Saratoga
Company Hack's Tackle & Outfitters
Contact
City Saratoga
Company Half Moon Lake Guest Ranch
Contact Frank Deede
City Pinedale
Company Hanna Outfitting
Contact Dave Hanna
City Jackson
Company Heart Six Ranch
Contact Mike Baumann
City Moran
Company High Country Flies
Contact
City Jackson
Company Jackson Peak Outfitters
Contact Charlie M. Petersen, Jr.
City Jackson
Company Jackson's Hole Adventures
Contact
City Jackson Hole
Company John Henry Lee

Outfitters
Contact John Lee
City Jackson
Company Johnson Outfitting
Contact Dean Johnson
City Cody
Company Keighley's Camps
Contact Mark Lantz
City Cheyenne
Company Kyle Wall's Trout Burn Guide Service
Contact
City Casper
Company Lazy TX Outfitting
Contact Clayton W. Voss
City Dubois
Company Lund Outfitting
Contact Kurt W. Lund
City Jackson
Company Medicine Bow Drifters
Contact
City Saratoga
Company Mooncrest Outfitters, Inc.
Contact Robert Model
City Cody
Company Old Glendevey Ranch, Ltd.
Contact Garth Peterson
City Jelm
Company Paintrock Adventures, LLC
Contact Todd Jones
City Hyattville
Company Paradise Guest Ranch
Contact Jim Anderson
City Buffalo
Company Petersen Outfitting
Contact Greg Petersen
City Pinedale
Company Press Stephens-Outfitter
Contact Press Stephens
City Dubois
Company Professional Big Game Outfitters
Contact Bud Nelson
City Jackson
Company Reel Women Fly Fishing Adventures
Contact
City Jackson
Company Ritz Sporting Goods
Contact
City Sheridan
Company Rocky Mountain Horseback Vacations
Contact
City Lander
Company Skinner Brothers Outfitters
Contact Robert Skinner
City Pinedale]
Company Snake River Fishing Trips
Contact
City Jackson
Company Solitary Angler
Contact Van Beacham
City Kemmerer
Company Sports Lure
Contact
City Buffalo
Company Spotted Horse Ranch
Contact Dick Bess
City Jackson
Company The Lodges of East Yellowstone Valley
Contact
City Wapiti
Company The Tackle Box
Contact Dean Coy
City Alpine
Company Thunder Mountain Outfitters
Contact Cameron Garnick
City Moran
Company Timberline Outfitters
Contact Craig P. Oceanak
City Cheyenne
Company UpStream Anglers & Outdoor Adventures
Contact
City Jackson
Company West Laramie Fly Store
Contact
City Laramie
Company Westbank Anglers
Contact
City Teton Village
Company Wind River Ranch

Contact Arthur Davenport
City Kinnear
Company Wycon Safari, Inc.
Contact Wynn Condict
City Saratoga
Company Yellowstone Outfitters Hunting & Fishing
Contact Lynn Madsen
City Afton
Company
Contact John E. Keiser
City Lander
Company
Contact Tom R. Montgomery
City Jackson

Canada

Alberta

Company "Must Be Nice" Drift Co.
Contact Tom Cutmore
City Calgary
Company Access - Alberta Outfitting & Guide Service
Contact Michael Terry
City Edmonton
Company Andrew Lake Lodge
Contact Glen Wettlaufer
City Edmonton
Company Andrew Lake Lodge & Camps
Contact
City Edmonton
Company Babala Stone Sheep Outfitters, Ltd.
Contact Randy Babala
City Cadomin
Company Bow River Troutfitters
Contact
City Calgary
Company Cheemo Lodge
Contact Ed Granger
City Innisfail
Company Cree Lake Lodge
Contact Vern & Gerri Biller
City Vermillion
Company Frontier Fishing Lodge
Contact Wayne Witherspoon
City Edmonton
Company Granger's Cheemo Lodge
Contact Clayton Granger
City Hardisty
Company Great Bear Adventures, Ltd.
Contact Ken Cotterill
City Calgary
Company Grist Haven Lodge
Contact Tony M. Kossey
City Cold Lake
Company Gypsy Lake Lodge
Contact Jeff Dodds
City Fort McMurray
Company Kingfisher Drifting, Ltd.
Contact Michael Truch
City Calgary
Company Lloyd Lake Lodge
Contact Richard & Mary Jean Pliska
City Fort McMurray
Company Magnum Outfitters
Contact Roy Thompson
City Peace River
Company Mawdsley Lake Lodge
Contact Glen Coulter
City Lethbridge
Company Mike Zelman & Sons Guide Service
Contact Mike Zelman
City Athabasca
Company Monod Sports
Contact
City Banff
Company Northeast Alberta Wilderness Outfitters, Inc.
Contact Charles Graves
City Ft. McMurray
Company Pawistik Lodge
Contact Scott Jeffrey

City Calgary
Company Poplar Ridge Outfitters, Inc.
Contact Harvey McNalley
City Cadogan
Company Rams Head Outfitters
Contact Stan Simpson
City Warburg
Company Redstone Trophy Hunts
Contact David & Carol Dutchik
City Cochrane
Company Ron Loucks Outfitting
Contact Ron Loucks
City Rocky Mountain House
Company Sven-Erik Jansson Associates
Contact Sven-Erik Jansson
City Edmonton
Company Tazin Lake Lodge
Contact Gordon Wilson
City Nanton
Company Team Whitetail Outfitting
Contact Darcy Zelman
City Athabasca
Company The Bow River Company
Contact Don Pike
City Calgary
Company Whispering Hill Trophy Hunters & Outfitters
Contact Jay Stewart
City Edmonton
Company Wolf Lake Wilderness Camp
Contact
City Calgary
Company Wolverman Wilderness Outfitters
Contact Walchuk & Degenhardt & Slager
City Grand Centre
Company
Contact Ted A. Horechka
City Dewinton

British Columbia

Company April Point Lodge
Contact Eric Peterson
City Campbell River
Company Ashnola Guide Outfitters
Contact Clarence Schneider
City Keremeos
Company Bear Lake Guides & Outfitters
Contact Dirk & Traute Schuirmann
City Prince George
Company Bear Paw Guide & Outfitters
Contact Dennis & Irene Smith
City Sinclair Mills
Company Beaverfoot Lodge
Contact Don Wolfenden
City Golden
Company Bella Coola Outfitting Co., Ltd.
Contact Leonard Ellis
City Bella Coola
Company Big Bay Marina & Fishing Resort
Contact Kay Knierim
City Stuart Island
Company Big Nine Outfitters
Contact Barry Tompkins
City Fort St. John
Company Blaine R. Southwick Outfitting, Ltd.
Contact Blaine Southwick
City Toad River
Company Blunt Mountain Outfitters
Contact Norm Blaney
City Kelowna
Company Bradford & Co. Guide Services, Ltd.
Contact Myles Bradford
City Dease Lake
Company Campsall Outfitters
Contact Hank Campsall
City Fort Steele
Company Canadian Adventure Safaris
Contact Odd Aasland
City Cranbrook
Company Chaunigan Lake Lodge

Contact
City Pitt Meadows
Company Christina Falls Outfitters, Inc.
Contact Darwin Watson
City Hudson's Hope
Company Coast Mountain Wilderness Lodge
Contact Ralph Voll
City Powell River
Company Collins Guiding
Contact Darrel A. Collins
City Quesnel
Company Columbia River Outfitters Guide Service
Contact
City Trail
Company Eagle River Guide Outfitting
Contact Eric Havard
City Iskut
Company Eaglecrest Guide Outfitters
Contact
City Sooke
Company Edmund Lake Lodge
Contact Herb & Anna Dyke
City Vernon
Company Elk Valley Bighorn Outfitters, Ltd.
Contact Robert Fontana
City Cranbrook
Company Equinoxe Angling Adventures.LTD.
Contact Pierre Morel
City Delta
Company Eureka Peak Lodge & Outfitters
Contact Stuart Maitland
City 100 Mile House
Company Fawnie Mt. Outfitters & Moose Lake Lodge
Contact John Blackwell
City Anahim Lake
Company Findlay Creek Outfitters
Contact Eric Godlien
City Invermere
Company Folding Mountain Outfitters, Ltd.
Contact Dale Drinkall
City Toad River
Company Fournier Brothers Outfitting
Contact Greg Fournier
City Quesnel
Company Frontier's Farwest
Contact Debbie Patterson
City Telkwa
Company Gemstar Outfitting
Contact Brian Schuck
City Golden
Company Glacier Peak Adventures, Inc.
Contact Gary Koopman
City N.Kelowna
Company Grizzly Lake Outfitters
Contact Ron Fitch
City Houston
Company Gundahoo River Outfitters, Inc.
Contact Art Thompson
City Muncho Lake
Company Horseshoe Creek Outfitters, Ltd.
Contact Ray Jackson
City Charlie Lake
Company Icha & Illgatcho Mountains Outfitters
Contact Roger Williams
City Anahim Lake
Company Indian River Ranch Guides & Outfitters
Contact Jamie Schumacher
City Atlin
Company Kasba Lake Lodge
Contact
City Parksville
Company Kawdy Outfitters
Contact Stan Lancaster
City Smithers
Company Kiniskan Outfitters
Contact Bruce Creyke
City Dease Lake
Company Kluachesi Lake Outfitting
Contact
City Fort St. John
Company Kluane Wilderness Lodge

Contact
City Kamloops
Company Klukas Lake Ranch
Contact Glen Kilgour
City Taylor
Company Larry Erickson's Alpine Outfitters
Contact Larry Erickson
City Manson Creek
Company Love Bros. & Lee Ltd.
Contact Ron Fleming & Brenda Nelson
City Hazelton
Company Lower Kootenay Guide Outfitters, Ltd.
Contact Don Bullock
City Creston
Company Monashee Outfitting
Contact Volker Scherm
City Revelstoke
Company Monroe Cattle Co.
Contact Mike Monroe
City McBride
Company Morice River Outfitting
Contact John Shepert
City Houston
Company Nanika Guiding
Contact Jim Tourond
City Burns Lake
Company Nimmo Bay Resort
Contact Craig Murray
City Port McNeill
Company Niut Trails Outfitting
Contact Eric Hatch
City Tatla Lake
Company North Coast Adventures, Inc.
Contact Wayne Price
City Galiano
Company North Country Jet Boat Charters
Contact
City Fort Nelson
Company Northern Woodsman Outfitting
Contact Les Allen
City Westbank
Company Northwest Fishing Guides
Contact Noel Gyger
City Terrace
Company Northwest Ranching & Outfitting
Contact Heidi Gutfrucht
City Hanceville
Company One Eye Outfit
Contact Mike McDonough
City Williams Lake
Company Opatcho Lake Guide & Outfitters
Contact Ralph Maida
City Prince George
Company Painter's Lodge
Contact Harley Elias
City Campbell River
Company Palliser River Outfitters
Contact Gordon Burns
City Wardner
Company Pitka Mountain Outfitters, Ltd.
Contact Colonel R. Anderson
City Fort Fraser
Company Purcell Wilderness Guiding & Outfitting
Contact Gary Hansen
City Kimberley
Company Quesnel Lake Wilderness Adventures
Contact Ken Davis
City Lac La Hache
Company Ram Creek Outfitters
Contact Steven Leuenberger
City Wardner
Company Rocky Mountain Lodge, Ltd.
Contact Henry Fercho
City Cranbrook
Company Rocky Mountain Outfitter, Ltd.
Contact
City Prince George
Company Sailcone Wilderness Fishing
Contact
City Royston
Company Salmon King Lodge
Contact Lucie Drovin
City Delta

Company Scoop Lake Outfitters, Ltd.
Contact Darwin Cary
City Kelowna
Company Shesley River Outfitters
Contact Rudy Day
City Telegraph Creek
Company Sikanni River Outfitters
Contact Doug Percival
City Pink Mountain
Company Sonora Resort
Contact Alan Moss
City Campbell River
Company Spring King Charters, Ltd.
Contact Ray & Ellen Hepting
City Kitimat
Company Steam Boat Mountain Outfitters
Contact
City Fort Nelson
Company Steiner Bros. Guide & Outfitting
Contact Ray Steiner
City Fraser Lake
Company Tahltan Outfitters
Contact Fletcher Day
City Smithers
Company Tetsa River Outfitters
Contact Cliff Andrews
City Fort Nelson
Company The Dolphins Resort
Contact Clint Cameron
City Campbell River
Company Thunder Mountain Outfitters
Contact Larry Bartlett
City Lac La Hache
Company Tincup Wilderness Lodge
Contact Larry Nagy
City Victoria
Company Trembling Pines Outfitter
Contact Roy Mulvahill
City Williams Lake
Company Tsuniah Lake Lodge
Contact Eric Brebner
City Williams Lake
Company Tsylos Park Lodge & Adventures
Contact Lloyd McLean
City Williams Lake
Company Tweedsmuir Park Guides & Outfitters
Contact Bob Nielsen
City Vanderhoof
Company Upper Stikine River Adventures, Ltd.
Contact Jerry Geraci
City Telkwa
Company Vaseux Lake Lodge
Contact Peter & Denise Axhorn
City Sooke
Company West Coast Outfitting
Contact Bob Welsh
City Port Alberni
Company West Kettle Outfitters, Ltd.
Contact Peter Grosch
City Beaverdell
Company Whatshan Guides & Outfitters
Contact Ken Robins
City Nakusp
Company Wistaria Guiding
Contact Gary Blackwell
City Burns Lake
Company Yohetta Wilderness Adventures, Ltd.
Contact Goetz Schuerholz
City Duncan
Company
Contact Tom Nichol
City 100 Mile House

Labrador

Company Cooper's Minipi Camps
Contact
City Happy Valley - Goose Bay
Company Crossroads Lake Lodge
Contact Bruce Woolfrey
City Wabush
Company Double Mer Fishing Camps Ltd.
Contact Howard Michelin

City Happy Valley
Company Grand Island Outfitting
Contact George Pardy & Junior Canning
City Labrador City
Company Hunt River Camps
Contact Clyde House
City Happy Valley - Goose Bay
Company Labrador Salmon Lodge
Contact
City Forteau
Company Lobstick Lodge
Contact
City Churchill Falls
Company Lucky Strike Lodge
Contact Dennis & Lorne Normore
City L'Anse au Loup
Company Miron River Outfitters
Contact Wayne Rodway
City Labrador City
Company Night Lake Lodge
Contact D.L. (Dave) Hollett
City Happy Valley-Goose Bay
Company Northern Lights Fishing Lodge
Contact Yves Ste. Marie
City Labrador City
Company Pinware River Lodge
Contact W. Arthur Fowler
City L'Anse au Loup
Company Powell's Outfitters
Contact Tony Powell
City Charlottetown

Manitoba

Company Aberdeen Lodge
Contact M. Nevakshonoff
City Fisher Branch
Company Agassiz Taxidermy & Outfitting
Contact Rick Liske
City Beausejour
Company Aikens Lake Wilderness Lodge
Contact Turenne & Lavack
City Winnipeg
Company Amphibian Lake Lodge
Contact Peter & Geri Czorny
City Winnipeg
Company Anama Bay Tourist Camp
Contact Alex Letander
City Gypsumville
Company Angell's Resort
Contact Gerry & Ruth Angell
City Flin Flon
Company Antsanen's Lodge
Contact Peter Antsanen
City
Company Arrow Lake Outfitters
Contact Wayne Ewachewski
City Shoal Lake
Company Athapap Lodge
Contact Stan Bowles
City Cranberry Portage
Company Atikaki Wilderness Camp
Contact Bob Jackson
City Pine Falls
Company Bakers Narrows Lodge Ltd.
Contact Dave & Gene Kostuchuk
City Flin Flon
Company Barrier Bay Resort
Contact Kevin & Gail Nally
City Seven Sisters Falls
Company Bator Boy Outfitting
Contact Geraldine & Michael Bator
City Gilbert Plains
Company Bear Lake Lodge
Contact Sandy Beardy
City Cross Lake
Company Betula Lake Resort
Contact Elmer & Yolande Bigelow
City Seven Sisters Falls
Company Big Buffalo Resort
Contact Lynette Ulrich
City Falcon Lake
Company Big Four Wilderness Camp
Contact Stan & Joan Wilson
City Cranberry Portage
Company Big Grass Outfitters
Contact tom & Judy Usunier
City Plumas

Company Big Northern Lodge & Outfitters
Contact John Eisner & Ian McKay
City Minitonas
Company Big Rock Hunting & Fishing Lodge
Contact Gus Borkofsky
City Gypsumville
Company Big Sand Lake Lodge
Contact Don & Lynn McCrea
City Winnipeg
Company Big Trophy Outfitters
Contact John Hatley
City Gillam
Company Big Whiteshell Lodge
Contact Henry & Diana Bergen
City Rennie
Company Bird River Outfitters
Contact Ron Alexander
City Winnipeg
Company Bloodvein River Outfitters
Contact Nick Arseniuk
City Lac du Bonnet
Company Boggy Creek Outfitting
Contact Maxwell Nemertchek
City Boggy Creek
Company Bolton Lake Lodge, Inc.
Contact Brian Dick
City St. Andrews
Company Breken Guided Trophy Hunts
Contact Ken & Brenda Maxymowich
City Dominion City
Company Brereton Lake Resort
Contact The Nedohins
City Winnipeg
Company Buffalo Point International Resort
Contact The Thunder Family
City Middlebro
Company Bull Moose Outfitters
Contact Albert & Terri de Lighte
City Ethelbert
Company Caddy Lake Resort
Contact Wayne Mooney & Shirley Whitehead
City Winnipeg
Company Call of the Wild Outfitters
Contact Nick Gorda
City Selkirk
Company Cameron Guiding
Contact Stew Cameron
City Forrest
Company Camp Hide Away
Contact Terry & Brenda Mihaychuk
City Lac du Bonnet
Company Canadian Trophy Lodges Ltd.
Contact Enns & Keller
City The Pas
Company Caribou Country Adventures
Contact Stan B. Suess
City Steinbach
Company Caribou Lodge
Contact Gervais & Martha Beaulieu
City Cranberry Portage
Company Carpenter's Clearwater Lodge & Outfitters
Contact Jim Lorden or Doug Sangster
City The Pas
Company Cats on the Red
Contact Stu & Dianna McKay
City Lockport
Company Chesley's Lodge & Resort
Contact Joe Isfjord & Bryan Gafka
City Petersfield
Company Childs Lake Lodge & Outfitters
Contact Brian & Joan Forbes
City Boggy Creek
Company Churchill River Lodge & Outfitters
Contact John & Barb L'Abbe
City Leaf Rapids
Company Claude's Fishing Huts
Contact Claude J. Lambert
City St. Laurent
Company Constable's Lakeside Lodge
Contact E. Constable
City Flin Flon
Company Cook's Camp
Contact Rene Cook
City Brochet
Company Crescent Beach Cottages & Motel

Contact Kevin Harbottle
City Whiteshell PO
Company Crowduck Lake Camp
Contact Nick & Bill Kolansky
City Winnipeg
Company D & O Soloway Outfitters Service
Contact Orville & Debbie Soloway
City Pine River
Company Diamond Willow Inn
Contact Leonard & Darlene Abromovich
City Snow Lake
Company Double M Guiding & Outfitting
Contact Mike Romaniuk
City Ethelbert
Company Duck Mountain Outfitters
Contact Leslie E. Nelson
City Minitonas
Company Dudman Farms
Contact Barry Dudman
City Onanole
Company Eagle Nest Lodge
Contact Fred & Jo-Anne Pedruchny
City Pointe du Bois
Company Eden Eagle Outfitters
Contact Gerald & Elaine Leforte
City Leaf Rapids
Company Einarsson's Guide Service
Contact Helgi Einarsson
City Gypsumville PO
Company Elbow Lake Lodge
Contact Jack Smith
City Swan River
Company Elk Island Lodge
Contact Paul & Gary Zanewich
City Winnipeg
Company Evergreen Resort
Contact Garry Morrish
City The Pas
Company Falcon Beach Riding Stables & Guest Ranch
Contact Murray & Marg Imrie
City Falcon Lake
Company Fishing Lake Lodge/Bissett Outfitters
Contact Byron Grapentine
City Bissett
Company Flin Flon Outfitters
Contact Rick Strom
City Flin Flon
Company Gammon River East Outcamps
Contact Bob Crockett
City Canada
Company George Lake Outfitters
Contact Rick Penner
City Pointe du Bois
Company Gods River Lodge
Contact Gods River Dev. Corp.
City
Company Golden Eagle Lodge
Contact Ross & Betty Sawyer
City Lynn Lake
Company Great Bear Trophy Lodge
Contact
City Winnipeg
Company Great North Lodge
Contact Glen Hoodle
City Flin Flon
Company Green Bay Resort, Inc.
Contact Sandy & Grant Fisette
City Whiteshell P.O.
Company Harrop Lake Camp & Outpost/Thunderbird
Contact Scott & Gwen Compton
City Winnipeg
Company Healey's Gods lake Narrows Lodge
Contact Sam & Marigold Healey John Jr.
City
Company Heartland Canada Discovery Tours
Contact Susan Sures & Dianne Clowes
City Winnipeg
Company Hobbs Resort
Contact Gib & Audrey Hobbs
City Grand Rapids
Company Indian Trail Outfitters
Contact Bob Cherepak
City Arborg
Company Inverness Falls Resort
Contact Stuart & Judy Cornell
City Rennie

Company Island Lake Lodge
Contact Darryl Heppner & Dennis Brears
City Island Lake
Company J & D Jumbo Outfitters/K. & C. Outfitting
Contact Jim Hoard & Kathy Hoard
City Pinawa
Company Jan Lake Lodge Co. Ltd.
Contact Richard & Marie-Paule Koopman
City Flin Flon
Company Jessica Lake Lodge
Contact Bill & Laurie Scarfe
City Rennie
Company Jim Dandi Promotions
Contact Jim Hewitt
City Winnipeg
Company K. D. McKay Outfitting
Contact Kenneth D. McKay
City Grand Rapids
Company K. S. B. Outfitters & Guiding Service
Contact Kenneth S. Biglow
City Thompson
Company Kaskattama Safari Adventures
Contact Charlie Taylor & Christine Quinlan
City Winnipeg
Company Kendall Point Lodge
Contact Darren Deason
City Pointe du Bois
Company Kenosewa Sipi Outdoor Adventures
Contact Ken Albert
City Norway House
Company Kettle Hills Outfitters
Contact Victor Gervais
City Minitonas
Company Keystone Resorts
Contact Barb & Lionel St. Godard
City West Hawk Lake
Company Kilman Rental Cottages
Contact Lorne & Myra Kilkenny
City Russell
Company Knee Lake A Resort, Inc.
Contact Phil Reid
City Winnipeg
Company Kum-Bac-Kabins
Contact Joyce Molyneaux
City Wanless
Company Kusstum Tours & Guide Service
Contact John R. Bilenduke
City Churchill
Company L & M Guides & Outfitters
Contact LeRoy Ramsay
City Brandon
Company Lake Manitoba Narrows Lodge Ltd.
Contact Lake Manitoba Narrows Ltd.
City Lake Manitoba Narrows
Company Lambert's Ice Fishing Services
Contact Yvon Lambert
City St. Laurent
Company Little Grand Rapids Lodge
Contact Ernie Janzen
City Winnipeg
Company Lone Wolf Campground & Outfitting
Contact Arnold Poirier
City Wabowden
Company Magson's Camp Outfitting Services
Contact Al & Mary Magson
City Lynn Lake
Company Manewan Enterprises Ltd.
Contact
City Flin Flon
Company Manfred Racine's Guiding & Outfitting Svce.
Contact Manfred Racine
City Boissevain
Company Mantagao Outfitters
Contact Buddy or Marlene Chudy
City Winnipeg
Company Matheson Island Lodge Ltd.
Contact Marc Collette
City East Selkirk
Company Matheson Lake Resort
Contact Larry Olson
City Winnipeg
Company Minor Bay Camps Ltd.
Contact Randy Duvell

City Winnipeg
Company Moak Lodge
Contact Glen & Len Heroux & Les Greig
City Eriksdale
Company Monkman Outfitting
Contact Bob Monkman
City Gillam
Company Mr. Walleye Taxidermy & Outfitter
Contact Robert R. Check
City East Selkirk
Company Munroe's Wilderness Outpost Camp
Contact Brian Dick
City Berens River
Company Muskwa Outfitters
Contact Ralph Merasty
City Brochet
Company Naturalistic Taxidermy Outfitters
Contact David Clark
City Brandon
Company Nejalini Lodge
Contact Al & Phil Reid
City Winnipeg
Company Nelson River Outfitters
Contact Bill Cordell
City Pikwitonei
Company Nelson's Gods Lake Lodge
Contact Nelson Tomalty
City Gimli
Company Nopiming Lodge
Contact Marge & Blaine Guenther
City Lac du Bonnet
Company North Country Lodge
Contact Jack & Georgia Clarkson
City Berens River
Company North Knife Lake Lodge
Contact Stewart & Barbara Webber
City Thompson
Company North of 49 Outfitters
Contact Lorne Weir
City Selkirk
Company Northern Angler Fly Fishing Adventures
Contact John & Tracy Yury
City Dauphin
Company Northern Spirit Lodge
Contact Greg & Michelle Petryk
City Cranberry Portage
Company Northwest Wilderness Adventures
Contact Brad Stoneman
City Lynn Lake
Company Nu-Cho Expeditions
Contact Tom Ellis
City Thompson
Company Nueltin Fly-In Lodges
Contact The Gurkes
City Alonsa
Company Nutimik Lodge
Contact Janet Wilson
City Seven Sisters Falls
Company Otter Falls Resort
Contact Gordon & Jackie Zechel
City Seven Sisters Falls
Company Outland Outfitting
Contact Jerry & Geraldine Cook
City Grand Rapids
Company Paint Lake Resort
Contact Bill & Barb Traviss
City Thompson
Company Penguin Resort
Contact Judy & Bob Partridge
City
Company Peter Wiebe Outfitting/ Grand Slam Outfitter
Contact Peter Wiebe & Barbara Wiebe
City Winnipeg
Company Petersons' Reed Lake Lodge
Contact Kathy & Corky Peterson
City The Pas
Company Pine Grove Cabins
Contact Eileen & Gary Hobbs
City Grand Rapids
Company Pine Island Lodge
Contact Brian Burgess
City Winnipeg
Company Pinewood Lodge
Contact Raquel & Jeff Lincoln
City Seven Sisters Falls
Company Plummer's Lodges
Contact Cameron Baty

City Winnipeg
Company Poplar Bay Park & Tourist Camp
Contact Barry & Linda Crawford
City Winnipeg
Company Pukisimoon Outfitters
Contact Fred Hobbs
City Grand Rapids
Company Red River Adventures & Outfitters
Contact Kim Meger
City Winnipeg
Company Ridge Country Outfitters
Contact Dean Randell
City Pinawa
Company River View Cabins
Contact Colin & Jean McKay
City Grand Rapids
Company Riverdale Tourist Camp
Contact Gerry & Georgette Roziere
City Lac du Bonnet
Company Riverside Lodge
Contact Ed Matwick
City Duck Bay
Company Rock Bottom Fishing Hole Outfitters
Contact Larry Bosiak
City Dauphin
Company Rod & Real Fishing Adventures
Contact Robert Stock
City Swan River
Company Rolly Outfitters
Contact Ron & Kelly Shykitka
City Benito
Company Rupertsland Guiding & Outfitting Services
Contact Werner Batke
City Winnipeg
Company Sasagiu Rapids Lodge
Contact Dorothy & Steve Samu
City Wabowden
Company Saskoba Outfitters
Contact B. Murray & G. Kostuchuk
City Flin Flon
Company Seal River Wilderness Adventures
Contact Mike & Jeanne Reimer
City Churchill
Company Seven Lakes Lodge
Contact Jack & Tom Kissock
City Portage la Prairie
Company Sharron's Outfitting Service
Contact Debi Hatch
City
Company Shining Falls Camps
Contact Ralph & Ruth Rutledge
City Selkirk
Company Silsby Lake Lodge
Contact Kip & Mickey Thompson
City Ilford
Company Silver Bear Creek Outfitters
Contact Bruce Crossley
City Grandview
Company Silver Birch Resort & Outfitters
Contact John Friesen
City Sprague
Company Silver Goose Lodge
Contact John F.Hatley
City Gillam
Company South Side Outfitters
Contact Rudy & Marion Usick
City Erickson
Company Sparrowhawk Outpost Camp
Contact Brett & Barry Arnason
City Winnipeg
Company Spence's Mantario Outfitters
Contact Steve Spence
City Bissett
Company Sportsman's Fishing & Hunting Lodge
Contact D & J Goran
City Sifton
Company Sportsman's Lodge
Contact Ruffo Schindler
City Winnipeg
Company Sturgeon Bay Outfitting Service
Contact Leonard & Terry Stagg
City Gypsumville
Company Summerberry Outfitting Services

Contact Peter & Doug McAree
City The Pas
Company Sutherland & Sutherland
Contact A.J. Sutherland
City Bowsman
Company T & A Johnston Outfitting
Contact T. Johnston
City Box 975
Company Tall Timber Lodge & Marine
Contact Kathy & Wayne Smith
City Lac du Bonnet
Company Tawow Lodge
Contact Jim & Hazel Corman
City Snow Lake
Company Ted Jowett Outfitting Service
Contact Ted Jowett
City Winnipeg
Company Tee-Pee Outfitters
Contact Donna & Letitia Hohle
City Leaf Rapids
Company Tent Town Outfitters
Contact M. Mahlberg
City Minitonas
Company Thompson's Guiding & Outfitting
Contact Glen Thompson
City Duck Bay
Company Three Lakes Camp
Contact George & Donna Hawes
City Flin Flon
Company Tonapah Lodge & Outfitters
Contact George & Jean Murnick Frank
City Cranberry Portage
Company Trail End Camp & Outfitters
Contact The Hrechkosys
City Pointe du Bois
Company Trapper Don's Lodge & Outfitting
Contact Don & Lynn McCrea
City Cowan
Company Trapper Mike's Outfitting Service
Contact Mike Snihor
City Thompson
Company True North on Kississing
Contact Tim & Val Matheson
City Sherridon
Company Unique Wilderness Adventure
Contact
City Lynn Lake
Company Utik lake Lodge
Contact Roger Whittington & George Dram
City Thompson
Company Vestby Angling Adventures
Contact Mark Vestby
City Roblin
Company Vickers Lake Outfitters
Contact Martin McLaughlin
City Snow Lake
Company Viking Lodge
Contact Ted Smith
City Cranberry Portage
Company Wamair Service
Contact William & Kathy Mowat
City Matheson Island
Company Washow Bay Lodge
Contact Ron Chekosky
City Arborg
Company Waterhen River Lodge
Contact Clarence & Della Popowich
City
Company Waterwolf Guide Service
Contact Stephen Ramsay
City Minitonas
Company Wekusko Falls Lodge
Contact Tony & Susan Brew Dwayne
City Snow Lake
Company Wellman Lake Lodge & Outfitters
Contact Linda & Alvin Wiebe
City Minitonas
Company West Hawk Lake Resort
Contact John & Carol Surowich
City West Hawk Lake
Company Westwood Lodge
Contact Tim & Emilie Lies
City Flin Flon
Company Whiskeyjack's Outfitting Service
Contact Jim Dudgeon

City Flin Flon
Company White Lake Resort Ltd.
Contact Hans & Hannelore Wutschke
City Rennie
Company Wild River Outfitting
Contact Harold Westdal
City Winnipeg
Company Wilderness Bear Guides
Contact Art & Craig Henry
City Woodlands
Company Wilderness Gardens Outfitters
Contact Fred Salter
City Lynn Lake
Company Wilderness Outfitters/ Burntwood Lake Lodge
Contact Larry Gogal
City Snow Lake
Company Youth Future
Contact Barry Lywak
City Koostatak

New Brunswick

Company Adair's Outfitting
Contact Larry D. Adair
City Kings County
Company Alpine Lodge
Contact Danny Stewart
City Blackville
Company Atlantic Adventures
Contact Brian McVicar
City St. George
Company Betts Kelly Lodge
Contact Keith Betts
City Doaktown
Company Black Rapids Salmon Club
Contact George Curtis
City Blackville
Company Black's Hunting & Fishing Camps
Contact Juanita Black
City Plaster Rock
Company Blueberry Hill Outfitters
Contact Ken & Lorraine Polley
City Sussex
Company Burnt Land Brook Ltd.
Contact Leroy G. Scott
City Boiestown
Company Bumtland Brook Lodge
Contact Joan & Barrie Duffield
City Boiestown
Company Cail's Private Salmon Pools on the Miramichi
Contact Stephen J. Cail
City Lincoln
Company Canoose Camps
Contact Thomas Mosher or Faith Sonier
City St. Stephen
Company Canterbury Hunting & Fishing
Contact Shawn Collicott
City Canterbury
Company Cape Lodge
Contact Donald E. Davis
City Hartland
Company Carolina Dorrington Hill Hunt Club
Contact
City Canterbury
Company Chickadee Lodge
Contact Vaughan Schriver
City York, Co.
Company Crouchers Outfitters
Contact Rod & Carl Croucher
City RR 8
Company Crow's Hollow
Contact Fred Amacher & Danny Roy
City Miramichi
Company Danny's Way
Contact Gerard Regan
City Miramichi
Company Dave Winchester's Sporting Camps
Contact Dave Winchester
City Hartland
Company Eagle's Nest Sporting Camp
Contact Arnold Drost
City Canterbury
Company Flo's Fishing Lodge
Contact Florence Lyons

City Doaktown
Company Forest Lawn Outfitter
Contact Brian How
City Bristol
Company Four Men Lodge of the Miramichi
Contact George Vanderbeck
City Red Bank
Company Four Mile Out Camp
Contact Allison R. Corbin
City Plaster Rock
Company Fundy Lodge
Contact Sid & Lynette Weinman
City St. George
Company Governor's Table Camp
Contact Hugh B. Smith
City Hartland
Company Green Acres Camp
Contact John Higgs
City Canterbury
Company Guimac Camps
Contact Ralph Orser
City Hartland
Company Harris Bar Lodge
Contact Amie Curtis
City Blackville
Company Hide Away Lodge
Contact Chuck & Danny Villeneuve
City Canterbury, Fosterville
Company Howard's Sporting Camps
Contact Glen Howard
City Plaster Rock
Company Interactive Outdoors
Contact Tim Bradley
City Pennfield
Company Juniper Lodge & Cottages
Contact Frank & Eileen MacDonald
City Juniper
Company Kelly's Sporting Lodge
Contact Carmon Kelly & Lorne MacDonald
City Fredericton
Company Kingsclear Outfitters
Contact Phil Atwin
City Fredericton
Company Lake Retreat Outfitter & Charters
Contact Rob Wilson
City Saint John
Company Little Bald Peak Lodge, Ltd.
Contact Al King
City Plaster Rock
Company Long Meadow Cabins
Contact Darren Johnston
City Harvey Station
Company Long's Hollow Outfitting
Contact J. Bonner Long
City Ludlow
Company Loon Bay Lodge
Contact David Whittingham
City St. Stephen
Company M&M's Whooper Hollow Lodge
Contact Martin & Marie Budaker
City Fredericton
Company MacFarlane Sporting Camps
Contact Dixon MacFarlane
City Millville
Company Malarkey Cabin Guiding Service
Contact Ray Dillon
City Zealand
Company Mamozekel Lodge & Cabins
Contact Shirley Mahaney
City Plaster Rock
Company May's Brook Camp
Contact Wilson H. Briggs
City Plaster Rock
Company Miramichi Fish Inn
Contact
City Blackville
Company Miramichi Gray Rapids Lodge, Inc.
Contact Guy A. Smith
City Oromocto
Company Miramichi Inn
Contact Andre Godin
City Red Bank
Company Mitchell Ledge Pool Camps
Contact Roger & Cynthia Mitchell
City Doaktown
Company Nash Bar Lodge
Contact Lorne & Kathleen Hawkins
City Blackville

City Doaktown
Company Nepisiguit River Camps
Contact Kenneth Gray
City Bathurst
Company Nerepis Lodge
Contact Reginald & Cecily Fredericks
City Westfield
Company North Lake Guiding Service
Contact Mrs. Edward Fredericks
City Canterbury
Company North View Hunting & Fishing Lodge
Contact Wayne DeLeavey
City Plaster Rock
Company North Woods Lodge
Contact Wade McVicar
City Back Bay
Company O'Donnell's Cottages & Canoeing
Contact Valerie O'Donnell
City Doaktown
Company Oak Mountain Lodge
Contact Clarence LeBlanc
City Penobsquis
Company Palfrey Lake Lodge
Contact Mrs. Larry G. Day
City McAdam
Company Perrin's Hunting & Fishing
Contact Blake Perrin
City Wirral
Company Pond's Resort
Contact Keith & Linda Pond
City Ludlow
Company Pond's...on the Miramichi
Contact
City Ludlow
Company Ponds Porter Kove Kamps
Contact Doreen L. Pond
City Ludlow
Company Riverside Lodge
Contact Kenneth Hayes
City Renous
Company Robichaud Outfitters
Contact Bernard Robichaud
City Richibucto
Company Sevogle Salmon Club
Contact Michael French
City Red Bank
Company Shogomoc Sporting Camps
Contact Muriel Way
City Nackawic
Company Slipp Brothers, Ltd.
Contact Ronald & Duane Slipp
City Hoyt
Company South Ridge Sporting Camp Ltd.
Contact William Prosser
City Juniper
Company Spencer's Fishing & Hunting Lodge
Contact Dell Spencer
City Boiestown
Company Spring Brook Camps
Contact Eugene O'Neill
City Sunbury Co.
Company Stoddard Hunting & Fishing Camp
Contact Clinton Norrad
City Boiestown
Company Sullivan's Fishing Camps
Contact Warren Sullivan
City Doaktown
Company Sunset Shangrila Fishing & Hunting Lodge
Contact Donald & Joan Lyons
City Doaktown
Company The Lyons Den
Contact Calvin & Mary Lyons
City Doaktown
Company The Old River Lodge
Contact Vicki & Alex Mills
City Doaktown
Company Tobique & Serpentine Camps, Ltd.
Contact Donald McAskill
City Plaster Rock
Company Tuckaway Lodge
Contact Vincent Swazey
City Boiestown
Company Wade's Fishing Lodge
Contact Joyce Holmes & William Bacso
City Moncton
Company Wauklehegan Outfitter
Contact Ronald J. Painter
City McAdam

Company Welovet Lodge
Contact Shawn Bowes
City Newcastle
Company Whetstone Creek Lodge
Contact Gerald & Marg Hallihan
City Renous
Company White Birch Lodge
Contact Bob Walsh
City Miramichi
Company Wilson's Sporting Camps, Ltd.
Contact Keith Wilson
City McNamee

Newfoundland

Company Adventure Lodges, Inc.
Contact Gerry Pritchett
City Gander
Company Adventure North, Ltd.
Contact Bill Murphy
City Corner Brook
Company Amalijek Lodge
Contact Melvin Jeddore
City Conne River
Company Angus Wentzell's Hunting & Fishing Camps
Contact Angus Wentzell
City Corner Brooks
Company Atlantic Salmon Sports Fishing, Inc.
Contact Bill Bennett
City Gander
Company Awesome Lake Lodge
Contact Len Rich
City Clarenville
Company Bayview Lodge
Contact George Hardy
City Rose Blanche
Company Beaver Lodge Ltd.
Contact Wayne Thomas
City Grand Falls-Windsor
Company Beaver Mountain Lodge/ Migules Mountain
Contact Dave Toms
City Bishop's Falls
Company Big River Camps, Inc.
Contact R. W. Skinner
City Pasadena
Company Birchy Point Lodge
Contact Mrs. Linda Mercer
City St. John's
Company Branch River Guide & Tour Service
Contact Doreen & Walter Corcoran
City Branch
Company Cal's Hunting & Fishing
Contact Calvin White
City St. George's
Company Canadian Northern Outfitters, Inc.
Contact Bill Lynch
City Grand Falls-Windsor
Company Caribou Pond Outfitting
Contact Baxter Slade
City Glenwood
Company Central Newfoundland Outfitters
Contact Bev & Gord Robinson Reg
City Grand Falls-Windsor
Company Conne River Outfitters
Contact
City Bay d'Espoir
Company Cow Head Outfitters
Contact Eileen Hynes
City Cow Head
Company Cross Pond Lodge
Contact Neil Lucas
City Port au Port
Company Eagle Mountain Lodge
Contact
City Corner Brook
Company Fishing Buddies Unlimited
Contact Alburt Furey
City St. John's
Company Gander River Guiding Services
Contact Rodney Torraville
City Gander Bay South
Company Gander River Outfitters, Inc.
Contact Terry Cusack

City St. John's
Company Gander River Tours
Contact Dan Stiles
City Gander Bay
Company Glen Eagles Tours & Charters
Contact Derm Flynn
City Appleton
Company Goose Bay Outfitters/Eagle River Trout
Contact Peter Paor
City Glovertown
Company Grand Hermine Park
Contact Edward Burke
City Wabush
Company Hare Brothers Outfitters
Contact Henry & Clayton Hare
City Burgeo
Company Heatherton Lodge
Contact Ed & Al Skinner
City Stephenville
Company Hideaway Lodge
Contact Robert Folkes
City Grand Falls-Windsor
Company Hynes Trout Fishing & Lodging
Contact Dan & Vera Hynesq
City Portland Creek
Company Indian Bay Connections
Contact Tony Rogers
City Centreville
Company Island Outdoor Adventures, Inc.
Contact Paul Dinn
City Goulds
Company Island View Cabins
Contact Leonard J. Ryan
City O'Regan's
Company James P.Gillam Outfitting
Contact James P.Gillam
City
Company Labrador Interior Outfitters Ltd
Contact Rick Adams
City Springdale
Company Labrador Sportsfish Ltd.
Contact Vince & Jim Burton
City Mount Pearl
Company Lake Douglas
Contact Albert Mitchell
City St.John's
Company Little Harbour Deep Lodge
Contact Cyril Pelley
City Springdale
Company Log Cabin Lodge
Contact George Pike
City Black Duck Siding
Company Long Range Mountain Hunting & Fishing
Contact Sharon Biggin
City Daniel's Harbour
Company Main River Lodge
Contact Gene Manion
City Corner Brook
Company Mayflower Outfitters
Contact Trevor & Ross Pilgrim
City Roddickton
Company Mitchell's Pond Hunting & Fishing Lodge
Contact Don MacInnis
City Highlands
Company Moosehill Cabins Ltd.
Contact Michael & Margaret Gillam
City
Company Mount Peyton Outfitters
Contact Don Tremblett
City Bishop's Falls
Company Newfoundland & Labrador Hunting Ltd.
Contact Roland Reid
City Corner Brook
Company Newfoundland Adventures Ltd.
Contact Todd Wiseman
City Pasadena
Company Northern Sports Fishing
Contact Aster Caines
City Portland Creek
Company Northwoods Ventures Outfitting
Contact Cyril Smith
City Corner Brook
Company Parson's Pond & Triple K Outfitters
Contact Roger Keogh
City Parson's Pond

Company Ray's Hunting & Fishing Lodge
Contact Raymond & Daphne Broughton
City Howley
Company Rifflin' Hitch Lodge
Contact Gudrid Hutchings
City Corner Brook
Company Saunders Camps
Contact Calvin Saunders
City Gander
Company Sea Pool Cabins
Contact Hugh Wentzell
City Portland Creek
Company Sea-Run Outfishing Adventures
Contact Scott Chafe
City St.John's
Company Snowshoe Lake Hunting & Fishing Inc.
Contact John & Ron Hicks
City Millertown
Company Sou'wester Outfitting
Contact Dean & Bonnie Wheeler
City York Harbour
Company St. Bernards Aviation Ltd.
Contact Kevin J. Hackett
City St. Bernards
Company Thorburn Aviation Ltd.
Contact Gene Ploughman
City Shoal Harbour
Company Tuckamore Wilderness Ldoge
Contact Barb Genge
City Main Brook
Company Twelve Acre Lodge
Contact Douglas Enterprises Ltd.
City St.John's
Company Twin Lakes Outfitters
Contact Don Pelley
City Grand Falls-Windsor
Company Victoria Outfitters
Contact Dave Evans
City St.John's
Company Viking Trail Outfitters
Contact Wallace Maynard
City Hawke's Bay
Company Viking Trail Outfitters
Contact Martin House
City Port au Choix
Company West Woods Outfitters
Contact Neil Sweetapple & Neil MacArthur
City Doyles
Company Wilderness Horizons
Contact Howard Hewitt & Lester Goobie
City Deer Lake
Company Young's Outfitting
Contact Stanley Young
City Grey River

Northwest Territories

Company Alcantara Outfitting
Contact Charles Bourque
City Fort Smith
Company Beaufort Delta Tours
Contact Willard Hagen & Dolly Carmichael
City Inuvik
Company Beaufort Outfitting & Guiding Services
Contact Tuktoyaktuk HTC
City Tuktoyaktuk
Company Blachford Lake Lodge
Contact Mike Freeland & Bob Stephen
City Yellowknife
Company Bluefish Services
Contact Greg Robertson
City Yellowknife
Company Brabant Lodge
Contact
City Hay River
Company Captain Ron's Boat Charters
Contact Ron Williams
City Yellowknife
Company Donovan Lake Outfitters
Contact Albert Jewell
City Fort Smith
Company Eagle Point Rentals

Contact Sally Paul
City Yellowknife
Company Eagle Tours
Contact Patricia Campbell
City Inuvik
Company Gameti Sport Fishing Outfitters
Contact Ron McCuaig
City Rae Lakes
Company Hume River Enterprises
Contact Charlie Barnaby
City Fort Good Hope
Company Husky Lake Cabin Rentals
Contact John Roland
City Inuvik
Company L.A. Outfitting
Contact Denesoline Corp. Ltd.
City Lutsel K'e
Company Lady Grey Lake Outfitters
Contact Karl Hoffman
City Fort Smith
Company Lennie's Guided Tours
Contact Archie Lennie
City Tulita
Company Megatrax Winter Snow Tours
Contact Alex Beaulieu
City Yellowknife
Company Modeste Outfitters
Contact Morris Modeste
City Deline
Company North Arm Adventures
Contact
City Yellowknife
Company Peterson's Point Lake Camp
Contact Margaret, Amanda & Chad Peterson Jim
City Yellowknife
Company Sandy Point Lodge
Contact Bruno Jaurnell
City Yellowknife
Company Saunatuk Fishing Lodge
Contact James & Sharon Gruben
City Tuktoyaktuk
Company Thubun Lake Lodge
Contact
City Rae-Edzo
Company Trout Lake Dene Lodge
Contact
City Trout Lake
Company True North Safaris Ltd.
Contact Gary Jaeb
City Yellowknife
Company Vern's Venture
Contact Vern Feltham
City Yellowknife
Company Watta Lake Lodge
Contact Robin Wotherspoon
City Yellowknife
Company West to North Tours
Contact Patty West
City Norman Wells

Nova Scotia

Company Big Intervale Salmon Camp
Contact Ruth Schneeberger
City Margaree Valley
Company Chute Pool Lodge
Contact Al Rothwell
City Dartmouth
Company Kaegudeck Lake Lodge
Contact
City Dartmouth

Ontario

Company 3 Mile Bay Tent & Trailer Park
Contact Vern & Helen Phillips & Family
City White Lake
Company Abram Lake Park
Contact The Pizziols
City Sioux Lookout
Company Agimac River Outfitters
Contact Harold St. Cyr

City Renfrew
Company Agnew Lake Lodge Ltd.
Contact Robert & Marlene Kennedy
City Webbwood
Company Ahmic Lake Resort
Contact Verna & Rob Hibbert
City Ahmic Harbour
Company Air Kenda
Contact Roy & June Bennett
City Gogama
Company Air-Dale Flying Service Ltd.
Contact
City Sault Ste. Marie
Company Albany River Outfitters
Contact Jerel & Sharon Johnson
City Pickle Lake
Company Alconsen Fly-In Outpost Camps
Contact Alex & Helene Bosse
City Elliot Lake
Company Allanwater Bridge Lodge
Contact Barney & Jane Jelinski
City Allanwater Bridge
Company Anderson's Lodge
Contact Dick Fahlman & Jackie Premack
City Sioux Lookout
Company Angus Lake Lodge
Contact Elizabeth & George Tamchina
City Temagami
Company Antler's Kingfisher Lodge
Contact Doug & Sandra Antler
City Deux Rivieres
Company Ara Lake Camp Ltd.
Contact Dick & Shirley Fayle
City Beardmore
Company Argyle Lake Lodge
Contact Chuck & Joan Fernley
City Schomberg
Company Arrowhead Camp
Contact Clyde Mason
City Nestor Falls
Company Artesian Wells Resort
Contact Paul & Barb Scidel
City Nolalu
Company Auld Reekie Lodge
Contact Doug & Cathie White
City Gowganda
Company Bain Lake Camp
Contact Beverly & Howard Dobbs
City Loring
Company Ballantyne's Indian Lake Lodge
Contact Scott & Leigh Ballantyne
City Vermilion Bay
Company Barkwick Camp
Contact Bill & Doreen Wickens
City Madawaska
Company Barr Woods Resort
Contact Burrows Family
City Haileybury
Company Basket Lake Camp
Contact Olga North
City Dryden
Company Bayview Camp & Cottages
Contact Barb & Mike Batsford
City Callander
Company Bear Paw Lodge
Contact
City Armstrong
Company Bear Trail Lodge
Contact Charlie & Kristine Haussermann
City Waldhof
Company Beaverland Camp
Contact The Dykstra's
City North Bay
Company Becca's Haven
Contact Phyllis & Rick Flewelling
City Temagami
Company Bending Lake Lodge
Contact Mike Muelken
City Ontario
Company Berglund's Outposts
Contact Wayne & Carol Berglund
City Ignace
Company Big Bear Camp
Contact Claude & Lucille Charbonneau
City Timmins
Company Big Hook Wilderness Camp
Contact Steve & Evie Hartle
City Red Lake
Company Big North Lodge
Contact Alex & Pat Rheault

City Minaki
Company Big Vermillion Lodge
Contact Jim & Doreen Kusick
City Hudson
Company Biloski Resort
Contact Bernie & Dorothy
City Thunder Pay
Company Birch Island Lodge & Air Service
Contact Gary & Margo Schroeder
City Little Current
Company Birch Island Resort
Contact Mike & Wendy Reid
City Minai
Company Birch Lake Lodge
Contact Barry & Edith Labine
City Red Lake
Company Birch Point Camp-Lodge
Contact The Greens
City Red Lake
Company Birch Point Resort
Contact June & Bob Gibbs
City Thunder Bay
Company Black Bear Camp
Contact Vicki & Robert Lowe
City Webbwood
Company Black Rock Resort
Contact Sverre & Hildur Kjevik
City Manitowaning
Company Blake's Wilderness Outpost
Contact John & Marie Blake
City Elliot Lake
Company Blue Fox Camp
Contact Dr. Paul R. Morgan
City Thornhill
Company Blue Mountain Lodge
Contact The Malott's
City Sudbury
Company Bonnie Lake Camping
Contact Tom & Paula Stephanie
City Bracebridge
Company Booi's Wilderness Lodge & Outposts Ltd.
Contact Jim & Tracy Booi & Family
City Red Lake
Company Border Outposts
Contact Dave Schneider
City Minaki
Company Branch's Seine River Lodge
Contact Carl & Joan Branch
City Atikokan
Company Brandts' Resort
Contact Wayne & Linda Brandt
City Nolalu
Company Brooks Cottages
Contact Chris & Christine Brooks
City Loring
Company Brown's Clearwater West Lodge/Outposts
Contact Barry Brown
City Atikokan
Company Brunswick Lake Lodge
Contact Marcel Dumais
City Etobicoke
Company Buck & Bingwood Cabins
Contact Brock & Brenda Chisholm
City Homepayne
Company Bull Moose Camp
Contact Tom & Shara Metzner
City Red Lake
Company Bullock's Gowganda Lake Camp
Contact Dave & Mary Bullock
City Gowganda
Company Camp Anjigami
Contact George & Elizabeth Young
City Wawa
Company Camp Can-USA
Contact Nelson & Brenda Leudke
City Temagami
Company Camp Gutelius on Dog Lake
Contact Mark & Marta Lamoureux
City Missanabie
Company Camp Horizon
Contact Denny & Ruth Dusky
City Field
Company Camp La Plage
Contact The Bedards
City Verner
Company Camp Lochalsh Ltd.
Contact Chris & Lynne Wilson
City Wawa
Company Camp Manitou
Contact Jerry Kostiuk
City Fort Frances

Company Camp McIntosh
Contact Jim & Madeleine Roger
City Dowling
Company Camp Michi Wawa
Contact Ken and Luanne Brezenski
City Ontario
Company Camp Midgard
Contact Manfred E. (Fred) Mueller
City Savant Lake
Company Camp Narrows Lodge
Contact Tom Pearson
City Fort Frances
Company Camp Raymond
Contact Fred & Barb Roth
City Lavigne
Company Camp Wanikewin Lodge
Contact Ken & Dee Baker
City Albn
Company Camp Waterfall
Contact Nancy & Rob Rummery
City Kenora
Company Camp Wenasaga
Contact Brian Pudil
City Ear Falls
Company Canada North Lodge Ltd.
Contact Mike & Julie Hoffman
City Ear Falls
Company Canadian Fly-In Fishing, Ltd.
Contact Jim Thomas
City Red Lake
Company Canadian Wilderness Camps & Outfitters
Contact Wolf & Gica Lehnhoff
City Kenora
Company Canadian Wilderness Outposts
Contact Jordie & Mitzi Turcotte
City Fort Frances
Company Cat Island Lodge
Contact Mike & Gaye Tamburrino
City Red Lake
Company Cedar Grove Camp
Contact Nancy & Casey Goodhew Bill
City Nipissing
Company Cedar Grove Lodge
Contact Gary Fleming
City Huntsville
Company Cedar Island Lodge
Contact Jim Moore
City Emo
Company Cedar Shores Resort & Wilderness Camps
Contact Bob Binkley
City Jellicoe
Company Century Lodge
Contact Rich & Kay Tyran
City Dryden
Company Chapleau Air Services & Sunset View Camp
Contact Lee Cole
City Capleau
Company Chapleau Lodge Resort
Contact Bob & Sally Landry
City Capleau
Company Chaudiere Lodge
Contact Tony & Betsy Stensen
City Monetville
Company Chimo Lodge & Outposts
Contact Peter Hagedorn
City Red Lake
Company Chisholm's Kaby Kabins
Contact Jim & Helen Chisholm
City Hornepayne
Company Christy's Cove Cottages
Contact Christina & Jonathan Wiersma Maike
City Britt
Company Cianci's Holiday North Lodge
Contact Frank & Lucy Cianci
City Red Lake
Company Clarks Camp
Contact Karla & Wayne Clark
City Vermilion Bay
Company Clear Lake Cottages
Contact Daniel & Deanne Cudmore
City
Company Cobb Bay Camp
Contact Henry Theelen
City Igance
Company Come By Chance Resort Ltd.
Contact Joe & Mary Albert & Ilona
City Nolalu
Company Como Lake Resort

Contact Lee Burk
City Chapleau
Company Cookie's Resort
Contact Jack & Cookie Armstrong
City Sioux Narrows
Company Coppen's Resort Limited
Contact Syd Coppen & Ed Plichta
City Fort Frances
Company Cormorant Lake Lodge
Contact Bob & Gale Extence
City Ear Falls
Company Crane's Lochaven Wilderness Lodge
Contact Eric Crane
City Noelville
Company Crawford's Camp
Contact Bob Rydberg
City Sioux Narrows
Company Crooked Lake Lodge
Contact Grant & Win Palmer & Hugh & Della Allan
City Alban
Company Crow Rock Camp, Inc.
Contact Wendel Dafcik
City Kenora
Company Crystal Harbour Resort
Contact Sandy Sundmark
City Sioux Narrows
Company Cygnet Lake Trailer Park
Contact Bill & Sandi Demkier
City Minaki
Company Deer Horn Lodge, Inc.
Contact Ruth, Jeff & Karen Chantler Dave
City Parry Sound
Company Deer Lake Cottages
Contact Stan & Anita Soloy
City Warren
Company Deer Trail Lodge
Contact Marie & Ian Seymour
City Vermilion Bay
Company Diamond Key Resort
Contact Dave & Maggie Powell
City Britt
Company Discovery Lake Lodge & Outpost
Contact Nichole & Kaylee Bohnen Paul
City Sioux Lookout
Company Dogtooth Resort
Contact Wayne & Patty Jones
City Kenora
Company Dolphin Motel & Cottages
Contact Beverley & Bayden Brownlee
City North Bay
Company Donnelly's Minnitaki Lodge
Contact Fran & Lil Donnelly
City Sioux Lookout
Company Drift-Inn Lodge
Contact Jeff & Morgan Laddy
City Nipissing
Company Duck Bay Lodge
Contact Dave & Sheree Swistun
City Sleeman
Company Dunc Lake Resort
Contact Theresa Burk
City Marathon
Company Duncan Lake Camp
Contact Ed & Faye Barnstaple
City Gowganda
Company Dunlop Lake Lodge
Contact Don & Pat Mackay
City Elliot Lake
Company Eagle Lake Lodge
Contact Orrie & Paula Colegrove
City Eagle River
Company Eagle Lake Sportsmen's Lodge
Contact Cindy & Jim Buhlman
City Vermilion Bay
Company Eden Camp Resort
Contact Tom & Joyce Jackson
City Thessalon
Company Edgewater Park Lodge
Contact Tom Thornborrow & Bob Harris
City Kearney
Company Ejay's Portage Bay Camp
Contact Evert & Jennie Cummer
City Ear Falls
Company Elk Cabins
Contact Rene Pelissier & Serge Marin
City Elk Lake
Company Elliot Lake Aviation Limited/Fishland Camp
Contact Bruno Rapp

City Elliot Lake
Company English River Fishing Adventures
Contact
City Grassy Narrows
Company s Birchdale Lodge Ernie & Lynn
Contact Ernie & Lynn
City Waldhof
Company Errington's Wilderness Islands
Contact Jr. & Doris Errington Al
City Sault Ste. Marie
Company Esnagami Wilderness Lodge
Contact Eric Lund
City Nakina
Company Esnagi Lodge
Contact Donna & Wally Leigh
City London
Company Evergreen Lodge Ltd.
Contact Mal & Pat Tygesson
City Eagle River
Company Ewok Cabins
Contact Harvey Barnes
City Sultan
Company Excellent Adventure Outposts
Contact Foron & Joyce Buckler Bob & Gale Extence
City Perrault Falls
Company Fin & Feather Resort
Contact Ron & Dee Clark
City Eagle Lake
Company Fireside Lodge
Contact Alan & Audrey Brandys
City Sioux Lookout
Company First Island Cottages
Contact Frank & Carol Yuhas
City Chapleau
Company Five Mile Lake Lodge
Contact Gary & Karen Pedersen
City Chapleau
Company Flayer's Lodge
Contact Hilding & Marion Flayer
City Ignace
Company Fletcher Lake Lodge
Contact Wayne & Jeanne Thompson
City Kenora
Company Flindt Landing Camp
Contact David & Louise Gish
City Savant Lake
Company Floating Lodges of Sioux Narrows
Contact Jim & Tanis Rebbetoy
City Sioux Narrows
Company French River Lodge
Contact Joe & Anne Ott
City Alban
Company Frog Rapids Camp
Contact Lawrence & Therese Bower
City Sioux Lookout
Company Frontier Lodge
Contact John & Betty Middleton
City Elliot Lake
Company Garden Island Lodge
Contact Norm & Val Paterson
City New Liskeard
Company Gardiner Outfitters & Air Service
Contact Ron & Shirley Barron
City Cochrane
Company Gawley's Little Beaver Lodge & Outpost
Contact Doug & Gayle Gawley
City Ear Falls
Company Ge-Kay-Da Wilderness Camp
Contact Colin & Liz Elkin
City Pointe au Baril
Company Georgian Bay Fishing Camp
Contact David Bulger
City Parry Sound
Company Ghost River Camp & Sturgeon River Camp
Contact Donna & Darrell Kartinen Alfred
City Sioux Lookout
Company Glen Echo Cottages
Contact David & Connie Waye

City Callander
Company Glenwood Cottages & Marina
Contact Joyce & Ken Fosberry
City McKellar
Company Gogama Lodge & Outfitters
Contact Madge & Dick Harlock
City Gogama
Company Goose Bay Camp
Contact A. Langford
City Ear Falls
Company Gosenda Lodge Ltd.
Contact Richard & Evelyn Glazier
City Timmins
Company Granite Hill Lake Resort
Contact Paul & John Smart
City Homepayne
Company Grant Outfitters
Contact Ted & Linda Grant
City Longlac
Company Gravel Lakes Cabins
Contact Sven & Shirley Lindfors
City Nolalu
Company Green Island Lodge
Contact Bob & Angie Korzinski
City Fort Frances
Company Green Lake Camp
Contact Charles Campbell
City Deux Rivieres
Company Green Wilderness Camp
Contact Linda & Warren Thibodeau
City Gogama
Company Green's Fly-In Outpost Camps
Contact Bob & Jack Green & Bernie Harapiak
City Red Lake
Company Grey Owl Camps
Contact Greg & Susan Swiatek
City Biscotasing
Company H&C Family Lodge
Contact Henri & Carole Savoie
City White River
Company Hache's Bear Camp Ltd.
Contact Camille & Marlene Hache
City Hillsport
Company Hagar's Cedar Point Resort
Contact Roger & Carol Henegar
City Perrault Falls
Company Happy Day Lodge
Contact Gil & Ruth Weber
City Chapleau
Company Happy Holiday Cottages
Contact Fred & Gladys Hinton
City Blind River
Company Happy Landing Lodge
Contact Geordy & Barb Roy
City Emo
Company Hawk Air
Contact Kelly & Mary Culhane
City Wawa
Company Hawk Lake Lodge
Contact Garry & Sandy Delton
City Kenora
Company Hearst Air Service
Contact George & Michael Veilleux
City Hearst
Company Hemp's Camp & Air Foleyet
Contact Richard & Evelyn Glazier
City Foleyet
Company Holinshead Lake Resort & Outposts
Contact Mitch Hagen
City Kakabeka Falls
Company Horseshoe Island Camp
Contact Don & Marjorie Hueston
City Matachewan
Company Horwood Lake Lodge
Contact Cindy & Barry Edwards
City Timmins
Company Huber's Lone Pine Camp
Contact Walter Huber
City Dryden
Company Hyatt's Manion Lake Camp
Contact Don & Brenda Hyatt
City Mine Centre
Company Icosa Village Corp.
Contact Lina & Henri Lacroix
City Port Loring
Company Ignace Outposts Ltd.
Contact Brad & Karen Greaves
City Ignace
Company Indiaonta Resort
Contact Herb & Vi Humphreys

City Atikokan
Company Inverlochy Resort
Contact Karl & Mai Saarna
City Nobel
Company Island 10 Fishing Retreat
Contact Ken Byberg
City New Liskeard
Company Island Lake Camp
Contact Gord & Ellie Mitchell
City Field
Company James Bay Outfitters & Air Service Ltd.
Contact Rob Lafleur
City Cochrane
Company John Theriault Air Ltd.
Contact John Theriault
City Sault Ste. Marie
Company Journey's North Outfitting, Inc.
Contact Nancy Kyro
City Geraldton
Company Kanip Kinniwabi
Contact Bill & Barb Beckham
City Wawa
Company Kanipahow Kamps Ltd.
Contact
City Chapleau
Company Kanukawa Outfitters
Contact Terry & Diane Carlin
City Deep River
Company Kap Outfitters
Contact Ron & Lise Marchand
City Kapuskasing
Company Kashabowie Outposts
Contact Gerri & Dave Sutton & Fern Duquette
City Thunder Bay
Company KCR Camp Limited
Contact Richard & Gloria Castle
City Kenora
Company Kenda Wilderness Lodge
Contact The Bennetts
City Gogama
Company Kennisis Lake Lodge
Contact Adelheid & Dan Buhl
City Haliburton
Company Ket-Chun-Eny Lodge
Contact The St. Germain's
City Temagami
Company Key Marine Resort
Contact Gil & Val Gariup
City Britt
Company Killarney Mountain Lodge
Contact Maurice & Annabelle East
City Killarney
Company Kimberley's Eagle West Resort
Contact Todd & Sean Steve
City Vermilion Bay
Company Kinogami Lodge
Contact Robert & Marilyn Plourde
City Chapleau
Company Knobby's Fly-In Camps
Contact Knobby & Bobbie Clark
City Sioux Lookout
Company L & M Fly-In Outpost
Contact Larry & Mary Adams
City Emo
Company Labelle's Birch Point Camp
Contact Dale & Linda Labelle
City Devlin
Company Lakair Lodge
Contact Kevin & Leslie Cameron
City Monetville
Company Lake Herridge Lodge
Contact Pat & Mike Thomas
City Temagami
Company Lake Kashabowie Lodge
Contact Dan & Irene Mado & Sons
City Thunder Bay
Company Lake Obabika Lodge
Contact The Herburger F Amily
City River Valley
Company Lake of the Woods Houseboats
Contact Noreen Luce
City Sioux Narrows
Company Land O'Lakes Lodge
Contact Christine & Robin Burke
City
Company Lang Lake Resort
Contact Howard & Racel Acton
City Espanola
Company Leisure Bay Holiday Resort
Contact Karl & Klaudia Gross
City Pointe Au Baril

Company Lindbergh's Air Service
Contact Brian Simms
City Cochrane
Company Loch Island Lodge Ltd.
Contact Andy & Amy Wilson
City Dubreuilville
Company Lochlomond Camp
Contact Larry & Deb Hadenko
City Longlac
Company Log Chateau Lodge
Contact Geoff & Jenny Pinckston
City Blind River
Company Long Point Airways
Contact The Wilsons
City Elk Lake
Company Long Point Lodge
Contact The Bowens
City
Company Lookout River Outfitters
Contact Bruce & Margaret Hyer
City RR#14 Dog Lake Road
Company Loon Haunt Outposts
Contact Bill & Louise Coppen
City Red Lake
Company Loon Lodge
Contact Moskwa Family
City Temagami
Company Lost Island Lodge
Contact Jim & Marlene Hayes
City Hudson
Company Lost Lake Wilderness Lodge
Contact The Dunkins
City Elk Lake
Company Louie's Outpost Hunting & Fishing Service
Contact Louie Horwath
City Blind River
Company Lucky Strike Camp
Contact The Bennings
City Lavigne
Company Lukinto Lake Lodge
Contact Bob & Faye Harkness
City Longlac
Company Lunge Lodge
Contact Wolfgang & Barbara Strafehl
City Monetville
Company Mache-Kino Fly-In Lodge
Contact Denis & Val Ladouceur
City Chapleau
Company Maiden Bay Camp
Contact Joan & Bill Hubbard
City Alliston
Company Makokibatan Lodge
Contact
City North Bay
Company Manitoba Trophy Outposts
Contact Brett & Judy Geary
City Red Lake
Company Manitouwabing Tent & Trailer Park
Contact Harry & Sandy Vandermeer
City Parry Sound
Company Maple Grove Cottages
Contact Reg & Lois White
City Mindemoya
Company Mar's Outfitting Service
Contact Marcel & Nancy Seguin
City Noelville
Company Marsh Bay Resort
Contact Jim & Debbie O'Brien
City Cobalt
Company Marten River Lodge
Contact The Cracknell's
City Marten River
Company Martin's Camp
Contact Bing & Dainne Hoddinott
City Nipissing
Company Mattice Lake Outfitters Ltd.
Contact Don & Annette Elliot
City Armstrong
Company Maynard Lake Lodge
Contact Dale & Laura Mychalyshyn
City Kenora
Company Mead's Spruce Island Camp
Contact Harv & Janna Sadlovsky Suzy Mead
City Kenora
Company Megisan Lake Lodge
Contact George & Brenda Nixon
City Willowdale
Company Memquisit Lodge Inc.
Contact Jeanne Trivett
City Monetville
Company Merkel's Camp

Contact Terry & Merrill Kluke
City Dryden
Company Meta Lake Lodge Ltd.
Contact Joe & Marg Strangway
City Nakina
Company Minakwa Lodge
Contact Etienne & Rejeanne deBlois
City Gogama
Company Minnehaha Camp Resort
Contact HArtley & Sherry Moore
City Loring
Company Missinaibi Outfitters
Contact Owen & Denyse Korpela
City Mattice
Company Mitchells' Camp
Contact Don & Mary Mitchell
City Spanish
Company Moose Horn Lodge
Contact Jeff & Heather Schuab
City Sioux Lookout
Company Moosewa Outpost
Contact Ivor & Brenda Horncastle
City Massey
Company Morest Camp Joan & Glen Currie
Contact
City Iron Bridge
Company Morin's All Seasons Resort Ltd.
Contact The Morins
City Gogams
Company Motel Bienvenue
Contact Ray & Pauline Dubreuil
City Dubreuilville
Company Motlong's Rod & Reel
Contact Dick & Alice Motlong
City Sioux Narrows
Company Mountain Cove Lodge
Contact Grace & Michael Piano
City Espanola
Company Mountain Home Lodge
Contact Warren Shewfelt & Julie Dale
City Marten River
Company Mountain View Camp
Contact Bill & Terry Buckley
City Blind River
Company Mountain View Resort
Contact Michael & Yvonne Schut
City Mindemoya
Company Nagagami Lodge
Contact
City North Bay
Company Naiscoot Lodge
Contact The Lutschers
City Pointe Au Baril
Company Nakina Outpost Camps & Air Service
Contact Don & Millie Bourdignon
City Nakina
Company Nanmark Cottages
Contact Terry & Liz Hyatt
City Callander
Company Nestor Falls Fly-In Outpost
Contact Dave & Michelle Beaushene
City Nestor Falls
Company Nielsen's Fly-In Lodge
Contact Don & Lynn Pursch
City Nestor Falls
Company Nipigon River Bear Hunts
Contact Bob Bearman
City Nipigon
Company Nipissing Lodge
Contact The Conrads & The Craftchicks
City Nipissing
Company Normandy Lodge
Contact Klaus & Wilma Brauer
City Wawa
Company North Country Lodge
Contact Ted Moyle
City Wawa
Company North Country Lodge
Contact Dale & Doreen Leutschaft
City Vermilion Bay
Company North Shore Lodge & Airstrip
Contact Tom & Chris Guercio
City Eagle River
Company North Spirit Lake Lodge Ltd.
Contact Bill & Valerie Nelson
City Red Lake
Company Northern Lights Resort
Contact Hermann & Lise Stroeher
City Loring
Company Northernaire Lodge

Contact Jane Burgess
City Evansville
Company Northland Outfitters
Contact
City Nakina
Company Northwest Flying Ltd.
Contact Jack Pope
City Nestor Falls
Company Nungesser Lake Lodge
Contact Bob & Rosie Kohlnhofer
City Red Lake
Company O'Sullivan's Rainbow
Contact Al & Donna Reid
City Nakina
Company Olivier's Fly-In Camps/ Horne Air Ltd.
Contact Maurice & Ruby Olivier
City Homepayne
Company Ontario North Outpost
Contact Barz & Clark
City Eagle River
Company Ontario Wilderness Houseboat Rentals
Contact Stewart & Yvonne Gill
City Morson
Company Open Bay Lodge Ltd.
Contact Basil & Pam Lemieux
City Upsala
Company Open Season Sometimes Sno'dInn
Contact Sheila Bliesath
City Wawa
Company Oskondaga River Outfitters
Contact Allan & Mary Ward
City Shebandowan
Company Owl's Nest Lodge
Contact Betty Ann & Wayne Hawthorn
City Alban
Company Parry South Air Service
Contact Dietmar Zschogner
City McKellar
Company Pine Beach Lodge
Contact H.C.Johnson
City Eagle River
Company Pine Cliff Lodge
Contact Richard & Kaylene Foley
City Dryden
Company Pine Cove Lodge
Contact Minnie Massicotte
City Noelville
Company Pine Grove Resort Cottages
Contact Bill & Carol Chambers
City Port Loring
Company Pine Point Resort Ltd.
Contact William & Arlene Haney
City Upsala
Company Pine Portage Lodge
Contact The Watson Family
City Wawa
Company Pioneer Lodge/Dog Lake
Contact Mike & Claude Gratton
City Wawa
Company Pipestone Fly-In Outposts
Contact Mike & Patti Henry
City Emo
Company Pipestone Point Resort
Contact Peter & Shirley Haugen
City Kenora
Company Placid Bay Lodge
Contact Dennie & Bev Shillinglaw
City North Bay
Company Pleasant Cove Fishing Resort
Contact The Bishops
City Pointe Au Baril
Company Polar Bear Camp & Fly-In Outfitter
Contact Billy Konopelky
City Cochrane
Company Polar Star Lodge
Contact Norah & Ross Finch
City Wabigoon
Company Pozniak's Lodge
Contact Robert & Cecile Fielding
City
Company Prairie Bee Camp
Contact Steve & Mary Rupp
City Capleau
Company Providence Bay Tent & Trailer Park
Contact Chick & Irene Cornish
City Providence Bay
Company R.aM Outfitters
Contact The Despres
City PO Box 2440

Company Rainbow Airways
Contact
City Dunchurch
Company Rainbow Cottages Resort
Contact Tony & Heather Kenny
City Bailieboro
Company Rainbow Point Lodge
Contact Bob & Gale Extence
City Perrault Falls
Company Red Indian Lodge
Contact Herb & Mary Anne Hoffman
City Sioux Narrows
Company Red Pine Lodge
Contact Garry & Cathy Litt
City Foleyet
Company Red Pine Wilderness Lodge
Contact James & Janice Bowden
City Haileybury
Company Riverlake Cottages & Campground
Contact Ed & Helen Larson
City McKellar
Company Riverland Camp & Outfitters
Contact Jay & Maryann McRae
City Madawaska
Company Rob's Canadian Wilderness Resort
Contact Rob & Sandy Brodhagen
City Dryden
Company Rockview Camp
Contact Susanne & Andre Rieser
City Callander
Company Rocky Shore Lodge
Contact Norm & Sue Cook
City Perrault Falls
Company Ross' Camp
Contact Pat & Wayne Howard
City Emo
Company Route Lake Lodge
Contact Hermann & Claudia Vogel
City Oxdrift
Company Royal Windsor Lodge
Contact Art & Olga Jalkanen
City Nipigon
Company Ryan's Campsite
Contact Robert & Jean Lucier
City Madawaska
Company Sac Bay Lodge Camp
Contact Fred & Heidi Wittwer
City Ignace
Company Saganash Outpost Camp
Contact Richard Landriault
City Kapuskasing
Company Samoset Lodge
Contact Ruth Hauta
City Monetville
Company Sand Bay Resort
Contact Bill & Barb Davis
City Nobel
Company Sandy Beach Lodge
Contact Wade & Tom Mitchell Roger
City Red Lake
Company Sandy Haven Camp
Contact Annette & Howie Thomas
City Sturgeon Falls
Company Schell's Camp & Park
Contact Don & Carolyn Hoshel
City Alban
Company Seagull Lodge
Contact Ed & Kevin Blondin
City Sturgeon Falls
Company Shining Tree Tourist Camp
Contact Bob & Sue Evans
City Shining Tree
Company Shooting Star Camp
Contact Shane & Betty Looby
City Metagama
Company Showalters Fly-In Camps
Contact The Showalters
City Ear Falls
Company Shuswap Camp
Contact Heinz & Gerda Loewenberg
City Monetville
Company Silver Poplar Grove Camps
Contact Bill & Gail Paul
City Hornepayne
Company Silverwater Lodge
Contact Mike & Heather Jeschonnek
City Temagami
Company Silverwood Fishing Lodge
Contact The Holl's
City Point au Baril
Company Slate Falls Outposts & Redpine Lodge
Contact Verne & Andrea Hollett

City Sioux Lookout
Company Slate Falls Vindar Outfitters
Contact Marjorie Chyk
City Sioux Lookout
Company Slippery Winds Wilderness Lodge
Contact Doug & Georgie Knipe
City Fort Frances
Company Snug Haven Resort
Contact Donna & Brian Graziotto
City Nobel
Company Sonny-Bob Lodge
Contact Bob & Pat Curtis
City Sault Ste. Marie
Company South Bay on Gull Rock
Contact Mary & Harry Spenceley
City Red Lake
Company Springhaven Lodge
Contact The Scales
City Point Au Baril
Company Stanley's West Arm Resort
Contact Marvin & Carol Wisneski
City Vermilion Bay
Company Stanton Airways
Contact John & Helen Stanton
City Severn Bridge
Company Stillwater Lake Airways Ltd.
Contact William & Lynn Krolyk
City Vermilion Bay
Company Stillwater Trailer Park
Contact Bill & Gina Barnes
City Nipigon
Company Sudbury Aviation Ltd/ No.Trails Outpost Camps
Contact Marg. Watson-Hyland
City Azilda
Company Sunbeam Bungalows Ltd.
Contact David Bain
City Callander
Company Sunny Hill Resort
Contact The Allinghams
City Barry's Bay
Company Sunset Cove Camp
Contact John & Louise Unsworth
City Nestor Falls
Company Sunset Cove Camp
Contact Doris & Franz Rittscher
City Callander
Company Sydney Lake Lodge
Contact John & Ute Finlayson
City Red Lake
Company Tama Kwa Vacationland
Contact Isolde & Herbert Krob
City Callander
Company Tata-Chika-Pika Lodge
Contact The Neils
City Gogama
Company Ted McLeod's Sunset Country Outfitters Inc.
Contact Ted McLeod & Lana Hurd
City Atikokan
Company Temagami Lodge
Contact Julia & Paul Forsyth
City Temagami
Company Temagami Riverside Lodge
Contact Roger Watson & Linda Dorr
City Field
Company Temagami Shores Inn & Resort
Contact The Bickells
City Temagami
Company Temple Bay Lodge Ltd.
Contact Bob & Peg Paluch
City Eagle River
Company The Island Lodge
Contact Bob & Chris Phillips
City Whitefish Falls
Company The Ogoki Frontier, Inc.
Contact Paul Boucher
City Thunder Bay
Company Thousand Lakes Resort
Contact George & Jenny Brown
City Thunder Bay
Company Timber Edge Camps
Contact Ron & Marg Lodge
City Sioux Lookout
Company Timberdoodle Lodge
Contact Neil & Brenda Smith
City Hornepayne
Company Timberidge Air & Outposts
Contact Corky Sischo
City Nakina
Company Timberlane Lodge
Manitoulin
Contact The Mackan Family
City Mindemoya

Company Tornado's Canadian Resorts Inc.
Contact Rogerson's Lodges
City Port Loring
Company Totem Lodge
Contact The Browns
City Sioux Narrows
Company Totem Point Lodge
Contact Sylvia & Joe Angi
City Noelville
Company Trail's End Lodge
Contact The Williams
City Emo
Company Tumblehome Lodge
Contact Ed & Shirley Giffin
City Clarendon
Company Twin J Hide-A-Way
Contact Jim & Judy Taziar
City Gogama
Company Twin Lakes Outfitters
Contact Bill Pocock
City Nakina
Company Uchi Lake Lodge
Contact Judy Henrickson
City Sioux Lookout
Company Vermilion Bay Lodge
Contact Gord & Susanne Bastable
City Vermilion Bay
Company Viking Outpost Cabins, Ltd.
Contact Hugh & Craig Carlson
City Red Lake
Company Vista Lake Outfitters
Contact Dennis & Evelyn Mousseau
City Savant Lake
Company Wakami Outfitters
Contact Marty & Ina Elliott
City Chapleau
Company Wakomata Shores Resort Ltd.
Contact James Burns & Norma Johnson
City Thessalon
Company Walsten Outpost Camps
Contact Neil & Kevin Walsten
City Kenora
Company Walton's Kay Vee Lodge
Contact The Waltons
City Hornepayne
Company Waltonian Inn Lodge & Cottages
Contact Nadia Day Frank & Thea Marusich
City Callander
Company Waterfalls Lodge
Contact Bob & Marilou Rogers
City Spanish
Company Welcome Lodge Nipissing
Contact Gary & Angela Martin
City Lavigne
Company West Arm Lodge
Contact Ray & Ron Pedneault
City St. Charles
Company White Pine Lodge
Contact Joseph & Mary Ellen Schaut
City Sioux Narrows
Company Whitefish Bay Camp
Contact Bob & Peg Hunger
City Nestor Falls
Company Whitefish Lodge
Contact John & Lorna Chiupka
City Wawa
Company Whitehaven Cottages
Contact Bill & Linda Strain
City Little Current
Company Whitewing Resort & Floating Lodges
Contact Dave & Bobbie McDonald
City Ear Falls
Company Wilderness Air Limited
Contact Bob Huitikka
City Vermilion Bay
Company Wilderness Lodge
Contact Judy & Eric Wismer
City Elliot Lake
Company Wilderness North
Contact
City Thunder Bay
Company Wilderness Outfitters
Contact Clark & Sandra Vanbuskirk
City Chapleau
Company Wildewood Fly In Lodge & Outpost
Contact Richard Kungle
City Savant Lake
Company Wiley Point Lodge
Contact Eric Brown

City Sioux Narrows
Company Williams Lake Lodge
Contact Peter & Kathy Stieglitz
City Dryden
Company Winnetou Resort
Contact Hank & Betty Thierauf
City Nobel
Company Witch Bay Canadian Outposts
Contact Randy & Cindy Thomas
City Kenora
Company Wogenstahl's Canadian Resort
Contact The Wogenstahls
City Vermilion Bay
Company Wolseley Lodge
Contact Jules Morin
City Noelville
Company Woman River Camp
Contact Dary & Diane Wilkinson
City Ear Falls
Company Woman River Fly-In Outposts
Contact Les & Sandy Schultz
City Ear Falls
Company Woodhouse Camp
Contact The Woodhouses
City Foleyet
Company Woods Bay Lodge
Contact Doris & Uwe Liefland
City MacTier
Company Wright Point Resort
Contact Joe & Carrie Whitmell
City Port Loring
Company Young Lake Lodge
Contact Steve & Debbie Vincent
City Ignance
Company Young's Wilderness Camp
Contact Perry & Carol Anniuk
City Nestor Falls
Company Yvon & Son's Bear Hunt
Contact Yvon & Gilles Goudreau
City Chelmsford

Prince Edward Island

Company Island Rod & Flies
Contact Stu Simpson
City Charlottetown
Company
Contact Brian Dempsey
City Charlottetown

Québec

Company Abitibi-Temiscaming Fly Fishing, Inc.
Contact Lou Cote'
City Macamic
Company Ashuanipi Hunting Outfitters
Contact Francis Rioux
City Ste. Francoise
Company Francine Melancon Milot
Contact
City Ste.-Anne-du-lac
Company George River Lodge, Inc.
Contact Pierre et Jean Paquet
City St. Augustin
Company Jupiter 12
Contact Gilles Dumaresq
City Quebec
Company Kenauk, The Seigniory at Montebello
Contact
City Montebello
Company Labrador 2BG Adventure Inc.
Contact Mr.F.Denis Boisvert
City St. Etienne de Lauzon
Company Les Entreprises Du Lac Perdu, Inc.
Contact Michel and Mary-Anne Auclair
City Sainte-Brigitte De Laval
Company Miwapanee Lodge Resort
Contact

City Kipawa
Company Moosehead Lodge
Contact Malcolm Taggart
City Messines
Company Oasis Du Gouin
Contact Jackie Leblanc
City Repentigny
Company Payne River /Tunulik River Fishing Camps
Contact Steve Ashton
City Baie D'Urfe
Company Pourvoire Lac du Blanc
Contact Linda Poitras
City Ste. Alexis des Monts
Company Pourvoirie Du Balbuzard Sauvage Inc.
Contact Annick Montagne/Willy Viens
City Senneterre
Company St. Paul's Salmon Fishing Club
Contact Jules Goodman
City Sillery
Company Tasiujatsoak Wilderness Camp
Contact Chesley & Cathy Andersen
City Chelseu
Company Ungava Adventures
Contact Sammy Cantafio
City Pointe Claire
Company Wedge Hills Lodge
Contact Diane Fortier
City Schefferville

Saskatchewan

Company 24 North Outfitters
Contact Phil Chalifour
City Leoville
Company Aerial Adventures
Contact Barry & Lana Prall
City Nipawin
Company Angler's Trail Resort
Contact Ivan & Elsie Fauth
City Beauval
Company Athabasca Camps
Contact Cliff Blackmur
City Saskatoon
Company Athabasca Fishing Lodges
Contact Cliff Blackmu
City Saskatoon
Company Athabasca Lone Wolf Camps
Contact Brian MacDonald
City Buffalo Narrows
Company Austin's Service
Contact Austin Tide
City Herbert
Company B & L Cabins & Outfitters Ltd.
Contact Blaine & Linda Cunningham
City La Ronge
Company Bait-Masters Hunting Camps
Contact Brain E. & Sylvia Hoffart
City Green Lake
Company Barrier Beach Resort
Contact Scott O'Bertos
City Tisdale
Company Bay Resort
Contact
City Prince Albert
Company Beaver Lodge Fly-Inn Ltd.
Contact Wellace & Elaine Johnson
City Spalding
Company Besnard Lake Lodge
Contact
City La Ronge
Company Beyond La Ronge Lodge
Contact Andy & Beatrice Fecke
City Melfort
Company Big Eddy Camp
Contact Solomon Carriere
City Cumberland House
Company Black Bear Island Lake Lodge
Contact Earl Mockellky
City Regina
Company Black Bear Outfitter
Contact
City Arran
Company Bloomfield's Ballantyne Bay

Resort
Contact George & Fran Bloomfield
City Rosthern
Company Boreal Camp Services
Contact Morton G. Harbicht
City La Ronge
Company Camp Kinisoo Ltd
Contact Christopher and Sheila Brown
City La Ronge
Company Can-Am Outfitters Ltd.
Contact Chris or Cindy Shea
City Brabant Lake
Company Careen Lake Lodge
Contact Jack & Eileen O'Brien
City Biggar
Company Caribou Creek Lodge Ltd.
Contact Dwight & Bev Whitley
City Meath Park
Company Churchill River Voyageur Lodge
Contact Terry Helary
City La Ronge
Company Churchill River Wilderness Camps
Contact Klaas & Norman Knot
City Medstead
Company Cree River Lodge Ltd.
Contact eter Evaschesen
City Melfort
Company Cuelenaere Lake Lodge
Contact Larry Cherneski
City Saskatoon
Company Cumberland House Outfitters Ltd.
Contact
City Cumberland House
Company Cup Lake Fishing Camp
Contact Lindsay & Barry Brucks
City Meadow Lake
Company D & D Camps Ltd.
Contact Dick Cossette
City Christopher Lake
Company Davin Lake Lodge
Contact Wes Borowsky
City Prince Albert
Company Dillon Lake Outfitting
Contact Arsene Nezcroche
City Dillon
Company Dobbin Lake Lodges
Contact N. Silzer & J. Motoshosky
City Regina
Company Elusive Saskatchewan Whitetail Outfitter
Contact Harvey McDonald
City Richard
Company Ena Lake Lodge
Contact A. Shane MacKinnon
City Prince Albert
Company English River First Nations Resort
Contact Alfred Dawatsare
City Patuanak
Company Flotten Lake Resort
Contact Abram & Paula Rempel
City Dorintosh
Company Foster Lake Lodge
Contact Trent Brunanski
City Wakaw
Company G & S Marina Outfitters
Contact Robert Schulz & Peter Gallo
City Strasbourg
Company Glen Hill's Trophy Expeditions
Contact Glen Hill
City Saskatoon
Company Granger's Cheemo Lodge
Contact Clayton Granger
City Hardisty, Alberta
Company Grayling Lodge
Contact C. Veikle & R. Brackenbury
City Cut Knife
Company Green Lake Lodge
Contact Karen & Bob Henderson
City Candle Lake
Company Grey Owl Camp Fly-In Ltd.
Contact Tom Schuck & Dick Panter
City Regina
Company Hasbala Lake Lodge
Contact
City Unity
Company Hatchet Lake Lodge
Contact George Fleming
City Prince Albert
Company Hawkrock Outfitters
Contact Allan Serhan
City Porcupine Plain

Company Hepburn Lake Lodge
Contact Dennis Callbeck
City Watrous
Company Hillcrest Motel & Outfitters
Contact Kelly & Debra Morrell
City Fort Qu'Appelle
Company Hilliard's Pine Island Camp
Contact Butch & Neva Hilliard
City La Ronge
Company J R Outfitters
Contact
City Nipawin
Company Jim's Camp - Nistowiak Falls
Contact James Daniel McKenzie
City Stanley Mission
Company Johnson River Camp
Contact Jean Graham
City La Ronge
Company Josdal Camps
Contact Tyrone Josdal
City Moose Jaw
Company K & P Outfitters
Contact S. Van Buskirk & S. Garrett
City Kyle
Company Katche Kamp Outfitters
Contact Bill & Jeanne Blackmon
City Saskatoon
Company Keeley Lake Lodge
Contact Gary & Gloria Callihoo
City Meadow Lake
Company Kenyon Lake Fly-In
Contact
City Saskatoon
Company Kevin Tourand Outfitting
Contact
City Nipawin
Company La Ronge Eagle Point Resort
Contact
City La Ronge
Company Lac La Peche Resort
Contact Eloise Vigeant
City Blain Lake
Company Lakeland Marine Rentals Ltd.
Contact Albin Walcer
City Nipawin
Company Lakeview Inn
Contact Wilbur George Bauer
City Loon Lake
Company Lindwood Lodge
Contact Gerry Lindskog
City La Ronge
Company Little Bear Lake Resort
Contact Dwayne Giles
City Prince Albert
Company Little Pine Lodge
Contact Wendy & Pat Tyson
City Chitek Lake
Company Long's 4 Seasons Resort Ltd.
Contact
City La Ronge
Company Lucky Lake Outfitters
Contact Willard Ylioja
City Lucky Lake
Company M & N Resort
Contact Wayne Chepil
City Waterhen Lake
Company Macoun Lake Island Lodge
Contact Harvey Nelson & Rodgeer Herman
City Dalmeny
Company MacSwaney's Cabins
Contact
City Nipawin
Company Maple Grove Resort
Contact
City Whitewood
Company Martin's Cabins
Contact Denis & Betty Martin
City St. Brieux
Company Medicine Rapids Resort
Contact Larry Stevenson
City Pelican Narrows
Company Mel-Sask Outfitters
Contact
City Melville
Company Mercer Outfitting
Contact Ken & Pat Auckland
City Big River
Company Michel Lodge
Contact Wayne & Kathy Berumen
City North Battleford
Company Minowukaw Lodge and Joe's Cabins

Contact
City Candle Lake
Company Mista Nosayew Outfitters
Contact Jeff Janzen
City Pelican Narrows
Company Moose Horn Lodge
Contact Marvin Peterson
City Prince Albert
Company Moose Range Lodge
Contact
City Hudson Bay
Company Mystic Magic Wilderness Lodge
Contact
City Denare Beach
Company Nagle Lake Outfitters
Contact Bob & Stella Rodwin
City Prince Albert
Company Newmart Fishing Resort
Contact Humen & Mauthe
City Saskatoon
Company Niska Hunting & Fishing Camp
Contact
City Moose Jaw
Company Nordic Lodge
Contact Donna Carlson
City Saskatoon
Company North Haven Lodge
Contact Jim Marple
City Meadow Lake
Company Northern Cross Resort Ltd.
Contact Jeff Jesske & Co.
City Goodsoil
Company Northern Echo Lodge
Contact Jim or Carol Eberle
City Pilot Butte
Company Northern Lights Lodge Ltd.
Contact Ted & Diana Ohlsen
City Weyburn
Company Northern Nights
Contact Bruce & Brian Basken
City Churchbridge
Company Northern Reflection Lodge
Contact Eddy Jones
City Dinsmore
Company Oliver Lake Wilderness Camp
Contact Michel Dube
City Prince Albert
Company Orban's Outfitting
Contact Darrell Orban
City Strasbourg
Company Overland Cross Country Lodge
Contact Wayne & Diane Elliott
City Denare Beach
Company Pardoe Lake Lodge
Contact Vern Hunt
City Prince Albert
Company Pelican Narrows U-Fly-In Ltd.
Contact Ray Fournier
City Saskatoon
Company Pickerel Bay Cabins
Contact Ray or Gail Twedt
City La Ronge
Company Pickerel Point Concessions
Contact
City Canora
Company Pierce Lake Lodge
Contact
City Pierceland
Company Pine Cove Resort
Contact
City Loon Lake
Company Pine Grove Resort
Contact Margaret Lucyshyn
City Saskatoon
Company Pipestone Lake Lodge Ltd.
Contact Marvin Bather
City Canwood
Company Pointer Lake Fishing Lodge
Contact Bryce Liddell
City Spiritwood
Company Prairie Outfitters
Contact Potter & Westin & Slabik
City Gull Lake
Company Pruden's Point Resort
Contact
City Nipawin
Company R & R Wilderness Lodge
Contact R.Jenson & R. Reylonds
City Outlook
Company Red's Camps
Contact Ron MacKay

City La Ronge
Company Rocky Lake Cabins
Contact Duane & Glenda Bohlken
City Hudson Bay
Company Russell's Churchill River Camps
Contact Jim Russell
City Sandy Bay
Company Selwyn Lake Lodge
Contact Gord/Mary Daigneault-Wallace
City Saskatoon
Company Shadd Lake Cabins
Contact Nancy McKay
City La Ronge
Company Silver Tip Outfitting
Contact Garry & Zay Debienne
City Nipawin
Company Simoneau's Outfitting
Contact
City Mistatim
Company Simpson's Sportsman's Lodge
Contact
City Spruce Home
Company Sisip (Duck) Outfitting Camp
Contact Robert McKay
City Cumberland House
Company Slim's Cabins
Contact Jim & Veronica Woods
City Creighton
Company South Bay Cabins & Services
Contact Percy Depper
City Saskatoon
Company Sturgeon Landing Outfitters
Contact
City Sturgeon Landing
Company T & D Amisk Cabins
Contact
City Creighton
Company Tawaw Cabins
Contact Emil & Merrel Berg & K. Wolffe
City Dorintosh
Company The New Canoe West Resort
Contact Harold Breault
City Cut Knife
Company Thistlethwaite Outfitting
Contact
City Stewart Valley
Company Thompson Lake Lodge/ Triple Lake Camps
Contact Mike Chursinoff
City La Ronge
Company Thompson's Camps, Inc.
Contact Garry Thompson
City La Ronge
Company Thunderbird Camps
Contact
City Pelican Narrows
Company Tobin Lake Resort
Contact Connie Anklovitch
City Nipawin
Company Trails End Outfitters
Contact Rolie Morris
City Nipawin
Company Triveet Lake Fly-In
Contact Stuart Warrener
City Saskatoon
Company True North Lodge
Contact
City Meadow Lake
Company Turtle Lake Lodge
Contact Maurice & Jeanette Blais
City Livelong
Company Twin Bay Resort Ltd.
Contact Ken & Naomie Selb
City Deschambault Lake
Company Twin Marine
Contact Curtis Lockwood
City Nipawin
Company Two Fingers Fishing Camp
Contact
City Regina
Company Two Spirit Guest Ranch & Retreat
Contact Lee Cryer & Denise Needham
City Regina
Company Vermillion Lake Camp
Contact
City Regina

Company Wadin Bay Resort
Contact Wayne Buckle & Audrey Miller
City La Ronge
Company Wally's Place
Contact Gen Assailly & Wally Nicklin
City Gerald
Company Waterhen Lake Store & Resort
Contact
City Waterhen Lake
Company White Fox Hotel Outfitting
Contact Robert Shatula
City White Fox
Company White Swan Lake Resort
Contact Gerry Wenschlag
City Meath Park
Company Wild Man Outfitters/Poplar Point Resort
Contact
City Big River
Company Wild Wings Outfitters
Contact R. Ross & B. Carter R. Button
City Swift Current
Company Wilson's Lodge
Contact
City Estevan

Yukon Territories

Company Barney's Fishing & Tours
Contact
City Tagish
Company Campfire Adventures
Contact
City Dawson City
Company Circle VH Outdoor Adventures
Contact
City Faro
Company Dalton Trail Lodge
Contact
City Haines Junction
Company Faro Yukon Fishing Tours
Contact
City Faro
Company Horizons North Ltd.
Contact
City Faro
Company Inconnu Lodge
Contact
City Whitehorse
Company Koser's Yukon Outback
Contact
City Ross River
Company Kruda Che Wilderness Guiding
Contact
City Hanes Junction
Company Oldsquaw Lodge
Contact
City Whitehorse
Company Otter Falls Wilderness Adventure
Contact
City Haines Junction
Company Pack Trails North Adventures
Contact
City Watson Lake
Company Paul's Fishing Tours - North of 60
Contact
City Whitehorse
Company Peacock's Yukon Camps Ltd.
Contact
City Whitehorse
Company Ruby Range Wilderness Lodge
Contact
City Whitehorse
Company Scott Lake Lodge
Contact Blaine & Susan Anderson
City Whitehorse
Company Sifton Wilderness Adventures
Contact
City Haines Junction
Company Snowy Mountain Safaris
Contact
City Faro

Company Takhini River Guiding
Contact
City Whitehorse
Company Taylor's Place Fishing Camp
Contact
City Watson Lake
Company Trophy Stone Safaris, Ltd.
Contact Curt Thompson
City Whitehorse
Company Widrig Outfitters, Ltd.
Contact Chris Widrig
City Whitehorse
Company Wilderness Fishing Adventures
Contact Russ Rose & Sheri Lockwood
City Carcross

Top Rated Questionnaire
Fly Fishing

Name of your Field Guide:_____
(Person that guided you in the field)

Date of Trip_____Location_____ Day trip ☐   Overnight trip ☐

Was this a Family Trip where your children were actively involved in the activities? YES ☐   No ☐

Technique used: _____

Species caught or observed: _____

Catch ☐   Catch and Release ☐

OUTSTANDING   EXCELLENT   GOOD   ACCEPTABLE   POOR/INFERIOR   UNACCEPTABLE

1. How helpful was the Outfitter (Guide, Captain or Lodge) with travel arrangements, fishing regulations, permits etc.?.. ☐ ☐ ☐ ☐ ☐ ☐

2. How well did the Outfitter (Guide, Captain or Lodge) provide important details that better prepared you for your fishing trip (clothing, equipment, information on the fish and the water, list of "take along", etc.)?................ ☐ ☐ ☐ ☐ ☐ ☐

3. How would you rate the Outfitter's (Guide, Captain or Lodge) office skills in handling deposits, charges, reservations, returning calls before and after your trip?.. ☐ ☐ ☐ ☐ ☐ ☐

4. How would you rate the accommodations (tent, cabin, lodge, etc.)?........... ☐ ☐ ☐ ☐ ☐ ☐

5. How would you rate the equipment provided by the Outfitter (Guide, Captain or Lodge) during your trip (boats, tackle, rods, airplanes, etc.)?...... ☐ ☐ ☐ ☐ ☐ ☐

6. How would you rate the cooking (quantity, quality and cleanliness of the service)?.. ☐ ☐ ☐ ☐ ☐ ☐

7. How would you rate your Guide's Attitude — Politeness — Disposition?..... ☐ ☐ ☐ ☐ ☐ ☐

8. How would you rate your Guide's knowledge of the area?........................... ☐ ☐ ☐ ☐ ☐ ☐

9. How would you rate your Guide's knowledge of the fish (feeding cycle, habits, type of flies to be used, etc.)?.. ☐ ☐ ☐ ☐ ☐ ☐

10. How were your fish prepared for trophy mounting and/or for the trip home? (For Catch and Release write N/A).. ☐ ☐ ☐ ☐ ☐ ☐

		Outstanding	Excellent	Good	Acceptable	Poor/Inferior	Unacceptable
11.	How would you rate the skills and the attitude of the Staff overall?.............	☐	☐	☐	☐	☐	☐
12.	How would you rate the quality of the waters?..	☐	☐	☐	☐	☐	☐
13.	How would you rate the quality of the fish?..	☐	☐	☐	☐	☐	☐
14.	How would you rate the flexibility of your Guide or Captain to meet your goal(s)?...	☐	☐	☐	☐	☐	☐
15.	How would you rate the overall quality of your fishing experience?...........	☐	☐	☐	☐	☐	☐

		Good	Fair	Poor
16.	How would you describe the weather conditions?......................................	☐	☐	☐

17. Did the Outfitter (Guide, Captain or Lodge) accurately represent the overall quality of your experience (quality of waters, fish, accommodations, etc.)?... ☐ Yes ☐ No

18. Did you provide the Outfitter (Guide, Captain or Lodge) with truthful statements regarding your personal needs, your skills and your expectations?.. ☐ Yes ☐ No

19. Would you use this Outdoor Professional/Business again?........................ ☐ Yes ☐ No

20. Would you recommend this Outdoor Professional/Business to others?..... ☐ Yes ☐ No

Comments: _____

_____

_____

_____

_____

_____

_____

_____

_____

_____

_____

_____

_____

_____

_____

_____

_____

_____

Will you permit Picked-By-You to use your name and comments in our book(s)? ☐ Yes ☐ No

Signature_____

Outfitters, Guides & Lodges by Fish Species

 Amberjack(s)

Westport Outfitters

 Arctic Grayling

Alaska Fish & Trail Unlimited
Beartooth Plateau Outfitters
George Ortman Adventure Guiding
Paintrock Adventures
The Complete Fly Fisher
Tracy Vrem's Blue Mountain Lodge
Wild Trout Outfitters

 Arctic Char

Alaska Fish & Trail Unlimited
George Ortman Adventure Guiding
George River Lodge
Tracy Vrem's Blue Mountain Lodge

Bass

 Largemouth Bass

G & W Guide Service
Tim Bermingham Drift Boat Guide
  Service
The Hungry Trout

 Smallmouth Bass

M & M's Whooper Hollow Lodge
Tim Bermingham Drift Boat Guide
  Service
The Hungry Trout
Tightlines
West Branch Angler & Sportsman's
  Resort

 Striped Bass

Chesapeake Bay Charter
The John B. Gulley Flyfishing Guide
  Service
Tim Bermingham's Drift Boat Guide
  Service
Westport Outfitters

 Barracuda

Fly Fishing Paradise

 Bluefish

Westport Outfitters

 Bonefish

Fly Fishing Paradise

 Dolly Varden

Esper's Under Wild Skies
George Ortman Adventure Guiding
Solitude River Trip
Tracy Vrem's Blue Mountain Lodge
Wilderness Outfitters

 Drum(s)

Capt. Doug Hanks
Capt. Mike Locklear
Chesapeake Bay Charter
Gone Fishing
Look-N-Hook Charters

 Mackerel(s)

Chesapeake Bay Charter
Westport Outfitters

Outfitters, Guides & Lodges by Fish Species

Northern Pike

Alaska Fish & Trail Unlimited
George Ortman Adventure Guiding
George River Lodge
Les Enterprises du Lac Perdu
Mike Wilson's High Mtn. Drifters
The Hungry Trout
The Reel Life
Tracy Vrem's Blue Mountain Lodge

Permit

Capt. Mike Locklear
Fly Fishing Paradise

Salmons

Atlantic Salmon

Gander River Outfitters
George River Lodge
Libby Sporting Camps
M & M's Whooper Hollow Lodge

Chinook (King) Salmon

Alaska Fish & Trail Unlimited
Bruce Slightom
Classic Alaska Charters
George Ortman Adventure Guiding
Serene Fly-Fishing Adventures
Sweet Old Boys
Tightlines
Tim Bermingham's Drift Boat Guide
  Service
Tracy Vrem's Blue Mountain Lodge

Chum (Dog) Salmon

Classic Alaska Charters
George Ortman Adventure Guiding
Tracy Vrem's Blue Mountain Lodge

Coho (Silver) Salmon

Alaska Fish & Trail Unlimited
Classic Alaska Charters
George Ortman Adventure Guiding
Sweet Old Boys
Tightlines
Tracy Vrem's Blue Mountain Lodge

Pink(Humpback) Salmon

Classic Alaska Charters
George Ortman Adventure Guiding
Tracy Vrem Blue Mountain Lodge

Sockeye (Red) Salmon

Alaska Fish & Trail Unlimited
Classic Alaska Charters
George Ortman Adventure Guiding
Tracy Vrem's Blue Mountain Lodge

Shark(s)

Chesapeake Bay Charter
Fly Fishing Paradise
Look-N-Hook Charters

Snapper(s)

Fly Fishing Paradise

Outfitters, Guides & Lodges by Fish Species

Snook

Capt. Doug Hanks
Gone Fishing
Look-N-Hook Charters
Salt & Fresh Water Fishing Charter

Tarpon(s)

Capt. Doug Hanks
Capt. Mike Locklear
Fly Fishing Paradise
Gone Fishing
Look-N-Hook Charters
Salt & Fresh Water Fishing Charter

Trouts

Brook Trout

Alpine Anglers
Beartooth Plateau Outfitters
Broken Arrow Lodge
Dragonfly Anglers
East Slope Anglers
Esper's Under Wild Skies
Fly Fishing Outfitters
Gander River Outfitters
George River Lodge
John Henry Lee Outfitters
Kelly Creek Fly Fishers
Les Enterprises du Lac Perdu
Libby Sporting Camps
Mike Wilson's High Mtn. Drifters
Paintrock Adventures
Rocky Fork Guide Service
The Battenkill Angler
The Complete Fly Fisher
The Hungry Trout
Tim Bermingham's Drift Boat Guide
    Service
Tite Line Fishing
Tom Loder's Panhandle Outfitters
Wild Trout Outfitters

Brown Trout

Alpine Anglers
Broken Arrow Lodge
Dragonfly Anglers
Eagle Nest Lodge
East Slope Anglers
Fly Fishing Outfitters
Grossenbacher Guides
Hatch Finders
Heise Expeditions
John Henry Lee Outfitters
Kelly Creek Fly Fishers
M & M's Whooper Hollow Lodge
Mike Wilson's High Mtn. Drifters
Paintrock Adventures
Rocky Fork Guide Service
Serene Fly-Fishing Adventures
The Battenkill Angler
The Complete Fly Fisher
The Hungry Trout
The John B. Gulley Flyfishing Guide
    Service
The Reel Life
The Reflective Angler
The Troutfitter
Tim Bermingham's Drift Boat Guide
    Service
Tite Line Fishing
Tom Loder's Panhandle Outfitters
West Branch Angler & Sportsman's
    Resort
Wild Trout Outfitters

Cutthroat Trout

Alpine Anglers
Beartooth Plateau Outfitters
Broken Arrow Lodge
Classic Alaska Charters
Dragonfly Anglers
Eagle Nest Lodge
East Slope Anglers
Esper's Under Wild Skies
Fishing on the Fly
Fly Fishing Outfitters
George Ortman Adventure Guiding
Heise Expeditions
John Henry Lee Outfitters
Mike Wilson's High Mtn. Drifters

Outfitters, Guides & Lodges by Fish Species

Paintrock Adventures
Rocky Fork Guide Service
Solitude River Trip
The Complete Fly Fisher
The John B. Gulley Flyfishing Guide
  Service
Tightlines
Tom Loder's Panhandle Outfitters
Wild Trout Outfitters
Wilderness Outfitters

Lake Trout

Alaska Fish & Trail Unlimited
Beartooth Plateau Outfitters
East Slope Anglers
George Ortman Adventure Guiding
George River Lodge
John Henry Lee Outfitters
Les Enterprises du Lac Perdu
M & M's Whooper Hollow Lodge
Mike Wilson's High Mtn. Drifters
Paintrock Adventures

Rainbow Trout

Alaska Fish & Trail Unlimited
Alpine Anglers
Beartooth Plateau Outfitters
Broken Arrow Lodge
Bruce Slightom
Dragonfly Anglers
Eagle Nest Lodge
East Slope Anglers
Esper's Under Wild Skies
Fishing on the Fly
Fly Fishing Outfitters
George Ortman Adventure Guiding
Grossenbacher Guides
Hatch Finders
Heise Expeditions
John Henry Lee Outfitters
Love Bros. & Lee
M & M's Whooper Hollow Lodge
Mike Wilson's High Mtn. Drifters
Paintrock Adventures
Rocky Fork Guide Service
Serene Fly-Fishing Adventures
Solitude River Trip

Sweet Old Boys
The Battenkill Angler
The Complete Fly Fisher
The Hungry Trout
The John B. Gulley Flyfishing Guide
  Service
The Reel Life
The Reflective Angler
The Troutfitter
Tim Bermingham's Drift Boat Guide
  Service
Tite Line Fishing
Tom Loder's Panhandle Outfitters
Tracy Vrem's Blue Mountain Lodge
West Branch Angler & Sportsman's
  Resort
Wild Trout Outfitters
Wilderness Outfitters

Steelhead Trout

Bruce Slightom
Fishing on the Fly
Serene Fly-Fishing Adventures
Sweet Old Boys
Tightlines
Tim Bermingham's Drift Boat Guide
  Service
Tom Loder's Panhandle Outfitters

Spotted Sea Trout

Capt. Mike Locklear
Chesapeake Bay Charter
Gander River Outfitters
Gone Fishing
Look-N-Hook Charters

Tuna(s)

Westport Outfitters

Index of Outfitters, Guides & Lodges
by State

Index of Outfitters, Guides & Lodges
by State

Index of Outfitters, Guides & Lodges
by State

Index of Outfitters, Guides & Lodges
by Province

Canada

Alphabetical Index by Company Name

About the Editor

Maurizio Valerio received a Doctoral degree Summa Cum Laude in Natural Science, majoring in Animal Behaviour, from the University of Parma (Italy) in 1981, and a Master of Arts degree in Zoology from the University of California, Berkeley in 1984.

He is a rancher, a writer and a devoted outdoorsman who decided to live with the wild animals that he cherishes so much in the Wallowa Mountains of Northeast Oregon. He has traveled extensively in the Old and New World, for more than 25 years. He is dedicated to preserving everyone's individual right of a respectful, knowledgeable and diversified use of our Outdoor Resources.